Y0-CBB-395

PITTSBURGH

PITTSBURGH A NEW PORTRAIT

FRANKLIN TOKER

University of Pittsburgh Press

For Ellen, passionate Pittsburgher

Published by the University of Pittsburgh Press, Pittsburgh, Pa., 15260
Copyright © 1989, 2009 University of Pittsburgh Press
All rights reserved
Manufactured in Canada
Printed on acid-free paper
10 9 8 7 6 5 4 3 2 1

Library of Congress Cataloging-in-Publication Data
Toker, Franklin.
  Pittsburgh : a new portrait / Franklin Toker.
    p. cm.
  Based on: Pittsburgh : an urban portrait. 1986.
  Includes bibliographical references and index.
ISBN-13: 978-0-8229-4371-6 (cloth : alk. paper)
ISBN-10: 0-8229-4371-9 (cloth : alk. paper)
  1. Pittsburgh (Pa.)—Description and travel. 2. Pittsburgh (Pa.)—Tours.
3. Neighborhood—Pennsylvania—Pittsburgh. 4. Historic buildings—
Pennsylvania—Pittsburgh. 5. Architecture—Pennsylvania—Pittsburgh.
6. Pittsburgh (Pa.)—Buildings, structures, etc. I. Title.
  F159.P64T65 2009
  974.8'86—dc22
  2009022903

Substantial portions of this book are adapted from a previous work by the author
titled *Pittsburgh: An Urban Portrait*, originally published by Penn State University
Press in 1986 and reprinted by University of Pittsburgh Press in 1989.

Book design by Landesberg Design

All maps were prepared by Robert Firth and Informing Design, Inc.,
© Informing Design, Inc.

Riverview Park

Millvale

Perry
Hilltop

19

279

Spring
Hill

Troy
Hill

65

Fineview

Washington's
Landing

28

ALLEGHENY RIVER

65

Manchester

Deutschtown

Polish
Hill

North
Side

The Strip

OHIO RIVER

279

579

The Hill

North Shore

51

Middle
Hill

West End

Point State
Park

Downtown

Lower
Hill

376

Uptown

19

Duquesne
Heights

The Bluff

376

Station
Square

Mt.
Washington

South Side Flats

376

South Side

South Side Slopes

19

Allentown

Mt. Oliver

Arlington

51

Beechview

McKinley Park

Morningside

Highland Park

Stanton Heights

Highland
Park

Lawrenceville

Larimer

Lincoln-Lemington

130

Garfield

Bloomfield

Friendship

East Liberty

Homewood

Upper
Hill

Shadyside

Mellon
Park

Point Breeze

Wilkinsburg

Oakland

Squirrel
Hill

Regent
Square

Schenley Park

Frick Park

Edgewood

SouthSide
Works

22
30

376

Greenfield

Swissvale

Hazelwood

Duck
Hollow

885

Homestead

Pittsburgh

M O N O N G A H E L A   R I V E R

PREFACE

How can the same city be both the most livable and the most leave-able in the United States? Meet twenty-first century Pittsburgh, where the quality of life keeps rising while the population keeps falling, now to half what it was in 1950. What accounts for this contradiction, and what explains Pittsburgh's resiliency?

The secret to Pittsburgh's strength lies in its neighborhoods. Every city has neighborhoods, but those in Pittsburgh strike visitors as particularly well defined. The revitalization of these neighborhoods and the development of river trails and new housing tell us more about the city than statistics can reveal. The neighborhoods kept Pittsburgh afloat through the collapse of the steel industry and the decades of economic uncertainty that followed, and it is their continuing strength that makes Pittsburgh unsinkable.

Beyond their manifest importance, there is a second reason why Pittsburgh's neighborhoods form the structure of this book. This volume's predecessor, *Pittsburgh: An Urban Portrait* (first published by the Penn State University Press in 1986 and then reissued by the University of Pittsburgh Press in 1989), is not only twenty years out of date, but it combined two books in one. The first was a survey of the city's buildings, and the second was an evocation of Pittsburgh as an urban experience. In 2005, the University of Pittsburgh

Press asked me to prepare a successor volume, and the Society of Architectural Historians followed with a request for a book that would assemble the formal and technical data on the city's main buildings. Those two requests allowed me to disengage the two halves of my earlier book, though some overlaps remain. One half became *Buildings of Pittsburgh*, published by the University of Virginia Press in 2007, and it represents, for me, a conversation among academics. *Pittsburgh: A New Portrait* represents a conversation among Pittsburghers — and anyone else who cares to join in — about the workings of a great but often overlooked city.

Readers wondering how this book differs from its predecessor will find that it has changed as much as its elusive subject has. Pittsburgh is "elusive" because it keeps changing while insisting that nothing has changed. Pittsburghers may be resistant to change, but the transformation in the urban landscape over the last twenty years is nothing short of radical. Gone — vanished almost without a trace — are a dozen of what were once the world's largest steel mills, along with all but a few score of the thousands of jobs they directly or indirectly created. U.S. Steel does continue to make some steel at Braddock and process coke at Clairton, and its corporate headquarters and those of a half-dozen other metals firms remain in town. But one could argue that the city's only unbroken link to steel is the Pittsburgh Steelers. This disconnect from steel is wrenching for yesterday's steelworkers, but in the end it may be a good thing. Half of Pittsburgh remembers nothing of its past, while the other thinks about it far too much.

Changes have been just as radical in Pittsburgh's other industries. The closing of the Newfield Mine ended two centuries of coal production in Allegheny County. Glass was first produced in Pittsburgh in 1795, but today only two of the former scores of glassworks are in production. PPG (the company has not called itself Pittsburgh Plate Glass in years) still manufactures glass upriver on the Allegheny, but its dozens of other factories straddle the globe.

Radical changes in the economy have produced a city that now looks profoundly different, and change is never easy. It was painful to see the landmark Chiodo's Tavern in Homestead flattened and replaced by a drugstore. It was even sadder when the wrecking ball claimed the East Hills Shopping Center, where Pittsburgh's white and African American communities came together to shop in the 1960s. But in urban affairs, as in forestry, what is lost clears the way for new growth. The demolition of houses for Pennsylvania Canal workers of the 1830s was a keen loss for the North Side, but it permitted construction of the PNC Park baseball stadium. Economic forces will eventually rebuild the East Hills Shopping Center or replace it with something else.

Commercial and industrial buildings were not the only familiar structures the city lost. While Pittsburgh's attention was elsewhere, many historic landmarks also disappeared. St. Peter's Episcopal Church in Oakland, dating from 1852, was torn down in the 1990s; the barge that architect Louis Kahn converted into an arts center was allowed to float away from Pittsburgh in 1996; and the city made no protest over the demolitions of a unique remnant of the Allegheny Arsenal or an important Bauhaus-style warehouse in the Strip. Just as foolishly, the majestic lobby of Mellon Bank was sadly defaced in the building's conversion to a short-lived Lord and Taylor department store.

Happily, other old buildings are still being used for new functions. On the North Side, young families live in condos and lofts recycled from the Heinz ketchup and food-processing plants; nearby, a hundred townhouses have replaced putrid slaughterhouses on Washington's Landing. In Lawrenceville, a century-old factory now makes robots for NASA, while the Mesta engineering plant in West Homestead gave birth to both the WHEMCO precision milling firm and Mestek computer services.

There is an equally remarkable amount of new construction in town, as scores of structures go up to serve the city's cultural and educational institutions. The University of Pittsburgh, Carnegie Mellon, and Duquesne, the three large universities here, have heavily invested in new buildings, while four other colleges — Robert Morris, Point Park, Chatham, and Carlow — have recently attained university status and unveiled ambitious growth plans. The streets of downtown Pittsburgh are filled with more concert-goers, students at technical and professional schools, and office workers than at any time past. In arts and entertainment, the city has spent several billion dollars on facilities for baseball, football, hockey, and basketball and a commensurate amount for new museums and theaters. A dramatic new convention center attracts visitors to the city, where a new airport welcomes them, a dozen new or soon-to-open hotels can accommodate them, and scores of new restaurants are ready to feed them. None of these features existed when the forerunner of this book was published in 1986.

It is difficult to imagine how the city and the region ever got along without the Pittsburgh High School for the Creative and Performing Arts (CAPA existed a generation ago but did not yet have the prominence it now enjoys Downtown), the Pittsburgh Parks Conservancy, the Pittsburgh Cultural Trust, the arts-funding Sprout Fund and the Regional Assets District, the Benedum Center, the Andy Warhol Museum, the Carnegie Science Museum, Theater Square, the Frick Art & Historical Center, and the Heinz History Center. No less impact has come in the last twenty years from rejuvenated institutions such as the Children's Museum, Phipps Conservatory, the aviary, the zoo, and the Mattress Factory art center. Equally significant projects are now under way: an immense nuclear research campus for Westinghouse in Cranberry; a hockey arena for the Penguins on the Hill; a subway extension from Downtown to the North Shore; Children's Hospital in Lawrenceville; the August Wilson Center for African American Culture, Downtown; the Three PNC Plaza skyscraper; and—like it or not—a gambling casino on the North Side. Add to this the half-dozen new or renewed Carnegie libraries in Downtown, the Hill, the North Side, Squirrel Hill, East Liberty, and the West End; the new Grant Street Transportation Center, the Pittsburgh Technology Center, upscale shopping facilities in East Liberty, the information technology (IT) start-ups, the cyber cafés, and the dozens of recently painted murals all over town, and one can start to grasp the extent of Pittsburgh's urban transformation.

The biggest news is that the city is bursting with housing initiatives despite having lost so many residents. In the last twenty years a half-dozen housing complexes have been developed, some so big they constitute whole neighborhoods. The first was Washington's Landing, on what was Herr's Island in the Allegheny River, with not only housing but sports facilities and light industry. Next came Crawford Square, Oak Hill, Bedford Hill, and the Legacy, developments that renovated or swept away the barrackslike housing on the Hill. The Brown's Hill Road slag heap on the edge of Squirrel Hill has been reshaped so that up to seven hundred new homes can be built at Summerset at Frick Park, and more houses will be going up where a coke works once stood in Hazelwood. Hundreds of residents have settled in subdivisions on the banks of the Monongahela in South Side, where belching smoke used to mark the Jones & Laughlin mills. (Trains still come through, but their harsh whistles are muted now.) The best-looking contemporary apartment block in the city has just gone up in Garfield, about the last district in which a longtime Pittsburgher would expect it.

The hottest of the housing markets is Downtown. With adaptive reuse development in full swing, the Carlyle, the Pennsylvanian, and Piatt Place have put condominiums where a bank, a railroad station, and a department store once operated. Together with new start-ups such as Encore on Seventh, 151 FirstSide, and the planned-on-paper RiverParc, these developments are giving the Golden Triangle an asset it has too often lacked since the Civil War: ordinary residents.

The facts marshaled above make clear the need for an update to my 1986 *Pittsburgh* book. Readers were generous in their reaction to that publication, demanding four printings from two different publishers. With its extensive coverage of African American districts like Homewood and the Hill, the earlier book was no whitewash, nor is its successor. I was pleased to have supplied Pittsburgh with a publication that could represent it in American and international publications. In his review of the book in the *New Yorker*, Brendan Gill memorably wrote, "If Pittsburgh were situated somewhere in the heart of Europe, tourists would eagerly journey hundreds of miles out of their way to visit it." The book even persuaded a few out-of-towners to settle here.

I hope this new *Pittsburgh* will continue to speak for the city, but it will do so with a different sort of language. The earlier book reflected the old Pittsburgh: dense, serious, businesslike, somewhat hard to read. This new portrait reflects the contemporary Pittsburgh: larger, more colorful, less serious, less crammed with detail. Like its predecessor, the new text keeps its focus on architecture and urbanism, but it wanders into certain personalities, certain anecdotes, and certain ordinary buildings that lack pedigrees. I have tried to write a book that could be read from cover to cover rather than picked at like a reference book, but it can still serve that purpose.

Another altered circumstance for this book is the changed climate of studies on Pittsburgh. When I was assembling data for the earlier work in the mid-1980s, there was little recent research. Two decades had passed since Stefan Lorant brought out *Pittsburgh: The Story of an American City* (1964), and it was nearly that long since James Van Trump and Arthur Ziegler compiled their pioneering *Landmark Architecture of Allegheny County, Pennsylvania*. (The "Further Reading" section lists these and most of the other major works on Pittsburgh.) Similarly, not until the 1980s did scholars begin to look carefully at the urban structure of Pittsburgh. In a more popular vein, Rick Sebak produced numerous films on Pittsburgh neighborhoods and themes for local public television station WQED.

Studies specifically about Pittsburgh's buildings also changed in the 1980s. Walter Kidney's *Landmark Architecture* presented much new data, some of which I incorporate here. New works on important local architects appeared. Barry Hannegan, of the Pittsburgh History & Landmarks Foundation, wrote essays on landscape design, and his colleague Al Tannler clarified questions about key buildings and architects. In 1997, Lu Donnelly, David Brumble, and I began to compile *Buildings of Pennsylvania: Pittsburgh and Western Pennsylvania*. I also wrote *Fallingwater Rising: Frank Lloyd Wright, E. J. Kaufmann, and America's Most Extraordinary House*, which is on its way to becoming a film.

The past thirty years have also seen the publication of works on the social, cultural, economic, and political shifts that affected physical changes in Pittsburgh. These works include new biographies of Andrew Carnegie, A. W. Mellon, Henry Clay Frick, and other prominent steel men; studies on the rise and fall of industries important to Pittsburgh; analysis of Pittsburgh's ethnic communities; and coverage of Pittsburgh's main literary and cultural efforts, including art collecting.

Just as welcome as this harvest of publications was the way Pittsburgh's scholarly institutions made their collections electronically accessible to the public. Early on, the Pennsylvania Department of the Carnegie Library of Pittsburgh put many images of its Pittsburgh Photographic Library online. The Historical Society of Western Pennsylvania created the Heinz History Center and put online an extensive database of its holdings. In the mid-1990s, the University of Pittsburgh began its Historic Pittsburgh project, which digitized hundreds of photographs and street atlases and made them available online along with data-searchable texts for such things as street directories of Victorian Pittsburgh and Stefan Lorant's historical chronology of the region. These changes meant that within a few minutes people could find the answers to questions that took me a whole day to resolve back in the 1980s.

Several new research and advocacy institutions have appeared on the scene since the 1980s. The Pittsburgh History & Landmarks Foundation continues the vital work it has been doing since 1964, but advocacy for the region's historic architectural legacy has been strengthened by Preservation Pittsburgh and the Young Preservationists Association of Pittsburgh. The Architectural Archives at Carnegie Mellon University now provides a home for thousands of architectural graphics, and the Heinz Architectural Center at the Carnegie Museum of Art has raised the region's consciousness on architectural design.

This community of curators and researchers has been uniformly generous in sharing ideas and images with me. That applies particularly to Marilyn Holt, Barry Chad, Cindy Ulrich, and Gilbert Pietrzak, who administer the Pennsylvania Department at Carnegie Library; to Al Tannler, Louise Sturgess, and their colleagues at the Pittsburgh History & Landmarks Foundation; to Tracy Myers at the Heinz Architectural Center; and to Martin Aurand at the Carnegie Mellon Architectural Archives. Special thanks go to Lu Donnelly for her connoisseurship of Pittsburgh architects, to Terri Baltimore and Mindy Thompson Fullilove for their insights on the Hill, to Jerry Andree and his staff for data on Cranberry Township, to Ron Baraff for sharing with me his knowledge of steelmaking, to Bob Regan for his statistics on the city's steps, to Chad Finer for photographing the Golden Triangle with me, and to my wife, Ellen, for her constant support. Some of my revisions were checked or amplified by the members of an undergraduate seminar I directed at the University of Pittsburgh in 2007, and three anonymous readers of an early draft were especially helpful with critiques and suggestions. The book might not have seen the light of day had it not been for the generous support of Richard M. Scaife and the Allegheny Foundation, and of Sheila and Milton Fine and the Fine Foundation.

By and large *Pittsburgh: An Urban Portrait* has done its job. It is time for *Pittsburgh: A New Portrait* to take over.

PITTSBURGH

INTRODUCTION: PITTSBURGH FROM THE GROUND UP

fig. 1.1
THE ALLEGHENY
AND THE
MONONGAHELA
FORM THE OHIO.
MURAL BY
RICHARD HAAS

The dramatic landscape around—and under—Pittsburgh began to form half a billion years ago. An ocean periodically covered the land, with sediment and the remains of plants and animals building up to form layers of stone. Although sometimes dry and sometimes flooded, the area was usually a vast swamp that extended from what is now eastern Pennsylvania all the way to Indiana. Between accumulated layers of sandstone, limestone, and shale, nature stored away natural gas, some of the world's purest oil, and an abundance of coal. Then, another dramatic event: between 200 million and 300 million years ago, according to recent research, the continental plate carrying Africa collided with the plate that included North America. This clash pushed up the Appalachian range—once as high as the Himalayas—including the Alleghenies.

Pittsburgh's landscape also boasts an abundance of water. The city's location at the confluence of the Allegheny, Monongahela, and Ohio rivers put it at one of the most vital nodes in North America. With the invention of steamboats, Pittsburgh had access to much of North America east of the Rockies. With further improvements in river navigation along the Mississippi and Ohio rivers, Pittsburgh had access to the Gulf of Mexico and the world's shipping lanes.

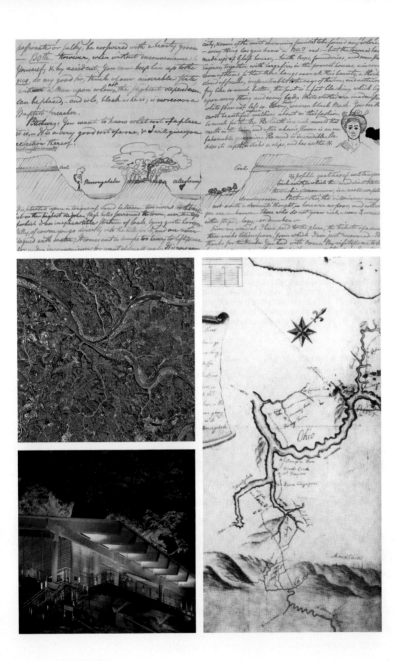

fig. 1.2
BENJAMIN LATROBE'S
1813 SECTION DRAWING
OF PITTSBURGH;
NOTE COAL SEAM

fig. 1.3
SATELLITE IMAGE
OF PITTSBURGH
HIGHLIGHTING THE
RUGGED TERRAIN
OF THE REGION

fig. 1.4
MODERN ENCLOSURE
AT THE MEADOWCROFT
ROCKSHELTER,
NORTH AMERICA'S
OLDEST KNOWN
PALEO-INDIAN SITE

fig. 1.5
GEORGE WASHINGTON'S
HAND-DRAWN MAP
OF THE FORKS OF THE
OHIO, 1754

The forces of nature moved with uncharacteristic speed in creating Pittsburgh's three rivers. During the last of the ice ages, from about seventy thousand to ten thousand years ago, glaciers crept to within forty miles north of Pittsburgh. (Moraine State Park gets its name from being the glaciers' closest point of approach.) The glaciers blocked the flow of a primitive form of the Monongahela River; its waters flooded and then eroded a broad plain through what are now the Pittsburgh districts of Braddock, Rankin, Point Breeze, Homewood, East Liberty, Shadyside, Bloomfield, Lawrenceville, and the Strip. The Monongahela eventually returned to its original bed, but the plain it had cut through the center of an otherwise hilly district prepared an ideal bed for the tracks of the Pennsylvania Railroad, which reached Pittsburgh in 1852. The railroad, in turn, transformed the farms along its path into sites for factories and homes for workers and millionaires in the booming post–Civil War period.

Geography is destiny. The almost accidental creation of the Alleghenies set up a barrier that forced Pittsburgh to develop in isolation from Philadelphia and the East Coast. Isolation did not deter the early Pittsburghers from prospering. They knew how to use the land, first growing crops on it and later exploiting the fossil deposits and minerals of western Pennsylvania to fuel new industries. For a hundred years Pittsburgh extracted the land's resources, grinding up sandstone to make glass, mining coal for making steel, and refining oil at the very beginning of a global industry.

The combination of a rugged but rich land and swift-flowing water advanced industry in other ways, too. A coal seam lay just below the surface of the land, where the erosive action of the three rivers revealed its presence. The architect Benjamin Henry Latrobe captured the dynamics of the coal seams and the rivers in a wonderfully concise section drawing he made of Pittsburgh in 1813.

Early industrialists built chutes into the side of Mount Washington to funnel coal to the glass and iron furnaces at its base. Had the hills met the rivers in steep banks, there would have been no place to build these industrial facilities. Fortunately, each river had eroded a broad flatland along its banks, as if made to order for an enterprising industrialist. Isaac Craig and James O'Hara were the first to use this natural feature for industrial production, setting up a bottle glass plant in 1795 on the Ohio River, opposite the Point. The Monongahela flatlands were developed in the mid-nineteenth century, with the industrialist B. F. Jones developing one bank and James Laughlin, his future Jones & Laughlin partner, building on the other. The bottomlands on the east and west banks of the Ohio became the industrial centers of Manchester and McKees Rocks, while the flatlands on the south bank of the Allegheny became the Strip. The Strip was an ideal place for iron foundries and strip mills and later for huge fruit and vegetable warehouses, now mostly used for other purposes.

Opposite the Strip, on the bottoms along the Allegheny's north bank, David Redick laid out Allegheny City (now Pittsburgh's North Side) in 1788. A generation earlier, in 1753, a young George Washington looked at the level point of land where the three rivers meet and knew he had discovered the ideal site for a British fort that would seriously challenge France's hold on the territory. On that military note, Pittsburgh's recorded history began.

There was of course considerable interest in the land at the Forks of the Ohio long before Europeans saw it. University of Pittsburgh anthropologists working at Avella, southwest of Pittsburgh, determined that Paleo-Indians occupied the Meadowcroft Rockshelter there for sixteen thousand years, the longest recorded sequence of habitation in the whole of North America. There is evidence of prehistoric construction in Pittsburgh, too. Some fifteen hundred years ago, Indians created a huge burial mound over a natural formation at McKees Rocks. The top of Grant's Hill in the Golden Triangle seems also to have served as a burial mound.

The timeline that culminates in twenty-first-century Pittsburgh is a long one, but the area's recorded history is actually rather recent. The first written accounts came from French, English, and Dutch explorers who made contact with the Delaware, Shawnee, and Seneca tribes in the area. The European-origin explorers could not have mapped western Pennsylvania without the Indians' sophisticated network of trails, which still serve as the basis for nearly all the important highways in the district. But the Indians had mostly abandoned the Forks of the Ohio by 1754, when British colonists began constructing Fort Prince George at the three rivers' confluence. The French demolished the stockade four months later and replaced it with Fort Duquesne, which they dedicated "under the title of the Assumption of the Blessed Virgin at the Beautiful River."

France intended to establish a settlement at the point of land and make it the nerve center and potentially the capital of an empire stretching from Montreal to New Orleans. This dream vanished when the British captured Fort Duquesne in November 1758 and three years later replaced it with Fort Pitt, named in honor of England's prime minister, William Pitt the Elder. It was one of the largest, most costly, and most elaborate English forts in the New World. General John Forbes named the garrison town around it Pittsbourgh, pronounced like Edinburgh, Forbes being a Scot.

Explanation
C . *Casemates under the Curtain*
D . *Powder Magazines.*
E . *Laboratories for the Artillery*
F . *Barracks for 700 Men.*
G . *Barracks for Officers.*
H . *Sally Ports from the Casemates*
K . *Low Town.*   L *The Gun*

fig. 1.6
SHAWNEE INDIAN
OF WESTERN
PENNSYLVANIA,
CA. 1750

fig. 1.7
PLAN OF
FORT PITT, 1760

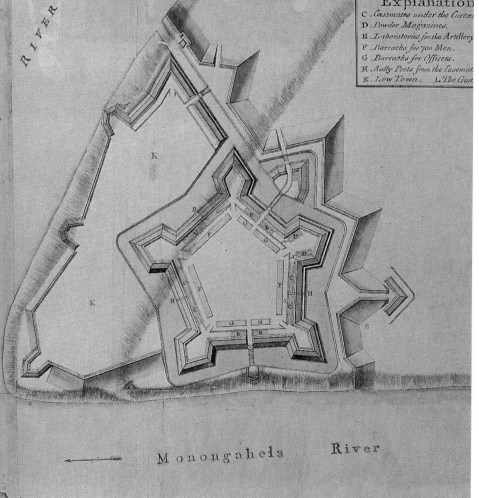

RIVER

Monongahela   River

fig. 1.8
EARLIEST KNOWN
PAINTING OF
PITTSBURGH, BY
GEORGE BECK, 1804

The town did not fare as well as the fort. For a decade it was a squatter settlement of shanties and log huts outside Fort Pitt. This rag-tag village was given a modicum of organization by British officer William Clapham, who in 1761 divided the settlement into an upper and a lower town, bisected by what is now Liberty Avenue. Grant and Market streets seem to have had a shadowy existence by that time, too. Most of the shanties were deliberately burned by the British commandant two years later in order to lift an Indian siege during Pontiac's Rebellion. It was the first of many instances of urban improvement by government edict.

The next year, 1764, the trader and surveyor John Campbell, who would later lay out Louisville, Kentucky, created the nucleus of an urban pattern called the "Military Plan" in four blocks along the Monongahela riverfront. One remnant of that plan can still be seen in tiny Chancery Street. But Pittsburgh could not move forward until a major dispute over ownership could be resolved. Three parties laid formal claim to the land on three occasions: the Delaware Indians in 1768, the Commonwealth of Virginia in 1779, and the heirs of William Penn in 1784. The Penns had made the strategic blunder of supporting England in the Revolution, but the Commonwealth of Pennsylvania allowed them to sell "the Manor of Pittsburgh" and several other holdings when their ancestral land grant was nullified. In haste, the Penns ordered Pittsburgh laid out in streets. The surveyors were George Woods and his teenage assistant, Thomas Vickroy; the time was 1784, eight years before Pierre L'Enfant produced his plan for the nation's capital city.

The surveyors faced several problems. One was the odd shape of the land, with its sudden rise of eighty feet at Grant's Hill, on the remnant of which the Allegheny County Courthouse now stands. A second was the surveyor's chain, which apparently was an inch too long for every ten feet. The third problem was the squatters, who used their muskets to persuade Woods to lay streets around rather than through the houses they had illegally built. Woods compromised by creating a triangular town, with one street grid parallel to the Allegheny, another parallel to the Monongahela, and an urban maze where the two grids clash on Liberty Avenue. The plan had its faults, but its tight geometry has kept the Triangle dense and lively for close to 250 years.

By inertia, if nothing else, the Woods street plan has taken on near-sacred status in Pittsburgh. Since 1784, the only significant changes have been the elimination of three streets to make way for Gateway Center in the early 1950s and of two short blocks for the construction of Oliver (now PNC) Plaza and PPG Place. Although the street plan of the Golden Triangle remained static, its building coverage changed with every generation. Overcrowding and the construction of factories next to residential buildings helped fuel the cholera epidemics of the 1830s and the Great Fire of 1845. The fire caused widespread damage and left twelve thousand Pittsburghers homeless.

To escape such urban dangers, hundreds of well-to-do families relocated to spacious villas on the Hill and in Oakland. Those districts became easier to reach after the railroad arrived in 1852 and the introduction of horse-drawn streetcars seven years later. Downtown lost its industrial plants and most of its churches and private residences to those newer districts and became primarily a commercial center.

9

fig. 1.9
MARKET SQUARE,
CA. 1796, AS
PORTRAYED IN AN
1852 PRINT

fig. 1.10
PITTSBURGH
AFTER THE GREAT
FIRE OF 1845

The young city could claim certain distinctions. In 1786, it got a newspaper (today's *Pittsburgh Post-Gazette*); by 1787, it had the beginnings of the University of Pittsburgh; and the next year, it became the seat of Allegheny County, which originally extended all the way north to Lake Erie. Until the 1820s, the city's wealth derived primarily from agricultural marketing and supplying thousands of settlers making their way west. The growth of Pittsburgh in its mercantile phase was steady but unspectacular: its population in 1850 was 46,601.

Despite the destruction of most of the Golden Triangle in the Great Fire of 1845 and the obliteration of nearly everything else by the construction of industrial plants, more of early Pittsburgh survives than one might suspect. A redoubt built at Fort Pitt in 1764, Beulah Chapel in Churchill, and the Burke Building on Fourth Avenue are good examples of late Georgian, Federal, and Greek Revival public architecture, respectively. Private architecture survives in even greater numbers: the Martin and Neill log houses in Squirrel Hill, both from the 1760s; a dozen wood and fieldstone houses in the South Hills and the North Hills; and two outstanding plantation houses. The older of these houses is Woodville, southwest of Pittsburgh, dating from 1785; the other is the Isaac Meason house of 1802 near Uniontown, about forty miles southeast of the city. Surviving photographs show monumental buildings designed by government architects Robert Mills, William Strickland, and John Haviland. Until the late 1980s, there was a fine building at the Allegheny Arsenal complex in Lawrenceville that could be linked to Benjamin Henry Latrobe, the most important designer of the early republic.

fig. 1.11
HOMEWOOD,
THE WILLIAM
WILKINS MANSION;
BUILT 1834,
DESTROYED, 1924

It was during the period from roughly 1840 to 1875 that Pittsburgh showed a decisive switch from a commercial to an industrial base both in its economy and its architecture. It was then that the city gained its worldwide reputation for smoke and soot—a perception that the passage of 150 years has failed to erase. The English novelist Anthony Trollope outlined the city's future reputation in the second volume of his travel observations, *North America*, published in 1862:

> Pittsburg is, without exception, the blackest place which I ever saw. …As regards scenery, it is beautifully situated, being at the foot of the Alleghany Mountains, and at the juncture of the two rivers Monongahela and Allegheny. Here, at the town, they come together, and form the River Ohio. Nothing can be more picturesque than the site.… Even the filth and wondrous blackness of the place are picturesque when looked down upon from above. The tops of the churches are visible and some of the larger buildings may be partially traced through the thick, brown, settled smoke. But the city itself is buried in a dense cloud.… I was never more in love with smoke and dirt than when I stood here and watched the darkness of night close in upon the floating soot which hovered over the house-tops of the city.… Certainly, Pittsburg is the dirtiest place I ever saw.

On the positive side, by the 1870s, Pittsburgh was the acknowledged "Forge of the Universe," turning out half the glass, half the iron, and much of the oil produced in the United States. In 1868, a Boston journalist, James Parton, reported finding fifty glass factories, sixteen potteries, forty-six foundries, thirty-one rolling mills, thirty-three machinery works, and fifty-three oil refineries in the city—some five hundred centers of production in all. Parton gave Pittsburgh its metaphorical title of "Hell with the Lid Taken Off" not to condemn the city, as Lincoln Steffens would employ it in 1904 in *The Shame of the Cities*, but in amazement at its scale and energy. It was this period also that saw the ethnic composition of the city shift from predominantly English and Scots-Irish, with some Irish and Germans, to a citizenry that was increasingly of Central and Eastern European birth.

The industrializing city began to speak a new visual language, too. One was that of the factories, which to Victorian Pittsburgh were more vital structures than its churches and public monuments. At this time, architects steeped in the classics were pushed aside by builders and engineers who were familiar with the iron and glass that Pittsburgh supplied in copious quantities. A visitor to Pittsburgh in 1852 commented, "There is a perfect mania here for

fig. 1.12
HENRY CLAY FRICK'S
COKE OVENS,
CONNELLSVILLE,
1886

improvements. Every day somebody commences to tear down an old house and put up a new one with an iron front." The best evidence of the region's early facility with structural iron is the Dunlap Creek Bridge in Brownsville, built in 1839 and America's first metal-arch bridge.

The architectural idiom of Pittsburgh's public buildings had begun to shift by about 1840, when the masculine and optimistic Greek Revival Style gave way to the more fantastic and escapist Gothic Revival. It also seemed as if the convulsive growth and industrialization had prompted the managerial class to seek house designs that transported them to an idyllic place, far removed from the environment they had created. The early Gothic Revival Style of the 1850s survives in four villas at Evergreen Hamlet, inspired by the publications of Andrew Jackson Downing, and in St. Luke's Church near Heidelberg. Minor buildings by the important Victorian designers John Notman and Frank Furness survive, though their major buildings in Pittsburgh have been destroyed.

In the 1880s, Pittsburgh's taste would change again, from Gothic to Romanesque Revival. On April 27, 1886, prominent American architect Henry Hobson Richardson rose from his deathbed and said, "If they honor me for the pygmy things I have already done, what will they say when they see Pittsburgh finished?" By "Pittsburgh," Richardson meant his Allegheny County Court-house and Jail, then as today acclaimed as the outstanding American building complex of the nineteenth century.

In aesthetic and social terms, the industrialization of Pittsburgh was not a change for the better. In 1852, Pittsburgh lost Liberty Avenue, its widest street, to the tracks of the Pennsylvania Railroad; they remained there until 1906. The unlovely aspect of Pittsburgh was not lost on the writer Willard Glazier, who described Pittsburgh in 1883 much more harshly than James Parton had fifteen years earlier: "Pittsburg is a smoky, dismal city, at her best. At her worst, nothing darker, dingier or more dispiriting can be imagined. The city is in the heart of the soft coal region; and the smoke from her dwell-ings, stores, factories, foundries and steamboats, uniting, settles in a cloud over the narrow valley in which she is built, until the very sun looks coppery through the sooty haze."

Glazier saw Pittsburgh at the beginning of its glorious but most notorious age, which ended with the deaths in 1919 of Andrew Carnegie and Henry Clay Frick, its two most representative figures. The half-century from 1865 to 1915 saw the creation of Pittsburgh's gigantic manufacturing complexes, beginning with Carnegie's Edgar Thomson Steel Works, in the satellite town of Braddock, in 1875. Other industries in the region built new mills that

fig. 1.13
ALLEGHENY COUNTY
COURTHOUSE
AS RENDERED BY
H. H. RICHARDSON'S
STUDIO, 1883

fig. 1.14
ENGINE OF INDUSTRY:
A PITTSBURGH BLAST
FURNACE OF THE LATE
NINETEENTH CENTURY

emulated the massive Thomson works until Pittsburgh's factories began to exceed in scale even the immense installations in England and Germany. H. J. Heinz centralized his food-processing operations in seventeen buildings on the North Side, and farther up the Allegheny, at New Kensington, Alcoa created the world's first complex for the production of aluminum. The huge glass plants of PPG stood upriver on the opposite bank of the Allegheny, at Creighton and Ford City. George Westinghouse commissioned factories of astonishing bulk for his electric works in East Pittsburgh, for his air brake plant in Wilmerding, and for his signaling works in Swissvale.

Around the turn of the twentieth century, the age of heroic industry reached a peak with the building of two spectacular plants. George Mesta constructed a machinery works in West Homestead, where he oversaw the world's largest presses and cutting dies. Then Jones & Laughlin produced its miles-long steelworks downstream on the Ohio at Aliquippa, with a meticulously crafted company town to house its workers.

This heroic era marked a peak in financial terms as well, as the various private cartels transformed themselves into publicly held corporations. In 1901, in an age that knew neither income tax nor severe inflation, Andrew Carnegie sold his steel-making operations to the forerunner of U.S. Steel for $492 million—the equivalent of nearly $50 billion today. Carnegie's personal take from the sale was about $350 million. The same transaction made instant millionaires of eighty-nine of Carnegie's top managers in Pittsburgh. Even more astute were the brothers A. W. Mellon and R. B. Mellon, the prime shareholders in Koppers, Carborundum, and Alcoa, and the major shareholders of Mellon Bank and Gulf Oil.

Fortunately, the industrialists who dominated the golden age of Pittsburgh had a good and sometimes excellent eye for architecture. From the Gilded Age, when the Beaux-Arts Style was in vogue (approximately 1890 to 1920, with a few designs from the 1930s), Pittsburgh still has buildings designed by George Post, Peabody & Stearns, Daniel Burnham, Bertram Grosvenor Goodhue, Ralph Adams Cram, John Russell Pope, and the moderately progressive Albert Kahn. Actually, of all the notable American architects of those decades, Pittsburgh lacks designs only from the pen of Louis Sullivan and Stanford White. (White had conceived but had not yet executed a statue base to stand opposite Carnegie Library when local resident Harry Thaw murdered him.)

Along with outside architects, Pittsburgh consistently produced its own capable designers. Carnegie and Frick, the Kaufmann family, and the Mellons gave their largest commissions to Pittsburgh-based architects, including Henry Hornbostel, Frederick Osterling, Alden & Harlow, Rutan & Russell, and Benno

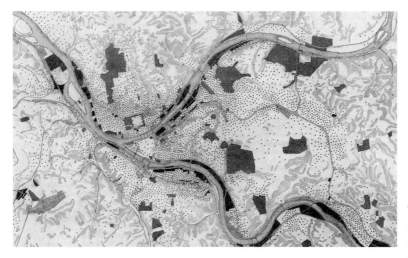

fig. 1.15
FREDERICK LAW
OLMSTED JR.'S 1910
STUDY; LIGHT GRAY
SHADING INDICATES
SLOPES TOO STEEP
TO BUILD ON

Janssen. Though local, all enjoyed national reputations and were regularly published in the major architectural magazines, as was Frederick Scheibler, a somewhat more unconventional designer of houses and apartment buildings.

The first years of the twentieth century were the proverbial best and worst of times for Pittsburgh. The city had been filling up with cash and capital at a prodigious rate, and its financial growth was matched by a population boom. The city welcomed the year 1900 with a population of 322,000, quadruple what it had been thirty years earlier. Thousands of immigrants poured into the region, many of them recruited in the villages of Eastern Europe by agents for Carnegie and Frick. Congress eventually banned this practice as industrial servitude.

The city was burgeoning in all its districts. The steel-making neighborhoods of the South Side, Hazelwood, Lawrenceville, and the Strip were appallingly crowded; the corporate-dominated boroughs and cities of Homestead, Braddock, East Pittsburgh, Turtle Creek, McKeesport, Duquesne, and McKees Rocks were little better. Pittsburgh remained a dark and unappealing town, particularly in winter. Streetlights burned around the clock, and soot was so pervasive that businessmen changed their white shirts two or three times a day.

Pittsburgh was also a tired town, dispirited with the bloody labor clashes in the Strip in 1877 and at Homestead in 1892, and embarrassed by the scathing indictment of social conditions in the Russell Sage Foundation's six-volume *Pittsburgh Survey* of 1909–1914. The Survey put the rates for typhoid fever and industrial accidents in Allegheny County as the highest in the nation. A few years later, the critic H. L. Mencken said of Pittsburgh,

> Here was the very heart of industrial America, the center of its most lucrative and characteristic activity, the boast and pride of the richest and grandest nation ever seen on earth—and here was a scene so dreadfully hideous, so intolerably bleak and forlorn that it reduced the whole aspiration of man to a macabre and depressing joke. Here was wealth beyond computation, almost beyond imagination—and here were human habitations so abominable that they would have disgraced a race of alley cats. I am not speaking of mere filth. One expects steel towns to be dirty. What I allude to is the unbroken and agonizing ugliness, the sheer revolting monstrousness, of every house in sight.

Not until the twentieth century was half finished would Pittsburgh seriously reform its worst environmental abuses, although it took its first steps in that direction around 1900. For the most part, the industrialists and civic leaders of the turn of the century preferred to engage in cosmetic urbanism, commissioning fine buildings that diverted attention from the real problems of the city. Carnegie led the way by funding his immense library, museum, and music hall in Oakland in 1890. Within two decades, Oakland, endowed with a huge flower conservatory, two fine university campuses, and a score of public halls and churches, presented itself as one of the best examples of the "City Beautiful" program of urban planning in the country. In the same years the business elite built five palatial railroad stations—one was by Philadelphia's Frank Furness, another by Chicago's Daniel Burnham—and a dozen of America's early skyscrapers. Pittsburghers enjoyed their buildings so much that a popular deck of cards in 1912 carried the images of fifty-two of them.

By 1900, the Golden Triangle was culturally and socially eclipsed by the Oakland district, but it retained its economic prominence in the region with the flood of cash unleashed on Pittsburgh by the creation of U.S. Steel. Carnegie's partner Henry Frick used some of his gains to erect four skyscrapers on Grant Street. A second partner, Henry Oliver (and his heirs), developed an equivalent block of holdings along Sixth and Oliver avenues. A third partner, Henry Phipps, created five more buildings where Sixth Street ended at the Allegheny riverfront. The Mellons followed with a half-dozen buildings of their own: their bank in 1924, skyscrapers for Koppers and Gulf around 1930, and Mellon Square and two more buildings in the early 1950s. Few Renaissance popes carved up Rome more effectively than these businessmen carved up Pittsburgh.

While the Golden Triangle developed within its boundaries, it also extended its dominance over the rest of the metropolitan district by becoming the focal point of the main roads in Allegheny County. This octopus configuration began to take shape with the arrival of the railroad in 1852, but its real impetus came in the first years of the motorcar, around 1900. Edward Manning Bigelow, the head of city planning (his actual title was more prosaic: public works director), created Schenley and Highland parks and four elegant motor promenades: Schenley Drive and Bigelow, Beechwood, and Washington boulevards. These fashionable roads rapidly spurred the development of residential Oakland, Squirrel Hill, Shadyside, Point Breeze, and Highland Park. Bigelow's four linked boulevards gave Pittsburgh an asphalt necklace, in a practical emulation of the "Emerald Necklace" of parks that Frederick Law Olmsted had given Boston a generation before.

In 1910, Frederick Law Olmsted Jr. proposed a fifth road to show off the Monongahela Valley as Bigelow Boulevard had highlighted the Allegheny; this road was eventually built in 1922–1927 as the Boulevard of the Allies. In the 1920s, the city also constructed Liberty Bridge and the Liberty Tunnels to link the Golden Triangle with the new suburbs south of the Monongahela River. Allegheny County simultaneously undertook construction of two other commuter roads to speed up traffic to suburbs in the Ohio and Allegheny river valleys.

The final arm of the octopus-like network of roadways was the Penn-Lincoln Parkway of the 1950s, which connected Pittsburgh to the Pennsylvania Turnpike on the east and to a new airport to the west. The road was built rather quickly, but it took another sixty years for local bureaucrats to give it the uniform designation of Interstate 376. The Parkway, the Crosstown expressway, and the rehabilitation of the Point had all been articulated in a master plan drawn up in 1939 by New York highway planner Robert Moses. The expansion of industrial research parks along the local expressways in the 1970s and 1980s affected but never eliminated the Golden Triangle's domination of the city and the county.

The years between the two world wars highlighted the romantic spirit in Pittsburgh's architecture, especially in terms of scale and exuberance. The grand scale derived from both the daunting topography and the colossal aspect of regional industry. A good example is George Richardson's Westinghouse Bridge (1932), whose record-breaking central span and concrete arches matched the heroic proportions of both the Turtle Creek Valley and the miles-long Westinghouse electric works nestled within it. A taste for the colossal and exuberant drove Charles Klauder's 535-foot-high Cathedral of Learning at the University of Pittsburgh and the adjacent Mellon Institute. Each of the sixty-two columns of the Mellon Institute is a single sixty-ton monolith of Indiana limestone. Their weight was so great that steel plates had to be set over the roadway manholes each time a column was brought to Oakland from the East Liberty railroad station. In the same years, Frank Lloyd Wright created for Edgar J. Kaufmann Sr. the ultimate Romantic fantasy home, Fallingwater, forty-five miles southeast of Pittsburgh.

While only one comparably ambitious building was erected in Pittsburgh after World War II—the Civic Arena, with its pioneering retractable dome—the city's taste for the colossal was evident in the reconstruction work undertaken during what was called the Pittsburgh Renaissance. After setting industrial production records in World War II, postwar Pittsburgh was an exhausted city, one that *Life* magazine called a sure candidate for the slag heap of history. Instead, under the leadership of the Allegheny Conference on Community Development, the city reversed its decline, throwing itself into planning for Gateway Center and Mellon Square, instituting smoke and flood control measures, and creating the first urban redevelopment authority in the nation. Encompassing a score of new skyscrapers and culminating in the construction of the U.S. Steel building in 1971, the Pittsburgh Renaissance still ranks as one of the most intensive reconstructions of any city center in history.

In the immediate prewar and postwar years, the city's leaders called in some of the most distinguished architects in the country. Among those who worked in Pittsburgh between 1930 and 1970 besides Wright (who built not only Fallingwater but a second Fayette County house) were Walter Gropius, Marcel Breuer, Mies van der Rohe, William Lescaze, Harrison & Abramovitz, Skidmore, Owings & Merrill, I. M. Pei, Edward Larabee Barnes, Hugh Stubbins, Johnson & Burgee, and The Architects Collaborative (TAC).

 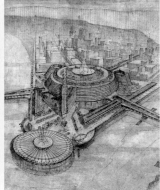

fig. 1.16
STEEL PLANTS
WITH DOWNTOWN
PITTSBURGH IN
THE BACKGROUND,
CA. 1950

fig. 1.17
FRANK LLOYD
WRIGHT'S
EXTRAVAGANT 1948
POINT PROPOSAL

What was lost sight of during Pittsburgh's Renaissance years was the distinctiveness of the city's architectural and urban legacy. Not only were important and potentially reusable buildings scrapped but entire neighborhoods were deemed expendable. The three worst mistakes of the Pittsburgh Renaissance were the misguided efforts that badly affected the Hill, the North Side, and East Liberty. Those three urban wounds have taken half a century to heal—and the remediation for the Hill is not yet finished.

The euphoria of the Pittsburgh Renaissance sent into oblivion many structures that should have remained as tangible links to the city's past. Four gigantic Jones & Laughlin mills disappeared: the Eliza Furnaces in South Oakland, alongside the Monongahela River; the South Side works on the opposite bank of the Monongahela; the LTV coke works in Hazelwood; and the mammoth Aliquippa works downriver on the Ohio. Gone, too, are the old U.S. Steel plants in both Homestead (a dozen ventilating stacks survive) and on the opposite bank of the Monongahela in Rankin (two blast furnaces were kept to serve as centerpieces for a planned National Historic Park of the Steel Industry). Upriver on the Monongahela, the world's most important tube works has vanished from McKeesport. Nearby, at Duquesne, the once towering Dorothy Six blast furnace is also gone.

The brownfields that remained after the domestic steel industry's collapse have been transformed to serve other purposes, or soon will be. Research parks and service centers have taken over most of the mill sites; shopping malls and housing occupy the rest. Today, begonias are the only plants you might find at the world-renowned Homestead works, where four generations of workers manufactured steel for navy battleships, the Panama Canal locks, and the Empire State Building. People running to movies, shops, and restaurants at the Waterfront or SouthSide Works see no tangible sign that men risked their lives working with molten steel on those very spots.

For the industrial installations still standing, the future looks either uncertain or grim. Among them is the Pennsylvania Drilling (Taylor-Wilson) plant in McKees Rocks; its construction was one of the world's pioneer achievements in the use of reinforced concrete. The same borough preserves— barely—the vast Pittsburgh & Lake Erie Railroad repair shops, where water now swamps the floors after each rain. The Westinghouse air brake plant in Wilmerding is still in operation, but how long it will survive is anyone's guess.

Among nonindustrial buildings in imminent danger is the New Granada Theater on the Hill. A 2008 emergency structural report on its condition may be a prelude to action on the building, which is in visible decay. In Larimer, pigeons fly in and out of the rose window at Our Lady Help of Christians

Church, and in Aspinwall the brick veneer is falling off the eccentric Frederick Sauer houses. In Homewood, Frederick Scheibler's triplet of the Syria, Kismet, and Nelda apartment buildings is disfigured by the loss of the Nelda to fire, and one wall of the Kismet is buckling to the point of no return.

Currently threatened with destruction are the grandiose Palladian-style Meason house near Uniontown, the Russian Orthodox cathedral on the Hill, the B'nai Israel synagogue in East Liberty, the Victorian shop fronts on lower Fifth Avenue opposite the new hockey arena, and the nearby Civic Arena on the Hill—yesterday's technical marvel now suddenly condemned as decrepit.

Other important structures suffer from abuse: Louis Kahn's offices and the *Tribune-Review* printing plant in Greensburg; Frederick Scheibler's Vilsack Row in Morningside; Frank Furness's elegant little railroad station in Edgewood; and two of Paul Schweikher's buildings: the Duquesne University student union building and station WQED in Oakland, both of which have lost their original steps.

Fortunately, there is another side to this story of neglect and deterioration: some of Pittsburgh's iconic monuments receive meticulous care. Extensive cleaning removed decades of industrial grime from both the University of Pittsburgh's Cathedral of Learning and the Carnegie museums and library. The Carnegie Museum of Art opened an elegant Heinz Architectural Center, and the Museum of Natural History built a soaring new home for its dinosaur exhibit. The Carnegie libraries in Braddock and Homewood were restored, and the Squirrel Hill branch was made over to produce new visual excitement; other new or restored libraries are on the way. Though much of the Mesta machine shop in West Homestead is gone, the sprawling house that the Mestas maintained nearby today looks as good as it did when fabled hostess Perle Mesta moved out, around 1925. The mansions that once housed such prominent families as the Schwabs, the Singers, the Kings, and the Fricks, as well as the Phipps Conservatory, the Schenley Park Visitors Center, and the entrance sculptures at Highland Park—all of these are once again in excellent condition. H. H. Richardson's Allegheny County Courthouse in Downtown is still suffering from neglect, but Courtroom 321 has been restored. Not merely restored but entirely rebuilt is George Washington's gristmill of 1776 at Perryopolis—a building that since the 1920s had existed only in photographs.

The task for Pittsburgh now is the remaking not just of certain buildings or blocks but of whole neighborhoods. Life is finally being coaxed back to the main urban battlefields—the Hill, the North Side, and East Liberty—not planned from above by industrialists in the Duquesne Club, as in the old days, but planted and nurtured by residents. Urban transformation is never a seamless transition, however. Shadyside has surrendered much of its charm in a relentless commercial makeover, Squirrel Hill has lost much of its retail activity to the Waterfront, and South Side has discovered that with its new prosperity comes a rowdy bar scene. The spottiness of Pittsburgh's urban health is also disturbing. The Strip and Lawrenceville are crowing at their revivals, and property values have jumped in Regent Square and Point Breeze, but there have been terrible losses on the Ohio at Aliquippa and in a dozen Monongahela Valley boroughs. The river towns of Braddock and Brownsville, once among the most characteristic industrial or commercial towns in western Pennsylvania, are both going begging for life support. Back in Pittsburgh, drive-by shootings dominate the news coming out of Homewood and Lincoln-Lemington, and it is a disgrace to see the African American community in Pittsburgh so marginalized in general.

READING PITTSBURGH AND ITS NEIGHBORHOODS

Cities are simultaneously visual environments, physical entities, and mental constructs, and so are the neighborhoods within them. You could even say that they achieve their greatest reality in the thousands of historical, cultural, and social memories stored away by their residents.

A neighborhood that succeeds as a distinct entity must have a strong sense of community, economic viability, and security. It also has a number of key visual characteristics, such as clear boundaries that separate it from other districts. It will also have a strong self-image, both visually and socially. A flourishing neighborhood typically has a strong central thoroughfare (the "main drag") that intersects with numerous side streets. A successful neighborhood also has significant monuments—not necessarily a bronze statue or war memorial but some structure or open place with high visibility that everyone in the neighborhood regards as exceptional. It may be a church, an old school, the borough hall, a fire hall, a Masonic temple, a movie theater, or some other commercial or even domestic element, so long as it is imposing enough and has been around long enough to project good memories.

Good neighborhoods have meaningful points of social interaction—visual backdrops that may or may not be "monuments" but are effective as meeting places. Such districts typically have particular colors, materials, or textures in common. And there will be visual "incidents"—things that stand out and break (and thus reinforce) the general pattern.

fig. 1.18
PITTSBURGH—
A CITY MADE UP
OF STRONG
NEIGHBORHOODS

fig. 1.19
ROWING ON THE
ALLEGHENY RIVER

Pittsburgh's neighborhoods meet these criteria in different ways. For "strong boundaries and clear separators," look at Downtown. The shape of the Golden Triangle, the earliest of Pittsburgh's neighborhoods, could hardly be more precise. It is shoehorned into a literal triangle shaped by the Monongahela and Allegheny rivers on two sides and Grant's Hill on the third. Grant's Hill has been whittled down considerably over the years, but the abrupt ending of Downtown's skyscrapers on that same line and the no-man's-land of the Crosstown expressway (Interstate 579) a block beyond tell visitors that they are leaving the town center as effectively as in the days when Grant's Hill was its original size.

Nearly all of the city's important neighborhoods have strong boundaries. South Side and North Side are bounded by rivers (the Monongahela and Allegheny, respectively) and hills (Mount Washington for the South Side, Troy Hill and Observatory Hill for the North Side). A dozen other Pittsburgh neighborhoods are bounded by channels eroded by glacial run-offs. Squirrel Hill is cut off from Oakland by Four Mile Run and from Regent Square by Nine Mile Run. Similarly, Highland Park is cut off from Morningside by Heth's Run and from Larimer by Negley Run. Elsewhere, Two Mile Run separates Lawrenceville from Polish Hill and Shadyside from Bloomfield and East Liberty. Squirrel Hill gets additional self-identify from its height: it seems like a miniature mountain to someone driving up from Shadyside or the banks of the Monongahela.

Troy Hill and Polish Hill have even steeper hills for their boundaries, while Shadyside is cut off from East Liberty by railroad tracks. Counterintuitively, perhaps, Shadyside also gains some identity by considering the fast traffic on Fifth Avenue to be one of its boundaries. Bloomfield attains some of its strong self-image from the fact that there is an excellent view of it from Oakland; Lawrenceville offers a similarly noteworthy view to motorists approaching it on the Washington Crossing Bridge. Greenfield also offers dramatic internal streetscapes, which can be viewed from either of its peaks.

As for the main drag and side street configurations, consider the side streets feeding into Butler Street in Lawrenceville, Liberty Avenue in Bloomfield, Second Avenue in Hazelwood, East Ohio Street in Allegheny East, or Chestnut Street in Deutschtown. Most elegant of all these thoroughfare connections is East Carson Street in South Side, a mile-long commercial and social conduit for the residential streets that feed into it.

As for monuments, whether architectural or cultural, one could argue that monuments and neighborhoods reinforce each other. The distinctiveness of a neighborhood's monumental structures may seem to detract from the collective style of a neighborhood, but the reality is different. Take Lawrenceville. Lawrenceville is all brick and frame houses, but if it were just that, it would not hold nearly as much interest for us as it does. Instead, it presents a pattern made up of a thousand small houses punctuated by fine churches, banks, a library, and a robotics factory. There is only one Doughboy Square and only one Iron City Brewery in Lawrenceville, but those two eccentricities, and a few more like it, are what make Lawrenceville a unique place.

For a stunning example of a monument that sums up a whole neighborhood, look no farther than the basilica of Polish Hill: Immaculate Heart of Mary Church. It advertises (or "brands," as one might now say) Polish Hill to outsiders, but it fosters even more pride in insiders. All monuments serve as visual incidents, emphasizing the sameness in a neighborhood by setting up a dramatic contrast between what is ordinary and what is monumental.

Most—though not all—monuments also nourish their communities by serving as points of social interaction. This is certainly true of the hundreds of structures built for religious services in the Pittsburgh area. St. Rosalia's in Greenfield even has a built-in piazza that is the perfect place to socialize after Mass. Similar gathering spaces are provided in scores of Carnegie libraries, union and volunteer fire halls, and sports venues. Oaklanders gather at the merry-go-round in Schenley Plaza (a perfect neighborhood monument even though it has been there only since 2007); Highland Parkers sun themselves by the reservoir; Squirrel Hillers stroll on the Schenley Park oval. Each of these neighborhood fixtures helps to reinforce the identity of the local community.

When thinking of a neighborhood in terms of colors, materials, and textures common to many of its structures, one might point to such examples as the serrated rhythm of the frame houses leaning over the slopes of Spring Hill, or the brick townhouses of the Mexican War streets area, always unified but never uniform, or the streets paved with bricks in Regent Square and Clairton, the stained-glass windows so common in Shadyside, or the Kool Vent aluminum awnings in the working-class parts of town. Among the best visual incidents that reinforce the otherwise cohesive appearance of a neighborhood are the gold-domed Orthodox churches in Homestead, Rankin, McKees Rocks, and Carnegie; the huge statue of St. Joseph the Worker hovering over the flat terraces of Munhall and clearly depicting a steelworker rather than a carpenter; the equally large statue of St. Benedict the Moor blessing the Hill; or the murals that the Sprout Fund has created in every district. Sometimes one building group serves more than one function. On Penn Avenue, the Lackzoom Acidophilus store is a visual incident, but the Plaza Theater in Bloomfield and the old Bageland in Squirrel Hill both were once visual monuments and social meeting places. The Plaza and Bageland have both been recycled for other uses now, but that process has given them something else in common, which is a sort of neighborhood archaeology. You can read decades of history in the façades of these structures, as the style of one era mutated into another.

One way to think of neighborhoods is to consider them pieces of the wider urban puzzle that forms a city. In this analogy, a city is born with one piece put in place and grows as pieces are added over time. Like some other major cities, Pittsburgh followed this logical growth pattern to a T, but with a critical difference. Some cities followed a particular blueprint as they grew. For example, Beijing grew outward from the Forbidden City in concentric squares; Moscow expanded from the Kremlin in concentric circles; Amsterdam added concentric pentagon after pentagon. Pittsburgh also grew outward from a core, but it threw away the blueprint and assumed a dizzying variety of forms. Downtown, the North Side, and South Side resembled triangles; the settlements along Penn and Fifth avenues took on the shape of trapezoids; Oakland puffed itself up as a square; the river valley settlements developed as rectangles; and suburbia has expanded Pittsburgh along a north-south axis. But at every moment, even when it sprawled, the city kept to a logical if not elegant urban layout.

Although Pittsburgh's geometric pattern of growth was not neatly confined to circles or squares or pentagons, it did proceed in identifiable units. One by one, eight pieces of the urban puzzle accumulated, and these eight pieces make up the next eight chapters of this book. In chronological order they are:

- the Golden Triangle at the Forks of the Ohio, laid out as a city in 1784;

- the North Side, on the opposite bank of the Allegheny, laid out in 1788;

- the South Side, on the opposite bank of the Monongahela, first industrialized in 1795;

- the neighborhoods along Penn Avenue, which began to develop on the flat ground east of Downtown around 1800, with the avenue eventually extending into a turnpike some nine miles long within the city and two hundred miles beyond its limits;

- the neighborhoods along Fifth Avenue, which started to expand through the hilly central strip of Pittsburgh beginning around 1810;

- Oakland, established three miles east of Downtown as an enclave for the wealthy when horsecars (carriages on iron rails, like trolleys, but pulled by horses) made it accessible after 1859 and then turned into an elegant civic center three decades later;

- the three river valleys, whose rapid industrialization began with Carnegie's steel mill in Braddock in 1875; and

- suburbia, beginning with some relatively small railroad-based colonies and greatly boosted by construction of the Allegheny and Ohio river boulevards in the 1920s, the turnpike and the Parkway in the 1940s, and the combining of the interstates into a sort of triangular beltway in the 1970s.

PITTSBURGH AT 250

Pittsburgh celebrated the 250th anniversary of its naming in 2008 and has marked half a century since the sweeping changes of the city's Renaissance. With some grim exceptions, contemporary Pittsburgh is generally well off, but the optimism that fed its industrial growth and the renewal of the Renaissance period has faded. The reason for the lack of a positive civic outlook is puzzling. After all, the RAND Corporation and Google have both opened substantial branches in the area, and Vivísimo (a search engine of global scope) is just one of hundreds of start-up businesses in information technology and biotech fields. Bill Gates thought enough of Carnegie Mellon to finance its newest venture in computer science. Nobody paid *Places Rated Almanac* to rate Pittsburgh as America's most livable city once, never mind twice (1985 and 2007).

Even more significantly, Pittsburgh has gone global a second time. The city had a tremendous global reach when it was an industrial power, but after its retreat from the world stage it has taken much prodding for it to reach out a second time. Globalization may seem highly negative if one views it as selling the city's businesses to overseas buyers. When the Westinghouse conglomerate broke up in the 1990s, an Italian firm bought the switching subsidiary and established a branch headquarters in Pittsburgh. Similarly, first a British and then a Japanese firm took over Westinghouse Electric.

But globalization has brought just as much to Pittsburgh that is positive. It was not the United States but China that launched the meteoric recovery of Westinghouse Electric with a half dozen orders for nuclear plants. Chemicals and pharmaceuticals giant Bayer gave the same impetus to the city by establishing its North American headquarters here. Globalization has also reinvigorated old Pittsburgh institutions. The University of Pittsburgh Medical

Center (UPMC) went global years ago, running its own organ-transplant complex in Sicily. Today, the University of Pittsburgh and Carnegie Mellon operate numerous branch campuses or programs in Europe and Asia. The international standing of Pittsburgh as a city with true global vision was confirmed in 2009, when the city was given a plum much desired the world over as the site of the G-20 Economic Summit.

Conservative though it is, Pittsburgh continually turns itself around. It was the city where venture capitalism was born, when Frick, Westinghouse, and Charles Martin Hall came to Pittsburgh after the Civil War and needed financing for their coke ovens, air brakes, and aluminum. After a long retreat from prominence in venture capital activity, today Pittsburgh ranks (in a PricewaterhouseCoopers study) as the second-fastest-growing region in the United States in venture capital for high-tech firms. The Pittsburgh Life Sciences Greenhouse has had particular success in bringing together investors and start-up bioscience companies. The speed with which Pittsburgh can reinvent itself may be best exemplified by bicycling; it took just two decades to go from one of the worst to among the best of American cities for the sport. The twenty-four miles of trails that now enhance Pittsburgh's waterfronts give a taste of the local cycling possibilities; dozens of old railroad trackbeds have been converted to bike paths. (Western Pennsylvania has more of these "rails-to-trails" than anywhere else in the nation.) From Pittsburgh you can now bike the uninterrupted 335-mile Great Allegheny Passage and the C&O Towpath to Washington, DC. Most city buses carry bicycle racks. Bikers in other cities know of Pittsburgh's excellent cycling, and at least a few have moved here just for that reason.

External changes to the city indicate that things are changing internally, too. With Pittsburgh's business community no longer as all-powerful as it was in the past, the city's generally conservative lifestyle has modified, too. In 1977, I had to usher the architectural critic Ada Louise Huxtable through the "ladies' door" at the Duquesne Club when we met for lunch, but thanks to social progress no one has used that door in years. Secure in its majority lifestyle, Pittsburgh today is more accepting of citizens who follow minority or unconventional lifestyles, probably because so much depends on their economic input. Andrew Carnegie was, and remains, the most important person in the history of Pittsburgh, but he died in 1919. Four of the most creative Pittsburghers in the decades since were the ecologist Rachel Carson, the playwright August Wilson, the artist Andy Warhol, and E. J. Kaufmann Sr., the man who built Fallingwater—a woman, an African American, a gay man, and a Jew. Newcomers, whether from foreign lands or other parts of the

fig. 1.20
THE FORKS OF
THE OHIO TODAY

United States, are still too few, but whoever arrives will find a welcome. A dozen Hindu and Buddhist temples and Muslim mosques, expressing this welcome visually as well as socially, have joined the steeples and golden domes erected by prior arrivals.

Despite these successes, Pittsburgh mysteriously persists in a sense of unease. The defining characteristic of industrial-era Pittsburgh was how hard it worked. That work ethic still exists, so the defining characteristic of twenty-first-century Pittsburgh seems to be how much it worries about itself. In 1995, a civic panel spent $222,000 to come up with a text that was supposed to define the city, but the result was nothing more than boilerplate booster-ism. Such an exercise defines the break between the old Pittsburgh and the new. The old Pittsburgh was rich enough to ignore the taunts of other cities and had no doubts about its place in the universe. The certitude that "all is well since all grows better"—the motto etched around the statue of Andrew Carnegie in Carnegie Institute—suffered a temporary eclipse after World War II, when Pittsburgh really was dying, but the city regained its confidence with the Pittsburgh Renaissance and the boom that lasted into the 1970s and 1980s. Certain developments early in the 1980s were troubling, especially when mammoth Gulf Oil capitulated to Chevron, a corporation just one-twentieth its size.

The collapse of the domestic steel industry in the 1980s was cause for real worry in the Pittsburgh region. A domino effect seemed to take hold, as the city lost one of its two newspapers, a dozen corporations downsized or left town, and the population continued to drop. This worrisome time for Pittsburgh lasted until about 2000. Although the worst of the downturn seems past (Pittsburgh counted 311,000 residents in 2007, with 2.35 million in its metropolitan area), the city remains uneasy about itself even when the news is good. In 2003, the mass-circulation *USA Weekend* asked readers to vote on the most scenic view in the country. The nighttime view of Downtown from Mount Washington came in second only to the Grand Canyon, but many in Pittsburgh thought the contest was fixed. The same lack of confidence emerged in 2006 from a study that tested how thirty American towns thought of themselves compared to what outsiders thought of them. In twenty-nine cities the locals had a higher opinion of the place than did outsiders; Pittsburgh was the sole exception.

What haunts Pittsburgh today is the sense that the city is not just post-industrial but post-heroic. For a hundred years it was the classic overachiever among American cities. How does a once-dominant force in world industry accept being no more than an average American town today? Carnegie, Frick,

Westinghouse, Heinz, the Mellons, the Rockwells, Gulf, Alcoa, and PPG were the global celebrities of their day. Pittsburgh gave, or rather sold, the world its first processed or mass-produced oil, steel, aluminum, and glass, and it perfected three other techniques just as critical to modern life. H. J. Heinz created the world's first hygienically packaged food, Westinghouse supplied alternating current electricity to supplant Edison's direct current version in every corner of the globe, and Jonas Salk perfected the first polio vaccine.

That historical record can never be taken away, but what on the scale of those achievements has come from Pittsburgh lately? The city's post-heroic malaise is compounded by another factor. The staggering productivity that once characterized Pittsburgh is rarely associated with it today. Andrew Carnegie's thousands of libraries around the world, Salk's polio vaccine, Rachel Carson's books, George Washington Ferris's carnival wheels, Stephen Foster's songs, Heinz ketchup, the Rockwell space shuttle, Andy Warhol's silkscreens— so much of what was produced in Pittsburgh now belongs to the world. The same issue applies to Pittsburgh-based philanthropies such as the Arthur Vining Davis, Heinz, Mellon, Scaife, and Carnegie funds, and it is even more painfully true of Pittsburgh's fabled art collections, seven of which have been moved elsewhere. Andrew Mellon's Renaissance canvases and Paul Mellon's Modern paintings are now in the National Gallery in Washington, DC, Duncan Phillips sent his exquisite Postimpressionist art to the same city, Henry Frick set up his Old Masters in New York, Paul Mellon left his British works to Yale, and Louise and Walter Arensberg installed their Dada and Cubist art in Philadelphia. Meanwhile, in the 1960s, G. David Thompson's brilliant collection of early Modern art (originally offered to Pittsburgh, but turned down) was scattered by auction to museums worldwide.

Despite the loss of industries, jobs, and cultural artifacts, Pittsburgh remains a remarkably cohesive town, its various elements coming together to find success. The early farmers distilled their grain into whiskey because it was easier to transport a few bottles and jugs rather than tons of grain over the Alleghenies to markets in the East. Making whiskey and beer required the manufacture of glass bottles, with fires fueled by local coal; the steel barons later used the same coal (refined into coke) to fire their blast furnaces. Heinz used Pittsburgh's glass and steel to package his foods, while Westinghouse applied the compressed air of the blast furnaces to power his railroad brakes and rail switches.

Cohesiveness is also the key to Pittsburgh's social life. The city is often cited as having the highest percentage of owner-occupied homes in the nation, which goes hand-in-hand with its strong work ethic and low divorce and crime rates. The richness of Pittsburgh's social fabric can also be seen in its landscape, not merely read in statistics. Sitting astride its hills and snuggled in its valleys are the ethnic neighborhoods outlined and preserved by the streams and gullies (Pittsburghers call them "runs" and "hollows") that form their natural boundaries. These ethnic communities include a substantial Arab presence in Oakland, and people of Slovak, Ukrainian, and Russian descent are still a significant group on the South Side, though outnumbered now by students and young executives who provide no discernible evidence of their ethnic heritage. Italians remain numerically significant in Mt. Washington, in Bloomfield, and in Junction Hollow, and there are still African Americans on the Hill, in Homewood, and in Manchester. People with German surnames still live on Troy Hill and Spring Hill and people with Polish names, on Polish Hill. One of American's most cohesive Jewish communities has flourished for a hundred years in Squirrel Hill, and many residents of the affluent boroughs of Fox Chapel and Sewickley Heights still carry the names of Pittsburgh's original Scots-Irish founders.

Though weaker than it once was, there is a distinctive civic identity to Pittsburgh. The population loss has forced churches all over town to be torn down or turned into condos, bars, or restaurants, yet religious observance in Pittsburgh still remains higher than the national average. (The Port Authority runs a special bus service on Sundays to get worshipers to churches on the Hill.) Any visitor will notice the local passion for sports—not just spectator sports and rooting for the Steelers in bars but also the abundant opportunities for golfing, boating, hiking, and biking. The city's cultural offerings show up just as notably in any national survey. Pittsburgh continues to eat certain cherished foods, like chipped ham and sandwiches that have french fries inside rather than alongside. And it continues to speak its own language: "redd up" for clean, "yinz" for you-all, "gumbands" for rubber bands or elastics, "anymore" for nowadays, and many other peculiarities of usage and accent, like the way television's Mr. Rogers pronounced *um*brella. The leading grocery chain is not called Giant Eagle but "th'iggle." "D'jeet yet?" one hungry Pittsburgher will ask another; "no, d'jyou?" And were Hamlet a Pittsburgher, his famed soliloquy would be reduced to "…or not…" because the verb "to be" is often dropped from constructions, as in something "needs fixed." Linguists regard these speech patterns as among the richest and most complex in the nation.

Perhaps the tight bond between the residents and their city and to each other may stem from the city's daunting topography. To span all of the rivers and valleys, Pittsburgh has 446 bridges, far more than Venice, Amsterdam, or

fig. 1.21
PITTSBURGH IS A
CITY OF BRIDGES:
THE MONONGAHELA
IN FOG

fig. 1.22
THE TWO ANDYS:
WARHOL AND CARNEGIE.
SMITHFIELD STREET
MURAL BY SARAH ZAFFIRO
AND TOM MOSSER, 2006.

St. Petersburg, Russia. To cut through the hills, Pittsburgh bored a score of tunnels; to get up and down the hills it erected 739 sets of public stairs, incorporating 45,415 individual steps. The city defines 323 of these public stairs as legal streets.

The topographic barriers can be inconvenient: the airport, for example, had to be built almost twenty highway miles from the Golden Triangle to secure enough flat land for its runways. But the hills also make Pittsburgh a forested city, since one-third of it is too steep to be built on and is covered with trees. Its topography helps unify Pittsburgh in yet another way. *USA Weekend*'s quest to find the most scenic view in the country hinted at one aspect of why citizens here are so loyal to Pittsburgh: they can see it, in its totality, anytime they drive up Mount Washington. Cities that can see themselves seem to display a stronger sense of cohesion than cities that cannot.

Pittsburgh's dramatic setting was for years answered by the heroic scale and complexity of its industry and architecture. This industry has always been larger than life, whether the product was steel, robots, or spacecraft. Pittsburgh fabricated the steel for Chicago's skyscrapers and engineered the Gateway Arch in St. Louis, trained the genius who designed the Brooklyn Bridge, and produced new copper sheets when the Statue of Liberty grew old. In the days when it was still a cauldron of smoke by day and fire by night, the Pittsburgh region tended to the raw and masculine, spawning, for example, some first-rate quarterbacks, including Joe Namath, Johnny Unitas, Joe Montana, and Dan Marino. But the environment equally nurtured musicians, photographers, filmmakers, and writers who were born in or did their best work while living here. These included composers Stephen Foster, Victor Herbert, and Henry Mancini; performers Oscar Levant, Lena Horne, Billy Eckstine, Erroll Garner, Art Blakey, Ahmad Jamal, Perry Como, Byron Janis, and Lorin Maazel; writers Willa Cather, Gertrude Stein, Mary Roberts Rinehart, George S. Kaufman, David McCullough, Annie Dillard, August Wilson, and Michael Chabon; engineers John Augustus Roebling and George Washington Ferris; pioneer African American painter Henry Ossawa Tanner as well as Mary Cassatt, Philip Pearlstein, Mel Bochner, and Andy Warhol; dancers Martha Graham and Gene Kelly; and actor Jimmy Stewart.

A good many of these artists put their specific focus on Pittsburgh. August Wilson set nine of his ten plays in Pittsburgh, and two of Michael Chabon's novels were about the city. For decades George Romero used the city, affectionately, as the background for his horror movies. Duane Michals, Luke Swank, Harold Corsini, Clyde Hare, Charles "Teenie" Harris, Herb Ferguson, and Walt Urbina are just a few of the numerous Pittsburgh photographers with international reputations, and the celebrated W. Eugene Smith did some of the best work of his career here. Thousands of canvases by the Wall brothers, John Alexander, Aaron Gorson, Johanna Hailman, Romare Bearden, Otto Koerner, and others have offered various artistic interpretations of the cityscape. The Spanish artist Felix de la Concha painted hundreds of views of Pittsburgh and Fallingwater, and the visual character of the city is being reinforced again by the murals going up in every quarter. Many arguments have been advanced to show how much Andy Warhol owed artistically to his birthplace.

Perhaps the most iconic image of Pittsburgh is the Pietà painted in 1933 by the self-taught John Kane, who set Mary's lamentation over the body of Christ in the middle of Oakland. You can easily make out the Cathedral of Learning, Carnegie Institute, and St. Paul Cathedral in the background. Such unselfconscious identification between an artist and a city parallels the love the medieval painters Duccio and Giotto bore for their hometowns of Siena and Florence, which they substituted for Christ's Jerusalem in their paintings. Not all Pittsburghers express their urban attachment as artistically as filmmaker George Romero or painter John Kane, but the bond between the city and its citizens remains passionate and deep.

Of the various categories of artists, it is architects who typically have the greatest power in shaping a city's image. Pittsburgh's topography and industrial infrastructure seem to have left an indelible mark on the engineers and architects who have built here. The old Pittsburgh was fortunate to have attracted talented architects, and that luck continues. Among contemporary designers who have built here are Robert Venturi, Richard Meier, Kallmann McKinnell & Wood, Kohn Pedersen Fox, Michael Graves, and Rafael Viñoly. There is also an important seminal work in nearby Greensburg by the master beyond school, Louis Kahn. With the exception of Viñoly, though, the practice of bringing architects of international importance to Pittsburgh has stalled of late.

Several hundred architects practice their profession in Pittsburgh today. The firms whose work is regularly published nationally include Astorino, Bohlin Cywinski Jackson, Burt Hill, Desmone & Associates, The Design Alliance, dggp Architecture, DRS, EDGE Studios, IKM, Tasso Katselas, Lubetz Architects, MacLachlan Cornelius & Filoni, Perkins Eastman, Pfaffman + Associates, Rothschild Doyno, Strada, Urban Design Associates, and WTW.

Unfortunately, the creativity expressed in the built environment and cultural scene does not extend to every sphere of activity, particularly in its adherence to traditional or outdated governing practices. The metropolitan area's political and fiscal capital is diluted because Allegheny County is divided into 130 separate municipalities. This is a drawback 364 days of the year, the exception being the Fourth of July, when each borough determinedly sets off its own fireworks. In addition, regional agencies do not seriously promote tourism. A score of first-rate sites just outside Pittsburgh (described in chapter 9) all go begging for visitors, except for Fallingwater (and Pittsburgh pays only perfunctory attention even to that masterpiece). Would other cities give a cold shoulder to the most architecturally famous house of the twentieth century?

A social worker might say that Pittsburgh needs to come to terms with its outsized past, and the city may be taking tentative steps in that direction by finally expanding its pantheon of heroes beyond Carnegie and Frick, Heinz and Westinghouse. One sign of this change is the naming of bridges. Over the Allegheny there are now bridges commemorating Roberto Clemente, Andy Warhol, and Rachel Carson, and over the Monongahela there are bridges named for labor leader Philip Murray and the Homestead Grays of the Negro League Baseball. Monumental sculptures or markers now depict native or adopted Pittsburghers such as baseball sensations Honus Wagner, Roberto Clemente, and Willie Stargell; writers August Wilson and Gertrude Stein; Gene Kelly; Steelers' founder Art Rooney; Mayor Richard Caliguiri; and television's Mr. Rogers. A new sculpture on Mount Washington recalls how important Pittsburgh was to George Washington, and vice versa.

The old Pittsburgh had terrible economic disparities, but with tremendous labor it forged itself into a highly distinctive place. It was a production center, and production (unlike services or the information industry) is tied to a place where workers, raw materials, fuel, and machinery can be coordinated. That type of integrated activity runs counter to the way businesses in the United States now organize themselves. Technology has made place or location far less relevant; a cell phone area code no longer instantly identifies what city a person is calling from, and emails and Web sites are often identified by no country or continent at all. But this national trend away from the importance of place may work to Pittsburgh's advantage. Since most of us no longer need to live in any specific place, why not move to Pittsburgh, where life is easy, the cost of living is low, the city is attractive, and the residents friendly and helpful? With all these positive qualities, Pittsburgh deserves to feel comfortable in its own skin. The city has been in transition for the past thirty or forty years, but it is time to realize that the transition is over: the Pittsburgh of the future is already here. Pittsburgh will truly be renewed when it accepts that its strengths are only built on the past: they are not imprisoned there.

DOWNTOWN: A GOLDEN TRIANGLE

fig. 2.1
THE GOLDEN
TRIANGLE

O f the various claims about who first likened downtown Pittsburgh to a Golden Triangle, one has primacy. After the Great Fire of 1845 ravaged the city's core, Mayor William Howard is said to have declared, "We shall make of this triangle of blackened ruins a golden triangle whose fame will endure as a priceless heritage."

The Golden Triangle nickname was already well established locally by 1914, when an article in the *Saturday Evening Post* gave it national publicity. The nickname was a good fit because the 255 acres bounded by Grant Street and the Allegheny and Monongahela rivers must count among the most gilded in the United States, having generated immense wealth. The Triangle constitutes a city in itself, with retail strips on Wood and Smithfield streets and Forbes and Fifth avenues, a government center on Grant, two churches and the Duquesne Club on Sixth Avenue, and extensive cultural facilities set among the cast-iron fronts and loft buildings on Penn and Liberty avenues.

The compactness of the Golden Triangle is a marvel in its own right: no two of its points are more than a fifteen-minute walk apart. The subway route from Grant Street to Gateway Center is so tiny that its entire length is shorter than the subway platform beneath Times Square in New York.

Being so small, downtown Pittsburgh is the preserve of pedestrians. In winter, they tend to stay indoors by using the subway and the tunnels, atriums, and interior streets of the new buildings. During the other seasons they move outdoors and enjoy Point State Park or Market Square, which has been hosting public gatherings since 1784. At noon every day, lunch crowds descend on Mellon Square, PPG Place, PNC Plaza, or the plazas set around the U.S. Steel tower and 625 Liberty. PPG Place was designed as a contemporary variant of Paris's Place Vendôme, but its main attraction now is a fountain that doubles in winter as an ice-skating rink.

The remaking of the Triangle during the Pittsburgh Renaissance of the 1950s was a closely guarded process, led by Richard King Mellon and Mayor David L. Lawrence with a largely self-taught staff under Park Martin, Wallace Richards, and John Robin. The upgrading of the Triangle in the 1980s (the so-called Renaissance II) was, by contrast, a technocratic rather than an autocratic process, with Mayor Richard Caliguiri and the Urban Redevelopment Authority devising the urban upgrades. The results were nevertheless substantial: the subway, cosmetic improvements to Grant Street, the first Lawrence Convention Center (even though it was a functional and artistic disappointment), Liberty Center, Oxford Centre, Mellon Center, PPG Place, Chatham Center II, Fifth Avenue Place, and 625 Liberty in the Triangle, with spin-off developments in the Strip, the South Side, and the North Side. These renewal efforts involved about five times as much building as in the original Renaissance projects in the 1950s.

fig. 2.2
THE FOUNTAIN
AT THE POINT

fig. 2.3
DOWNTOWN,
LOOKING WEST TO
THE OHIO RIVER

In the twenty-first century the Triangle is undergoing a different kind of change. No longer just a place to which business people commute, it has recently become home to some three thousand residents, with up to five times that number projected to move Downtown in the decade beginning in 2010. Across the whole of Downtown and in the adjacent Strip, dozens of older buildings have been converted to student dormitories, apartments, or condominiums.

Parking remains a hurdle to Downtown redevelopment, not so much in its scarcity as its cost. (However, you can park all day in downtown Pittsburgh for the price of a half hour in midtown Manhattan.) Retail is spotty: the suburban malls get most of the trade, and the only large department store still in Downtown is the Macy's that was Kaufmann's for 135 years. Only one movie theater remains from the dozen of a century ago. Overall, though, entertainment and the arts are flourishing Downtown. The Pittsburgh Cultural Trust now manages five updated theaters and concert halls in the Triangle: Heinz Hall, Benedum Center, the Byham and O'Reilly theaters, and the Harris Theater, an art cinema. Finally diversified from its old state as a purely business center, the Triangle's current health is vigorous: where it leads, the rest of Pittsburgh will follow.

fig. 2.4
THE MONONGAHELA
WATERFRONT

THE POINT AND THE MONONGAHELA RIVERFRONT

I n 1868, Boston journalist James Parton wrote of Pittsburgh, "On that low point of land, fringed now with steamboats and covered with grimy houses, scarcely visible in the November fog and smoke, modern history began." Not everyone would agree with Parton that "modern history" first announced itself in Pittsburgh. Events of some importance also took place in Williamsburg, Boston, and Philadelphia, not to mention Athens, Florence, and Runnymede. But the juncture of the Monongahela and Allegheny rivers—known as the Forks of the Ohio in the eighteenth century—was the setting for three milestones. At that spot in 1758, North America was secured for the British and not the French. In 1875, Andrew Carnegie's revolutionary steel mill secured the industrial might of the world for the United States and not Europe. In 1945, there began one of the most striking rebirths of any city in the country.

The fifty-nine acres at the Forks of the Ohio are today split between Point State Park and Gateway Center, together encompassing twelve office and residential towers, four bridges over land and water, two military strong-holds, and one of the world's more vivid fountains. The views across the water to the South Side and North Side capture the industrial history of Pittsburgh, while on the land side stands Gateway Center, the starting point for the city's rebirth in the 1950s. It is not much of an exaggeration to say that without Gateway Center, the city might have withered to an unrecognizable husk of its former glory.

The British intended Fort Pitt to be their stronghold in North America, and its construction became the first great accomplishment in Pittsburgh. When a military engineer, Captain Harry Gordon, devised it in 1759, he had the benefit of three centuries of advancement in the science of fortifications, going all the way back to Renaissance Italy. Gordon gave the fort the shape of a slightly irregular pentagon with five pointed bastions. The bastions mini-mized cannon fire from direct broadside hits on the long sides and helped pin down enemy troops before they could storm the walls. Two of the bastions had walls nearly fifteen feet high and seven and a half feet thick. Those solid stone walls were faced with 1,244,160 bricks. The fortress walls were keyed to the kinds of attacks the British anticipated: on the land side, from which infantry would attack, the walls were of brick and stone; facing the water, across which cannon would fire, there were earthworks to absorb the blows. Inside the fort was a parade ground with casemates (underground rooms framed in timber), magazines, and housing for a thousand men; outside was a moat with a drawbridge and an earthen embankment. The bricks were made locally, the stone was quarried locally, and the timber was planed at a stream in Pittsburgh's West End that has ever since been known as Saw Mill Run.

Luckily, the greatest fort England ever built in the Western Hemisphere was put to the test only once, in Pontiac's Rebellion of 1763. Despite its elegance, the fort had major problems. The river-oriented earthworks eroded badly in the spring floods, and none of the bastions proved effective against snipers.

In 1764, dismayed by the fort's poor performance, Colonel Henry Bouquet constructed five redoubts outside its walls to catch snipers in crossfire; one of them survives. Fort Pitt and the other four redoubts were allowed to tumble into ruins just one generation after the French threat ended. When the Grenadier, Music, and Flag bastions were rebuilt in the 1950s, their plans and details were based on archaeological observations. Nonetheless, experts later found fault with the restoration: the Music Bastion was not accurate, the bricks in the walls being mostly modern, and the moat opposite the Hilton Hotel was narrower and shallower than the original. These charges were used as justification for filling in the moat in 2008 in order to expand the area for concerts and other public events.

The Block House, as Colonel Bouquet's surviving pentagonal redoubt is misnamed, still carries his name and the date 1764 inscribed over the door. It retains its original sandstone base, a complete rim of wooden girders, and coursed common-bond brick walls. Iron cranking plates in the walls support the upper floor, and the diminutive building bears a modern pyramidal roof of wooden shingles. This glimpse into American colonial history is the oldest surviving structure in Pittsburgh.

By the first decades of the nineteenth century, Fort Pitt had been so thoroughly vandalized that even the earthen ramparts were gone. A few voices suggested that the Point could be turned into the city's first park, but the fate of the site was sealed in 1854, when the Pennsylvania Railroad built the Duquesne Freight Depot directly over the ruins. It would take nearly a century for the city and state to redevelop the Point for shared use as a historic park and an office complex. In 1947, while the development of Gateway Center was being debated, Edgar J. Kaufmann gave Frank Lloyd Wright a new commission (they had partnered to create Fallingwater a decade earlier). Kaufmann wanted renderings for a circular megastructure thirteen levels high and one-fifth of a mile in diameter, with a helical auto ramp that would have been four and a half miles long. Pittsburgh shied away from this oversized vision of the future, which would have obliterated the historical relics

fig. 2.5
FORT PITT BLOCK
HOUSE, THE
OLDEST STRUCTURE
IN PITTSBURGH

at the Point, but it did adopt Wright's ideas for a colossal fountain and twin bridges crossing the rivers close by. This episode supports the idea that history repeats itself, since John Augustus Roebling had proposed a double suspension bridge for the Point a century earlier.

George Richardson, who engineered the Fort Pitt Bridge over the Monongahela and the Fort Duquesne Bridge over the Allegheny, was a master of bridge design during his forty-year career in Pittsburgh and Allegheny County. Richardson and his design team transformed what might have been a potentially ugly overpass connecting the two bridges into a luminous portal of three ultrathin stretched barrel vaults. The tensioning of the prestressed reinforcing rods in the concrete vaults was so complex that the final calculations of 1962 were personally overseen by the celebrated French bridge builder Eugène Freyssinet just before his death that same year.

The eye-catching element in Point State Park turned out to be not its fort but its fountain. All of the planners who had eyed the Point for a hundred years imagined some focal element here. For Wright, it was a fountain; for Robert Moses, a shining beacon; for other visionaries it was a colossal sculpture—of a steelworker, an allegorical Meeting of the Waters, or the legendary steelworker Joe Magarac. (Legend holds that Magarac—which is Slovak for "jack-ass"—was the strongest steelworker in Pittsburgh. According to the tale, he would measure the consistency of a ladle of molten steel by tasting it and ended his life by leaping into a blast furnace to upgrade the quality of its iron ore.) What emerged in 1974 was a geyser that normally jets about 150 feet high but can rise—to challenge all aquatic records—to more than 300 feet. It spews 6,000 gallons of water a minute from a 100,000-gallon hidden reservoir fed by an aquifer some 50 feet below ground. (This so-called "fourth river" is a staple of Pittsburgh trivia quizzes.) The fountain was not the only way to accentuate the Point, but since the old Pittsburgh had its columns of fire and smoke, there is some appropriateness to this play of waters as a symbol for the cleaner city of today.

Until the 1990s, Pittsburgh was the only city with structures designed by both of the grand Kahns of American architecture: Albert and Louis. In the 1930s, the industrial architect Albert Kahn put up an important component of the Heinz factories on the North Side, and in 1976, Louis Kahn (no relation) designed the American Wind Symphony's barge *Point-Counterpoint II*, which for several decades was docked on the Allegheny River frontage of the Point. Kahn's barge would float down the Ohio and Mississippi rivers for concert tours in the summer. The floating concert hall and musicians' dormitory was clad in burnished steel, and with its huge portholes, it looked like a

fig. 2.6
FOUR GATEWAY
CENTER

fig. 2.7
UNITED
STEELWORKERS
BUILDING

silver flute gliding over water. Since 1996, the symphony has chosen to sail Kahn's barge in different waters; it now takes music through the heart of North America and as far away as Europe.

Gateway Center, with the earlier Gateway Plaza and later Equitable Plaza, was more than a postwar investment by the Equitable Life Assurance Society; it was a leap of faith in the future of Pittsburgh and—in a way no longer imaginable—a demonstration of the healing power of modern architecture. Conceived in 1947, One, Two, and Three Gateway were among the most talked-about buildings after World War II because, apart from New York's Rockefeller Center, so large a single-blueprint commercial complex could be found nowhere else in the world. Also making the leap of faith were the corporations that signed up as tenants: Jones & Laughlin Steel, PPG Industries, People's Gas, and Westinghouse, which made their commitments on the basis of nothing more than a sketch.

The design of these cruciform towers represented a tug of war between the traditionalists Otto Eggers and Daniel Higgins, both involved with John Russell Pope in the design of the National Gallery and the Jefferson Memorial in Washington, and the progressive Irwin Clavan, who in the same years designed cruciform-tower housing estates in New York. Behind Gateway Center also lies the exemplar of Le Corbusier's towers-in-the-park scheme for Paris in 1922. Between seven and fifteen cruciform towers were originally projected for Pittsburgh, all in traditional brick and limestone. At the last minute the designs were respecified for stainless steel, but scarcities because of the Korean War resulted in the use of chrome-alloyed steel.

When building resumed in Equitable Plaza, across Liberty Avenue, from 1955 to 1968, the landscape architects used a more informal site plan. However, the continuous perimeter podium they created makes this half of Gateway Center more difficult to enter from the adjoining streets. The Verizon Building and the Pennsylvania State Office Building on the plaza are conventional office slabs, but the bold shape of Four Gateway, with its long glass tower and extruded stainless-steel service wing, is a fine expression of mid-century modernism.

One of the criticisms of Gateway Center (especially in Jane Jacobs's *The Death and Life of Great American Cities*) is the way it turned its back on the larger city. Fifth Avenue Place, on the opposite side of Stanwix Street, was the first building in thirty-five years to create a visual link with the Gateway complex rather than standing back from it, as the PPG and Riverfront Center, at 20 Stanwix Street, complexes do.

Opposite Fifth Avenue Place, at the corner of Stanwix and Penn, stands a still fondly remembered remnant of Downtown's retail history. The structure that for a century housed the Joseph Horne Company department store is today Penn Avenue Place and serves not shoppers but the Highmark medical insurance group (also the main tenant in Fifth Avenue Place). The exterior is handsome in a conventional Beaux-Arts way, while the interior was once striking in its high Tuscan Doric columns with gilded moldings—all now stripped away. The elaborate brass window surrounds at ground level are not there just for show: Horne's was devastated by the St. Patrick's Day flood that struck Pittsburgh in 1936. Afterward, these fittings were added so that enormous brass plates can be placed over the windows to keep the Allegheny out, should it rise that high again.

Three important buildings complete Equitable Plaza toward the Monongahela bank. The United Steelworkers Building is the main monument to organized labor in Pittsburgh, the city in which the Iron & Steel Workers Union (predecessor of the American Federation of Labor) was organized in 1876. The union headquarters building, originally constructed for IBM, is also a milestone in skyscraper architecture; it shattered a long-held dogma of skyscraper construction whereby the exterior walls generally did not support any of the load. For this skyscraper, however, U.S. Steel instead fabricated an exterior load-bearing wall in place of a conventional "curtain" wall. During construction, the three different types of steel in the exterior walls were painted red, white, or blue to designate their different structural roles. The midcentury slickness of the design can at times be cloying, but particularly at night the thirteen-story diamond-faceted walls of stainless steel hover alluringly over the heavy concrete base.

The union building faces a mildly Gothic brick-faced St. Mary of Mercy Church on the opposite corner of Boulevard of the Allies and Stanwix. A harmless legend—possibly even true—holds that the church stands just where the first Mass in Pittsburgh was celebrated in 1754. Behind the United Steelworkers' tower, overlooking the Monongahela's bank at Stanwix Street at the corner of Fort Pitt Boulevard, stands the former world headquarters of Westinghouse Electric Corporation. The dark gray anodized aluminum slab for what was then one of Pittsburgh's corporate mainstays was less progressive in design than the same company's research centers built in the 1950s and 1960s at Churchill and Monroeville. Nonetheless, Westinghouse was technically distinguished by its pioneering integration of the lighting, heating, and air-conditioning systems and by having the world's first talking elevators, developed by Westinghouse, of course.

Riverfront Center, at the opposite corner of Stanwix Street and Fort Pitt Boulevard, takes a more informal approach to corporate architecture: a skewed hexagon wrapped in sunscreens of Italian travertine. The appearance of sunscreens in Pittsburgh marked the final confirmation of the efficacy of its stringent pollution controls: in pre-Renaissance Pittsburgh, few people worried about overexposure to the sun.

First Side is a finely scaled district comprising the dozen blocks along the Monongahela waterfront from Stanwix to Grant streets and from Fort Pitt Boulevard to the Boulevard of the Allies. Its western end, between Stanwix and Market streets, follows John Campbell's provisional plan of 1764. The layout of First Side was shaped a second time by the Great Fire of 1845, which leveled most of it, and a third time by the enlargement of Second Avenue into the Boulevard of the Allies, in 1922. The resulting traffic flow cut First Side off from the rest of Downtown, which helped preserve it. Its richly detailed shops and warehouses, with dramatic views of the Monongahela River and Mount Washington, are now being enhanced by 151 FirstSide, an eighteen-story tower on the waterfront that was the first new condominium in the Golden Triangle since the Pittsburgh Renaissance.

Architecturally, the most consistent block remaining from the old Golden Triangle is the 100 block of Market Street between the Boulevard of the Allies and First Avenue. Here, except for two gaps, both sides of the street are packed with commercial structures that have residential lofts on the top floors. The buildings are largely mid- and late nineteenth-century substitutes for shops and warehouses that were lost in the fire of 1845.

Whatever fate held in store for Pittsburgh in 1784, surveyor George Woods was sure it would be linked to the Monongahela, so he drew most of his 490 lots as narrow strips on the numbered avenues parallel to the Monongahela. In consequence, scores of First Side's towers have double façades that stretch from one avenue to another. This feature is particularly evident in the 200 block of Fort Pitt Boulevard, between Market and Wood streets, where a dozen of the best old commercial buildings front on both the Monongahela and First Avenue. For a hundred years, until 1955, the riverbank was a single broad levee, where steamboats would pick up and disgorge passengers and freight. The steamboat and barge trade was so voluminous at Pittsburgh that for a century the city claimed to be the world's busiest inland port; in some quarters that claim persists.

The Conestoga Building at the corner of Fort Pitt Boulevard and Wood Street got its name from the westward pioneers who bought covered wagons in the Conestoga Valley of Lancaster County and then brought them across the

Alleghenies to Pittsburgh, where they embarked by boat for the West. Though shorn of its elaborate cornice, the Conestoga Building survives as one of the oldest steel-frame buildings in town.

Most of the nearby structures on the riverfront predate the Conestoga by a generation, and several feature cast-iron fronts. Two examples of the latter are 235 and 239 Fort Pitt, where iron elements were bolted over traditional brick and wood façades. Closer to the Point, at number 231, is an elegantly restored Italianate brick and stone façade. The old four-story warehouse at 227 Fort Pitt Boulevard now stands as a contemporary evocation of the oriel fronts or narrow bay windows that once overlooked many of Pittsburgh's streets a century ago.

Wood Street unfolds its architectural character block by block from the Monongahela to Liberty Avenue, offering excellent examples of architectural styles popular after the Great Fire of 1845. One block in from the river, at the corner of Wood Street and First Avenue, stand four Beaux-Arts skyscrapers (two with matching façades on the Boulevard of the Allies), which in their *gravitas* suggest Pittsburgh's consciousness of being midway between Chicago and New York, with the power of the first tempered by the urbanity of the second. At 101–103 Wood Street there survives another of Pittsburgh's cast-iron fronts, this one from about 1860. Despite a lifeless retrofitting in the 1980s, the iron-stamped Gothic façade provided some inspiration for the design of the neighboring Wood-Allies Garage on the Boulevard of the Allies. That nine-level steel-deck cage begins with a red neo-Romanesque brick base and ends as a parody of the fake Gothic pinnacles of PPG down the block.

After two blocks that are predominantly Beaux-Arts in character, Wood Street switches its architectural code at the intersection with Boulevard of the Allies to Art Deco in the twenty-one-story main building of Point Park University (the university uses Wood Street as the central promenade of its urban campus). What failed once as an athletic club and again as a hotel today succeeds as a leading center for the performing arts. With thirty-five hundred students, Point Park University is a major component of the Golden Triangle educational offerings. An estimated forty thousand students can be found Downtown on weekdays, a projection that is accurate if it also encompasses Duquesne University, on the edge of Downtown.

The blocks farther inland introduce other architectural styles: late international style for the YWCA at Third Avenue, and mid-Victorian for a set of storefronts beyond Fourth Avenue at 409, 411, 413–415, and 417 Wood Street. The second to last of these has been the home of Weldin's stationers since 1883; the current classically inspired façade is a redesign from 1905.

The construction in 1979–1984 of a world headquarters for PPG Industries had significant impact not just on the lower blocks of Third and Fourth avenues but for the whole of Downtown. PPG Place occupies five and a half acres in a complex of eight elements that occupy or touch six city blocks. The central element is the half-acre open plaza, with a forty-story glass tower in the center and five uniformly detailed low-rise structures around it. Between the tower and the Gateway Center complex on Stanwix Street lies the three-story Wintergarden atrium, while a second atrium below Two PPG Place is home to restaurants and specialty shops. Everything is sheathed in uniform mirror glass, with twenty thousand pieces of silver PPG Solarban in the tower alone. In winter, the outdoor plaza becomes a skating rink; the rest of the year children enjoy the user-friendly "water feature" fountains around the central obelisk.

The creation of PPG Place in 1984 was an American corporation's outstanding act of generosity toward its home city. Pittsburgh Plate Glass was founded half a block away in 1883 by John Pitcairn and John B. Ford. Today, it is the largest producer of glass in the world, as well as a giant in paints, plastics, and chemicals. When the company considered building a headquarters tower near its birthplace on Market Street, it knew that it would be relatively easy to buy only the half acre it needed. But what PPG really wanted was to upgrade the whole district in the manner of Rockefeller Center, so it purchased an area ten times larger than needed for its own building. It was a daring move, considering the financial and political risks involved. Another daring move was the selection of Philip Johnson's unconventional Postmodern Gothic design for the PPG office tower. It marked only the second time in the postwar era (after Johnson's design for the AT&T headquarters in New York) that an American corporation had chosen fantasy over the staid International School Style for its public image.

The obvious precedent of the PPG design is the Victoria Tower at the Houses of Parliament in London, though it is only about half the height of PPG's 635 feet. There was also a local model: the Cathedral of Learning at the University of Pittsburgh. PPG's tower is a brilliant apparition when seen from outside the Triangle, for example, from West Park on the North Side. Unlike the Cathedral of Learning, which has a rich variety of surface and texture, the PPG tower tends to the monotonous at close range. The interior, with its soaring lobby and repetitive arches, is visually unyielding, although handsome with its deep-red glass paneling. Despite these blemishes, PPG Place

fig. 2.8
PPG Place

fig. 2.9
OBELISK AND
FOUNTAIN AT
PPG PLACE

was one of the best twentieth-century additions to the Pittsburgh skyline. Those few who are truly unhappy with the glass tower should not throw stones, especially inside the lobby, where closed-circuit television cameras watch from behind one-way glass.

In the last three decades of the nineteenth century, profits from oil, iron, glass, coal, coke, and steel made Pittsburgh second only to New York in terms of amassed capital. The two-block stretch of Fourth Avenue from PPG Place up to Smithfield Street, intersected by Wood Street, was once home to the dozen banks that stored this capital. Pittsburgh still has high importance as a financial center, but the oil and stock exchanges and most of the banks that made Fourth Avenue an erstwhile rival to Wall Street were torn down years ago. The most distinguished of these vanished structures was Frank Furness's quirky but lovable Farmers' Deposit National Bank as well as the Bank of Pittsburgh, the latter a close approximation of the New York Stock Exchange. Constructed in 1896, the Bank of Pittsburgh came down in the 1940s, although its columns survive in Jefferson Memorial Cemetery in suburban Pleasant Hills.

As the oldest commercial building and the only externally intact Greek Revival structure in Downtown today, the Burke Building at 209 Fourth Avenue has seen it all. Built in 1836, and for a time serving as a bank, it stood for a decade before the Great Fire skirted it by a few feet in 1845. The building's owners were the Irish-born lawyers Robert and Andrew Burke; their architect, John Chislett, was born in England in 1800 and schooled himself in the Neoclassical traditions seen in the buildings of Bath. Chislett came to Pittsburgh around 1833 and was the city's dominant architect during the mid-nineteenth century. The Burke Building today resembles a domestic more than a commercial design: a brick structure faced in sandstone, Doric columns at the door, and a four-square plan with fireplaces and a central stair hall. With windows elongated almost to doors in the manner popularized by Thomas Jefferson, it is uncompromisingly elegant.

The trio of the Benedum-Trees, Investment, and Arrott buildings on Fourth Avenue just below Wood might recall the fortified towers of medieval Bologna or San Gimignano. The rhythm for the group was set by the Arrott, at the corner of Fourth and Wood. Its designer, Frederick Osterling (1865–1934), was both prolific and quarrelsome, but he was a generally brilliant designer in Pittsburgh for nearly half a century. His range of styles included Romanesque, Classical Revival, and modern Gothic. Osterling's design for an insurance magnate demonstrates the usual academic sequence of a large-scale base intended for retail purposes, then a shaft of office floors in rusticated brick patterning, and a cap of four stories with tall arched windows and an exuberant copper cornice. The lobby is an equally impressive mix of marble, mosaic, and brass.

Three years after Osterling designed the Arrott, the Machesney tower rose at 221 Fourth Avenue; it was later renamed the Benedum-Trees Building after the oilmen Michael Benedum and Joseph Trees bought it. At nineteen stories, Benedum-Trees was only slightly lower than the Arrott, and it clearly responded both to the Arrott and to the now-vanished Bank of Pittsburgh in its dramatic base of Corinthian columns and oriel windows, an aggressively vertical terra-cotta shaft, and an enormous overhanging entablature complete with lions and florid curved brackets. The Investment Building at 239 Fourth Avenue went up in the 1920s, making it a generation younger than the towers left and right of it. Its brick shaft is a total abstraction without ornament, but at the top the corners are sliced away to reveal a set of elegant obelisks, powerful enough to catch the eye of Philip Johnson when he designed his Neoclassical obelisk for PPG Place down the block.

Point Park University Center is an adaptive reuse of a group of six banks that once clustered together in the 400 block of Wood and up Fourth and Forbes avenues. The first two banks were the Freehold Building and the Real Estate Trust Company on Fourth Avenue, both from the 1890s. These were joined at the corner of Fourth and Wood in 1901 by the People's Savings Bank, a fifteen-story tower that mirrors the Arrott tower across Wood Street. It might be called competent rather than remarkable except for the brilliantly handled semi-circular stairwell inside and the raised brick panels that are randomly scattered on the exterior, giving the building the appearance of a decaying Roman ruin. The bank's most delicious feature is its two dramatic reliefs of industrious bees, easily inspected from the sidewalk.

In 1902, the Colonial Trust Company cut sideways through the block to create a fourth building, with twin Renaissance-style façades on Fourth and Forbes avenues; what was supposedly the world's longest bank lobby ran in between. In 1926, the dual façades became a trio when the lobby was extended as a T-shape and fronted with a severe Ionic pediment at 414 Wood. The sixth and last piece of the puzzle fell into place the next year, when a new building linked the Wood Street façades of the People's Bank tower to the Colonial Trust. In 1976, prominent Argentina-born designer Rodolfo Machado, who was working for the IKM Partnership and taught at Carnegie Mellon, came up with a cool, minimalist design for a shopping mall project that would amalgamate these buildings. The design scheme was widely praised but underfunded, and an inexpensive alternative design was used instead. When that mall went bankrupt, the complex underwent a final renovation in 1997 and

fig. 2.10
BURKE BUILDING

fig. 2.11
PEOPLE'S SAVINGS BANK

fig. 2.12
DOLLAR BANK

fig. 2.13
ARROTT BUILDING

fig. 2.14
TIMES BUILDING

2.10
2.11   2.13
2.12   2.14

emerged as the Point Park University Center. What sounds like a depressing chronicle has ended on an uplifting note: the interior columns and the lilting volumes of the interior are just short of breathtaking. A grand staircase on the right enables viewers to inspect the magnificent gold-paneled ceiling.

Fourth Avenue is marked by a particularly pleasing visual consistency today. Because of that quality, twenty-four of its buildings were incorporated into a National Register of Historic Places district in 1985. The south side of the 300 block of Fourth, from Wood to Smithfield streets, originally had a sequence of four banks and a newspaper office. The three turn-of-the-century banks at 306, 312, and 324 Fourth were the Union National Bank, the Commonwealth Trust, and Keystone Bank—all predictably sober except for the beautifully articulated Keystone Bank, where a light court was recessed in the façade and garlanded above by a bridgelike arch. The three towers were eventually amalgamated into the Union National Bank, whose core structure was converted into the Carlyle, a luxury condominium residence, in 2007. The first fourteen floors of standard units and four top floors of double-sized apartments sold at such a satisfying rate that the developers purchased the Commonwealth Building for conversion into an additional sixty residences.

The upper end of the same Fourth Avenue block is considerably less sober. The evolving social and business attitudes in mid- and late nineteenth-century America can be discerned by comparing the efflorescence of the earlier Dollar Bank, at the upper corner intersecting Smithfield Street, to the straitlaced Union National, at the lower corner intersecting Wood. Dollar Bank, dating from 1871, with wings added in 1906, is the ultimate in public relations architecture; it is a building that is all doorway. The red sandstone façade features a sumptuous pair of double columns guarding the door with the help of two dozing lions. Its designer, Isaac Hobbs, was a fashionable Philadelphia architect and architectural publisher whose conception of the bank shows at once what was both splendid and hopeless in Victorian architecture. The ornament is vigorous, learned, and delightful, but the essential lines of the façade are drowned by the Baroque and Italianate details.

The imbalance of the part and the whole, so characteristic of American architecture after the Civil War, was the problem that would occupy H. H. Richardson, who was just beginning his architectural career when Dollar Bank went up. Frederick Osterling, Richardson's long-distance pupil (there is no indication the two designers ever met), captured the simplifying ability of his "master" reasonably well in the four-story Times Building alongside Dollar Bank, at 336 Fourth Avenue. The patron here was the publisher, civic powerhouse, and GOP political boss Christopher Lyman Magee, for his newspaper, the *Pittsburgh Times*. Now sensitively restored inside, this eight-story Romanesque Revival tower has façades on both Fourth and Third avenues, with the former enlivened by particularly fine grotesque carvings that are replicated in the dimly lit interior of the building.

What was once a solid line of buildings on the north side of the 300 block of Fourth Avenue is now broken by a parking lot, but even so, this view shows how good architects can make their structures distinctive without destroying the wider unity of a city block. The flagship of this upper block is the Standard Life Building at 345 Fourth Avenue, dressed in deep red Roman bricks and terracotta plaques. The Standard Life skyscraper "talks" to People's Savings at the lower end of the block with its exaggerated detail on the upper floors, particularly the colossal arch stones set over the top windows. To the left of Standard Life is the earliest building of this cluster, the Fidelity Trust Building from 1889, at 341 Fourth. It begins well with a base of two massive arched doors and a dwarf mezzanine of three rectangular openings with colonettes, but in the upper floors the façade changes rhythm at almost every level, as though slices of a half dozen different buildings had been stacked atop one another.

In 1898, a decade after the construction of the Fidelity Trust Building, Henry Clay Frick summoned the dean of American architects, Daniel Burnham, to build the small Union Trust Company (now the Engineers' Society) at 337 Fourth, immediately next door. This little Greek temple, with a podium of deeply channeled blocks below and severe Doric columns above, was the first of eleven projects that Burnham drew up for Pittsburgh—more than he created for any city except his native Chicago. Next door to Burnham's monument, local architect Charles M. Bartberger built a considerably more accomplished structure for his Industrial Bank, at 333 Fourth Avenue. Bartberger was the German-trained son of the prolific German-born Charles F. Bartberger, who in terms of volume was one of Pittsburgh's top architects from the 1850s to the 1880s. Charles M. in turn trained his own son, Edward W. Bartberger, who lived until 1968. Thus, three Bartberger generations practiced architecture in Pittsburgh for well over a century.

Charles M. Bartberger appears to have thought carefully about eighteenth-century Neoclassical precedents before crafting a Beaux-Arts synthesis for the Industrial Bank. The architectural languages of the Englishman Nicholas Hawksmoor, the Frenchman Claude-Nicholas Ledoux, and the German Peter Speeth seem to predominate. For dramatic effect, Bartberger capriciously overscaled elements like the triglyphs, some of which suddenly and irrationally droop down onto the masonry surface. Every element of the façade "speaks" as well as looks the part it was meant to play: the public banking hall below is marked by the two-story sweep of the entrance arch, and the board-room above is denoted by fat colonettes. Finally, Bartberger was subtle and amusing in his contextual references. The single perky acroterion (stylized plant leaf) on his pediment mimics the five that Burnham used with dour seriousness next door, while the combination of arch below and dwarf mezzanine above is a tribute to the same feature in the Fidelity Trust, two doors away. The Industrial Bank design was Bartberger's finest hour. Perhaps he knew it; at any rate, when the opportunity came, he seized it.

SMITHFIELD STREET AND DOWNTOWN RETAIL

The name Smithfield Street constitutes a tribute to the little-remembered Revolutionary War captain Devereux Smith (1735–1799), who was a personal friend of George Washington and operated a successful Indian trading firm with Ephriam Douglass. Smithfield began as an ordinary cross-street like Wood, but when a bridge connected it to the South Side in 1818 it became richer and larger in scale, and its small, early buildings were cannibalized by bigger ones. There are, nonetheless, some worthy survivors. One is the elegant Adam-style Americus Club (now the Pitt Building) at the corner of Allies and Smithfield. Built in 1918 in the English Neoclassical Style of the late eighteenth century, the clubhouse's left side was amputated four years later when the narrow old Second Avenue was transformed into the Boulevard of the Allies. Two other lively survivors stand at 110 and 112 Smithfield. The first is a High Victorian Gothic commercial block, dated 1881, which presents itself with all the pugnacity of a piece of Eastlake furniture. It is a marvelous sight in the sparkle of its blue, red, and light brown tiles. The second standout is the L-shaped former home of Engine Company No. 2, a former firehouse from 1900 that introduces an Art Nouveau flavor to the neighborhood. It stands three stories tall, with a bleached white granite base and two stories of beautifully dressed sandstone.

The intersection of Smithfield Street and Fifth Avenue is the busiest in town and is among the most significant for its architecture. The prime building here is Macy's Department Store (Kaufmann's until 2006), while on the three other corners stand the old Mellon Bank headquarters, the early high-rise Park Building, and the Swindall-Rust headquarters, formerly the Frank & Seder Department Store, which provides a Classical counterweight to some of its more architecturally unruly neighbors. The elaborate clock at the Macy's corner proclaims the importance of the store: at close to a million square feet, its significance is not merely architectural but social and even cultural.

fig. 2.15
KAUFMANN'S CLOCK

fig. 2.16
MACY'S, FORMERLY
KAUFMANN'S

The Macy's store offers a prime recollection of three figures tightly woven into the fabric of Pittsburgh: Edgar Kaufmann Sr., Benno Janssen, and Frank Lloyd Wright. Brothers Morris, Henry, Jacob, and Isaac Kaufmann arrived in Pittsburgh from Germany in the years after 1860, and by 1871, they had a flourishing trade on the South Side. Around 1877, the Kaufmanns moved their store to this prestigious corner, and in 1885, the year Morris's son Edgar was born, they enlarged it into the "Big Store." The corner of the store now standing at Smithfield and Forbes was built for the Kaufmanns in 1898 by Charles Bickel and borrows motifs from the Romanesque and Classical Revivals, as well as from the Chicago school of Louis Henry Sullivan and his colleagues.

Edgar Kaufmann Sr. (1885–1955), universally known as E. J., took charge of the firm in 1913 and had the socially prominent architect Benno Janssen design a new terra-cotta block to replace the store built in 1885 at the corner of Smithfield and Fifth. A few years later Kaufmann purchased the first of fifteen hundred acres for a country retreat near Pittsburgh that Frank Lloyd Wright made world famous as Fallingwater. Janssen designed an extension of the store on Forbes Avenue at Cherry Way a few years later. In 1930, he modernized its ground floor interior in Art Deco Style, with piers of black Carrara glass and murals by Boardman Robinson. Critics regarded it as the most beautiful store in America—and the most profitable. It marked Kaufmann's first step toward Modernism.

The glass and murals are long gone from Kaufmann's/Macy's, and so is the office that Wright built for Kaufmann in 1936 and 1937 (contemporary with Fallingwater) on the store's tenth floor. Wright designed the furniture and paneling for this sumptuous suite, including a cypress plywood mural, and he selected the wall fabrics himself. The office served Kaufmann for twenty years, until his death in 1955, after which his son Edgar Jr. had it dismantled and shipped to London's Victoria and Albert Museum, where it is a star attraction.

Architect Benno Janssen (1874–1964) is undeservedly forgotten today, even though a recent biography offers excellent coverage of his body of work. Janssen was born to a German-American family in St. Louis, enrolled at the École des Beaux-Arts in Paris in 1902, and soon after came to work in Pittsburgh. He was the best academic designer Pittsburgh ever had, on a par with or superior to Carrère & Hastings, Horace Trumbauer, David Adler, Charles Platt, and the host of others who took care of wealthy Americans' architectural needs before and after World War I. Kaufmann was Janssen's most loyal client. He gave him nearly a dozen commissions and even lived in

Janssen's own home in Squirrel Hill before ordering a new house from him in Fox Chapel.

Janssen's career reminds us of Kaufmann's importance as a patron of architecture for many years before he built Fallingwater. Kaufmann commissioned buildings from Janssen, Wright, the Bauhaus-associated Richard Neutra (for Kaufmann's Palm Springs winter retreat, the outstanding example of American midcentury modernism), Joseph Urban (a swimming pool at the Irene Kaufmann Settlement on the Hill), and the important Pittsburgh architects Mitchell & Ritchey (for the Civic Arena in the lower Hill District). After Janssen retired in the 1930s, Kaufmann switched his architectural allegiance to Wright, and together the two men planned Fallingwater in 1934 and 1935.

Kaufmann's architectural patronage reminds us in turn of how important Frank Lloyd Wright (1867–1959) was to Pittsburgh and vice versa. Kaufmann was Wright's outstanding patron. Their partnership lasted twenty years and yielded nearly a dozen uncompleted projects in addition to those that were realized. The unfinished projects included Kaufmann's sponsorship of Wright's Broadacre City model, which was exhibited at Kaufmann's immediately after being shown in 1935 at Rockefeller Center; Wright's extensive sketches for a megastructure at the Point; the Rhododendron Chapel, meant to rise on the grounds of Fallingwater; another winter house (Wright intended it to outshine the one already built by Neutra); a hillside apartment on Mount Washington; and a planetarium and parking garage next to Kaufmann's store. Though disappointingly little came of it, the partnership of Wright and Kaufmann was one of the most intense collaborations of artist and patron in the history of American art.

AN ARCHITECTURAL PARADE ON FIFTH AVENUE

Fifth Avenue was for years Downtown's primary retail and entertainment corridor, but the free parking offered by the suburban shopping malls and theaters forced the street into decay. The throngs seen in old photographs of Fifth Avenue will never return, but in the meantime, there is heartening progress, with several excellent buildings waiting to be reutilized. The Park Building, at the corner of Fifth Avenue and Smithfield, is a design triumph by the then-dean of American architects, George B. Post. Completed in 1896, it was the third or fourth of Pittsburgh's steel-frame skyscrapers. Post's local patrons were David and William Park, operators of the Black Diamond Steel Works and major investors in Pittsburgh real estate. The site was appropriate; the Pittsburgh Iron Foundry went up at this intersection in

1805, and soon thereafter it cast the cannons that Commodore Perry fired on Lake Erie during the War of 1812 as well as the ones Andrew Jackson used at the Battle of New Orleans in 1815.

For the Parks, Post recast the design for his earlier Havemeyer Building in New York, but the Pittsburgh variant was substantially more interesting. The base is simplified and strong, and the nine identical middle floors are well articulated through corner windows. But the joy of the Park Building is in the thirty *telemones* or Atlases that are (seemingly) crushed by the weight of the top cornice. The telemones are cast in terra cotta and were originally polychromed. Pittsburgh has always loved them, perhaps because these mythological creatures straining at their work symbolize the hard physical labor that for so long characterized the city's work force.

The 300 block of Fifth Avenue, from Smithfield down to Wood Street, was for a century home to another of Pittsburgh's innovative skyscrapers. At 335 Fifth Avenue master piano salesman Samuel Hamilton erected the ten-story Hamilton Building in 1889 to a height of 125 feet. The building was a traditional masonry structure, not steel frame, but it was the last word in late Victorian commercial expression. A few doors down from where the "piano" skyscraper once stood is the structure that ate it up: Piatt Place, at the corner of Fifth Avenue and Wood Street. This was originally the Lazarus Department Store. When it went up in 1998, it was the first new American downtown department store in decades, though it failed almost immediately. The adaptive reuse given the structure in 2007 yielded another sixty-five luxury condominiums to house a growing Downtown population. The rest of the complex features street-level boutiques and restaurants.

fig. 2.17
PARK BUILDING

The final blocks of Fifth Avenue, from Wood Street to Liberty, offer an intriguing mix of late nineteenth- and late twentieth-century Pittsburgh. On the street's south side are arrayed a number of hearty survivors from the early retail days. The double-unit commercial structure at 214–218 Fifth Avenue is an Italianate cast-iron front from the 1860s or 1870s, with large glass panes and interlacing floral designs stamped out in iron molds. Farther down the street stand two particularly good examples of retail and office blocks from the early twentieth century: the Buhl Building at 205 Fifth Avenue from 1913, decked out in ebullient blue and cream terra-cotta plaques, and the Diamond Building (formerly the Diamond National Bank), from 1904, at the intersection of Fifth Avenue and Liberty. The latter rises twelve stories high and is topped by the most dramatic Beaux-Arts copper cornice in the city. The handsome block bends backward from its central entrance to fit into one of the triangular lots embodied in the quirky city plan of 1784.

OLIVER PLAZA AND PNC PLAZA

The closing of the tail end of Oliver Avenue between Wood and Liberty in the 1960s created a trapezoid block on which now rise four tall towers. The earliest of these was One Oliver Plaza, a thirty-eight-story glass-and-steel box standing on a base of dark granite at the Sixth Avenue angle of the trapezoid. At the Fifth Avenue end of the block stands One PNC Plaza, built as the Pittsburgh National Bank Building in 1972. This replaced an Italian Renaissance tower that Daniel Burnham erected for the predecessor First National Bank. One PNC Plaza was conceived as a glass slab, with a service core that is clad in pearl-gray granite. It does its job well, but at thirty stories, the current building is merely three floors higher than the 1912 tower it replaced, leading one to question the notion of architectural obsolescence.

Two PNC Plaza was squeezed between the One Oliver and One PNC Plaza towers in 1976. Although handicapped by weak linkage to the streets in front and behind them, the two interlocking mirror-glass octagons of Two PNC manage an elegant solution to an overbuilt site. The octagonal geometry of these twin towers relates well to the polygonal shape of the former Meyer and Jonasson department store, the low-rise neighbor at 606 Liberty Avenue. Meyer and Jonasson got its odd shape because it conformed to the old course of Oliver Avenue before it was filled in below Wood Street.

The technologically advanced Three PNC Plaza was Downtown's first high-rise in a generation. Its environmentally friendly materials and energy-efficient cooling and heating systems won it a LEED (Leadership in Energy

fig. 2.18
THREE PNC PLAZA

and Environmental Design) certificate from the U.S. Green Building Council. The bank's twenty-three stories encompass residential condominiums, an underground parking garage, office space (mainly for the venerable Reed Smith law firm), and a hotel. Construction of the tower is one more indication of the modest resurgence of Pittsburgh's business community.

69

MARKET SQUARE

The history of Pittsburgh is written out in buildings in every part of the Golden Triangle, as seen in First Side and in the palatial skyscrapers on Fourth Avenue that still speak of Pittsburgh's wealth in the early twentieth century. Visitors nonetheless get their best feel for old Pittsburgh in and around Market Square. Much of the square's pedestrian traffic comes from its utility as a walkway between PNC Plaza, a block to the north, and PPG Place, a block to the south. But even in its current weakened state—we can always hope for a better one—Market Square can still claim to be the heart of Downtown.

fig. 2.19
MARKET SQUARE

The square was the sole open space in George Woods's 1784 street plan. Over the years it was the site of a courthouse, a city hall, and a sequence of market buildings that came down only in 1961. Historically the square (western Pennsylvanians traditionally call a space like this a diamond) was always meant to be paved and built on, not green and open as the present pseudo-restoration has it. A better alternative would be to get rid of the quadrants, cover the central square with glass over a gigantic neon map of Pittsburgh, and invite citizens to dance there every night.

The diamond's perimeter buildings pretty much summarize Pittsburgh's architectural history: Gallagher's Pub and Ryan's Ale House (2 and 3 Market Place) from the Civil War era, a fragment of glassy PPG Place at the southwest quadrant, and a restaurant decked out in Tudor Revival. Two of the better citizens of the square are Nicholas Coffee and the Landmark Tavern, which dates to 1902. The former displays a tall Chippendale front crowned by a neon coffee cup with steam wafting out; this joking reference to Philip Johnson's Chippendale-topped Sony Building in New York serves also as an efficient device to give height to the façade and elegance to an urban gathering place that sorely needs it.

The best recent news for Market Square is the Downtown YMCA (along with apartments overhead) taking over the shuttered G. C. Murphy store where Market Square fronts on Forbes Avenue (the rebuilt complex goes by the redundant name of Market Square Place). Like the new housing and dining opportunities for the pioneers who are moving Downtown, the Y's move to put exercise facilities at the heart of the Golden Triangle may be the tipping point in decades of effort to get Pittsburghers to move Downtown.

MELLON SQUARE AND THE SIXTH-OLIVER CORRIDOR

The creation of Mellon Square (bounded by Smithfield Street, William Penn Place, and Oliver and Sixth avenues) was an inspired mix of altruism and self-interest. The Mellons had been a presence in Downtown since Judge Thomas Mellon resigned from the bench in 1869 and opened a bank, saying that any man who could not get rich in Pittsburgh within ten years was a fool. Mellon's first bank was a masonry building at 514 Smithfield Street, roughly opposite what is now the square, but in 1873, the judge put up a more imposing cast-iron front that featured a statue of his hero, Benjamin Franklin.

Serene and majestic on the outside, Mellon Bank has covered the block of Smithfield between Fifth Avenue and Mellon Square since 1924, but it has been destroyed inside. The long and airy banking hall, one of Pittsburgh's prime architectural and social spaces, vanished in 1999 when its short-sighted owners and an overeager city hall let Lord and Taylor rebuild it as a *faux*-Manhattan emporium. Fifteen tons of Italian marble in each of the Ionic columns was smashed and hauled away, leaving just their steel cores. Gone was the vast basilicalike space of the hall, sixty-five feet tall and two hundred feet long; gone were the aisles coffered and painted deep blue with speckles of gold leaf; gone was any hint that the world's earliest venture capitalists once operated out of Pittsburgh. Befitting its place as the heart of Mellon operations, the hall commemorated A. W. and R. B. Mellon with portraits and inscriptions on the walls of the vault. After Lord and Taylor's quick demise a few years later, the now banal interior awaits some new use.

Banking was always just the visible tip of the Mellon money machine. Their investments in coal, coke, steel and its chemical by-products, oil, aluminum, real estate, and transportation were far more lucrative than what they earned as bankers. Until the appearance of megabillionaires in computers and securities in the 1980s and 1990s, the Mellons of Pittsburgh were among the wealthiest families in the world, in a league with the Fords, the Rockefellers, and the du Ponts.

The family headquartered its business ventures on Smithfield Street until three of those firms required their own headquarters. At the end of the 1920s, Gulf and Koppers moved two blocks away, to Seventh Avenue. Alcoa tried to bolt from the family circle and build in New York after World War II, but Richard King Mellon had not backed the Pittsburgh Renaissance only to see it scorned at home. He quashed the move to New York, and he and his more worldly cousin Paul Mellon conceived a grand complex that would house Alcoa and the expanded bank operations in twin towers facing each other across a park. Construction of Mellon Square and its underground parking garage required demolition of a full city block, but it paid off handsomely in sight lines to all the surrounding buildings. Apart from creating a place in which its perimeter buildings might preen, Mellon Square holds up well as a period piece from the mid-1950s, when "organic" and "modern" were words architects could still use without stumbling. The design in Venetian terrazzo appears today somewhat thin in the manner of the Eisenhower years, but the trees and fountains have aged well, and Kenneth Snelson's *Forest Devil* sculpture in stainless-steel pipes provides welcome animation.

Around Mellon Square rises a particularly impressive grouping of twentieth-century skyscrapers. On the Oliver Avenue or southern edge of the square rise the Mellon Bank of the 1920s, described above, and Citizens (originally Mellon) Bank, a postwar financial tower on the upper edge of the square. On the square's western edge stands the Oliver Building, from 1910, and at its northwest corner the Heinz 57 Center, headquarters for Heinz North America. The structure was for decades a Gimbel's department store, and before that Kaufmann & Baer's, originally built by some breakaway Kaufmann cousins to rival the main Kaufmann store. At the corresponding northeast corner stands what was for years the Philadelphia Traction Company block, put up in 1902 by the transportation mogul P. A. B. Widener.

All of these perimeter buildings carry architectural distinction, but the most successful and renowned of them is the Regional Enterprise Tower, erected in 1953 as the Alcoa Building (the corporation handed it over in 1998 to a consortium of nonprofit organizations). Using aluminum wherever possible, Alcoa's thirty-story tower is radically lighter and more efficient than buildings of comparable size. Its curtain wall was not constructed piece by piece but prefabricated in aluminum sheets that contained both windows and the floor zone. The windows swing open in special rubber gaskets, so the building's exterior requires minimal cleaning and maintenance. Inside, the same spirit of radical innovation prevailed: aluminum furniture, aluminum piping and wiring, aluminum air-conditioning ducts, and an airy and fanciful lobby. This list of distinctions briefly propelled Alcoa to top rank among postwar skyscrapers, but it was evidently too futuristic for the national design community, which shunned it for thirty years until Richard Meier returned

fig. 2.20
REGIONAL
ENTERPRISE TOWER,
MELLON SQUARE

fig. 2.21
ALUMINUM SPIRE,
SMITHFIELD UNITED
CHURCH

to the prefabricated aluminum skin for his high-tech style in the 1980s and 1990s. Even locally, later building designs ignored Alcoa's precedent, except for the Porter Building. Half a block uphill on Grant Street, it looks (as the cliché goes), like the box Alcoa was shipped in.

NORTH OF MELLON SQUARE

The four blocks north of Mellon Square, marked by several narrow eighteenth-century streets, encompass an eclectic mix of architectural survivors. The most gracious of these is the Allegheny H-Y-P Club (formerly the Harvard-Yale-Princeton Club) on William Penn Place at the corner of Strawberry Way. It occupies one of the two plain brick rectangles that were built in 1894 as worker housing, then remodeled in High-style Georgian in 1930 by the academic classicist Edward B. Lee. The H-Y-P Club uses only the right block for its clubhouse; the left block houses nonprofit organizations linked to the adjoining Regional Enterprise Tower.

The end wall of the tiny court that separates the two blocks incorporates relics from schools back East: two columns salvaged from Appleton Chapel at Harvard and six stones of uncertain provenance from Princeton and Yale. Overhead is the fantastic sight of the rose window and aluminum spire of Smithfield United Church. Until women were admitted to the club in 1980, only two female guests had been officially entertained there. The actress Cornelia Otis Skinner was one, Mae West the other. West remarked on the occasion, "It's rather difficult for me to think up things to say to Harvard-Yale-Princeton men collectively. Of course, I can think of plenty to say to men individually."

Neighboring the club and a little downhill from it, at the corner of 620 Smithfield Street and Strawberry Way, stands Smithfield United Church of Christ, the sixth home of a congregation founded in 1782. This highly successful example of a modern inner-city church stands only a few hundred feet from the original site granted it by the Penns in 1787. Smithfield United is one of three Downtown works—another two dozen are in Oakland—by Pittsburgh's outstanding local architect, Henry Hornbostel (1867–1961). A New Yorker who came to Pittsburgh in 1904 to build the campus of the Carnegie Technical Schools, predecessor to Carnegie Mellon, Hornbostel stayed thirty years as a designer and sometimes dean of the Carnegie Tech School of Applied Design. Hornbostel had excellent credentials: he graduated from Columbia University in 1891, spent four years at the École des Beaux-Arts (where he was known as *l'homme perspectif* for his brilliant drawings), taught at Columbia, worked for Stanford White, and was runner-up in the competition to design the campus of the University of California at Berkeley. Though Pittsburgh was his main base, Hornbostel continued as an active architect in New York through the 1920s. The Hell Gate, Queensboro, and Manhattan bridges are his most prominent monuments there, but he also created a campus for Emory University in Atlanta and did civic buildings in Albany, New York, and on the West Coast.

The contrast of spiritual and mundane values is the key to understanding Hornbostel's approach to the design of the Smithfield Church. He placed the church hard against the sidewalk to integrate it uncompromisingly with the city and used standard industrial materials to erect it: steel, limestone, and poured and cast concrete. The main floor, right off the street, is not a sanctuary but a gym, complete with showers and locker rooms. The congregation has used it for various purposes over the years, including a daycare center and a dormitory for the homeless. The sanctuary, one floor up, is rich in its wood trim, stained glass, and lavish plaster fan vaults. Higher still, on the roof, Hornbostel used aluminum for his filigree spire—an early use of that material for structural purposes and an unforgettable vision that parallels the contemporary Watts Tower in Los Angeles.

A newcomer to Smithfield Street, at number 612, is the Downtown branch of Carnegie Library, a facility that gives new life to a neglected block. This small but always crowded library speaks volumes, with "Library" in oversized letters that span the entire height and width of the glass façade. What animates this end of Smithfield Street even better is a droll mural, painted in 2006 by Sarah Zeffiro and Tom Mosser, at the intersection of Smithfield and the narrow Strawberry Way, above the Wiener World hot-dog shop. *The Two Andys* presents civic heroes Andy Warhol and Andy Carnegie under hairdryers, in the most striking of the two dozen murals put up around Pittsburgh in recent years by the Sprout Fund.

THE SIXTH-OLIVER CORRIDOR

Three corridors have left their imprint on the Golden Triangle: the nine blocks of the Cultural District, along Penn and Liberty avenues; the collection of government and corporate entities along Grant Street; and the three-block stretch of Sixth and Oliver avenues that connects the Mellon and PNC banking powerhouses. This last corridor is august: it preserves memories of the Mellons and the Olivers, the Duquesne Club, two of Pittsburgh's oldest churches, a Brooks Brothers, and a Saks Fifth Avenue.

It is also perfect in its symmetry, with Mellon Square to the east and PNC Plaza to the west, two Daniel Burnham skyscrapers at the ends of the district, two venerable churches in the middle, and an Indian burial ground along its central axis.

The Trinity Church burial ground originated in a small hillock that must have been one of the few dry spots in the Triangle when the Allegheny River flooded it each spring. The French, knowing that American Indians had used it, took the hillock over for their own burials from 1754 to 1758, the years in which they held Fort Duquesne at the Point. The British and Americans added more graves, and by the time of the last burial in 1854, about four thousand recorded bodies and far more unrecorded ones rested there. The graveyard left its mark on the toponomy of Pittsburgh, too. The French called the processional way leading to the cemetery the Allée de la Vièrge, for the Blessed Virgin Mary, but the name "Virgin Alley" caused sufficient embarrassment that it was changed in 1904 to Oliver Avenue.

Henry W. Oliver (1840–1904) was one of the Scots-Irish capitalists who led Pittsburgh to dominance in the age of industry. His initial firm, founded in 1863, manufactured nuts and bolts. He reincorporated that firm in 1888 as the Oliver Iron & Steel Company, and he eventually controlled much of the rich Mesabi iron ore range in northern Minnesota. Oliver reaped millions from J. P. Morgan's buyout of Carnegie Steel in 1901, and he proceeded to invest it Downtown. Before he died in 1904, he commissioned Daniel Burnham to build a department store at the lower end of this block. A few years later, Oliver's heirs commissioned the Oliver Building from Burnham as a memorial to the industrialist. Burnham produced a wider, deeper, taller version of his building for H. C. Frick of a few years earlier. Its base of grayish pink granite Doric columns is well if coldly handled, while the main façade above is a mass of cream terra cotta covering a full acre and a half on the Smithfield Street façade alone. The cap to the building consists of three stories of banded Corinthian pilasters and an exuberant cornice line 347 feet in the air.

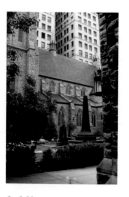

fig. 2.22
Trinity Cathedral
and Graveyard

The interior decoration of the Oliver Building is carried out with similar élan: white marble with dark splashes of bronzework in the lobby and Honduras mahogany trim in the offices upstairs. The heirs were satisfied enough to ask Burnham for still more buildings, including a memorial bathhouse next to the Oliver ironworks on the South Side (still standing, but in the end designed by another firm). These properties were later capitalized into the realty holding company that built Oliver Plaza (now absorbed into PNC Plaza) sixty years later.

When the Penn heirs carved up the town in 1784, the sacredness attached to the burial ground on Sixth Avenue made it the obvious choice for the three free lots they doled out to the Episcopal, Presbyterian, and German-Evangelist congregations. The Presbyterians and Episcopalians are still on the block; the German and Evangelist congregations are only a few hundred feet away.

Sixth Avenue's Trinity Episcopal Cathedral and First Presbyterian Church are both monuments with impeccable design pedigrees. Trinity's first and second churches of 1787 and 1805 were farther down the block, on Liberty Avenue; the third church was built on this site in 1824 by the rector, John Henry Hopkins, who published an engraving of his design locally in 1826, then nationally in his *Essay on Gothic Architecture* in 1836. The present Trinity Cathedral was designed forty years later by Gordon Lloyd, an English-born architect from Detroit who had been trained both in the archaeological and rhetorical variants of the Gothic Revival. The latter taste manifests itself in the bold massing of the octagonal spire over the Trinity tower. Inside, the feeling is not English but decidedly American, and the interior assimilates several features of the late style of Richard Upjohn, to whom the church has occasionally been attributed. Trinity is a ravishingly austere building inside, with compound piers and archivolts of gray stone standing out against the cream white walls, and deep brown diaphragm arches soar across the nave. If Gordon Lloyd was this good (not even his obituary suggested he was), all honor to him!

First Presbyterian Church, on the opposite side of Trinity's graveyard, is the successor church to one that was redesigned and expanded by Benjamin Henry Latrobe in 1812 and to a later Gothic Revival design by Charles F. Bartberger at midcentury. The designer of the present building, Theophilus P. Chandler Jr., was a practiced Philadelphia architect with excellent social connections both in that city and in Boston. In Pittsburgh he was the favored architect of the Thaw family, which resulted in commissions to erect three Presbyterian churches. The challenge to Chandler in 1905 was that the church must look good against the backdrop of Trinity while upholding Presbyterianism in the most intensely Presbyterian city in the country. His response was a much more showy design than Trinity's, with double towers in front and a fantastic march of gables and pinnacles on the side aisle flanking the cemetery. The interior is distinguished by rich and structurally daring woodwork and by fourteen stained-glass windows by Tiffany—outstanding even in a city that abounds in some of the best stained glass in the country. Remarkable, too, is what looks to be an apse behind the altar but operates as a pair of enormous doors that swing open to provide additional space.

The two churches on Sixth Avenue have a host of architecturally pleasing neighbors. The open-air pulpit in front of First Presbyterian, an unusual Medieval feature, points directly across the street to the most powerful of these neighbors, the Duquesne Club. The club moved to this location in 1879, six years after its founding, and a decade later erected its present Richardsonian Romanesque brownstone façade. Inside the Duquesne Club are scattered fifty-four dining rooms, mainly private suites maintained by major Pittsburgh corporations. The role played by the club in the development of Pittsburgh since 1873 can be exaggerated, but not by much. One explanation offered for the peculiar bunching of skyscrapers in certain parts of the Triangle is that the corporate CEOs prefer not to build too far from the Duquesne clubhouse on Sixth Avenue. In a study of civic leadership in Pittsburgh in 1958, Arnold J. Auerbach polled the executive committee of the Allegheny Conference on Community Development, with these results: twenty-four of the twenty-five members belonged to the Duquesne Club, nineteen to the Mellon-centered Rolling Rock Club at Ligonier, and thirteen to the Fox Chapel Golf Club.

Next door to the Duquesne Club is the former German Savings and Deposit Bank, now the Granite Building. This Romanesque Revival bank has to be accounted among the most sumptuously textured buildings in Pittsburgh, though in the end it becomes a fairly tedious catalogue of all the shapes and textures granite can assume.

The 300 Sixth Avenue Building, at the corner of Wood, completes the Sixth Avenue sequence as the counterpart terra-cotta slab to the Oliver Building at the top of the block. It served for a generation as McCreery's Department Store, then from the 1940s to the 1960s as the Spear & Company store. Not having a particularly strong design to begin with, the building was further compromised by an unsympathetic rehabilitation. The new base did, however, include one superb feature: *The Puddler*, an illuminated stained-glass mural of an ironworker. It was installed in 1942 and today is one of the prime icons of the city.

fig. 2.23
THE PUDDLER

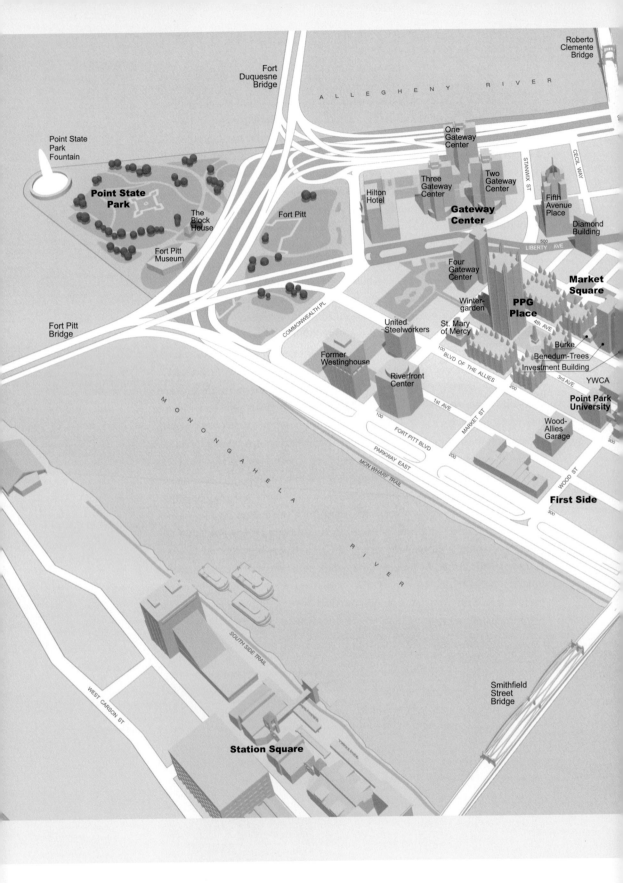

Roberto
Clemente
Bridge

Fort
Duquesne
Bridge

A L L E G H E N Y   R I V E R

Point State
Park
Fountain

**Point State
Park**

The
Block
House

Fort Pitt
Museum

Fort Pitt

Fort Pitt
Bridge

COMMONWEALTH PL

One
Gateway
Center

Hilton
Hotel

Three
Gateway
Center

Two
Gateway
Center

STANWIX ST

CECIL WAY

Fifth
Avenue
Place

**Gateway
Center**

Diamond
Building

LIBERTY   AVE

500

Four
Gateway
Center

Winter-
garden

St. Mary
of Mercy

**PPG
Place**

4th AVE

**Market
Square**

United
Steelworkers

Former
Westinghouse

Riverfront
Center

100   BLVD OF THE ALLIES

Burke

Benedum-Trees

Investment Building

3rd AVE

YWCA

**Point Park
University**

1st AVE

MARKET ST

200

100

FORT PITT BLVD

Wood-
Allies
Garage

WOOD ST

300

PARKWAY EAST

200

300

First Side

M O N O N G A H E L A

MON WHARF TRAIL

R I V E R

SOUTH SIDE TRAIL

WEST CARSON ST

Station Square

Smithfield
Street
Bridge

Andy Warhol Bridge

Rachel Carson Bridge

The Strip

Heinz History Center

10th ST BYPASS

FT DUQUESNE BLVD

CAPA High School

David L. Lawrence Convention Center

SMALLMAN ST

PENN AVE

Byham Theater

Cultural District

Renaissance Pittsburgh Hotel

O'Reilly Theater

Theater Square

Benedum Center

Wood St Gallery

PENN AVE

Westin Convention Center Hotel

Liberty Center

Grant St Transportation Center

The Pennsylvanian

LIBERTY AVE

Heinz Hall

625 Liberty

Keenan

Clark

Harris Theater

LIBERTY AVE

Moorhead Federal Building

Gulf Building

Federal Reserve Bank

MLK JR. EAST BUSWAY

Post Office/ Federal Courts

Two PNC

One Oliver Plaza

Granite

STRAWBERRY

Heinz 57 Center

7th AVE

Bell Telephone

Koppers Building

U.S. Steel Tower

Mellon Arena

Three PNC

One PNC

300 6th Ave

Duquesne Club

Smithfield Church

WAY

Regional Enterprise Tower

WM. PENN PL

Harvard-Yale-Princeton Club

First Presbyterian Church

Oliver Building

Trinity Cathedral

Mellon Square

6th AVE

First Lutheran Church

Piatt Place

OLIVER

AVE

Arrott Building

WOOD ST

300

FIFTH AVE

Park Building

Former Mellon

Citizens Bank Building

Wm. Penn Hotel

Mellon Center

6th AVE

CENTRE AVE

The Bank Tower

FORBES AVE

Macy's

Union Trust

The Carlyle

4th AVE

Former Industrial Bank

SMITHFIELD ST

400

Frick Building

FIFTH AVE

3rd AVE

Times Building

Dollar Bank

Allegheny County Courthouse

Former County Jail

CROSSTOWN BLVD

SMITHFIELD ST

400

BLVD OF THE ALLIES

Oxford Centre

GRANT ST

City-County Building

DIAMOND ST

FORBES AVE

County Office Building

1st AVE

CHERRY WAY

Grant Building

4th AVE

400

3rd AVE

COURT ST

ROSS ST

BLVD OF THE ALLIES

Duquesne University

500

2nd AVE

PNC Firstside

1st AVE

ELIZA FURNACE TRAIL

LIBERTY BRIDGE

Municipal Courts

County Jail

Downtown

2.24
2.25   2.26
2.27

THE CULTURAL DISTRICT AND THE ALLEGHENY RIVERFRONT

For nearly two centuries, the ten city blocks of the Penn-Liberty corridor carried the slightly bawdy or at least lively ambiance of a port, which was the area's main function. In 1760, Penn Avenue became the western terminal of the Forbes Road that went to central Pennsylvania, and by 1820, it served as the terminal of the new turnpike to Philadelphia. Nine years later the first barges reached Pittsburgh on the Pennsylvania Canal, and in 1852, Liberty Avenue was repaved with tracks to become the western terminus of the Pennsylvania Railroad. Until the railroads declined in the 1950s, the Penn-Liberty corridor was the dominant center of Pittsburgh's hotel, entertainment, and wholesale trades. After a generation of neglect, Penn-Liberty has come back to life as the Cultural District, vigilantly watched over by the Pittsburgh Cultural Trust. Conceived by H. J. Heinz II, the trust became one of several Pittsburgh concerns supported by his daughter-in-law, Teresa Heinz Kerry. Entertainment crowds are now an everyday sight as patrons leaving various special events stream from the Lawrence Convention Center, CAPA, Heinz Hall, and the Benedum and Byham theaters.

Sixth Street, the start of the Cultural District, is not to be confused with Sixth Avenue, though it invariably is. While only two blocks long, with half of its length devoted to parking garages, Sixth Street has always been lively because it is the major link between the Golden Triangle and the North Side, on the opposite bank of the Allegheny River. The critical building for the street and the district was Heinz Hall, formerly the old Penn Theater but renovated and renamed in 1971 to become the spark that breathed life into the Penn-Liberty corridor after years of decline. The sumptuously *faux-rococo* Penn Theater opened in 1926 during the glory years of vaudeville and the movies. Marcus Loew's movie palace gradually lost its clientele and went dark in the mid-1960s, until its conversion into the concert hall boosted the performing arts all over Pittsburgh. Under the careful tutelage of William Steinberg, André Previn, and longtime Pittsburgher Lorin Maazel, the Pittsburgh Symphony moved into the top rank of American orchestras.

Pittsburgh responded hungrily to these cultural and architectural offerings, and a plaza was constructed alongside Heinz Hall a decade later as a second amenity. The restoration of Heinz Hall was not flawless, but it captured the right mix of Hollywood theatricality and contemporary performance needs. Ornamental terra cotta was newly fabricated for the exterior, while inside Heinrich Keilholz, one of the world's leading acousticians, molded five tons of plaster into an acoustical reflector over the stage. Opera, ballet, and musicals were so well received that the Pittsburgh Cultural Trust took on the restoration of the nearby Byham (formerly Gayety, then Fulton), Benedum (formerly Stanley), and Harris (formerly porno) theaters and the construction of the O'Reilly Theater.

The link between Sixth Street and the North Side evidently fascinated Henry Phipps, because he commissioned five office towers on or near the Allegheny riverbank between 1900 and 1930. Phipps (1839–1930) was a poor North Side boy who grew rich as bookkeeper and then business partner to his neighbor, Andrew Carnegie. In 1901, he abandoned Pittsburgh for New York after selling his Carnegie Steel shares to J. P. Morgan. Unlike the stereotype of the Gilded Age businessman, Phipps had a conscience. He built flower conservatories on the North Side and in Oakland, established a fine natatorium in the Golden Triangle, commissioned a rent-subsidized model apartment block for his old North Side neighbors, and gave a fortune to Johns Hopkins University in Baltimore for tuberculosis research.

The strength of his roots may well have been the reason why Phipps had so many building investments in clear view of the North Side. (News reports of his day alluded to two more building projects for the north bank of the Allegheny, which would have cemented the whole district as Phipps's personal fief.) Phipps's Bessemer and Manufacturers' buildings, the latter incorporating the natatorium, have been replaced by parking garages, but the Fulton Building still stands, transformed in 2001 into the elegant Renaissance Pittsburgh Hotel. The distinctive seven-story, open-mouth arch fronting Phipps's sky-scraper is the perfect "portal" building for Pittsburgh, and the shape may have influenced the open bracing design of the bridge built at the end of Sixth Street in 1925 (now the Roberto Clemente Bridge). The Renaissance Pittsburgh is distinctive, too, for some Louis Sullivan–style exterior ornament and the disarming luxury of its marble-clad, skylit lobby. There is good reason to believe the persistent legend that Phipps originally intended the building to function as a hotel, not the office building it became. The gloriousness of this space seems to have suggested the next move for Phipps and his clan: first Pittsburgh, next Manhattan, and then on to their greatest building coup as kingpins in the Florida land boom of the 1920s around Palm Beach.

Theater and opera patrons entering the lobby of the Byham Theater on Sixth Street have no way of knowing that the lobby belongs not to the Byham but to the Renaissance Pittsburgh Hotel that looms over it. The explanation probably lies in the shifting of the Pennsylvania Railroad freight line in 1906, from Liberty Avenue to an elevated line along Fort Duquesne Boulevard. The introduction of the tracks blocked direct access to the Byham (the Gayety then), which was given a new lobby within the Fulton Building. It was probably the noise of the trains that induced Henry Phipps to turn his intended hotel into office space.

Fort Duquesne Boulevard was freed from the elevated trains in the late 1940s, and it is now a fine, tree-lined promenade. The street also provides a vision of fulminating Bessemer converters, but this is only in the trompe l'oeil mural painted by Richard Haas in 1993. The mural shows Haas at the top of his form, with a clever juxtaposition of real and painted windows and doors. On the right side of the mural is a special treat: Haas's rendering of the Allegheny and Monongahela rivers joining to form the Ohio. The Haas mural reminds us of the national importance of Pittsburgh's three rivers. It was on the Allegheny riverbank, between the Clemente Bridge and the Convention Center, where in 1803 Captain Meriwether Lewis supervised the construction and launching of the "keeled boat" that he then navigated down the Ohio and Mississippi rivers to St. Louis. By this act, Pittsburgh can claim to have launched the Lewis and Clark expedition, at least informally.

The Allegheny riverbank provides a perfect viewpoint from which to take in the identical "Three Sisters" bridges, one of the lyrical sights of the city. These went up in the 1920s at the ends of Sixth, Seventh, and Ninth streets and were renamed in the late 1990s to commemorate Roberto Clemente, Andy Warhol, and Rachel Carson. The first Sixth Street Bridge dated from 1819; its replacement by John Augustus Roebling stood from 1859 to 1892, with a third bridge from 1892 to 1925. Some fragments of the north abutment of Roebling's structure are still embedded in the Roberto Clemente Bridge. The "Three Sisters" bridges were rebuilt in the 1920s and 1930s as part of a massive highway and bridge program that made Pittsburgh the world center of bridge technology for that time. The bridges are the best public sculptures in the city, with a palpable lightness that comes from their special quality as self-anchoring suspension structures. The parabolic curves of their cables seem to lift the bridges effortlessly over the broad river with the consummate grace of a pole vaulter.

83

fig. 2.28
ANDY WARHOL BRIDGE

fig. 2.29
BRIDGES OVER
THE ALLEGHENY

fig. 2.30
THEATER SQUARE

fig. 2.31
LOUISE BOURGEOIS
SCULPTURES IN
KATZ PLAZA

SEVENTH STREET

Seventh Street is no more important than the other cross-streets in the Penn-Liberty district, but it has some particularly good buildings that have survived. Two of these rise dramatically near the river's edge. The Homes Building at 121–123 Seventh, from around 1905, is a bright and scrupulously maintained Chicago-school commercial block. Across the street, at 130 Seventh, stands the Century Building, a twelve-story reinforced concrete shaft ornamented with green jade terra cotta and several dozen grimacing heads. Developers are converting this Beaux-Arts office building into three stories of retail and office space, with another nine floors of mixed-income apartments. The 151-unit Encore on Seventh apartments opened at the corner of Seventh Street and Fort Duquesne Boulevard in 2007, when Downtown's first grocery store in decades also opened for business. In the works, pending financing, is a housing initiative of still greater ambition: the Pittsburgh Cultural Trust's RiverParc, which is planned to stretch along the riverfront from Seventh to Ninth Street and from Penn Avenue to the Allegheny riverbank, encompassing 700 housing units. When the mix of residential, commercial, and cultural concerns is complete (the current projected date is around 2015), there will no longer be any question of sustaining neighborhood life Downtown.

Were the Pittsburgh Cultural Trust to adopt a single-word motto, it might be "synergy." Recognizing that one or two facilities would fail to reverse the entertainment drain from the Golden Triangle, the trust opted for half a dozen. On Seventh Street at Penn Avenue stands one of their best catches, the Benedum Center for the Performing Arts. Born in 1928 as the Stanley Theater, the Benedum was twinned at birth with the Clark Building next door, erected by movie mogul James Bly Clark. The Clark is a 1920s update of the earlier Frick and Oliver buildings, created as a base for Clark's extensive movie operations—he owned large chunks of MGM, Warner Brothers, and Paramount—and to provide an exchange for the Pittsburgh jewelry trade. The Hollywood interests have moved out, but a good number of jewelers are still there.

More in the public eye than the commercial block is Clark's movie theater, restored and enlarged in 1987 as an opera house. The Benedum's calm Adamesque exterior belies its considerable size (once four thousand seats, now reduced by one-third) and lavish interior decoration. Typical of the 1920s, it had a gigantic Wurlitzer organ, frescoes in the stair halls, and a six-ton amber crystal chandelier that was assembled by eight men working in

85

sixteen-hour shifts for a week. When it was the Stanley Theater, it attracted all the popular music stars, from Al Jolson to Frank Sinatra. As the Benedum, it supports a hectic schedule of musicals, the Pittsburgh Ballet Theatre, and the Pittsburgh Opera.

Rounding out the venues for the arts and entertainment around the intersection of Seventh Street and Penn Avenue are two plazas, a legitimate theater, and a handsome parking garage. The complex goes by the overall name of Theater Square and incorporates the O'Reilly Theater, from 1999, and the adjacent parking garage of 2004. The playhouse, home to the Pittsburgh Public Theater, is a trifle heavy on Neoclassical theory and casual about sight lines and audience involvement, but the parking garage is superb: by turns brilliantly blue and amber, it has the nobility of an Egyptian temple front.

Two plazas face each other at the intersection of Seventh and Penn. One is nameless and hosts art installations that last about a year (the most notable was an assemblage of Pittsburgh façade relics by the Russian sculptor Anatoly Kiradov). The other is Agnes Katz Plaza, with its groves of trees, a towering Louise Bourgeois fountain, and eerie eyeball seats on which visitors are invited to sit.

The architectural king of Seventh Street was, and in a way still is, Colonel Thomas J. Keenan, founder in 1884 of the defunct *Evening Penny Press*, which evolved into the *Pittsburgh Press*, now also defunct. Keenan was a major Downtown developer with a good sense of urban dynamics. He placed his Keenan Building at the corner of Seventh and Liberty so adroitly that a century later his tower is still a stand-out. Keenan's tower consists of a base with sculpted portraits of George Washington, William Penn, and Andrew Carnegie; a brick shaft of eighteen stories enveloped in cream terra cotta; and an early example of a poured-concrete dome. The dome was Keenan's window on the world, and he used it as a luxurious penthouse. Rumor had it that he did not live there alone, however, and a generation of proper Pittsburgh ladies crossed over Liberty Avenue rather than come too close.

LIBERTY AVENUE

Building for building, Liberty Avenue would have to be accounted one of the richest streets in Pittsburgh, though it is the rare pedestrian who examines it that closely. A good starting point for viewing the Liberty Avenue streetscape is 625 Liberty Avenue, adjoining Heinz Hall Plaza. This structure was commissioned in 1984 by Allegheny International, which was a remake of an old specialty steel company that became a conglomerate of advanced technology companies and consumer-oriented firms, such as Sunbeam and Oster. Through some maneuvers that could work only in a closely intertwined business community like that of Pittsburgh, Allegheny International agreed to build in Penn-Liberty if the nearby Stanley Theater would change its bookings from rock music to opera. Allegheny International self-destructed after the civic leaders accepted this bargain, but the tower went up anyway.

The tower, now called 625 Liberty, was designed by one of the most successful architectural firms of the 1980s: Kohn Pedersen Fox, which came up with a retail arcade at ground floor and a setback shaft of thirty stories above, colored and ornamented in the Postmodern mode of those years. The design is lively and distinctive, upbeat but elegant. In a contextual bow to its neighbors, the tower is masonry-clad rather than metal or glass skinned. Its height parallels Two PNC across the street, while its cap reflects the Art Deco top of the Allegheny General Hospital on the North Side. The tower also salutes the nearby Allegheny River, with a crown resembling a simple arched bridge.

fig. 2.32
625 LIBERTY

The adjacent blocks of Liberty Avenue, particularly the side toward the Allegheny River between Seventh and Tenth streets, preserve some notable late Victorian building stock, generally constructed without the intervention of any architect but still impressive. These were wholesale loft buildings, seven to ten stories in height, which took advantage of deliveries directly off the Pennsylvania Railroad trains that came down this street until 1906. Today, mostly professional offices or residences occupy the upper floors.

The earliest examples of the construction that survives in this area are the cast-iron fronts from the later nineteenth century, beginning with the double stores at 805–807 and 927–929 Liberty Avenue, from the 1860s. One can still read the foundry stamp on the first façade: "Anderson & Phillips, 150 Water Street, Pgh." Other cast-iron fronts follow at 951–953 Liberty, with vases of flowers in low relief.

The heyday of cast iron as a structural material was brief, particularly in Pittsburgh, where the many people working in the metal trades knew that cast-iron buildings were brittle and even volatile if subjected to fire. Such buildings also tended to be monotonous, relieved only by bits of Gothic or Italianate detail. For these reasons Pittsburgh continued to ship cast-iron prefabs all over the Midwest but built few for itself after the 1870s. Pittsburgh's preferred commercial style in the 1870s was the elaborate High Victorian Gothic, sometimes incorporating cast-iron mullions within a brick or stone front, at other times only simulating the material for effect. Good examples are the six-story loft at 811 Liberty and a storefront dated 1881 at 820 Liberty, with segmental arches and exaggerated keystones in the manner of the Philadelphia designer Frank Furness. Set among these older buildings is the Harris Theater at 809 Liberty. A venue for independent and art films and the occasional live performance, the Harris is hard to miss because of its bold blue marquee.

Then come the Victorian high-rises, notably the sequence from 901 to 925 Liberty Avenue, which once constituted a continuous row of lofts broken only by a single alley. The sequence was later interrupted by a fire at 917–919, but it is still a dramatic thing to see these massive sandstone blocks marching in step. Particularly striking are the Maginnis Building at 913–915 Liberty and the Ewart Building at 921–925, both from 1891.

fig. 2.33
LOFT BUILDINGS,
LIBERTY AVENUE

The opposite side of the same blocks similarly constitutes a faithful record of mid- to late nineteenth-century commercial life, with other period styles interlaced at random. Among the heartiest of these survivors is the small triangular building at the intersection of Wood Street and Liberty and Sixth avenues. Now used by the Port Authority of Allegheny County, it served for half a century as Azen's Furriers, but it went up in 1928 as the Monongahela National Bank. We can trace its construction history back even further because the building sits on one of the dozen quirky triangles that George Woods drew up in his city plan of 1784. In 1805, this triangle became the second home of Trinity Church, which, evidently inspired by its site, took the shape of an octagon. What exists today is the last gasp of Art Deco used in 1947 when the structure was remodeled into Azen's. When the Port Authority created its subway in the 1980s, it remodeled the block yet again. The structure emerged from this second rehabilitation with sleek Neoclassical-style columns at ground level, a Sol LeWitt marble-and-slate mural on the mezzanine level below, and the Wood Street Galleries above. The galleries host interdisciplinary exhibitions from artists across the world, so the new use for the building brought Pittsburgh both transportation and art.

fig. 2.34
AUGUST WILSON
CENTER

Another happy accommodation of architecture and urbanism takes place two blocks down Liberty at another of George Woods's triangles, this one at the intersection of Liberty, Smithfield, and Seventh Avenue. Here the triangle carries the Triangle Building of 1884, by Andrew Peebles. We know Peebles primarily from this work and from his fine First Lutheran Church on Grant Street, since he lost the Allegheny County Courthouse design competition to H. H. Richardson in 1883 because he failed to get his drawings in on time. Peebles used cast iron for his multitude of columns on the Triangle Building: the walls combine brick and stone trim for effects of texture that metal could not provide. Especially effective is the sense of "live" masonry as the stone lintels appear to split as though they are being forced upward by the purely fictive pressure of the paired columns below them. As in the best work of Frank Furness, the Triangle Building presents a metaphorical picture of a structural system at work, and we respond to it emotionally.

The adjoining block of Liberty creates still another of Woods's triangles, this one where William Penn Way cuts through. This triangle, too, holds just one building: the August Wilson Center for African American Culture. The center celebrates the many African American contributions to Pittsburgh and is named for Wilson, the preeminent American dramatist at the end of the twentieth century. The curved shape on the building alludes to the billowing sail on a slave ship like those that brought the ancestors of Pittsburgh's African American community to America.

L ike any other triangle, the Golden Triangle has three apexes, but since the south and west corners end in views of water, only the northeastern angle formed by the intersection of Liberty and Grant streets presents a significant architectural backdrop. The cluster of buildings there begins on Penn Avenue, where the commercial structures are in slightly later architectural styles than are those on Liberty. The self-confident Beaux-Arts idiom predominates. The General Nutrition Building, which houses a Pittsburgh-based company that is a leading retailer of vitamins and supplements, was originally the Spear & Company Department Store. The Arbuthnot Stephenson Building at Penn and Garrison Alley was also previously a store, as was the Eiben & Irr Building, at 940 Penn. Many of these structures are now condominium or apartment buildings.

Handsome as they are, these blocks of Penn Avenue form a commercial canyon that gives no hint of the Allegheny River just a block away. This disregard for the Allegheny riverfront explains the significant visual impact that the Pittsburgh Public High School for the Creative and Performing Arts (CAPA) had on the district when the structure went up in 2003 at the corner of Ninth Street and Fort Duquesne Boulevard. A well-preserved neighborhood like the Golden Triangle sometimes carries with it the dangers of over-contextualization: designing new buildings with an overeager linkage with their older neighbors. The design team that worked on CAPA walked that tightrope without a single misstep. The four-story curved glass atrium on CAPA's water side gives an architectural wink to the same configuration at Alcoa, across the river. In the same fashion the tumult of whites and reds along CAPA's Ninth Avenue façade imitates a neighboring structure, now incorporated into the complex, that dates from 1915. But nothing about CAPA is servile: it is a raucous celebration of creativity, just like the four hundred adolescents who study inside. And the on-the-cheap theater inside beats Michael Graves's posh O'Reilly Theater hands down.

One block up along the Allegheny is another welcome bit of glitz: the David L. Lawrence Convention Center, also from 2003. This replaces the first try at such a center, from 1981, which was so inadequate that it was torn down scarcely more than fifteen years later. The earlier center had the same site alongside the Allegheny River, but it turned its back on the river and used the water's edge for nothing more than its loading docks. The dull exterior conveyed no sense that this was an important civic monument, so we can be grateful its life was short.

To help the city do better the second time, the Heinz Endowments sponsored an architectural competition, which was won by the internationally prominent Argentinian, Rafael Viñoly, who works out of New York. Viñoly's witty catenary-curve homage to Pittsburgh's bridges held the promise of being Pittsburgh's boldest design statement since the Cathedral of Learning at the University of Pittsburgh arose in the 1920s.

Much of the convention center's promise was fulfilled, but not all. Unforgettable was the vision of water that was to have flowed down the glass roof and cascaded into the Allegheny River—a Fallingwater redux. The water was supposed to have kept down internal temperatures, which was probably an impractical concept, but the visual payoff of the waterfall would have been tremendous. The cascade was overruled as costly and frivolous (it also might have distracted or even showered drivers on Fort Duquesne Boulevard), and the complex also lost its proposed rooftop promenade, which would have offered a riverside view even to people who had not paid admission to the building. The art component has not really paid off, either: with the changed rooftop configuration, Jenny Holzer's twin threads of text about Pittsburgh, rendered in blue electronic strips, lack an audience, and the installation has largely become a throwaway. Pittsburgh can still cheer its convention center as the world's largest LEED-certified building, but the city basically blew its chance to build something truly great.

The adjoining Liberty Center was developed in 1987 as a convention center hotel plus a half million square feet of office and retail space. The original occupant of the site, in 1829, was the Pittsburgh terminal of the Pennsylvania Canal. Since the convention complex had to satisfy multiple viewpoints down two sides of the Golden Triangle, it was configured as two towers and several low structures, giving its rectangular footprint the more dynamic feeling of a triangle. The elevations are straightforwardly late modern in style: they are slightly historicist at the base, where they mirror the

91

fig. 2.35
CAPA, A MAGNET
HIGH SCHOOL FOR
THE CREATIVE AND
PERFORMING ARTS

fig. 2.36
DAVID L. LAWRENCE
CONVENTION CENTER

Romanesque and academic revival façades facing them, then turn corporate high tech at the point where they soar over the surrounding buildings.

At the opposite corner of Eleventh Street and Liberty Avenue, the Grant Street Transportation Center has given the city a new bus terminal and office space that should develop into a significant visual endpoint to this apex of the Triangle.

Another transportation nexus stands on the uphill side of Liberty Avenue, at a dramatic setback from the juncture of Liberty and Grant Street. Like every public building, the recycled Union Station (at some points in its life called Penn-Union), now the Pennsylvanian Apartments, is part architecture and part politics. Pittsburgh had a strong dislike for the Pennsylvania Railroad, which it regarded as an eastern monopoly that bled Pittsburgh as it fattened Philadelphia. This vigorous and self-confident pile of brick and terra cotta was designed to mollify such resentment, which had been fanned into a white heat in the Pittsburgh railroad riots of 1877. In that notorious labor uprising, the rail workers protested their perceived exploitation by setting fire to millions of dollars' worth of structures and equipment.

The architect in charge of the replacement terminal was Daniel Burnham, Pittsburgh's favorite outsider and the leading designer in the country at the time. The patron was the railroad's president, Alexander Cassatt. A native of Pittsburgh like his famous artist sister, Mary, Cassatt understood local sentiment. Also like Mary, Alexander Cassatt had an artistic bent, which he demonstrated by building three of the best railroad stations in the country: McKim, Mead & White's Pennsylvania Station in New York, Burnham's Union Station in Washington, and this one, which opened in 1902. Henry Clay Frick was by then among the biggest stockholders in the railroad, and he too weighed in on this design as central to his own agenda for improvements to Grant Street.

Burnham had been awarded the Union Station commission in 1898, and he responded with a low-lying structure that had a rectangular cab stand in front. This concept he shelved — it would surface later as the key to his

fig. 2.37
ROTUNDA OF THE
PENNSYLVANIAN,
FORMERLY
UNION STATION

Washington station—in favor of a twelve-story skyscraper with a fantastic domed rotunda that combined imperial Roman scale and a whiff of Art Nouveau in its surface decoration. (Pittsburgh architectural historian James Van Trump suggested that Burnham appropriated the design from the main gate of the Paris Exposition of 1900, by René Binet.) The station—apartments since the early 1990s—is adequate, but the rotunda is one of the best things Burnham ever did. For half a century the rotunda worked perfectly as a city gate, beckoning travelers from Grant and Liberty with its bejeweled terra-cotta ornament and the voluptuousness of its supple curves.

COMMERCE AND GOVERNMENT ON GRANT STREET

I t took two centuries of urban doctoring to bring Grant Street to its present state of coherence. In 1829, the city filled in the tongue of Hogg's Pond that cut Grant Street at its midpoint (the fill was the earth that came from the digging of the Pennsylvania Canal tunnel under Grant's Hill). In 1832, 1846, and 1912, Grant's Hill was progressively leveled until it was reduced to a manageable stump. In 1927, a second hindrance to the remaking of Downtown was resolved with the dismantling of the Pennsylvania Railroad freight depot, at the corner of Grant and Seventh Avenue. Only then could Grant Street blossom into a showcase of government and corporate architecture. Today, repaved in brick and granite, it is Downtown's most handsome architectural promenade.

Grant Street begins with three large but muted federal government buildings. It comes as no surprise to find the federal presence so marginalized in Pittsburgh; since the Whiskey Rebellion of Pittsburgh-area farmers in 1794, the city has tended to ignore Washington (and Harrisburg) and concentrated on city and county government alone. The William S. Moorhead Federal Building commemorates the region's Democratic member of the U.S. House of Representatives from 1959 to 1979. It stands twenty stories tall at the intersection of Grant and Liberty but is so bland that it has scant visual impact.

Then come two federal buildings that went up when Andrew W. Mellon served as secretary of the treasury in the Harding, Coolidge, and Hoover administrations, from 1921 to 1932. These are the New Post Office and Federal Courts Building on the full block of Grant from Liberty to Seventh, and, facing it, the Federal Reserve Bank of Cleveland (Pittsburgh branch). The last consists of an office tower and a banking hall with fine interior decoration in Aztec and Egyptian motifs. The exterior is clad in marble and aluminum and punctuated by imposing if chilling heraldic reliefs in Art Deco Style.

As a government administrator, Mellon was able to secure funding for the Federal Courts and Federal Reserve buildings, but in the same years he also commissioned two corporate towers at the intersection of Grant and Seventh Avenue. These were the Koppers Building, in 1929, and the Gulf Building, three years later. The two public and two private commissions were born at the same place and at the same time because Mellon took immediate advantage of the removal of the railroad freight depot in 1927. It is hard to imagine that Mellon would have had either the time or the inclination to get personally involved in the art of architecture, but there is evidence that he did. A letter survives in the Frank Lloyd Wright Archives to show that in the late 1920s or early 1930s Mellon and E. J. Kaufmann Sr. had a significant dialogue on the architectural style that would be used in the Federal Courts Building.

The two corporate towers represent Mellon's foresight as one of the shrewdest venture capitalists in the country. The copper-roofed Koppers Building (an architectural pun) was for years home to a giant construction materials firm that owed its origins to Heinrich Koppers, who had invented a coke oven that trapped blast-furnace emissions and recycled them into useful by-products. Mellon took control of Koppers's invention, which eventually replaced traditional beehive coke ovens. The Koppers tower is a set-back Art Deco rendering of a U-shaped French château. The lobby inside is faced in green, brown, and red marble, with bronze metalwork. The mailbox is a miniaturized Koppers Building, with stylized pineapples and an exaggerated roof, while the pilaster strips take on elements of Greek, Egyptian, Aztec, and Mayan designs.

A. W. Mellon's nephew, William Larimer Mellon, controlled Gulf Oil, the company created to profit from the immense Spindletop oilfields in Texas at the turn of the twentieth century. Pittsburgh's connection with oil at the corner of Grant and Seventh actually went back half a century earlier, when, in 1854, Samuel Kier erected on this spot the world's first refinery for making illuminating oil. At forty-four stories and nearly six hundred feet, the Gulf Building was the tallest in Pittsburgh for almost half a century, but its visual impact is playful rather than domineering. The form is svelte and the materials are pearl gray and light-gray granite. After the Soldiers and Sailors National Military Museum and Memorial Hall and the Carnegie Museums in Oakland, the stepped-pyramid top is the city's third and most effective recall of the Mausoleum of Halicarnassus, one of the seven wonders of the ancient world. The Gulf Building's pyramid takes on a 1920s twist as it rises up in broad terraces that are illuminated with banks of lights at night and topped by an electric weather beacon. The lobby is severely Classical in motif, with the main

fig. 2.38
GRANT STREET
SENTINELS: MELLON
CENTER, U.S. STEEL,
KOPPERS BUILDING,
GULF BUILDING,
FEDERAL COURTS

corridor laid out in modular compartments of deep red and yellow posts and lintels, like a well-appointed Etruscan tomb. The building is no longer associated with oil: Chevron sold it in 1985 after it swallowed up Gulf. Professional and commercial offices moved in, and so did a family of peregrine falcons, which have made their home on the top decks since 1991 — confirmation of Pittsburgh's cleaned-up environment.

A few doors down Seventh, at numbers 416–420, Verizon preserves the ancient Bell Telephone of Pennsylvania Building, claimed to be the oldest telecommunications facility in the nation. It was designed as a switching hall in 1890 by Frederick Osterling; the architect's monogram can be seen on the second pier to the right, aping Richardson's signature on the county courthouse a few years before. At seven stories, Osterling's building is high but not strictly speaking a skyscraper, since it contains no steel and is supported by thick, bulging walls. Bell added an eleven-story skyscraper behind, on Montour Way, in 1905, then more additions in 1908 and 1930, and finally a nuclear-bomb resistant box of 1969 on Grant Street. By that time, the corporation's preferred style had changed to late international school.

The United States Steel Corporation was founded in 1901 by J. P. Morgan as the first billion-dollar corporation in America. The firm was in its heyday as "Big Steel" in 1971 when Harrison & Abramovitz and Abbe designed the U.S. Steel tower for the corner of Grant and Seventh Avenue. The Heinz world headquarters and the UPMC health care group share the building today, but the structure remains an advertisement for steel.

Architectural advertising is an old tradition in Pittsburgh, going back to 1892, the year in which the Carnegie Building left its steel cage standing naked in the sky for six months so people could gape at it. Westinghouse was all electric, PPG all glass, Alcoa all aluminum. But since exposed steel corrodes and is prohibited by fire codes, U.S. Steel used Cor-Ten, a steel invented in 1934. This specialty steel solved the corrosion question because it self-rusts, forming a protective coating around the steel (but not only the steel; a good stretch of Grant Street is covered in rust as well). The fire liability of exposed steel was also solved by filling the eighteen main girders around the building with half a million gallons of water and antifreeze. If attacked by fire, the liquid solution would dissipate its heat by convection and so resist flames for four hours.

The U.S. Steel tower works as a triangle, with three walls of office space set around a braced core. The building is large enough, at sixty-four stories, each with an acre of floor space, that extreme changes in temperature would cause the vertical columns on the exterior to expand and contract as much as nine inches. A building that tall would also sway in strong winds. U.S. Steel engineers solved both of these problems with an innovative "hat" built into the top two stories. Whenever the tower is buffeted by wind loads or extreme changes in temperature, the hat tightens the exterior frame all the way down to the base. Regrettably, the same imagination was not applied to the styling of the building, which looks more like a mechanical diagram than architecture. The only point at which the inner drama of the engineering becomes an architectural drama is in the two-story lobby, where cross-braced girders cut crazily through terrazzo walls. The U.S. Steel tower is a building that commands respect for its engineering and sensitivity to urban design, but it is a hard structure to love.

The U.S. Steel tower acquired a similar younger sibling one block to the south in 1983: One Mellon Center, a fifty-four-story steel-clad Pittsburgh headquarters for the Bank of New York Mellon Corporation. The tower was originally designed to house the Dravo Corporation, an industrial engineering company, which explains the peculiar "bustle" effect at the back: this area was meant to serve as the expansive drafting rooms that engineers use but bankers do not. Mellon completed the tower when Dravo hit financial reversals.

Mellon Center is a competent building, but it may try too hard to be a good architectural neighbor. Its color and its modified mansard roof echo the Union Trust across the street, its material conforms to that of the U.S. Steel tower, and its general proportions replicate those of Richardson's courthouse tower across Fifth Avenue. This concern for contextualization never really paid off, which has always given the Mellon Center a somewhat isolated feel on Grant, even with the financial services facility that it added behind it on Ross Street. A bank as rich as this one ought to *look* rich.

In the nineteenth century, Grant Street was all churches, as befitted a Victorian promenade. Only First Lutheran Church remains, at the corner of Strawberry Way, opposite the U.S. Steel tower. The tower on this eccentric, handcrafted High Victorian Gothic design begins as a squat shape in irregularly coursed brownstones, lifts up to a high lancet belfry with a dwarf arcade at the top, reaches a crescendo in four gables with clock faces, then soars in a slate-covered needle to 170 feet. The effect is lively and colorful, the color reinforced by pink mortar between the stones (perhaps a subliminal touch copied from Richardson's courthouse). The interior is less remarkable, though well conceived for a cramped site; the Good Shepherd window by Frederick Wilson of the Tiffany Studios bathes everything in the radiance of its opalescent glass, and Grant Street suddenly seems far away.

In a lordly gesture, one developer put up all of the structures in the next three blocks on the north side of Grant Street, though he saw himself as the "patron": Henry Clay Frick. There can't be much doubt that Frick (1849–1919) was one of the outstanding giants in a city that produced so many around the turn of the twentieth century. Indisputably canny in business and in collecting art, Frick ran his life and his affairs with a determination worthy of Genghis Khan. But he overreached himself on Grant Street.

The drama of Frick's life began in West Overton, forty-five miles southeast of Pittsburgh. Nearby were the coal fields of Connellsville that Frick eventually turned into the largest coking operation in the world. Frick's forty thousand beehive ovens reduced coal to coke to make it burn many times more fiercely when used at the blast furnaces in Pittsburgh. His mastery of coke made him both Carnegie's most important partner and most dangerous rival. In 1892, Carnegie left to Frick (who was chairman of Carnegie Steel) the task of crushing a strike at the Homestead works, which cost a dozen lives. From New York, the anarchist Emma Goldman dispatched Alexander Berkman to assassinate Frick. Berkman gained entry to his office, shot Frick in the neck and back, and stabbed him in the leg and hip, but Frick finished his day's work as he sat bleeding at his desk—his legendary sangfroid uninterrupted. The Homestead strike hardened Frick's rivalry with Carnegie, and the two wrangled for years over Frick's due share of Carnegie's empire. At the end of his life, Carnegie sought reconciliation with Frick, who told his emissaries, "Tell Mr. Carnegie I'll see him in Hell." The retort was perhaps less harsh than it sounds, however. It was a sarcastic greeting that enemy soldiers would yell at each other in the Civil War, and both Frick and Carnegie would have remembered it.

Frick also battled Carnegie's architectural legacy at every chance he got: on Grant Street; in Point Breeze, where Frick moved alongside estates owned by Carnegie and his brother Tom; in Oakland, where Frick purchased land with the intent of overshadowing Carnegie's museum; and on Fifth Avenue in Manhattan, where their two homes still stand as the last word in opulence.

The sale of the various Carnegie companies to J. P. Morgan in 1901 gave Frick the millions he would for decades pour into his twin delights: paintings and buildings. Frick's astonishing collection of paintings is deservedly famous, but he loved to put up buildings, too. Besides the mansion that is now the Frick Collection in Manhattan, he financed a score of structures in Pittsburgh. Frick got into fine architecture in the 1890s with his house in Point Breeze and the original Union Trust in Downtown. By 1900, he was in high gear and had chosen Grant Street to make a dazzling architectural statement. Grant already had two superb visual anchors in the Allegheny County Courthouse and Penn Station. Frick determined to put up a line of skyscrapers between them.

Frick's first building on Grant Street, from 1902, was the Frick Building, directly opposite the county courthouse. The site had a major impediment: John Notman's St. Peter's Episcopal Church of 1852. The congregation sold their church to Frick in 1901 but obliged him to rebuild it stone by stone in Oakland, where it stood another ninety years until its second destruction around 1990. Frick was determined to get this particular piece of land on Grant because by building his proud tower (with Daniel Burnham, his favorite designer) he would darken and humiliate Andrew Carnegie's headquarters in the Carnegie Building, which stood immediately behind the site, on Fifth Avenue (that building was replaced in 1952 by a Kaufmann store annex). Frick supposedly swore that he was putting up his tower to look down—he used a more emphatic verb—on Mr. Carnegie. Frick's desired metaphor would actually have been possible, since Frick's private bathroom on the twenty-first floor hovered right over Carnegie's headquarters. Frick hired Burnham again in 1905 to design the Allegheny Building, alongside the Frick Building at 429 Forbes Avenue, a maneuver that deprived the Carnegie Building of light from the south after Frick's first tower had cut it off from the east.

Unfortunately, in all of this architectural infantilism the big loser was not Carnegie, who by then spent his time in either New York City or Scotland, but the courthouse. That building had been conceived as the benevolent and protective tower for the whole of the Golden Triangle, but just fifteen years later it was dwarfed and emasculated by Frick's massive high-rise across the street.

Whatever his nefarious motives, Frick procured a fine building, arguably Burnham's best work. The granite-over-steel skyscraper was the first in which Burnham overthrew the cumbersome base-shaft-cap formula for a sleek unornamented tower of cold elegance. What Burnham learned here he used with profit a year later in the nearly identical elevation of the Flatiron Building in New York. The Flatiron has a more memorable footprint, but its barnacled skin looks crocodilian compared to that of the Frick.

The Frick Building's interior is particularly fine. It has two lobbies; the lower one was created out of a basement in 1912 when the city cut twelve feet off the "hump" that remained of Grant's Hill, leaving the original lobby high in the air. That lobby is guarded by two lions—the work of Alexander Phimister Proctor, which influenced the later lions at the New York Public Library—and dominated at the end by *Fortune and Her Wheel*, John La Farge's stained-glass window of a maiden gliding over rough waters. Immediately below the window stands a white marble bust of Frick by Malvina Hoffman, a close friend

fig. 2.39
HENRY CLAY FRICK'S
FOUR SKYSCRAPERS

fig. 2.40
WILLIAM PENN
HOTEL LOBBY

fig. 2.41
FRICK MEMORIALS:
HIS STATUE BUST
AND JOHN LA
FARGE'S *FORTUNE*

of Frick's daughter, Helen. For half a century that bust passed the nights hooded in black velvet—a gesture both of reverence and protection from vandalism. A gold-plated gas jet in the form of a bare-breasted nymph stands a few feet to the right, ready to light up cigars for Frick and his friends, while to the left stands a set of fine turn-of-the-century telephone booths rendered in brass and San Domingo mahogany. The offices upstairs were similarly lavish in their appointment, none more so than room 1926, Frick's personal suite, which for sixty years was home to his daughter Helen's charitable trust. Like her father, Helen Clay Frick (1888–1984) had great affection for Pittsburgh even during the decades she lived elsewhere. One of her ties to the city came to light in Martha Sanger's biography of Helen Frick, which revealed that Henry secretly deeded the tower to her in 1901, while it was still under construction. The skyscraper's new owner was only thirteen.

After putting up his first tower, Frick continued to assemble properties on Grant Street, though twice more he was bedeviled by churches. In 1902, he bought and destroyed Third Presbyterian Church, and he eventually erected the William Penn Hotel on that site. In 1903, he bought St. Paul's Cathedral, and on that site a decade later he would locate the Union Trust.

Now came Frick's great vision, which would have enriched not only him but also Pittsburgh. Frick evidently kept a close watch on Daniel Burnham's plan for downtown Cleveland, unveiled in 1903 as the "Group Plan." It featured a half-mile-long mall that would have terminated in a new railroad station. Circumstantial but persuasive evidence suggests that Frick intended to replicate this arrangement in Pittsburgh, turning the thousand feet of Grant Street between the county courthouse and Penn Station into either a green mall or a parade of noble buildings. In the end, neither Pittsburgh nor Cleveland realized their ambitions. Cleveland got its mall but not a new train station; Pittsburgh got a train station but not Frick's mall.

Frick kept up his efforts on Grant Street nonetheless. For his Union Trust of 1917, where Grant meets Sixth Avenue, Frick chose Gothic over the more usual Classical Style. Some have hypothesized that this move was a nostalgic gesture to St. Paul's, the Catholic cathedral that had stood on the site, but there were more practical reasons. The construction of the Woolworth tower in New York in 1914 had made Gothic newly fashionable for commercial work, and the use of the style for the Union Arcade (it was built as a shopping mall originally) may have been calculated to appeal to a female clientele. Tradition insists that Frick was advised to accept a Lowlands-style (Flemish/ Dutch) design by his art dealer, Lord Joseph Duveen, who was himself of Dutch ancestry. Burnham was dead by this time, but Frick obtained excellent work locally from Frederick Osterling and the latter's draftsman, Pierre Liesch. Liesch, a native of Luxembourg, was well placed to concoct an approximation of a Flemish guild hall.

The Union Trust makes a highly individual statement. It is clad in white terra-cotta plaques and carries an efflorescence of trefoil hood molds projecting out as a cornice line. The roof line is lively without being busy, and it culminates in a forest of dormers, with two chapel-like elevator shafts poking out at top. Internally, the Union Trust is among the most glamorous of Pittsburgh's Downtown buildings. The four-story open shopping arcade was closed when business conditions no longer warranted it, but a stained-glass Cyclops eye still glowers from the top of the central light well, ten stories up.

Frick's architectural promenade on Grant Street ended with the William Penn Hotel, although he got his close friend P. A. B. Widener to erect another corporate building in the adjoining block. The hotel sits on the block between Grant and Mellon Square. Its main entrance is on William Penn Place, since that was the block that went up in 1916; the Grant Street half did not appear until 1929. Determined as usual, Frick vowed to make this the finest hotel in the country. He stole the chef from the Plaza in New York, the maître d'hôtel from the Savoy in London, and the chief clerk from the Bellevue Stratford in Philadelphia. The hotel functioned as a sumptuous—and air-conditioned— clubhouse, with lavish public rooms below and a cafeteria, dormitory, and library on the top floors for servants accompanying the guests. Frick reserved the presidential suite for himself when he was not staying in his Point Breeze or Manhattan mansions.

When the second block, on Grant, went up after Frick's death, it involved Joseph Urban, the chief set designer for the Metropolitan Opera and the Ziegfeld Follies. The Urban Room on the seventeenth floor of the William Penn Hotel is awash with black Carrara glass, ceiling-height windows draped in orange velour, and a frescoed ceiling. This Art Deco masterpiece, as well as the lobby and restaurant, was restored to flawless elegance in a massive restructuring of the hotel that also brought to light a relic of Americana that properly belongs in the Smithsonian but now sits somewhere in the manager's office: the original bubble machine invented by Lawrence Welk when he played there in the 1940s.

Not every scholar cites the Allegheny County Courthouse and Jail as the most distinguished American building of the nineteenth century, but a great many do. Some architects (Philip Johnson was one) call this absolutely the best building in the United States. The courthouse does give the impression of being a near-perfect building. It was a near-perfect solution to a difficult

fig. 2.42
LIGHT WELL, UNION
TRUST BUILDING

fig. 2.43
UNION TRUST ROOF

design problem and was in perfect compliance with the allocated budget. (Allegheny County was so pleased with this accomplishment that it proclaimed the budget, to the penny, on massive brass plaques in the lobby.) It also stands as the perfect tribute to architect Henry Hobson Richardson, who is memorialized in a third-floor tablet that reads, in part, "He left to his country many monuments of art, foremost among them this temple of justice."

The courthouse is unequivocally a nineteenth-century building in its eclectic style, its technology, and its structural system, but it transcends its era. Richardson's design was marred here and there: by the removal of its entrance stairs during the widening of Grant Street (today one enters through the former basement); by the dry interior detailing specified after Richardson's death in 1886 by Shepley, Rutan & Coolidge, a firm whose principals had been his pupils; and by the poor care that generations of bureaucrats have given it. But it is hard to imagine a building that corresponds more closely to what the client wanted from it and what the city and the nation needed it to be—a symbol of justice in the turbulent days when America was coming of age as an industrial power.

When Richardson reluctantly entered the design competition for the courthouse in 1883, the immediate need was to replace John Chislett's Greek Revival courthouse of 1842, which had stood on Grant's Hill until it was destroyed by fire. The specific requirements were complex: a welter of courtrooms, administrative offices, politicians' suites (some with secret stair access), and public counters where citizens could pay their taxes and record their properties, their passports, and their newborn babies. The county commissioners laid out the main lines of the building in the competition program, and it was they, not Richardson, who designated the basic shape of two hundred by three hundred feet, with a jail on the trapezoid block behind. It was also they who insisted on the building's spacious courtyard. It was Richardson, however, who assembled the various components of the project in such masterly fashion. To the basic concept and shape of a Renaissance palace (on one of his preparatory sketches, now at Harvard, Richardson wrote, "Get Farnese"), he added details taken from nearly two dozen historical precedents.

Among these precedents were the superposed arches of the courtyard elevation, which are taken from the Roman Pont du Gard, in southern France; the two back towers are copies of the early Renaissance campanile in Venice's Piazza San Marco; the front tower details are from the Romanesque collegial church at Torres in Spain; the acanthus leaf cornice all around the building is taken from Notre Dame in Paris; and the plan of the jail, with its central octagon and extended arms, is a remake of the fifth-century monastery of

fig. 2.44
ALLEGHENY
COUNTY
COURTHOUSE,
TOWER TOP

fig. 2.45
COURTHOUSE
INTERIOR
STAIRCASE

Kalat Siman in Syria. Other details stem from French, German, Italian, and Spanish Romanesque precedents. The idea of the bridge between the courthouse and jail is borrowed from the Bridge of Sighs in Venice, but the form is that of the Rialto Bridge.

With all of its learned precedents, the courthouse might have become a Victorian horror, but it emerged instead as a well-organized office building, its functions horizontally layered in a complex programmatic sequence. The public offices are at ground level, the main courtrooms on the third floor, and the administrative offices on the top floor. Through this horizontal layering, Richardson ran a complex set of vertical conduits: a grand staircase in front; four elevator shafts (each with a dog-leg stair tower wrapped around them); and pneumatic tubes so paperwork could be passed quickly between the first and third floors. Richardson made the tower on Grant Street three hundred feet high because in it he placed the fresh air intakes for his ventilation system: foul air was expelled from the courthouse through the two back towers. The offices and courtrooms were then arrayed around the courtyard so that no part of the building was deprived of natural illumination.

There are other indications of Richardson's painstaking concern for functionality, too. The old courthouse having burned, the new one was built to be fireproof, and it was likely one of the early buildings fitted for electricity. Richardson designed it as a three-story structure but provided for the possibility of inserting two mezzanines if later needed; today the building has the maximum five floors. Though the interior suffers from bureaucratic neglect, in 1988 the architectural historian Lu Donnelly promoted the restoration of Courtroom 321, and it was achieved to thrilling effect. Most evocative of all are the box girders: they are clad in leather that is itself held in shape by gold-leafed rivets.

What is most admirable about the courthouse design is the way Richardson addressed both the physical and the metaphysical aspects of the problem. One example of that dual success is the double role of the front tower, as both vent intake and symbolic guardian of the city. The *tourelles* (half towers) on the long sides also have a dual purpose: in functional terms, they house both the judges' chambers and the jury rooms set between the courtrooms. In symbolic terms, the *tourelles* and the gaping arches between them represent city gates. (Richardson probably got the concept from the Roman Porta Nigra, in the German city of Trier, or from the main gates of Rome.) Justice is thus the guardian of the city.

Finally, the courthouse exemplifies the elusive attribute that every architect strives to achieve in his or her buildings: the expression of place—what the Romans called *genius loci*. The courthouse does not merely stand in

fig. 2.46
ALLEGHENY COUNTY
COURTHOUSE
AND JAIL COMPLEX

2.47
2.48
2.49   2.50

fig. 2.47
A RESTORED
COURTROOM IN THE
ALLEGHENY COUNTY
COURTHOUSE

fig. 2.48
COURTHOUSE
TOURELLES

fig. 2.49
FORMER JAIL,
ROSS STREET

fig. 2.50
JAIL INTERIOR

Pittsburgh; it *is* Pittsburgh. Richardson thrilled to the vitality of the city, which he captured perfectly in the abstract rhythms of the courtyard walls, and the cyclopean scale of the granite blocks in the jail. The genius of the courthouse is the culminating genius of many traditions that Richardson saw as united in the Pittsburgh of the 1880s. Even Richardson's choice of stone expressed his vision of Pittsburgh as the center point of the country: granite hauled in from Massachusetts for the outside, limestone from Indiana on the inside.

The courthouse also stands at a center point in terms of its technology. It ranks among the last of the great stone palaces that began with the Romans and among the earliest of modern office buildings. But its range as the culminating building of the nineteenth century goes even further. Functional and artistic, poetic and profound, the courthouse complex represents the marriage of the Classical and the Romantic—the two fundamental wellsprings of Western civilization.

Four nearby buildings complement the courthouse in different ways. The closest physically is the former jail on Ross Street, now used for juvenile hearings. In this structure it is Richardson's perimeter wall (extended in 1908 by Frederick Osterling, who also expanded two cellblocks) that takes your breath away, but his interior rotunda is impressive, too. The erstwhile jail still teems with crime stories, notably that of Mrs. Soffel, the warden's wife who sprang the murderous Biddle Boys from jail in 1902.

More stories abound nearby on Fourth Avenue, in Frederick Osterling's morgue, of 1903. This Medieval block is close to Richardson's work in spirit because it used to stand directly opposite the jail until it was moved in 1928. What dislocated the morgue was the construction that same year of the County Office Building on Ross Street, a utilitarian administration building with a few Medieval touches.

The true successor to Richardson's design work on Grant Street is not Medieval but Classical in spirit. This is the City-County Building of 1917, on the opposite side of Forbes Avenue from the courthouse. This is both the city hall of Pittsburgh and an overflow for the county's administrative and judicial offices. Here Henry Hornbostel solved a problem even more intractable than the one presented to Richardson a generation earlier. He had to not only accommodate the same confusing mix of justice, politics, and taxes but also placate the collective egos of both the city and the county politicos who would share the building.

Hornbostel's solution neither mirrored nor challenged Richardson but brought into being a structure that was both amiable and elegant in its own language. The three huge portico arches and the three-story Doric colonnade

fig. 2.51
CITY-COUNTY
BUILDING

ensured that the building would be understood at once as a public monument. Internally, the building also announces its grand and ceremonial purpose through Hornbostel's ingenious vaulted and side-lit corridor, which reveals the full nine-story height of his central light-well. Like every Beaux-Arts architect, Hornbostel sought to convey the inner essence of the institutions he worked for: in the noble and even inspiring chambers of the City-County Building, he lifts us from the indignity to the dignity of civic life.

Indifferently maintained, the City-County Building gained an important treasure in the moving sculpture of Mayor Richard Caliguiri that has stood in the entrance portico since 1990. It is by Robert Berks, creator of the noted Albert Einstein statue on the Mall in Washington.

Henry Hornbostel seems to have known that his Grant Building of 1929, one block closer to the Monongahela riverfront, would be among his last monumental structures in Pittsburgh. In 1927, in the prospectus brochure for it, Hornbostel included a fantasy drawing that portrayed the skyscraper looming over all his other Pittsburgh buildings, including a church and two synagogues, his campuses for the University of Pittsburgh and Carnegie Mellon, and his bridges, hotels, and monuments. In the Grant Building, the old Beaux-Arts master assumed the last of his many styles: a lively, almost garish Art Deco of limestone, brick, and Belgian granite. This plan was tamed considerably between conception and execution and became tamer still as most of the ornament was shaved off over the years. The present lobby arrangement from the 1980s, an update of Hornbostel's original, is a combination of architectural nonsequiturs in the ironic grammar of ornament of a Michael Graves or Robert Venturi. Externally, the building remains a powerful sight, with its dramatically proportioned setbacks resembling a giant's throne.

The forty-six-story Oxford Centre, opposite the Grant Building, creates a successful duet with it because it, too, exploits the power of geometry in its two interlocking octagons of silver-painted aluminum and glass. Oxford serves as the headquarters for many professional firms and corporations but also provides an atrium lined with high-fashion shops and an athletic center and clubhouse set over its parking garage. Neither structurally nor stylistically innovative, Oxford nonetheless has the self-confidence that makes for good contextual architecture.

The architectural treasures of Grant Street conclude with two columns (always called pylons) that mark the intersection of the raised part of Boulevard of the Allies and Grant Street. The American eagles atop the bundled columns and the two Miss Liberty sculptural reliefs flanking the ramp were both carved in 1922 by Frank Vittor, and they repay close examination.

111

fig. 2.52
LOBBY, CITY-COUNTY BUILDING

A street as fine as Grant demands some kind of flourish where it joins the banks of the Monongahela—something equivalent to the way Penn Station closes the opposite end. The city once had such a flourish, just a block away, in Frank Furness's Baltimore & Ohio terminal, but that was torn out in 1955. The needed flourish is now missing, unfortunately, but five relatively recent structures on First Avenue provide partial compensation.

The earliest of the five to go up was the current Allegheny County Jail, from 1995. This successor to the old jail will never follow Richardson's into the architectural history books, although it garnered some function awards from penologists. Pittsburgh mostly regards this costly "Hilton-on-the-Mon" with disdain because of the visual pollution it creates as one drives into town. Richardson's reputation has nothing to fear from it.

fig. 2.53
THE COURTHOUSE
TOWER AMID
OXFORD CENTRE
(LEFT) AND MELLON
CENTER (RIGHT)

A much better design emerged in the Pittsburgh Municipal Courts Building that the Astorino firm rushed to completion alongside the jail in 1995. This tiny courthouse facility is physically linked to the jail, since it holds night courts and preliminary hearings for detainees around the clock, but its design philosophy could not be more different. The jail is nakedly utilitarian in intent, with a pseudo-historical veneer derived from Duquesne University's Old Main on the hill above. By contrast, the Municipal Courts Building is a sincere attempt to revive the Beaux-Arts message of institutional dignity. Despite its low budget and a miserable site below the Liberty Bridge, the Courts Building gives a coloristic flourish on the exterior walling, a winsome plan (an approximation of a tetraconch, with two pointed ends and two curved sides), and a setting of low-key nobility for the dispensing of justice. Light pours four floors down from central skylights, revealing the essential shape of the building the moment one enters it. The main courtroom is noble in a proletarian way, too, with good natural light and as much wood paneling as the budget would allow. Justice is treated with true dignity here—not just for the judges but for the accused. It is a design that does not take respect for granted; it earns it.

fig. 2.54
FIRST AVENUE
LIGHT RAIL STATION

In 2001, the Astorino firm did a competent job of fitting PNC Firstside Center, a large, multifunction complex, into a difficult site at the intersection of Grant Street and First Avenue, designing its riverside façade to mimic the curved ramps of the Parkway (I-376). In the same year IKM Inc. produced two more structures for an even more difficult site: a triangular wedge set between the Panhandle Bridge (which carries LRT or Light Rail Transit system cars to and from the south suburbs) and the 1920s Liberty Bridge. The resulting First Avenue Garage and Station combines a six-level garage with a stop on the T (the LRT). The garage and T-stop proffer an elegance far exceeding their commonplace function, combining a distinctive metal roof-top shed, a luminous six-level atrium for the elevators, a full-glass façade for the escalator, and two marvelous free-form canopies.

The half-dozen new structures along First Avenue give cause for optimism for the future of the Golden Triangle. They demonstrate that new Downtown buildings need not be, and perhaps should not be, definitive architectural statements. The Triangle is still in a state of development, rather than comple-tion, and its best years may lie ahead of rather than behind it.

113

3 THE NORTH SIDE: A RIVAL CITY

fig. 3.1
SCULPTURAL
FRAGMENTS FROM
PITTSBURGH'S
LOST BUILDINGS
AND BRIDGES

Pittsburgh's North Side stands at an acute junction today. For a century, the name "North Side" referred to a dozen fairly modest neighborhoods, such as Manchester or Troy Hill, that were home to residents of various races, classes, and heritages. Now the North Side is filling up with museums, sports facilities, offices, housing, and even a gambling casino, and these new forces refer to the district as the North Shore. Which way will the neighborhood identity go: traditional North Side or edgy North Shore?

The area long known as the North Side was visited as early as the 1740s by traders from eastern Pennsylvania who took note of the broad flat land that provided a good venue for meeting American Indians. In 1783, the Commonwealth of Pennsylvania set aside the so-called Depreciation Lands for Revolutionary War veterans, who were awarded back pay in farmland instead of cash. (The idea of paying war veterans with land instead of cash is an old one, going back to at least the Roman Empire.) The next year, Pennsylvania paid Alexander McClain and Daniel Leet to survey a reserve tract of three thousand acres that would be bounded on the south by the Allegheny River and on the west by the Ohio River. On that tract, Allegheny City was laid out in 1788 as the seat of a new Allegheny County that would stretch as far north as Lake Erie. But Allegheny City never got to be a county seat; Pittsburgh grabbed that status for itself.

In the end, the destiny of Alleghenytown (as its residents usually called it) was industrial and not pastoral. Few if any veterans settled there, and many of the lots ended up being used as factory sites. For a hundred years, the North Side yielded an industrial produce of astonishing variety: cotton textiles, glass, rope, flour, oil, salt, woolens, carriages, wagons, coaches, plows, sleighs, boats, paper, saddles, harnesses, boots, shoes, pottery, brassware, springs, locomotives, and cast-iron bathtubs.

It was the cotton textile mills that inspired the weaver William Carnegie to make his difficult trek from Dunfermline, Scotland, in 1848. Carnegie's wife, Margaret, stitched shoes for a North Side cobbler, while his son Andrew changed bobbins in a cotton mill. Before its forced annexation to Pittsburgh, Allegheny City constituted a flourishing municipality in its own right. It lured the University of Pittsburgh, briefly, before that institution moved across town to Oakland. Allegheny City put up a famous astronomical observatory and had its own roster of celebrated citizens. The latter included the industrialists Carnegie, Heinz, Benjamin Franklin Jones, William Thaw Jr., and Henry Oliver; the scientists John Brashear and Samuel Pierpont Langley; and the writers and artists Willa Cather, Gertrude Stein, Robinson Jeffers, Mary Roberts Rinehart, Mary Cassatt, Martha Graham, and Bartley Campbell. Around 1900, Brighton Road and Ridge Avenue claimed more millionaires than any other two blocks in the world.

After a century of neglect, the contemporary North Side is proving to be a fascinating laboratory, not for science or technology but for the process of rehabilitation and repopulation of its old neighborhoods—a process with results that are relevant elsewhere in the nation.

fig. 3.2
WEST PARK

OLD ALLEGHENY

The founder of Old Allegheny was, technically speaking, Benjamin Franklin. It was he, as president of the Supreme Executive Council of Pennsylvania, who in 1788 commissioned David Redick, a surveyor from neighboring Washington County, to lay out Allegheny City. Redick was far from enthusiastic about the chosen site, writing to Franklin that "[the land] abounds with high hills and deep hollows, almost inaccessible to a surveyor.... It would have been far more suitable for residents of the moon, than farmer or settler."

Redick nonetheless worked the best acres of the North Side into a square of thirty-six blocks, each 240 by 240 feet and each subdivided into four smaller lots. He left the four central blocks empty, for public use, and also provided a common grazing land of 102 acres that surrounded the little city's boundaries. Redick's design was most likely based on New England town plans, like that of New Haven, Connecticut, but its ultimate source may have been the Bible. The forty-eight Levitical cities of ancient Israel were similarly described as squares surrounded by common pastureland in roughly the same proportion as Allegheny, but at twice the scale.

Redick's designated grazing area faced the threat of competing uses, none more menacing than the laying of the Pennsylvania Railroad tracks through West Park in 1852. Still, a surprising three-quarters of the original pastureland survives today, ringed in part by the Mexican War streets, where the veterans were supposed to have their agricultural out-lots, smaller than farms but intended for sustenance.

Old Allegheny disappeared not from war or pestilence but by being gobbled up by Pittsburgh in 1907. The decades of neglect that followed should give pause to western Pennsylvania's current crop of annexation enthusiasts. What remained of Old Allegheny suffered from the unexpected consequences of urban renewal, which began during the economic boom of the 1950s but diminished in the turbulent racial atmosphere of the 1960s.

The renewal was driven by Alcoa, which cut out the heart of Allegheny City by razing 518 old buildings. That gaping hole now presents itself as Allegheny Center, bounded by a ring road bearing the names North, East, South, and West Commons. At its center lies the failed Allegheny Center Mall from the 1960s, condemned to an early death by its clichéd and dreary retail layout and its isolation atop an ugly parking garage. North of the former mall (now offices) stand a half-dozen low office towers and a set of apartment blocks.

No one could have foreseen that the best part of the development would turn out to be the adjacent Allegheny Commons East, from the 1970s. What began as a rent-subsidized development was more successful in architectural and human terms than the upscale townhouses in the counterpart Foster Square (now the Allegheny) on the west side of Allegheny Center. Allegheny Commons East takes its architectural motifs from medieval Italian hill towns such as Gubbio or Viterbo and, like them, ingeniously weaves its streets and ramps though the buildings. Its density is substantial: 136 housing units on just three acres, or about nine times the density ratio built into the 1930s Chatham Village. But the Commons clearly benefited from Chatham Village in its internal focus and modest but gracious design vocabulary.

The urban redevelopers of the 1960s allowed just three relics of Old Allegheny to survive in the heart of the new development: the Carnegie Library, Buhl Planetarium, and Allegheny City Post Office. What is now called the Carnegie Library–Allegheny Regional Branch, from 1889, was the first of Andrew Carnegie's libraries not strictly linked to any of his industrial installations. Its design emerged from a national competition, with Carnegie personally involved in the selection. His choice of Smithmeyer & Pelz was almost inevitable after the firm won the competition for the Library of Congress. Instead of being in the Classical mode, as is their Washington library, this architectural idiom replicates that of Richardson's Allegheny County Courthouse, although in a far less interesting way. The library tower is fine, but elsewhere the massing of forms is arbitrary and confusing rather than enlivening, and the treatment of the stone is flat. The adjoining Carnegie Hall (the first to carry that celebrated name) was imaginatively reworked in 1976 and served for years as the home of the Pittsburgh Public Theater until that organization relocated Downtown in 1999. Now the hall serves the New Hazlett Theater, founded in 2004 as a nonprofit organization to serve small arts groups. Alongside the library stands Daniel Chester French's *Labor*, the central figure from a partly rebuilt monument that Carnegie commissioned in 1904 in memory of James Anderson. Anderson was the ironmaster who opened his private library to the "working boys" of Allegheny City, an act of generosity Carnegie never forgot.

The whole of the next block west of the library was reserved for the Buhl Planetarium and Institute of Popular Science, an Art Deco evocation of the values that Carnegie had sought in his library fifty years earlier. This is a sleek, low building from the 1930s, with fine sculpted reliefs and walls rendered in smooth limestone over a rusticated base. For years, the planetarium offered a yearly cycle of star shows and hands-on exhibits of science phenomena, but then it closed in 1991.

fig. 3.3
ALLEGHENY
COMMONS EAST

fig. 3.4
THE FIRST
CARNEGIE LIBRARY,
NORTH SIDE

The next block west had a once-empty structure, too, in the Allegheny City Post Office. The recycling of this monument into the Old Post Office Museum was one of the first triumphs of the Pittsburgh History & Landmarks Foundation (PH&LF). The building is a handsome, if somewhat cold, mixture of classically derived motifs, culminating in a double-shell dome that is imposing on the exterior but intimate inside. Next door, PH&LF assembled a striking garden of sculptural and architectural fragments from lost Pittsburgh buildings, notably Charles Keck's astonishingly scaled bronze reliefs from the Manchester Bridge of 1915.

The stepchild in this group is the Children's Museum of Pittsburgh, which took over the empty planetarium to its left and the post office to its right and linked them with what it calls the "Green Museum" in 2004. This steel-and-glass structure, the largest silver-class LEED-certified museum in the country, is notable for its environmentally friendly design and construction, making the building itself a teaching tool. The highlight is Ned Kahn's butterfly design of glass panels that form a wind sculpture by day and an illuminated lantern by night.

The common grazing ground that once encircled Allegheny survives, in the main, as West Park. Beginning in 1826, the commons was dominated by the mass of William Strickland's Western Penitentiary (modified by John Haviland in 1835), before a new jail went up in Woods Run in 1887. The grounds were then organized into the first urban park in western Pennsylvania. Today the park offers residents a small artificial lake, Lake Elizabeth, along with playgrounds, tennis courts, and a farmers' market. A family street stand has been selling peanuts, popcorn, and ice balls at the park since 1934.

fig. 3.5
SPANISH-AMERICAN WAR MEMORIAL, WEST PARK

Today the commons is free of buildings, except for the National Aviary, which houses more than six hundred exotic and endangered birds in a remake of the flower conservatory that Andrew Carnegie's business partner Henry Phipps gave Allegheny City in 1887. Three public monuments also stand in the park: an equestrian George Washington statue from 1891; a columnar Civil War soldiers' monument transferred to its current location from what is now the campus of the Community College of Allegheny County (CCAC); and the best of the lot, Charles Keck's Spanish-American War memorial of 1914. The torpedo tube and armored porthole that are represented as sinking in a pool of water are actual relics from the submerged USS *Maine*. Keck also designed the memorial tablets in the severe brick exedra wall behind the memorial. The effect is startlingly evocative: a testimonial to the horrors of war that entirely avoids glorifying it.

fig. 3.6
MEXICAN WAR
STREETS

THE MEXICAN WAR STREETS AND ALLEGHENY WEST

Across West North Avenue from West Park lies the Mexican War streets district, incorporating about three hundred houses on a dozen city blocks. It was the impending destruction of these homes that gave birth to the Pittsburgh History & Landmarks Foundation in 1964 as one of the early ventures in historic preservation in the United States. In this instance, it sought the preservation not merely of individual buildings but of a whole neighborhood. The Mexican War streets homes were built from the 1850s to the 1890s on small (generally twenty feet wide) lots parceled out by General William Robinson Jr. on streets he named for the heroes and battle sites of the U.S.-Mexico War, in which he had fought. The two-story pre–Civil War houses are generally tied to the Greek Revival Style, while the post–Civil War houses are typically three stories high, often with mansard roofs. The homes were designed for a higher social stratum than were the equivalent rows on the South Side, Lawrenceville, or the Hill. The residents were professional people, prosperous artisans, or the owners of businesses in downtown Pittsburgh, which after 1859 they could reach in minutes by horsecar.

The rowhouses of the Mexican War streets decayed into boardinghouses or flophouses by the mid-1960s, but the district held such little importance to the wider city that no one bothered to demolish them. The Pittsburgh History & Landmarks Foundation restored many, and it sought to sustain the local African American community when white professionals began moving in. A substantial gay and lesbian community also moved into the area and became the driving force behind a surge in home refurbishing. The YMCA at Monterey and North Avenue, the Mattress Factory (discussed below), and the neighborhood churches have helped to transform what would have become a reverse ghetto into a flourishing biracial neighborhood.

There are hundreds of fine houses in the Mexican War streets district, but among the standouts are 516 West North Avenue (at the corner of Monterey, circa 1870), with the plan of an Italianate home but ornamented with old-fashioned Federal details; a Queen Anne house at 1201 Resaca Place, at the corner of Eloise, with a pyramidal fishscale roof and a delightful corner turret; and its counterpart at 1201 Buena Vista, an exuberant Richardsonian Romanesque brownstone of around 1890, with a three-story bay that terminates in an open loggia and conical roof. The servants' quarters and carriage house behind this slab-shaped mansion are conceived instead in the earlier Queen Anne style, in wood.

Not many American cities contain a functioning monastery in their midst, as Pittsburgh does on the South Side, and fewer still preserve alms-houses, which is essentially what the Allegheny Widows' Home on North Taylor Avenue was until 1983. The three-story Greek Revival main building was erected in 1838 as the Orphan Asylum of Pittsburgh and Allegheny. In 1866, it also became a home for Civil War widows, and six years after that the City of Pittsburgh constructed rowhouses on three sides of the main build-ing, where widows could live with their families in small townhouses. The institution continued in that mode for more than a century. In 1984 and 2006 the complex was rehabilitated under HUD section VIII funding as federally subsidized housing for the elderly and disabled.

For close to a century on Sampsonia Way, workers made Stearns & Foster mattresses in a tall building that dated from around 1870. Its abandoned shell was taken over in the 1980s to become the Mattress Factory, a center that is hailed worldwide for installation art, and two new additions followed. Room-size exhibits, both permanent and temporary, demand and repay long spells of contemplation: one label outside a pitch-dark gallery advises viewers that they may not be able to discern anything in the gallery until they sit inside for half an hour.

Rising high above the domestic rooftops, the eastern boundary of the Mexican War streets district is guarded by Engine Company No. 3 at the corner of Arch Street and Jacksonia. This colorful firehouse from 1877 is a pleasing amalgam of High Victorian Gothic and Italianate details. Except for the loss of the octagonal cupola over the tower, the building is intact and enjoys a new life as a gallery.

Also fronting West Park, but on a diagonally opposite corner from the Mexican War streets district, the smaller but richer Allegheny West constitutes just a dozen blocks in the trapezoid formed by West North Avenue, Brighton Road, and Ridge and Allegheny avenues. The houses in Allegheny West are some of the most distinguished in town, and the neighborhood boasts two of Pittsburgh's best churches as well. A good introduction to the neighborhood is provided by the three-story brick townhouses called McIntosh Row, at the corner of Western Avenue and Brighton Road. Greek Revival details still pre-dominate in these townhouses, though the date is late for that style, around 1865. McIntosh Row's basic lines were transposed into a more luxurious scale by the residences at the end of the row: a set of two Italianate double houses at 814 and 816 Western, and two single townhouses at 818 and 820 Western. McIntosh Row's ground-floor windows were elongated during restoration in 1979, which makes them "incorrect" but no less elegant. Though wrong

stylistically, the windows add to the marketability of a block that would otherwise have invited destruction.

The Joshua and Eliza Rhodes house (now the Parador Inn, at 939 Western Avenue), from around 1866, with porch and wing added in 1875, is an excellent example of a wealthy individual's "modest" mansion in the decades before Frick, Heinz, and Westinghouse put up homes of monstrous size. Joshua Rhodes made his "modest" fortune in public transportation. The Caribbean-style bed-and-breakfast that now occupies Rhodes's home preserves its twenty-two rooms and its twenty-seven-hundred-square-foot ballroom in an adjoining carriage house. The latter comes complete with a tin ceiling and hardwood floors, an update from the 1920s. The Rhodes house treats you to its fine touches at every turn, starting with the exquisite leather-clad walls and the delicately tiled floor of the entrance vestibule.

For mansions of the later Gilded Age, from the 1880s through World War I, one need look no farther than Brighton Road, overlooking West Park, and the houses around the corner on Ridge Avenue. The great majority of the architectural dinosaurs once standing here have disappeared, but one impressive survivor is the Benjamin Franklin Jones Jr. house, where Ridge Avenue meets Brighton Road. This is a forty-two-room Tudor fortress of concrete reinforced with steel, which was the family product. By 1908, when the house went up, Allegheny City had lost its independence, and the Jones family left in 1931 to live year round at their summer estate in Sewickley Heights. The Jones house now belongs to the community college across the street; its looks were more institutional than domestic to begin with, and it is almost indistinguishable from the Tudor pile of what used to be the Western Theological Seminary alongside it.

At the west end of the same block stands the William Penn Snyder house at 850 Ridge, at the corner of Galveston Avenue, from 1911. Divided into offices for an insurance broker, this mighty townhouse belongs to the species that many a Pittsburgh millionaire constructed in Manhattan but only a few built here. A light-toned brownstone, the Snyder house aims at the general impression of an eighteenth-century Paris *hôtel* but reveals its true era with the automobile garage doors on Galveston Avenue. The interior is largely finished in marble, with superbly carved overdoor decorations and jambs in mahogany. The house cost nearly a half-million dollars to build (something like $15 million today), but the Snyders left it after only a few years when they joined the retreat to Sewickley Heights. The next block is dominated by the Byers-Lyon house at 901 Ridge, a somewhat artless hodgepodge of Italian and French Renaissance motifs set around a courtyard that was supposedly modeled on the Alhambra. Now part of the Community College of Allegheny County, this double house of ninety rooms and fourteen baths for a father and his daughter cost even more than the Snyder house.

The William Thaw Jr. house at 930 Lincoln Avenue, a block closer to the Allegheny, is an architectural palimpsest of the years 1875 to 1900, with the original Romanesque Revival building on the right, a later segment with an unusual recessed porch in the middle, and a third wing in Colonial Revival Style on the left. The brickwork triangles on its crow-step Dutch gable are a detail borrowed from Richardson's Emmanuel Episcopal Church a few blocks away. The charming Italianate house with a verandah next door at 940 Lincoln was home for almost fifty years to Art Rooney, founder of the Pittsburgh Steelers.

Two streets parallel to Lincoln, away from the Allegheny riverfront, lies Beech Avenue, with an engaging series of three-story houses from the late nineteenth century, many adorned with spacious verandahs. Two famous names attach themselves to houses here. Gertrude Stein (who, as she wrote, "always remained firmly born in Allegheny, Pa") was born in 1874 in the richly adorned two-story Italianate brick house at 850 Beech; Mary Roberts Rinehart lived for years in a substantial brick house one block over, at 954 Beech, at the corner of Allegheny Avenue. It was in this house in 1907 that Rinehart wrote *The Circular Staircase*, one of America's pioneering mystery novels.

Separated by a city block and six years in date, two distinguished Allegheny West churches take diametrically opposed positions in both architectural and ideological terms. Calvary United Methodist Church at the corner of Beech and Allegheny represents the best in the luxurious churches of the High Victorian Gothic Style. Everything about the church inside and out is rich, textured,

fig. 3.9
GERTRUDE STEIN HOUSE

and comfortable, so that to enter it is to intrude on a sumptuous private drawing room. The sanctuary is dominated by a wooden barrel-vaulted ceiling that converges over the space in a complex sixteen-sided vault reminiscent of the octagon crossing at Ely Cathedral in England. The making of the Resurrection, Ascension, and Apocalypse stained-glass windows was directly supervised by Louis Comfort Tiffany, who exhibited the latter two as his best work at the Chicago World's Fair in 1893, prior to their installation at Calvary United Methodist. Though it seats eight hundred, Calvary is lucky to attract two dozen worshipers on any given Sunday. Undaunted, the church board has made great strides in maintaining and restoring their architectural treasure.

Honesty of design is not Calvary's strong point. What appear on the outside to be small half-octagonal side chapels protruding from the nave turn out to be mere conversation points inside, with no liturgical function at all. Exterior gables around the apse simulate radiating chapels that you also will not find inside. Calvary actually has no apse at all; what reads as such on the exterior turns out to be an apse-shaped Sunday school inside.

Henry Hobson Richardson's Emmanuel Episcopal Church at the corner of West North Avenue and Allegheny looks at first glance to be the power plant for Calvary. It is an unpretentious brick building (neighbors call it the "bake oven") that cost only twenty-five thousand dollars to construct—under 1 percent of the expense lavished on Richardson's contemporaneous courthouse. While the courthouse exults in its complexities, Emmanuel is reductionist and minimalist—perhaps more than any American church of the nineteenth century.

If the richness of Calvary is one of vocabulary, then the richness of Emmanuel is one of syntax. Here Richardson ignored the spire and the transept—the twin crutches of church design—and conceived Emmanuel with nothing more than the vividness of the brickwork and the power of a severe triangular gable set low on a canted base. The brickwork designs are more intricate than any Richardson had designed before, which shows his trust in his Pittsburgh laborers. The designs entailed five concentric circles of brick around each of the three entrance arches, then a zone of complex basket weave on the gable wall above, and finally *muisetanden*, or "mouse teeth," infill triangles along the gable edge. One can imagine that Richardson appropriated this feature from Dutch colonial architecture in the Hudson River Valley, a domain he knew well from working on the New York State capitol at Albany.

To the shape, texture, and color of the exterior, Richardson added his expertise at rhythmic groupings. The interior of the church, with its three bays demarcated by laminated wood arches, is admirably expressed outside in the rhythm of the windows. Entering the dynamic space of this church, the worshiper feels enwrapped in a spiritual cocoon. Richardson got the commission in August 1883 from the chair of the church's building committee, the Honorable Malcolm Hay, assistant postmaster of the United States. Richardson's selection for this relatively modest building was almost certainly helpful in smoothing the way to the commission he won a few months later for the Allegheny County Courthouse—a job that was literally a hundred times more costly.

Not surprisingly, only a few of the scores of mansions that once existed in Allegheny West are still standing. It was fortunate that what swallowed many of them up was the Community College of Allegheny County, which has demonstrated its commitment to both new architecture and old. CCAC enrolls more than sixty thousand students on four campuses. In turning the long slope facing Ridge Avenue into CCAC's North Side Campus in 1973, Tasso Katselas faced a challenge not so different from the one resolved by Henry Hornbostel in his Acropolis-style campus for the University of Pittsburgh in 1908. Katselas's solution was different from Hornbostel's, though, since the invoking of historical precedents was not popular in the 1970s. Nor did the economics of maintenance allow Katselas to produce a multitude of smaller buildings, as Hornbostel had projected in Oakland. Katselas created instead a sequence of interlocking buildings in poured and cast concrete with a textured brick facing. Not everyone loves it, but the complex maintains itself well, and by now it is a North Side icon. One can usefully compare it with the more mellow Institutional Style Katselas adopted in 1985 when he designed the Bidwell Training Center and Manchester Craftsmen's Guild at 1815 Metropolitan Street, about a half-mile away.

MANCHESTER, PERRY HILLTOP, OBSERVATORY HILL, AND FINEVIEW

The once-independent town of Manchester was founded in 1832 alongside Allegheny City, on the east bank of the Ohio River. Its name was a double augury: to prosper in the production of cotton cloth, as did Manchester in England, and to rival the earlier town of Birmingham on what is now Pittsburgh's South Side. Manchester flourished for about a century, overcoming the shift of cottons to the South and to New England and annexation, first by Allegheny City, in 1867, and then forty years later by Pittsburgh. It is bounded by Bidwell, Chateau, Franklin, and Foulsey streets and by Columbus and West North avenues.

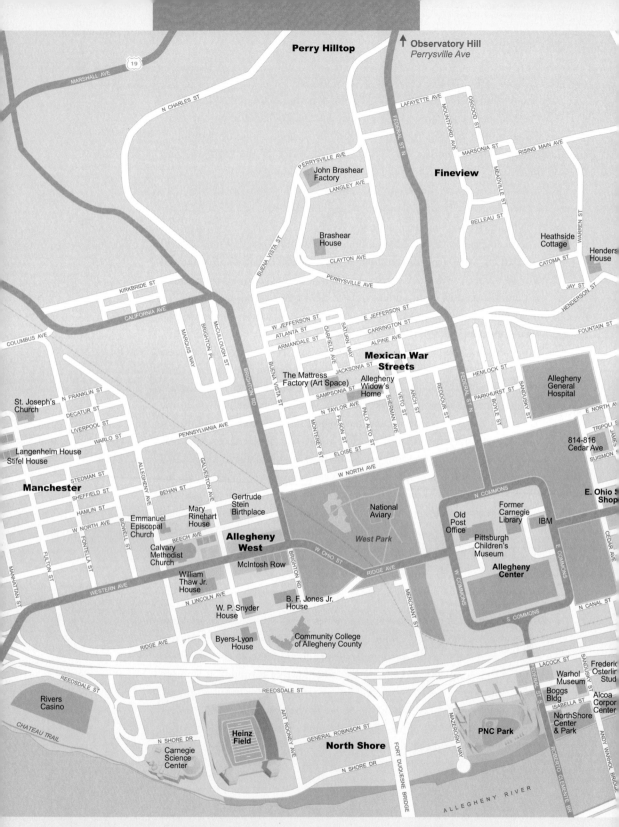

Perry Hilltop

↑ Observatory Hill
Perrysville Ave

MARSHALL AVE

19

N CHARLES ST

LAFAYETTE AVE

MOUNTFORD AVE

OSGOOD ST

Fineview

PERRYSVILLE AVE

MARSONIA ST

John Brashear
Factory

LANGLEY AVE

MEADVILLE ST

RISING MAIN AVE

WARREN ST

BELLEAU ST

Brashear
House

CLAYTON AVE

Heathside
Cottage

CATOMA ST

Henders
House

BUENA VISTA ST

PERRYSVILLE AVE

JAY ST

HENDERSON ST

KIRKBRIDE ST

FOUNTAIN ST

CALIFORNIA AVE

MARQUIS WAY

BRIGHTON PL

McCULLOUGH ST

W JEFFERSON ST

E JEFFERSON ST

COLUMBUS AVE

ATLANTA ST

CARRINGTON ST

ARMANDALE ST

GARFIELD AVE

SATURN WAY

ALPINE AVE

**Mexican War
Streets**

HEMLOCK ST

Allegheny
General
Hospital

BUENA VISTA ST

The Mattress
Factory (Art Space)

JACKSONIA ST

Allegheny
Widow's
Home

SAMPSONIA ST

VETO ST

ARCH ST

REDDOUR ST

FEDERAL ST N

PARKHURST ST

BOYLE ST

SANDUSKY ST

St. Joseph's
Church

N FRANKLIN ST

DECATUR ST

N TAYLOR AVE

FILSON ST

PALO ALTO ST

SHERMAN AVE

E NORTH A

LIVERPOOL ST

MONTEREY ST

TRIPOLI

JAMES

WARLO ST

PENNSYLVANIA AVE

ELOISE ST

SUISMON

Langenheim House
Stifel House

W NORTH AVE

814-816
Cedar Ave

STEDMAN ST

Manchester

ALLEGHENY AVE

BEHAN ST

Gertrude
Stein
Birthplace

National
Aviary

N COMMONS

Former
Carnegie
Library

IBM

**E. Ohio S
Shop**

SHEFFIELD ST

Mary
Rinehart
House

Old
Post
Office

HAMLIN ST

BIDWELL ST

GALVESTON AVE

Emmanuel
Episcopal
Church

BEECH AVE

**Allegheny
West**

Pittsburgh
Children's
Museum

E COMMONS

CEDAR AVE

W NORTH AVE

FONTELLA ST

Calvary
Methodist
Church

McIntosh Row

West Park

W COMMONS

**Allegheny
Center**

FULTON ST

William
Thaw Jr.
House

BRIGHTON RD

W OHIO ST

N CANAL ST

MANHATTAN ST

N LINCOLN AVE

B. F. Jones Jr.
House

RIDGE AVE

MERCHANT ST

WESTERN AVE

W. P. Snyder
House

S COMMONS

Byers-Lyon
House

Community College
of Allegheny County

RIDGE AVE

LACOCK ST

SANDUSKY ST S

Frederic
Osterlin
Stud

REEDSDALE ST

Warhol
Museum

Boggs
Bldg

ISABELLA ST

Alcoa
Corpor
Center

Rivers
Casino

REEDSDALE ST

FEDERAL ST S

NorthShore
Center
& Park

CHATEAU TRAIL

ART ROONEY AVE

GENERAL ROBINSON ST

MAZEROSKI WAY

PNC Park

ANDY WARHOL

N SHORE DR

**Heinz
Field**

North Shore

FORT DUQUESNE BRIDGE

ROBERTO CLEMENTE BR

Carnegie
Science
Center

N SHORE DR

ALLEGHENY RIVER

The North Side

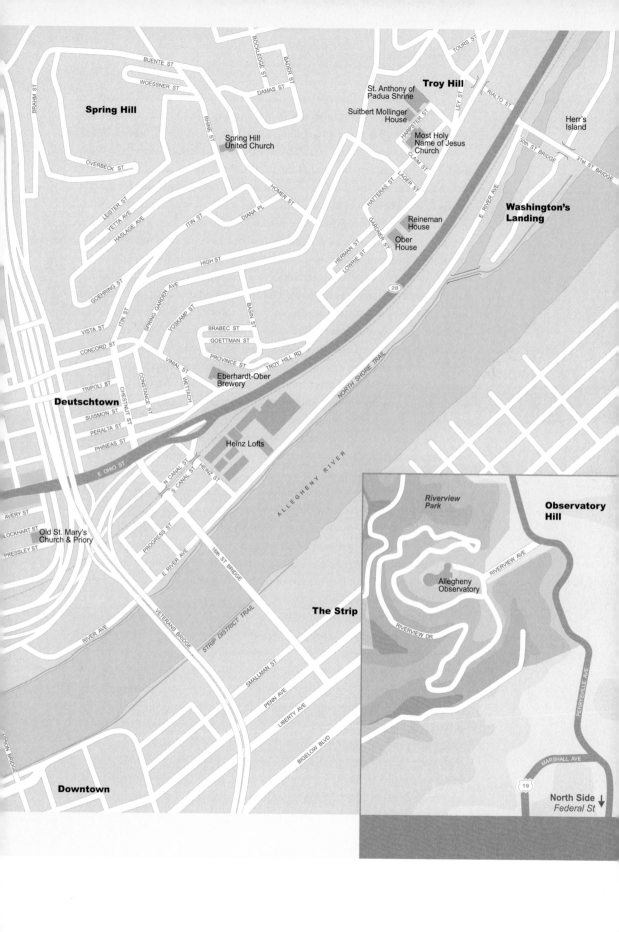

Manchester's decline started at the beginning of the twentieth century, when it was severed from the rest of the North Side by what are now the Conrail tracks. Then, in the 1960s, construction of the Chateau Street Expressway (state route 65) cut it off from the industrial plants on the Ohio River. Its population dropped from fifteen thousand to about twenty-five hundred. Many of the residents by then were African Americans forced out of the Lower Hill district in the 1950s. By the 1960s, it was effectively a slum.

Manchester is hardly free of problems today, but beginning in the 1970s, the area dramatically turned itself around with an unusual experiment in both social and architectural engineering. The rebirth of Manchester followed the discovery by the Manchester Citizens' Corporation that it could rehabilitate hundreds of homes using federal loans or subsidies if they were certified according to historic district guidelines. The Urban Redevelopment Authority of Pittsburgh secured about $25 million in federal housing monies, the Pittsburgh History & Landmarks Foundation set the rehabilitation guidelines, and the restoration firm of Tom Mistick & Sons renovated hundreds of structures. As a result, Manchester now glows with restored façades on North Sheffield, Pennsylvania, and Liverpool streets and on cross-streets such as Manhattan, Fulton, and Allegheny.

The main portal that gives access to the fifty blocks of Manchester is the intersection of Allegheny and West North avenues. The intersection includes an empty lot, symbolic of the unfinished business that still needs to be addressed in Manchester. But a half-block away are dozens of restorations that show the new spirit of the place. The three-story, U-shaped double house at 1313–1315 Allegheny Avenue, between West North and Sheffield streets, is festooned with gingerbread detailing and resembles a Mississippi steamboat. Its two best features are a lovingly restored entablature of minuscule brick brackets flanking four panels of basket-weave terra cotta and an elaborate spindled verandah.

The 1100 and 1200 blocks of West North Avenue from Bidwell to Fulton contain fine three- and four-story Italianate and Second Empire townhouses of the late 1860s and early 1870s. Especially good examples are at 1102, 1110, 1112, and 1116–1118 West North. The double house at 1203–1205 West North Avenue has been superbly renewed, its dark blue porch supported by fanlight-shaped brackets and ornamented with glass discs imported from France. Another double house at 1211–1213 West North Avenue features six individual gables crowning the third-floor windows. The mansions farther on toward the Ohio riverfront reflect still another wave of prosperity in Manchester in the 1880s and 1890s. The townhouses at 1229 to 1241 West North Avenue are excellent examples of the Romanesque Revival, while the delicately detailed

Wertheimer-Sipe house at 1220 West North, from 1892 and later, is a fine example of Queen Anne. Particularly witty is the balance of a conical tower of brick on the right and a shingled polyhedron of wood on the left. The homes at 1328–1334 West North Avenue, at the corner of Manhattan Street, are typical of the neighborhood in having stylistic kinship but never uniformity in their different variants of Italianate Style. At right angles to this row, the unbroken row of wooden homes at 1015–1027 Manhattan bespeaks an earlier time and a lower caste; workers lived here, not managers.

Sheffield Street, a block over, was mainly built up during the 1880s and 1890s, when the Queen Anne Style was in vogue. The street later decayed badly, but the double house at 1324–1326 Sheffield, between Manhattan and Fulton streets, has emerged radiantly from restoration, with a renewed mansard roof and endearing checkerboard fretwork on the gables.

The 1200 block of Sheffield between Fulton and Fontella was rebuilt according to three different ideologies of renewal. Several of the elaborate old double houses on the north side of the block have been given a period restoration: 1220 Sheffield, for example, was superbly restored and now awaits only its cast-iron cresting. On the opposite side of the block sit a half-dozen split-level houses from the 1970s, the result of a give-the-people-what-they-want philosophy that produced suburban houses in the middle of an urban context. They seem unloved and are already deep in decay. On the north side of the same block are fourteen award-winning passive solar houses erected in 1983–1984 in collaboration with the Department of Architecture at Carnegie Mellon. Here, too, the intent was to create something intimate and enjoyable for the tenants or purchasers but in an architectural language that would mirror more faithfully the density of the surrounding blocks and some of the decorative detailing of the older homes.

Pennsylvania Avenue, one block over, reflects the same generational approach to urban redevelopment. The homes on the 1200 block were plowed under and replanted with suburban split-levels in the 1970s, while the houses of the 1300 and 1400 blocks were preserved and renovated as they were. The most interesting home on the street is the William G. and Mary Lea Frazier house at 1414 Pennsylvania, between Manhattan and Chateau. This Italian-style villa with its imposing tower was constructed in 1876 in the manner of designs published some years before by Andrew Jackson Downing and Samuel Sloan. The mansion has had only four owners in 110 years: late in the twentieth century it was known as Calliope House, for the spirited gatherings of folk musicians that were held here. Today the building houses a school for bagpipers.

Left and right of the Frazier house on the north side of the block are more villas of the same period, plus a suburban interloper of the 1970s, while the south side of the street harbors modest two-story frame and brick worker housing. The affluent character of the patrician side of the block is splendidly upheld by the Fraziers' back-to-back neighbor, the James Anderson house (today a hospice) at 1423 Liverpool, between Chateau and Manhattan. Though it is only haphazardly documented, it appears that the ironmaster James Anderson, Carnegie's lending-library benefactor, built the house around 1830. What makes the year hard to pin down was the radical resurfacing of the house in 1905, which turned an authentic house of the early republic into a Georgian Revival fake. Nonetheless, the distinctive two-story porch may be original late Georgian rather than fake Georgian. Anderson's father, William, was a professional builder who had worked on the White House in the 1790s; he may have guided his son on this unusual feature.

The 1300 block of Liverpool is one of the glories of Manchester. After decades of neglect, its spiky rows of Second Empire and High Victorian Gothic mansions have now been brought back to life. This exceptionally vivid block, with one bright verandah outshining the next, was known as "North Jerusalem" to its neighbors in the 1880s because of the high proportion of Jews living on the street. The Jews of Manchester and Allegheny founded the original Concordia Club not many blocks away, in 1874, a year after they were excluded from the new Duquesne Club. The North Side had two synagogues, only one of which remains standing, though the building is now a church in Deutschtown. Edgar J. Kaufmann Sr., builder of Fallingwater, was part of the Jewish mercantile aristocracy that lived on or near this street.

Of special note are the Stifel house at 1319 Liverpool, from 1885, and the Gustav Langenheim house at 1315 Liverpool. Constructed in 1884, the Langenheim house was designed by Frederick Osterling, then just nineteen years old, on the cusp of a long and profitable career as one of Pittsburgh's most important architects. In the 1980s, the Langenheim house was reconfigured to provide eight rent-subsidized apartments for the elderly. The façade consists of three stories of brick shot through with curved lintels of stone and brick that continue as wraparound stringcourses. Its style is High Victorian Gothic with a bow to Queen Anne in its incongruous Corinthian-topped pilasters. Frank Lloyd Wright would have loathed it, but the way each element of the building grows from a preceding one is nothing if not organic.

The Liverpool streetscape ends with St. Joseph's Church, from 1898, at the corner of Liverpool and Fulton streets. Now the spiritualist Original Church of God Deliverance Center, its gabled corner tower—currently shorn

fig. 3.10
LIVERPOOL STREET
TOWNHOUSES

fig. 3.11
ALLEGHENY
OBSERVATORY

fig. 3.12
VIEW OF DOWNTOWN
FROM FEDERAL
STREET, FINEVIEW

of its needle spire—lifts above the rooftops of the neighboring mansions to provide the main landmark of central Manchester.

Manchester is all flats, but as is the case everywhere in Pittsburgh, hills are close by. A short but lively ride up to Perry Hilltop and Observatory Hill shows off radically different neighborhoods. Perry Hilltop derives its name from an incident in the War of 1812, when Commodore Oliver Hazard Perry used Perrysville Avenue—then called the Franklin Road, and the Venango Indian Trail before that—to transport the supplies used in his victorious naval battle with the British on Lake Erie. Today these 1,000 hilltop acres provide a lush setting for about fifteen thousand Pittsburghers who enjoy breathtaking views from their often-picturesque frame houses on the steep hillsides. As is often the case in Pittsburgh, the greenery of Perry Hilltop was the gift of nature rather than of human foresight: the ninety-six acres of Uniondale Cemetery and the 275 acres of Riverview Park are verdant today only because nothing could be built on such steep slopes. Still, the natural topography has been intelligently tended, and Riverview Park remains thickly forested. Careful planning inserted hiking trails, picnic groves, and a swimming pool without spoiling the setting.

At the higher reaches of Perrysville Avenue, the modest Perry Hilltop neighborhood gives way to the grander Observatory Hill and its great monument, the Allegheny Observatory. This University of Pittsburgh facility, constructed from 1900 to 1912, continues to serve as one of the world's eminent astronomical centers. It occupies an elegant palace of buff brick walls and terra-cotta columns and breathes the tranquility of eighteenth-century Enlightenment architecture.

The fame of the observatory was established even in its first home (this is its second), because as early as 1861 it already possessed the thirteen-inch refractor telescope that a group of Pittsburgh businessmen purchased for it. The observatory was also nationally known because it was an early timekeeper for the railroads and the federal government. Its director was Samuel Pierpont Langley, later called to head the Smithsonian. Langley was an aviation pioneer, too; his unmanned heavier-than-air machine took to the air before that of the Wright brothers.

Langley was succeeded by James Keeler, whose sightings on Observatory Hill established that the rings surrounding Saturn were composed of particles rather than being solid. Keeler's successor, John Brashear, was a self-taught genius. He was a South Side millwright who ground lenses as an avocation and later produced telescopes for observatories all over the world. Brashear established the world standard for the length of the meter, and through the application of his telescopes other scientists were able to discover hundreds of planets.

It was Brashear who built the two other celebrated instruments that are housed under the observatory's domes: the thirty-inch Thaw refractor telescope, regarded as the most accurate of its type in the world, and the thirty-one-inch Keeler reflecting telescope, which photographs the spectra of the stars in double and multiple star systems. Allegheny Observatory's staff entered the computer age a generation ago as specialists in astrometry, which plots the mathematical coordinates of the stars by computer simulation. Two-thirds of the known star distances have been determined through astrometrical calculations on the Thaw telescope.

Brashear helped solve the immense technical problems presented in the design of the observatory. Each of the telescopes was set below its own dome, with movable floors below the Thaw and Keeler instruments to allow viewers or cameras to look through them comfortably no matter how they are angled. For perfect accuracy, the two telescopes were built on independent foundations of bedrock and do not touch the observatory walls. But the observatory is no spartan lab. It was exquisitely and even palatially finished in costly woods and marbles that were mainly financed by the industrialist William Thaw Jr. It even boasts a fine stained-glass window of Urania, the Muse of Astronomy. Nor is it a building devoid of the human spirit. At the base of the Keeler telescope is the somber crypt that contains the tombs of Keeler and his son and of John Brashear and his wife, Phoebe. Brashear's epitaph (from a poem by Sarah Williams) reads, "We have loved the stars too fondly to be fearful of the night."

For those who prefer not to commune with the memory of Brashear in the crypt, there are recollections of him in two buildings in the Perry Hilltop neighborhood. Brashear's telescope workshop still stands at 2016 Perrysville Avenue, about a mile and a half south of the Allegheny Observatory. A long and narrow brick box, it is not devoid of ornament, but the design seems principally driven by the need to maximize light. Around the bend, at 1801 Clayton Avenue, stands the house that William Thaw Sr. built for Brashear in the 1880s. Both the home and the factory were immediately adjacent to the original observatory, which was in use until 1912. Also on this hilltop, the University of Pittsburgh (then Western University of Pennsylvania) erected an entire campus of Romanesque Revival buildings, which was convenient for Brashear when he served as university chancellor pro tem in 1901–1904. The Brashear house is made of wood that imitates rusticated masonry blocks. It is a beguiling building, with a fine three-panel oriel lookout over an elaborate porch. Fittingly for the visionary Brashear, it yields a view that encompasses not only Pittsburgh but half the horizon as well.

The adjoining neighborhood of Fineview is so small that its entire shopping district consists of two corner stores. Fineview occupies its own hilly outcrop a quarter of a mile east of the intersection of Perrysville Avenue and Federal Street, at an average elevation of four hundred feet above the Allegheny. This is the most intractable of Pittsburgh's hilltop neighborhoods; public steps rather than roads seem to predominate. In the nineteenth century, the central area, known as Nunnery Hill, was served by an eleven-hundred-foot-long funicular, one of four that brought residents up the hills of North Side.

Three homes in Fineview are particularly remarkable. One is the one-story Heathside Cottage, built around 1865 at the intersection of Catoma Street with Myler. It was originally the home of Colonel James Andrews, but it was later pressed into service as the lodge for the gatekeeper of the Catholic cemetery up the hill. It was Andrews who built the piers for the early-1870s Eads Bridge in St. Louis, a huge leap forward in bridge technology. Andrew Carnegie provided the iron for the bridge, and the two men were in close touch (family legend says Carnegie courted one of Andrews's daughters). The architect of the brick cottage may have been Joseph Kerr, who was associated with Andrews in the construction of Pittsburgh's midcentury post office. The structure has been restored so that its bricks serve as their own ornamentation; above sits a fishscale slate roof and lacy carving in the barge-boards. Particularly gracious outside are the hood molds and diamond-pane windows set in the three-panel bay; inside, the detailing is miniaturized and luxurious.

A moment's walk downhill from Heathside Cottage stand two other Gothic Revival structures: the imposing Henderson house at 1516 Warren Street, from the 1860s, and a contemporary board-and-batten wooden cottage at 1521 Warren Street, at the corner of Lee. The tiny Henderson cottage, with its cross-gable plan and ogive-arch porches, is the more compelling of the two, close in spirit to the four cottages created in 1851 at Evergreen Hamlet, roughly two miles farther upstream on the Allegheny River.

The ten-room Henderson house consists of ashlar blocks elegantly set off with finely worked sandstone quoins. Like the cottage opposite, the plan of the house is cross-gabled, but it also incorporates sets of staggered axes. Next to it stand a carriage house and a springhouse in the same elaborate style. The rehabilitated building provides seven apartments, so in its second century, the Henderson house continues to be a useful member of this fascinating hillside community.

fig. 3.13
QUEEN ANNE-
STYLE DOUBLE
HOUSE,
CEDAR STREET

DEUTSCHTOWN, SPRING HILL, AND TROY HILL

The neighboring districts of Deutschtown, Spring Hill, and Troy Hill are geographically distinct: the first is all flats, the two others, all slopes. But together they constitute the heart of Pittsburgh's German community. Deutschtown (or, more prosaically, East Allegheny) is a flat area of about 250 acres comprising several dozen city blocks. Its core lies between Allegheny Commons and the Heinz plant on the Allegheny River. Formerly a major center for the tanning, meatpacking, and beer industries, Deutschtown decayed with the collapse of its economic base. Like the Mexican War streets and Manchester districts, it owes its current rebirth to the high quality of its housing stock, which includes fine examples of Romanesque Revival and Queen Anne.

Ethnic ties are still strong in this district, though less binding than in the era before World War I, when Deutschtown had the major share of the seventy German singing societies in town. It is still the headquarters for the Teutonia Männerchor, whose colorful headquarters in pseudo-German half-timbering survives at 857 Phineas Street. Founded in 1854, the club still promotes German singing and dancing in its activities and celebrations.

While the primary language of Deutschtown was German, it was also a haven for Croatian immigrants, who called the area east of Chestnut Street Mala Jaska, or Little Jaska, for the region near Zagreb where many of them were born. It was no less a haven for African Americans, who flocked to the Avery Institute (destroyed several decades ago in the construction of the off-ramps from I-279), established by the manufacturer Charles Avery in 1849 as an educational, social, and religious center for the community.

Most of Deutschtown consists of quiet residential streets such as Cedar, with its score of proud townhouses overlooking East Park, between Suismon and Pressley streets. The best of these townhouses is the Queen Anne–style double house built for two brothers at 814–816 Cedar. It brings together walls of deep red pressed brick, a stubby, slate-covered mansard roof, two pyramidal towers decked out in fishscale patterns, and ornamental molded brick. The façade stretches over five bays in a receding/projecting rhythm, with a passageway in the middle that leads to servants' quarters in the rear. A bonus on the façade is three reliefs from Greco-Roman mythology: Medusa in a fine panel on the second floor, Neptune on the stringcourse above, and a radiant Minerva at the top. The house appears to date from the late 1870s or the 1880s and may be the work of the Charles Bartbergers, father and son, who specialized in scenographic fronts like these.

Many of the same details used by the architect or builder of 814–816 Cedar appear a short walk away at 602 Pressley, between Cedar and Nash. This is a three-story mansard-roofed house with a central frontispiece that seems to staple itself onto the second floor with corbeled brackets. Here again the ornament is in molded brick: two portrait heads flanking a hoary lion. The gable is lovingly articulated in a series of raised brick circles that recall similar ornament in wood in the contemporary houses of Manchester. Some of the qualities of this and the Queen Anne house at 814–816 Cedar were captured in the 1980s in the thirty-two three-story townhouses of Deutschtown Square, bounded by Avery, Cedar, and Lockhart streets. This was one of the first developments to bring young urban professionals into this staid neighborhood.

For those who want to buy the real thing in nineteenth-century town-houses for a fraction of the cost of these imitations, many are still available at the upper end of Deutschtown, in the six blocks centered at the intersection of Chestnut and Tripoli streets. In this area, frame dwellings alternate with brick rows, with houses packed together as tightly as the bright red bricks in the roadway. Tellingly, nearly all of the hundreds of tiny homes are in good shape except for those on Suismon Street between Chestnut and Madison. The cause of this dereliction of architectural duty is easy to locate. The I-279 expressway blasted through this neighborhood in the 1980s, and what was broken up so violently cannot be easily restored.

The homes of Deutschtown are enlivened by the presence of three imposing institutions: one charitable, one religious, one industrial. The most visible of these is Allegheny General Hospital. For decades this was the most fashionable charity in Pittsburgh, as can be read in the names on the donor plaques in the lobby. The society connection is also evident in the outer dress of the hospital. When the architects, York & Sawyer, designed Presbyterian Hospital in Oakland in the 1930s, their design there was sober Beaux-Arts. For Allegheny General, they flirted instead with Art Deco and produced something that was both more light-hearted but more significant for the Pittsburgh skyline.

Allegheny General Hospital, constructed in 1936, was large for its time—twelve hundred rooms in a skyscraper of seventeen stories of yellow industrial brick. Its design exploits the dramatic contrast with Fineview Hill immediately behind and gives special emphasis to the Greek temple that crowns it. This marvelous feature is floodlit at night and seems to float like a vision of Valhalla through the Pittsburgh sky. (The best viewing spot turns out to be not on the North Side but two miles away, on Liberty Avenue in Lawrenceville.)

For the passerby at street level, the best part of the hospital is the entrance portico, which is three bays long and both rib- and barrel-vaulted internally. Its columns are radiant shafts of granite and marble and terminate in basket capitals or highly stylized acanthus leaves in an architectural mix that is part

fig. 3.14
CHESTNUT STREET,
DEUTSCHTOWN

Venice, part Constantinople, and part Cecil B. de Mille. Externally, the porch sallies forth with an arched corbel table infilled with blue and green terra cotta; the frieze depicts medical pioneers in the guise of Byzantine saints.

Another neighborhood monument, at 614 Pressley Street, is the Priory and Grand Hall, which is the deconsecrated St. Mary's Roman Catholic Church of 1854. Its architecture offers a fascinating glimpse into the social history of Pittsburgh (and America) in the mid-nineteenth century. The church was constructed without windows because of the constant vandalism of virulent anti-Catholic partisans during the ascendancy of the Know-Nothing Party. Almost as if to answer that bigotry, St. Mary's proudly hewed to its German and Catholic heritage in two broad Romanesque-style towers that originally terminated in bulbous Bavarian domes.

The achievement inside is even more remarkable for a working-class immigrant parish. Four giant columns support a Greek cross of transverse barrel vaults that rise sixty-five feet at the center to an umbrella vault and skylight. One of the sources for the design was evidently German Baroque, but the other was probably Christopher Wren's intimate churches for London, like St. Mary-at-Hill. The Grand Hall is the name assumed by the erstwhile church when it was restored to serve as a venue for weddings, banquets, and charity events.

Who designed this small masterpiece? The only part of the church that is documented is the 1906 addition of a vestibule by the architect Sidney Heckert. The local attribution of the church to the second pastor of the congregation, Father John Stiebl, is possible but unlikely. Amateur architects, like the parish priest would have been, rarely think in terms of sophisticated volumetrics like those of the Grand Hall. The Redemptorist Fathers, the religious order that built the church, were known to hire top architects such as Robert Cary Long Jr., who designed their convent in Baltimore after his brief stay in Pittsburgh. The architect of the 1854 St. Mary's may well have been Charles F. Bartberger, who would have just arrived from Germany and been busily at work on both old St. Paul's Cathedral on Grant Street and the convent of the Passionist Fathers on Mount Washington.

Next door sits the former priory that the busy local architect Henry Moser added in 1888. This is a lively and ingenious solution to a dark, cramped site. Deconsecrated now, this important and moving complex has gained vigorous new life as a twenty-four-room European-style hotel with Victorian- and Edwardian-style furnishings and decorations.

The towering industrial monument of North Side is the Heinz Foods complex, where the Sixteenth Street Bridge meets the Allegheny waterfront.

Henry John Heinz had the same relationship to food that Henry Ford had to the automobile: he invented no single product but instead changed the way the world lived by packaging and marketing food better than anyone in history. Heinz was born on the South Side in 1844, the son of two recent German immigrants. He grew up in Sharpsburg, three miles upstream on the Allegheny from the future site of his factory. There he entered his father's brickmaking concern before branching out in 1869 to grow horseradish on the family land. Like Thomas Mellon in the same year, Heinz could not help but flourish (though he went bankrupt early on) because everything he needed for bottling and canning his foods was available in Pittsburgh: the glass, the corks, the pottery crocks, and the tin-coated steel cans.

Even the inspiration for his "57 Varieties"—among the most famous and the most instantly recognizable slogans in the history of marketing—seems to have come from the streets of Pittsburgh. In his old age Heinz recounted that he had modeled his slogan on one he had seen in 1892, while riding an elevated train in New York. In that sign a manufacturer had advertised his twenty-one different styles of shoes. Apart from an improbable gambling reference to "lucky seven" (Heinz was a staunch Presbyterian), Heinz never explained why he had fixed on the number fifty-seven, which was neither the number of products (more than sixty) he sold by 1892 nor the number of the Manhattan street where the elevated train had stopped (Twenty-eighth). The number fifty-seven was evidently so deeply stuck in Heinz's subconscious that he could no longer pull it out. Where had he come by it?

Perhaps the answer lies in the place of invention: a public train moving past a sequence of numbered streets, not in New York but in Pittsburgh. Heinz lived not far from Pittsburgh's Fifty-seventh Street, which was—and still is—the last in a long line of numbered cross-streets along Penn Avenue and Butler Street that ends opposite his hometown of Sharpsburg. The Robert Fleming Bridge on the Allegheny River between Sharpsburg and Pittsburgh is designated the Sixty-second Street Bridge because in 1867, when the streets received their numbers, sixty-two streets were projected to run along the Allegheny riverfront. But only fifty-seven streets were actually built; what would be the theoretical Sixty-second Street, opposite the bridge, is just a lane.

Heinz knew that sequence of fifty-seven streets intimately, even painfully. For six days a week during the 1870s and 1880s he would leave his home in Sharpsburg, cross the bridge to Pittsburgh, and take the five-mile, fifty-seven-block ride on the horsecars of the Citizens' Passenger Railway to his office and plant on Second Avenue in the Golden Triangle. Fifty-seventh would have been the first Pittsburgh street that greeted Heinz in the morning and the last to salute him in the evening, on a trip he took perhaps five thousand times. It was a number his subconscious would never let him forget.

In 1889, Heinz moved production from the Golden Triangle to the Allegheny's north bank, where he built the world's first modern food-processing complex. The Deutschtown site gave him both water and rail access since it sat between the tracks of the Pennsylvania and the Pittsburgh & Western railroads. The industrious German-Swiss neighborhood was also ideal for recruiting the fifteen hundred male and two thousand female employees he would eventually employ.

In the initial phase of the factory's development, there were seventeen buildings; eventually there were thirty-two. The architect behind their design is unknown, but the most likely candidates are Frederick Osterling, who built Heinz's Point Breeze mansion during the same years the factory buildings were constructed, and Robert Maurice Trimble, also a Pittsburgh architect, who designed the nearby Sarah Heinz House. Heinz himself oversaw the construction of these Romanesque Revival blocks in his production complex, demanding walls of the finest glazed and pressed brick and solid concrete and stone foundations, which were generally three and a half feet thick. Once, dissatisfied, he ordered an entire factory covered with new walls because he deemed the original brickwork substandard. The buildings contained kitchens; plants for bottling, packing, and canning; an electricity plant with its own dynamos; a restaurant; an indoor swimming pool; a gymnasium; and classrooms for employee self-betterment. Newspapers called the stable building "an equine palace" and reported in awestruck tones on its cork floors imported from England, its steam radiators, its warm hoof baths for tired horses, its hospital wing, and its "jail" for those horses prone to kicking.

Today, about a dozen of these original buildings survive. The Sarah Heinz House announces the whole complex on East Ohio Street with a luxurious Tudor-style settlement center that still serves the children of the neighborhood district. Immediately below the Conrail tracks the plant itself begins, with the enormous Employee Service Building (at the corner of Heinz and Progress streets) that the famed industrial architect Albert Kahn designed in 1930 to blend with the earlier buildings. It once contained a lavishly appointed auditorium for employee presentations and dining rooms for male and female employees. Farther down on Progress Street stand the Meat Products, Bean, and Bottling buildings, all in the same austere industrial style but with corner turrets and handsome corbel tables. Opposite them rises the Cereal Building. Farther inside the complex are two more buildings by Albert Kahn: the

fig. 3.15
HEINZ LOFTS

fig. 3.16
HEINZ PLANT

Administration Building in reinforced concrete, an early building on which Heinz's favorite mottoes are rendered in stained glass, and the Administration Annex from the 1930s, a severe industrial white-brick building facing the Allegheny.

By the time the firm produced twelve hundred varieties, it had commissioned three International Style buildings from Skidmore, Owings & Merrill. These classics from the 1950s included the Research Building on the Allegheny waterfront, the eight-million-cubic-foot Warehouse Building, and Gordon Bunshaft's highly publicized Vinegar Works on East Ohio Street, with its refined glass curtain walls.

Today, Pittsburgh's schoolchildren can no longer take the "pickle tour" that they and fifty thousand adults a year used to enjoy. The Heinz Company retains close ties to the city of its birth, but it no longer makes food in the old plant. Some food production is still carried out in Pittsburgh, but not by Heinz, and for the most part the historic industrial site is now living quarters. In 2005, five of the manufacturing buildings became the Heinz Lofts, complete with a rebuilding of certain towers and the replacement of ironwork that had been removed. The five condominium buildings are linked by sky bridges and retain their original names: Shipping, Meat, Bean, Cereal, and Reservoir.

About three thousand Pittsburghers live on Spring Hill, which has an average elevation of 450 feet above the Allegheny waterfront. The hill is cut off from the rest of the city by the East Street and Spring Garden valleys. Spring Hill's population was as German as the street names Rhine, Kaiser, and Goehring suggest, and it is fastidiously neat in its white frame houses and Italianate brick homes of the mid- and late nineteenth century. The hill is wholly residential, except for a few churches. The Spring Hill United Church of Christ on Rhine Street is the smallest but most memorable of these. Built of red brick, this curious structure with a miniature crow-step gable and pseudo–flying buttresses recalls Dutch or northern German architecture of the fifteenth century as understood in the age of Art Nouveau.

One can see but not directly reach Troy Hill from Spring Hill; to do so, one must descend to Spring Garden Avenue and then head up Troy Hill Road. Standing at the base of that road is the Brewery, an imaginative reworking of the old Eberhardt-Ober Brewery that went up in 1852 and was rebuilt in 1897. Across the street stands another brewery relic, and behind the main plant are some vestiges of the old beer vaults that had been cut into the hillside. Almost all of the breweries in Pittsburgh—in Spring Hill, in Lawrenceville, and on the South Side—were located next to hills or in valleys in order to have access to hillside vaults like these. The Brewery employs

fig. 3.17
TROY HILL SKYLINE,
FROM THE
ALLEGHENY RIVER

authentic German brewing techniques and engages in two different kinds of "fermenting": one is literal, in that the company is a microbrewery run by a descendant of the first German to settle in Pennsylvania, and the other is figurative: most of the old building is rented out to start-up high-tech companies.

Troy Hill is the second most isolated of Pittsburgh's neighborhoods (for inaccessibility, nothing beats Duck Hollow, described in chapter 6). The village of New Troy, named for the New York State hometown of the area's original landowner, Elizabeth Seymore, was founded in this locale in 1833, but in its first ten years it attracted nothing but cemeteries. One of these, Voegtly Cemetery on Lowrie Street, is the site of an annual Memorial Day commemoration with bands and a parade.

During those Memorial Day events, one can almost see the gregariousness of the old German community, with its *Turnvereins* (gymnastics clubs) and *Liedertafeln* (singing societies). The railroad repair shops and the Heinz plant at the base of the hill brought in a few new settlers each year, and the occasional devastating flood down on the Allegheny floodplain induced still more residents to seek homes on Troy Hill's windswept plain. By 1900, when it still had its own trolley run and inclined plane, Troy Hill reached its peak population of ten thousand. It is home to about twenty-five hundred people today.

Troy Hill Road follows a long but comfortable grade for half a mile along the escarpment of a steep cliff; over it, like silent sentinels, peer white frame houses. At the crest of the hill stands a funeral home that was once the John Ober house, a rare Pittsburgh example of the so-called "stick style." Built in 1877, it was purchased a few years later by one of the partners in the Eberhardt-Ober Brewery. The skin of the building is composed entirely of wood siding that has been arranged in fishscale and diamond patterns, while the corners and stringcourses stand out boldly as wooden strips. The Ober house has an Italian villa plan closely resembling that of the contemporaneous

Frazier house in Manchester, but details like its detached and bracketed eaves reveal links to the fashionable houses that were being built at the same period in Newport, Rhode Island. More exuberant still is the Reineman house, two doors away at 1515–1517 Lowrie Street. This huge double house of the 1870s in brick and wood trim has been meticulously preserved, from its spindled verandah to its mansard slate roof, excepting only the loss of its wrought-iron cresting.

The home of Troy Hill's most celebrated inhabitant has also come through the years unscathed. The Suitbert Mollinger house (today the rectory of the Most Holy Name of Jesus Church, at the intersection of Harpster Street and Tinsbury) is a richly crafted Second Empire house of brick with elaborate door and window surrounds of stone. It was built in 1876 by Mollinger, a wealthy Belgian nobleman who, after a stay in Padua for medical and theological studies, became a priest and settled in Pittsburgh. The house was superbly crafted throughout, but its glory is the dining room. There, Mollinger's massive oak furniture, crystal chandelier, carved ceiling medallion, and animal and bird murals are preserved in an atmosphere of sanctity.

Next door, at 1704 Harpster, stands the reason for Mollinger's renown: the Shrine of St. Anthony of Padua, erected in the 1880s. The exterior of this light sandstone Gothic Revival chapel with flanking needle spires is picturesque, though visually less exciting than similar Pittsburgh designs of the time. But it is the inside that makes the chapel unique in the New World. St. Anthony's harbors some five thousand relics of early Christian saints and martyrs that Mollinger purchased in Europe, together with yellowed (but now digitally archived) attestations of authenticity. The presence of such a bountiful harvest of relics once drew thousands of pilgrims to the top of Mount Troy. The miracles that were proclaimed with regularity at the shrine have ceased now, but the collection is still a fascinating sight. A half-block away, where Claim Street meets Harpster, stands the Most Holy Name of Jesus Church, a gaunt Germanic brick structure with a tall central tower that is powerfully effective against the open hilltop.

The American cities that were most strongly influenced by their German populations—Milwaukee, St. Louis, Cincinnati, and Pittsburgh—all had in common superb waterfronts and hearty appetites for food, beer, and architecture. In the case of Pittsburgh, the food industry was solidly centered in the North Side even before H. J. Heinz located his plant there. There are several reminders of slaughterhouses in the district. One is Rialto Street, known for a century as Pig Hill because farmers would drive their pigs down its slopes to be butchered. Not for the faint hearted, Rialto descends 370 feet to East Ohio

fig. 3.18
VOEGTLY
CEMETERY,
TROY HILL

fig. 3.19
SHRINE OF
ST. ANTHONY
OF PADUA

Street and the Thirty-first Street Bridge at a 24 percent grade. There are four even steeper streets in Pittsburgh, but Rialto is vertiginous enough to give drivers the sensation that they are flying down a track—and rightly so, since it exactly parallels the old track bed of the Mount Troy inclined plane.

149

THE NORTH SHORE

O ne of the issues that Pittsburgh has only recently begun to address is the reclamation of its waterfronts. At this moment, the most interesting developments are on the North Shore, which is a riverfront crescent stretching three miles, from the Thirty-first Street Bridge to the West End Bridge. This zone was particularly hard hit by the flight of industry, and it is instructive to see what kinds of functions, from housing to gambling, are being established in order to draw people back. Herr's Island, reached by a ramp off the Thirty-first Street Bridge, serves as a microcosm of the larger district. The island is a three-quarter-mile-long wedge in the Allegheny River that begins a few hundred yards from the base of Troy Hill. The stockyards and slaughterhouses of Herr's Island once made it the most revolting place in the whole of Pittsburgh. Right through the 1960s, when slaughtering was taking place, the stench could be detected as far as Stanton Heights, two miles away. Some of the island's stockyards were connected with its slaughterhouses, but most were holding pens for the livestock being transported on the Pennsylvania Railroad's main line between Chicago and New York. In the days before refrigeration cars, meat had to be shipped from the Midwest to the East Coast "on the hoof." The cattle needed a breather on the long trip east, and Herr's Island provided that opportunity, if little else. After the invention of refrigeration, the specialized function of the island became unnecessary, and it declined until it reached a semi-ruined state in the late 1960s.

The transformation of Herr's Island into Washington's Landing (George Washington almost died in 1753 when he slipped on an ice floe nearby) began in the 1980s with its acquisition by the Urban Redevelopment Authority of Pittsburgh. In 1989, the authority created a master plan that projected a community of housing and light industry with riverside trails, a marina, and a rowing center. Under its newly sanitized name, the forty-two-acre island has brilliantly fulfilled those early hopes. The similarity of the homes is monotonous, but they have a nice beachhouse flair, and the trails and marinas afford a perfect place to commune with the Allegheny River. The once hideous environment is now so wholesome that it was chosen for the headquarters of the Western Pennsylvania Conservancy, which operates Fallingwater.

fig. 3.20
RIALTO STREET, ONE OF PITTSBURGH'S MANY STEEP CLIMBS

fig. 3.21
WASHINGTON'S
LANDING

fig. 3.22
ALCOA CORPORATE
CENTER, BETWEEN
CLEMENTE AND
WARHOL BRIDGES

Washington's Landing is a major feature on the Three Rivers Heritage Trail, a significant project in the continuing effort to restore and protect the riverfronts. This pedestrian trail for cyclists, walkers, and runners begins at Washington's Landing and extends along the riverfront all the way to the West End Bridge. With the completion of the West End Pedestrian Bridge, a platform that will hang from the main bridge structure, hikers and bikers will effortlessly connect with a parallel trail along the Monongahela, toward and beyond Station Square.

About a mile downriver on the Allegheny from the old Heinz factories stands the beguiling Alcoa Corporate Center, set between the Andy Warhol and the Rachel Carson bridges.

The main seat of the company since 1998, this structure was an early instance of a building that integrates itself into a riverfront. The seductive curve of the façade mimics that of the river and the jogging trail alongside it. The aluminum skin and sunshields keep up the tradition of advertising Pittsburgh's products in corporate skyscrapers.

Facing the back of Alcoa stands the Frederick Osterling architectural studio at 228 Isabella Street, a block from the Rachel Carson Bridge. Currently the center of MAGLEV technology in Pennsylvania, which hopes to construct a magnetic-levitation bullet train between Pittsburgh and Philadelphia, this diminutive building from 1917 presents a glass façade of Gothic trefoils in the manner of Osterling's Union Trust Building, Downtown. When it was Osterling's studio, it provided an elegant reception room above and a large drafting hall below. Osterling's studio ranks among America's earliest glass-fronted buildings, and it speaks volumes about architects' social and economic position in Pittsburgh society early in the twentieth century.

fig. 3.23
FREDERICK OSTERLING'S STUDIO, ISABELLA STREET

Between the next set of bridges, the Andy Warhol and the Roberto Clemente, lie the linked complexes of the NorthShore Center and Allegheny Landing Park—the former being the main sparkplug as well as the origin of the district's new name as the North Shore. The complex dates from 1984, and it was a significant gesture in bringing Pittsburgh back to the waterways that gave birth to it. For the open space between the new buildings, private foundations subsidized an art park dotted with sculptures. Sculptors of the initial works placed in the park were Ned Smythe, George Sugarman, and Isaac Witkin; the cast-bronze image of two construction workers, created by George Danhires and titled *The Builders*, was added later. The result is a grassy knoll that recalls the Neoclassical Porta della Ripetta landing in eighteenth-century Rome. The two low-rise buildings flanking the park were designed in pronounced horizontality to reinforce the riverbank setting. Their dark maroon brick is similarly keyed to the older buildings around it, particularly to the bold Romanesque-Classical warehouse at the corner of Isabella and Sandusky that was renovated into Four NorthShore Center. Though a harder-edged design, the Alcoa Service Center, which joined the complex in 2000, reveals a similar concern for contextualization.

Around the corner, at 117 Sandusky Street, an elegant old warehouse became the Andy Warhol Museum in 1994. This terra-cotta high-rise commercial block was built in 1911 for the Frick and Lindsay plumbing supply business. Later, it housed the Volkwein Music concern, a sheet-music and instrument distributor that has somehow stayed in business (today located near the airport) for a century. The Volkwein block lost its cornice at one point, but a replica of the original was cast in fiberglass. A series of six cornucopia-shaped consoles drip onto the building like giant snails from the top stringcourse. The interior of the building was gutted and transformed into nineteen galleries on six floors that would exhibit the work of Warhol, the enormously influential Pittsburgh-born artist. The concrete piers and floors take on a serenity that well complements the provocative images on the walls. Not to be missed is the "pillow room," where visitors are encouraged to bat inflated pillows through the air. The Warhol exhibits keep changing, and the museum offers related exhibits on themes in contemporary art. Outside, one catches a nice interplay between the museum's cool interiors and the high-tech exterior of the SMS Schloemann-Siemag headquarters, across Sandusky Street at number 100.

The current form of the North Shore began to take shape around 1970, when it was designated as the site for Three Rivers Stadium, to serve the Pirates, after they abandoned Forbes Field, and the Steelers, after they abandoned the University of Pittsburgh stadium, both sites being miles away, in Oakland. The stadium site on the north bank of the Allegheny opposite the Point was already sanctified because the Pirates' first home, Exposition Park, stood there more than a century ago. At that ballpark, in 1903, the Pirates played Boston in the first World Series.

Pittsburgh took to Three Rivers Stadium only tepidly, however, and it was demolished even before the mortgage was paid off to make way for PNC Park and Heinz Field. PNC Park, facing the Allegheny waterfront alongside the Roberto Clemente Bridge, was designed as an urban ballpark in the mode of the classic Wrigley Field and Fenway Park—and Pittsburgh's own Forbes Field. The stadium is a steel structure with terra-cotta tiled pilasters and large masonry arches. An uncommon two-deck design seats 38,496 in a field that faces the river and the Downtown skyline. PNC Park and Heinz Field both

fig. 3.24
ANDY WARHOL
MUSEUM

fig. 3.25
PNC PARK, HOME
OF THE PIRATES

fig. 3.26
WATER STEPS,
NORTH SHORE
RIVERFRONT PARK

opened in 2001. The steel-framed, horseshoe-shaped Heinz Field also offers to sixty-five thousand fans excellent views across the water. Both the Steelers and the University of Pittsburgh Panthers play football here, before bright yellow seats that approximate the Steelers' black and gold—colors that come from the coat of arms of William Pitt, first Earl of Chatham.

Of the two sports venues, the baseball stadium is the more ingratiating, with some heartfelt symbolism. Just inside the left-field entrance, life-size bronze statues represent seven greats of Pittsburgh's two Negro League teams: the Homestead Grays and the Pittsburgh Crawfords. These include the legendary Josh Gibson, Satchel Paige, Cool Papa Bell, and Smokey Joe Williams—all of whom have taken their places in the Baseball Hall of Fame in Cooperstown, New York. Three outstanding Pirates stand as larger-than-life-size statues at three nodal points around the field: Honus Wagner by the main entrance, Willie Stargell outside the left field entrance, and Roberto Clemente outside the center field gate, near the Allegheny River and the bridge that carries his name. Clemente was not only a brilliant and beloved player, he was a humanitarian who died in 1972 while flying relief supplies to

fig. 3.27
HEINZ FIELD,
CAPITAL OF THE
STEELER NATION

earthquake-ravaged villages in Nicaragua. At the base of his statue are inserted relics of "sacred ground" (as the inscription says) from his birthplace in Puerto Rico, from old Forbes Field, and from the demolished Three Rivers Stadium.

The future development of the North Shore depends on the structures that are planned for the area between the two arenas. Year by year, barren parking lots are giving way to hotels, restaurants, and office buildings for firms like Del Monte Foods and Equitable Resources. This pace of construction has proceeded with a rhythm that should quicken after 2011, when Pittsburgh's subway cuts underneath the Allegheny from the Golden Triangle. Meanwhile, the lively North Shore Riverfront Park, with its riverwalk, docking areas, and engaging Water Steps, forcibly demonstrates Pittsburgh's determination to return to its rivers.

Two final buildings complete the transformation of North Shore before it ends at the West End Bridge, about a mile northwest of the Point. The Carnegie Science Center stands on the bank of the Ohio River, just west of Heinz Field. Its hands-on exhibits, planetarium, and OMNIMAX Theater educate visitors about science and technology, while in the river itself are a World War II submarine and two floating classrooms that use the Ohio as the basis of their enrichment curriculum. Nothing commemorates Andrew Carnegie himself in the science center named for him, but a visitor seeking some sign of his boyhood environment need walk just one block, to 1106 Reedsdale Street, in the shadow of Heinz Field. Carnegie lived on Reedsdale (then named Rebecca Street) in the 1850s. For the time being, trapped in the end wall of the tall warehouse next door, there survives the ghostly vision of two brick stories, an attic, and a high chimney—all that survives from a house that would have been just like Carnegie's.

The battle of North Side and North Shore will come into sharper focus with the start-up of the Rivers Casino around 2010. The focus of the two-story glass-and-steel structure will be on a cylindrical atrium that will house nightclubs, restaurants, and shops in an interesting vision of the future, if not the one Ben Franklin had in mind. With so many attractions concentrated here, the North Side threatens to overtake Oakland as Pittsburgh's prime civic center—sweet revenge for the many humiliations inflicted on the district since 1788.

THE SOUTH SIDE: REAL PITTSBURGH

fig. 4.1
OLD PITTSBURGH:
THE MONONGAHELA
FLOWS BETWEEN
SMOKING STEEL
MILLS, 1940S

The topography of Pittsburgh seems straightforward: a North Side and a South Side, an East End and a West End. Although neatly and verbally linked, each area is proudly independent of and even indifferent to its opposite. Those in the East End have no idea how to get to the West End, and scrappy South Siders would have no wish to be twinned with the more stately North Side.

Of the latter two districts, it is the South Side that best reveals its nature from a distance. A visitor in a glass skyscraper in the Golden Triangle can turn and observe cable cars—actually funiculars, known in Pittsburgh as inclines—scaling the long hill south of the Monongahela at two different points. The hill itself demands attention: it rises 450 feet and stretches unbroken for five miles, from Beck's Run near Homestead to Saw Mill Run in the West End. Since 1851, this hill has been called Mount Washington, on the reasonable assumption that it was from its heights that Washington surveyed the Golden Triangle in 1753. The early settlers of Pittsburgh just called it Coal Hill, and for decades it smoked from uncontrolled fires deep within its mine shafts.

Draped over most of the length of the Mount Washington cliff are hundreds of brick and frame houses, many reached by winding public steps rather than roads. At the base of the hill is the densely settled floodplain of

Old Birmingham, or South Side proper, while closer to Downtown lies the entertainment and commercial development of Station Square. On the gentle back slopes, Mount Washington divides into a dozen semi-suburban communities, some lying within the boundaries of the City of Pittsburgh, others outside.

What eventually became South Side and Mt. Washington were both included in a three-thousand-acre royal grant to Major John Ormsby in 1770 for his military services in the French and Indian War. Ormsby was content to farm this land, but in 1811, his son-in-law, Dr. Nathaniel Bedford, and Bedford's business partner, Isaac Gregg, laid out that part of it by the Monongahela River as the village of Birmingham. The name recalled Bedford's industrial hometown in England, but he must also have seen it as an augury. Bedford named the longest streets of Birmingham for his daughter, Josephine; his wife, Jane; and her sisters, Sidney, Sarah, and Mary. He named Bedford Square for himself and Carson Street for a sea captain friend of his. Those names and the village's street plan have survived intact for more than two centuries.

South Side industrialized early, with James O'Hara and Isaac Craig producing glass there by 1795 and most of Pittsburgh's seventy-six glass factories, responsible for half the national output, operating there in the nineteenth century. The American Iron Works (the core of what would become Jones & Laughlin) opened its cold-rolling mill there in 1853. In 1859, Graff, Bennett & Company began making pig iron at the Clinton Iron Works, where Station Square now stands. It was Pittsburgh's first successful blast furnace (an earlier Shadyside furnace had failed in the 1790s), followed the same year by Jones & Laughlin's Eliza Furnaces, on the north bank of the Monongahela.

Making iron and steel transformed the South Side from a genteel village into a cauldron of activity. Its population shot up from a few hundred to about thirty thousand (about twice what it is today), and its ethnic composition changed from German and Scots-Irish to Eastern European. Until the 1970s, one could still find numerous separate parishes serving Ukrainian, Croatian, Polish, Serbian, Russian, Lithuanian, and Slovak congregations, but today many have merged. Nonetheless, *kiszki, kielbasa,* and *halubki* are on sale at the food shops along East Carson Street, and the ladies at St. John the Baptist and St. Vladimir's churches still sell their handmade *pyrohy* every Thursday.

No steel is produced on the South Side now, and the only Steelers visible here are the ones televised in the several score bars on East Carson Street. In the 1980s, South Side turned itself into Pittsburgh's mecca for art and antiques, but those galleries were swept away by the profusion of eating and drinking places now found inside the Victorian storefronts. The food is French, Spanish, Arab, Mediterranean, and generically Continental; the shopping specialized; the nightlife entertainment respectable and homegrown. Whether upscale at the SouthSide Works or fourth-generation traditional on the flats of Old Birmingham, South Side presents a vivid cross-section of post-industrial Pittsburgh.

OLD BIRMINGHAM, EAST CARSON STREET, AND THE SOUTH SIDE SLOPES

The 964 acres of Old Birmingham, the core of South Side, are divided about equally between the "flats" and "slopes"—the Monongahela River floodplain and the terraces where Mount Washington levels sufficiently to accommodate several hundred houses. The division of Old Birmingham into two camps was both topographical and social in origin, since the dividing point was the railroad at the base of Mount Washington: Germans above, Eastern Europeans below. The dichotomy of flats and slopes has an architectural dimension as well: the slopes are covered in clusters of white frame cottages, the flats in red brick rowhouses. Whether on the flats or the slopes, the inhabitants of Old Birmingham are marked by their strong communal feelings. Excepting student tenants, to a degree rare in urban America today, much of South Side's life revolves about its homes and handsome churches.

There are many entry points to the South Side, but visitors must avoid the Fort Pitt and Liberty bridges, which lead to tunnels through Mount Washington and never connect with South Side at all. The Fort Pitt and Liberty tunnels (known locally as "tubes") were cut when their corresponding bridges were built, while the Mount Washington Transit Tunnel was bored through in 1904 to bring trolleys to the southern suburbs. There is also a fourth tunnel, the Wabash, which has been rehabilitated for automobile traffic. This was cut through in 1904 as part of a scheme by George Gould, son of the high-living financier Jay Gould, to break the monopoly of the railroads, which controlled freight traffic in Pittsburgh. The bridge and railroad terminal that were once served by this tunnel are long gone, but the bridge piers still rise starkly out of the Monongahela, as if inviting a new use.

There are four more bridges that span the Monongahela from South Side. The most venerable is the Smithfield Street Bridge, from 1883, which leads into Station Square, at the western end of South Side. The current bridge is the successor to Pittsburgh's first bridge, a wooden structure from 1818, and

fig. 4.2
PHILIP MURRAY
BRIDGE

to a wire-based suspension bridge constructed by John Augustus Roebling in 1846. Smithfield is the longest and most graceful variant of a rare bridge configuration called the lenticular or Pauli truss. The fisheye shape of its trusses and their strengthening by both vertical and diagonal members made lenticular truss bridges exceptionally sleek and stable, but only a few are left in the world today.

Visually, the Philip Murray Bridge (for years simply the Tenth Street Bridge) may be the most inviting of this quartet, its taut but poetic suspension cables lithely suspended from two high steel portals. Farther upriver stands the efficient but brusque Birmingham Bridge and, still farther upriver, the Hot Metal Bridge and the SouthSide Works.

The Philip Murray Bridge brings cars directly into East Carson Street, South Side's main thoroughfare, but taking a few detours offers some worthwhile experiences. Bedford Square, the heart of South Side, lies two blocks east of the Murray Bridge. The square is small and segmented by the cross-cuts where South Twelfth and Bingham streets cut through. When Nathaniel Bedford laid out the square around 1810, his model was Pittsburgh's cramped Market Square, not London's elegant Bedford Square. Bedford put up the first local market house in 1813; the present South Side Market House is the fifth on the site. One of just two market buildings still standing in Pittsburgh, it serves today as the South Side Recreational Center. The homes on the perimeter of Bedford Square represent the typical mix of South Side's domestic architecture: small rowhouses of two stories and an attic, from the decades before or immediately following the Civil War, plus some High Victorian Gothic houses of three full stories or two stories with a mansard-roof attic.

fig. 4.3
DECORATIVE
BRICKWORK, OLD
GLASSHOUSE ON
BINGHAM STREET

Bingham Street, leading out of Bedford Square, was the center of glass-making in America in the last half of the nineteenth century. Some glass-houses had been in this area since shortly after 1800; others moved to the South Side after being devastated by the Great Fire of 1845 in the Golden Triangle. The dominant firm was Bakewell, Pears & Company, which was founded by the transplanted Englishman Benjamin Bakewell in 1808 and soon enjoyed a worldwide reputation for flint houseware glass. Presidents James Monroe and Andrew Jackson regarded Bakewell glass as the equal of any European service, and both ordered it for the White House.

The Bakewell glasshouses occupied a full block of Bingham Street between South Ninth and South Tenth streets and the Monongahela water-front until the site was redone for Henry Oliver's ironworks. The Oliver Bathhouse at the corner of South Tenth Street and Bingham was originally sketched out by Daniel Burnham as one of his multiple commissions from the Oliver estate, but the building went up only in 1915, after Burnham's death, so local architects MacClure & Spahr were in charge of the project. Their style was Jacobean Revival, with dolphins on the top floor to symbolize the structure's aquatic purposes. Opposite the long side of the bathhouse stands the Bedford School Lofts, a noble three-story block from 1850 that now houses eight condominiums. The severe lines of the old school show how effective the language of the Greek Revival was in Pittsburgh even at midcentury.

At the corner of South Ninth and Bingham streets, the structure that was once one of the factories for the U.S. Glass Company today serves as part of the Salvation Army. Expanded in 1891 to the size it is today, this building was the headquarters of a consortium of a dozen smaller glassworks that briefly rivaled PPG. Its north wall, thirty-two bays long, reflects the older Romanesque Revival mode of factory construction. Some of the architectural details are in fact idiosyncrasies peculiar to Frank Furness, whose influence in Pittsburgh reached its height in 1888 with the construction of his B&O Railroad terminal Downtown.

Two churches are crucial to the visual makeup of East Carson Street. St. John the Baptist Ukrainian Catholic Church, at the corner of Carson and South Seventh Street, was originally, in the 1890s, a standard American Protestant church and housed a Lutheran congregation. It was only in 1917 that it became a striking symbol of Pittsburgh's Central and Eastern European communities, when the new congregation remodeled the sanctuary to form a cross-in-square shape that is traditional in Byzantine religious architecture. St. John the Baptist has one gilded dome and seven turquoise domes that recall not only St. Mark's in Venice but the *pysanka* eggs distributed at Easter by the Ukrainian community. The churches of Pittsburgh's Central and Eastern European community have a long and complex history, with some of them being Orthodox, others Roman Catholic, and still others following the Eastern Rite of the Catholic Church. These differences are rooted in the vast and ethnically varied expanses of the former Austro-Hungarian Empire, with Pittsburgh's immigrants coming from many different parts of that empire.

The smaller but still beguiling presence at 1005 East Carson, near South Tenth Street, is the former Cleaves Temple Christian Methodist Episcopal Church, from 1913. The red bricks and the white overscaled Ionic portico, the bright orange towers, and the onion-topped domes heighten the impact of this dashing little church. Three congregations—first Ukrainian Presbyterians, then Eastern Rite Catholics, and finally Methodists—worshiped here, in a denominational flux that underscores the bittersweet process of assimilation

fig. 4.4
St. John the
Baptist Ukrainian
Catholic Church

in old working-class neighborhoods like the South Side. The structure's current function also speaks to the inevitability of change; it is now a piano bar.

The major thoroughfare of South Side is the twenty-block-long East
Carson Street, one of the better preserved commercial streets in America.
The several hundred buildings in the streetscape between the Murray and Hot
Metal bridges make this a primer of styles from the nineteenth century to the
Great Depression. Three eras predominate: Civil War Italianate, with elabo-
rate hood molds (there are good examples in the 1200, 1300, and 1700 blocks
of East Carson); High Victorian Gothic from the 1870s and 1880s, with brack-
eted cornices (an excellent but modernized example is the former Ukrainian
Home, now a bar, at 1113 East Carson Street); and Art Deco from the 1930s.
Good examples of Art Deco are 1121 and 1214 East Carson, with Art Deco
storefronts at 1510, 1605, and 1734. Most of these buildings now house bars
or entertainment spots, the direction in which South Side is evolving.

A few banks lend some sobriety to this exuberant architectural scene:
the Iron and Glass Bank at 1114 East Carson, from 1926, styled to match
its name (though it is now First National); the Classical-style Carson City
Saloon at number 1401 (originally a Mellon Bank, and the German Savings
and Deposit Bank before that), from 1896; and PNC (originally People's
Trust) at 1736 East Carson, from 1902. The fine George Trautman house,
in High Victorian Gothic, stands immediately behind PNC, at 94 South
Eighteenth Street. A block away, the terra-cotta-fronted Maul Building at
Carson at Seventeenth Street was put up by the president of the German
Savings and Deposit Bank in 1910.

fig. 4.5
EAST CARSON STREET

fig. 4.6
A TEXACO STATION
IS NOW A POPULAR
RESTAURANT

fig. 4.7
SOUTH
THIRTEENTH STREET,
LOOKING UP TO
ST. MICHAEL'S CHURCH

fig. 4.8
ST. ADALBERT'S ROMAN
CATHOLIC CHURCH

fig. 4.9
TYPICAL SOUTH
SIDE RESIDENTIAL
STREET

4.5
4.6
4.7   *4.8*
4.9

Of all of the adaptive reuses on the South Side, the most engaging involves not a historic building but the Texaco station on Carson at Twenty-fourth Street, now operating as the Double Wide Grill. The gas pumps and all the classic garage attributes are still there, backed up by a huge mural of South Side life.

The side streets in South Side provide their own architectural accompaniment to the main theme sounded by East Carson Street. On the short numbered streets between the riverbank and the base of Mount Washington, and on the long streets named for John Ormsby's daughters, stand hundreds of houses in unbroken rows. Though preservationists are not yet scrambling to protect them, the Kool Vent aluminum awnings that predominate should be certified at some future point as the world's largest ensemble of the genre. The awnings were custom built and custom colored and featured special angled side louvers that withstood the wind-shear effect that tore away ordinary awnings. They were invented and patented in Pittsburgh in 1942 and then marketed nationally through licensees. Although the rest of the country enjoyed them, too, Kool Vent awnings became a Pittsburgh specialty. Installed at the rate of some two dozen a day for forty-one years until production stopped in 1983, the awnings today adorn the windows and stoops of thousands of Pittsburgh homes. They were particularly important in the South Side, Bloomfield, and Lawrenceville, where rowhouses offered less individuality than the detached homes of fancier Pittsburgh neighborhoods.

Towering over the rowhouses are a dozen deconsecrated churches. Most are now condominiums, but the Civil War–era Birmingham Methodist Church at Bingham and Thirteenth became the City Theater. The main sanctuary now seats an audience of 270, while the social hall functions much as it always did, with a side passage to the Hamburg Theater for more experimental works. Though it now houses a public relations firm, the Talmud Torah Synagogue, built in the 1920s at 1908 Sarah Street, close to Twentieth Street, still proclaims the Ten Commandments in Hebrew over the main door.

Closely tied to South Side's rowhouses are its ethnic community centers. The spiritual home of the Polish community is the striking twin-towered St. Adalbert's Church, from 1889, hard by the railroad tracks at the dead end of South Fifteenth Street. It was a complete social center, with church, rectory, and Polish-language school. The Falcon Auditorium on South Eighteenth Street, between Sarah and Carey Way, was for a century the Polish community's secular home. It was housed in a severe Romanesque Revival building of the 1870s that was previously a Methodist church. Today redone as apartments, it has lost the auditorium in which Ignace Paderewski raised an army of Polish-speaking men in 1917 as part of the Allied cause—a crucial step in the rebirth of modern Poland. Two blocks away, at 1721 Jane Street, a German social club of the 1870s was recycled into the Lithuanian Hall. This tentatively Classical Revival structure was upstaged in 1908 by its annex, where overscaled corbel brackets testify to the widespread influence in Pittsburgh of Art Nouveau.

These neighborhood churches and clubs frequently were located on street corners, for greater visibility. The South Side Presbyterian Church, at the corner of Sarah and South Twentieth streets, follows that formula in a broad, twin-towered façade terminating in a Palladian arch in the belfry of its asymmetrical left tower. St. Casimir's Roman Catholic Church and adjacent school, at the corner of Sarah at South Twenty-second Street, is the oldest Lithuanian-oriented parish in the city. It takes advantage of another corner site by raising two towers on high, square shafts of brick with rusticated brick quoins. The tower belfries are marked by Neobaroque paired columns set diagonally on the corners.

Sustenance of a less spiritual sort came to Old Birmingham from two rambling complexes on opposite sides of South Twenty-first Street, just below the rise of Mount Washington. One was the Duquesne Brewery at South Twenty-first and Mary, a rich collection of Romanesque Revival and modern designs from the late nineteenth to the mid-twentieth century. The complex now provides accommodation for a dozen artists' studios and galleries, plus a garage-door fabricator whose shop has not yet succumbed to gentrification. Atop the former brewery's roof, a gargantuan clock from 1933 provides the neighborhood and half of Pittsburgh with accurate time.

The postindustrial South Side is ideal territory for new housing on or near the Monongahela waterfront. The site is flat, quiet (except for the CSX trains that still pass by), secluded but safe, and easily reached on foot from Downtown or the Bluff. Duquesne University students live in South Side in considerable numbers, though they have to cross the river and climb up the Bluff to attend classes. If, as mentioned in the introduction to this book, a visitor to Pittsburgh in 1852 was struck by "a perfect mania" for putting up cast-iron shop fronts, then the perfect mania in the city today is the housing going up on South Side.

Most of these developments stand on the site of the South Side works of Jones & Laughlin Steel (in its last years part of LTV Steel), which once stretched between East Carson Street and the river from South Twenty-fifth through South Thirty-third streets. The Twenty-fifth and Twenty-sixth street blocks of the old site are now given over to businesses at River Park Commons and to

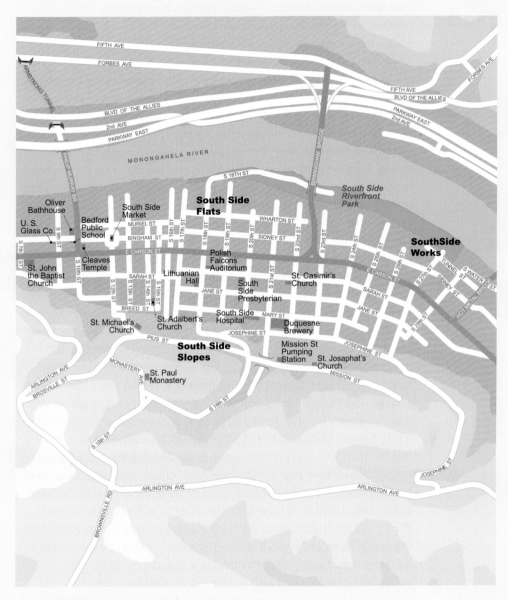

The South Side

apartment living at the Carson Street Commons. More extensive townhouse complexes include Fox Way Commons, New Birmingham, and Riverside Mews, closer to the Monongahela banks, between South Sixteenth and South Eighteenth streets.

Several amenities have been preserved or are being developed with the idea of turning mere housing developments into traditional-style neighborhoods, along the precepts of "new urbanism." The restoration of many of the century-old rowhouses means that not every house in sight is just three years old. Preservation efforts also encompass shop fronts, such as an especially attractive sequence of eleven Romanesque Revival buildings in the 2200 block of East Carson Street. A necessary amenity for any thriving neighborhood is provided by the shopping center, including a grocery store, on South Twenty-second Street, in the shadow of the Birmingham Bridge. This retail center, on the site of the old Levinson Steel fabricating plant, is dishearteningly suburban in character, but it has been kept small in scale, and its presence ensures that local families can buy essentials without having to rely on a car. Another amenity is Southside Riverfront Park, which consists of eight blocks of revitalized woods on the Monongahela riverfront, from South Eighteenth Street (the access point) to South Twenty-sixth. Another fine amenity here is the 1908 Carnegie Library branch on East Carson Street, next to the Birmingham Bridge.

The best news coming out of South Side today is SouthSide Works, a mixed-use development that since 2000 has replaced the core of the Jones & Laughlin South Side works. The firm had its origins on this site in 1853, when Benjamin Franklin Jones and Samuel Kier expanded the small ironworks firm of Bernard Lauth & Brother and became the American Iron Works. Jones, Kier, and Lauth began their combined operations with a daily output of seven tons. Kier left the group and became involved in a variety of business ventures, including outfits making pottery, firebricks, and canal boats, and he was a pioneer in oil refining. In 1855, his role at the American Iron Works was taken over by the banker James Laughlin. The South Side mill began to produce steel in two Bessemer furnaces in 1883. By 1900, fifteen thousand men were pouring three thousand tons of steel a day at the mill.

Nothing can bring the fiery red glow of the Bessemer converters back to the South Side sky, but what might have been a depressing brownfield today bustles in a thirty-four-acre mix of more than a dozen buildings and a million square feet of housing, retail, entertainment, and office space. The first tenants of SouthSide Works were the administrators of the UPMC Sports Performance Complex in the Quantum I building (the sports facility itself belongs to a separate forty-acre development farther upstream). Quantum II, on East Carson Street at Hot Metal Street, captures the details and massing of a Second Empire building for its retail and corporate tenants, while more retail, housing, entertainment, and parking spreads out from a *faux* town square at the intersection of South Twenty-eighth and Sidney streets. Not every decision here was necessarily the right one, but SouthSide Works' density, its integration with the preexisting street grid, its assimilation of the dominant old architectural forms, and its stress on urban versus suburban features has made it an authentic Pittsburgh neighborhood, despite its artificially accelerated pace of development.

The South Side slopes touch the flats, but they constitute a world unto themselves. A bridge over the Conrail tracks at South Twelfth Street leads up a steep ramp and to the superbly sited St. Michael's Roman Catholic Church, at the corner of Pius and Brosville streets. In the Middle Ages the faithful believed that Saint Michael, mightiest of the archangels, felt most at home if his altars and sanctuaries were erected at great heights, which explains why churches bearing his name were often perched atop mountains or surmounted by exceptionally high spires. Pittsburgh's German Catholic immigrants evidently remembered this tradition when they built a church dedicated to St. Michael on this dramatic terrace overlooking Old Birmingham. The best features of the church are the superb site, the high needle spire, and the sequence of exquisitely molded brick buttresses along Pius Street. The style is German Romanesque—the so-called *Rundbogenstil*—which, in combination with the hillside and the river below, suggests that the building would look quite at home in the German countryside. Today the deconsecrated church building serves as the aptly named Angel's Arms Condominiums.

Not so powerful as the gaunt church but more lovable is the later St. Michael's rectory behind it. Especially seductive are its two circular towers, which are recessed into the left and right corners and topped by elegantly swirled metal domes. The church and rectory are only two elements in a complex that also included a community center, a large convent residence, and a school for girls, all on Pius Street. Since 1910, the auditorium at 44 Pius Street has been the site of annual Lenten presentations of *Veronica's Veil*, an Oberammergau-style passion play that engages 150 South Siders as actors.

Still higher up, the summit of Monastery Avenue is crowned by St. Paul of the Cross Monastery. This flourishing monastic complex on the crown of Mount Washington is the oldest of the twenty-eight houses in America where Passionist Fathers live and work. It consists of a broad Romanesque-Gothic church with monastic buildings on three sides. Inside, the style switches from

fig. 4.10
HOT METAL BRIDGE

fig. 4.11
VILLAGE SQUARE,
SOUTHSIDE WORKS

fig. 4.12
HILLSIDE HOUSES,
SOUTH SIDE

Medieval to a stunning German Baroque hall-church, with three naves of equal height divided by sturdy, deeply fluted composite columns rendered in imitation marble. The chancel is the high point of the interior, consisting of a coffered barrel vault over a continuous entablature that in turn rests on pilasters and cruciform piers—an arrangement that reflects the double duty of the building as both a community church and a monastic chapel.

Monastery and South Eighteenth streets wrap around St. Paul of the Cross Monastery in the manner of a circular ramp ascending around a Crusader's castle. The "castle" lacks the traditional water-filled moat, but it is just as effectively cut off by two bridges on Mission Street. Mission is one of those long, terraced South Side streets that seem to flourish in harsh isolation. It is heralded by the handsome Beaux-Arts-style Mission Street Pumping Station, from 1910, and is intersected at right angles by Sterling Way and Eleanor Street, both so steep that they have steps instead of sidewalks, plus handrails for winter conditions.

The guardian of Mission Street, near Sterling, is St. Josaphat's Roman Catholic Church, from 1916, which is also being redeveloped into condominium residences. It is a severe brick structure, originally built for the neighboring Polish community, and mingles recollections of old Europe (a Romanesque Revival porch and a high tower with bell-and-onion dome) with stylistic elements taken from the emerging modern movement. Sterling Way continues uphill for several blocks to one of the multiple peaks of Mount Washington. The houses are widely spaced amid lush gardens complete with rabbits hopping along narrow lanes. Viewing those gardens and the steelworkers' hard-won houses is a somewhat surreal part of the Pittsburgh experience. You can palpably sense the determination that for two centuries has sustained the South Side against its habitual adversaries of steep hills and life-threatening employment.

There is a protocol about industry and workers in Pittsburgh. Industry cannot climb hills as steep as the slopes of South Side, but workers' houses can. So the workers of Pittsburgh put their mark on the almost-inaccessible hilltops with their homes and turned the steepest land into cemeteries. The most dramatic of these resting places is St. Michael's Cemetery on South Eighteenth Street, just below Arlington Avenue. These twenty-six acres began to receive the remains of workers (and some capitalists) as early as the 1860s. The headstones are artistically carved, especially the earliest ones, with inscriptions in German. Looking out, one has a vast panorama of Pittsburgh: to the left, the U.S. Steel tower in the Golden Triangle; to the right, Oakland and the University of Pittsburgh's Cathedral of Learning. The workers of Pittsburgh have earned their scenic place of rest.

fig. 4.13
PUBLIC STEPS,
PIUS STREET

fig. 4.14
COBBLESTONES,
ELEANOR STREET

fig. 4.15
SMITHFIELD STREET
BRIDGE

STATION SQUARE AND MT. WASHINGTON

The richness of South Side in topographic, social, and architectural terms stems from its isolation, or at least its separation, from the rest of Pittsburgh. But one enclave of South Side encourages access. That is Station Square, a forty-acre riverfront development stretching between the Smithfield and Fort Pitt bridges. Begun in 1975, Station Square marked the first moment in more than a century that Pittsburgh grasped the visual and social potential of its rivers, as opposed to their commercial and industrial uses. The commercial return from this investment has been good though not spectacular for its several score shops and restaurants, but the "urban return" from Station Square has been most fruitful of all. It extended the retail and social boundaries of the Golden Triangle to encompass both banks of the Monongahela, in the process significantly altering the buying and entertainment habits of middle-income Pittsburgh.

The creation of Station Square (the name is standard redevelopment hype—there is neither a working station nor a square) was guided by the Pittsburgh History & Landmarks Foundation and funded by Pittsburgh philanthropist Richard Scaife. The site had been a freight yard that was established in 1877 by the tiny but profitable Pittsburgh & Lake Erie Railroad, to which was added a passenger terminal a generation later. Today the railroad is part of CSX, and the terminal serves as the Landmarks Building.

fig. 4.16
PITTSBURGH &
LAKE ERIE RAILROAD
TERMINAL,
NOW PART OF
STATION SQUARE

The terminal is a wonderful relic of old Pittsburgh. What appears to be a square building is in fact a trapezoid, because Beaux-Arts propriety demanded a north face parallel to the Monongahela and an east face parallel to the Smithfield Street Bridge. The mark of this excessive concern for architectural decorum is the peculiar wedge-shaped vestibule, a necessary device to steer visitors along the centerline of the building. The old waiting room on the lower level was renovated in 1977 by the Detroit restaurateur Chuck Muer as the Grand Concourse. This palatial room, with its barrel vault of stained glass, forms one of the most dynamic spaces in the city, although everything that looks to be marble is simply painted plaster. The only genuine thing is the side revetment on the grand staircase, for which the working drawings specified "real marble."

Behind the old terminal are additional early twentieth-century railroad buildings that now serve as office, retail, and entertainment space, while tourist attractions include a ten-ton Bessemer converter, an Art Deco diner, and a fleet of Victorian trolleys and railroad cars. The best of the secondary buildings is Commerce Court, a reworking of a 1917 seven-story steel-frame warehouse. The interior design is perhaps a bit too reminiscent of something one might see in Las Vegas, but the brooding exterior lines of the warehouse were retained, and those long brick walls give the complex a solid visual anchor. Farther downriver is the dock for the Gateway Clipper fleet, the largest excursion boat operation in the country and another major step in getting Pittsburghers back to the water. The waterfront had long been a place to avoid; Mayor Tom Murphy regularly told audiences in the 1990s that his mother would always warn him to be home before dark and to stay away from the rivers. More than anyplace else, it was Station Square that helped Pittsburghers defy both of those taboos.

The Monongahela Incline of 1870 and the Duquesne Heights Inclined Plane of 1877 are among the world's oldest working funiculars and the only survivors of the seventeen that once served a half-dozen Pittsburgh neighborhoods. It is fitting that they serve not only tourists but also commuters because they were inspired by the human-powered coal inclines that had operated on Mount Washington in earlier decades. The engineer for the Monongahela Incline was John J. Endres, who assembled a remarkable group of collaborators for the project. John Augustus Roebling calculated and fabricated the cables, and Endres hired two special assistants: one was his daughter Caroline, one of the nation's first woman engineers (her sister Bertha was one of the first female architects); the other was his future son-in-law, Samuel Diescher. Diescher built or rebuilt ten Pittsburgh inclines, designed still more inclines as well as steel mills all over the United States, launched boats in South America, and assisted Pittsburgh's George Washington Ferris in the spectacular debut of the Ferris Wheel at the Chicago World's Fair of 1893. He was also chief engineer for the Duquesne Incline.

The Monongahela Incline is the shorter of the two surviving funiculars—635 feet, compared to the Duquesne's 793 feet—but it is steeper (with a 35 percent grade, compared to the Duquesne's 30.5 percent). Both inclines are powered by electricity now and not by steam as they were in the past, but the Duquesne Incline retains its original cable drum and wooden-toothed drive gear. Its cabins are also original relics of Victoriana. The four incline stations—the two lower stations on West Carson Street are of brick, and the two upper stations on Grandview Avenue are of wood—are all delightful period pieces. The Duquesne Incline's lower station connects to a pedestrian bridge over East Carson Street, while its upper station is packed with curios of Pittsburgh's transportation history. Each incline has carried about 100 million passengers without accident. The ride up is thrilling, the ride down terrifying; one is obliged to try both.

You can reach the summit of Mount Washington by the two inclines, by the 1920s-era McArdle Roadway off Liberty Bridge, or by the tortuous East Sycamore Street, which branches off Arlington Avenue above its intersection with East Carson. Anyone ascending the heavily forested slopes of the hill will find them little changed from George Washington's time, although the future president might have seen forty-pound turkeys waddling through the woods or caught twenty-pound perch in the Monongahela. At the summit, lookouts

fig. 4.17
Duquesne Incline

on Grandview Avenue present a vivid panorama of the Golden Triangle and the Monongahela and Ohio rivers.

Grandview Avenue is an interesting architectural promenade in its own right. It dates from 1861, the year Mt. Washington was organized as a borough, which was eleven years before Pittsburgh annexed it along with a dozen other boroughs, villages, and townships south of the Monongahela. Two neighborhood enclaves survive from those early years. One is a worker neighborhood of tiny houses packed into the saddle of land crisscrossed by Shiloh Street and Virginia Avenue; the other is a middle-class neighborhood of genteel late Victorian houses along Maple, Virginia, and Bigham. At the corner of Grandview and Maple avenues four Queen Anne rowhouses with chromatic corner turrets have survived; a stone marker indicates that they were constructed in 1880. Within the upper curve of McArdle Roadway, at the intersection of Grandview with Merrimac, stands another superbly preserved Queen Anne house complete with turret and octagonal gazebo.

A few blocks over, still on the lip of Mount Washington, the apartment block at 1000 Grandview is competently designed but elicits some regret from architectural connoisseurs, who recognize the address as the one designated for Frank Lloyd Wright's Pointview Apartments. This was one of a notable series of never-built Pittsburgh projects that Wright created in the 1940s for E. J. Kaufmann, and working drawings for 1000 Grandview had already been produced when the project was abandoned in 1953. The plans were detailed enough that they could be executed tomorrow—as several local designers still dream of doing. Not far away on Grandview, the block between Plymouth and Oneida streets carries the Trimont Condominiums, a Wright-like twenty-five-story block that emerged in 1985 as a riff on Wright's unexecuted Pointview design.

These same blocks of Grandview also contain some good public buildings. Outstanding are the small, Classical-styled Carnegie branch library at 315 Grandview and the dramatic though thin Gothic Revival St. Mary of the Mount Church, at 403 Grandview. Two blocks in from Grandview stands Grace Episcopal Church, at the intersection of Bertha and West Sycamore. This impressive stone sanctuary in early English Gothic dates from 1926, but a predecessor wooden chapel served the landed gentry of Mt. Washington as far back as 1852.

The Gothic Revival Style survives on Mount Washington in secular as well as in sacred architecture. The four clapboard Daniel Hilf houses on Volk's Way, a little alley next to 224 Kearsarge, are Gothic in spirit though not in explicit style and show the possibilities of good vernacular worker housing at even the smallest scale and budget. Hilf, a Bavarian immigrant, put these houses up around 1910. There is another modest but affecting house some blocks away at 1732 Greenleaf Street, at the corner of Bradley, probably surviving from the 1850s, when Mt. Washington was still farmland but about to witness factory construction at the base of the hill.

Chatham Village is a housing complex that is famous the world over, though almost unknown in Pittsburgh. Just three blocks from Grandview Avenue, it is acclaimed in urban planning circles worldwide as a supreme achievement in low-cost housing. These houses—the name celebrates William Pitt, Earl of Chatham—were built by Pittsburgh's Buhl Foundation from 1932 to 1936 to accommodate 216 families on seventeen acres of steeply sloping ground, with another thirty acres retained, mostly to remain wooded but with a portion reserved for a playground. For two decades Chatham Village was considered a model for federally subsidized housing in the country, though none of the copies ever matched the original's quality.

Although the architecture of Chatham Village is a gracious, simple Georgian, the real star is the layout. Exploiting ground so hilly it was regarded as unsuitable for any sort of building (and thus could be acquired at low cost), famed urbanists Clarence Stein and Henry Wright laid out three clusters of houses around miniature village greens. Each cluster subdivides into smaller groups of two to eight houses, with parking either in integral garages or in hidden garage rows on the periphery of the village.

The social center for the complex is the Thomas Bigham house, from 1844, on Pennridge Road. Now called Chatham Hall, the house has simple lines and brick walls that inspired the design of the neighboring rows, and it

fig. 4.18
CHATHAM VILLAGE

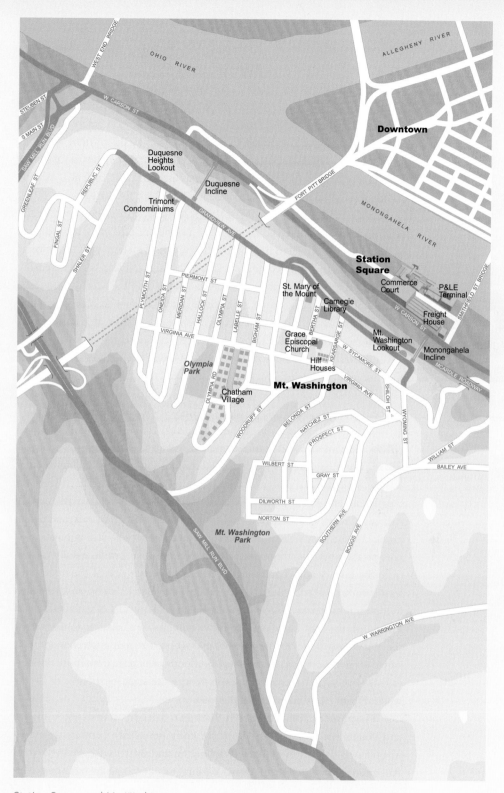

Station Square and Mt. Washington

has some fame in its own right as the most important of Pittsburgh's half-dozen stops on the Underground Railroad that slaves followed to freedom. Stein and Wright had devised middle-class housing projects before Chatham, including their more celebrated Greenbelt in Maryland, but none achieved more social and financial success than this one. Occupancy has always been 100 percent, first as rental property, then as a cooperative, and now as condominiums. More than a few families have lived here for decades.

Half a mile west of Chatham Village, Grandview Avenue ends in the neighborhood of Duquesne Heights, but not before offering a second panoramic view of Pittsburgh. At Grandview's intersection with Sweetbriar Street, the three rivers come into sharp focus and there is an especially dramatic view of the North Side, the Ohio River, and the nearby Duquesne Incline. Since 2006, visitors at this scenic overlook have been accompanied by a set of bronze sculptures depicting George Washington in a tense *tête-à-tête* with the Seneca leader Guyasuta. More excitement comes from the heart-in-your-mouth descent down the back of Mount Washington via Republic and Greenleaf streets to West Carson Street and the West End Bridge.

fig. 4.19
JAMES WEST'S
POINT OF VIEW
REPRESENTS
A 1770 MEETING
BETWEEN
WASHINGTON
AND GUYASUTA

THE BACK SLOPES OF MOUNT WASHINGTON

Being an unequal confederation of villages, Pittsburgh gives neighborhoods such as Oakland, Shadyside, and Squirrel Hill more than their fair share of attention and other districts less. The villages on the plateau and back slopes of Mount Washington, particularly Allentown, Arlington, Knoxville, Beltzhoover, Beechview, Brookline, Carrick, and Overbrook, are the least well known in proportion to their size and population—now totaling seventy thousand. This low communal profile results mainly from the history and economics of the area, which is one of the newer and least commercially developed districts of the city. But it may be explained also in topographic terms, since the key to prestige in any city is visibility, and in Pittsburgh the back slopes of Mount Washington are invisible to the rest of the city. Flying over Pittsburgh, even a longtime resident might remark with surprise on these "back slopes" neighborhoods, which are even more difficult to make out as they merge imperceptibly with the adjacent suburbs of Brentwood, Dormont, Whitehall, and Baldwin.

The portal roads into these Mt. Washington neighborhoods are Arlington and Warrington avenues, which in the early nineteenth century served as turnpikes to the nearby towns of Washington and Brownsville, Pennsylvania. Arlington Avenue curves up Mount Washington alongside the track bed of an inclined plane that was abandoned in the 1950s. Many of the small frame houses along its path are raised to fit against the hillside, as though on stilts. The character of this casual street changes dramatically at the crest of the hill, where Arlington intersects Warrington Avenue and Allentown begins.

Allentown, named for the butcher Joseph Allen, and Beltzhoover, named for its major landowner, Melchor Beltzhoover, were both laid out after the Civil War by the developers Benjamin McLain and his son-in-law, Thomas Maple. Like Nathaniel Bedford a generation before, McLain and Maple named the main cross-streets for their children. The settlers of Allentown were German artisans who came up the hill to escape the polluted South Side, commuting to the city either by trolley or by the three inclined planes that once scaled the four-hundred-foot bluff to these neighborhoods. The center of this artisans' hilltop village was its commercial core on Warrington Avenue, a strip that has lost much of its color today as its residents (today numbering about three thousand) find less fatiguing places to live. But Allentown left behind impressive relics from the hundred years in which it flourished. The three-story commercial block at 816–818 Warrington Avenue well represents the economic history of the neighborhood. It was boldly fashioned in the High Victorian Gothic Style, probably in the 1880s, with elaborately stepped corbels and wide segmental arches, then reclad at street level in the 1930s in Art Deco black glass.

The double spires of St. George's Roman Catholic Church, from 1910, loom like France's Chartres cathedral over the small brick and frame houses on Allen Street, at the corner of Climax. Especially dramatic is the view over the church a few blocks uphill, where Climax and Knox streets intersect with Arlington Avenue. The social and physical cohesiveness of Allentown is dramatically revealed each year on Good Friday, when teenagers from St. George's put on togas and Roman centurion armor and replicate Christ's procession to Calvary.

Monumental architecture like St. George's is the exception in these modest neighborhoods, but there is another singular building about a mile farther down Arlington Avenue. The Arlington Fire Station at the intersection with St. Patrick Street, dating from the 1980s, is unexpectedly handsome for a utilitarian structure. The home of Dispatch 22 derives its power from the severe geometry of its rhomboid plan and the contrast between the glass-encased fire engine room and the concrete block of the firefighters' living quarters behind it. In back of the station, the firefighters have box seats for Little League games that are played there all summer.

fig. 4.20
WAY OF THE CROSS, ANNUAL PROCESSION IN ALLENTOWN

185

The main artery of the area, Warrington Avenue, snakes a dozen blocks downhill to its end at Saw Mill Run Boulevard (state route 51 south). The street follows a circuitous course that in turn parallels the streambed of Saw Mill Run: highway and stream together trace out the southern perimeter of Mount Washington. A number of transportation routes conjoin at this point. Warrington Avenue, the Mount Washington Transit Tunnel, and the Liberty Tunnel all feed into Saw Mill Run within an eighth of a mile of each other. In this vicinity, what had been the Washington Pike assumes the name of West Liberty Avenue (truck route 19 south) and becomes a busy thoroughfare of used-car dealerships. Immediately uphill West Liberty intersects Pioneer Avenue, a pleasant street that cuts through the semi-suburban neighborhood of Brookline.

The areas today occupied by Brookline and Overbrook (the names recall those of wealthy suburbs of Boston and Philadelphia, respectively) were farmland until 1908, when both neighborhoods were laid out by A. P. Haaz, a land speculator. The two developments and the adjoining neighborhoods of Banksville, Beechview, and Carrick were so remote from Pittsburgh that, until they began to prosper as trolley suburbs in the 1920s, much of the land had to be sold at bargain rates for use as cemeteries. The main link road here is Brookline Boulevard, which is long and spacious and has the diagonal parking characteristic of a shopping mall. One side of the boulevard has been commercially developed, with stores below and apartments with Spanish tile roofs above; the other side is largely given over to houses perched on high broad lawns. If these dormitory communities are unexciting for some, they are just right for others; the home burglary rate in Overbrook is exceptionally low.

The architectural highlights of the back slopes of Mount Washington are the recreational facilities in Brookline Memorial Park. The land for the park was given to the city by developers who could not make any money from the acreage because of its steep slopes and poor subsurface conditions. In the 1980s, the forlorn park was provided with a swimming pool and baseball diamonds. A limited vocabulary of colors and elements kept the project within its narrow budget and harmonized with the rows of tract houses from the 1930s and 1940s, which stare down on the park like spectators. The materials for the pool—glazed concrete block, glass block, and brick—are handled with a severe totemic aspect, like the ruins of a southwestern pueblo.

The extraordinary element in the park is the Sam Bryen Arch, which serves as the portal to two baseball diamonds. The "arch" is no more than a gap between a garage and a maintenance shed, but its designers turned it into something profound, in both shape and function. Probably based on the Lion Gate at Mycenae, the arch consists of glazed concrete block over a mauve base, a sturdy concrete lintel, and two concrete columns. The wall rises to embrace a concrete block that is inscribed with high-minded aphorisms from the *Little League Handbook of Fair Play*. To the left, a long wall shelters niches that are being filled over the years with plaques proclaiming the winning teams in Brookline's Little League. It is wonderful to find a suburban monument that is at once stark and lush, classic and pop, complex and contradictory.

Yet another of the old country roads that branch off Arlington is Brownsville Road, the old Birmingham & Brownsville Macadamized Turnpike, which led to the important Monongahela port of Brownsville. Some of the tollgates on this road lasted as late as 1900; today, the road mainly serves as a shortcut to the Carrick and Brentwood neighborhoods.

The northern portion of Brownsville Road divides the working-class neighborhood of Knoxville from the independent borough of Mt. Oliver. Knoxville was a fruit farm established early in the nineteenth century by the Reverend Jeremiah Knox. His descendants turned the family farm into a housing development in the 1870s, but its modest housing stock today dates mainly from the early twentieth century. The neighborhood landmark here is Paul Schweikher's Knoxville branch of Carnegie Library, from 1966, at 400 Brownsville Road, at the corner of Matthews. This strikingly self-contained cement-block structure, complete with steel-mesh security grilles that are locked at night, pulls back from the street by means of two deeply recessed vestibules that muffle traffic noises. The library receives its natural lighting not from the street but from two gray metal hoods that rise fortresslike from the central block of the building and terminate in skylights. The design of the library is elitist rather than populist in tone, since its shrinks from contact with the rag-tag architecture of the street and sets itself up as a sanctuary of learning for those neighborhood residents who want one.

Carrick is an old pike town farther down Brownsville Road from Knoxville and Mt. Oliver. A middle-class district of twelve thousand inhabitants today, it had a brief moment of affluence at the turn of the twentieth century, as the wealthier South Side families abandoned that crowded zone for something more refined. One remnant of this period is the Boulevard, an elegant promenade of Queen Anne and Colonial Revival houses that opens off Brownsville Road opposite South Side Cemetery.

Farther south, Brownsville Road crosses the Pittsburgh city limits and becomes the main arterial of the independent borough of Brentwood, a semi-suburban district that was carved out in 1915 and is now home to ten thousand residents. Here the "city suburbs" of Pittsburgh end, and the independent suburbs of the South Hills begin.

PENN AVENUE: FIRST FOUNDRIES AND FIRST SUBURBS

fig. 5.1
JUDY PENZER'S
*THE BRIDE OF
PENN AVENUE,*
GARFIELD

The distance from the Strip, an industrial district on the south bank of the Allegheny, to the eastern suburb of Monroeville is about twelve miles by air and nearly twice that if one drives. The psychic distance is perhaps even greater. The Strip and Monroeville care nothing about each other, and they are separated by about twenty other neighborhoods, all similarly detached. But all of these neighborhoods are in fact linked by Penn Avenue. This linkage was forged by nature: in a city marked by hundreds of hills, this chain of neighborhoods along Penn Avenue sits on land that is basically flat. Penn Avenue is actually a remnant of the original nineteenth-century Pennsylvania Turnpike, known in its early days as the Greensburg, Harrisburg, or Philadelphia turnpikes, and it rambles all the way.

Whoever drives the full length of Penn Avenue traverses almost the whole of "mainland" Pittsburgh, an area that holds half of the city's land mass and population. This is a historic route, based not only on the turnpike but also on old American Indian trails that were used either in General Edward Braddock's failed assault on Fort Duquesne in 1755 or in General John Forbes's successful capture of that fort in 1758. Like most Indian trails, Penn Avenue is relatively level because it follows a temporary channel the Monongahela carved out during the last ice age.

Pittsburghers never gave a name to this riverbed (one could call it the Monongahela Plain) because at first they failed to recognize it as such. But it was an obvious feature to the scouting parties of the Braddock and Forbes campaigns and on two other occasions when it proved a godsend. The first came in 1852, when this unique flat route through Pittsburgh was chosen for the Pennsylvania Railroad track bed, which still runs between the Strip and Wilkinsburg. The second occasion came in 1983, when the Pittsburgh bus system used a portion of the railroad's right-of-way for a dedicated bus lane that moves commuters in and out of Downtown in about twenty minutes.

The Monongahela Plain determined which neighborhoods would be the first to develop. Wilkinsburg, seven miles east of the Golden Triangle but linked to it by rail, was a flourishing village by 1860, while Squirrel Hill, three miles closer to Downtown but without a rail link, was still only half settled as late as 1910.

The Monongahela Plain not only encouraged industrial development but also was able to generate income. There was scant profit to be made in urban development on the hilltops of Pittsburgh, where all the homes had to be custom built to the unique topography underneath them, but building rows of cheap houses on a flat plain was both easy and lucrative. Scions of several pioneer families, particularly the descendants of one Caspar Taub, made fortunes by cutting up their ancestral estates into the smallest possible lots. One branch of the Taub clan, called the Winebiddles, squeezed a respectable fortune from their lands in Bloomfield, Friendship, and Garfield. Later descendants did even better, slicing up their great-great-grandfather's land with such exactitude that they laid the foundations of a colossal fortune. History has forgotten their links to the Taubs and the Winebiddles and remembers them for themselves: the Mellons.

THE STRIP AND POLISH HILL

The Strip has gone by a variety of names, among them Bayardstown, O'Harasville, and Denny's Bottoms. It was first a wooded riverbank, then in turn a residential area, a manufacturing center, a wholesale and produce distribution point, and finally a destination for shoppers. Like most Pittsburgh districts, the Strip defines its three hundred acres with precision: its boundaries are Eleventh Street and the Golden Triangle on the west, the Allegheny River on the north, the wooded slopes of the Hill on the south, and Doughboy Square and the packed rowhouses of Lawrenceville on the east. From its earliest development, the Strip has functioned like a giant industrial assembly line, with functionally linked businesses sprouting up to serve other businesses.

In this literal strip of a mile and a half along Penn and Liberty avenues an important part of the world's industrial history was born. In 1773, James O'Hara, Pittsburgh's pioneer manufacturer, bought most of the land included in the Strip, and that land plus a stretch of the Allegheny waterfront to Lawrenceville nurtured the growth of the earliest iron foundries in Pittsburgh. It was in the Strip that Thomas Armstrong cornered the world market on the production of cork, and it was here, too, that George Westinghouse and Charles Martin Hall, aged twenty-one and twenty-two, respectively, nurtured their revolutionary inventions of air brakes and aluminum into major industries. When James Parton, so astonished at the industrial strength of Pittsburgh in 1868, crafted his metaphor about Pittsburgh being hell with the lid taken off, he was not talking about the Carnegie and Jones & Laughlin mills on the Monongahela, which were still a decade or more in the future, but about the mills in the Strip.

The Strip was a transportation nexus, even in its earliest days. By the 1790s, it was part of the right-of-way of the earliest road to Philadelphia. In 1806, speculators secured the right to create an improved turnpike from Pittsburgh to Harrisburg, and by 1815, the first fifty miles were in use, giving passage to thousands of wagons. Within three more years the entire Pittsburgh-Harrisburg turnpike was opened to travel. In the next decade the Strip also served as a terminal point for goods transported on the Pennsylvania Canal, which connected Pittsburgh and Philadelphia via the Allegheny and Susquehanna rivers. When technology rendered the canal obsolete at mid-century, its function was taken up by the Pennsylvania, Junction (later Baltimore & Ohio), and Allegheny Valley railroads, all of which cut through or linked to the Strip.

The story of the Strip is one of human as well as industrial triumph. It and the adjoining neighborhoods of Lawrenceville, Polish Hill, and Bloomfield once housed thousands of workers who needed only their feet and minimal travel time to arrive at their factory jobs. The residents of the rowhouses on the Hill also had quick commutes during the decades when it was linked to the Strip by an incline. Almost all early Pittsburghers were English or Scots-Irish, but around 1800, the Irish arrived. It was in the Strip in 1808 that they built St. Patrick's, the city's first Catholic church. The Strip later became the point of entry for German, Polish, and Slovak immigrants, most of whom lived alongside its factories in long stretches of brick rowhouses. The Strip has few residents today, but an idea of its former population density can be

191

fig. 5.2
A REMNANT OF
THE CRUCIBLE
STEEL FOUNDRY

conceived from the rows of Greek Revival and Second Empire houses surviving on the 2500 block of Penn Avenue and on Spring Way, on Twenty-seventh Street at the corner of Mulberry Way, and on the 2900 block of Penn.

The struggle to create a livelihood was bitter for the workers in the Strip, even though the district was touched at least twice by living saints. John Neumann was pastor of St. Philomena's Church in the 1830s, and fifty years later Mary Katharine Drexel served as a novice with the local convent of the Sisters of Mercy. Most of the Strip's churches left the district when its houses gave way to industrial plants, but two remain. St. Stanislaus Kostka, at Twenty-first Street and Smallman, was founded in 1875 and built in 1892 as the mother congregation for the several hundred thousand western Pennsylvanians of Polish origin. This powerfully detailed and splendidly sited church closes the five-block-long piazza (actually a former rail switching yard) from the Sixteenth Street Bridge to Twenty-first Street with the self-possession of a Renaissance cathedral. St. Stanislaus is elaborate and capacious inside, with rich frescoes of biblical and Polish history. It enchanted the archbishop of Krakow when he visited the parish, before he became Pope John Paul II. At 1711 Liberty, St. Patrick's Church was rebuilt in severe dress in 1935, although permitting itself a high conical tower that recalls the heroic Irish monasteries of the Dark Ages, complete with a fragment of the Blarney Stone inside. Not so lucky was the mother church of the Slovak community in the region: St. Elizabeth of Hungary, at 1620 Penn Avenue, which ended up as a nightclub. Restored externally, this winsome building matches an entrance porch and window pediments from American house architecture with the central tower of a fortified church that might be found in Eastern Europe. Today these churches are but grace notes to the main anthem of the Strip, which is sung to commerce and industry.

A new element came to the Strip in 1996, when the Senator John Heinz Pittsburgh Regional History Center took over an icehouse at 1212 Smallman, between Twelfth and Thirteenth streets. This muscular structure was built in 1898 to house blocks of ice that the Chautauqua Lake Ice Company would cut and haul from western New York every winter. Delivery came by direct railroad access through the corner of the building. Still vivid are its low masonry vaults and the riveted steel beams that supported the weight of the ice blocks once piled on the floors inside.

Today the Heinz Center records history, but during the Civil War the adjacent neighborhood blocks made history, too. A Hampton Inn now rises on the adjacent block of Smallman and a research center sits by the riverside, but in the nineteenth century the Fort Pitt Foundry sprawled over a half-dozen

fig. 5.3
OPEN-AIR MARKET
IN THE STRIP

blocks from Smallman Street to the Allegheny riverbank. The foundry claimed it was capable of pouring the largest masses of iron in the world, a claim confirmed by Thomas Jackson Rodman, superintendent of the nearby Allegheny Arsenal, who cast his gigantic, eighty-ton Rodman cannons there. The first of Rodman's cannons was cast in October 1863, with a length of twenty feet and a weight of about 114,000 pounds. The gun cast in February 1864 was even longer; its weight was 160,000 pounds in the rough before being shaped to a mere 116,496 pounds. Reputedly the longest gun in the world, it was capable of blasting cannon balls a distance of three miles. Some historians assert that it was the might of these cannons that deterred the British and French from entering the Civil War on the side of the Confederacy—an action they had seriously contemplated before being deterred by these monsters of death.

The Strip is more sedate today, its visual character fixed at its west end, toward Downtown, by tall loft buildings such as the former Byrnes & Kiefer Company at 1133 Penn Avenue, recycled as professional offices in 1984 but still impressive in its sandstone façade in Richardsonian Romanesque Style. At 1201 Penn, in the adjoining block, what was the old Sack Store Fixture building now stocks office furniture in a vividly articulated Romanesque Revival warehouse with staring lunette windows punched deep into its thick walls.

What makes the Strip the most alluring of the Pittsburgh industrial districts today is its devotion to food, which it has distributed to the rest of the city since the Pennsylvania Railroad tracks were ripped out of the Golden Triangle in 1906. The railroad then relocated its food sheds to the Strip, in switching yards that stretched a half-mile, from Thirteenth to Twenty-first Street. Later, trucks came into the Strip, particularly after the construction of

fig. 5.4
CIVIL WAR
CANNON,
ARSENAL PARK

fig. 5.5
SIXTEENTH
STREET BRIDGE

the Sixteenth Street Bridge in 1923. This lovably pompous structure was designed by Warren & Wetmore, architects of Grand Central Station in New York, with James Chalfant as engineer. It owes its exuberant bronze seahorse ornaments to sculptor Leo Lentelli.

It was to coordinate trains and trucks that the mammoth Pennsylvania Railroad Fruit Auction & Sales Building was erected in 1926. The building covers five blocks in length, but it is relieved by touches of Art Deco on the caps of its miniature buttresses. Rail traffic to Pittsburgh had just about ceased in 1983, but the City of Pittsburgh had the structure renovated that year to ensure a base for the local produce trade. The far end of the structure, diagonally opposite St. Stanislaus, houses the galleries and workshops of the Society for Contemporary Craft, which introduced a note of cultural diversity in the Strip.

Shoppers seeking fruits, vegetables, plants, and imported foods cherish the market atmosphere that animates the ramshackle Federal, Greek Revival, and Italianate houses (and much of the sidewalk) on Penn Avenue between Seventeenth and Twenty-first streets, with lesser intensity as far as Twenty-eighth Street.

Starting at six each morning these blocks thrive with the rhythm of a Middle Eastern bazaar. The classics among the restaurants and take-out places in the Strip are DeLuca's for breakfasts, Wholey's and Benkovitz for fish, and the all-night Primanti Bros. for colossal sandwiches, but a dozen other places guarantee good eating as well. Lidia's Pittsburgh serves authentic Italian food by PBS cooking-show host Lidia Bastianich; Eleven serves American food and has the largest wine cellar in the city; Kaya's serves Caribbean and African fare; and the Spaghetti Warehouse attracts a college crowd with vast portions of pasta at moderate prices. The food stores with the largest cult following are Parma Sausage, Rubino's, Galioto's, and Weisberg's for fruit and vegetables; Stamoolis Brothers for pita bread, phyllo dough, and spanakopita; Pennsylvania Macaroni Company; the Pittsburgh Cheese Terminal; Panini Bakery; and Sam Bok Oriental Foods. Dessert is available all day at Klavon's Ice Cream in a 1920s ice cream parlor on Smallman Street, at the corner of Twenty-ninth, with jukeboxes that were last updated a generation ago.

With the arrival of so many consumer-based firms in the Strip, shipping and light industry has retreated nearer to the Allegheny waterfront, particularly to a bumpy road that since 1856 has paralleled the Allegheny Valley Railroad tracks. Officially Railroad Street, the road is always called AVRR. Used by a number of industrial companies today, the majority of these buildings were erected by the Kloman-Phipps works, which merged after the Civil

War into Andrew Carnegie's Union Iron Mills, or Park Brothers & Company, later the Black Diamond Steel Works. A unique survivor here is the Park Brothers firm's elegant counting house at 2949 Smallman, at the corner of Thirtieth, now housing a Web site design studio. Other sheds belonged to the Union Iron Mills and survive today as the Ralph Meyer Company on both sides of Smallman between Thirty-first and Thirty-second streets. These brick basilicas, now 150 years old, are supported internally by triangular trusses of wood or their iron replacements.

The industrial facilities that now strike us as museum pieces were once the cutting edge of nineteenth-century technology. This fact is driven home by the plaque at 3220 Smallman that commemorates the site of the Pittsburgh

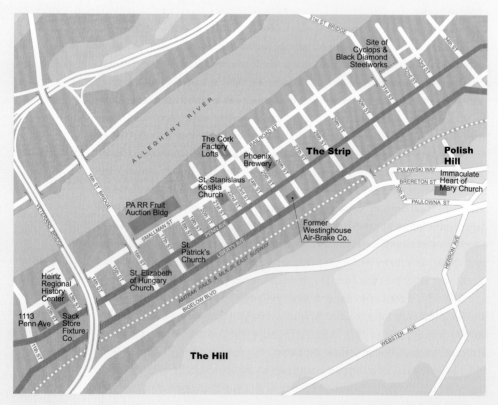

The Strip and Polish Hill

Reduction Company, later known to the world as Alcoa (legend holds that the name was changed because of confusion with a Pittsburgh garbage disposal firm). The first-ever ingots of commercially made aluminum were poured at this site on Thanksgiving in 1888.

A few streets away, at 2401–2425 Liberty Avenue between Twenty-fourth and Twenty-fifth streets, stands the block-long plant erected in 1870 for the Westinghouse Air-Brake Company. Until George Westinghouse invented the air brake, the potential for rail travel was greatly hamstrung by the crude brakes that had to be set by hand in each car. Westinghouse solved the problem by applying to it the new invention of compressed air. He then moved from upstate New York to Pittsburgh to find financial backers who would begin production of his invention, as Charles Martin Hall did a decade later for his aluminum manufacturing process.

Westinghouse constructed this handsome factory, twenty-five bays long, as the last word in industrial design, then labored frantically with his employees to satisfy the worldwide demand for his invention. In five years the plant turned out two thousand locomotive brakes and seven thousand car brakes. In 1871, a year after production began, Westinghouse made Saturday a half-holiday; he was the first employer in the United States to do so. World demand continued to be so intense that this plant, big as it was, gave way to another on the North Side in 1881, and then in 1890 to a third plant, many times larger, at Wilmerding. Westinghouse and John Augustus Roebling were probably the two most inventive figures ever to come out of Pittsburgh. By the year 1914, when Westinghouse died, his companies controlled fifteen thousand patents.

After Westinghouse sold the plant, the facility had various functions, such as a stage-set assembly facility for the Civic Light Opera Company. In 1987, in a nice twist, the factory that was emblematic of nineteenth-century high-tech became the home of Red Zone Robotics. For about a decade Red Zone manufactured robots that could perform in environments where humans could not, such as nuclear disasters. The Pittsburgh Opera is the main tenant here today.

As late as 1940, the Strip was home to more than 4,000 residents, but when industrial corporations such as Alcoa pulled out, so did their workers. The Strip became little more than a shantytown, to the point that the 2000 census enumerated just 266 residents. That figure has now doubled or tripled, as industrial installations have been turned into housing. One of the earliest of those initiatives is the Brake House at the corner of Liberty and Twenty-fifth streets, which developers created in 2002 by carving eighteen lofts out of a subsidiary part of the Westinghouse Air-Brake factory. The renovations accentuated the steel beams and masonry of the original, and semi-transparent movable walls give residents both privacy and a generous supply of natural light. Renovation has also transformed an abandoned Civil War–era schoolhouse at the corner of Smallman and Thirty-first Street into the fourteen luxury units of the Schoolhouse Lofts, each twenty-six hundred square feet in area and with fourteen-foot ceilings.

A few blocks farther from Downtown, the six-story Phoenix Brewery (later the Otto Milk Company), at Smallman and Twenty-fourth streets, from 1893, offers a good example of the more showy industrial architecture toward the end of the nineteenth century. The old Phoenix Brewery building features a stone platform and three sturdy Classical arches of brick at its base, three stories of elongated Romanesque arches above, and a corner tower with a pressed-brick phoenix rising from the flames. The half-Classical, half-Romanesque look constitutes a sort of Queen Anne school of industrial architecture, which was used to ennoble not only this brewery but three other key breweries in town, on the South Side, the North Side, and in Lawrenceville.

fig. 5.6
THE ARMSTRONG
CORK FACTORY,
NOW RESIDENTIAL
LOFTS

The building that once produced beer and bottled milk has yielded about sixty living units, in the second-largest housing development in the Strip.

The most difficult of these conversions was that of the Armstrong Cork Factory on the block of AVRR between Twenty-third and Twenty-fourth streets. This immense factory on the river's edge, ten stories high, owes its existence to Thomas Armstrong, a clerk in a Pittsburgh bottleworks who applied new mechanical techniques to the age-old trade of cutting corks. Armstrong's first factory on the site, built in 1879, gave way a quarter of a century later to this sequence of a dozen buildings as his company pioneered the use of cork as a building material. Armstrong Cork began to build on this site with masonry load-bearing walls, then switched to steel frames with brick veneer. Stylistically, the factories evolve from Romanesque Revival to a kind of industrial classicism, with three-story pilasters of brick crowned with Ionic capitals.

When Armstrong Cork left, the complex stood empty for decades. The sticking point delaying its conversion was the need to provide parking, a situation that was finally resolved in 2007 when a new garage and retail building were constructed on the opposite side of AVRR. The 297 rental units and thirty-five different floor plans of the Cork Factory Lofts offer not only the now-expected amenities of a fitness center, business center, outdoor pool, hot tub, and garden patio with fire pit but also a community room with bar, library, fireplace, pool table, and game table in the old engine room.

What almost killed the Strip a century ago was its own success: it was too small to contain all the flourishing enterprises to which it had given birth. Now reconciled to its smaller scale and reoriented to service, consumer sales, and housing, the area is undergoing a vigorous economic and architectural rebirth. With its population rising fast, the Strip is one of Pittsburgh's most dynamic neighborhoods.

At Liberty Avenue and Twenty-eighth Street, a broad roadway leads across the railroad tracks and upward into Polish Hill. Beginning in 1885, Polish immigrants who worked in the foundries and mills of the Strip settled in such numbers in the neighborhood they called Polskie Gory that its 139 acres were filled up by World War I. The neighborhood's frame and brick houses sometimes clung to such steep hillsides that they could be reached only by long flights of wooden or concrete steps. Today some fifteen hundred homesteaders live in this narrow district that is bounded on the north and east by the gully of Two Mile Run, with Bigelow Boulevard overhead and the Conrail tracks below. The day of the monolithic ethnic neighborhoods in Pittsburgh is over, however.

In 1905, the men of the neighborhood, skilled from their work in the iron foundries, steel mills, and glass factories, constructed the majestic Immaculate Heart of Mary Church at 3058 Brereton Street. The land purchased by the congregation was rich in scenic potential, being immediately below the new carriage drive on Bigelow Boulevard and at the crest of Brereton and Dobson streets, with sight lines extending several miles down the Allegheny Valley. The church remains the best sited of any in Pittsburgh, but at a cost: the hillside was so precipitous that normal placement of the nave was impossible; you enter the church expecting to see the nave stretching in front of you. Instead, you make a sharp left turn and then face the nave. In addition, the structure had to straddle the hill, its length running along the spine of the ridge. Immaculate Heart of Mary is an amalgam of two or even three architectural precedents. From the back it looks like St. Peter's in Rome, even to the detail of Michelangelo's peculiar attic windows; from the front it could be Borromini's Sant'Agnese on Piazza Navona in Rome; inside, it has the feel of Christopher Wren's City Churches in London.

A few doors downhill from the church, at 3028 Brereton, stands a once-splendid survivor of a different moment in the life of Polish Hill. The original function of this spacious four-story brick structure is written in gold letters over the door: EMMA KAVFMANN CLINIC. This is all that remains of the University of Pittsburgh's medical school before it moved to Oakland. The school itself was at the corner lot, downhill; this free health clinic was put up in 1896 by Isaac Kaufmann in memory of his late wife. Isaac and Emma Kaufmann's daughter Liliane grew up to marry her cousin Edgar Kaufmann (Pittsburgh being such a small town) and ended up as the stylish hostess of Fallingwater.

Today the houses shoehorned onto the streets of Polish Hill are a varied lot: frame rowhouses, detached brick homes, a few suburban-style ranches, and new townhouses. The earlier homes stand three and four stories tall, either of brick or clapboard that has given way to aluminum siding or imitation brick. The ground floor is often a shop, but a tiny archway gives promise of a garden behind. The homes are oriented for the best views over the Allegheny Valley, even if they must crane around their neighbors to get it, like spectators at tennis. Walking on Paulowna, Herron, Brereton, or Dobson streets, and on Pulaski or Flavan ways, one can only be moved by this proud community that never amassed material wealth but "made good" on this hillside on its own terms a century ago.

fig. 5.7
IMMACULATE HEART
OF MARY CHURCH,
POLISH HILL

fig. 5.8
SIDEWALK BRUNCH,
LAWRENCEVILLE

fig. 5.9
HOUSES,
LAWRENCEVILLE

LAWRENCEVILLE, BLOOMFIELD, FRIENDSHIP, AND GARFIELD

Just below Polish Hill, Lawrenceville distinguishes itself with an eclectic mix of tradition, culture, creativity, and expressionism. In what has very recently become an artisans' haven, visitors have a wide choice of the arts, from dance to pottery. But the old neighborhood was radically different. Lawrenceville was always important, but it was for decades less cohesive than its neighbors along Penn Avenue, and its participation in the Pittsburgh Renaissance was limited because of that absence of cohesion. One of the largest of the city's neighborhoods, with thirteen hundred acres, its limits are well defined only on the north and south, by the Allegheny and by Two Mile Run. On the west and east Lawrenceville trails off without punctuation into the Strip and Bloomfield, respectively. Its character, too, is mixed: the flat land is industrial and the slopes residential, with a population of ten thousand.

Lawrenceville is the only part of Pittsburgh that one might be able to envision inhabited by American Indians. A number of whites, George Washington included, visited the Delaware village of "Shannopin's Town" on Butler Street, but the natives had gone by the time Joseph Conrad Winebiddle started a tannery in the area in 1771. In 1814, Colonel William Foster purchased 121 acres between the roads to Butler and Greensburg (Butler Street and Penn Avenue today) and laid out a village. He named it Lawrenceville to commemorate Captain James Lawrence, the naval commander who had died the year before with the shout of "Don't give up the ship!" Lawrenceville was large enough to become an independent borough in 1834; in 1868, it was one of many districts incorporated into Pittsburgh.

Because it merges without any noteworthy demarcation into its neighboring districts, Lawrenceville suffered in the past from poor visual identification. Now on the rise, the neighborhood sees the need to brand itself more aggressively, and in 2008, it expended a considerable sum in erecting locally made "entering Lawrenceville" signs at five key entry points. But one entrance portal, at least, outshines that of any neighborhood in town. This is Doughboy Square, at the intersection of Butler Street and Penn Avenue. In the nineteenth century, this was the Forks of the Road, where the turnpikes to Butler and Greensburg split. In 1921, Pittsburghers began calling this triangle Doughboy Square for the neighborhood war memorial that stands there. The square has a lessened intensity today because of the demolition of some of its constituent buildings, but it still has a strong architectural and social character. The floridly Beaux-Arts Pennsylvania National Bank was recycled in 1992 by Desmone & Associates Architects for its own quarters. It serves as a majestic triangular backdrop to the Doughboy, with the curious curved buttresses on the left side giving a hint of Art Nouveau.

Doughboy Square's neighbors are a lively bunch, too. One standout is a muscle-bound Romanesque Revival undertaker's castle of 1888, at 3441 Butler, which was a garage for a time and is now a design studio. A few doors away, at 3339 Penn, is the former Engine House No. 25, with finely modulated brickwork characteristic of the late nineteenth century. The building went up in 1896, ceased serving as an ambulance-dispatch station in 1986, and was empty for a decade. Now it flourishes as a photographic studio and an informal museum of photos and memorabilia about the baseball player Roberto Clemente. This triangle of worthy civic buildings ends at 3445 Butler with the former Lawrenceville Bathhouse, which opened in 1904 as part of a string of public gifts from Henry Phipps. The building had eighteen showers on the first story and ten tubs on the second; on a typical Saturday, several thousand millworkers and their families would line up outside.

One of the prominent visual monuments of Lawrenceville stands a few blocks over at another fork in the road, where the sprawling Pittsburgh Brewing Company (originally Iron City Brewery) stands at 3340 Liberty Avenue, next to the Herron Avenue Bridge that links Lawrenceville and Polish Hill. Pittsburgh Brewing was once the third largest beer trust in the United States, and it still has an important standing nationwide. In 1962, the brewery joined with Alcoa to create a significant landmark in American material culture: the first pop-top can. The dozen buildings of the brewery all date from the second half of the nineteenth century, some as early as 1866, when Edward Frauenheim and Leopold Vilsack built Iron City here. The Queen Anne–style administration building dates from around 1888 and is a finely detailed brick structure featuring a bust of Ceres, goddess of grain, with sheaves of wheat for hair.

On the opposite side of Liberty stand two other Lawrenceville landmarks: the Lawrence Square Apartments at 3417–3429 Liberty, a triangle of worker flats from the end of the nineteenth century that wraps around the former site of the Iron City wagonworks, and what was the Italian Romanesque-style St. John the Baptist Church at 3501 Liberty. The latter's beautifully rendered polychromed façade, vividly striped (though now truncated) campanile, and exuberant brickwork make for a superb experience visually, but declining attendance at worship closed this parish, and the building now serves as a pub: the Church Brew Works.

There is nothing historic about the row of frame cottages, now mostly resurfaced in metal or vinyl, that lead uphill on Liberty from this former church, but one might pause here to ask why fortune has so recently and warmly smiled on Lawrenceville. Lawrenceville currently bills itself as a "back to the basics" neighborhood and reminds the rest of Pittsburgh that it offers affordable housing, the convenient Butler Street business district, and easy access to work, shopping, and play in Downtown, Shadyside, and Oakland. The prime asset of Lawrenceville is that it has a house to fit any budget. Large single-family brick homes dominate the eastern part of Lawrenceville, toward Bloomfield, while residents closer to Downtown find inexpensive homes in the old worker complexes or in their modern counterparts around Doughboy Square.

One does not think of Lawrenceville as having mansions, but there are a few. The one standing at 3600 Penn Avenue, opposite Thirty-sixth Street, has a historic marker in front that commemorates the composer Stephen Foster. William Foster chose this commanding site on the Greensburg Pike in 1814 for the "White Cottage" that was designed for him by Benjamin Henry Latrobe. There, on July 4, 1826—the day presidents John Adams and Thomas Jefferson both died—William's son Stephen was born. Failing to prosper in Lawrenceville, the father moved the next year to the North Side, where America's most significant early composer spent much of his life. It was a brief life—thirty-eight years—and its end coincided with the destruction of the White Cottage, which was replaced in 1864 by the Second Empire mansion that now stands there, built by Andrew Carnegie's early partner, Andrew Kloman. Fifty years later, in 1914, the Pittsburgh philanthropist James Park bought the mansion as a refuge for Stephen Foster's aged and impoverished daughter, Marion Foster Welch. In the 1980s, music returned to the site when, for a decade, the house served as a residence for musicians in the American Wind Symphony.

For years, another old house at 3414 Penn was erroneously pointed out as the Foster birthplace. Henry Ford, to whom history was "more or less the bunk," came to Pittsburgh in 1934, heard the tale—but ignored the Foster family descendants who tried to warn him about the suspect pedigree of the second home—and bought the counterfeit house for his Greenfield Village in Dearborn, Michigan. Today, Greenfield Village has stopped insisting that it has the real thing and merely calls the fraudulent house "associated with Stephen Foster."

Diagonally across Penn Avenue from the Foster site, at the corner of Penn and Thirty-seventh Street, stands an apartment block that gained its fame in another way. Held up by a bricklayers' strike in 1903, its builder, John Fink, constructed it out of coal ashes that were mixed with cement and

fig. 5.10
ENGINE HOUSE
NO. 25,
LAWRENCEVILLE

ground brick, then poured into a wooden framework. The innovation gave the block an obvious name: the Cinderella Apartments.

St. Augustine's Roman Catholic Church on Thirty-seventh Street between Bandera and Butler is a large Munich-style Romanesque Revival church squeezed into a narrow site. It is nonetheless the visually dominating point in Lawrenceville because of its high towers and octagonal crossing dome. The hammer and tongs sculpted among the instruments of the Passion over the entrance would have been artifacts of daily use for the German millworkers who constituted the bulk of this parish congregation. Another half-dozen buildings on the same block support the activities of the church and the Capuchin friars who minister to it.

Fisk Street, four blocks east of Thirty-seventh, is another good introduction to the public and private architecture of Lawrenceville. Wedged into this narrow way is the imposing Lawrenceville branch of Carnegie Library, the first branch in the Pittsburgh library system and the prototype for several Carnegie libraries in other cities. Carnegie's libraries in Pittsburgh were typically placed close to his industrial installations. He remembered Lawrenceville for his early success with the Lucy Furnace. This library was the first in the world to

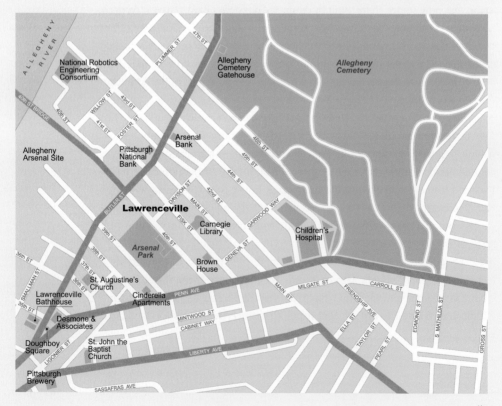

Lawrenceville

have a children's section, and the building plan is particularly gracious and efficient, with the book stacks radiating like spokes in the half-circle of the apse. The portal is especially fine, with gray terra-cotta plaques set in alternation with thin courses of Roman brick. Diagonally across the street at 294 Fisk is the Civil War–period Brown House, a Gothic Revival brick cottage with fantastic drooping gingerbread designs on the gables.

Western Pennsylvanians who grumble that their region is shortchanged in the Defense Department budget can only lament the passing of the Allegheny Arsenal. The arsenal operated from 1814 to 1907 on a campus set between Thirty-ninth and Fortieth streets, from Penn Avenue down to the Allegheny riverbank—all land sold to the government by Stephen Foster's father. The arsenal produced ammunition through four wars; during the Civil War, its twelve hundred workers cast thirty thousand bullets a day. But tragedy accompanied this industrial boom. In 1862, an explosion rocked the arsenal, killing approximately eighty employees, including many young girls. The nearby Allegheny Cemetery carries a monument in their honor.

The dozen core buildings at the arsenal were planned in 1813 by Benjamin Henry Latrobe, the designer responsible for the best parts of the interior of the nation's Capitol and the exterior of the White House. At the request of steamboat pioneer Nicholas Roosevelt, Latrobe had come to Pittsburgh in 1811 to design the *New Orleans*, the first steamboat ever built inland. At the arsenal site, Latrobe laid out the thirty-acre grounds and designated the main structures in a sequence of vivid drawings conserved today in the Library of Congress. Construction was supervised by Colonel Abraham R. Butler at the cost of $300,000—considered a fortune at that time. In 1825, the year when the Marquis de Lafayette visited the city and took breakfast in the arsenal with his old Revolutionary War comrades-at-arms, its buildings constituted one of the best Neoclassical groups in the country. In 1907, the upper portion of the arsenal grounds became Arsenal Park, but a half-dozen early buildings survived until the 1950s. Just two are visible today: the L-shaped, barrel-vaulted powder magazine buried in the hillside of Arsenal Park and a nearby brick structure incorporated into Allegheny County's Clack Health Center.

Until recent years there was a third survivor, the most important of the lot. This was the machine shop that stood immediately adjacent to the Washington Crossing Bridge. Its material was simple brick, but its sandstone entablature, Doric capitals atop severe pilasters, and elegant proportions gave it the majesty of a Greek temple. The "temple" was cut back in 1923 to make room for the bridge, but it survived until 1990, when its owner—ignoring my own personal plea—demolished it. Without proof, one cannot be sure that the machine shop was the work of Latrobe either in design or construction, but a structure that looked so noble despite the ill-treatment it had endured clearly had an excellent pedigree, and now it is gone.

Apart from its specifically military role, the Allegheny Arsenal holds importance as the first rationally laid-out factory complex in Pittsburgh. Its hundreds of workers resulted in a construction boom in Greek Revival houses in Lawrenceville in the 1830s and 1840s. Scores of those homes survive around the intersection of Thirty-eighth and Foster streets and elsewhere in the lower town, each marked by severe stone lintels over the windows and some having sidelights by the doors. As Lawrenceville expanded eastward, toward Bloomfield, the new homes added the Italianate lintels fashionable in the 1860s and later the High Victorian Gothic corbel brackets of the 1880s. But the sense of intimacy on its crowded streets was never lost.

The arsenal determined that Lawrenceville's future would be in industry, a fair amount of which can still be detected between Butler Street and the river. One of the main mills here was the precursor of the H. K. Porter Locomotive Works, which opened in 1866 on Harrison Street between Forty-ninth and Fiftieth streets. A dozen low brick structures of that complex survive, having been put to other uses.

fig. 5.11
CMU's NATIONAL
ROBOTICS
ENGINEERING
CONSORTIUM
RESIDES IN A
CONVERTED
FACTORY

A second colossal mill came into operation in 1877 on the Allegheny riverbank between Fifty-first and McCandless streets. This was Carnegie, Kloman & Company's Lucy blast furnace, named for Carnegie's sister-in-law, Lucy Coleman. The Lucy Furnace engaged in a fierce production race with the Isabella Furnace, across the river in the milltown of Etna, until it hit the phenomenal output of fourteen hundred tons of steel a week in 1881. Though worn out, Lucy was not demolished until 1937. Vestiges of the Crucible Steel works and Heppenstal Forge also remain near that site, between the AVRR line and Hatfield Street, between Forty-third and Forty-eighth streets, today being redeveloped as the Lawrenceville Technology Center. The industrial tradition of Lawrenceville continues at the National Robotics Engineering Consortium, where Fortieth Street meets the Allegheny River. This is an inspired 1996 reuse of the old Epping-Carpenter Company factory that was erected in 1898 by Samuel Diescher, Pittsburgh's celebrated incline engineer.

The engine that is driving Lawrenceville's dynamic revival is design, particularly the 16:62 Design Zone that encompasses Butler Street as part of a coordinated marketing strategy from Sixteenth Street in the Strip through Lawrenceville and parts of Bloomfield. Beginning in 2000, fifty design-oriented firms opened in or relocated to these blocks, many in the immediate vicinity of Butler and Main streets. Butler serves as the commercial thoroughfare of Lawrenceville, the way East Carson serves the South Side or East Ohio Street the North Side. The architectural streetscape on all three thoroughfares is essentially interchangeable: the stores are jammed together, three or four stories high, their styles reflecting the national taste in architecture in the decades after the Civil War.

Pride of place on Butler Street is centered in its ornate bank buildings: the Arsenal Bank, in High Victorian Gothic mode at Butler and Forty-third streets and now a gift shop, and the elegant PNC Bank, built as the Metropolitan National Bank, at Butler and Forty-first streets. The latter is a hushed Beaux-Arts temple of mammon, its eight stained-glass windows depicting the principal gods of Pittsburgh industry.

Along with the specialized shops and design studios are the murals that add color to an already vibrant community. One of these, with a game-based theme, adorns the Crazy Mocha coffee shop at 4032 Butler Street, near the Fortieth Street Bridge, and the 5100 block of Butler Street carries Kevinn Fung's Sprout Fund–supported mural, *Wheeling Heliocentric Orrery*.

Hatfield Street, two blocks below Butler toward the river, is another recent player in Pittsburgh's art scene, with galleries lining its six-block length from Forty-fourth to Fiftieth streets, in the shadow of the old mills. A good boost toward synergy in the emerging arts community came in 2007 with the conversion of the Ice House on Forty-third Street into artists' studios.

Butler Street takes a significant jog just beyond its intersection with Forty-seventh Street, where it skirts the three hundred acres of Allegheny Cemetery. In chronological order, it ranks as sixth among the early rural cemeteries of the United States, after earlier projects in Boston, Philadelphia, Brooklyn, and elsewhere, but it is not the least of these in terms of historic and artistic interest. Like the Stanton Heights neighborhood that lies east of it, this cemetery was part of the Bayard and Croghan summer estates. Having been part of these privately owned retreats, the gorges and peaks of today's cemetery escaped being ground down into city streets, and a genuine romantic spirit was thus preserved. John Chislett was the designer of both the grounds and the gatehouse in the 1840s; the Gothic chapel on the lower grounds dates from 1870 and the gatehouse on Penn Avenue, from 1887. In 1903, William Falconer, formerly the main landscape architect for the city, embarked on a new job and revised parts of Chislett's grounds scheme.

Within the cemetery grounds lie eighteen mayors of Pittsburgh; some international celebrities, such as the playboy Harry Thaw, singer/actor Lillian

fig. 5.12
ALLEGHENY
CEMETERY
GATEHOUSE

Russell, and composer Stephen Foster; and a host of industrial kings of Pittsburgh in mausolea ornamented with fine Tiffany windows. Briefly making his appearance among them was A. W. Mellon, who was buried here in 1937 but later disinterred by his son Paul for reburial in Virginia.

One long block from the cemetery's upper gatehouse, on Penn Avenue at Forty-fourth Street, stands Children's Hospital of Pittsburgh. This is the city's first billion-dollar construction and one with profound implications for the future of Lawrenceville and the adjacent community of Bloomfield.

The first impact of this vast structure is visual: it towers over its two neighborhoods, though its impact is lessened by its colorful detailing and the way its mass is broken up into a half-dozen separate components. But the economic and cultural repercussions of moving Children's Hospital from Oakland to Lawrenceville are even more profound. Even before it opened in 2009, the project significantly pushed up the price of Lawrenceville's houses, in extreme cases to quintuple what they had been. The impact of having three thousand new employees in the neighborhood was not limited to economics but spilled over into the local cultural and even gastronomic scene. Before the year 2000, leisurely brunches on the sidewalks of Butler Street, which are commonplace now, would have been as likely as baptisms taking place on the Strip in Las Vegas.

Bloomfield is a feast as rich to the eyes as the homemade tortellini and cannoli in its shop windows are to the stomach. Along with two subdistricts, Bloomfield stretches along Penn and Liberty avenues from the Bloomfield

Bridge to Negley Avenue in East Liberty, and from Garfield Hill on the south to the dip of Two Mile Run and the Conrail tracks on the north. Its 658 acres encompass three hamlets: Bloomfield proper, with its nine thousand residents, mainly Italian in origin, with roots in five specific towns in the Abruzzi region; Friendship, with fifteen hundred residents, many of them German in origin, living in the triangle between Liberty and Penn; and Garfield, with some five thousand residents, mainly African American, living around Penn Avenue and the streets laid over Garfield Hill.

The urban organization of Bloomfield departs from the Pittsburgh norm in having subdistricts that are socially and topographically distinct and also in having not one but two arterial streets. Penn Avenue is the older of the two by a century, and it is markedly narrower and quieter, as befits a matron some two hundred years old. The second, Liberty Avenue, was not laid out until the 1880s, about the time Italian immigrants began to arrive in Bloomfield; its hundred-foot width gave it the aspect of a market street from the beginning. Liberty is lined with two solid walls of three-story shop fronts with apartments overhead. Many shops bear German names such as Hinnebusch and Mentzer at the cornice line or datestones from the late nineteenth century. The side streets off Liberty feature well-maintained rowhouses along almost impossibly narrow streets. Houses rarely go on sale here; they are instead passed down through families, and grandchildren typically live just blocks away from grandparents, aunts, uncles, and cousins.

While Penn and Liberty brought cross-traffic through Bloomfield, the deep gorge of Two Mile Run cut it off from the Hill and Oakland until 1914, when the first Bloomfield Bridge opened. The linking of the two neighborhoods was symbolized by a wedding held at its center point. Seven decades later, in 1986, the current successor bridge was inaugurated by a second wedding, by then a secure part of Bloomfield lore.

The junction with Bloomfield Bridge marks the start of the distinctive commercial strip on Liberty Avenue, which gets festooned with Italian flags in summer and sparkling lights in winter. The fire hydrants and curbs are also painted in the colors of the Italian flag—red, green, and white. But other cultures can play this game, too. For years the Bloomfield Bridge Tavern promoted itself as "the finest Polish restaurant in Little Italy." The tavern's parking lot is decorated with tributes to Polish war heroes and communities while inside the fare is not pizza or pasta but *pierogi*, *haluski*, and *czarnina*.

Breaking up the commercial spirit of Liberty Avenue are two public monuments. The older is St. Joseph's Roman Catholic Church at Liberty and

fig. 5.13
CHILDREN'S HOSPITAL
OF PITTSBURGH,
LAWRENCEVILLE, VIEWED
FROM BLOOMFIELD

fig. 5.14
THE HEART OF
BLOOMFIELD:
ST. JOSEPH'S
CHURCH

fig. 5.15
STOREFRONTS,
LIBERTY AVENUE,
BLOOMFIELD

Pearl, from 1886. Its architect, Adolphus or Adoulf Druiding, was Hanover born and trained, then practiced in St. Louis for thirty years after his immigration to the United States in 1865. He got the commission for St. Joseph's, which was then a German-speaking parish, after constructing St. Vincent's Abbey in Latrobe, east of Pittsburgh. Druiding's tan Gothic Revival brick walls are deeply pointed and crisply patterned, and his two asymmetrical towers rise dramatically above Liberty.

At the far end of the same block is another neighborhood monument: the Plaza Theater, at 4765 Liberty near South Mathilda. The Plaza is an engaging mix of Beaux-Arts (that style's detailing is still visible in the windows and cornice on top) and Art Deco, the latter applied in a partial remodeling in the 1930s—a sure sign the neighborhood was still flourishing. There are no more shows for the Plaza now that it's a modest coffeehouse and sandwich shop, but its striking design still plays an important scenographic role down the length of Liberty Avenue.

It requires only a moment to step from the crowded ambiance of Liberty Avenue to the quiet elegance of Friendship, the late nineteenth-century community organized by Caspar and Harriet Winebiddle on a portion of the six hundred acres their ancestors had assembled a century before. The "friendship" in the name was supposedly one between Joseph Conrad Winebiddle, whose land it was, and the descendants of William Penn.

Characterized by large and attractive Victorian homes and wide streets, Friendship was farmland until trolley lines were extended into the area after the Civil War. The handsome streets, particularly Winebiddle, South Pacific, and South Atlantic, testify to the rising numbers and wealth of the middle managers in Pittsburgh firms around 1900. The streetscapes of Friendship document the beginnings of corporate culture as much as the high towers in Downtown. The houses are solid four-squares, many of them in Colonial Revival design with telltale Palladian windows for the upstairs front bathroom. The plans and details are virtually identical to those of homes in Shadyside, Highland Park, and Squirrel Hill, the three other neighborhoods where corporate managers settled in great numbers between 1890 and 1910.

Some Friendship homes were architect designed, but the great majority were simply produced by developers. The formulas at 316 and 328 Roup Street, for example, are identical. The best of the older homes in Friendship is the Henry Lynch house of 1868, at 201 South Winebiddle, at the corner of Coral. It is a textbook example of a Second Empire mansion, with a central tower and asymmetrical wings under mansard roofs. Lynch's mansion housed the Ursuline Academy from 1893 until 1993, then became a banquet and meeting facility. Now it has been recycled again as the Waldorf School of Pittsburgh, with college students getting academic credit for participating in its restoration.

Among other happy results, the restoration project turned up the intriguing possibility that the prominent architect Isaac Hobbs may have designed the house. Hobbs was in Pittsburgh in the same years the house was going up, and he knew Lynch as a director of the downtown Dollar Bank, the architectural project that had brought him to town.

The Winebiddle house at 340 South Winebiddle is a good example of the later Romanesque Revival homes found in the area, while the High Victorian Gothic, with characteristic touches of Queen Anne ornament, is best exemplified by the Charles M. Bartberger house at 408 South Pacific. Bartberger designed the home for himself in 1883. Along with Osterling's studio on the North Side and Hornbostel's two dozen buildings in Oakland, it serves as an important document of the culture of the Pittsburgh architectural community in the expansionist years from around 1880 to around 1920. Bartberger stamped the building three times: his monogram is on the gable, the Masonic seal is on the second floor, and his coat of arms is on a stained-glass window

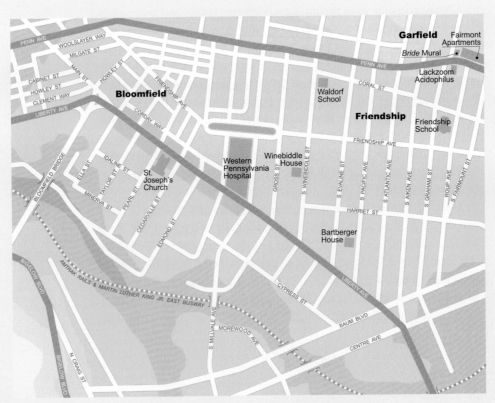

Bloomfield

fig. 5.16
LYNCH HOUSE,
NOW THE
WALDORF SCHOOL

on the upstairs landing. Everything about the house suggests an owner whose social aspirations exceeded his budgetary reach. The interior detailing is fastidious to the point of claustrophobia, as though one of the marble palaces of Newport had been caught in a rainstorm, and shrank.

The Winebiddle lands were parceled out from west to east, so the homes toward East Liberty display later turns in style: a large New England Colonial home with an overscaled gambrel roof at the corner of Friendship and South Aiken, a Renaissance Revival mansion with links to the Prairie School Style at 240 South Graham, and the Colonial Revival twins at 316 and 328 Roup. These homes are grand, but since they were constructed just before the age of the motorcar, they do not have garages. Among the fine homes is the heart of the Friendship subdistrict: the Friendship School, on Friendship between South Graham and Roup. This accomplished Beaux-Arts palace is characterized by ornamental columns and corner pilasters of terra cotta and by windows that are broadly grouped, almost in strips.

One thing not obvious on the streets of Friendship is the way most of the older mansions have been internally subdivided into apartments. The tenants are often graduate students, teachers, and undergraduates who routinely discover spaces with original ornamental woodwork, polished hardwood floors, and stained-glass windows. After decades of being down on its luck, Friendship is returning as one of Pittsburgh's desirable neighborhoods. As is true on the North Side, much of the energy comes from the gay community, which is spearheading the conversion of many big houses from rentals back to single-family homes. On good days the residents are drawn from once-elegant streets like Cedarville and Gross to meet on Friendship Avenue or on the benches at

Friendship Park. Playing ball may be contrary to posted regulations, but it is still important here, as is the art of conversation.

The land that would become Garfield was first developed by Joseph Conrad Winebiddle in 1771 and annexed to Pittsburgh in 1868. The largely empty land was laid out in streets in 1881 and named after James Garfield, the U.S. president inaugurated and assassinated that year; the sale of its lots occurred on the day he was buried. Garfield's lower streets, just off Penn Avenue, are monotonous rows that barely acknowledge their hilly site, but the upper streets are curved and shady and lined with pleasant brick cottages—as well as severe rows of subsidized housing. Some views are breathtaking; from the crest of Fern Street, one can see half the city.

The streetscape along Penn Avenue has a diverse number of restaurants and shops. Much of the housing stock is mundane, but there are many formerly elegant structures in the long rows of Queen Anne townhouses, with verandahs, on the 5100 and 5200 blocks of Penn from North Evaline to North Atlantic streets. Then comes a sight so unexpected as to be surreal: at the end of a row of yet more Queen Anne townhouses comes an ordinary brick wall at 5439 Penn Avenue, at the corner of North Graham. In 1992, Judy Penzer, a New Yorker who loved Pittsburgh, painted *The Bride of Penn Avenue* on that wall. Her work, incorrectly but lovingly known as the "Garfield Bride," gained acceptance particularly after Penzer died in a tragic air accident in 1996. Unfortunately, the painting is holding up poorly and has already required conservation work. Michelangelo's Sistine Chapel Ceiling it is not, but it is inspiring to contemplate the no-longer-young African American bride leaving a verandah that is identical to those of the adjacent houses.

Art has taken hold in Garfield, not just in this mural but in other media as well. Garfield is home to the Upstairs Theater, an intimate theater that features local performers and is close to the Rogers School for the Creative and Performing Arts, where some of the city's muralists have studied. There is a concerted effort to reuse the empty storefronts on Penn Avenue as galleries, studios, and artists' residences. The Dance Alloy Theater has been active in Garfield for years, and the Pittsburgh Glass Center at the corner of Penn and South Fairmount avenues has deftly recycled a three-story car dealership and garage into one of the world's premiere facilities for glassblowing. This studio of course builds on one of the oldest of the city's artisanal traditions.

Though it may be counterintuitive, it is not entirely surprising that the most imaginative apartment construction of early twenty-first-century Pittsburgh has gone up in Garfield: the Fairmont Apartments at 5461 Penn Avenue, at the corner of North Fairmount. A passerby cannot help but be

fig. 5.17
FAIRMONT
APARTMENTS,
PENN AVENUE

immediately taken by the urban commitment of this housing complex, which expresses itself in several ways. One is in the generous allotment for ground-floor retail stores, which gain emphasis by being placed between huge diagonal struts, with three living floors canted out overhead. Another comes in the slightly raucous colors and rhythms of the façades, not endless and bland like a palace but broken up and edgy, like most of Penn Avenue. The final remarkable feature is, of all things, the parking lot. This does not take up frontage on Penn Avenue (like the nearby Children's Home lot does) but is set firmly and invisibly behind the apartments, accessed by an archway. One has to think of Frank Lloyd Wright's challenge to his apprentices: would their new building not merely suit the preexisting environment but actually improve it? In the Garfield neighborhood, the answer is a resounding yes.

Garfield has one last aesthetic curiosity for us: directly opposite *The Bride of Penn Avenue*, and just up from the Fairmont Apartments, stands the old Lackzoom Acidophilus store at 5438 Penn, near South Graham. This small building (now almost derelict) is as remarkable for its bizarre name as for its luxurious Classical terra-cotta façade, complete with cherubs. It dates from around 1920 and was the modest progenitor of the formidable Pittsburgh-based General Nutrition Corp. This sunny, quirky building must in its odd way be accounted one of the delights of Penn Avenue.

EAST LIBERTY, HIGHLAND PARK, AND MORNINGSIDE

The urban renewal turmoil that afflicted East Liberty is better known than similar horrors on the Hill and the North Side because it affected not just residents but also nonresidents of the zone. Outsiders used to come here in the thousands to shop, eat, or pray, when prewar East Liberty was the third most important commercial center in Pennsylvania after downtown Philadelphia and downtown Pittsburgh.

The end of East Liberty might have been foretold by its beginning. The district is a classic example of a "piketown," a settlement that developed step by step with the roads and transportation systems that passed through it. The first of these highways were the Forbes Road and Greensburg Pike to Philadelphia, and later the transportation systems that developed were the railroad, the horsecar, the trolley, and the automobile. There is much to be learned from East Liberty, particularly from its struggle to overcome the urban renewal specialists who nearly killed it in the 1960s. Its early urban history yields a special bonus, though: the little-known story of the foundation of the Mellon fortune, not in oil or aluminum but in land, specifically, huge parcels along Penn Avenue.

Most Americans probably think of the Mellons as being straight out of a Horatio Alger short story, in which a decent, hard-working young man goes from rags to riches. That legend does apply to the Mellons, in part; the banker and art collector A. W. Mellon was the son of Thomas, who had lifted himself out of the dire poverty that had forced the family out of Northern Ireland. Most people tend to forget, however, that A. W. Mellon's mother, Sara Jane Negley, belonged to a clan that controlled some thirty-three hundred acres of choice Pittsburgh land—nearly everything that today comprises the neighborhoods of East Liberty, Highland Park, Larimer, Lincoln, and Homewood.

The story of the Mellons' land acquisition is as simple as the workings of compound interest. It begins with the German immigrant Caspar Taub, who in 1762 was granted 303 acres in the Highland Park district by Colonel Henry Bouquet in exchange for a promise to deliver one-third of his crops to feed Bouquet's soldiers at Fort Pitt. Taub's daughter, Elizabeth, married Joseph Conrad Winebiddle Sr., who owned even more land in Lawrenceville and Bloomfield. In the third generation, the Winebiddles' daughter, Barbara Ann, married Jacob Negley, who thus controlled nearly all of the land from Highland Park to Point Breeze.

Around 1810, Jacob Negley laid out the town of East Liberty on his land (in England, a "liberty" referred to land just outside the city that was reserved for grazing; Pittsburgh once had a North and West Liberty as well as an East Liberty). A few years later, Negley paved and widened the two-mile stretch of the Greensburg Pike that ran through his land. The street where he lived was and is called Negley Avenue, and Negley Run was once a fast-flowing stream that powered his gristmill. He later built a new steam-powered gristmill on higher ground.

In 1843, Negley's daughter Sara Jane married Thomas Mellon, who derived the foundation of his fortune from Negley land. Mellon used his wife's land in four ways: he sold it outright, he built houses on it, he offered mortgages on it, and he foreclosed on property when the mortgages were not repaid. Mellon also involved himself in numerous transportation ventures connected with this land. In 1859, he was one of the main proponents of the two horsecar lines that connected East Liberty to the Golden Triangle, one going through Oakland, the other through Lawrenceville. When the lines were electrified in 1892, East Liberty became the trolley nexus of Pittsburgh.

The Mellons played no less a role in East Liberty's last spurt of growth early in the twentieth century, when it became the center of Pittsburgh's motor culture. In 1913, Thomas Mellon's grandson, William Larimer Mellon, who was head of Gulf Oil, built one of the world's first drive-in gas stations on

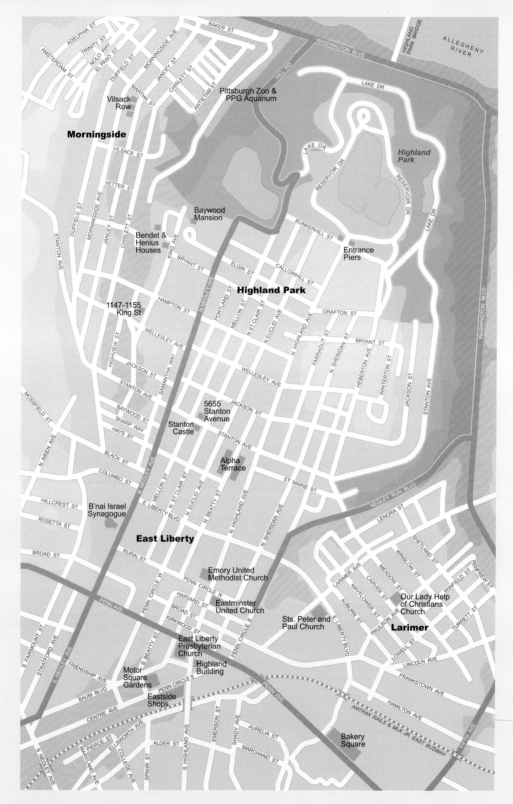

East Liberty and Highland Park

Mellon land at the intersection of St. Clair Street and Baum Boulevard. The next year Gulf published the world's first map specifically drawn up for motorists.

A dozen car or parts dealers opened on Baum Boulevard in the first years of the twentieth century. In 1916, Henry Ford took advantage of this concentration to erect a Ford car-assembly plant at the corner of Baum and Morewood, where one can still read "Ford Motor Company" atop a handsome terra-cotta front. (Ford had allegedly first offered the Mellons a partnership to make cars in Pittsburgh rather than in Detroit, but they laughed him off.) Some of the area's earliest Model Ts were manufactured, sold, and serviced in East Liberty, its Ford facility being one of a group of assembly plants the company built around the country. A useful feature of the East Liberty Ford plant is the way it ramps downhill to the adjacent gully, making it easy to load automobiles on railroad flatcars parked on the tracks. The plant is being recycled to form part of the UPMC cancer research and care facilities on the opposite side of the tracks.

Baum Boulevard's role in the auto industry left the neighborhood with another important structure. The Chrysler Sales and Service Building (now Day's Baum Boulevard Dodge Chrysler Jeep), where Baum Boulevard meets Roup, projects its streamline moderne cylindrical tower for views down both Baum and Negley Avenue. It went up in 1934 following the designs of Albert Kahn, the leading industrial architect of the twentieth century. Kahn put up factories and showrooms like this all over the country; the design of this Chrysler dealership derives from Kahn's Chrysler Sales and Service Building in Detroit. Even though this building is not an original that he drew up for Pittsburgh, Kahn's corner siting of the structure at the nexus of three streets could not be better.

Most Pittsburghers are less familiar with East Liberty's urban history than they are with its urban renewal gone haywire. Beginning in 1960, Pittsburgh's Urban Redevelopment Authority pumped $68 million into the center of this

fig. 5.18
HIDDEN MASTERPIECE: ALBERT KAHN'S CHRYSLER DEALERSHIP

five-hundred-acre district. In the process, it destroyed fifteen hundred old houses and created two thousand new housing units in apartments and town-house clusters; it plowed under a dozen old roads and opened up a dozen new ones; and it transformed a tight urban knot into a fake-suburban shopping mall.

In the process, Penn Avenue was itself junked. In its place, developers put in the pedestrian (in both senses of the word) Penn Mall, with four adjacent streets hijacked into becoming Penn Circle East, North, West, and South. Instead of drawing people in, Penn Circle diverted would-be shoppers away from stores, hastening the decline of East Liberty from a vital community to a neighborhood struggling with poverty and its own identity.

Even though East Liberty had weakened as a retail center before this aggressive redevelopment, the cure was worse than the disease. The number of shops in East Liberty declined from 242 in 1963 to 98 in 1977, although the number has now rebounded. From 1960 to 1970, the population fell from twelve thousand to nine thousand, and it continues to decline.

Today, most of the straitjacketing street grid and the banal street furniture of the 1960s have been ripped out, and streets are returning to the traffic patterns they had in the booming 1940s. Everything is being done to encourage a return to the irregularity and unstructured casualness that marked the district when it was a flourishing community. Half or more of the 1960s housing units have already been demolished or radically rebuilt, and in 2005, the neighborhood celebrated the demolition of the East Mall and Liberty Park high-rise housing towers. The community is now embracing housing solutions that involve the adaptive reuse of smaller buildings and creating new spaces for the retail economy that is coming back to Baum Boulevard and Penn and Centre avenues.

The irony is that the architectural fabric of East Liberty in the bad years of the 1980s and 1990s, with its empty lots where high-rises once stood and so many car dealerships, warehouses, and storefronts stood vacant, allowed for the incubation of new developments in a way that more intact neighborhoods could not. Large-box retail stores like Home Depot, Trader Joe's, Whole Foods, and Borders have enjoyed outstanding success because East Liberty's continuing importance as an urban nexus put their operations where half of Pittsburgh could get to them.

While some household-name retail chains simply insinuated their suburban mall aesthetic into East Liberty, others were sensitive to the existing architectural fabric. Whole Foods, for example, recycled the Witt-Gateway warehouse on Centre Avenue, and Trader Joe's took over the Wheeler Paint

Company building on Penn. By linking intriguing architectural elements, human scale, color, and openness, most of the new stores have maintained connections to the neighborhood street grid. Especially successful is a grouping of buildings called Eastside, at the intersection of Penn Circle South and Highland Avenue, where East Liberty's vigilant long-term nonprofit community development group worked with a developer to create four lively retail buildings, the design of which included parking and other amenities. The pioneer stores are now being joined by an unconventional two-level Target store at the intersection of Penn Avenue and Penn Circle South.

The latest project to revive East Liberty is also a makeover. This is Bakery Square, a redevelopment of the blocks-long Nabisco Bakery of 1917 on Penn Avenue, one long block from its intersection with Fifth. Here the colossal Nabisco cracker plant is being turned into office, retail, and hotel space. Dark brick with cream-colored accents, the Nabisco plant worked as a visual anchor not just for East Liberty but also for adjacent Shadyside, Point Breeze, and Larimer. The complex will provide a major infusion of capital and jobs for these districts, though nothing will ever replace the glorious smell the bakery once produced.

The vigorous rebirth of East Liberty has inflicted on its residents something the quarter has not experienced since Taft was president: growing pains. The destruction of the high-rise apartments opened East Liberty to the rest of the city, visually and psychologically, but it also shuffled a good many residents to other parts of town. Those residents still in place have reason to fear that developers will chip away at their community until it becomes just an appendage to Shadyside, the wealthy quarter just one set of train tracks away.

The main visual and social anchor remaining in the neighborhood is the East Liberty Presbyterian Church on Penn at South Highland. It is the most luxurious of the half-dozen buildings the Mellon clan gave Pittsburgh during the Depression, exceeding in fastidiousness even the Cathedral of Learning and Mellon Institute. Its designer was Ralph Adams Cram, who in the 1930s led the last of several Gothic revivals in American architecture. Cram regarded East Liberty Presbyterian as his masterpiece; whether it was or not, the church ranks among the most lavish commissions any American architect landed until Richard Meier designed the Getty Center in Los Angeles half a century later.

Pittsburgh old-timers called the church the "Mellon fire escape," implying that the clan was building it for the redemption of their souls. Richard B. and Jenny King Mellon are buried in a marble chamber off the nave. Like

fig. 5.19
EAST LIBERTY
PRESBYTERIAN
CHURCH

Etruscan sarcophagi, full-size sculptures of the Mellons once covered the tombs, with R. B. Mellon looking particularly startling in a business suit. In a more theologically learned era, the mausoleum doors were thrown open only one day a year, at Easter. Today, the mausoleum doors remain open all year long, and the effigies of the two Mellons have been whisked away.

East Liberty Presbyterian is only indirectly a Mellon monument. As the fifth church to have stood on the land that Jacob Negley donated for a house of worship in 1819, it is actually a Negley monument, and it was designed to reinforce the Mellons' standing among Pittsburgh's landed aristocracy. Since the neighborhood was already decaying by 1930, Cram placed the greatest emphasis on a three-hundred-foot-high Spanish Gothic spire that can be seen all the way from Bloomfield to Homewood—roughly the area the Mellons' various ancestors originally owned. The impact of the church on its neighborhood is not merely visual but also social. Cram designed it to be both church and community center, with classrooms, a gym, and bowling alleys. Today, the church drives East Liberty's social life. It runs tutoring for local students, provides food and shelter to the homeless, and works closely with East Liberty Development Council for the quarter's economic redevelopment. The congregation also makes a special effort to reach out to Pittsburgh's gay and lesbian community, which assembles in the sanctuary by the hundreds each year for a sing-along Christmas concert.

fig. 5.20
R. B. Mellon tomb

After half a century of decline, it is remarkable that the core blocks of East Liberty retain as much polish as they do. The first instance of this resilient architecture stands immediately opposite the Mellons' church, in the thirteen-story Highland Building on Highland, just off Penn. It is one of the many skyscrapers developed by Daniel Burnham for Henry Clay Frick and was formerly twinned by a Mellon skyscraper that has given way to the suburban-style bank next door. Curiously, for the Highland Building Burnham copied features from two buildings by his nemesis, Louis Sullivan. Sullivan's Carson Pirie Scott store in Chicago contributed the detailing of the bead-and-reel ornament channeled through the terra-cotta skin, and his Guaranty Building in Buffalo inspired the swooping cornice. Vacant for decades, the Highland Building is slated to return to life as a hotel.

The three blocks of Penn Avenue from Beatty to Sheridan present more good news. The expansive Richardsonian Romanesque-style Liberty Building at 6101 Penn Avenue offers refurbished office space, a smart row of three Art Deco shop fronts from the 1930s is holding its own, and the restored façade of the former Regent Theater at 5941 Penn newly sparkles as the Kelly-Strayhorn Theater. The theater was renamed for East Liberty–born

fig. 5.21
MOTOR SQUARE
GARDENS

entertainers Gene Kelly and Billy Strayhorn and offers hope for a cultural as well as economic revival of the district.

Two blocks west of the East Liberty core, at the intersection of Baum Boulevard and South Beatty, stands the vast Motor Square Gardens, the Mellons' second most prominent monument in the area. The Mellons built it in 1900 as the East Liberty Market House to spur lagging home sales in their housing subdivisions in the area. But the structure was luckless: it failed as a market house around World War I, failed as a sports arena in the 1920s, failed as a Cadillac showroom in the 1960s, and failed as an indoor shopping mall and food court in the 1980s. Finally, the right reuse program came along, and it has been a branch of the AAA motoring club for two decades.

The Mellons' market marries the exposed steel girders of an industrial interior with an enormous skylit dome and thermal windows showy enough for a Roman emperor on the outside. Inside, most visitors will feel some excitement when confronted with the enormous volume and dynamic structure that is reminiscent of the iron-and-glass concourse of the old Pennsylvania Station in New York.

The remaining skyscape of East Liberty is dominated about equally by churches and business blocks. This combination is not surprising, since East Liberty was always a commercial crossroads rather than a government or cultural center. Either intentionally or through timidity, the urban planners left most of East Liberty's churches intact. After East Liberty Presbyterian, the most prominent was Sts. Peter and Paul Roman Catholic Church at 130 Larimer Avenue, between East Liberty Boulevard and Broad Street. The prototype of this church for a German congregation was probably the Gothic St. Elizabeth at Marburg. This near-replica recalls the towering original in the leap of its twin spires but not in its lackluster detailing nor the concrete blocks that masquerade as *faux* stone. It is a pity to report that the church is now shuttered and deteriorating.

Substantially better off, at the intersection of Highland and Penn Circle North, is the Eastminster United Presbyterian Church, a vigorous Romanesque-style sanctuary for an inner-city church distinguished by its imaginative programming. Visit it just before Christmas to watch the three wise men coming to the outdoor Nativity on real camels.

Emory United Methodist Church at 325 North Highland is one of East Liberty's few successful buildings from the urban renewal era of the 1960s. It is a sort of modern Romanesque attire for a congregation that has been present in the neighborhood since 1832, and it is genuinely handsome. A few blocks to the north and west stand two more churches that function like sentinels, marking out the line of East Liberty's boundary with Highland Park. One is the traditionally styled Colonial Revival chapel at the Pittsburgh Theological Seminary. The school's extensive campus at 616 North Highland Avenue was originally the farm where Charles Lockhart began refining kerosene and ended up owning a major block of Standard Oil. The other sanctuary is the dramatic half-Byzantine, half-Renaissance B'nai Israel synagogue at 327 North Negley Avenue, opposite Rippey. The synagogue creates a blaze of color against the east slope of Garfield Hill and provides an equally memorable space inside. In 1996, the congregation left the complex to the Urban League of Pittsburgh, which installed a charter school in the 1950s schoolhouse next door.

The B'nai Israel synagogue is a case study in the tweaking of architectural precedents that old-style designers delighted in. The porch is an industrialized version of the Pazzi Chapel in Florence; after entering through the door, one can access the sanctuary by climbing up double ramps that mimic those inside Hadrian's Tomb in Rome; inside, one comes face-to-face with the voluminous interior of the Pantheon. Were architectural wit enough to guarantee preservation, B'nai Israel would have survived another century.

Highland Park was first planted in crops by settlers in the 1770s. Alexander Negley, the main proprietor of the area, took out a warrant on his "Fertile Bottom" farmland in 1778 for 300 acres north of what became East Liberty. Negley's son Jacob enlarged his holdings here after he married Barbara Ann Winebiddle in 1795. Then, in 1837, county surveyor Robert Hiland cut Highland and Negley avenues through the Negley homestead, and the district received a version of the surveyor's own name (albeit a bit gentrified). This community of seven thousand residents on 1,000 acres presents an urban paradox. Three of the neighborhood area's four sides are dead ends, bounded on the west by the steep slopes of Heth's Run, on the east by Negley Run and Washington Boulevard, and on the north by the Allegheny River. Similar geographic isolation proved crippling to the neighborhoods of Manchester, Garfield, East Hills, and Homewood, but the paradox is that it made Highland Park flourish, as one can see from its score of handsome streets and a thousand of the best houses in Pittsburgh. The answers to the paradox lie north and south of Highland Park. To the north lies the actual park: 360 acres that Edward M. Bigelow bought for the city in 1893 and Christopher Magee further developed with his Pittsburgh Zoo in 1898. To the south lies East Liberty, the heart that for a hundred years pumped into Highland Park whatever urban amenities the community did not develop on its own.

While the vitality of most East End neighborhoods is intensified by inter-action between the residential and commercial areas (think Oakland, Shady-side, East Liberty, and Squirrel Hill), the vibrancy of Highland Park lies in the exact opposite. In the early nineteenth century, the East End was all farm-houses and estates. What transformed it was the streetcar, which allowed easy passage into booming East Liberty at the end of the same century. By the time the automobile became common around 1915, Highland Park was almost entirely filled in as a residential district, with just a handful of shops on Bryant Street. It was too intensively settled and well established for the auto-mobile to wreck it.

After Robert Hiland did the initial subdividing of the Negley farmland, the current street pattern took shape little by little until it was complete in the 1880s. Here and there, architectural survivors serve as reminders of what Highland Park looked like in that gilded era. From the earlier period there is a much-changed brick farmhouse, now at the intersection of Heberton and Grafton streets, that was built around 1819 by Mary Ann Berkstresser Negley. The Pittsburgh Parks Conservancy uses the building for office space and summer camp activities.

A half-dozen of Highland Park's homes testify to its industry-based prosperity after the Civil War. A modest forerunner is the Tim house of 1861 at 1317 North Sheridan Avenue. This Italianate design was a villa, not a farmhouse, since J. W. Tim was a daily commuter to business Downtown via the East Liberty railroad station a mile away.

The best of Highland Park's old mansions is Baywood, at 5501 Elgin Street off North Negley, with vast grounds, formal gardens, and even castles. The builders were the glass magnate Alexander King and his wife Cordelia, parents of Jenny King Mellon, progenitor of the Scaife branch of the Mellon clan. Baywood dates from around 1872, and it remained in the King family for decades. Then, around 1946, the natural bowl-shaped feature on the King estate was proposed as the site for an open-air amphitheater to house the Civic Light Opera. The idea so infuriated Robert King that he struck a bar-gain with Mayor David Lawrence: he donated the land to the city in 1949 on the condition that no new public structure be constructed. King's adroit maneuver saved Highland Park from urban upheaval, but the same project went on to ruin the Hill. King lived in his mansion until his death in 1954, when it became the King Cultural and Conservation Center.

Baywood returned to private ownership in 1994. The white paint came off the red brick; the balconies, the trim, and the sixteen-foot-high gilded finial on the roof reappeared; and help was extended to the four castellated towers

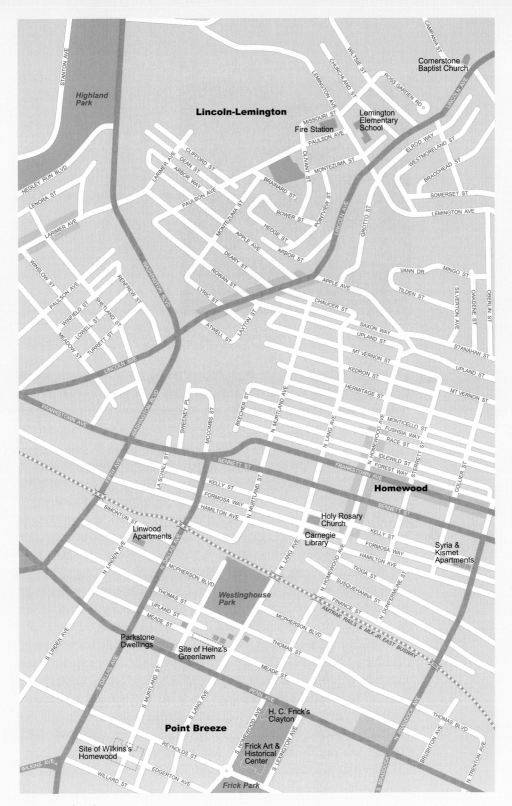

Homewood and Point Breeze

fig. 5.22
BAYWOOD

("King's Folly" to his neighbors) that King had put up in 1898. Only one of the castles could be restored; the other three had fallen into a more romantic ruin than King intended.

Highland Park's growth spurt in the streetcar age is well epitomized in Alpha Terrace, a collection of two dozen rental townhouses on both sides of the 700 block of North Beatty Street. Several Mellon cousins constructed it on what had been the Rumbiddle plantation, building the east terrace in 1889 and the west terrace in 1894. The west side of the development is Romanesque Revival in solid granite, a probable reflection of H. H. Richardson's court-house Downtown. The east side is more fanciful Queen Anne in style, with shingled walls above a stone base. Access to the community was initially lim-ited by gates at its north and south ends.

Still more numerous than these survivors are the houses that were built after 1890, when Christopher Magee laid the trolley lines. The reason for Magee's civic gift of the Pittsburgh Zoo might well be understood if one con-siders those trolley lines; having the zoo at the north end of the tracks boosted ridership on his trolleys. Dense blocks of homes went up northward from East Liberty and outward from the Highland Avenue artery. Homes from this period are often turreted, shingled, bracketed, and trimmed in vivid col-ors, most notably along Stanton Avenue. The Queen Anne–style homes in the 800 block of Mellon Street probably date from this streetcar era, with three especially eye-catching restored homes sporting shingled turrets. The Shingle-style house at 5811 Stanton, between North Euclid and North Beatty, has also been beautifully painted and maintained.

The wonder of the age was Rowanlea, the mansion and estate of Carnegie's partner Alexander Peacock, from 1892. It occupied the block at the corner of Highland Avenue and Bryant, but it was too huge to be recycled into homes for ordinary mortals, so it was demolished and all that suggests its lavishness today are some surviving gateposts. However, there are still some opportunities for house-spotting nearby. Always the subject of curiosity is Stanton Castle at 5652 Stanton Avenue, at the corner of St. Clair, a twentieth-century medievalizing brick house that features a low segmental arch at its center. Across the street, at 5655 Stanton Avenue, stands the exquisitely shaped Shingle-style house that architect William Fraser built for himself in 1891. The Flemish Renaissance–style Elliot house at 935 North Highland went up the same year, all in brick, with pressed brick trim and Flemish scroll gables on the front and sides. Typical of the slightly later Colonial Revival homes of the era is the 1901 Sebastian Mueller house at 944 Sheridan Avenue, built for a brother-in-law of H. J. Heinz and rather elegant in its "Roman" brick and Queen Anne trim.

An era of even greater creativity in house design was unfolding between the two world wars. Domestic architecture from the early twentieth century is well represented in Highland Park by the row of five houses from 1914 at 1147–1155 King Street, below Bryant; their probable designer was Frederick Scheibler. The low roof slope of these houses is appealingly lifted up on splayed bungalow piers. Around the corner, at 5525 Beverly Place, Frederick Scheibler's Klages house of 1922 seems to have mimicked the low roof slope on King Street and then taken on additional Romanesque masonry details. A similar move to the picturesque shows up a little farther north, in the Lillian Henius house at 1315 Cordova Road, near the corner of Bryant and King. This part-fieldstone, half-timbered, and pseudo-thatched cottage was drawn up in 1918 by the local progressives Kiehnel & Elliott for an artist whose studio took over the top floor. Close by, another picturesque stand-out is the Bendet house at 1321 Cordova Road. This Mother Goose cottage of around 1927, with its high-pitched shingle roof and conical entrance, presents a rare example of one Pittsburgh house parodying another. The subject of the parody was Benno Jannsen's just-completed house for E. J. Kaufmann in Fox Chapel. The developer of this little property was Kaufmann himself, through his Kaufmann Development Company, and the architect, Theodore Eichholz, worked for Kaufmann. Eichholz eventually abandoned such architectural jokes and ended his career in the 1940s with commissions for huge hospitals and the Greater Pittsburgh International Airport.

fig. 5.23
BENDET HOUSE,
CORDOVA ROAD

A half-dozen houses by Frederick Scheibler survive on the streets of Highland Park and in a fascinating house row in nearby Morningside, which makes this an appropriate point at which to commemorate the designer who was the main force in bringing modern architecture to Pittsburgh.

The life of Frederick Gustavus Scheibler Jr. (1872–1958) is an almost exact chronological parallel to that of Frank Lloyd Wright (1867–1959), but the two modernists had little in common apart from their passionate love of creating human shelter. The grandson of a German bookbinder, Scheibler was born and lived his whole life in Pittsburgh, almost never leaving western Pennsylvania either to travel or to build, though he oversaw one project in California. His architectural education was no less parochial: an apprentice-ship in 1888 with Henry Moser, several more years with the minor architect J. Lewis Beatty, then his own career as an independent designer for twenty-five years. He had little interaction with his colleagues; he is not even pictured among the thirty-two architects who bought their way into the pages of *Palmer's Pictorial Pittsburgh* in 1905. But through magazines, Scheibler knew what his English, German, Austrian, and American colleagues were design-ing in the years 1900–1920, and he could study their renderings firsthand in the annual exhibits of the Pittsburgh Architectural Club at Carnegie Institute. The architectural world knew about Scheibler, too; his works were published nationally and even overseas, in Germany and Austria.

Scheibler designed several hundred homes in Pittsburgh, notably in Morningside, Shadyside, Squirrel Hill, Point Breeze, Wilkinsburg, and

Homewood, as well as in Highland Park. With some practice, one can distinguish them fairly easily from the work of two other Cottage-style designers of the era: Edward B. Lee and Edward J. Weber. Scheibler's homes are generally adaptations of European prototypes, especially the English Free Style of C. F. A. Voysey, C. R. Mackintosh, and M. H. Baillie-Scott, and the Vienna Secession School. He transformed these prototypes into an American vision that over the years became more Romantic than the originals. His career was marked by a proto-Modern phase from about 1905 to 1915, when he was in some ways even ahead of the International Style architects. Then followed a second, more Romantic interpretation of the earlier themes, which continued to about 1925. Scheibler's national and international reputation had largely evaporated by 1915; by 1925, even in Pittsburgh, few remembered him.

The park at Highland Park, which opened to the public in 1893, now encompasses 380 acres of land and features the Pittsburgh Zoo and PPG Aquarium, two reservoirs, and a playground in addition to other traditional park attractions. The mural painted at the intersection of Bryant and North St. Clair streets in 2003 recalls the park's main entrance at Highland Avenue when it first opened, with its "City Beautiful"–inspired pillars, statues, fountain, and walkways. Extensive work by determined residents in 1996 brought the fountain and reflecting pool back to life, although the fountain now has a circular brick patio with park benches, an arrangement similar to that of Schenley Fountain in Oakland.

If the Italian sculptor Giuseppe Moretti had qualms in answering Edward M. Bigelow's call to come to Pittsburgh, which he did in 1895, his assignment at the Highland Park entrance piers ought to have settled them. Between 1896 and 1900, at the end of Highland Avenue, Moretti had a dream commission, and he executed it flawlessly. Sumptuous paired Ionic columns carry heroic bronze laurel-wreathing figures on top of the piers and American eagles and lamp-holding nymphs at the base.

Moretti did a second park entrance at the eastern end of Stanton Avenue, where the name of the street changes to Lake Drive. His work there is the *Horse Tamers*, represented by the mythical twins Castor and Pollux. The execution is flawless, although the heroic classicism of the two groups is a bit lost on their middle-class surroundings, with tennis courts on one side and modest brick bungalows on the other. Still, the group allows Highland Park to emulate Rome, which has two sets of the same subject, going back to lost Greek originals. Taken together, the two sculpted entrances to Highland Park show off the American Renaissance at its best.

The preservation of Highland Park's open-air Reservoir No. 1, from 1879, reflects the lengths Pittsburghers will fight to preserve their green space. Stringent environmental regulations of 1998 required that all Pennsylvania reservoirs be covered with a plastic bubble. This promised hideous consequences for citizens who use the three-quarter-mile walkway around the reservoir. Opponents of the bubble raised enough awareness on the issue to fund a multimillion-dollar micro-filtration plant, completed in 2002, that allowed the reservoir to remain open to the skies. For technical reasons, Reservoir No. 2 was not exempted from the regulation requiring a cover and is now hidden under a huge blue plastic sheet.

The waste from the filtration plant—heavily chlorinated water—needed to be purified before it could be released into any natural waterway or source. The original plan was to aerate the water as it flowed over a concrete channel that ran from the plant to Lake Carnegie. The Highland Park community again argued for a better solution, which it achieved in the form of a high-tech "babbling brook" that sends the water over pebbles, rocks, and other organic materials on its way to Lake Carnegie. The inflow of clean water in turn benefits the lake, which had a tendency to stagnate.

The major institution here is the Pittsburgh Zoo and PPG Aquarium, successor to the Beaux-Arts–style zoo that opened in 1898. The zoo was rebuilt in the 1980s to simulate the various animals' natural habitats, and in the 1990s, an educational complex went up, followed by a forty-five-thousand-square-foot aquarium with an eye-catching wavelike roof, in 2000.

An excursion into this urban park tells us something about the people living in this neighborhood. They rescued the park three times in a decade: by restoring its grand entrances, saving the reservoir from disfigurement, and avoiding the unsightly water filtration channel that experts told them was inevitable. Such efforts prove their civic-mindedness, as does the revitalization of their neighborhood. Perhaps not coincidentally, Highland Park also has the most even racial balance of any quarter of the city. It may be the most civilized corner of Pittsburgh.

Morningside, set on a long narrow plateau between Highland Park and Stanton Heights, has been something of a secret ever since its founding. Even more than Bloomfield, Morningside is a neighborhood of predominantly Italian heritage. Every August, the community celebrates the two-day St. Rocco Festival, beginning with an Italian mass at St. Raphael Church and ending with a procession, singing, dancing, food, and fireworks.

Farmland until the 1870s, the area that became Morningside grew after streetcar tracks were put down on Chislett Street, and the years from 1915 to 1930 saw a huge population influx. The architectural character of the neighborhood is perceptibly different from that of Highland Park: the houses are smaller and lack the turrets, brackets, colored shingles, and third stories that distinguish the residences of the older neighborhood. In compensation, Morningside's hundreds of simple brick porches give it a comfortable and inviting ambiance.

Morningside also preserves an architectural treasure, though just barely. The eighteen units of Vilsack Row, at the intersection of Jancey Street and Martha, are among the best early-modern homes in Pittsburgh. Frederick Scheibler erected these five-room townhouses in three separate rows for the Vilsack estate in 1912. They have deteriorated over time, and most now bear mismatched porches. The central group was arbitrarily rebuilt and lost the dramatic scallop below the roofline that is one of the best features of the row. Still, what is left on the side units has an uncompromising geometric boldness. The complex derives its power from a simple projection-recession rhythm that is intensified by the massive simplicity of its arched entrances and strip windows.

fig. 5.26
VILSACK ROW,
MORNINGSIDE

It is unfair but inevitable in the presence of a provincial masterpiece like Vilsack Row to ask how this work compares to those of Wright and the Prairie School in the Midwest or of Gropius, Mies, Le Corbusier, and the beginnings of the International Style in Europe. Vilsack Row is so simply composed in brick, stucco, and wood trim that it appears to leapfrog over Wright's designs and finds its main parallel in the contemporary concrete houses of Irving Gill on the West Coast. Whatever its parentage, the economy of scale and materials shown in this project, the social concern it manifests for worker housing, and the foreknowledge of what architects would be designing a half-century afterward make Vilsack Row one of the revealing documents of early modernism in the United States.

Stanton Avenue first links Highland Park to Morningside, then climbs uphill as the delimiting border of the separate district of Stanton Heights. Here, the 1830s and 1840s, the Croghans and Schenleys lived in luxury at Picnic House in the years when Queen Victoria was still a girl. But their summer estate was taken over by a golf club, and around 1947, it was laid out as an inner-city suburb. Like Morningside, Stanton Heights is exclusively residential and makes use of the neighboring communities of East Liberty and Bloomfield for its commercial needs.

LARIMER, LINCOLN-LEMINGTON, HOMEWOOD, AND EAST HILLS

The neighborhoods of Larimer and Lincoln-Lemington are contiguous but do not actually touch: Larimer is positioned alongside East Liberty, while Lincoln-Lemington is a world entire to itself. The theorem of isolated neighborhoods being unstable neighborhoods finds certain exceptions in Pittsburgh, but this is not one of them. Larimer's sole organic link is to East Liberty because it is cut off from Highland Park by Negley Run and from Lincoln-Lemington by the deep gully and fast traffic of Washington Boulevard.

Larimer takes its name from William Larimer, who made a fortune in the railroad industry and built a manor house overlooking East Liberty on what is now Larimer Avenue. The Larimer neighborhood was settled in the first wave of Italian immigration at the same time as Bloomfield was being settled, in the 1880s. It particularly appealed to those families who were already prosperous enough to buy freestanding houses with gardens. The Italian-origin community has all but disappeared today, although a few shops with Italian names stand at the intersection of Larimer and Meadow streets, in what otherwise is a predominantly African American neighborhood.

A few blocks down Meadow, at number 6513, stands the community's once-great monument, Our Lady Help of Christians Church, but this exuberant double-towered Italian Baroque structure of 1898 is now deserted. This sad sight all too well represents Larimer itself, which is among the poorest quarters of Pittsburgh and is weighed down heavily by drug violence and unemployment.

Like the communes of medieval Italy, where the upkeep of the bridges was critical to survival, Larimer depends on bridges to maintain its link with Lincoln. The three bridges over Washington Boulevard are among the more powerful sights of the city. The earliest of the three, from 1903, is the Pennsylvania Railroad Bridge that carries the Conrail tracks over Lincoln Avenue, on the east side of Washington Boulevard. The bridge consists of six ponderous arches that are faced with stone over an internal structure of concrete. Under the northernmost of those six arches, at a right angle to the bridge, pass the two semi-elliptical stone arches of the Lincoln Avenue Bridge of 1906. A quarter of a mile farther to the north, Washington Boulevard is crossed again by the elegant Larimer Avenue Bridge, a concrete structure of 1912.

In the gully itself, at the intersection of Washington Boulevard and Negley Run, stands a strange building with the character of a circus prop. It is the blackened five-story tower of the firefighter training school that is set on fire again and again to simulate actual fire conditions. Its purpose is serious, but its architecture provides one of the more incongruous sights in the city.

fig. 5.27
LARIMER AVENUE
BRIDGE, PAINTING
BY JOHN KANE,
1932

With a population of approximately five thousand, the Lincoln neighborhood, with its Belmar and Lemington subdistricts, was once an attractive area high on a plateau that overlooks the Allegheny Valley to the north, Negley Run and Highland Park to the west, Penn Hills to the east, and the flats of Homewood to the south. Its arterial road, Lincoln Avenue, is not what one generally finds in the older neighborhoods of Pittsburgh. It twists through the area with the breeziness of a suburban highway (it eventually leads to the suburb of Penn Hills) rather than affecting the sobriety of a city street.

Homes in Lincoln are mainly of World War I vintage. They are more generously spaced out in this modest African American neighborhood than they are in wealthier neighborhoods such as Shadyside. But good—or more precisely, previously good—housing cannot by itself create a vital neighborhood. Buffeted by drug violence and weighed down by unemployment, Lincoln has been in slow decline for decades.

Lincoln has an undeniable individuality all the same, some of it stemming from its hills and near-suburban character and some from several monuments of first-class architectural importance. The first of these is the Lincoln-Larimer Fire Station, at the corner of Lemington Avenue and Missouri Street, the most striking building in a decayed community. This 1908 firehouse by Richard Kiehnel and John Elliott is intact, save that the large doors at some point were altered from arches to straight lintels—actually a design improvement. A careful look at this building will reveal the influence of Frank Lloyd Wright. One can make out Wright's general ideas in the crisp horizontal lines and the uncompromisingly strong vertical tower and in some of the decorative details in the window embrasures. Kiehnel had worked in Chicago and so knew Wright's early works there, such as Unity Temple; also, being German-born, he would have had at least some awareness of the Vienna Secession Building, which seems to have had a secondary impact on the fire station design. But the firehouse is fiercely original and stands up well to anything other modernist pioneers were producing in America or Europe.

The Lemington Elementary School at 7060 Lemington Avenue, opposite Paulson, is the most striking school in the city in decorative terms. The school is constructed of beige industrial brick but has Classical proportions, so the piers between the windows simulate the approximate height and girth of the columns in a Greek temple. The main building is capped by a frieze of brown, cream, blue, red, and green terra-cotta tiles, which creates a similar evocation of the triglyphs and metopes of a temple entablature. The blaze of color in the two large polychromed reliefs over the main entrance evokes still other cultures: those of Islam, the Aztecs, and Hollywood. Unfortunately, the school is currently closed.

A few blocks to the northeast, at the corner of Lincoln and Campania avenues, stands the grandiose Cornerstone Baptist Church. It was constructed in 1928 as St. Walburga's Catholic Church for the Sisters of Divine Providence and for a primarily German congregation. The parish was closed and the building passed to the African American community in the 1960s. It is a flamboyantly sited hillside building of finely dressed but irregularly coursed sandstones of varied hues and has an inviting open space in front of its façade. The tower, with its onion-shaped dome, is especially memorable.

There are many ways to enter Homewood. The most vivid way is to turn off Penn Avenue at one of the three underpasses that cut below the Conrail tracks at North Homewood, North Dallas, and North Braddock avenues. This was the way Albert Wilkes entered it in *Sent for You Yesterday*, John Edgar Wideman's PEN/Faulkner award-winning novel set in Homewood's African American community: "Through the deep shadow under the railroad bridge and he knew he was in Homewood again." It is the way of approaching Homewood that most forcefully shuts out the white world and embraces that of the African American.

One can also enter Homewood from Frankstown Avenue, another old route that leads from East Liberty to the eastern suburb of Penn Hills. A third entry point is a visual one—and the most dramatic—and that is to view all of Homewood from the top of Brushton Hill, where Brushton Avenue intersects with Mohler and Upland streets. (Brushton was a Homewood subdistrict that once had its own railroad stop.) This is the only point in Pittsburgh where it is possible to see a neighborhood in its entirety, down to every last house and garage. The outlines of the Cathedral of Learning and of several

VISITORS–PLEASE
REPORT TO OFFICE

fig. 5.28
TERRA-COTTA
DETAIL, LEMINGTON
SCHOOL

fig. 5.29
HOMEWOOD, FROM
BRUSHTON HILL

Golden Triangle skyscrapers impinge on the skyline, too, but they are so far away that they could never transcend Homewood's isolation. Looking down on Homewood, even the most prosaic traveler might imagine himself or herself as the explorer Balboa, gazing over the Pacific.

Homewood is exceptionally flat for Pittsburgh; consequently, it was the perfect place to build thousands of houses for workers. The land once belonged to James Kelly, a civic-minded entrepreneur who was also a major landowner in Wilkinsburg, Point Breeze, and Edgewood before the Civil War. To finance a town on the Homewood site, Kelly borrowed from Judge Thomas Mellon. Mellon foreclosed on Kelly after the Panic of 1873 and financed the subdividing of lots for scores of tiny houses built in strips parallel to Frankstown Road. The lots sold for about sixty-five dollars each, the homes for a few hundred dollars more. The Pittsburgh atlas of 1886 gives a sense of the frenetic pace of construction, showing as it does the dotted lines of three dozen more blocks that were just then being carved from what had been the Homewood racetrack. By 1910, the entire valley was filled with those monotonous houses.

At one time, Homewood's population had been diverse: well-to-do business owners, Irish immigrants working in the nearby railyards, jockeys or workers from the racetrack, members of B'nai Zion Synagogue or the Homewood African Methodist Zion Church, founded in 1871. African Americans became more prominent among the neighborhood's residents in the Depression, but they constituted only 22 percent of the population as late as 1950. That number soared to 66 percent by 1960, when the urban renewal of the Lower Hill forced families into Homewood. By then it had become a classic ghetto.

Two long-ago events sparked changes that impact Homewood to this day. The first was the assassination of Martin Luther King Jr. in 1968, which caused riots in Pittsburgh and throughout the nation; the second was the Civil Rights Act. The impact of the latter did not immediately affect the neighborhood, but it ultimately had the more profound effect. For the first time, middle-class African Americans were empowered to buy homes in neighborhoods such as Penn Hills and Monroeville, outside their traditional districts, and many did. This flight resulted in a drastic reduction in Homewood's population. Around 1950, Homewood had its peak of 34,355 residents. By 1960, that figure was only 30,523, and just three years later, in 1963, it was only 24,000. By 1980, Homewood's numbers had dropped to about 15,000 and by 1990, to 11,500. Some of the decline paralleled shutdowns in the steel industry, but much of it was driven by the increase in crime and gang wars.

"Catastrophic disinvestment" is the euphemism favored by urban planners for the kind of vacancy that is the prime characteristic of Homewood today. At the once-busy Frankstown Road, numerous lots are simply fields, and once-crowded streets such as Tioga are nearly vacant. Unsurprisingly, the population has dipped below ten thousand as residents leave for better neighborhoods.

Homewood's worst years might be behind it now, so its current prognosis for the future is cautiously optimistic. The East End Community Collaborative, Operation Better Block, and other agencies have launched an initiative to update the parks and public areas and to improve residential areas. There is already some visually interesting architectural detail in the neighborhood, such as the red-brick tower and the metal core in the rent-subsidized Bennett Place of 1988 at the intersection of Bennett and Sterrett streets. Some good older blocks are being restored, such as the 7000 block of Bennett, with its hillocks topped by neatly kept homes and lawns. Homewood also preserves buildings by Frederick Scheibler: his Syria and Kismet Apartments at 7430–7434 Bennett, from 1904, enhance the street with their two-story porches approximating Greek temple fronts. But Nelda, the third unit of the triplet, burned to the ground, and Kismet is tottering.

Homewood preserves certain public buildings that would be handsome additions anywhere. The Homewood branch of Carnegie Library, at the corner of Hamilton and Lang avenues, is one of the most elegant in the city. It was the system's largest branch when it opened in 1910 and among the most original of all the system's locations. Carnegie himself had lived just six blocks from it, though that was half a century before its construction, and across the tracks. Still, Carnegie seems to have linked himself to the building in a special way, purchasing the site himself and allocating $150,000—the equivalent of several million dollars today—for the best possible result. The interior shows it, in its quarter-sawn oak paneling, moldings and casework, the fancy cornices, the pilasters with linenfold panels, and the stained-glass and clear windows that allow sunlight to flood the library. Carnegie's investment has clearly paid off: this branch library sparked the careers of writers Annie Dillard (as she recalls in *An American Childhood*), August Wilson, John Edgar Wideman, and Albert French. Consummately handsome also is Holy Rosary Roman Catholic Church, at the corner of Kelly and Lang, from 1928. It is the best façade of Ralph Adams Cram's three churches in town, with seemingly real but structurally superfluous flying buttresses and a thrillingly flamboyant rose window. The interior is austere but dramatic in Catalan Gothic.

fig. 5.30
CARNEGIE LIBRARY,
HOMEWOOD

fig. 5.31
HOLY ROSARY
CHURCH

Should Homewood ever regain its urban health, it will owe its good fortune in large part to the generous instincts of architects or patrons such as Scheibler, Cram, and Carnegie. The rest of Homewood was built as cheaply as traffic would bear, and a bad urban legacy, like a good one, will long endure.

Homewood did something rare for an inner-city district: it cloned itself as a suburb. The most ambitious attack on the problems of Homewood was the creation of East Hills, an enclave east of Homewood that became available in the 1960s when Turner Dairy moved its cows to greener pastures in Penn Hills. On the vacated pasture nearly a thousand housing units were then built, mainly garden apartments and townhouses that were laid out to achieve maximum privacy on winding hillside streets like East Hills Drive, Wilner Drive, and Robinson Boulevard.

The development worked well in architectural terms, but it was undermined in urban and social terms by the isolation of the site from all parts of the city except Homewood. Predictably, the residential makeup soon shifted from racially mixed to uniformly African American. Today, many of these houses from the 1960s, some of which were boarded up before they were ten years old, have been rehabilitated inside and brightened up in pastel colors outside.

fig. 5.32
EAST HILLS
HOUSES, RECENTLY
RESTORED

Two civic centers were established for the East Hills development, but unfortunately both are defunct. One was the East Hills Elementary Magnet School at 2150 East Hills Drive. This loosely grouped series of two- and three-story pavilions, each articulated by a distinctive feature on its roof, was regarded by parents all over Pittsburgh as one of the best schools in the city. When it opened in 1966, and for a decade thereafter, the school was racially balanced, but this balancing act demanded so much energy that at the moment the school is closed.

The other civic complex was the East Hills Shopping Center, built in the 1960s off Frankstown Road. This was a mall that took twenty years to get on its feet, and now 90 percent of it has been demolished. Difficult to reach and impossible to see because it sits high on a hilltop, the mall was a manifestation of Pittsburgh's "Acropolis complex"—its penchant for bulldozing hilltops into flat sites for large structures, other instances being on the North Side, the Hill, and Oakland. But the developers of these complexes forgot that the original Acropolis is imposingly visible from almost anywhere in Athens, whereas the shopping mall was nearly invisible. East Hills Shopping Center went bankrupt in the face of competition from glittering emporia to the south and east. Now just 10 percent is left, used for a school and child care facility.

Can these bones of long dead commerce be revivified? Wal-Mart's "Jobs and Opportunity Zones" program has committed itself to build a

148,000-square-foot Supercenter if the shopping center ever reopens. Wal-Mart further promises to work with neighborhood businesses and suppliers to spur job creation and economic development and to employ some four hundred people. There are hundreds, maybe thousands of American communities that cringe in horror when they hear Wal-Mart is coming to town, but Pittsburgh's East Hills is not one of them.

POINT BREEZE, REGENT SQUARE, EDGEWOOD, AND SWISSVALE

Penn Avenue runs parallel to Homewood, though not through it; nonetheless, it provides a link for it and all the East End neighborhoods. The last three miles of Penn Avenue within Pittsburgh's limits cut broad and straight through Point Breeze as the street aims for the first town east of Pittsburgh, which is Wilkinsburg. It was in Point Breeze that Penn Avenue turned itself into one of the most opulent millionaire rows of nineteenth-century America. Armstrong, Heinz, Frick, and Westinghouse—the kings of cork, pickles, coke, and electricity—lived in Point Breeze; so did Andrew Carnegie, his mother, his brother, his cousin George Lauder, and a half-dozen of his partners. The entertainer Lillian Russell lived in this neighborhood, and the Thaws and R. B. Mellon resided around the corner, aggregating a minimum of three dozen millionaires when that term meant something significant.

This area through which the last of Pittsburgh's Penn Avenue runs was known at different times as Point Breeze or as Homewood. Point Breeze was the name of a tavern that stood from 1800 to 1886 at the intersection of Penn and Fifth avenues; Homewood was the 650-acre estate where Judge William Wilkins lived in a mansion not much smaller than the White House. In the autobiography Andrew Carnegie composed just before he died in 1919, he wrote of "the stately mansion at Homewood, which was to the surrounding district what the baronial hall in Britain is or should be to its district—the center of all that was cultured, refined and elevating."

Wilkins's Homewood mansion played a crucial role in the architectural and social history of Pittsburgh, and it remained an object of curiosity even after it was replaced in 1924 by the dozen brick homes that stand today at the intersection of Edgerton and Murtland. William Wilkins (1779–1865) was a banker, a judge, a diplomat, a U.S. representative and senator, the American ambassador to Russia, and secretary of war in President John Tyler's Cabinet. His brother-in-law, George Dallas, was vice president to President James K. Polk. What brought Wilkins to Point Breeze was still another title: president of the Greensburg Pike (now known as Penn Avenue). Taking up the position as pike president, Wilkins moved to the area and bought the hundreds of acres that today make up both Frick Park and Homewood Cemetery. He built the Homewood mansion around 1836. Although he claimed to have designed it himself, the plan was evidently assimilated from Minard Lafever's *Modern Builder's Guide* of 1833, and some professional architect must have at least consulted on the project.

Who was that architect? Wilkins knew at least four competent designers: Philadelphia's William Strickland and John Haviland, both of whom worked in Pittsburgh in the 1820s and 1830s; Pittsburgh's John Chislett, who in 1834 had built the Bank of Pittsburgh, of which Wilkins was the leading director; and Robert Mills, the chief federal architect when Wilkins was a Cabinet member. There seem to have been several models for this huge house. Its conceptual model was the Hermitage, the mansion built outside Nashville by President Andrew Jackson, who was Wilkins's political mentor. Wilkins specifically likened the architecture of his house to Thomas Jefferson's Monticello, because, like Monticello, it was filled with gadgets. Another trail leads to Baltimore (a city Wilkins visited at length when he was courting his first wife), where the name Homewood was originally applied to the estate of Charles Carroll Jr., which is now part of Johns Hopkins University. The Baltimore and Pittsburgh Homewoods fit well together in general configuration, each with a porticoed front, recessed passages, and reemergent wings. This would have been the footprint that Wilkins gave his professional architect to develop into a house, unless, as he always insisted, he really did draw the plans himself.

Point Breeze was remote from Pittsburgh when Wilkins moved there, but by 1860, it was served by two railroad stations and was the ideal location for Pittsburgh's men of business. Among the first to arrive was Andrew Carnegie, in 1862, with a residence on Homewood Avenue not far from that of his friend Judge Wilkins. When the aristocratic Wilkins died in 1865, Homewood and its grounds were divided among his four daughters. The mansion and a one-eighth share of the land (eighty acres) were then purchased by Carnegie's partner and mentor, William Coleman, the coal and oil king. The move decisively signaled the transfer of power in Pittsburgh from the pioneer aristocracy to the new iron and steel elite. Then, in 1867, Coleman married off his daughter Lucy to Carnegie's younger brother, Tom. The Shingle-style house that stands today at 222 Carnegie Place was Tom and Lucy Carnegie's carriage house, a fragment of a fine estate that Andrew gave them as a wedding present when he departed Pittsburgh for New York that same year.

The flowering of Point Breeze was glorious but short-lived. The Westing-house, Heinz, and Carnegie estates were cut up in the 1920s; the Mellon, Thaw, and Armstrong houses came down in the 1940s and 1950s. Today, the uninitiated will see almost nothing of the Gilded Age on Penn Avenue apart from H. C. Frick's house, but a little detective work will quickly reveal where other estates used to be, the way the location of Tom and Lucy Carnegie's home was uncovered. A dozen cul-de-sacs were once private driveways, while clues to other estates can be seen in wrought-iron fences, such as the one on the north side of Penn between North Murtland and North Lang, which marks the block where H. J. Heinz's mansion, Greenlawn, used to stand. The elaborate Queen Anne shingled cottage at 209 North Lang was used by the Heinz estate manager, the cinderblock structure at 7033 Meade Place is the garage in which Heinz stored his prized fleet of limousines, and the odd house at 7035 Meade served as private storage for his watches and curios.

Other surviving mansions or mansion fragments along Penn Avenue include a considerable house of 1898 on the 7100 block (renumbered as 201 Osage Lane) that is chopped up into low-cost apartments and called the Cloisters. Another was the Gables, home of the Horne's department store mag-nates at 7418 Penn, now the Reformed Presbyterian Theological Seminary.

George Westinghouse's mansion, Solitude, built in 1871 and the first house in Pittsburgh to have electric lights, was demolished in 1918 when its ample grounds became Westinghouse Park. An archaeological dig here in 2006 yielded remnants of the mansion, the remains of a two-hundred-foot underground tunnel that led to Westinghouse's personal laboratory, and traces of the four natural gas wells (one of which was sixteen hundred feet deep) that Westinghouse drilled in 1883 to supply his house with gas. Westinghouse became so fascinated with gas that he invented the gas meter, developed a piping system to supply his neighborhood with gas, and eventu-ally founded the Equitable Gas Company. Two houses that Westinghouse built as gifts around the year 1900 also survive: one for his son at 201 North Murtland, another for his personal physician at 7100 Thomas Boulevard. Under their Renaissance detailing, neither is far from Prairie School designs, their walls made of the same long "Roman" bricks that Frank Lloyd Wright made famous in his Chicago-area houses in the same years.

Just one Point Breeze mansion survives in its glory today: Henry Clay Frick's Clayton, on Penn Avenue at South Homewood, now a public museum of his life. The estate calls itself the Frick Art & Historical Center, the centerpiece of which is the Frick Art Museum, a Brunelleschian villa of Alabama limestone with an intimate collection of Renaissance panels and bronzes. Besides Frick's

251

fig. 5.33
REMNANTS OF
THE HEINZ ESTATE,
PENN AVENUE

mansion there is a museum that showcases turn-of-the-twentieth-century private transportation vehicles, including Frick's 1914 Rolls Royce, a playhouse and bowling alley built for the Frick children, a flower conservatory, and a retainer's house that has been recycled as a restaurant.

Whatever your thinking about robber barons, and whatever your reaction to the heavy taste that dominates Clayton, it is riveting to see up close a whole lifestyle that is so far removed from today. It is not so much the physical as the social context that confronts visitors here. One learns, for example, that social conventions required Adelaide Howard Childs Frick to change her clothes up to six times a day. She worked for weeks on the luncheon she hosted for President Theodore Roosevelt in 1902, but the luncheon was for men only, so Adelaide never even met her eminent guest. Tours of Clayton emphasize its "upstairs/downstairs" contrasts: the kitchen and butler's pantry (seven servants kept up the twenty-three rooms) give way to the breakfast and dining rooms, the fastidious entrance hall, the reception room, and the parlor for lady visitors. The paintings (Hogarth, Gainsborough, Goya, and Monet) are good, but the glimpses of late-Victorian family life are what make the tour memorable.

It is not by coincidence that Clayton remains while other mansions in the area have disappeared, for few men in America gave more thought to their public persona than Frick. Frick's daughter, Helen, also spent most of her life polishing her father's memory until it shone with flawless luster (she lived in New York but returned to Pittsburgh to die in Clayton). She spent millions to turn back time and restore her father's mansion to its state as of around 1900, so Clayton remains today much as it was when Frick left Pittsburgh in 1914 for his greater mansion in New York. At its core is an Italianate villa from around 1870 that Frick bought in 1882. There was an initial remodeling in 1883 by Andrew Peebles and a second one by Frederick Osterling eight years later, ultimately producing the more-or-less French château we see today.

With Judge Wilkins dead and Andrew Carnegie residing in New York and Scotland, Frick played the lord of Point Breeze. He began to buy large parcels of the Wilkins estate, beginning at his back door on Reynolds Street and extending south through the gully of Nine Mile Run until he acquired several hundred acres. Around 1900, Frick commissioned Daniel Burnham to design an art gallery for the Beechwood Boulevard end of the estate, but in the end Frick took his Raphael and his Bellinis, Holbeins, and Rembrandts to New York, saying that Pittsburgh's smoke would damage them. No one seems to have pointed out that Frick, the king of coke, contributed more smoke than anyone else.

fig. 5.34
CLAYTON,
HENRY CLAY FRICK'S
MANSION

fig. 5.35
CLOTHESLINE,
CLAYTON

Today, most of Frick's estate survives as Frick Park, the largest in the city's park system. The rustic but noble pavilions at the park entrance on Reynolds Street are by the Beaux-Arts master John Russell Pope; they date from Helen Frick's presentation of the park to the public in 1935. Deep in the park lies Nine Mile Run, a tributary of the Monongahela River that mostly flows underground in culverts but in the park remains exposed.

In 1911, Fredrick Law Olmsted Jr. advised the city to develop Nine Mile Run into parkland, but instead, from 1922 until the 1990s, two hundred acres adjoining what is today Frick Park were covered by slag dumped by the Duquesne Slag Products Company. The Nine Mile Run watershed restoration that began in 2001 was ambitious: restoration of the stream and wetlands was completed in 2006, but the slag will never leave. As Frank Lloyd Wright said regarding any architect's mistakes, the city is planting over it.

There are few millionaires among the eight thousand residents of Point Breeze today, but this lively and racially balanced community and the adjacent Regent Square together provide much to attract young homeowners. The focus of preservation efforts in Point Breeze is not on the millionaire rows but on such architecturally varied streets as Linden, Reynolds, Hastings, and Gettysburg, or McPherson and Thomas boulevards, which were laid out in 1885 in imitation of the grand boulevard design that Baron Haussmann had created for Paris some years earlier.

fig. 5.36
MILTON STREET,
REGENT SQUARE

In Regent Square stand a half-dozen borderline-modern works by Frederick Scheibler. Typical are the Linwood Apartments at the corner of McPherson and North Linden, a three-story brick structure coated in Portland cement. Constructed in 1907 without any ornament, it bears unmistakable kinship with the Viennese work of Joseph Maria Olbrich and Adolph Loos. The broad white planes and their contrast with the wood trim also recall contemporaneous works by Frank Lloyd Wright. Peculiar to Scheibler however, and much in keeping with Pittsburgh, is the expression of structure: the bowing of the two-story wooden piers holding the balconies, the concealed/revealed steel beams sunk into the soffit of the ground-floor porches, and the graphic detail of the dowel ends protruding through the piers, as though ready to slip.

The same concern for mass, projection, and detail animates two more Scheibler apartment buildings in Point Breeze, both from the years 1905–1908. One is 201 East End Avenue, at the corner of Tuscarora, and the other the masterly Old Heidelberg Apartments at 401–423 South Braddock, at Waverly. The 201 East End block is less daring than the Linwood Apartments because of the more traditional pediments over the porches and the conventional Art Nouveau detail of the wave motif over the central door. Scheibler's skill as a decorator is more apparent in the Old Heidelberg block, with its art glass, mushroom wall reliefs, and stumpy piers on the third floor, with heart-shaped capitals borrowed from Olbrich.

Scheibler's architectural transition from rationalist to romanticist can be followed in three other groups of his work in Point Breeze. These are a three-unit rowhouse of 1913, around the corner from the Old Heidelberg, at 420–422 East End Avenue; two houses of 1910 and 1918 at 579 and 584 Briarcliff Road, on the hill that overlooks the intersection of Forbes and Braddock avenues; and three detached cottages at 7506, 7508, and 7510 Trevanion Street in the Regent Square–Swissvale neighborhood, constructed in 1905, 1917, and 1915–1916, respectively.

These designs prepare us for the overt picturesqueness of Scheibler's last major work: the Parkstone Dwellings from 1922, at 6937–6943 Penn, near North Murtland. The irregularly coursed schist walls, the exaggerated slope of the slate roof, and the pronounced decoration of the giant mushrooms and mosaic "rugs" on Parkstone's balconies give evidence of Scheibler's growing discomfort with the modern movement. By 1922, Pittsburgh's leading modernist architect seems to have looked into the future—and decided not to join it.

Regent Square is a neighborhood of mind, not of boundaries, since it intermingles segments that legally belong to Pittsburgh, Swissvale, Edgewood, and Wilkinsburg. The land was originally part of the William Wilkins estate, then became a grid-based subdivision known as the Devon Plan. Though it is one of the smaller communities of the East End, Regent Square radiates with activity and a tight-knit village ambiance. The neighboring Swisshelm Park is another small community of two-story brick houses, albeit with a more suburban feel.

The civic center of Edgewood is particularly impressive. Its landmark is First Presbyterian Church of Edgewood at 120 East Swissvale Avenue, with its unusual Medieval German Westwerk of two huge towers and a bridge-arch between them. Opposite is a stylish war memorial and the Edgewood Municipal Building, a picturesque grouping of a Cotswold-style tower and outbuildings.

Adjacent to the war memorial stands the Shingle-style Edgewood Railroad Station, where East Swissvale Avenue meets the Conrail tracks. Its site was the heart of Edgewood when, from 1864 to 1964, half the working residents commuted to the Golden Triangle on the Pennsylvania Railroad each day. A note in the *Philadelphia Inquirer* from the year 1902 cites the author of this modest structure as the celebrated Frank Furness, and there is little reason to doubt it. Furness built scores of suburban railroad stations, as

fig. 5.37
OLD HEIDELBERG
APARTMENTS

fig. 5.38
PARKSTONE
DWELLINGS,
PENN AVENUE

well as central stations in Philadelphia and Pittsburgh. Even on a tiny budget, and despite his being in decline by 1902, Furness was incapable of delivering a dull building. Admirable in this one is the tight symmetry of the T-shaped plan, the way the shingles of the upper wall are battered out from the bricks of the lower wall, and the complex rake of the shingled roof. Even the support system for the long shed at trackside goes far beyond what was demanded. It consists of eight sets of back-to-back iron quadrant arches—just the kind of detail Furness soaked up thirty years before from his reading of Eugène-Emmanuel Viollet-le-Duc's *Entretiens sur l'Architecture*. What a pleasure to discover a surviving building by the master who had such influence on Pittsburgh architecture in the late nineteenth century.

Among the other public monuments of Edgewood is the combined C. C. Mellor Library and Edgewood Club on the far side of the tracks, at the corner of West Swissvale and Pennwood avenues. Diminutive in size, it combines a library, a community center, and a swimming and tennis club with a Mediterranean sophistication appropriate to a wealthy suburb. Exactly fitted to its triangular plot, the building is a white stucco mass held low to the ground, with a bright Spanish tile roof and pergola and a line of stubby columns on the Swissvale Avenue side—altogether one of the best public buildings in the city, given its complicated location.

fig. 5.39
EDGEWOOD
RAILROAD STATION

Edgewood also contains many of Pittsburgh's finer homes, set on lush tree-named side streets such as Locust, Maple, Hawthorn, Chestnut, Elm, Linden, Walnut, and Beech. It is the best place in the city to study the Shingle Style or the various revival modes that followed in the 1910s and 1920s. Three fine homes of the early twentieth century on Maple Avenue provide a sample of Edgewood's riches: at 200 Maple, a Prairie School house of sober lines and characteristic eaves; at 361 Maple, an imposing Georgian Revival mansion; at 431 Maple, a Craftsman-style stucco house by architect Charles Barton Keen.

The half of Edgewood that lies on the Pittsburgh side of the railroad tracks is older than the farther half. The Pittsburgh half was laid out in 1864 by John Grazier on land purchased from James Kelly, with a plan designed to maximize the romantic vistas of its curving streets. It is in this vicinity that West Swissvale Avenue ends in two dozen homes that form one of the most handsome Victorian clusters in the city. Outstanding are the Gardner-Bailey house of 1864 at 124 West Swissvale, an Italianate farmhouse of flush wood siding carrying an eccentric square cupola that gives it an air of majesty far beyond its modest scale, and the Grubbs-Kerr house at 235 West Swissvale, a board-and-batten home from the time of the Civil War.

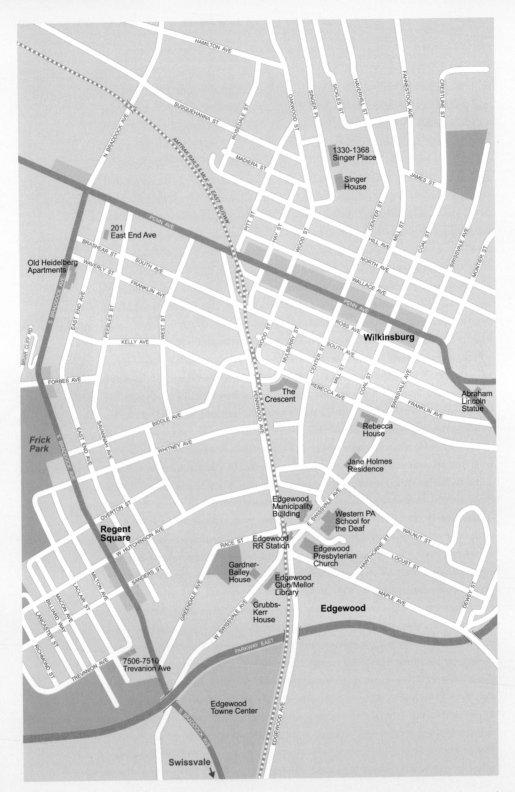

Regent Square, Wilkinsburg, and Edgewood

At the foot of West Swissvale Avenue is an intersection with I-376, affording quick access either to the Golden Triangle to the west or to the eastern suburbs of Pittsburgh. Braddock Avenue also cuts through Nine Mile Run here, linking Edgewood to Swissvale. The latter, a residential-industrial town of nine thousand, has as one of its main landmarks George Westinghouse's brick-and-concrete Union Switch & Signal factory, now part of the Edgewood Towne Center mall, near the intersection of Braddock Avenue and the Conrail tracks. The original complex began operations in 1886; the society architect Benno Janssen added the administration building—all that remains of the plant today—in 1917. The shopping center consists of locally owned stores as well as national franchises and saves East End residents from having to drive out to the suburban malls.

WILKINSBURG

A borough of about nineteen thousand citizens, Wilkinsburg is a working-class town served by the last stretch of Penn Avenue. Like Edgewood and Swissvale, the town merges so imperceptibly into the contiguous parts of Pittsburgh that it is a suburb in a legal sense only. The area has been identified by four names in its bicentennial history: "Jewstown," after Levy Andrew Levy included the area in his warrant for 266 acres in 1765; "Rippeyville," from the name of its leading tavern-keeper two decades later; "McNairstown," after Colonel Dunning McNair laid it out as a village in 1790; and Wilkinsburg, after 1812. It was moving toward a merger with Pittsburgh in the mid-nineteenth century but instead incorporated itself as an independent borough in 1887. Wilkinsburg's best years were the 1920s and 1930s, when it had a large commuter population living near the Pennsylvania Railroad line. The line still cuts through Wilkinsburg, but trains no longer stop there. Wilkinsburg declined along with rail travel in general, but it should eventually revive as a new generation discovers its low-cost housing and the convenience of an express bus lane to Downtown.

The buildings are generally modest, but the town is conservative enough to have preserved several vernacular "monuments" that would have been torn down elsewhere. Among them is a Depression-era diner at 7714 Penn (actually within the Pittsburgh city limits). Now a sandwich shop, it keeps alive at least the image of the last functioning streamline-style diner in the city. Wilkinsburg also preserves a handsome train station, a neocolonial borough building and post office, a half-dozen good commercial buildings in its downtown, and the Crescent apartment complex. This last, at 724–734 Kelly

Avenue, south of Rebecca, is an ambitious sequence of commercial and housing units that were tied together around 1904 by an amateur designer who had evidently seen a photograph of the "crescents," or curved townhouse rows of London or Bath. Today, this ambition is mocked by the Crescent's current dilapidated state, but the Pittsburgh History & Landmarks Foundation is working toward its restoration.

North of Penn Avenue, at 1318 Singer Place, on the slope of Wilkinsburg Hill, stands the best Gothic Revival home in Pittsburgh. The construction of the John Singer house in 1863–1869 was, along with William Coleman's take-over of the Wilkins mansion, a striking indication of the wealth of Pittsburgh's early ironmasters. Singer made his fortune in iron and chose to spend it in baronial splendor on a thirty-acre estate with a large ornamental lake and private chapel, of which only this mournful castle remains. The thirty-five-room house cost seventy-five thousand dollars, twenty to fifty times the price of a decent-sized home at the time. The popular Joseph W. Kerr may have been the architect, although the plan and elevations could easily have been derived from the Victorian pattern-books of such architects as Isaac Hobbs or Samuel Sloan or from the fashionable *Godey's Lady's Book and Magazine*. Alternatively, Singer might have commissioned a plan from some national figure. If family tradition is correct that he supplied iron to Thomas U. Walter for the construction of the Capitol dome, then Walter (a Gothic enthusiast in his spare time) might have had some connection to the project.

fig. 5.40
JOHN SINGER
MANSION,
WILKINSBURG

The walls of the Singer house are of sandstone, hammer dressed and regularly coursed, with finely polished ashlar blocks as quoins. The steeply pointed roofs are covered in hexagonal-shaped slate, arranged in fishscale and variegated designs, and the eaves and some windows carry ornamental stone bargeboards that drip almost menacingly with spindled lacework. Everything is just as rich inside, and it is not irrelevant that another family tradition states that Singer brought artisans over from London, since decoration on the Houses of Parliament had ended in exactly the same years that his house was under construction.

Conservative and tranquil by comparison is the neighboring row of twenty homes by Frederick Scheibler at 1330–1368 Singer Place, from 1914. Sitting just a few blocks away and also effectively situated against the slope of Wilkinsburg Hill is a wood frame Gothic Revival villa of the 1860s at 813 Hill Avenue, near the corner of Mill. Still highly impressive, though stripped of ornament now, it appears to copy designs from Isaac Hobbs's book, *Villas and Cottages*, a popular design source in Pittsburgh.

A few blocks to the east, Hill Avenue intersects with Swissvale Avenue, which is Wilkinsburg's main cross-street and its link to Edgewood and Swissvale. At this corner a set of impressive civic monuments offers some idea of what Wilkinsburg was like in its glory days: Rebecca House, at 900 Rebecca Avenue, and the adjoining Jane Holmes Residence, at 441 Swissvale Avenue. The original title of the first institution was the Home for Aged Protestant Women; that of the second was the Sheltering Arms Home for Aged Protestants. Both carried on their charitable functions until 2008: the first as the Three Rivers Center for Independent Living, and the second as the Jane Holmes Residence and Gardens. By that year, the two institutes had new quarters in the suburbs, so the buildings are now awaiting other tenants. Both of these rambling structures are in the Italianate Style, with the broad verandahs that marked their building type in the years after the Civil War. Their benefactors were two cousins with identical names: "Baltimore Jane" Holmes and "Pittsburgh Jane" Holmes—banking heiresses who gave away millions of dollars (in today's values) before the robber barons raised the monetary standards in philanthropy still higher. A block south on Swissvale at the corner of Walnut, within the boundaries of Edgewood borough, stands the Western Pennsylvania School for the Deaf, a Beaux-Arts building with eight overscaled Ionic columns and a top-heavy porch.

The end of Wilkinsburg's commercial strip is marked by a fork in the road: Penn Avenue to the left, Ardmore Boulevard to the right. At the fork itself stands a heroic reminder of the town's early involvement in highways. This is Alonzo Pelzer's life-sized copper statue of Abraham Lincoln—the result of thousands of copper pennies donated by Wilkinsburg's schoolchildren in 1916. The Great Emancipator holds a document in his left hand, but what it says is irrelevant, because the main function of this statue is to be a metaphorical highway sign indicating a fork in Penn Avenue. The Lincoln statue was placed here around the time of World War I because it was where Penn intersected with the then-brand-new Lincoln Highway (now Ardmore Boulevard and state route 30) that leads across Pennsylvania to Philadelphia. The left-hand road, still designated Penn Avenue, begins a long climb up Wilkinsburg Hill and eventually enters the borough of Churchill and merges into the Penn-Lincoln Parkway (I-376) and the 1940s Pennsylvania Turnpike, itself something of a historical relic.

FIFTH AVENUE: UPHILL AND UPSCALE

fig. 6.1
GWINNER-HARTER
HOUSE, FIFTH
AVENUE, SHADYSIDE

Of all the city's streets, Fifth Avenue has had an impact on Pittsburgh second only to Penn Avenue's. Just as Penn Avenue and the railroad combined to create a string of neighborhoods from the Strip and East Liberty out to Point Breeze and Wilkinsburg, so Fifth Avenue and the horsecars and streetcars that ran on it gave birth to the four highly important inner-city suburbs of the Hill, Oakland, Shadyside, and Squirrel Hill. Though much diminished as a provider of public transportation today, Fifth Avenue still weaves a common thread through about a third of the city's land mass.

Penn Avenue and Fifth Avenue had another significant difference in that the former became a thoroughfare through the inevitability of geography, while the latter became one by fiat. There was no Fifth Avenue in Pittsburgh's East End at first, because what ultimately became that thoroughfare began as an unconnected sequence of local streets. These were Beelen's Field, Watson's Field, and Braddock's Field roads in Uptown and Pennsylvania Avenue in Oakland. Not until the 1850s did financiers amalgamate the various local streets into the Farmers' and Mechanics' Turnpike, which stretched the five miles from the Golden Triangle to Point Breeze.

Fifth Avenue played a crucial role in the early years of public transportation in Pittsburgh. In the 1840s, it carried a coach service from the Golden

Triangle to the Hill. In 1859, the omnibus carriages were given rails, and as horsecars, they made the ride up Fifth Avenue into Oakland with enough speed that the line was extended in 1872 into Shadyside and East Liberty. Still later, in 1889, Fifth Avenue was used for a third mode of public transportation, when tracks for steam-driven cable cars were laid down its length, all the way to Point Breeze. The cable cars proved unequal to Pittsburgh's hilly terrain, however, and the project failed after just four years.

Then came the innovation that truly made Fifth Avenue an urban artery: the electrified trolley. The trolleys were installed on Fifth Avenue as far as Shadyside and East Liberty in 1892, and they reached Point Breeze four years later. For half a century, Fifth Avenue functioned as one of the principal streetcar routes in Pittsburgh. The four streetcar suburbs that developed along Fifth Avenue were all annexed to Pittsburgh in the 1860s, but each formed a distinct identity. The Hill became the nerve center of African American life, Oakland became a civic center, Shadyside a WASP enclave, and Squirrel Hill heavily Jewish. Excluding Oakland for the moment, the three "suburbs" and their offshoots treated in this chapter continue to focus internally on their residents rather than reach outward to the city as a whole. They defy John Donne's poetic declaration and remain islands entire of themselves.

THE BLUFF, UPTOWN, AND THE HILL

The Bluff is the first neighborhood demarcated by Fifth Avenue and by the less significant Forbes Avenue. The Bluff lies just east of Downtown, but because of its high elevation, it is not observable from all parts of the Golden Triangle. From the towers on Grant Street, however, if the angle is right, the Bluff stands out with clarity and considerable drama. It is no Mount Washington in height, but, in 1759, the British did consider it among the alternative sites for Fort Pitt.

Known at first as Ayer's or Boyd's Hill, the Bluff is a mile-long flat plateau with a commanding view of the Monongahela River. Today, it is a crowded neighborhood of four thousand people that pulls together the early settlements of Pipetown, Riceville, and Soho. The street grid here was drawn up around 1830, with the majority of the extant houses dating from the decades immediately following that exercise. The district grew enormously with the installation of the Fort Pitt Incline, which from 1882 to the 1930s gave steelworkers quick access from Bluff Street to their jobs in the mills on Second Avenue.

For much more than a century the Bluff has been home to two institutions of signal importance: Mercy Hospital and Duquesne University. Nothing now remains of the original Mercy, the first hospital in Pittsburgh, which builder Haden Smith put up in 1847 at Locust and Pride streets for the Catholic Sisters of Mercy. Until the 1980s, one could spot an occasional turret or cornice on Mercy's Second Empire and High Victorian Gothic buildings, but these have now been sacrificed in the name of medical progress.

That portion of the Bluff closest to Downtown has been occupied since 1878 by Duquesne University, a foundation of the Germany-based Fathers of the Holy Ghost. Today, Duquesne educates approximately ten thousand undergraduate and graduate students and is distinguished in liberal arts and its schools of law, music, and communications. Several campus buildings are outstanding: Old Main is a dramatic six-story High Victorian Gothic brick block of 1884, and the Duquesne University Student Union is a 1967 Brutalist but surprisingly gracious poured-cement structure with a dramatic two-story gathering place inside.

The signature campus building is the Richard King Mellon Hall of Science, from 1968. Proportioned like a Greek temple, the black steel structure is the only work in town of Chicago's Ludwig Mies van der Rohe. It presents a vision that works well for campus residents but is most exciting when seen from the slopes of South Side. From that vantage point you can better imagine it as a Greek temple perched atop an academic acropolis.

Uptown uses Fifth Avenue as its centerline, but the district has less definition than the Bluff because it acts like a trough or a saddle, about one and a half miles in length, separating that neighborhood from the Hill. Uptown serves as a corridor between the Golden Triangle and Oakland and consists of hundreds of nineteenth-century rowhouses on Fifth and Forbes avenues and their cross-streets. To these were added scores of commercial blocks, which in the early twentieth century accommodated more wholesale distributors of dry goods than any similar complex between New York and Chicago. Uptown decayed in the 1950s and 1960s, along with the decline of the Hill and the

fig. 6.2
THE BLUFF, AS SEEN FROM THE GRANT BUILDING

fig. 6.3
MELLON HALL OF SCIENCE, DUQUESNE UNIVERSITY

wholesale trade itself; today, it is a marginal though still promising part of the city's urban revitalization.

Along with the occasional distinguished old rowhouses on Fifth and Forbes avenues, and on side-streets like Tustin and Miltenberger, Uptown preserves the imposing Fifth Avenue High School on Fifth at Dinwiddie, from 1894. This handsome transitional Romanesque-Gothic Revival structure in orange brick carries a repeated surface pattern that was called "diaperwork" during the era of Victorian architecture. Construction of the school was an attempt to reach out to Pittsburgh's foreign-born population, since the ward was populated entirely by immigrants. It was the first fireproof school in Pittsburgh and remains a hearty survivor, recycled in part to house a home-improvement service.

The revival of the school and restoration of some adjacent homes sparked the transformation of several lower Fifth Avenue storefronts into law offices. Around 2000, Uptown seemed ready to reassume its status as the proud link between the Golden Triangle and Oakland. But its transformation stalled, and the current impetus for reviving Uptown is the new eighteen-thousand-seat Consol Energy Center on Fifth Avenue between Washington Place and Crawford. Development rights for the hockey arena district include the potential destruction of Mellon Arena and its replacement by a complex of office buildings, stores, restaurants, a hotel, housing units, and parking.

A two-mile ridge sheltering about eleven thousand inhabitants, the Hill stretches from the Golden Triangle to Oakland and is one of the more creatively evoked neighborhoods in the country. There are so many memories stored in this neighborhood that the Hill seems to have two realities: its physical presence and a separate existence in the mind. It was on the Hill that Stephen Foster was taken by his nanny to church services and thus had his main encounter with African American life. Numerous Pittsburgh writers and art-

fig. 6.4
THE HILL,
VIEWED
FROM STRIP

ists, including Willa Cather, have described life on the Hill. The Hill did not greatly impress William Sydney Porter, who lived here in 1901 after a stint in prison. Still using his prison name of O. Henry, he wrote that his new home was the "low-downdest" hole on earth and its inhabitants "ignorant, ill-bred, contemptible, boorish, degraded, insulting, sordid, vile, foul-mouthed, indecent, profane, drunken, dirty, mean, depraved." The Hill emerged in more elevated form in the *Hill Street Blues* television series, which was conceived by a producer and actors trained in Pittsburgh. More significantly still, August Wilson used the Hill as the setting for all but one of his monumental cycle of ten plays on African American life.

The Hill has always been diverse because it began as a confederation of three different hills and three separate villages. It was a waystop for all the ethnic groups in Pittsburgh, particularly Germans, Italians, Russians, Slovaks, Armenians, Syrians, Lebanese, Greeks, and Chinese, and it was the cradle for two groups present for generations: Pittsburgh's African Americans, now numbering ninety thousand citywide, and its Jews, currently about a third that number. This social diversity always gave the Hill a radical strain, first as a center of abolitionist sympathies and later as a hotbed of socialism. Oral tradition insists that both David Ben-Gurion and Leon Trotsky proselytized for their causes on what was for years known as "Jews Hill."

The African Americans who reside on the Hill represent a community that was part of the founding of Pittsburgh in 1758. But western Pennsylvania's links with Virginia meant that slaves were also present. Slaves numbered 150 in the census of 1790; most, but not all, were free within a generation. It was runaway slaves who established the settlement of Hayti on the Lower Hill and its first African American church, both by 1818. On the Middle Hill—an amalgam of Gazzam's, Goat, and Ruch's hills—was Lacyville; on the Upper Hill (known also as Coal, Quarry, or Herron Hill) was the village of Minersville. Nonetheless, for its first hundred years, the majority population on the Hill was German and Scots-Irish. Newcomers in the 1880s were mainly Eastern and Central European, and primarily Jewish, and by the 1940s its residents were predominantly African Americans. This African American community went on to become one of the most stable in the United States. By the early twentieth century, it included business owners, small manufacturers, and about sixteen hundred steelworkers; the *Pittsburgh Courier* was for decades the most respected African American newspaper in the country. Today, two centuries after it was first established, the Hill remains the heart of Pittsburgh's African American community, even as that community has spread out to a score of urban and suburban neighborhoods.

Like Pittsburgh's other streetcar suburbs, the Hill has no industry and plays no significant role in commerce beyond its local retail stores. The last product manufactured there was the smoked fish that until the 1990s was still being cured in wood-fed ovens at Cantor & Smolar's on Bedford Avenue. What the Hill produced, and produced abundantly, was people. Main-stage entertainers such as Adolph Menjou, Lena Horne, Oscar Levant, Billy Eckstine, Erroll Garner, Art Blakey, George Benson, Ray Brown, Lou Christie, Kenny Clarke, Roy Eldridge, Walt Harper, Earl Hines, Ahmad Jamal, Billy Strayhorn, Maxine Sullivan, Stanley Turrentine, and Mary Lou Williams all got their start on the Hill.

The Harlem Renaissance poet Claude McKay called the Hill "the cross-roads of the world" for its array of arts and entertainment. The documentary film *Wylie Avenue Days* well encapsulates the glory years of the Hill from the 1930s to the 1950s, with its hot spots, clubs, restaurants, African American–owned businesses, gathering places, and rituals. That film was one of the early sources to recount the remarkable career of Charles "Teenie" "One Shot" Harris, who photographed happenings in the community from the 1930s through the 1970s. Harris's first nickname came from his ample girth; Pittsburgh mayor David Lawrence gave him the second because he never used more than one frame at each shoot. Starting at the *Pittsburgh Courier* in 1936, Harris was present whenever anything exciting — or ordinary — happened on the Hill. His nearly 100,000 images of African American life, kept today in the Carnegie Museum of Art and the *New Courier* archives, constitute a staggering achievement.

A second influential artist from the Hill was Samuel Rosenberg. Rosenberg started by painting portraits but moved on to depictions of the Hill during the Depression. His social realist canvases captured the essence of his neighbor-hood, and he influenced three about-to-be-famous students at Carnegie Tech (now Carnegie Mellon): Andy Warhol, Mel Bochner, and Philip Pearlstein. The most recent creative spirit to come from the Hill, and the most influential of all, was the Pulitzer Prize–winning playwright August Wilson (1945–2005). Wilson's father was a German-American baker named Frederick Kittel; his mother was Daisy Wilson, whose own mother had come to Pittsburgh from North Carolina on foot. "You can't just be alive. Life don't mean something unless it got meaning," says one of Wilson's characters in *Joe Turner's Come and Gone*, and he proved it in his own remarkable life. Growing up on the Hill, Wilson dropped out of school and educated himself in the Carnegie libraries there, in Oakland, and in Homewood. Winning a Pulitzer Prize and a Tony for *Fences* in 1985 spurred Wilson on to the heroic sweep of his ten-play

fig. 6.5
BOYHOOD HOME
OF PLAYWRIGHT
AUGUST WILSON

cycle, one for each decade of the twentieth century, all but one set on the Hill. Wilson's childhood home stands at 1727 Bedford Avenue, opposite Roberts. The sight is incongruous, with a historic marker hailing Wilson in front and a derelict shell behind. (Plans are under way to restore it as a writers' retreat.) The house is a miniature Hill in itself: the African American Wilson family owned it, and still does; a Jewish family ran a market in front, while Italian-Americans repaired watches next door.

The Hill retains its old configuration of three subdistricts: the Lower Hill, now entirely redeveloped, from the Golden Triangle up to Crawford Street; the Middle Hill, from Crawford to Herron Avenue, on the fringe of the University of Pittsburgh campus; and the Upper Hill, from Herron to Bigelow Boulevard.

The Lower Hill

The reconstruction of the Lower Hill began in 1955. In an area of 100 acres, 1,300 buildings housing 413 businesses and 8,000 residents, nearly all African Americans, were displaced by the Urban Redevelopment Authority when the area was amalgamated into the Golden Triangle. Protesters shouted that "urban renewal is Negro removal!"

Even forgetting for the moment the devastating social impact of the Lower Hill redevelopment, its success could only be judged as minor. The new complex failed to graft on to the Golden Triangle because of the intrusion of the Crosstown expressway (I-579) and the misalignment of the two areas' street grids. Some bad luck also dogged the Lower Hill redevelopment,

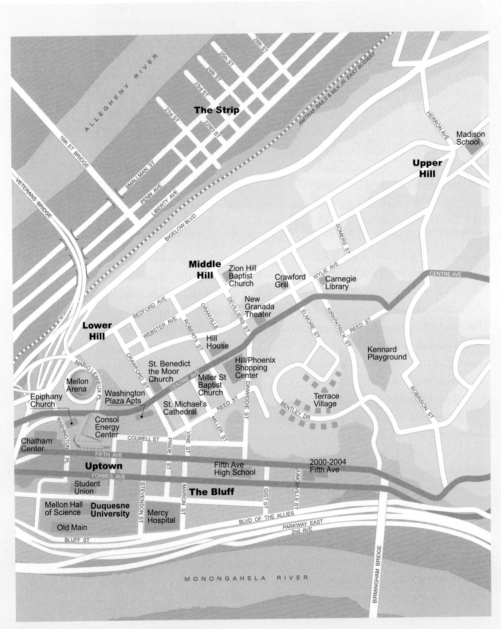

Uptown and the Hill

particularly the bankruptcy of William Zeckendorf, one of its major players, and the decision by the Heinz foundations to locate their new concert hall in the Golden Triangle rather than on the Hill. But the major cause of its failure was the animosity between the developers and the African American community. When that animosity boiled over as part of the nationwide race riots of 1968, it ended Pittsburgh's dream of a cultural acropolis on the Lower Hill.

In Genoa, the thirteenth-century church of Santissima Annunziata bears the nickname "del Vastato" (the destroyer) because it was so large that its construction annihilated the parish it was meant to serve. History may also bestow that title on Mellon Arena, if it survives (current plans are to tear it down after 2010). What was then called the Civic Arena opened in 1962, but its origins go back to the 1940s and Edgar Kaufmann's enthusiasm for summer opera outdoors and frustration with summer rain showers. An early scheme by Kaufmann's architects (Frank Lloyd Wright hungered for the commission but never got it) proposed a cable-supported tent that, depending on the weather, could open and close like a Japanese fan. They looked for a site, but Oakland, Squirrel Hill, and Highland Park all protested "not in my back yard." The Hill had no powerful civic voice to offer protest, so it was selected for the construction scheme that had by then evolved into a retractable dome that would shelter eighteen thousand spectators. The Urban Redevelopment Authority then weighed in with an earlier project that aimed at the clearance of the Lower Hill.

The arena's stainless steel dome, 415 feet in diameter (a world record at the time of its construction), is composed of eight sections that are supported by a cantilevered tripod—technically a space-frame box girder—that holds six of the sections when they are swiveled back. Each section weighs 220 tons; rolling all six back takes a little over two minutes—and provides the spectators inside with an unforgettable experience. Electric cables and a jumbo monitor currently make it impossible to open the arena roof, though nothing structural stands in the way.

The arena's operas quickly gave way to musicals, and the musicals gave way to hockey and the occasional rock concert. Now construction of the hockey arena on Fifth Avenue has condemned the building to death before its fiftieth anniversary. The planning debacle was double-edged: it first killed a flourishing community and then denied a brilliant achievement of twentieth-century engineering the acclaim it deserved. But architecture is always like that: to achieve greatness demands more than the solution of technical problems.

All that is left of the Lower Hill today is Epiphany Roman Catholic Church on Washington Place at Centre Avenue, a strongly articulated Romanesque Revival structure in deep red brick with plentiful terra-cotta trim outside and

fig. 6.6
CONSOL ENERGY CENTER, NEW HOME OF THE PENGUINS

fig. 6.7
MELLON ARENA

a richly frescoed interior. The quite agreeable Beth Hamedrash Hagadol–Beth Jacob Synagogue, from the 1960s, stood alongside the church on Colwell Street, in the old Jewish district, for just under half a century before it was gobbled up for the new hockey arena on Fifth Avenue. Now the congregation, an amalgamation of two dozen synagogues that had built on the Hill since 1873, houses itself in a Fifth Avenue storefront.

About half the Lower Hill is now parking lots, since most of the apartment towers that were proposed never materialized. Of two that did materialize, some famous names in the late International Style were involved in their design: William Lescaze for the Chatham Center apartment-office-hotel complex on Washington Place at Fifth Avenue, and I. M. Pei for the Washington Plaza Apartments on Centre Avenue at Crawford Street. Efficiently planned and beautifully textured in poured concrete, Pei's tower of four hundred units is the epitome of the refined design of the 1960s, but it looks forlorn by itself, since the Zeckendorf bankruptcy in 1962 canceled plans for the other towers.

The Middle Hill

The Middle Hill extends a mile and a half from Crawford Street to Herron Avenue along the three long residential streets of Wylie, Webster, and Bedford and a commercial strip on Centre Avenue. The Middle Hill is the only place in Pittsburgh that affords views of both the Allegheny and the Monongahela valleys, and it began in the 1830s as a fine residential suburb of estates and Greek Revival mansions. It received a regular street pattern and several hundred townhouses just before the Civil War, when its prestige was still high. A census taken in 1877 listed three hundred professionals—doctors, lawyers, and judges among them—as Middle Hill residents. The bounteous Italianate mansion standing at 3323 Webster, in the Upper Hill, is one of scores of residences that still testify to those halcyon days. In the 1600 block of Bedford Avenue, toward Downtown, there are also some High Victorian Gothic and Romanesque Revival townhouses. Among the best preserved groups on the Hill are a row of Italianate homes in the 1600 block of Webster Avenue, near Roberts, which tradition says were erected by Judge Thomas Mellon when he lived there in the 1850s.

The majesty of the Hill begins in its topography. Looking up from the Sixteenth Street Bridge you can appreciate the sheer cliff that separates the Hill from the Strip below. Human ingenuity overcame the cliff with the construction in 1883 of the Penn (or Seventeenth Street) Incline at Seventeenth Street. So long as that incline functioned (it ceased operating in 1953), the Hill was linked to ample food and ample jobs in the Strip. The residents of the Strip got a bonus, too: the upper station of the incline on Arcena Street doubled as a dance hall.

Now the two neighborhoods share nothing in common but some decaying public stairs down the cliff, some scars on the rock face where the incline tracks used to run, and the four concrete piers on Arcena Street that once anchored the tracks into the hillside. The informal overlook that the incline left on Arcena Street—just minutes from August Wilson's home on Bedford, via Ledlie Street—offers one of the great views of Pittsburgh and the villages huddled on the Allegheny Valley hillsides opposite.

The dismembering of the Penn Incline was one of several episodes that isolated the Hill. Another was the erection of mammoth housing blocks in the 1940s, which put a barrier between the Hill and Oakland. A third episode—the worst—was the destruction of the Lower Hill. Each event lowered the quality of life on the Hill, and the quality of its housing stock declined correspondingly. One incongruous sign of this decline are several score suburban-style ranch houses from the 1970s on Roberts Street and scattered in other pockets on the Hill. Well intended, they had nothing to do with the historic patterns of architecture on the Hill, and many have already been destroyed.

The Middle Hill retains a significant number of monumental structures. The most striking of these is St. Benedict the Moor Roman Catholic Church on Centre Avenue at Crawford. This elaborate Gothic Revival structure was built in 1894 for the German-based Holy Trinity parish. It changed its name to St. Brigid's when the parish's members became predominantly Irish and took its present name in 1971 to reflect its mostly African American membership. St. Benedict's was an integral meeting place for civil rights demonstrations in the 1950s and 1960s, and the marches and protests against the urban redevelopment of the Lower Hill usually began on this corner. To honor these struggles, the walled-in plaza of Freedom Corner was created opposite the church in 2001, with an evocative design etched in marble by Carlos Peterson. The corner provides a memorial and a commemoration in its inscriptions, but its prime role is to create a venue for future large-scale meetings.

A block and a half to the southeast is St. Michael's Russian Orthodox Cathedral at 43 Reed, at the corner of Vine, notable for its high flight of wooden steps ascending to its glittering interior. The church has lost its congregation, however, and the future of this dignified but diminutive structure is not promising.

In the same few blocks are a half-dozen synagogues that now serve as churches for the African American community. All are easily identified by Hebrew inscriptions on cornerstones, on the façades, and inside. Two of the

most interesting are the Miller Street Baptist Church at 23–25 Miller, opposite Foreside, which still carries its original cornerstone with the date 1905
and, high up on the façade, the name Beth David in Hebrew, and the monumental domed Zion Hill Baptist Church on Webster Avenue at the corner of
Erin, which was the former Kether Torah–Agudas Achim Synagogue. All of
these congregations migrated long ago to Squirrel Hill or the East End. At
110 Erin, halfway between Webster and Centre, the Enon Baptist Church
took over the Anshe Lubovitch synagogue, which, to judge from the quiltlike
patterning in the brick, was probably erected by the men of the congregation
themselves. Both here and in Zion Hill Baptist Church, ritual *mikvah* baths
survive in the basement, recycled as baptisteries.

Worship was just part of the Jewish community here. The classes, social
programs, and sports of the Blakey Program Center at 1908 Wylie take place
inside the Hebrew Institute building of 1915. Restoration of the institute's
brickwork removed the covering that for half a century had hidden its elaborate
split-pediment entrance, and the Hebrew lettering is thus visible once more.
The educational programs here were highly progressive, emphasizing secular
as much as religious culture, and culminating in the basketball court that is still
in use on the top floor. The Blakey commemorated in the center's name is not
the musician Art Blakey, incidentally, but his community activist cousin Bill.

Considerably more secular than the Hebrew Institute were the Turkish
baths once found all over the Hill and the socialist meeting halls. None of the
former seems to have survived, but you can still see the Labor Lyceum of the
Arbeter Ring/Workmen's Circle on Miller Street, opposite the Miller School.
Both the school and the lyceum are currently boarded up, but the lyceum's
high-relief corner plaque of 1916, though half smashed, still boldly exhorts,
"Workers of the World, Unite!"

Other meeting places that survive include the First Mosque of Pittsburgh,
at 1911 Wylie between DeVilliers and Granville, which went up in 1899 as a
Carnegie library, its shelves crammed with Yiddish books and newspapers.
When the library moved out, various social agencies moved in, and today
Carnegie's proud motto, "Free to the People," is emblazoned just inches from
the Arabic inscription announcing the building's current use. A new branch
of Carnegie Library went up in 2008 at the epicenter of the Hill, the intersection of Centre Avenue with Kirkpatrick and Mahon streets. On a fairly
narrow, angular, and sloping site, the library opens up to the street with a
corner room dedicated to August Wilson. One complete wall carries an
enlargement of a 1923 map of the Hill, with notes on Wilson's real and fictive
locations in his life and in his plays. A few minutes' walk away, at 2001 Wylie,

the historic Ebenezer Baptist congregation worships in a towering new building that in 2006 replaced a Gothic Revival structure from 1931 and earlier structures going back to 1874.

The Hill once had two supremely important social centers. The more cerebral was the Irene Kaufmann Settlement at 1835 Centre Avenue. Built for immigrant Jews but open to everyone, it was one of the glories of the settlement house movement, with several dozen classrooms, public baths, sewing rooms, gyms, and assembly halls. Swimmers had their own palace at the facility: a fantastic poolhouse in Art Deco Style. The designer that E. J. Kaufmann brought in for the poolhouse was Joseph Urban, an intimate friend as well as hired hand of publishing tycoon William Randolph Hearst. The main building and Urban's swimming pool are gone, but a more sedate auditorium from 1928 survives. In place of the landmark settlement house there now stands the James F. Henry Hill House Center, dramatic in its laminated wooden girders.

The other social gathering place to which Hill residents flocked for decades was the New Granada Theater, on Centre Avenue at DeVilliers. It was designed by Louis Bellinger in 1927 as a meeting hall for an African American lodge of the Pythian Temple; its renovation into a theater and nightclub was entrusted to Alfred M. Marks in 1937. The result: an elaborate Art Deco entertainment palace with a façade of enamel metal plaques that once blazed with color. Now shuttered, the New Granada is a storehouse of memories of the vaudeville performers, Yiddish actors, and African American jazz musicians who entertained there on alternate nights. While everyone agrees that the New Granada must reopen, and there have been a few steps in that direction, it is less obvious who will advance the millions of dollars it would cost.

The creator of the New Granada, Louis Bellinger, is a story in himself. Bellinger was the first African American architect in Pittsburgh, and the theater is the most prominent of a score of projects he did in Wilkinsburg, Hazelwood, and other neighborhoods, many involving the updating of rental properties. But one ought not forget Alfred Marks, either. Designer of a string of federally funded projects in the 1930s, Marks was the one who cloaked the ground floor in those brilliantly hued metal panels that give the New Granada its striking color and verve. Though entirely by coincidence, the sequential contributions of Bellinger and Marks to this temple of popular culture epitomize the easy multiculturalism for which the Hill was famous.

This note of diversity is sounded still another time nearby, at what was for years the most famous building on the Hill: the second Crawford Grill at 2141 Wylie Avenue, at the corner of Elmore. What was once the ornate

Sochatoff Building of 1917 was transformed into the nationally renowned jazz club that routinely hosted Sarah Vaughan, Nat King Cole, Miles Davis, and all the jazz greats who came through Pittsburgh or grew up here. That first Crawford Grill fell victim to the leveling of the Lower Hill. Its second home, on Wylie, fell victim instead to changing tastes and white patrons' reluctance to trek up to the Hill. It sits vacant, for now.

It would be numbing to stagger through the Hill hearing nothing but "here used to be...." Fortunately, there is good news coming out of the Hill today, although context requires one last dip into the bad old days. In 1940, the Pittsburgh Housing Authority completed two public housing projects on the Hill: the large Bedford Dwellings, a series of cul-de-sacs north of Bedford Avenue, and the mammoth Terrace Village (an umbrella term that also encompasses its Allequippa Terrace subdivision). The monotonous brick blocks covered the land from Bedford Avenue to Herron Avenue, especially on the new and artificially winding Bentley and Burrows drives. The designers were Marlier, Lee, Boyd, and Prack—typical of the antimodernists who ruled the Pittsburgh building world between the two world wars.

Terrace Village was the second largest of the pioneer federal housing projects in the United States and important enough that President Franklin Roosevelt himself came to open part of it in 1940. The list of rules for the residents, unimaginable today, included lights out at 10:00 p.m., no pets, no signs, no laundry in the windows, and no cooking of cabbage. In all, there were 3,073 housing units in the 155 buildings on the Hill, with an enlargement in the 1960s to 3,727 units in 191 buildings.

Ironically, the blocks were largely modeled on the award-winning Chatham Village, and the landscape architect for the complex, Theodore Kohankie, was a Chatham Village holdover. Terrace Village was made by leveling Gazzam's, Goat, and Ruch's hills, which were cut down and used to fill in the valley that is now Kirkpatrick Street. (The extensive earthmoving uprooted a coal seam that provided two years of free winter fuel for the project.) But the earthmoving also created a barren site where the natural topography had once been rich and varied. Worse, it made Terrace Village into an enclave that was detached from the street grids of Oakland and the Hill. The housing development became an orphan to both of the older centers.

Terrace Village still exists, on paper, but the old blocks are no more. In 1996, renovation of some of the blocks was entrusted to Perfido Weiskopf Architects, who immediately made some salutary changes: the flat roofs of the blocks were given gables, and each rental unit now has two floors, like the Hill's old two-story houses (before, the units were laid out horizontally, like suites on one floor of a hotel). Lighting, signage, gates, and lawns were put into service to render the old complex private and safe. Other blocks closer to Oakland were torn down and, in 1998, replaced by the Oak Hill development.

The most encouraging housing developments on the Hill today are at least in part market driven and thus not entirely subsidized. On the 1800 block of Bedford Avenue, Bedford Hill is creating new rowhouses with a sensitive appreciation of the old context in color, texture, height, and architectural rhythm. Another kind of continuity comes from the multifunction complex called the Legacy, on the block bounded by Centre and Wylie, Erin and Elmore. This community facility opened in 2008 with shops on the Centre Avenue front and the Lou Mason Jr. Apartments on the Wylie Avenue side. In the latter development, Rothschild Doyno Architects broke what could have been a monotonous block-long front by capturing the in-and-out rhythms of the old Hill streetscape, as they did in their higher-budget Fairmont Apartments in Garfield, but more modestly and in some ways more engagingly. There is no forgetting of "the legacy" at the Mason Apartments because the twelve pavilions in alternating tan and brown brick carry the names of such Hill jazz greats as Erroll Garner, Earl "Fatha" Hines, Billy Eckstine, Art Blakey, Ahmad Jamal, George Benson, Stanley Turrentine, and Walt Harper.

The most visible part of the Hill's revitalization is also the oldest. Crawford Square is a highly successful experiment in "new urbanism" that grew from a small nucleus of new houses put up in 1991 on Crawford Street, alongside what is now the Freedom Corner plaza. Its 140 homes and 350 rental units eventually stretched from Crawford and Centre up to Roberts and Webster avenues, and its spin-offs now encompass both sides of Centre, with more coming. The courtlike streets and clusters of Crawford Square attract a wide range of homeowners and renters, some paying market rate, others receiving subsidies, and all varied in age and race. The development is a financial, urban, and social success, although old-time Hill residents understandably wince when they hear newcomers giving their neighborhood address not as the Hill but Downtown.

Sugartop (Upper Hill)

The Middle Hill ends with an appreciable valley at Herron Avenue, east of which Sugartop begins. That nickname for the Upper Hill says it all. In Lena Horne's old neighborhood, a few middle-class African Americans live in the occasional old mansion, but most families occupy small, well-tended newer homes. The main landmark is the elaborate Madison School at Milwaukee and Orion streets, from 1902, by Daniel Burnham's apprentice, Ulysses

Peoples. The intersection of Milwaukee and Adelaide streets marks the peak of Sugartop, from which you can see nearly every part of East End Pittsburgh. That high point is close to the Hill's eastern slope, through which runs Blessing Street, the winding road that connects the Upper Hill with Bigelow Boulevard and the Bloomfield Bridge. The linked Robert E. Williams Park and Herron Hill Reservoir serve as a general community meeting place. The progression from the slums of the Lower Hill to the tenement blocks of the Middle Hill and the green avenues of the Upper Hill is almost an emblematic outline of the American dream.

SHADYSIDE

Shadyside has always seen itself as a village. The image was valid in the 1850s, when Shadyside was a settlement of not more than twenty families on the Pennsylvania Railroad line. The village image is still much cultivated in Shadyside today, and with some validity, because the neighborhood pulled back from the trajectory taken by Homewood, its near twin in size and topography.

Ironically, Shadyside flirted with industry early on, but the experiment was not a success. In 1792, the Alsatian immigrant George Anshutz teamed with Anthony Beelen and William Amberson to create the first blast furnace in Pittsburgh, on what is now Amberson Avenue. Operations soon ceased because it was uneconomical to import all the iron ore from Armstrong County.

Shadyside nearly industrialized a second time, when the Pennsylvania Railroad came through in 1852. The local landholders, led by the intermarried Castleman, Aiken, and Amberson clans that had owned most of Shadyside since 1780, instead carved up their estates in a way that would avoid transforming them into a town filled with worker housing. The lots were not too narrow, which meant Shadyside would not join Bloomfield, Lawrenceville, and Homewood as a workers' suburb. They were not too grand, and so they would avoid the fate of the white elephant mansions of Point Breeze and not get chopped up into apartments. Even the heavy traffic that eventually surrounded Shadyside on four sides was turned to advantage. Today, Fifth Avenue on the south, the Conrail tracks on the north, Penn Avenue on the east, and Neville and Craig streets on the west seem to form a protective cordon around the district.

A current map reveals much about the settlement of Shadyside in the crucial years just before and after the Civil War. The Aiken land was subdivided in the 1850s into a few broad estates in the half-mile between Neville

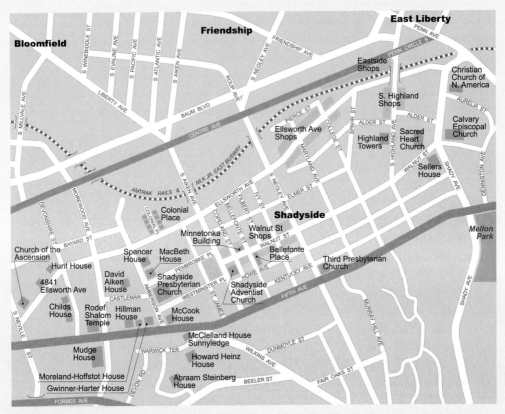

Shadyside

on the west and Aiken Avenue on the east. In the 1860s, Judge Thomas Mellon and other entrepreneurs transformed what had been the old McFarland estate, from Aiken to College Street, into narrow lots of twenty-five by one hundred feet. Last to be developed was the eastern half of Shadyside, from College to Penn Avenue, easily recognized today by a grid that is set on a divergent axis. This area was developed in the 1870s and 1880s by the local businessmen who had their estates there.

The different ways of dividing up the old estates gave results that are still striking. For example, it is highly instructive to examine the long block of Aiken Avenue from Ellsworth to Walnut. Because the two sides of the street were developed by different landowners, the left, as you look toward Fifth Avenue, is crowded with modest houses while the roughly contemporaneous homes on the right side approach mansion status.

Today, Shadyside counts about fourteen thousand residents on 750 acres and is the wealthiest district per capita in Pittsburgh. Four religious denominations erected their most opulent houses of worship here: the Roman Catholic Sacred Heart, Calvary Episcopal, Shadyside Presbyterian, and Rodef Shalom Temple. The area's various congregations are arrayed in fine symmetry. Ascension and Calvary Episcopal churches mark Shadyside's boundaries west and east; Shadyside Presbyterian and Third Presbyterian mark its midpoints north and south. The denominations are roughly equal in social terms, but a liturgical distinction reveals their different origins. The Presbyterians translated the old Latin version of the Lord's Prayer passage "dimitte nobis debita nostra sicut et nos dimittimus debitoribus nostris" as a reminder to forgive their debtors, because many of their Presbyterian forefathers were merchants. The early Episcopalians or Anglicans derived their wealth from land, so they translate the same passage as an exhortation to forgive those who trespass against them.

A visitor coming to Shadyside from Oakland finds a sequence of buildings that continues the monumental tradition of Pittsburgh's civic center. The most prominent of these is Rodef Shalom Temple, at Fifth and Morewood, from 1907. This little-studied building for a congregation that dates from the 1850s must count as one of the premier synagogue designs in the United States. Its language is entirely different from that devised for colonial-era Jews by Peter Harrison or postwar Jews by Frank Lloyd Wright, but the same proficiency has been achieved. What the congregation sought here was a house of worship that would relate it in some way to everyone who used or merely glanced at it. It would thus not be alien to the other public monuments of Oakland but be akin to them in scale and richness. It would not deny the

fig. 6.12
RODEF SHALOM
TEMPLE

heavy industry of Pittsburgh, in which the congregation vigorously participated. Instead, it affirms industry in its common yellow Kittanning brick and in its probable model, which was the railroad station completed the decade before at Bucharest. Unlike most premodern synagogues, there is nothing artificially Moorish here, although the dazzling colors—now faded—on the terra-cotta bands hint so strongly of eastern origins that passersby know instinctively that this is not a church.

Outside, Rodef Shalom is divided into three component parts: the squared dome, which seems modeled on the Great Synagogue of Rome from 1901; the sanctuary cube; and the ornamented doorway. Inside, a visitor finds the same basic shapes and motifs, but the decoration here is enriched with Sullivanesque ornament and a skillful handling of natural and artificial light. The architect Henry Hornbostel was evidently pleased with his building, and he bestowed on it two small monuments that encapsulate the whole history of architecture. Left and right of the façade rise two small light standards, with baskets through which are growing shoots of acanthus. Hornbostel did not specify his intent for these light standards, but surely they are meant to portray the origin of the Corinthian capital, as recounted two thousand years ago by the Roman architect Vitruvius.

Within a block or two of Rodef Shalom stand five other monumental structures. The former First Church of Christ, Scientist, on Clyde Street between Fifth and Ellsworth, now a school, is a small but powerful Neoclassical temple marked by an elegant Ionic porch. Its designer, S. S. Beman, gained fame for his Chicago skyscrapers and the industrial town of Pullman, Illinois, but his accomplished work in the Classical Style was also prominently on view at the Chicago World's Fair and in the string of Christian Scientist churches he built in many cities, culminating in the Mother Church of 1904 in Boston. The effect of this tiny shrine expertly set at a concave turn on Clyde Street is assuredly theatrical, but First Church is one of those buildings where the viewer does not mind being seduced.

Holy Spirit Catholic Church, Byzantine Rite, at Fifth and Clyde, is also dramatic in its oblique siting and triplet of sky-blue onion domes, but the effect is diminished by an internal conflict in the design between its modernist and traditionalist components. Fortunately, no such equivocation about traditional and modern approaches affects two public buildings on the opposite side of Fifth Avenue. Central Catholic High School at 4720 Fifth Avenue recalls a late Gothic city or castle gateway. Clad in richly accentuated bricks in the tradition of William Butterfield and John Ruskin, it adds greatly to the scale and color of the street. Next door to Central Catholic stands what might

fig. 6.13
VITRUVIAN GASLIGHT
AT RODEF SHALOM

have been an intrusion to Shadyside: the poured-concrete radio and television studios of WQED Multimedia at 4802 Fifth Avenue. WQED is the oldest public broadcasting station in the country, known to countless children as the home of *Mister Rogers' Neighborhood*. This distinguished building from 1970, one of a half-dozen Paul Schweikher designed while he taught in Pittsburgh in the 1960s, reflects the completion of the designer's pilgrimage from the International Style of the 1930s to the New Brutalism popular after the 1950s. To Schweikher, Brutalism was a formal rather than a philosophical position, and WQED emerged as a sensitive building both for its users and for those who pass by it. The structure is cavernous but does not lose sight of human scale or human delight. The concrete, for example, was poured with special care, and the design presents educational television as the equivalent of, or successor to, the libraries, colleges, and churches that upheld civilization in the past—exactly the message of the neighboring institutions in Oakland. Unfortunately, the main WQED staircase was ripped away and replaced with a frilly mesh.

The last of the portal buildings to Shadyside on its western border is the Episcopal Church of the Ascension, where Ellsworth Avenue meets Neville Street. This imposing mass of irregularly coursed sandstone is dominated by an enormous Tudor Gothic tower. Inside is an exquisitely finished nave, sumptuously articulated with an open timberwork roof and enriched by elegant side aisles and subsidiary chapels—the perfect abode for late Victorian society at prayer.

The blocks around the Church of the Ascension and Rodef Shalom display some excellent domestic architecture from the closing decades of the nineteenth century. Yet a visitor on this block, as is so often the case around Pittsburgh, will marvel at the extraordinary degree to which even the most affluent streets have homes crowded together. We can understand crowded streets in Pittsburgh's older and poorer neighborhoods, but what explains the crowding in the newer and generally prosperous Shadyside, Highland Park, Point Breeze, and Squirrel Hill? Perhaps the crowding has its origins in a theory of the little-remembered nineteenth-century reformer Henry George. In *Progress and Poverty* and other works, George argued that inequality in the distribution of wealth could be eradicated by a single tax based on the value of land alone. The theory was widely praised in late nineteenth-century America and nowhere more than in Pittsburgh. In Pittsburgh, the wealthy families embraced George's concept enthusiastically but perversely. The city taxed land at twice the rate of buildings, and for a good while it did not tax homes in the East End at all. So Pittsburgh's gentry built the biggest possible mansions on the smallest possible lots.

fig. 6.14
TAYLOR HOUSES,
BAYARD STREET

fig. 6.15
CIVIL WAR–ERA
MANSION,
ELLSWORTH AVENUE

Almost any street in Shadyside is an architectural revelation, starting toward its western limit with the finely crafted Taylor houses at 4735 and 4737 Bayard Street, between Neville and Devonshire. These twin wood-frame homes are Greek Revival in style and must count as the oldest structures in the district. The farmer Charles Taylor put 4737 Bayard up in 1842 for himself (for years it carried that date on a side wall), and he then built 4735 Bayard for his two daughters. The parallel 4700 block of Wallingford between Neville and Devonshire was developed a good deal later, and so it preserves a dozen Queen Anne–style mansions of the 1890s.

Ellsworth Avenue has always been one of the main showpieces of Shadyside's thoroughfares. An especially hardy survivor is the Italianate villa at 4841 Ellsworth Avenue, near Devonshire Street. This remarkable building was part of the Aikens' estate in the 1870s, and it was probably they who built it, around 1860. The original ten acres have been reduced to just an acre or two now, but that is still enough to allow for a pool and private tennis courts. The Victorians called this style "Italian bracketed," and it was popularized in Andrew Jackson Downing's *The Architecture of Country Houses*, from 1850. That means that, handsome though the house is, it was the product of a builder rather than an architect. The highlight of the design is the verandah that wraps around three sides; at the midpoints of the side walls, high brick transepts cut through the house as though it were a church. A block east stands the Alfred Hunt house from the 1970s, at the corner of Ellsworth and Devonshire. In this mansion for an Alcoa heir, aluminum was used wherever possible, even in its raw form; anorthosite boulders containing aluminum ore form its base.

Devonshire, the cross-street that links Ellsworth and Bayard with Fifth Avenue, may be the most handsome street in Pittsburgh. Along its length are more fine Victorian-era homes, starting with the New England Colonial shape of the Childs house at 718 Devonshire, from 1896 (both the family

fig. 6.16
MID-VICTORIAN
FARMHOUSE,
ST. JAMES STREET

fig. 6.17
ENGLISH-STYLE
COTTAGE,
AMBERSON
AVENUE

and the architects, Peabody & Stearns, were originally New Englanders). The Childs house is followed by an elaborately textured Queen Anne house at 808 Devonshire and then a somber Romanesque Revival–Queen Anne house at 820 Devonshire, with blackened sandstone walls and wooden porches and gables.

The middle segment of Shadyside, between Devonshire and Negley, has more interesting houses. The oldest homes surviving in this area are two Gothic Revival frame cottages around the corner from each other, one at 920 St. James Street, the other at 5302 Westminster Place, both from the 1860s. Slightly later is the Italianate David Aiken Jr. house at the dead end of 5020 Amberson Place, from 1864. Aiken was the lord of Shadyside: Shadyside Presbyterian Church was founded in his villa in 1866. When the Aiken lands were divided up a generation later, the house was given a stucco finish to harmonize it with the smooth walls of the homes that had gone up around it.

It was a little girl growing up a few doors away, in the Charles Spencer house at the corner of Amberson and Pembroke, who tells us better than any atlas about changes in Victorian Shadyside. The girl was Ethel Spencer, whose childhood memoir was posthumously printed as *The Spencers of Amberson Avenue*, a recollection describing unpaved streets, cattle grazing on lawns, and woods everywhere. The Spencers were an upper-middle-class family (the father worked for Henry Clay Frick) who built their house in 1886, just as Shadyside was shifting from farmland and orchards to a town with a street grid. The Spencer home stands alongside the George MacBeth house at 717 Amberson, put up two years earlier. Both of these excellent Queen Anne houses have a scalene quality, as though their upper walls were imitating the smooth-scaled skin of a fish. As always in the Queen Anne Style, the buildings seem restless, with multiple gables, multiple inserts and projections, and a highly complex sequence of planes. The people of that era needed lots of room; the Spencers were a family of nine, plus servants.

More Shingle-style and Queen Anne–style homes follow around the corner in the 5200 and 5300 blocks of Westminster Place, beyond Shadyside Presbyterian Church. The double house put up by William Gardner at 914–916 St. James Street, from 1890, is a huge brick pile with brilliant texturing. It was also a multipurpose structure, with half of it intended to serve as a home for the Gardners and half for their tenants, and all of it serving as an advertisement for Gardner's business, which was bricks.

As the great estates were being divided up among the younger generation, the Spencers' architect, George Orth, drew up a "mass" housing project of sorts on Colonial Place, a block from the corner of Amberson and Ellsworth. In this short dead-end block next to the railroad tracks, Orth and others put up five pairs of mirror-image houses in 1897. The result is a triumph of Victorian eclecticism: nine hybrids (a tenth house was destroyed) combining elements of Renaissance Revival, Dutch Colonial, and Georgian architecture. At 5135 and 5201 Ellsworth, Orth erected monumental twin houses with columned porticos that seem like the sentries of Colonial Place. Number 5135 Ellsworth is the Edward V. Babcock mansion, where a Pittsburgh mayor entertained seven U.S. presidents and a bevy of foreign potentates over the years. Babcock (1864–1948) later served as a county commissioner and was responsible for the creation of Allegheny County's North Park and South Park. Diagonally opposite on Ellsworth, Pitcairn Place encloses fifteen more houses in the spot where a family rich in Pennsylvania Railroad and PPG stock once had a single home.

These blocks of Shadyside kept filling up with mansions until changing social mores (and the difficulty of finding reliable servants) ended that lordly style around World War I. One of the last of these palatial residences is the beguiling Louis Brown house at 704 Amberson, from 1913. This is a poured-concrete structure, but its pseudo-thatched roof creates an artful simulation of an English cottage. Directly opposite, and from the same year, stands the Roy Hunt house of 1913, at 5050 Amberson Place. This restrained horizontal villa for an Alcoa heir came from the drafting table of Maximilian Nirdlinger, a designer who had earlier worked for Frank Furness in Philadelphia and then settled in Pittsburgh to take advantage of the many work opportunities.

The status of "millionaire row" was anything but stable in American cities. That a street could keep its prestige for eight hundred years, the way Via Tornabuoni has in Florence, is foreign to American urban dynamics. So Pittsburgh first thought of Penn Avenue in Point Breeze as its millionaire row, but later it seemed to be Ridge Avenue in Allegheny, and still later Fifth Avenue in Shadyside. The concentration of tycoons in Shadyside was thinner than in the city's other millionaire rows, but the two miles of Fifth Avenue, from Neville, the western boundary with Oakland, to Penn Avenue, the eastern border with Point Breeze, made it collectively more impressive.

Fifth Avenue was endowed with its first mansions in the 1850s and its last in the 1920s. The last was one of the most interesting: the Pauline and Edmund Mudge house (now Mudge Graduate House of Carnegie Mellon) at the corner of Fifth and Morewood avenues. This Neoclassical design featuring an elegant double-bow façade in smooth limestone was probably influenced by the contemporary work of the English architect Sir Edwin Lutyens. Internally, Mudge House is a diagram of a jazz-age marriage, with a "his" wing on the north and an equivalent "hers" wing at the south end of the upper corridor.

A half-dozen important mansions can be seen on Fifth Avenue between Morewood and Wilkins, with the tone being set by the Hillman house at 5045 Fifth Avenue. This Second Empire mansion was built for the steamboat king James Rees around 1878, then reclad for the Hillmans in Neo-Georgian Style by E. P. Mellon in 1922; today, it is subdivided into condominiums. Next door, the Moreland-Hoffstot house at 5057 Fifth—still a single-family home—is an elegant terra-cotta variant of the huge mansions of Newport, Rhode Island.

Well set back on a fine lawn, the Gwinner-Harter house at 5061 Fifth is an especially elaborate Second Empire mansion that was built around 1871 for prominent lawyer and lay churchman William B. Negley. In 1911, the stone contractor Edward Gwinner bought the house and reconfigured it inside and out. Rebuilt with certain modern touches after a fire in 1986, it still serves as a private home. Across Amberson Avenue, at 925 Fifth, stands the baronial Willis McCook house, an industrialist's Tudor castle that is scheduled for conversion into a twenty-two room bed-and-breakfast called the Amberson.

fig. 6.18
SUNNYLEDGE,
FIFTH AVENUE,
SHADYSIDE

The outstanding house on this section of Fifth Avenue is Sunnyledge, located at the corner of Fifth and Wilkins and now the Sunnyledge Hotel. This combination house and office for society doctor James McClelland was completed in 1887 by H. H. Richardson's disciple, Alexander Longfellow Jr. In brick, it parallels the spatial envelope in which Richardson enwrapped two other brilliant homes in the same decade: one in wood for the Stoughton family in Cambridge, Massachusetts, and one in stone for the Glessner family in Chicago. At forty-nine thousand dollars, the McClelland home was quite inexpensive by Pittsburgh's millionaire standards, since William Thaw paid fifty times more for the house he put up farther east on Fifth Avenue in 1889. Still, it was expensive for the times; Theodore Roosevelt's contemporaneous Sagamore Hill on Long Island cost just one-third as much. The links between Sunnyledge and Richardson's Glessner house were discovered just a few years ago, when account books revealed that the balusters for both Sunnyledge and the Glessners' house came from the same batch of millwork (at a cost of one dollar apiece), since Richardson's heirs were completing both houses simultaneously after the master had died.

Shadyside also extends south of Fifth Avenue into several hamlets on the slopes of Squirrel Hill. One of these is Morewood Heights (known at other points in its history as Devonshire or Wilkins Heights), which is reached by narrow lanes off Wilkins, Forbes, and Beeler streets. Among the score of excellent homes on this private hilltop, the most lavish is the Howard Heinz house at 5090 Warwick Terrace, in Jacobean Revival Style from the 1920s. The most inventive home on this hillside is the small but brilliant Abraam Steinberg house at 5139 Penton Road at Dorset, uphill from Beeler. This is one of several score homes built in the Pittsburgh area in the interwar and postwar years by Peter Berndtson and Cornelia Brierley, two architects trained in the Taliesin Fellowship by Frank Lloyd Wright. The house, from 1952, integrates circles and rectangles as the two basic geometries of the design, which is centered on a wedge-shaped courtyard in the middle. It is fascinating to watch how Berndtson (and, in the conceptual stage at least, Brierly) inserted a sequence of ramps in the house, which parallel in a minor key the ramps that Wright was designing for his Guggenheim Museum project in New York in the same years. The Steinberg House stands on a sloping and heavily wooded site, its brick walls battered outward in close empathy with the land it sits on.

In the first years of the twentieth century, some of the Shadyside upper middle class moved into apartments, as they had a decade earlier in Oakland. Two of the best of these apartments, modern in style rather than the usual historicist design, were put up by Frederick Scheibler. One that everybody

sees but nobody stops to look at is his Minnetonka Apartments at 5425–5431 Walnut, at the corner of Copeland, from 1908. One of Scheibler's rare commercial buildings, it carries two floors of living quarters over its ground-floor shops. This is a svelte, complex design with a Classical bias but without a Classical vocabulary, and it mirrors Viennese work of the same period. Highly effective is the way the main entrance breaks from the straight façades into a half-cylinder, inviting shoppers inside. Walnut Street itself has been expressive of changing times, shifting from what had at first been a street of houses into modest storefronts and then, in the 1980s, into the current sequence of boutiques, restaurants, furniture stores, coffee shops, and boxy chain stores.

Half a dozen blocks to the east stands Scheibler's Highland Towers at 340–342 South Highland Avenue, from 1913. This four-story brick apartment building shows Scheibler's work at the point in his career when he was most influenced by Frank Lloyd Wright. The proportioning of the volumes and the decorative tiles on the surface certainly recall Wright. Like Wright, too, Scheibler was interested in the spareness of Japanese buildings, which he recalls in the broad fenestration of the central block. Along with these debts to Wright, there is a close connection between Scheibler and the Dutch architects of the Amsterdam school and the De Stijl movement. The strongly Expressionist and even Cubist aspects of Highland Towers never impinge on its functionality. Each floor contained four apartments (subdivided into smaller units today) of eight large rooms, including a room off the kitchen to house the maid.

Where did the other servants for Shadyside's mansions live? There is no need to guess, since accommodations built for servants—among other workers—are still being used as residences, which stand as two packed brick rows (now with some gaps) on both sides of the 5800 block of Pierce, between College and Maryland streets. The rows, with the wail of the trains immediately behind them, resemble the backstreet mews of London or the stoops of Baltimore, but updated: the stoops here are not made of marble but of concrete block.

The churches of Shadyside form a kind of visual parade, much as its mansions do. The one with the best visibility is Third Presbyterian, on Fifth and Negley. Third Presbyterian is a mountainous sandstone Gothic structure with a rush of pinnacles, and it gives the sensation of being an entire city in itself. Funding for this superbly rich building came in equal parts from Henry Clay Frick, who paid to have the congregation's Downtown church destroyed to make way for his William Penn Hotel, and from Josiah Thaw, whose notorious brother, Harry, entered into tumultuous matrimony with Evelyn Nesbit in this church on April 4, 1905. The church interior is alternately severe and rich, with its unplastered sandstone walls enframing some of the best stained glass in America. Represented here is the decorator Louis Comfort Tiffany; the fresco painter Kenyon Cox; and William Willett, one of the two Pittsburghers (the other was Charles Connick) who were central to the revival of Gothic-style stained glass in America.

A half mile to the west, at the corner of Amberson Avenue at Westminster Place, Shadyside Presbyterian Church rises massive and pyramidal in sandstone blocks that were black with soot for a century but are now snow white. Shadyside is a powerful restatement of Trinity Church in Boston, the early masterpiece of H. H. Richardson. This Pittsburgh variant by his disciples has much more ample windows than its Boston model, perhaps intended to catch whatever light was available from the dark sky over Pittsburgh a century ago. Both churches are cruciform in plan, their interiors supported by four powerful arches. Shadyside Presbyterian will remind West Coast residents of still another design by the same firm: the chapel at Stanford University.

Shady Avenue, the thoroughfare of eastern Shadyside, gave its name to the neighborhood because of its importance as the link to East Liberty to the north and to Squirrel Hill on the south. The homes in this area tend to be newer than those in central Shadyside and to a degree more exuberant, especially the Shingle-style house at 424 Denniston Avenue, at the corner of Kentucky, from 1892. The texturing of its dark brown shingles and the arbitrary mix of gable ends, porches, oriel windows, projecting bays, and a corner *tourelle* are most effective.

At the intersection of Shady and Walnut streets stand two more distinguished churches. The better known is Calvary Episcopal Church by Ralph Adams Cram, from 1907, a dramatic limestone pile in thirteenth-century English Gothic that also weaves in a half-dozen other historical periods. Calvary

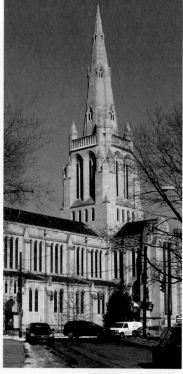

6.22
6.23   6.24
6.25

dominates its corner with the enormous block of the central crossing tower and a needle spire that is brutally but dynamically set atop it. The interior glass is inventive and casts a rich light on the rough texture of the timber roof and austere stone walls. Cram was forty-three years old when he completed Calvary, and it is a landmark of the mature period of his career.

The superbly preserved Francis Sellers (or Sellers-Carnahan) house, an 1858 Italianate villa at the same corner, served for generations as Calvary's rectory, but it has reverted to private ownership in recent years. The grounds are greatly curtailed from the ten acres Sellers began with but still convey a good sense of Shadyside when it was a rustic village.

It is worth noting that Sacred Heart Church, at the same intersection, is better related to its site than is Calvary and carries out some of Cram's objectives better than he did himself. One has the impression that Cram's design for Calvary, fine as it is, was mailed from Boston by someone who had only a haphazard knowledge of its intended placement, whereas for Sacred Heart, architect Carlton Strong appears to have sat pondering the site for days, like a painter before his easel. The two fine churches at the corner of Walnut and Shady have a third partner in the dynamic but less sophisticated Shady Avenue Christian Assembly (originally Shady Presbyterian Church) at 241 Shady Avenue, at the corner of Aurelia, from around 1890. This dramatically articulated Romanesque Revival–Queen Anne design incorporates some of the most vivid brickwork in the city.

Aurelia, the side street along this church, is a solid wall of elaborate Queen Anne homes. The writer Willa Cather, who contributed so much to literary Pittsburgh during her residency from 1896 to 1906, used Aurelia as the model for Cordelia Street in her short story "Paul's Case." Cather wrote of it, in some irony, "It was a highly respectable street, where all the houses were alike and where business men of moderate means begot and reared large families of children ... all of whom were as exactly alike as their homes."

Aurelia leads to the Village of Shadyside complex, which transformed a vacant nine-acre site into 215 housing units divided among sixty-seven townhouses and seven condominium blocks. The new townhouses, set between Penn Avenue and Aurelia itself, relate well to their Victorian prototypes and restore an urban density to an area that had lost it in earlier redevelopment schemes. The result is a nondialectical solution to the problem of creating instant tradition in architecture. The project could be called "Learning from Shadyside" (in the manner of Robert Venturi's *Learning from Las Vegas*) because it sums up the essence of an especially handsome residential colony.

fig. 6.26
TOWNHOUSES,
MURRAY HILL
AVENUE,
SQUIRREL HILL

SQUIRREL HILL AND GREENFIELD

Squirrel Hill is such a stereotypical bedroom community that one might expect little distinction in its architecture or its residents. But that would be a mistake, for beneath a conventional exterior, Squirrel Hill has always had an impressive roster of notables. Its famous residents have included Harry Thaw, Gene Kelly (his dance studio survives at 5824 Forbes Avenue), Jonas Salk, and five of the most important Mellons: A. W. and his son Paul; R. B. and his son Richard King Mellon; and Gulf founder William Larimer Mellon. The women of Squirrel Hill were even more impressive. Two were noted for literature and science: Willa Cather, who lived on Murray Hill Avenue around 1900 while teaching high school English, and the environmentalist Rachel Carson, who boarded in a Chatham University dormitory in the 1920s. Two other Squirrel Hill women were involved in sensational criminal cases: Evelyn Nesbit, the "girl in the red velvet swing," notorious for her entanglement in the murder of her former lover Stanford White by her husband, Harry Thaw; and the tragic heiress Sunny von Bülow, born in Shadyside as plain Martha Crawford. Two international socialites living in Squirrel Hill were famous simply for being famous: Perle Mesta and Marjorie Merriweather Post.

Squirrel Hill is a neighborhood of surprises. It has no significant history, yet it preserves two log houses from the eighteenth century and a cemetery in which American Indians are buried. It produces little of significant artistic or aesthetic value (witness the boring mural on lower Murray Avenue), but among its homes are designs by Walter Gropius, Richard Meier, and Robert Venturi. This largest and most populous Pittsburgh neighborhood (24,900 residents living on 2,500 acres) is tightly united though also sharply divided: north of Forbes Avenue lies its wealthy Scots-Irish and German-Jewish half; south of Forbes lies its middle- and working-class half of tiny rowhouses and kosher food shops and restaurants.

Squirrel Hill has a feature that is unique among Pittsburgh neighborhoods and a rare phenomenon anywhere: in a literal sense, it turned itself around. Today, Squirrel Hill "faces" north and west, toward the residential neighborhood of Shadyside and the college town of Oakland, respectively. But in the 1760s, what was a pioneer settlement of farmers and Indian traders faced south on the Monongahela River, toward what is now Homestead. Its center of activity was the present-day intersection of Brown's Hill Road and Beechwood Boulevard. Nearby, in what is now the 3400 block of Beechwood, John Turner staked out his estate, Federal Hill, in 1778,

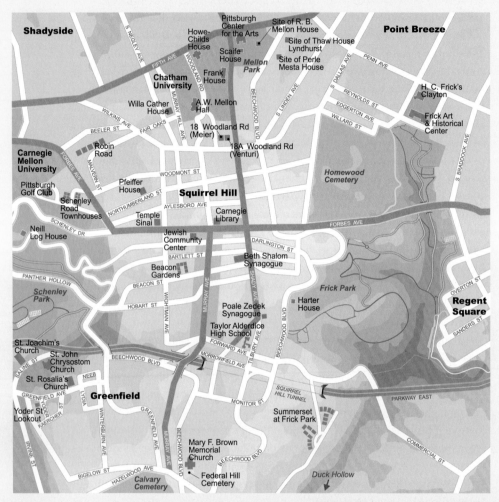

Squirrel Hill

including the cemetery that survives on Beechwood at Federal Hill Street. Also close by, at a sharp bend of Beechwood Boulevard, William "Killymoon" Stewart built a tavern in 1819 that hosted generations of travelers to Pittsburgh until it was destroyed after World War II. Because of its inaccessibility—only three minor lanes led uphill from Shadyside, Hazelwood, and the Monongahela shore—Squirrel Hill would remain estates and farms until late in the nineteenth century.

Two recent developments are once again pulling Squirrel Hill toward its roots on the Monongahela. One is positive in impact, the other negative. The positive change is the new housing estate, Summerset at Frick Park; the negative is the Waterfront, a jumbo shopping mall on the Monongahela River that has challenged Squirrel Hill's retail trade.

Squirrel Hill opened up to the north and west with the introduction of the electric trolley along Forbes and Murray avenues in 1893; it was basically a convenient stop on the way to the new industrial satellite of Homestead. The area became fashionable with the creation of Beechwood Boulevard a decade later, and it turned populous in the 1920s, when the Boulevard of the Allies linked it to the Golden Triangle. The trolley sparked the building of hundreds of large, nearly identical "cookie-cutter" homes for the middle managers of the steel companies, homes like those on Shady and Denniston avenues near Aylesboro. The opening of Beechwood Boulevard after 1903 encouraged the building of mansions on Squirrel Hill's eastern border, which became an extension of the millionaire row in Point Breeze. A bit later, thousands of new residents, mainly from Oakland and the Hill, moved into the modest rows of brick homes on the cross-streets of Murray Avenue, south of Forbes. By the 1930s, Squirrel Hill was filled; not more than a few score homes were built until the 1990s, when construction started up again.

fig. 6.27
HOMES FOR MIDDLE
MANAGERS,
DENNISTON AVENUE

Squirrel Hill is defined geographically as the area lying between Schenley and Frick parks and between Fifth Avenue and the Monongahela River. No one thinks of Squirrel Hill as a river town today because the south edge of the settlement declined in vigor as its west and north edges expanded toward Oakland and Shadyside.

The earliest land access to Squirrel Hill came through Shady Avenue, which ascends a hill just above Fifth Avenue. The neo-Georgian mansion of the Pittsburgh Center for the Arts gives Squirrel Hill a prominent visual point of entry at the corner of Fifth and Shady avenues. That mansion, the former Charles Marshall house, was donated in 1945 to what is now Pennsylvania's largest arts center, which holds classes, lectures, and exhibits. The center's auxiliary building is the former Alan and Sarah Scaife house, a Tudor Revival mansion of 1904 that was rebuilt in 1927 as a wedding present from Sarah Scaife's father, R. B. Mellon, whose own estate occupied the ten acres that now constitute Mellon Park, next door.

The Mellon house was probably the largest ever built in Pittsburgh: twenty-two servants maintained its organ, its sixty-five rooms, the Tiffany windows that are exhibited today in the Carnegie Museum of Art, the lavish marble that was later recut to provide altars for St. Peter's Church in New Kensington, and the stunning formal gardens. Richard B. Mellon built it in 1907; his son Richard King Mellon briefly lived there after his father died, then had it destroyed in 1941. An idea of the sumptuousness of the structure is provided by the surviving carriage house, the wrought-iron spiked fence by Samuel Yellin, and the remaining gardens. The terraced Renaissance garden was augmented in the late 1920s by the landscape architect Gilmore D. Clarke of New York, who returned to work in Pittsburgh twenty years later on the very different commission for Gateway Center. The Mellon house sat on its hillock with a bent axis that gave it the best possible sightlines on both Fifth Avenue and Beechwood Boulevard. In the 1930s, when R. B. Mellon held the purse strings for both the Cathedral of Learning and East Liberty Presbyterian Church construction projects (they interested him far more than they did his brother, A. W. Mellon), he could watch both those gigantic monuments going up from his bedroom window. This was perhaps the only viewpoint in Pittsburgh from which both buildings could be seen—and R. B. might have made that a condition of their design.

Pittsburgh's ruling class used to run motorcar races along the curves of Beechwood Boulevard as soon as that fine road was laid out in 1903; that activity might have been a condition of its design, too. Today, Beechwood is a pleasant street, even magnificent in stretches, but so many of its mansions are gone that it seems a promenade of architectural ghosts. One of the best was Beechwood Hall, home of civic leader William Nimick Frew, which from 1902 until the 1930s stood alongside the Mellon estate on Fifth Avenue. A good approximation of its grandeur survives in the ponderous neo-Georgian mansion inside a wrought-iron fence at 1054 Beechwood; this structure was evidently intended to house a Mellon relative or retainer. On the opposite side of Beechwood Boulevard, thirty-two modest postwar homes are crowded into the grounds that used to mark Lyndhurst, the mansion that railroading tycoon William Thaw Sr. built in 1889, the last year of his life.

The name Lyndhurst derived from a mansion built by Alexander Jackson Davis at Tarrytown, New York, that was purchased in 1880 by the railroad mogul Jay Gould. Pittsburgh's Lyndhurst was a huge Gothic mansion that spread over its hill and seemed to resemble a half-dozen different buildings glued together. Containing forty-two rooms, it cost $2.5 million—the same price as Richardson's courthouse and jail and ten times the cost of the eight-story German Savings and Deposit Bank on Sixth Avenue, Downtown.

The builder of Lyndhurst, William Thaw Sr., fathered ten children in two marriages. His offspring represented the best of the Pittsburgh industrial elite. Three of the boys—William Jr., Benjamin, and Josiah—were respected community leaders; one of the daughters became the Comtesse de Perigny and another, the Countess of Yarmouth. Although he inherited only a few million dollars of the family fortune, younger brother Harry obscured all the illustrious deeds of the clan when he murdered the prominent architect Stanford White in 1906.

William Thaw Sr.'s widow, Mary, lived at Lyndhurst until her death in 1929 (the legend that she bankrupted herself paying for Harry's legal defense is groundless). A slight impression of all of this estate's magnificence can be acquired today from a view of the powerful brick surrounding wall along Lyndhurst Drive, off Beechwood Boulevard. An intriguing Queen Anne miniature house with diamond-pane windows and a scalloped upper story at 1065 Lyndhurst Drive was the Thaw family playhouse; a part of their stables stands alongside, at 1071 Lyndhurst.

William Thaw was not the only builder on Beechwood Boulevard to die before he could enjoy his house. Several hundred yards uphill on Beechwood, the dead-end Beechwood Lane marks the grounds on which George and Perle Mesta constructed their immense limestone Neoclassical residence in 1925. George died the same year; Perle, who survived him by half a century, eventually sold it, and it survived another few decades as a Catholic retreat before it was torn down. The garage and caretaker's house still survive, as does the Mestas' current domicile, which is the Mesta mausoleum in nearby Homewood Cemetery.

Had decisions been made differently, the marvel of Squirrel Hill would have been Henry Clay Frick's art museum. Subconsciously, Frick never left Pittsburgh, and he lies buried with the Mestas and the Heinzes in Homewood Cemetery. By the time Frick took his paintings to New York in 1914, his art collection was so fine that only the king of England, the czar of Russia, and the princes of Hesse and Liechtenstein outdid him in private galleries, and only the National Gallery in London, the Louvre, and the Vatican among public museums could hold a candle to his assemblage. Until 1905, Frick intended to showcase his paintings in a museum that Daniel Burnham was designing for him on Beechwood Boulevard. Burnham made site plans and probably produced the fountain basin that survives just inside the Squirrel Hill entrance to Frick Park, at a sharp bend in Beechwood Boulevard, as well as the entrance pavilions. Instead, Frick left his anecdotes to Pittsburgh and his paintings to New York.

The termination of Frick's museum scheme and the destruction of the Mellon, Frew, Thaw, and Mesta houses make Beechwood Boulevard one of those nostalgia-filled, bittersweet corners of Pittsburgh. But what you can still see is impressive—a lively mix of Spanish Revival, Tudor, and Colonial Revival houses. An even better visual treat awaits on the campus of Chatham University, which stretches along Woodland Road between Fifth Avenue and Wilkins.

Immediately after the Civil War, a half-dozen related families of Pittsburgh's industrial elite built houses on the fifty-five forested acres that now serve as the Chatham campus. The families living on that land were joined there in 1869 by a woman's college (only the fourth such in America) that was the predecessor to Chatham University. It was here that Rachel Carson graduated with a bachelor of science degree in marine biology in 1929, before embarking on her pathbreaking career in ecology. Today, Chatham occupies a score of buildings; some it built for itself, while others are the Shingle-style mansions it inherited.

The oldest home on the Chatham campus is Willow Cottage, the Howe-Childs house on Fifth Avenue at Woodland. The university purchased and meticulously restored this clapboarded house of the late 1860s, but not before an unusual legal wrangle developed between the City of Pittsburgh and the family that then owned it and wished to destroy it; the owners lost.

The largest home in this vicinity is Andrew W. Mellon Hall, halfway up Woodland Road. The mansion was constructed in 1897 for the steel millionaire George Laughlin; A. W. Mellon tripled it in size twenty years later, employing his nephew E. P. Mellon as architect. What had been a *faux*-Tudor house now received trainloads of authentic Tudor and Jacobean work that had been retrieved from manor houses in England. Among the luxurious additions Mellon made to the house were a solarium, an all-aluminum office (including aluminum drapes, destroyed along with the rest of the metallic decor), and a bowling alley and swimming pool vaulted in Guastavino tile. Paul Mellon occupied the house for a few years after his father's death in 1937, then turned it over in 1941 to Chatham, which uses it for administrative offices.

What shocked Woodland Road residents in the late 1930s was not the death of A. W. Mellon but the construction in 1939–1940 of the avant-garde Frank house by Walter Gropius and Marcel Breuer, at 96 East Woodland. Gropius had just come to the United States to teach at Harvard, and the

Frank house was only his second building in America, the first being his own house at Lincoln, Massachusetts. Regarded as little more than a curiosity at the time, and generally overlooked today although it is one of the half-dozen major buildings of the International Style in the United States, the Frank house deserves a thorough investigation. What is fascinating in social terms about this modernistic house is how it functions in the same mode as the earlier mansions on Woodland. Just like the Mellon house, for example, it has a porte-cochère, an elaborate reception vestibule, salons and drawing rooms, servants' quarters, and an indoor swimming pool. The house also bears the clear imprint of its patrons, Robert and Cecilia Frank. They were close friends of Edgar and Liliane Kaufmann, and they had watched the building of Fallingwater from its inception. For the house on Woodland Road, Cecilia Frank ran the interior design, while her husband, an engineer, oversaw all aspects of construction. Robert Frank insisted that the house be welded (steel buildings were then typically riveted) so as not to disturb his neighbors with the sound of rivet hammers.

The Frank house sits on a thickly wooded rise and consists of three parts: the three-story entrance pavilion, a gently curved two-story bow window over a fieldstone base, and a long wing with a recessed porch and a projecting hangar for the swimming pool. It is a contradictory building by reason of its size, which links it to the nineteenth rather than to the twentieth century, and in the mix of materials: fieldstone, concrete, glass block, and stainless steel. Gropius and Breuer inserted some eloquent passages in its façade, like the concrete stair reinforcement (a pure piece of Cubist sculpture), but its industrial hardness makes it problematic as a human habitation even now, decades after it was built.

One can usefully contrast Gropius's Frank house with the Frank Giovanitti house, which the famed architect Richard Meier (best known for the Getty Center) designed in 1983 with a Neo-International Style vocabulary at 118 Woodland Road, near Wilkins. The house, which received global praise, is a Cubist theorem that glistens in pure white stucco and porcelain-clad steel panels. It creates an extension of its hillside with a grassy patio that masks the garage underneath. An isolated gateway points across this patio to the public rooms of the house, with private accommodations on two levels above and below.

At exactly the same moment, Robert Venturi, the prophet of populist architecture, was putting up the Betty and Irving Abrams house right behind, at 118A Woodland Road. Venturi's response to the hilly site was to yield to nature, rather than to synthesize human and natural forms, as Meier did.

fig. 6.28
FRANK HOUSE

fig. 6.29
GIOVANITTI HOUSE

fig. 6.30
HOUSE WHERE
WILLA CATHER
LIVED, 1180 MURRAY
HILL AVENUE

fig. 6.31
ABRAMS HOUSE,
SQUIRREL HILL

He set the house over a creek that ran through the old estate. Allusion to the creek possibly shaped the form of the house, which resembles a mammoth paddlewheel digging itself out of a trough. The structure is clad in green and white wooden clapboards, enamel panels, and stucco. The cacophony of materials and its irregular fenestration and profile make an unforgettable contrast to Meier's Cartesian purity next door. Venturi disavowed the house after several tussles with Betty Abrams, but later, seeing it constantly cited as one of his masterpieces in domestic design, he embraced it.

Bordering the Chatham University campus on the west, and accessible through a side outlet of Woodland Road, stands an ample Colonial Revival house at 1180 Murray Hill Avenue, where Murray Hill meets Fair Oaks. From 1901 to 1906, the writer Willa Cather lived there as a guest of the family of Judge Samuel McClung. The seven years that Cather spent teaching and editing a magazine in Pittsburgh were especially fruitful in her development as a writer, and Cather reciprocated by giving Pittsburgh a prominent role in her short stories of these years. To honor this good feeling, for many years a group of Cather devotees met to dine in this house each December 7, her birthday. Murray Hill Avenue would be a fine street even without Cather's historic presence, however; its charm is considerably enhanced by the irregularities that have developed over the years in its Belgian block roadbed, and it boasts a lovely sequence of speculator Queen Anne houses with eyebrow dormers in the manner of H. H. Richardson.

Fair Oaks, at right angles to Murray Hill Avenue, is a good representative of the prosperous interwar period in Squirrel Hill. West of its intersection with Wilkins Avenue, the street enters the Murdoch Farms district, which was dairyland until the early twentieth century. The most interesting homes here are five Cotswold-style houses grouped together on Robin Road, a private lane that opens off Fair Oaks near its juncture with Malvern Avenue. All five were built in the late 1920s by Benno Janssen and William Cocken on a precipitous slope that descends toward Beeler Street, with special emphasis on the slate roofs and the textured walls of stone and brick.

The homes in Squirrel Hill are somewhat less venturesome than contemporary houses in Shadyside or Highland Park, but still interesting. The Renaissance-style Marcus Aaron house at 5564 Aylesboro Avenue, at the corner of Wightman, stands close to a massive three-story Roman brick mansion at 5605 Aylesboro that somehow meshes the progressive Prairie School with the regressive Colonial Revival. A half block down the slope, the English-style Louis Kingsbaker house at 5530 Aylesboro is an accomplished building in the Voysey manner, with an exaggerated chimney that terminates in an obelisk.

There are a few modern houses in the district, too. The Speyer house at the corner of Wightman and Northumberland is a Miesian block in cool gray brick, glass, and steel that Mies's Pittsburgh-born associate, A. James Speyer, designed in 1963 for his mother. Standing out a good deal more violently from its older neighbors is the Pfeiffer house at 5553 Northumberland, near Wightman. It was constructed in 1982 by Arthur Lubetz, who made obvious reference to Gropius's nearby Frank house with his use of industrial materials such as stainless steel and aluminum siding (the house was built for an Alcoa executive). The house is split in two by its steps, by its windows, and by its main chimney, so that its appearance is not structural but antistructural. While most buildings emphasize what holds them together, this one proposes an architectural entropy that makes one reflect on structure both in architecture and in domestic life.

If the Pfeiffer house constitutes a metaphorical split, around the corner one finds a literal split in the Myler house, by the celebrated Bertram Grosvenor Goodhue, as it is now divided into two separate homes at 1331 and 1333 Bennington Avenue. When Mary Dennison Myler gave this commission to Goodhue in 1921, he provided a long wing to meet both her needs and those of her daughter's family. This dual purpose created the fault line along which the building was cut in 1980, when no one wanted anything that big.

Schenley Park, across Forbes Avenue from Murdoch Farms, was the setting for the Pittsburgh Golf Club in 1896 and for the beautifully articulated Jefferson-style portico for the 1905 addition. Then protests arose against a private club's use of a public park, and a second golf clubhouse went up closer to Forbes. On the way to the club stand sixty-two neo-Georgian townhouses that have been packed, a little too energetically, in the Schenley Road development at the dead end of Northumberland Street. The construction of this housing complex was the most radical change in the topography of Squirrel Hill in the half century before the creation of Summerset at Frick Park. Two mansions had occupied the site; the larger was the seven-acre estate of the retailer Nathaniel Spear, which comprised a fine house by Henry Hornbostel and a Japanese garden with ponds and a picturesque bridge. Several proposals for high-rise condominiums had been defeated by the neighbors, who only reluctantly accepted this instant imitation of London's Downing Street. The result is inferior in imagination to the Village of Shadyside and can scarcely be compared with Chatham Village two generations ago, but it represents a general victory for neighborhood self-determination.

Schenley Park preserves two affecting relics of pioneer days in Pittsburgh. One survivor is the Robert Neill log house in the Schenley Park golf course, on Serpentine Drive. The assumption once was that this house was from the

1780s, but deed research at Carlisle (seat of Cumberland County, which at the time encompassed all of western Pennsylvania) now points to a construction date in 1769. The builder was Ambrose Newton; Robert Neill purchased the house in 1774. Living about five miles from the Point, the five members of the Neill family were taking their lives in their hands every time they stepped out of this doorway. The *Pittsburgh Gazette* for July 2, 1789, for example, carried the news that two young men who had gone fishing two miles from the Point were killed by Indians.

About a half-mile away, between Schenley Park's tennis courts and its swimming pool, stands a second log house associated with Ambrose Newton, on Overlook Drive. This house probably also dates from the 1760s or 1770s. The Neill house is the more interesting of the two log houses, however, and consists of massive wooden planks infilled with mud and small fieldstones. The logs (faithful replicas, in the main) are notched at the ends and show the marks of the adze that hewed them. Internally, the building is a single room with an attic loft.

fig. 6.32
NEILL LOG HOUSE,
SCHENLEY PARK

Forbes Avenue is the main thoroughfare between Schenley and Frick parks, but Beacon Street also links the two. Beacon is the continuation of Boulevard of the Allies out of Schenley Park, and both its name (from the Brahmin outpost in Boston) and width suggest that it was expected to develop into a neighborhood of great mansions. It ended up instead more like a failed Beechwood Boulevard, for the most part lined with ordinary middle-class houses. Something very good lies in the midst of this mediocrity, and that is Beacon Gardens at 5635–5663 Beacon, near Wightman. These simple linked units in common industrial brick went up to a design by Frederick Scheibler in 1914. Each of these perfect little houses is enlivened inside by exquisite natural lighting and detailing in the best Craftsman Style.

A half-block east, Beacon intersects Murray Avenue, a commercial district that continues around the corner on Forbes. The appeal of the dozens of food stores that make a hillside market out of Murray Avenue is strictly gastronomic; the stores themselves offer little of visual interest, although the layering of buildings that has taken place in the last two generations is often instructive. The storefront that houses twin restaurants at 2120 Murray Avenue, for example, seems at first glance to be nondescript. But if one looks above the storefront, one can see that the property began life around World War I as a Tudor-style mansion. In the 1930s, the neighborhood changed so drastically that a moderne storefront was built into the hillside in front of the house. The storefront was given a Miesian remodeling in the 1950s, when thousands of customers shopped at what was then the Bageland store. The moderne ornament was given a regilding (unfortunately already faded) when the structure was split in two around 2000, so almost a century of change is now visible just at that one address.

Shady Avenue, parallel to Murray, carries three large structures from the 1920s that are more typical of "monumental" architecture. The first of these is the Taylor Allderdice High School from 1927, whose columnar Classical bulk dominates the intersection of Shady and Forward avenues for motorists using Shady to enter Squirrel Hill from Downtown. (A later athletic facilities building dilutes what was once a dramatic impact.) Uphill, Poale Zedek Synagogue also takes advantage of prominent sightlines as it looks down at motorists entering the intersection of Shady and Tilbury avenues. A few more blocks up Shady, the same towering effect comes from Beth Shalom Synagogue at the intersection of Shady and Beacon, one of the highest peaks in the city.

For the most part, the dozen other synagogues in Squirrel Hill are more modest in ambition. Many, like Young Peoples Synagogue at 6401 Forbes, at the corner of Denniston, are ingenious adaptations of Tudor Revival mansions from the 1920s or earlier. The most impressive of the house-synagogues is Temple Sinai, at the intersection of Forbes and Murdoch. This was the mansion built for the oilman John Worthington just before World War I, to which the congregation added a modernist wing in the 1960s. Beautifully preserved is the Worthingtons' garden, which the landscape historian Barry Hannegan has linked to a 1904 garden design by Sir Edwin Lutyens for the English estate Hestercombe, in Somerset. Grand or modest, these houses that became houses of worship all over Squirrel Hill mix, and hence reinforce, the special qualities of both domestic and ecclesiastical architecture.

The central focus of Squirrel Hill is the intersection of Forbes and Murray, where one finds the colorful brick Jewish Community Center, with its engaging Hebrew-lettered clock tower; the severe stone pile of Sixth Presbyterian Church, from the 1890s; and the prima donna of the neighborhood, the Squirrel Hill branch of Carnegie Library. The library was established in 1972 on the second floor of a building that housed a bank on its ground floor. When Arthur Lubetz redesigned it in 2006, he tore out the front courtyard—a gracious idea that had not worked—and projected a glazed lobby over the walls of the old space. Hundreds of patrons who never knew the library existed flocked to use it, with the 75 percent increase in usership making it the busiest unit in the citywide system. The experience is both high-tech, in the raised floor system that allows perpetual upgrades to the computer banks, and old-fashioned, in the leisurely manner in which users locate books in alcoves rather

fig. 6.33
POALE ZEDEK
SYNAGOGUE,
SQUIRREL HILL

fig. 6.34
TAYLOR ALLDERDICE
HIGH SCHOOL

fig. 6.35
WATER GARDEN AT
TEMPLE SINAI,
SQUIRREL HILL

fig. 6.36
CARNEGIE LIBRARY,
SQUIRREL HILL

than stacks and then (if they wish) squeeze into window boxes to read them, like Alice in Wonderland in her gargantuan phase.

The last stretch of Beacon Street, uphill from Murray, climbs to the peak of Beacon Hill, some five hundred feet above the Monongahela River, then ends beyond Shady Avenue in a rich colony of houses that includes Rosewall, a neo-Georgian block at 6530 Beacon where heiress Marjorie Merriweather Post lived in the 1950s and 1960s with her fourth husband, Pittsburgher Herbert May.

A few blocks downhill, Beacon intersects Beechwood Boulevard at Homewood Cemetery. This, Pittsburgh's second most prestigious burial ground, was carved from William Wilkins's 650-acre estate. The cemetery layout dates from 1878; the entrance complex is from 1923. In Homewood's 205 shaded acres are buried H. J. Heinz I, II, and III, H. C. Frick and his daughter, Helen, the musician Erroll Garner, the photographer Charles "Teenie" Harris, baseball great Harold "Pie" Traynor, the Mestas, and a score of Mellons. The collective cenotaph for the Frick family was personally designed in 1905 by Daniel Burnham for Henry Clay Frick. Many of the deceased lie in fine mausolea with Tiffany windows. Pittsburgh's most astute collector of modern art, G. David Thompson, was also buried here, in 1958, and a stainless-steel cast of Constantin Brancusi's *Bird in Space* (1924) was commissioned in 1961 to stand tall above the grave. Sadly, Thompson and Pittsburgh lost that fine part of his legacy when the Brancusi piece was hacked off in an act of vandalism in 1990.

The last stretch of Beechwood Boulevard winds about two miles from Homewood Cemetery toward the Monongahela. A half-mile from the cemetery, past the fine pavilions at the entrance to Frick Park, stands the Harter house at 2557 Beechwood, near Forward, built in 1923 and one of the best of Frederick Scheibler's attempts at organic architecture, complete with pseudo-thatched roof.

An overlook opposite 3024 Beechwood, farther south, seems to have been specifically located to give a dramatic view of the steelworks that then stood on the far bank of the Monongahela at Homestead. Three-quarters of a mile beyond, Beechwood curves back on itself and enters the district that, two centuries ago, was covered by John Turner's Federal Hill estate. This area is home to the oldest congregation in Squirrel Hill: the Mary S. Brown Memorial Methodist Church, at the corner of Beechwood and Federal Hill Street. The church serves as custodian to the cemetery next door, with its Indian graves and recollections of the early pioneers—an almost unimaginable step back in time.

fig. 6.37
HOMEWOOD
CEMETERY

Another half-mile toward the Monongahela, Beechwood splits, with the right-hand side becoming Brown's Hill Road, which in turn splits, the left segment becoming Old Brown's Hill Road, one of two entrances to Summerset at Frick Park. (An alternate entrance is reached via Beechwood and Commercial Avenue.) This part of Squirrel Hill is the newest, and the most ambitious housing estate in Pittsburgh in decades has taken shape on the most unlikely of sites: the Brown's Hill slag heap. From 1922 to 1982, the blast furnaces across the Monongahela in Homestead dumped their slag there.

The Urban Redevelopment Authority purchased the slag dump in 1997 in order to build 710 single-family homes, townhouses, and luxury or medium-range apartments. The project was named Summerset after the estate Colonel James Burd patented on the site by in 1760. The project has radically trans-formed the hillside above Nine Mile Run, which separates Squirrel Hill from the neighborhood of Swisshelm Park. So far, none of the homes have sunk into the slag (which was artificially hardened), and the various firms design-ing the houses have exercised generally good judgment in offering some variety in terms of placement, footprint, colors, materials, and finishes. As in Pittsburgh's parallel "instant neighborhoods" on the Hill, the South Side, and Washington's Landing, there is something a bit bizarre in the forced old-fashionedness of all the lawns and porches, as if building sets for *Ozzie and Harriet* or *Leave It to Beaver*. Interestingly, Summerset's homes have no backyards. The focus groups assembled by the planners acknowledged that Squirrel Hill backyards were almost never used, so Summerset omitted them.

Another surprise awaits on Old Brown's Hill Road: the tiny community of Duck Hollow, the most sequestered of all of Pittsburgh's neighborhoods. After a few twists and turns and a bridge over the mouth of Nine Mile Run,

fig. 6.38
SUMMERSET AT
FRICK PARK

fig. 6.39
GREENFIELD

Old Brown's Hill Road leads into this tiny settlement, which is bounded by a grass-covered section of the slag heap, an indeterminate hillside, some railroad tracks, and the Monongahela riverbank. The neighborhood's informal greeting tableau consists of plastic swans, presumably more socially elevated than a line of ducks. The twenty or so houses make up a patchwork—each is actually a different color—of homes and families that have banded together to keep their community alive. Another twist of the road brings one at last to the Monongahela, the font from which Squirrel Hill sprang. One is so far from Pittsburgh at this point that the amateur anglers on the banks could be fishing in the Mississippi, the Thames, or the Seine, were it not for the bulk of the Homestead Grays Bridge and the signs on the public trashcans that exhort everyone to keep Squirrel Hill litter free.

On a map, Greenfield looks nearly identical to Hazelwood because it shares with that more barren district the shape of a curved triangle formed by the Parkway, Beechwood Boulevard, Brown's Hill Road, and a deep bend in the Monongahela. But Greenfield is topographically indivisible from Squirrel Hill. It began as one of the several summer colonies to which rich Pittsburghers would flee to catch breezes off the Monongahela, and a scattering of farmhouses and Queen Anne mansions still dots its slopes. Overwhelmingly, however, Greenfield's homes date from the explosive growth of the steel industry after the Civil War, and several thousand of them are proudly maintained by their Italian-, Irish-, and Russian-descent owners.

The community's arterial roadway is Greenfield Avenue, a former trolley line that, with certain permutations, links Greenfield to neighboring Squirrel Hill and Hazelwood and to the distant Golden Triangle. The more inaccessible slopes of Greenfield were covered with houses only in the 1950s, when the Eliza Furnaces and the Jones & Laughlin coke works at Hazelwood were still going full blast. In those years, Greenfield Avenue had not one but two movie theaters. What better evidence of a golden age could there be?

At the midpoint of Greenfield Avenue's steep descent to the Mon stands St. Rosalia's Church, at the corner of Greenfield Avenue and Lydia. This modern adaptation of Romanesque Style is set back on its own piazza, which creates a fine sense of theater for a mainly Italian-origin parish. The interior is a single cavernous barrel vault covered in fresco, as an Italian church ought to be. Behind the church stands the Greenfield Elementary School of 1923, another of the Kiehnel and Elliott partnership's striking early-modern designs.

Greenfield is built like a two-horned pyramid, which creates extraordinary views from almost every street. From Bigelow Street, Winterburn, or an ironically named alley called Parade, the Downtown skyscrapers come into sharp focus, though they are five miles away. There are no more steelworks to be seen upriver and downriver on the Mon, and the nighttime glow they cast is gone as well, but on Yoder Street one is rewarded with a thrilling panorama across Schenley Park into Oakland.

In terms of the local topography, Greenfield Hill is unusual in having those two peaks rather than one. The peaks seem to hail each other from a distance, and anyone who stands at the top of Hoosac Street or Coleman Avenue has the odd sensation of viewing a neighborhood from within. These internal views vividly convey the depth of feeling in Pittsburgh's insular neighborhoods. In the predecessor to this volume, I observed that young urban professionals had not yet discovered Greenfield. Today they have, and Greenfield is filling up with young twenty-somethings enjoying the convenience of city living without the pain of Squirrel Hill rents or Shadyside mortgages.

Behind St. Rosalia's one can look a hundred feet down to the community known as the Run, or Russian Valley. The first name comes from nature: this is the end of Four Mile Run, named for the stream so powerful in eons past that it carved out a great hollow between Oakland and Squirrel Hill. The second name, Russian Valley, comes from a misunderstanding of the name Ruska Dolina (Rusyn Valley), because the uphill Greenfielders mistook the resident ethnic Carpatho-Ruthenians, or Rusyns, for Russians.

Today, Big Jim's Restaurant, the social center of the Run, and several score frame houses still spread out vividly under the Swinburne Street and Parkway bridges. One of the two churches in the Run, the tiny wooden St. Joachim's on Boundary Street at Four Mile Run Road, still serves a Polish and Slovak community. The second shrine, St. John Chrysostom Byzantine Catholic Church, at the intersection of Saline Street and Anthony, was built in the 1930s by Rusyn immigrants. Its triple-barred gold crosses sparkle over the I-376 expressway that invaded this quiet valley in the 1950s. What draws curiosity-seekers to St. John Chrysostom church is the knowledge that Andy Warhol was once part of its congregation. Warhol was baptized in 1928 in a predecessor church, but every week he would walk over the Swinburne Street Bridge, down Greenfield Avenue, and devotedly worship here. Some art historians claim it was the gorgeously frescoed walls that inspired Warhol to become, after Picasso, the most influential artist of the twentieth century.

317

fig. 6.40
THE RUN,
GREENFIELD

fig. 6.41
ST. JOHN
CHRYSOSTOM
CHURCH

OAKLAND: THE NERVE CENTER OF EDUCATION AND CULTURE

fig. 7.1
Aerial view of
Oakland with
Downtown
in the distance

Pittsburgh has not just one vital center but two: the Golden Triangle, at the meeting of the three great rivers; and Oakland, cradled on a high plateau three miles to the east. The nerve center of education and culture for western Pennsylvania, Oakland fills to overflowing a tight wedge of land a mile long and roughly a quarter of a mile wide. It is sharply cut off from the rest of Pittsburgh by the gullies of Junction and Panther hollows to the east, the flatlands by the Monongahela River to the south, and Herron Hill to the north and west.

Oakland's seven hundred crowded acres contain three universities, a dozen hospitals, and thousands of students, but it is far more than a college town. It represents an attempt at the end of the nineteenth century to create a new face for Pittsburgh when the city had so decayed that it required a shimmering alter ego miles away. The giants of Pittsburgh industry and culture focused on Oakland for only two decades, from 1890 to 1910, but those were the crucial years in which many American cities rebuilt themselves in the spirit of the "City Beautiful" movement in urban planning and the Beaux-Arts Style in architecture. For Pittsburgh, these were also years of judgment, if not years of atonement, when the city was targeted by the muckraker Lincoln Steffens and by the six-volume *Pittsburgh Survey* as the most corrupt and socially repressive city in the United States. Pittsburgh's civic leaders responded to those attacks not by eradicating their severe social problems but by creating Oakland.

The limestone terraces that form the Oakland plateau were settled in successive waves. The first settlement began after the Penn family sold the 5,766-acre Manor of Pittsburgh in the 1780s and 1790s. A generation later, the healthful climate of this farmland district became a refuge for several score wealthy families who sought to flee the cholera epidemics that swept the Golden Triangle in the 1830s. More gentry abandoned Downtown after the Great Fire of 1845, but industrialization followed them to Oakland with the inauguration of the Jones & Laughlin mill in south Oakland, in 1859. The district's annexation to Pittsburgh followed a decade later.

Oakland might have become one of the crowded but colorful worker neighborhoods of Pittsburgh, comparable to Bloomfield or Lawrenceville, had it not been for a woman who clung to its past and four men who fashioned its future. The woman was the heiress Mary Schenley; the men were Andrew Carnegie, the developer Franklin Felix Nicola, the designer Henry Hornbostel, and the educator John Bowman. Born in 1826, Mary Elizabeth Croghan Schenley was barely out of her teens when she inherited hundreds of acres of choice land in central Pittsburgh that her grandfather James O'Hara started to amass before the Revolutionary War.

Although she owned so much of it, Mary Schenley did not choose to live in Pittsburgh. At fifteen, she eloped with a captain in the British army who was twice widowed and three times her age. She passed the remaining sixty-two years of her life in England and France, and when she died in 1903, she had not set foot in Pittsburgh for forty years. But she remained loyal to the city of her birth, and in 1889, Schenley gave four hundred acres to create Schenley Park as the eastern boundary of Oakland.

The decisive move in the creation of Beaux-Arts Oakland was made the next year, when Andrew Carnegie siphoned off ten acres of Schenley Park for construction of his library, museum, and music hall. Carnegie quadrupled the size of the complex in 1907, and the Scaife, Mellon, Bruce, Hillman, Heinz, and other endowments enlarged it again with the addition or restoration of a dozen galleries between 1974 and 2007.

Carnegie's patronage of Oakland was a challenge to other industrial leaders to endow the area with buildings of equal magnificence. Had the city's exhibition hall moved to Oakland from the Golden Triangle, as almost happened, Oakland would have become the dominant city center.

No planning document survives for what one might call the invention of Oakland, and probably none was ever drawn up, but there is one tantalizing record of its two main visionaries conversing about how to shape it. The *Pittsburgh Post* of May 9, 1890, reported that Andrew Carnegie made his way up Herron Hill (as the Oakland end of the Hill was called), and there, like Moses gazing over the Promised Land, he selected the site of his future library. Sharing that moment with Carnegie was the city's public works director, Edward Manning Bigelow, who had also ascended the mountain, along with other politicians and civic worthies.

The program for Oakland was straightforward: create a civic center commensurate with the city's wealth. This goal derived from a subtle rivalry with the World Columbian Exposition, which was held over a six-month period in Chicago in 1893 and which was announced in April 1890, just before Carnegie and Bigelow climbed Herron Hill. The Chicago world's fair took America by storm in its lavishness, its bold planning, and the grandeur of its replicas of imperial Roman buildings. In 1894, Carnegie published his analysis of the fair in *Engineering Magazine* as "Value of the World's Fair to the American People." It requires no great stretch of the imagination to assume that he intended Carnegie Institute to act as a perpetual fair for art and natural history. Carnegie's partner, Henry Phipps, created a huge flower conservatory in 1893 that was not only the symbolic successor to Horticultural Hall at the Chicago fair but a shelter for many of the plants that had been on view there. Plus, the campus of the Carnegie Technical Schools (now Carnegie Mellon) was built between 1903 and 1922 in the shape of the Chicago fair's midway. Thus did the buildings and streets of Oakland concretize the vision of a more glorious America that had been fleetingly raised in Chicago.

The man who effected the transformation of Mary Schenley's cowfields into Pittsburgh's "City Beautiful" was Franklin Felix Nicola (1860–1938). A wealthy Clevelander from a Revolutionary-era dynasty (German in origin despite the Italian name), Nicola sought to create in Pittsburgh a suburb-in-a-city parallel to what was being achieved in Cleveland Heights. He acquired some of Mary Schenley's land while the heiress was still alive, and on it in 1898 he opened the Schenley Hotel. Carnegie, Henry Clay Frick, A. W. Mellon, George Westinghouse, and H. J. Heinz were among the hotel's shareholders. The hotel survives in superb condition, renovated to serve as the University of Pittsburgh's student union.

In 1905, Nicola's Schenley Land Company bought the remaining Oakland portions of the Schenley estate, and Nicola laid out a model city with a separate character for each of its four quarters. The residential quarter (Schenley Farms) accommodated ninety-six houses on one level, with another thirty-nine on a terrace above. The educational quarter began taking shape in 1908, originally as a vast Acropolis-like scheme for the University of Pittsburgh, proposing scores of magnificent buildings to be ranged along the brow of Oakland Hill (which is actually Herron Hill but ever since 1920 or so has been called Oakland Hill). The monumental quarter eventually housed the Soldiers and Sailors Memorial Hall and Museum and a half-dozen other civic institutions, while the social quarter produced headquarters for a half-dozen private clubs or interest groups.

With the exception of the two university campuses (Nicola was not involved with Carnegie Mellon), monumental Oakland was largely complete by 1910, and it was magnificent. It is best represented today by the twenty blocks of Fifth Avenue from Rodef Shalom Temple (discussed earlier, as part of Shadyside), past St. Paul Cathedral, Mellon Institute, the Cathedral of Learning, the Soldiers and Sailors Memorial and the hospitals, and concluding with Carlow University.

Some structures have been lost since Carnegie and Nicola's time, above all Forbes Field, but others—in the case of the medical sector, too many others—have gone up in their place. But Oakland's growth has come with a price, as numerous residential streets have been gobbled up by charitable institutions. Still, there has been a resurgence of the "people's Oakland" in recent years, with the revitalization of Craig Street into a funky and eclectic dining and shopping district, the reclamation of Schenley Plaza from parking lot to green space, and the opening of restaurants serving international foods in south Oakland. The four founding fathers and the mother of Oakland would certainly be surprised and at times dismayed to see what the district is today, but in its general lines it has become what they envisioned: one of the prime civic centers in the nation.

THE UNIVERSITY OF PITTSBURGH

Most Pittsburghers see Oakland as a college town in the midst of the city. Carnegie Mellon and Carlow University mark the eastern and western limits of this town, respectively. At its heart are encamped the fifty thousand students and employees of the University of Pittsburgh and its affiliated hospitals. The university was born Downtown in 1787 as the Pittsburgh Academy; only after several changes of name and site did it settle on Franklin Felix Nicola's forty-three acres in Oakland, in 1908. Along the way, the university took care to educate Thomas Mellon and his sons Andrew and Richard, who would later reward it with major funding for the Cathedral of Learning.

Today an acclaimed research institution, the University of Pittsburgh is noted for strong departments in the humanities and the natural and social sciences. Its faculty innovations include heavier-than-air aircraft before the Wright brothers, the Salk polio vaccine, synthetic insulin, and pioneer heart and liver transplants. The university's endowment is measured in billions; it outdraws Harvard and Stanford in federal research funding, ranking sixth in funding from the National Institutes of Health. *The Top American Research Universities* numbers the university in an equal-rank cluster of the top seven public research facilities in the country.

The university's fifty major buildings on 132 acres constitute a pleasant and sometimes beautiful campus, but with Forbes and Fifth avenues running through it, it is resolutely urban. For a variety of reasons, it abandoned the 1908 "Acropolis" project of Henry Hornbostel, which called for one of the more dramatic college settings anywhere. The scheme was one more manifestation of the overreaching ambition of early twentieth-century Pittsburgh to have the biggest and most dramatic of everything. It called for sixty buildings to rise in terraces several hundred feet up Oakland Hill, whose brow would have been crowned by a full-scale reproduction of the Forum of Trajan in Rome. (Instead, the Veterans Affairs Medical Center has been standing on the summit since the 1950s.) Giant escalators were planned to move students up and down the hill. In addition to its ancient prototypes in Athens and Rome, the campus project followed two newer models: the World's Fair at Chicago in 1893 and the winning scheme in 1897 for the *premier grand prix* at Paris's École des Beaux-Arts, when architect Hornbostel was still in attendance there. The project might seem outrageous to us today, until one recalls that it was abandoned in favor of the still more preposterous Cathedral of Learning.

The university had built only a few of the planned scores of Greco-Roman buildings in the Acropolis scheme when John Bowman (1877–1962) was appointed university chancellor in 1921 (he served through 1945). Bowman effectively killed that scheme when he decided to put up just one structure—one that would be the most extravagant college building in the world. A native midwesterner, Bowman came to Pittsburgh in the same year that Bertram Grosvenor Goodhue began to build the Nebraska state capitol in Lincoln as a towering beacon rising four hundred feet over midwestern cornfields. Bowman needed a building of comparable brilliance to exalt the importance of the University of Pittsburgh over an industrial landscape that had little use for education. (It was a prophetic move, since the decline of steel in Pittsburgh has made the university and its medical center offspring the city's largest employers.) Bowman found the answer to his quest in the Cathedral of Learning. Originally projected to rise fifty-two stories, the Cathedral would have been the tallest building in Pittsburgh and the second-tallest skyscraper in the world, after Manhattan's Woolworth Building.

To realize his astonishing vision, Bowman needed a site and an architect. The Mellons provided the former, in fourteen acres of prime land at the heart of Oakland that had been owned by H. C. Frick. The choice of designer fell on Charles Klauder, a Philadelphian who had assisted James Gamble Rogers in planning the Gothic dormitories at Yale and then worked independently for Princeton. Bowman's memoirs record that he passed over Ralph Adams Cram because he was too fussy and Bertram Grosvenor Goodhue because he was dying. Edward Purcell Mellon (a secure pipeline to Mellon money) served briefly as Bowman's architect until the two had a falling out.

There had never been such a tall education building before, although the Université de Montréal later came close, and Stalin's Moscow State University topped it. Klauder was obliged to choose his prototypes from a disparate lot. What Beaux-Arts architects called the *parti* (the basic building image) derived from the Harkness Tower at Yale, on which he had assisted Rogers. To this he added elements from the plan and elevation of Goodhue's Nebraska state capitol and from the winning and runner-up entries to the *Chicago Tribune* tower competition of 1922. Undoubtedly influential, too, was Cass Gilbert's Woolworth Building in New York, for its deft handling of scale, its so-called modern Gothic Style, and even its nickname, the "Cathedral of Commerce." By 1925, the Art Deco Style had arrived from Paris, and this new style also left a strong imprint on Klauder's design, particularly in the aluminum strips between the windows. Aluminum was always a good thing to include in a Mellon-financed building; R. B. Mellon had a model of the Cathedral cast in it.

Chancellor Bowman unveiled his spectacular progeny in 1925 as the "Tower of Learning," but John McMahon, a Scots-born draftsman in Klauder's studio, muttered instead that it was a "Cadral of Larnin'," and the name stuck. The steel framework was begun in 1926, and work continued through October 1929, just days before the stock market crashed. To ensure that the building would not be truncated in the Depression, Bowman ordered the four floors of the base left bare of stonework until the full height of the building was reached. Some seventeen thousand adult Pittsburghers and ninety-seven thousand schoolchildren (who gave their dimes in exchange for fancy certificates) contributed to the project, which reached completion inside and out in 1937.

Frank Lloyd Wright was partially accurate when he scorned the Cathedral as "the world's largest keep-off-the-grass sign." In functional terms, the building never worked well, and it was increasingly turned into administrative offices.

fig. 7.2
CATHEDRAL OF
LEARNING,
SYMBOLIC HEART
OF THE UNIVERSITY
OF PITTSBURGH

fig. 7.3
COMMONS ROOM,
CATHEDRAL
OF LEARNING

fig. 7.4
CHINESE NATIONALITY
ROOM, CATHEDRAL
OF LEARNING

fig. 7.5
IRISH NATIONALITY
ROOM, CATHEDRAL
OF LEARNING

In the sense of providing an urban ambiance, however, the Cathedral is a triumph. The forty-two-story, 535-foot elevation can be monotonous when seen head on, despite the setbacks and Gothic tracery, but when seen obliquely on Fifth or Forbes avenues from the east (the routes A. W. and R. B. Mellon took from their homes in Squirrel Hill), the composition sparkles with corner pinnacles that bud, bloom, and vanish into thin air.

Yet this aesthetic success was only secondary to Bowman, whose objective in building the Cathedral was to dominate the whole of Pittsburgh, physically and psychologically. In this sense, the building succeeded beyond all expectation. For three-quarters of a century Bowman's tower has blazed as the most audacious structure in the city. For millions of working-class parents in western Pennsylvania, education means getting their children into the Cathedral at the University of Pittsburgh.

Klauder's aptitude for the extravagant was unleashed even more inside the Cathedral than outside. In the Commons Room, he concocted one of the great architectural fantasies of the twentieth century. This immense room, one hundred feet wide and two hundred feet long, looks and acts like a cavern in a coal mine, calling Pittsburghers back to their carbonite commercial roots. The style of the Commons Room is fifteenth-century English perpendicular. It is technically Gothic in construction, since the stone shafts and the rib vaulting sixty feet above the floor are self-supporting, but the massive central piers are just screens for the structural steel that holds up the tower above.

The Commons Room is always quiet despite its use by thousands of students every day, because the "stones" between the ribs are actually Guastavino acoustical tiles. The carving by local artisan Joseph Cattoni provides a botany lesson in indigenous western Pennsylvania plant life. The wrought-iron gates and decorative metalwork were fashioned in Philadelphia by Samuel Yellin—regarded as the finest worker who ever touched that metal. The Cathedral interior is remarkably intimate for its size, from its warm green Vermont marble floors to the Gothic tracery that appears unexpectedly every few floors. The Honors College on the thirty-fifth floor (not a public space, but hospitable to visitors) offers excellent views over Oakland and the whole of Pittsburgh.

In the midst of this Gothic reverie, the Cathedral preserves on its ground floor a heroic reminder of the mother of Oakland, Mary Schenley, in the gilt-stucco ballroom and oval antechamber from Picnic House, the family home that stood about a mile and a half away in Stanton Heights. The rooms were executed in 1835 by Philadelphia carver Mordecai Van Horn and are regarded as among the most lavish Greek Revival designs in America. Tradition holds that Schenley's father put up these frivolous rooms specifically to lure Mary back to Pittsburgh.

Also special are the two dozen "Nationality Rooms" conceived in the 1920s by sociologist Ruth Crawford Mitchell as a means of linking the university with the cultures of Pittsburgh's steelworking immigrant families. Guided tours give a fascinating if occasionally fantastic view of global architecture through these period reproductions. They range from fifth-century BCE Athens through eighth-century China, Renaissance Italy, and Napoleonic France (bending the rules a little, since the room styles are supposed to pre-date the university's founding in 1787). In years past, University of Pittsburgh students and faculty would recite the whole of James Joyce's *Ulysses* in the Irish Room every Bloomsday (June 16). Mitchell supervised the completion of the Irish Room in 1957, after which came a thirty-year slump during which no new rooms were added. This jam was broken by the Israel Heritage Room, after which a dozen new rooms followed. All of the rooms are interesting, but particularly enchanting are the Greek and Swedish rooms and the Syria-Lebanon Room, which was once the library of an eighteenth-century Damascus villa.

The grounds around the Cathedral were intended to carry a thicket of Oxford-style quadrangles, but in the end they were left luxuriously green except for memorial buildings to two quite different sons of Pittsburgh: Stephen Foster and H. J. Heinz. Klauder's Stephen Foster Memorial was completed in 1937 in the shadow of the Cathedral. It is a combination of two theaters, a social hall, a research library, and a dodecagonal shrine to the composer.

A tiny blip compared to the Cathedral, Heinz Memorial Chapel, from 1938, seems to leap bolt upright 253 feet from the flat campus lawn to the top of its copper *flèche*. In setting, detailing, and emotional impact, the Heinz chapel holds its own against better-known college chapels, such as those at Harvard, Duke, Princeton, and the University of Chicago. This chapel shows Klauder as a master at mixing sources of inspiration. The way the chapel leaps up like a mountain is a rerun of the architectural darling of the interwar years, the island abbey of Mont Saint-Michel. Klauder took the dimensions of the chapel and its function as a bejeweled vessel from the thirteenth-century Sainte-Chapelle of Louis IX in Paris. A third model, the church of Saint-Maclou at Rouen, served for the unusual convex entrance. Once inside, one cannot help but be impressed by the richness of the stone and wood carving and the luminescence of the stained glass. The double lancet windows in the transept, seventy-three feet high, are claimed to be the highest anywhere; the quality and iconographic inventiveness of the designs are equally regarded as preeminent in twentieth-century work.

fig. 7.6
STAINED GLASS:
HEINZ CHAPEL

fig. 7.7
HEINZ CHAPEL,
UNIVERSITY OF
PITTSBURGH

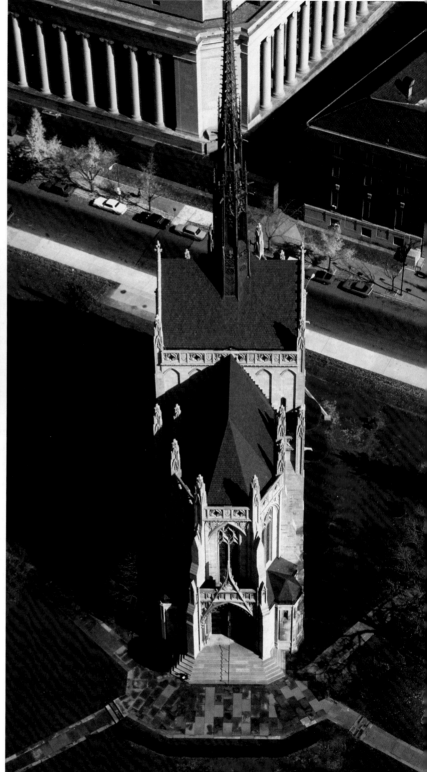

The fabricator of the glass was the Pittsburgh artist Charles Connick, who learned his trade in local glasshouses and later became a leader in the rediscovery of the principles of making Gothic stained glass. Connick later moved his studio to Boston, where these windows were designed. This prodigious show of glass—about a quarter of a million separate pieces—would have pleased H. J. Heinz, who loved stained glass and did much to promote its rebirth in Pittsburgh. It recalls Heinz in another way as well: his success in food processing came from his scrupulous quality control and his flair for advertising. Both of these traits he combined in his decision to market his products in clear rather than the usual frosted glass bottles, so customers could see how pure his foods were. The cornerstone of his empire was horse-radish, but Heinz's prosperity was truly built on glass.

Mellon Institute, the former Young Men's Hebrew Association (YMHA), and the Board of Education building, all on Bellefield Avenue, are the best of the dozen handsome buildings that ring the Cathedral grounds. The building that houses the Mellon Institute, a division of Carnegie Mellon, is an astonishing performance in scale and architectural fantasy, almost equal to the Cathedral itself. It was one of five huge buildings (along with the Cathedral of Learning, the Gulf and Koppers towers Downtown, and East Liberty Presbyterian Church) that the Mellons financed during the Depression. At Mellon Institute, it was R. B. rather than his brother A. W. Mellon who delighted in the mountain of construction details, even driving at the head of the procession when some of the institute building's columns were brought through the Oakland streets. The brothers had founded the Mellon Institute together in 1911 as the world's first research and development center for industry. After it outgrew two earlier buildings, Richard Mellon prepared a third home that might outlast the centuries. This third Mellon Institute stands on Fifth Avenue at Bellefield; the architect was Benno Janssen, and construction lasted from 1930 to 1937.

Janssen's prime model was probably Karl Friedrich Schinkel's Altes Museum in Berlin, from 1823. That structure has the same configuration of a hollow square fronted by a heroic Ionic colonnade and cut in two by an axial hall. The same model had already been used west of Pittsburgh for the Greek Revival capitol in Columbus, Ohio, and on the East Coast by Guy Lowell at the Boston Museum of Fine Arts. But the precedent that probably meant more in terms of Mellon dynastic interests was Robert Mills's Treasury Building of 1836 in Washington. The heroic Ionic colonnade at the Treasury Building conveyed an architectural message the Mellons were particularly anxious to send. In 1931, the ten-year reign of A. W. Mellon as secretary of

fig. 7.8
MELLON
INSTITUTE

the treasury was coming to an end. In the flush of the Roaring Twenties, Mellon had seemed to be a genius, but now critics in Congress were snapping at his heels, and tax-evasion proceedings had just started against him. Perhaps Mellon quieted his critics by exchanging elements from his separate lives in Pittsburgh and Washington. For Washington, he built the National Gallery of Art, sending it numerous paintings from his home in Pittsburgh. For Pittsburgh, he built Mellon Institute, which bore the face of his Treasury Building in Washington.

Benno Janssen designed Mellon Institute to the ultimate standard of all Classical Revival buildings: the Parthenon in Athens. The entrance façade on Fifth Avenue closely follows the length of the Parthenon, and Janssen replicated the façade on the other three sides, even though one faced nothing more than a back alley. The colonnades, with slit windows behind them, rise five stories while the building digs down to bedrock (to minimize vibration in scientific experiments), which is three stories below. Scientific experimentation of a different mode continues in the institute today. The Pittsburgh Supercomputer Center supports one of the most powerful cyber-based research networks anywhere on the globe.

Having matched the Parthenon, the Mellons then exceeded it in one spectacular gesture. At the Parthenon, the architect Ictinus, like all Greek and most Roman builders, could only construct columns by fitting together drums of marble. The Mellon Institute columns are not drums but single chunks of Indiana limestone. They were quarried as solid 125-ton monoliths, then slimmed to their final weight of sixty tons. Even their capitals weigh five tons apiece—all these weights being without equal anywhere in the world. To ensure justness of proportions at such a mammoth scale, a full-size replica of the corner and two columns was secretly constructed of plaster and wood in a cornfield in the Allegheny Valley, north of Dorseyville. R. B. Mellon was thus able to see what he was getting, and probably to ensure that no one else would get a sneak peek, the fifty-thousand-dollar mock-up was removed two weeks later.

Two stately buildings alongside Mellon Institute sit in its architectural shadow, though each predates both the institute and the Cathedral of Learning. The Board of Education at 341 South Bellefield is a graceful Renaissance palace of 1927 with exquisitely beveled limestone blocks and Michelangelo-style windows. The middle building on the block, at 315 South Bellefield, is the old YMHA, now the University of Pittsburgh's Bellefield Hall. The president and mainstay of the YMHA in 1924, its construction year, was the mercurial E. J. Kaufmann Sr., master of the family's department store in Downtown.

Kaufmann was no passive philanthropist; he oversaw every element of the Y's design and construction.

It would have been brilliant of Kaufmann to have picked Frank Lloyd Wright to design the Y in 1924, the way he chose him to create Fallingwater a decade later. But in 1924, Kaufmann, a Jew, was still trying to negotiate his place in WASP society, and in those circles, radical modernism was beyond the pale of good taste. Benno Janssen was the obvious choice as architect not only because of his closeness to the Kaufmanns (he designed their store and their various Pittsburgh homes) but also because he had already proved his mettle at clubhouse architecture two blocks away, at the Pittsburgh Athletic Association.

With his mastery of architectural history, Janssen forged an unlikely match: the stone arch at the YMHA parallels that of the early Renaissance Palazzo Piccolomini delle Papesse in Siena, while the Flemish-bond brick-work and high basement recall monuments like Stratford, the eighteenth-century Thomas Lee house in Virginia. This improbable combination works well both in form and in function. The high attic profile, for example, hides a flat expanse of roof where two generations of Y patrons could sunbathe in privacy. The same mix of practicality and art extends to the interior, which carries both sports facilities and one of Pittsburgh's most storied concert halls. Here, Marian Anderson, Arthur Rubinstein, Isaac Stern, Jean-Pierre Rampal, and a host of other music luminaries made their Pittsburgh debuts. Eight squash courts are positioned directly over the hall, but sports enthusiasts are entreated not to play while concerts are in progress below.

Visitors to Bellefield Hall might wonder at the large blank lunettes on the upper lobby walls. The blanks were intended for murals, a technique of great interest to Kaufmann (his son, E. J. Kaufmann Jr., studied painting in Mexico). In the early 1940s, Kaufmann Sr. commissioned the Mexican painter Juan O'Gorman, a colleague of the muralists Rivera, Orozco, and Siqueiros, to fill those blanks. O'Gorman came to Pittsburgh to paint a full series, but the Y board was not enchanted with his Marxist imagery and preferred the walls bare.

On the far side of Forbes Avenue stand another half-dozen university buildings, arranged around Schenley Plaza. In one corner of the plaza stood the much-loved Forbes Field ballpark from 1909 to 1971. It was built by Barney Dreyfuss, who had forged the old Allegheny baseball team into the Pirates—a name bestowed in 1891 by Philadelphia newspaper reporters who accused Pittsburgh of stealing player Louis Bierbauer. The old stadium can be seen regularly in telecasts of MGM's 1951 baseball classic, *Angels in the Outfield*, and many Pittsburghers still feel its spirit hovering over the buildings now occupying that site. A good chunk of the high brick outfield wall as well as home plate are preserved intact today; the latter (actually a replica) is encased in the ground floor of Posvar Hall. On October 13 each year, diehard Pirates fans gather at the 457-foot line of left field to play tapes of the Pirates' winning home run in the 1960 World Series.

After coal magnate John Hillman donated the land bordering the stadium to the University of Pittsburgh in the 1950s, architect Max Abramovitz prepared a master plan for a sequence of classroom and professional buildings that would replace the stadium once it was razed. Between 1967 and 1978, four buildings were constructed on or near the ballpark site: Hillman Library, David L. Lawrence Hall, the Law Building, and Posvar Hall. None of the four is important as architecture, although Hillman, at least, creates a functional environment as a research and undergraduate library for its users and its several million books.

The university's more recent buildings have fortunately been superior to those four in design sensitivity and practicality. The glass-walled Mervis Hall on Roberto Clemente Drive houses the university's business school. Its stark roofline was out of place in the Victorian environment of Bouquet Street when Mervis went up in 1983, but the turrets and steeples that once rose nearby have been replaced by lackluster university dormitories today. Otherwise, Mervis works well, and the scalloped recess in the façade softens the hardness of the glass and asserts an entrance in a way many all-glass structures forget to do. The gentle russet tone of the accents in the glass echoes the nearby outfield wall of Forbes Field. The effect is businesslike, as the designers intended, but also unexpectedly serene.

After almost a century as a glorified parking lot, Schenley Plaza is a green oasis today. For millennia the area was a gully, which the nineteenth century knew as St. Pierre's Ravine. In a practical move, the ravine was filled in from 1911 to 1913 with earth that was being removed a few blocks away from Oakland Hill as part of the laying out of the Schenley Farms neighborhood. Sealing off the ravine and constructing the Schenley Fountain were both part of a scheme to establish Schenley Plaza as a visual link with Schenley Park. A host of interested parties initially clashed over designs for the plaza, but by 1917, a plan was in place. It was formal, symmetrical, and used the proposed Schenley Fountain as its focal point. The plan also employed a great amount of asphalt, a feature that ensured it would spend the rest of the twentieth century as a full-scale parking lot. Only in 2006 was the plaza reclaimed as green space by the Pittsburgh Parks Conservancy. Today it includes a huge lawn and an entertainment tent as well as food kiosks. The plaza still does not function as a prelude to Schenley Park, which is a full block as well as a bridge away, but it works well on its own as a place for students and families to gather, eat, and enjoy each other's company.

The Mary Schenley Fountain sits near, rather than actually in, Schenley Plaza for some curious reasons. In 1898, before anyone thought to fill in the gully, the city erected a fine stone arch over the far end of St. Pierre's Ravine and called the new span the Bellefield Bridge. The bridge got buried—literally—in 1915 when the gully was filled in, and the arch thus had no further use. Three years later, it was found expedient to construct the Schenley Fountain over that subterranean broad arch (had the fountain been placed over the newly filled-in earth, it would have wobbled and sunk like a house built on sand). Today no viewer would suspect the fountain's exotic construction history because it seems to occupy a natural place in front of the Frick Fine Arts Building, but the buried bridge—last glimpsed in 2008—is a top item among Pittsburgh's urban legends.

Victor Brenner, sculptor of the fountain called *A Song to Nature*, was a Lithuanian Jewish immigrant who a decade earlier had designed the Lincoln penny. (At approximately half a trillion produced, it is the most widely circulated image in history.) Brenner's fountain evokes the rebirth of nature through the asymmetrical opposition of the earthbound Pan hibernating and the spirit of Harmony, who wakes him with a song on her lyre. The sculpture fails to achieve its objective of organizing the loose space of Schenley Plaza, but as an independent object, it works extremely well—a tribute to a style in which artists could work with nature and allegory without embarrassment.

fig. 7.9
SCHENLEY
FOUNTAIN

Since 1965, the main visual pointer from Schenley Plaza to Schenley Park has not been the Schenley Fountain but the neighboring Renaissance villa of the Henry Clay Frick Fine Arts Building. This is one of three local showcases for the Fricks' art collections, along with the Frick mansion and the Frick Art Museum in Point Breeze. In 1925, Helen Frick founded what is now the Henry Clay Frick Department of the History of Art and Architecture at the University of Pittsburgh. The growth of the department proved unexpectedly vigorous, so to house it properly, she sought out the successors to the firm of Carrère & Hastings for a replica of the Italian palazzo they had constructed for her father on Fifth Avenue in New York.

After shooting down one proposal after another for almost forty years, Helen Frick eventually gave the nod to Kenneth Johnstone, a modernist more comfortable in concrete than Carrère. Johnstone merely tweaked the scheme (an adaptation of the Villa Giulia in Rome) that the academic firm of Eggers and Higgins had already come up with before they dumped Frick as a client. The Frick Fine Arts Building consists of a series of classrooms, a richly appointed library, art galleries grouped about an open cloister, and a forty-five-foot-high octagon capped by a pyramidal roof. The cloister is one of the delightful sights of Pittsburgh. Its walls hold a series of fresco reproductions that the restorer Nicholas Lochoff had prepared in Italy for the Moscow Museum of Fine Arts. Stranded in Florence by the Bolshevik revolution, Lochoff appealed to the connoisseur Bernard Berenson, who recommended to Helen Frick the purchase of the fresco reproductions. The sumptuousness of the cloister and the library, the aura of Berenson and Frick that hangs over the building, and the scholarly art exhibits in the galleries make the Frick Fine Arts Building a rewarding place to explore.

fig. 7.10
CLOISTER AT THE
FRICK FINE ARTS
BUILDING

At the diagonally opposite corner of Schenley Plaza sits an elegant ten-story skyscraper with a handsome veneer of thin, tawny-brown Roman bricks; inside, it shows off a succession of lavish public suites that were brought back to life after decades of decay. This was Franklin Nicola's old Schenley Hotel, and its conversion into the William Pitt Student Union involved balancing student needs with old memories. Those memories included legends of national trendsetters such as Diamond Jim Brady and Lillian Russell, who had lived or partied there; visits from every president from Theodore Roosevelt to Dwight Eisenhower; and the death on April 21, 1924, of world-renowned Italian stage actress Eleonora Duse, the most famous person ever to die in Pittsburgh (Andy Warhol may be buried in Pittsburgh, but he expired in New York). In 1925, local author Haniel Long wrote a poem about her, "Duse Dies in Pittsburgh." Some of its lines recall:

The divine Duse. An old woman then,
but still the most shining woman in all the world.

They kept her alive with oxygen in other cities
so she might die in Pittsburgh. Death
had something in mind; brought her the long leagues from Italy
so she might die in my city.

She wouldn't stop in Indianapolis;
said she had heard that "Spittsburgh" was a nice city,
insisted on going through to Spittsburgh,
died there, crying for the boat to take her home.

fig. 7.11
PITT STUDENT
UNION,
FORMERLY THE
SCHENLEY HOTEL

The building's restoration program was functionally and philosophically complex. It called for the conservation of the public rooms as period pieces, the conversion of the hotel rooms above into state-of-the-art student activity offices, and the creation of new dining and recreation rooms in the old basement. The response of the restoration architects to this basically schizophrenic program was a basically schizophrenic building: luxuriously and meticulously Belle Époque on the main floor, functionally modern in the office floors above, and extravagantly Postmodern in the basement below. What one sees today could be mistaken for a collaboration of Stanford White with radical designers like Giulio Romano for the old rooms or Robert Venturi for the new ones. Inside the basement the decor is pleasurably surrealistic: fat tubular columns with triple necking grooves, as though visitors had stumbled unaware into a gigantic Palladian pinball machine.

The University of Pittsburgh campus divides into a lower portion around the Cathedral of Learning and Schenley Plaza and an upper campus north of O'Hara Street, with buildings on Bouquet and De Soto streets bridging the two parts. The most significant of those intermediary buildings are the seven blocks of undergraduate dormitories that were once the luxurious Schenley Apartments, which Franklin Nicola added in the 1920s behind his Schenley Hotel.

Between O'Hara Street and the top of Oakland Hill survive several buildings from the University of Pittsburgh's 1908 "Acropolis" scheme. Thaw Hall and Allen Hall (the first home of the Mellon Institute) on O'Hara Street still stand as the baseline for what was intended to be a colossal sequence of temples marching uphill. Just up the hill, Eberly Hall was not part of the 1908 scheme, but it follows the basic lines of the master plan. A yellow brick road behind O'Hara survives to suggest the main outlines of what never got built.

The architectural prima donna on O'Hara Street today is not one of the old buildings but an escalatorlike structure that houses the Learning Research and Development Center at 3939 O'Hara Street. The LRDC is recognized worldwide in the fields of language comprehension and computer applications in educational research. The 1970s building is shaped like a giant staircase against the hillside because it was meant to act like one: the bare patch still visible on the right side of the lobby was designed to carry a huge escalator to hoist students up to the proposed dormitory complex above. The dormitory towers were finally built in the 1990s and in the early twenty-first century, but there was no further thought given to resurrecting the escalator scheme. The upper campus is still growing; in 2002, the Petersen Events Center (which includes a hill-climbing escalator) at the top of De Soto Street replaced a football stadium from the 1920s.

With acclaimed doctors, surgeons, and researchers such as Jonas Salk, Benjamin Spock, Erik Erikson, and Thomas Starzl practicing medicine or conducting research at the University of Pittsburgh, Oakland's medical and health research powerhouse does not lack for eminence. But after three-quarters of a century of growth in its tiny confines, it is seriously overbuilt. The hope is that the crowding will be alleviated with the relocation of Children's Hospital to Lawrenceville and selected research facilities to neighborhoods such as Shadyside.

If one studies this mass of buildings closely enough, there is some distinguished architecture as well as important medical history to be found. On De Soto Street, halfway up Oakland Hill, lies the center of the complex: the octopus-shaped UPMC Presbyterian–University Hospital. Downhill, on Fifth Avenue, are the subsidiary Falk Clinic and the former Children's Hospital buildings. The architect E. P. Mellon participated in the design of all three of these 1930s towers in his role as watchdog for the Mellons' philanthropic and commercial buildings.

On the fringe of the medical superblock, at the corner of De Soto and O'Hara, stands the Art Deco–style Detre Building. It houses the Western Psychiatric Institute, a world leader in psychiatry and the facility where Spock and Erikson collaborated in their study of troubled children. A somewhat look-alike Art Deco counterpart on Terrace Street, but not so tall, is Jonas E. Salk Hall, the former Municipal Hospital. It was in this facility that Jonas Salk, a research professor of bacteriology at the University of Pittsburgh from 1949 to 1954, developed and perfected the Salk polio vaccine. The research was done in labs on the ground floor and in the basement. Salk and his team used rhesus monkeys in the work, and for years the walls bore paw prints from the occasional animal that scampered out of its cage.

On the steep hillside west of Presbyterian stands UPMC Montefiore Hospital, a neo-Georgian structure from 1929 that originally descended the slope in three terraces but now lies buried under later additions. Wiser heads prevailed in the adjoining block at Carlow University, where a dozen late Gothic Revival red-brick structures have gone up since the 1920s without such overcrowding. The wooded stretches of hillside between the buildings still convey a faint suggestion of what made Oakland so desirable a location in the first place.

CARNEGIE MUSEUMS, SCHENLEY PARK, AND CARNEGIE MELLON

That Andrew Carnegie (1835–1919) had a genius for business is clear from his career. A boy of thirteen when his penniless family sailed from Scotland in 1848, Carnegie required only twenty years to amass a first fortune in railroads, a second fortune in oil, and a third—and much larger—fortune from iron bridges and steel. But Carnegie had no less genius when it came to public relations. He was probably richer than any of the other robber barons of turn-of-the-twentieth-century America except John D. Rockefeller, but while such names as Morgan, Frick, and Ford are recalled today either equivocally or with distaste, Carnegie—for many people—represents a model industrialist.

The skill in public relations that Carnegie would one day demonstrate worldwide was first seen on a grand scale in Pittsburgh with his gifts of the Carnegie Museums and Carnegie Mellon University. Carnegie gave away some $350 million (billions of today's dollars), including twenty-five hundred libraries and seven thousand church organs the world over. But none of these gifts bears such a personal mark as the immense Carnegie Library and Carnegie Museums of Pittsburgh, which incorporate a library, two museums, and a music hall. The complex stretches five hundred feet along Schenley Plaza and eight hundred feet on Forbes Avenue—long enough that city buses have to make two separate stops in front of it. This eight-acre complex is the grandest monument of Beaux-Arts planning in the city and was recognized as such outside Pittsburgh, too. The authoritative 1911 edition of the *Encyclopaedia Britannica* featured the Carnegie complex as the exemplar of the modern museum.

For Pittsburgh, the importance of the Carnegie Library and Museums (these include the Carnegie Science Center and the Andy Warhol Museum on the North Side) go beyond their size. Culturally, Carnegie Institute (the founding name has been supplanted by "Carnegie Museums") marked the end of the Dark Ages for a town that had wealth but little culture before the institute opened in 1895. Its impact on Pittsburgh was extensively recorded by Willa Cather, both in her personal correspondence and in her short story "Paul's Case," which Cather partly set in the library and music hall.

Today, the museums of art and natural history, the music hall, the lecture hall, and the library, with its nineteen branches, support more varied activities than any American cultural institution except the Smithsonian. The Carnegie complex was equally important to Pittsburgh in urban terms, since it was the most important building to arise beyond the original city in the Golden Triangle. So remote from Downtown that it had to produce its own heat and electricity, it pointed the city in a new direction, both physically and spiritually—an important change for a city that until then had been interested only in production. Carnegie's gift not only effectively gave birth to Oakland but also encouraged the expansion of the residential quarters of Shadyside, Highland Park, Squirrel Hill, and Point Breeze.

The design competition announced in 1891 for Carnegie Library was the most heralded contest in American architecture in its day. It drew 102 entries and thirteen hundred drawings from ninety-six architects in twenty-eight cities. The victory of the Longfellow, Alden & Harlow firm was no surprise, since their design of the Duquesne Club two years before gave them entrée with anyone who counted in Pittsburgh. That partnership (Alden & Harlow alone after 1896) is forgotten today, but in the years 1890 to 1910, its volume of business rivaled those of the top design offices in New York. The firm's success was based on a combination of the social skills and connections of Alexander Longfellow (a nephew of the poet), who had apprenticed with both Richardson and Stanford White; the design skills of Alfred Harlow, another White disciple; and the managerial skills of Frank Alden, Richardson's job superintendent for the Allegheny County Courthouse project.

Richardson's courthouse had been dedicated with acclaim just three years before the museum competition, but rather than serving up an exclusively Richardsonian design for the Carnegie competition, the partners indulged in the lighter eclecticism popularized by McKim, Mead & White, particularly that seen in the firm's Villard houses in New York, from 1882. The partners looked west as well as east and were evidently also quite taken by many details of Henry I. Cobb's Newberry Library in Chicago, from

339

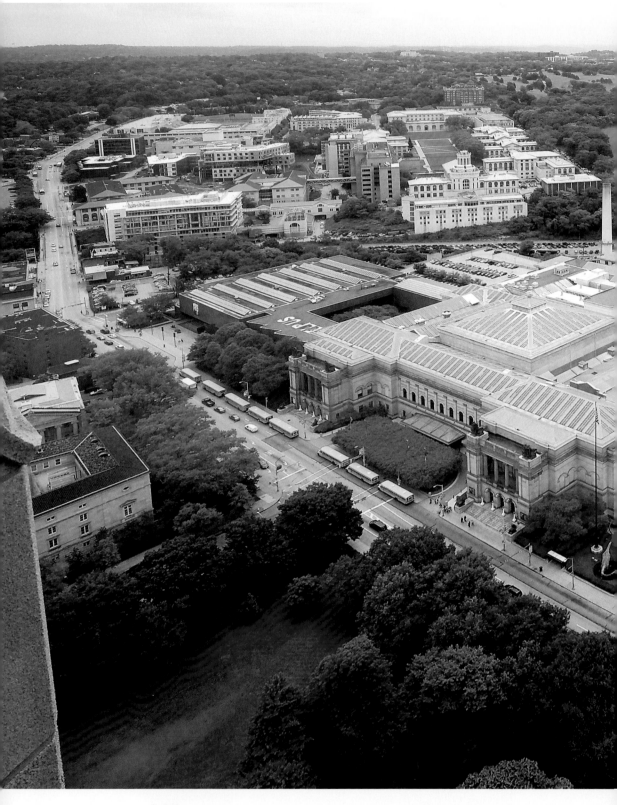

fig. 7.12
CARNEGIE INSTITUTE
COMPLEX, WITH
CARNEGIE MELLON
UNIVERSITY IN THE
DISTANCE

1887. The inspiration for both of those neo-Renaissance compositions was the fifteenth-century Medici Palace in Florence, the appropriation of which was always a nice compliment to a powerful patron. The names of the twenty-four authors that are carved above the windows on Schenley Plaza were personally approved by Carnegie, who was a voracious reader and probably knew at least one book or play by each. In the museum's 1907 addition, names from the literary pantheon were joined by several score more names in art, science, and music.

As was so often the case in Beaux-Arts designs, the interior plan of Carnegie Library was taken from an entirely different historical source from that of the exterior. The plan seems to reflect the eleventh-century double-transepted and double-apsed basilica of St. Michael at Hildesheim, Germany. The apse at the back—the one pointing toward Schenley Drive—serves today as the children's library. A much larger apse once boldly projected toward Forbes Avenue and was crowned with twin Venetian bell towers that copied the two located Downtown at the courthouse. Decades ago, James Van Trump convincingly argued that the precedent for this grand interior was Gabriel Davioud's Palais du Trocadéro in Paris, from 1878. The apse on Forbes Avenue was masked by the 1907 addition, which required demolition of the two bell towers. Internally, the original semicircular shape is retained in Carnegie Music Hall.

Inside Carnegie Library, the ground-floor rooms are laid out with alcoves and Palladian-arched screens in the manner of a large but intimate private house. The most successful element from a restoration in 2004 is a bamboo-surrounded outdoor reading deck, which was carved out of a previously unused exterior courtyard. Upstairs is a sequence of large rooms, most with skylights that over the years were closed and roofed over. Beginning in 1896, the Carnegie Institute was the site for the world's second international exhibition

fig. 7.13
CARNEGIE
MUSIC HALL
CONCERT

of modern art: the Carnegie International. The two-thousand-seat music hall on Forbes Avenue features an impressive half-Pantheon dome inside, recalling the pure geometric style of Neoclassical France. The music hall is rarely dark: among its users are the Three Rivers Brass Band, the Pittsburgh Chamber Music Society, the Drue Heinz Lecture Series, and the International Poetry Forum. Audiences at the last have heard readings by Anne Sexton, Archibald MacLeish, Siobhan McKenna, John Ciardi, Yevgeny Yevtushenko on his first visit to the United States, and Princess Grace of Monaco.

In 1898, Andrew Carnegie read about extraordinary dinosaur fossil discoveries in Wyoming, and he financed an expedition to secure for Pittsburgh what would eventually amount to one of the world's outstanding collections of such finds. He also resolved to quadruple the size of his library to include permanent galleries for art and natural history. These decisions resulted in the vast extension along Forbes Avenue, which Alden & Harlow did in 1907. The designers retained the earlier rhythm of pillow-shaped ashlar stones in Cleveland sandstone at the base, but they gave the new work the massiveness of form and scale that had in the meantime appeared at the Chicago World's Fair in 1893. To mask the transition between the two parts of the building, an enormous pivot was created in the pyramidal-capped roof of the Hall of Architecture, which broods over the whole.

Inside, the new parts of the museum raised the spatial and textural articulation of the old portions to a level of operatic sumptuousness. Six thousand tons of European marble decorate these halls, a good deal of it coming from the quarry that supplied Pentelic marble for the Parthenon in Athens. The building contains about four miles of marble wainscoting in all, justifying Philip Johnson's quip that there may be more Sienese marble in the Carnegie Institute than is left in Siena.

The most exuberant of the interior spaces is the music hall foyer, built around a colonnade of mammoth Giallo Antico marble columns. The entablature and the ribs penetrating the cove ceiling are covered in sheets of gold leaf; the whole follows the general rhythm of Michelangelo's ceiling in the Sistine Chapel. The foyer is presided over by a life-size gilded bronze statue of Carnegie seated on an Ionic throne topped by finials of Scottish thistles. Around the base is carved his favorite motto: "All is well since all grows better."

Carnegie's spirit can be caught even more vividly in two rooms alongside Forbes Avenue: his feminine side in a beautifully stenciled Venetian drawing room to the right as one enters the building, and his masculine side in the dark mahogany boardroom (briefly glimpsed in the movie *Flashdance*) to the left, with his rolltop desk still in use.

fig. 7.14
GRAND STAIRCASE,
CARNEGIE MUSEUM
OF NATURAL
HISTORY

fig. 7.15
ARCHITECTURE
HALL, CARNEGIE
MUSEUM OF ART

The back-to-back museums are rewarding to explore, both for their exhibits and the visual experience of the enormous corridors and rooms en suite. Some ten thousand examples of natural history material are on display, with twenty times that number kept in reserve for scientific study. The Hall of Dinosaurs, which houses the third-largest collection of dinosaur fossils in the United States, includes a *Diplodicus carnegii* and an *Apatosaurus louisiae*, named after the patron and his wife. The Hall of Dinosaurs was expanded in 2007 when an atrium was carved out of a previously open courtyard (the adjoining library stacks provide the best views). The fossils were remounted in more accurate poses, along with replica plants from corresponding eras.

The expansion of the Carnegie Museum of Art came a generation earlier, in 1974, with construction of the Scaife Galleries. This important architectural commission went conditionally to Charles Luckman (Louis Kahn was also interviewed), then definitively to Edward Larabee Barnes, who laid out the main exhibit spaces in the cool white mode of the late International Style.

The painting collection in the Museum of Art is strong on Impressionism and Postimpressionism and particularly good on American art between the world wars. The collections include works by Pittsburgh-born artists Mary Cassatt, Andy Warhol, Philip Pearlstein, and Mel Bochner. The newest addition to the art museum is not an external appendage but the internally carved out Heinz Architectural Center, off the balcony of the Hall of Sculpture. This building within a building contains galleries, a study room, a library, and offices on three floors that are shoehorned into what had been a single gallery and its skylights. Among the built-in architectural antiquities here are two handsome copper dormer windows that were recovered from the New York mansion of Carnegie himself.

Downstairs, in the unforgettable Hall of Architecture, the Carnegie shows off a collection of "dinosaurs" of a different sort: reproductions of ancient buildings. To connoisseurs and children alike, this assemblage of plaster casts is often the most appealing part of the complex. Carnegie had no special feeling for the pictorial arts. Ever the democrat, he disdained the Old Masters that Frick and Mellon were collecting and favored instead modern works that he called the "Old Masters of Tomorrow." The art form that suited him best was the plaster cast, since casts of famous buildings and sculptures appealed to his passion for education. In close contact with the head of fine arts at the museum, Carnegie financed a search for approximately twelve hundred of the best models in architecture and sculpture, which were then cast in plaster for the Pittsburgh museum. For five years an army of agents

fig. 7.16
DINOSAUR HALL

throughout Europe worked to secure these casts, some being made from pre-existing molds, others created just for Carnegie. Two men were kept busy in Pittsburgh just translating the foreign-language telegrams that were coming and going overseas.

The major triumph of Carnegie's agents was the cast of the Romanesque abbey church of Saint-Gilles-du-Gard, which at eighty-seven feet is the longest in the world. The Saint-Gilles-du-Gard façade was cast in 195 separate molds that were transported from Marseilles on three different steamships. On a world scale, the quality of the Pittsburgh collection exceeds that of the Musée Nationale des Monuments Français in Paris and is second only to the Victoria and Albert Museum's cast collection in London. To house the collection, Alden & Harlow prepared a hall 126 feet square, 76 feet tall to its inner skylights, and 137 feet to its outer skylights. The skylights are stepped up, like that wonder of the ancient world, the Mausoleum of Halicarnassus. The effect of the casts and the colossal space is little short of hypnotic. If a single room could be said to represent the power and ambition of the Gilded Age in Pittsburgh, this is it.

The Carnegie complex may or may not be the best architecture in Pittsburgh, but there is no question that Schenley Park represents the city's best in landscape architecture. The most meaningful starting point for a visit to Schenley Park is just outside Carnegie Library's main entrance. Although one might expect to find another testimonial to Carnegie at this site, instead there stands a memorial stele to Christopher Lyman Magee (1848–1901). This is an odd choice because it was Magee, the political boss of Pittsburgh, and his partner William Flinn whom Lincoln Steffens singled out as the most corrupt politicians in the country, according to his book *The Shame of the Cities* (1904). But Magee got along well with Carnegie, and he smoothed the way for Carnegie's takeover of eight acres of city property, which explains his commemoration here. It was also Magee's street railway that transported workers from their slum neighborhoods to enjoy the amenities of Oakland.

The Magee memorial is a superb product of the artistic movement of 1875 to 1915 known as the American Renaissance. The base was conceived by Stanford White but executed after White's death by Henry Bacon; the sculptor was Augustus Saint-Gaudens. Today's memorial is actually a partial bowdlerization of the original concept, however. A photograph taken in the Saint-Gaudens studio in New Hampshire documents the sculptor's intent to crown the stele with a large bust of Magee. Somebody—perhaps Carnegie—evidently vetoed the bust, so atop the stele instead is a politically correct—or at least innocuous—Classical anthemion.

347

fig. 7.17
CHRISTOPHER
MAGEE MEMORIAL

Carnegie had no particular role in the creation of Schenley Park, but it, too, fitted into his urban scheme since the city initially did not put in a bridge over the Junction Hollow gully that ran alongside the museum at Forbes Avenue. That meant that anyone wishing to walk from Carnegie Institute to Carnegie Mellon University had to pass through Schenley Park.

Schenley Park is the great natural drama of Oakland. But that great drama is preceded by the little drama of Junction Hollow. The hollow, separating Schenley Park from the rest of Oakland, is a 150-foot-deep gorge and was known to early Pittsburghers as Four Mile Run. It originated in one of many runoffs when the prehistoric Monongahela River coursed through Oakland in the last of the ice ages. The old name derived straightforwardly from its distance from the Point; the current name refers to the tracks of the Pittsburgh Junction Railroad that were laid here in 1884–1886. The railroad tracks duck underground just north of Forbes Avenue and run for about five blocks under Neville Street through the Schenley Tunnel.

Junction Hollow works as a kind of mirror in which Carnegie's museum and university can admire each other. The mirror was almost obliterated in 1963, when the Oakland Corporation, a consortium of the University of Pittsburgh, Carnegie Mellon, and other players, proposed to build into the depths of Junction Hollow an enormous research center. The master plan (by New York's Harrison & Abramovitz) stumbled badly at the outset by willfully erasing the name Junction Hollow and replacing it with the more alluring name of Panther Hollow, a separate gully that intersects the former one a bit farther south. About a mile long, "Oakland upside-down," as the proposed structure might be termed, would have filled Junction Hollow with seven stories of building, leaving a tunnel for railway tracks and a motor expressway at the bottom. Five thousand scientists would have joined the University of Pittsburgh and Carnegie Mellon to make this the world's largest research unit. But the promise of federal funding died with President Kennedy, and Panther Hollow joined the list of Pittsburgh's unrealized dreams.

fig. 7.18
JUNCTION
HOLLOW

fig. 7.19
PANTHER HOLLOW,
SCHENLEY PARK

Junction Hollow supports a jumble of frame houses that cling to its sides despite all the laws of gravity. Above it rises Henry Hornbostel's splendid Hamerschlag Hall at Carnegie Mellon, with the huge chimney and arch that catch the eye of anyone looking over from the Carnegie Museums. Below the Schenley Park Bridge is an evocative relic of the early days of Oakland: the Bellefield Boiler Plant, which for years also powered the dynamos that gave the museum complex its own electricity. Readers of Michael Chabon's *The Mysteries of Pittsburgh* will recognize the boiler plant as Pittsburgh's "cloud factory." The plant still receives coal through its own trestle entrance from the railroad tracks. It no longer creates electricity, but it continues to supply steam heat to a dozen neighboring institutions.

The story of the creation of Schenley Park is almost as long as the millions of years it took nature to shape it and as short as the transatlantic race that decided who would get the land on which it now sits. What is now the park was the heart of Mary Schenley's inherited estate, complete with the two eighteenth-century log houses that still stand toward Squirrel Hill. In 1889, Pittsburgh's director of public works, Edward Bigelow, rushed his lawyer to London, just ahead of a commercial realtor, to persuade Mary Schenley to give the land to Pittsburgh as a park and not to sell it for housing. Under Bigelow's guidance, Schenley Park was enhanced with the addition of Phipps Conservatory, an artificial ice rink, a band shell, a racetrack, an electrically operated water organ, and boating facilities on the artificial Panther Hollow Lake.

Bigelow then directed the design of four bridges to give the city access to the new park. Two of these (the Forbes Avenue and Charles Anderson bridges) are replacements for earlier structures, but the Schenley Park and

Panther Hollow bridges are originals from the 1890s, and they arch over their respective gullies just as Bigelow intended. The Panther Hollow Bridge comes complete with a quartet of fine bronze panthers by Giuseppe Moretti. (Panthers were hunted in the local woods until the early nineteenth century.) Bigelow had enticed Moretti from Siena to play the role of his court sculptor in Pittsburgh; between 1895 and 1923, he ennobled public works of all sorts with his art.

When one enters Schenley Park, it is possible not only to appreciate the legacy of Edward Manning Bigelow in the abstract but also to see an image of the man himself. Sculpted by Moretti in 1895, this statue stands on a high pedestal on a small island at the park entrance. Bigelow was part of the audience when the statue was unveiled, which gives some idea of his lack of modesty. But the unusual tribute was not undeserved. Bigelow not only secured Schenley Park for the city but also built Grant Boulevard (today Bigelow Boulevard) to link it to the Golden Triangle three miles away. Bigelow Boulevard was part of Bigelow's overarching "emerald necklace" scheme that linked Schenley, Frick, and Highland parks by means of Bigelow, Beechwood, and Washington boulevards, plus a refurbished Butler Street that returns motorists Downtown along a fourth dramatic promenade.

As is true of Schenley Park's apparent model, New York's Central Park, which was laid out thirty years earlier, its scenic vistas and dramatic contrasts were not designed by nature; they had to be coaxed out of the land by human ingenuity. The ingenious artist of this effort was another Bigelow import, the Scottish landscape designer William Falconer, who between 1890 and 1895 shaped the land in the tradition of the eighteenth-century Romantics and bestowed on it long serpentine carriage drives. Particularly successful is Flagstaff Hill, an artificially banked-up amphitheater that is ringed with trees. It is the city's premier spot for kiting on windy days, and it efficiently hosts the movies, concerts, and plays that are presented during summer.

Schenley Park has become increasingly more important to the cultural life of Pittsburgh in recent years. The dilapidated Schenley Park Visitors Center was turned into a fine meeting place by the Pittsburgh Parks Conservancy, and the park itself comes alive for Carnegie Mellon's buggy races, for the Vintage Grand Prix that has antique cars racing through the rambling driveways, and the Race for the Cure, in which almost fifty thousand breast cancer survivors and their friends participate annually. Biking in Schenley Park is also popular. After cyclists ride through the park they can connect to the Eliza Furnace Trail and bike to Downtown. However, bikers ought to be careful to steer clear of the wild turkeys that make their home in

fig. 7.20
FLAGSTAFF HILL,
SCHENLEY PARK

fig. 7.21
PHIPPS CONSERVATORY

Junction and Panther hollows. They can congregate on the bike trails by the score, and while wonderfully picturesque, they have no use for cyclists.

Dreamlike and fantastic, Phipps Conservatory stands on the far side of Schenley Drive from Flagstaff Hill. In plan, this is the most intricate Beaux-Arts building in the city, with a succession of major and minor axes and cross-axes in the manner of a vast nineteenth-century insane asylum. On a national scale, Phipps is much more than architecture; complete by 1893, it was the first permanent demonstration of a large-scale enclosed botanical garden in the United States, and its two and a half acres still rank as the largest greenhouse in the country. It was probably the only American conservatory of its time with such precise climate control that it could grow its most sensational exhibit: the Victoria lilies, large and resilient enough that visitors could step onto them like rafts.

The conservatory's pavilion roofs rise in billowing curves over the ogive vaults of the long halls to create the proper note of Kublai Khan exoticism, while three bronze sculptures sound grace notes nearby: Frank Vittor's colossal *Christopher Columbus*, from 1958; Giuseppe Moretti's *Hygeia* of 1922; and John Massey Rhind's *Robert Burns* of 1914, the last mainly paid for by Andrew Carnegie himself.

In 2005, the entrance to Phipps was redesigned with new landscaping and a welcome center. The design makes the best use of limited space by digging down for a Renaissance-inspired courtyard garden and lobby entrance and by topping the multilevel welcome center with an expansive glass dome. The dome is inspired by the conservatory's Victorian wings, while the new greenhouses and the tropical forest glasshouse at the back are sweepingly abstract.

A few moments' walk into the fertile glen near Phipps offers a reflection on Pittsburgh's most original millionaire. A pond, a jet of water, a gilded bronze youth, and a set of narrative reliefs constitute the Westinghouse Memorial, from 1930. The sculptors were Daniel Chester French and Paul Fjelde; Henry Hornbostel and Eric Fisher Wood were the architects. The conception of this memorial presented a thorny problem. Unlike memorials to heroes such as Paul Revere, whose glorious deeds are known to all, the Westinghouse Memorial had to rehabilitate the memory of someone who had died humiliated, forgotten, and alone. George Westinghouse (1836–1914) was one of the most versatile inventors in American history, ranking second only to Thomas Edison in the number of patents he filed during the 1870s and 1880s. From his Pittsburgh laboratory, Westinghouse invented air brakes, signals, and switches to make railroad travel safer and more efficient; he created the first gas and electric meters and shock absorbers; and he was a pioneer in

natural gas, compressed air, electric machinery, and alternating-current electricity. But the Westinghouse firm had been snatched from him by New York
bankers in the 1907 recession, and the inventor retreated to the Point Breeze
estate he had prophetically named Solitude years before.

Fifteen years after the death of Westinghouse, sixty thousand employees
around the world gathered funds to create a memorial to him. When Henry
Hornbostel was hired to coordinate the monument, he realized that it had to
be both an icon and a narrative and serve not merely to depict the deceased
but to document him, even to set the record straight. Hornbostel's response
was to stop up a small stream and set a weeping willow (the Neoclassical sign
of grief) and six black Norwegian granite benches (as aids to meditation)
around a pond, with a monumental exedra as focus. The exedra holds a portrait medallion of Westinghouse flanked by a worker and a scientist. Six plaques
document his exploitation or development of the railroad air brake, steam
turbines, signaling systems, the harnessing of Niagara Falls for power, and
the alternating-current system of electricity. Opposite, emerging from the
pond as though in a magic boat, stands French's penetrating characterization
of an idealistic youth studying what made Westinghouse great. It is a memorial that does more than commemorate; it redresses the slights of history and
gives peace to the dead.

The year 1900 was a good one for Andrew Carnegie. He reorganized his
steel companies prior to selling them the next year to J. P. Morgan; he sought
plans for the enlargement of Carnegie Institute; and he promised the mayor
of Pittsburgh he would build a school of applied industries if the city would
provide the land. The Carnegie Technical Schools held its architectural competition in 1904, opened in 1906, changed its name to Carnegie Institute of
Technology in 1912, to Carnegie-Mellon University in 1968, and to Carnegie
Mellon in 2000. Carnegie Mellon has had a meteoric rise among world universities in recent years, emerging from the pack to run alongside or ahead of
powerhouses like MIT and Stanford as a premier center for computer science,
robotics, and artificial intelligence. As one of the "new Ivies," it attracts students
from around the world, with a full 20 percent of the student body coming
from outside the United States.

Finding the right site for Carnegie's school was no problem. Christopher
Lyman Magee aided Carnegie a second time, volunteering his Chadwick
Farm, a thirty-two-acre cabbage patch on the opposite side of Junction
Hollow from Carnegie Institute. The portion of the land toward Schenley
Park was long and flat—ready-made for a campus. But the portion toward
Forbes Avenue seemed useless: part was cut through by a deep ravine, and

fig. 7.22
WESTINGHOUSE
MEMORIAL,
SCHENLEY PARK

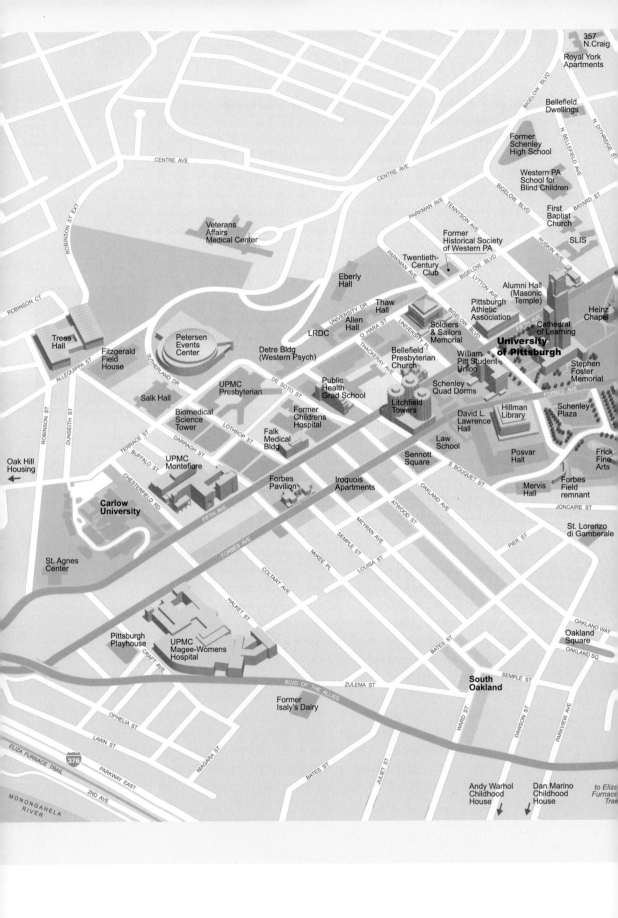

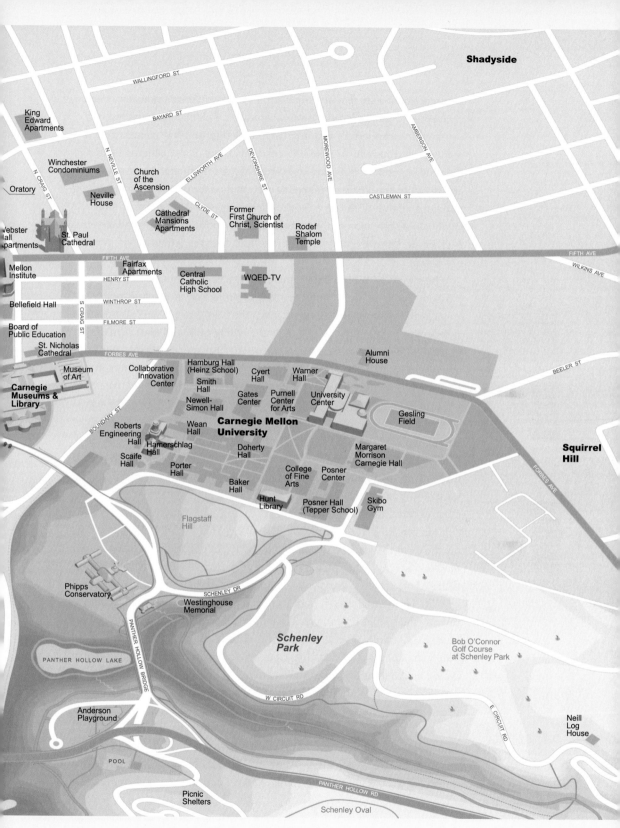

Shadyside

WALLINGFORD ST

BAYARD ST

King
Edward
Apartments

Winchester
Condominiums

Oratory

Neville
House

Church
of the
Ascension

Cathedral
Mansions
Apartments

Former
First Church of
Christ, Scientist

Rodef
Shalom
Temple

Webster
Hall
Apartments

St. Paul
Cathedral

ELLSWORTH AVE

CLYDE ST

DEVONSHIRE ST

MOREWOOD AVE

AMBERSON AVE

CASTLEMAN ST

FIFTH AVE

WILKINS AVE

Mellon
Institute

Fairfax
Apartments

HENRY ST

Central
Catholic
High School

WQED-TV

FIFTH AVE

N NEVILLE ST

N CRAIG ST

Bellefield Hall

WINTHROP ST

Board of
Public Education

FILMORE ST

St. Nicholas
Cathedral

S CRAIG ST

FORBES AVE

Alumni
House

BEELER ST

Museum
of Art

Collaborative
Innovation
Center

Hamburg Hall
(Heinz School)

Cyert
Hall

Warner
Hall

Carnegie
Museums &
Library

Smith
Hall

Gates
Center

Purnell
Center
for Arts

University
Center

Newell-
Simon Hall

Gesling
Field

Roberts
Engineering
Hall

BOUNDARY ST

Wean
Hall

**Carnegie Mellon
University**

Hamerschlag
Hall

Scaife
Hall

Doherty
Hall

Margaret
Morrison
Carnegie Hall

**Squirrel
Hill**

FORBES AVE

Porter
Hall

Baker
Hall

College
of Fine
Arts

Posner
Center

Hunt
Library

Posner Hall
(Tepper School)

Skibo
Gym

Flagstaff
Hill

Phipps
Conservatory

SCHENLEY DR

Westinghouse
Memorial

**Schenley
Park**

Bob O'Connor
Golf Course
at Schenley Park

PANTHER HOLLOW LAKE

PANTHER HOLLOW BRIDGE

Anderson
Playground

W CIRCUIT RD

E CIRCUIT RD

Neill
Log
House

POOL

Picnic
Shelters

PANTHER HOLLOW RD

Schenley Oval

Oakland

part rose about sixty feet in a small hill. The hill would be graded away half a century later, but for decades it was inviolate; A. W. Mellon lived on top of it.

Henry Hornbostel's winning campus design of 1904 concentrated on the level land next to the park. Even today, most of the campus buildings fit in the superblock bounded by Forbes Avenue, Margaret Morrison, Tech, and Frew streets. Hornbostel's solution combined features of several campus traditions, above all the new Rockefeller-sponsored University of Chicago (itself a transformation of the midway grounds of the 1893 World's Fair), the McKim-designed Columbia University, and Thomas Jefferson's University of Virginia.

As always with Hornbostel, there are fascinating mutations. Jefferson's pavilions here emerge as industrial blocks projecting at intervals from two long assembly-line spines. A viewer reads the Carnegie Mellon campus both as Jefferson's academic village and as the rolling mills and blast furnaces of Carnegie Steel. Both Jefferson and Hornbostel intended students to look out over a steep slope at the end of the campus. The view chosen by Jefferson was the bucolic Shenandoah Valley; Hornbostel was obliged to work with the train tracks in Junction Hollow. Both designers seemed to regard their end vistas as unfinished business that was left for students at the university to complete: westward expansion in the first case, industrial expansion in the second. The sense of changing times is underlined also in the choice of the central focus of the two campuses. Jefferson chose a Pantheon-inspired rotunda, symbol of past knowledge; Hornbostel chose a boiler plant with a tremendous smokestack.

Hamerschlag Hall (originally Machinery Hall), from 1912, introduces the theme of the campus building as a learned but often ironic comment on the architecture of the past. The motif of paired pilasters flanking a deep niche comes from Leon Battista Alberti's Sant'Andrea at Mantua, designed in 1470. Hornbostel used it both front and back in Hamerschlag Hall and at several other points on campus. On top he created his finest gesture: a circular Roman temple of Venus, wrapped in slightly risqué fashion around a tall yellow smokestack. To extend the exotic sources further, Hornbostel probably picked up the spiral staircase twirling around the smokestack from the eighth-century Great Mosque at Samarra. The Venus Temple at Tivoli had already inspired several notable buildings in turn-of-the-twentieth-century New York, so there was nothing especially creative in Hornbostel's use of the Roman source at Carnegie Mellon until his last step, when he made it into a smoking temple. Carnegie Mellon's temple no longer smokes, but when it did, it recalled the similar designs of Claude-Nicholas Ledoux or of Benjamin Henry Latrobe that incorporated smoke, such as Latrobe's Philadelphia Waterworks of 1800. Like their work, Hornbostel's is in the best tradition of "speaking architecture." It bespeaks his wish that Carnegie Mellon would unite art and technology just as he had coupled Venus and Vulcan.

The center of activity on the early campus was the one-eighth-mile-long corridor that slopes through Porter Hall and Baker Hall. Setting the corridors at a 4.25 percent grade facilitated Hornbostel's accommodation of the long buildings to the slope of the land, which falls off steeply enough that Carnegie Mellon students run freewheeling buggy races in the adjoining roadways. The corridors—ceremonial parade routes of industrial civilization—are Hornbostel's real triumphs. The railings are cast-iron pipes, the color accents emerge from different grades of factory brick, and the ceiling is a gently curved segmental barrel vault. The culmination of the design is a self-supporting three-story spiral staircase of Guastavino tile set in a languorous curve that may be the sole sign of lassitude in the whole institution.

On the opposite side of the Porter-Baker building is the parallel spine of Doherty Hall and Wean Hall. Hornbostel kept adding to his campus design at a keen pace until 1922, by which time Carnegie was dead and most of the intended buildings had been constructed. When construction resumed forty years later, the aluminum-dressed Hunt Library and Warner Hall were visual adversaries of the old. Fortunately, it was a Hornbostel student, Dahlen Ritchey, who in 1971 filled in another major gap in his master's scheme with Wean Hall. Of finely poured (and some cast) concrete, and with a large projecting auditorium that continues the line of Hornbostel's pavilions, Wean is a good model of gracious but nonservile contextualism.

Hornbostel obviously enjoyed translating Leon Battista Alberti into an industrial idiom, but on the two occasions when the program allowed it, he enthusiastically dressed his buildings in finer cloth. The first chance came in 1907, in his design for Margaret Morrison Carnegie Hall, the women's college named for Carnegie's adored mother. The building is set on a side street at an oblique angle to the male-dominated campus mall. It is further distinguished by its motherly, or at least feminine, half-oval forecourt of paired Doric columns that mirrors a reciprocal half-oval recession in the façade itself.

In 1996, the Margaret Morrison building was vertically expanded by the addition of a seven-thousand-square-foot penthouse called the Intelligent Workplace. Housing the university's Center for Building Performance and Diagnostics, this living laboratory tests innovations in building enclosure, interiors, heating and cooling, and telecommunications. The goal is to generate environments that meet people's physical and psychological needs. The

7.23
7.24   *7.25*
7.26

steel-and-glass penthouse does not conflict with the older building below; actually, it captures some of the spiritual quality of the best of modern design, going back to the Crystal Palace in London. In this and in all its recent buildings, Carnegie Mellon also demands a commitment to green and sustainable architecture.

Hornbostel's slightly later (1912 and 1916) College of Fine Arts has the tall wings and low projecting central pavilion of a seventeenth-century French palace, but its detailing (visible especially on the underside of the cornice) also draws from Louis Henry Sullivan. The college cuts into a hillock and so appears low and horizontal when approached from Forbes Avenue, as Hornbostel's presentation drawings envisioned. The five niches along the front of the building serve up architectural details in Gothic, Greek/Hellenistic, Roman, French Renaissance, and Egypto-Islamo-Indian styles. Achille Martini, the original sculptor, quit the job to join the Italian army in World War I, but the university completed about 95 percent of his work in 1993.

It is instructive to reflect on the close parallels in physical size, student-body size, and curriculum between the College of Fine Arts and Walter Gropius's Bauhaus at Dessau, which opened a decade later. Hornbostel embraced neither the industrial idiom nor the open plan that attracted Gropius, yet for this building he integrated the five arts as creatively as Gropius did in Dessau. Hornbostel placed the sculpture studios in the basement, a theater and exhibition hall on the main floor, music practice rooms in the mezzanine, drafting halls for architecture and design in the upper stories, and painting studios in the skylit attic. For years the attic held loges—tiny compartments in which architecture students were locked up while *en concours*, competing in design problems the way Hornbostel (and academics such as H. H. Richardson before him) had competed while attending the École des Beaux-Arts in Paris. Like that famous French institution, the College of Fine Arts recalls the glory of art in frescoes, plaster casts, and building plans inlaid in the floor. At one's feet lie images of the Egyptian temple of Horus in Edfu, the Parthenon, Chartres Cathedral, and Michelangelo's design for St. Peter's. The last plan lacks its four front columns—but the Beaux-Arts always did have an arbitrary take on history.

Hornbostel's work at Carnegie Mellon was essentially complete by 1930, and the campus remained little changed for much of the twentieth century except for the addition of Wean Hall and some buildings on Forbes Avenue. That construction drought ended with a new master plan in the mid-1980s. A new axis, perpendicular to the Forbes Avenue mall (traditionally called "the Cut") and pointing to the intersection of Forbes Avenue and Margaret

Morrison Street, became the center line for the construction of the new East Campus in 1987. The first phase of the new campus yielded Gesling Stadium, the backside of which doubles as a parking garage, several athletic fields, and a chain of residence halls. The new buildings emulate Hornbostel's concern for axes and enclosure, while their yellow factory-brick walls emerge as crisp and scaled-down versions of his Beaux-Arts confections.

The next phase of construction was perpendicular to the East Campus axis, along the Cut. Hornbostel had initially designed a viaduct to span the gully—an idea that died in Pittsburgh but may have influenced Bertram Grosvenor Goodhue's thousand-foot causeway approach to the San Diego Exposition of 1916. The hill on which A. W. Mellon lived was eventually graded and the gully largely built over. The dominant building now is the University Center of 1995, which likewise echoes Hornbostel's use of material and his aesthetics. The main impact comes from the twenty-one openings defining its massive loggia, which extends 420 feet along the Cut. The rhythmic cadence of the openings reminds some observers of the Uffizi Gallery in Florence. The University Center terminates in a rotunda at its south end, which softens its severity and links it to the portico that went up nearby at Margaret Morrison Hall a hundred years before. Completing the implied quadrangle along the Cut is the Purnell Center for the Arts, erected opposite the University Center in 1999. A parallel building project nearby yielded the Posner Hall extension to the business school and a fine garden called the Kraus Campo, a collaboration between conceptual artist (and Carnegie Mellon alumnus) Mel Bochner and the landscape architecture firm of Michael Van Valkenburgh Associates.

The East Campus and the quadrangle along the Cut constituted an enormous building campaign by any standards, but other parts of the Carnegie Mellon campus were also rebuilt around the year 2000. One neglected area had been the jumbled descent into Junction Hollow, which was partially upgraded in 1987 with the addition of a physical plant building and revised again in 1996, when Payette Associates hung Roberts Engineering Hall on the escarpment directly below Hamerschlag Hall. The brow of the building, constructed of concrete, metal, and glass, now incongruously carries the prow of the USS *Pittsburgh*, which formerly emerged from the same hillside. From a purist's standpoint, the new building detracts from the grandeur of the Hornbostel masterpiece at the crown of the cliff, but the architects succeeded in responding to the existing architecture and making the building mostly unobtrusive and well suited to its difficult site.

At different times the university also built on the Forbes Avenue side of campus: in 1984, putting up the Cyert Computing Center, and in the next two decades, adding two more structures on the Junction Hollow slopes. Next to Hornbostel's U.S. Bureau of Mines building (today Carnegie Mellon's Hamburg Hall, from 1912) stands the Gates Hillman Center (in full, the Gates Center for Computer Science and the Hillman Center for Future-Generation Technologies), sited in a natural ravine that previously broke up the prevailing campus building grid. The Gates Hillman Center uses a skewed axis and angled exterior walls to link with these preexisting buildings, at least visually, though its slate-and-zinc skin finally departs from the tone set by Hornbostel's yellow brick.

Visitors to Carnegie Mellon cannot miss the distinctive *Walking to the Sky* sculpture by alumnus Jonathan Borofsky that was installed on Forbes Avenue in 2006 to predictable controversy. The arrangement of human figures (carefully rendered as multiethnic) walking up a one-hundred-foot pole was planned for the intersection of the Hornbostel Mall and the Cut, but the site was dropped in favor of the one on Forbes rather than challenge Hornbostel's vista and the supremacy of the Hamerschlag tower. Many regard this as the best sculpture in Pittsburgh. Others see it as merely provocative, but even this dispute reveals an intensity most public art never manages to achieve even after decades, let alone in a few years.

NORTH OAKLAND

The central crossing of Oakland is not an intersection of streets but of blocks, specifically, the twelve-block east-west arm on Fifth Avenue from Morewood to Thackeray, and the eight-block north-south arm along Craig Street from Forbes Avenue to Baum Boulevard. This is neither Carnegie nor Mellon territory, though it owes much to both dominions. It was mainly crafted by Franklin Nicola, who drew up its urban blueprint in the 1890s and carefully tended it for nearly half a century. Today, its elegant synagogue and churches, its clubs, civic buildings, apartments, and select homes, make it a model inner-city suburb.

The planning of central Oakland actually began a generation before Nicola appeared, in a middle-class community of the 1850s whose remnants survive today in the boutiques and restaurants of Craig Street between Forbes and Fifth avenues. Originally part of the substantial Oakland estate of the English-born settler James Chadwick, the Craig Street area was subdivided once in the 1840s, when it was purchased as a suburban retreat by publisher

363

Neville B. Craig, and again a decade later when Craig sold much of it to a land-speculation company headed by Edward Dithridge.

Dithridge erected a turreted brick mansion on Fifth Avenue between Bellefield and Dithridge streets, with a series of other princely houses around it for other members of his family. He laid out the cross-streets of Henry, Winthrop, and Filmore and carved up the south half of Bellefield (the name under which the land was patented in the eighteenth century) into lots for about a hundred small houses set between Craig and Neville streets and Fifth and Forbes avenues.

The style of houses such as those at 4612 and 4614 Henry Street might without contradiction be called vernacular Greek Revival, since they were erected by untutored builders decades after the Revival Style had gone out of fashion on the East Coast. The homes along Filmore Street, particularly the sequence of 4628 to 4638 Filmore, were built in the 1870s in Italianate or High Victorian Gothic dress. Their size and elaboration indicate a change of target market: not workers or even the middle class but the upper middle class.

The gentrification of Craig Street in the late 1970s and the 1980s stemmed from its ideal placement as a short cohesive district between the two major drawing points of Carnegie Institute and St. Paul Cathedral and from the adaptability of the large mansions and townhouses erected there a century before. What used to be fashionable Second Empire and Queen Anne drawing rooms now serve as coffeehouses, restaurants (some of which serve organic food), specialty shops for everything from Indian groceries to Irish jewelry, and countercultural medical arts such as hypnosis, midwifery, and acupuncture. Patrons spill out to sidewalk tables on sunny days, making Craig one of the vibrant spots of Oakland.

St. Paul Roman Catholic Cathedral is the most prominent of a half-dozen Downtown congregations that migrated to Oakland early in the twentieth century. At the crossroads of Fifth Avenue and Craig Street, the sanctuary was put up in 1906 with Frick money from the sale of the old cathedral on the site of the Union Trust in Downtown. The designers, from Chicago, were specialists in building Gothic Revival churches for Catholic parishes across the country. St. Paul is a hybrid of an unusual French Gothic plan of six towers and four side aisles plus an overlay of English and German features in the elevation—an accurate reflection of its polyglot diocese. The flora and fauna carved into the limestone façade are all native to America. The cathedral quality of St. Paul is strengthened by its attendant diocesan buildings, particularly Synod Hall around the corner on North Craig and the rectory at the corner of Dithridge. Nearby are a parish house, a convent, and a school.

fig. 7.27
St. Paul Cathedral,
Oakland

Leaving behind its traditional constituency of churches, shops, and apartment houses, central Oakland began in the early 1980s to welcome a wave of high-tech firms that were drawn to its position halfway between Carnegie Mellon and the University of Pittsburgh. Immediately in front of St. Paul, at 4500 Fifth Avenue, stands the Software Engineering Institute, built in 1987. This houses a Defense Department collaboration with Carnegie Mellon that was a key element in making Pittsburgh a world capital in software expertise. Diagonally across Fifth Avenue, at Bellefield, high-tech and religion coexist in Bellefield Towers, a 1980s glass-walled and polychrome structure designed for high-tech and biotech companies. A solitary square tower of rough-hewn and irregularly coursed sandstone stands in front, a remnant of the old Bellefield Presbyterian Church. That congregation's successor Community of Reconciliation today worships in a special precinct of Bellefield Towers.

Another of the stylish neighborhood churches in Oakland is St. Nicholas Greek Orthodox Cathedral at the corner of Forbes and Dithridge. Originally the First Congregational Church, until 1921, this is an unusually vigorous design in yellow industrial brick preceded by a dramatic Ionic portico. The interior of St. Nicholas should not be missed as an architectural paradigm of America itself: a cool Protestant interior heated up by a blazing iconostasis.

The First Baptist Church at the corner of North Bellefield Avenue and Bayard, a block north of Fifth, is probably better known outside Pittsburgh than in town as a master work by Bertram Grosvenor Goodhue, America's most creative Gothic Revivalist of the twentieth century. In 1910, he beat sixty other contestants in a national design competition for the church. The building went up in 1912, but the congregation was formed a century earlier and at first used the Monongahela River for baptisms. The interior of First Baptist has the richness of materials, textures, and volumes that keeps Goodhue's reputation high today. On the outside, the power of the elevation and massing stems from its forced compactness, so that the church rises up as a sheer vertical cliff of limestone and glass. Unfortunately, neither the plan nor the elevation of First Baptist works to best advantage on this site, which is too open and detached from the street on one side and too close on the other to the University of Pittsburgh's poured-concrete School of Information Science, an eight-story Expressionist exercise in the style of California's William Pereira.

Close to First Baptist, at Bayard Street and Dithridge, stands the Pittsburgh Oratory, housing an array of Catholic groups and presenting in its façade an even newer essay in Gothic Revival, from 1997. This wonderfully rich evocation of a medieval English college could be called Gothic Revival revival, considering how difficult it is to find the budgets and the workmanship for such elaborate historical projects today. In 2007, the Oratory added a detached element to this complex at 211 North Dithridge, half a block away: a ninety-foot-high clock tower of brick, with decorative lozenges of blackened bricks standing out from the red. The tower is square, with corner pinnacles, and is home to the Gailliot Center for Newman Studies, which now houses the most important collection of writings by John Henry Cardinal Newman anywhere outside England.

Multifamily buildings existed in American architecture from the time of the early republic, but only in the late nineteenth century did an apartment type reach sufficient respectability that society leaders would live in it. Conservative Pittsburgh never wholly approved of apartments except as pieds-à-terre for country residents, but, ever the pioneer, Franklin Nicola broke some of this prejudice with his Schenley Hotel of 1898, which many of the Pittsburgh elite used as a residence. Nicola followed in the 1920s with the massive Schenley Apartments next to the hotel, rendering buildings of such luxury that anyone who lived there was automatically assumed to be both rich and prominent.

Oakland preserves scores of apartment buildings from different eras, several of which stand out as good representatives of their type or period. In 1925, Henry Hornbostel and Eric Fisher Wood set the trapezoidal Webster Hall Apartments at the bend in Fifth Avenue at North Dithridge, to make its eleven-story bulk appear even larger than it is. It was created as an athletic club of four hundred residential units, then became a hotel and finally an apartment building.

Down the block is the elaborately Tudor Hampton Hall at 166 North Dithridge, near Bayard, with just fifty-four apartments. More attuned to modernism, although ornamented with coats of arms, Scottish strapwork, and terra cotta, are the Fairfax at 4614 Fifth Avenue and Cathedral Mansions at 4716 Ellsworth Avenue. The modernist aesthetic partially enunciated in these prewar buildings and in Webster Hall is fully pronounced in two postwar apartments just west of the Cathedral Mansions: the Le Corbusier–inspired Neville House at 552 North Neville Street and the jade tile–clad Winchester Condominiums at 540 North Neville. The Astorino firm picked up the progressive taste that informed those buildings when it added the Metropolitan Shadyside condominiums on the opposite side of Neville Street in 2007.

367

The Irish immigrant builder John McSorley was responsible for two of Oakland's best apartment blocks. The King Edward Apartments, a Tudor Revival block on Bayard Street at Melville, from 1914, was followed a decade later by an additional Art Deco wing on Craig. Farther from the center of Oakland, and rising high above it, are the Royal York Apartments at Bigelow Boulevard and Dithridge. Developer McSorley had worked as a builder in Toronto and Chicago before coming to Pittsburgh, so his apartments combine the names of distinguished Toronto hotels with the luxury of Chicago's Gold Coast. The Royal York is one of the best Art Deco designs in the city, with buff tile walls beautifully molded into Egyptoid strips suggestive of bundled papyrus columns. The apartment was angled to give its inhabitants spectacular views across Oakland to the south and to the north across Two Mile Run into Bloomfield.

Some of the newest and oldest of central Oakland's apartments are within sight of the Royal York. Bellefield Dwellings on Centre Avenue, between Bellefield and Dithridge, went up in 1904 and was one of the earliest society apartments in the city. It was promoted by Robert C. Hull and Francis T. F. Lovejoy (a junior partner of Andrew Carnegie) as the most luxurious of its type in the country. The Bellefield astonished Pittsburghers with integral garages in the basement; mahogany woodwork and tapestry mosaics in the lobbies; and wall safes, telephones, refrigerators, and direct-access passenger and service elevators for every apartment. Such interior luxuries were suggested on the outside by the vigorous color massing of the Jacobean Revival brick walls, which makes the whole block look like a private château. Still a pleasant and sunny block, it serves today as federally subsidized housing for the elderly.

The most specialized of Oakland's apartment blocks is the William S. Moorhead Tower on North Craig Street at Baum, a sixteen-story slab that accommodates 142 apartments for the blind. The building mixes practicality and whimsy on the outside, with concrete block and poured concrete that has been stuccoed over and painted bright yellow. The blocky mass of the tower is relieved by a stepped parapet at the top, a vertical glazed strip indicating the location of the elevator lobbies, and a ground-floor *aedicula* that signifies in the most basic way the path to the main door. The scale is excellently handled, so those decorative touches are neither overpowering nor mincing compared to the massiveness of the building itself. Of special importance to the blind inhabitants are ingenious features such as changes of texture in the floor and walls and piped-in music for orientation toward the elevators, creating what designer Arthur Lubetz calls "a nonvisual conception of space."

369

fig. 7.28
LUBETZ ARCHITECTS,
CRAIG STREET,
OAKLAND

Given Pittsburgh's traditional work ethic, it is fitting that the city's pioneer essay in Postmodernism was the 1982 recycling of an old garage into the Arthur Lubetz Architectural Office at 357 North Craig. A generation after it went up, the Lubetz office continues to surprise, and gratify, passersby. Lubetz made clear that he was extending the old garage by adding a second skin to it on the parking-lot side. The best part of the addition is the underbelly of the staircase, in which a spectator understands the positive-negative volume of the deep steps as though in one of the fetchingly ambiguous prints of M. C. Escher.

The "second skin" concept continues in three separate segments along the parking-lot façade, each with an elegant thin wall made of fine concrete blocks. The blocks are cemented together with pink mortar, recalling the exquisite pointing of the granite blocks in H. H. Richardson's courthouse Downtown. On the front, the same pink mortar holds in place glass blocks of different sizes and rhythms. The whole effect, both the vocabulary and the grammar of ornament, is one of the richest in town.

Franklin Nicola died close to insolvency in 1938, leaving an estate of just $2,216, but he had lived to see his vision of an Oakland civic center come to fruition. He reasoned that a neighborhood with public monuments but without inhabitants would be no neighborhood at all, so he developed other parts of Mary Schenley's estate as apartments, clubhouses, and private residences. In 1905, he designated the portion of the Schenley cow pasture bounded by Parkman Avenue and Bigelow Boulevard as a residential quarter for ninety-six houses, which he called Schenley Farms. East of this quarter, several buildings already stood from the years before Nicola's arrival, primarily the Western Pennsylvania School for Blind Children, at Bigelow and Bayard, from 1894. Among the most important structures to go up during Nicola's tenure as neighborhood entrepreneur was the mammoth Schenley High School on Bigelow at Centre, in 1916.

What distinguished the Schenley Farms development was the care taken to place the best architecture within the best urban context. On top of his initial investment of $2.5 million in land, Nicola spent another $1.5 million (figures approaching an aggregate of about $100 million today) on improvements to the streets. He insisted on underground wiring, which even now is rare in Pittsburgh; dense planting of shade trees; and construction of a huge retaining wall to secure Parkman Street against the hillside slope that bends around it. The construction standards set by Nicola were unheard of outside housing for the very rich. For twenty thousand to thirty thousand dollars, purchasers got thirteen-inch-thick brick walls with insulating air chambers, hardwood floors, finished basements, brass pipes, hot-water radiators recessed beneath windows, integral ducts for vacuum cleaning, four telephones per house, stained glass, and elaborate woodwork. An additional thirty-nine houses, still elegant but more modest, were created by Nicola in Schenley Farms Terrace on the hillside above, fronting on Centre Avenue and Bigelow Boulevard.

Lacking clients for his risky venture, Nicola employed architects to build eleven model houses on the west side of Lytton Street in 1906, then advertised them as a come-on for the sale of the remaining lots. By 1909, half of the ninety-six lots had been filled; by 1920, the group was complete.

fig. 7.29
SCHENLEY
FARMS

The homes of Schenley Farms constitute a remarkable ensemble, not just for Pittsburgh but for any city. The homes were less advanced in style than in technology, yet in that respect, too, they are an interesting lot. Contrary to most upper-middle-class suburbs before World War I, just one house exhbits the Beaux-Arts Style. In a few cases—for example, 204 Tennyson, by the progressive firm of Kiehnel & Elliott—local architects emulated their Prairie School colleagues in Chicago. For about a third of the houses, the models were based on the work of contemporary British architects of the so-called English Free Style, particularly Sir Edwin Lutyens, C. F. A. Voysey, C. R. Mackintosh, and M. H. Baillie Scott. Some designs instead recalled the work of the earlier Richard Norman Shaw. The other half more predictably depended on the various revivals: Tudor, Colonial, Georgian, Neoclassical (including some learned details from the French Claude-Nicholas Ledoux and the Americans Thomas Jefferson, William Thornton, and Benjamin Henry Latrobe). A half-dozen houses dared to be simply vernacular. Nicola's advertising invariably referred to Schenley Farms as a model community, but for once he was too modest: compared to housing conditions in the rest of the country around 1905, it bordered on the utopian.

On the border of residential Schenley Farms, between Bigelow Boulevard and University Place, stands a singular Oakland icon. In 1907, a national design competition was held to create the Soldiers and Sailors Memorial Hall and Museum. The contest attracted famous entrants such as Cass Gilbert, John Russell Pope, and Ernest Flagg, but it was won by Henry Hornbostel, who was already well known in town. Hornbostel designed this long-delayed tribute to Allegheny County's Civil War veterans to face Bigelow Boulevard, as the competition demanded, but he persuaded the county commissioners to allow him to rotate it ninety degrees to address the more compelling vista on Fifth Avenue.

Soldiers and Sailors Memorial Hall opened in 1910 with a design that is as vigorous though not so suave as Henry Hornbostel's Rodef Shalom Temple or his College of Fine Arts building at Carnegie Mellon University. Its strength lies in its deft solution to a complex program that called for meeting rooms, a memorial, an auditorium that would seat twenty-five hundred people, and a banquet hall for the thinning ranks of Civil War veterans. As always, Hornbostel showed a good eye for structural solutions. The four slopes of the pyramidal roof—an allusion to the Mausoleum of Halicarnassus—are rendered in poured concrete. The banquet hall is carried over the void of the auditorium on a hidden bridge truss—an acknowledgment of a static liability that nonetheless calls for caution when the room is used for dances.

fig. 7.30
Soldiers & Sailors
Memorial Hall
and Museum

fig. 7.31
Pittsburgh Athletic
Association

The main ventilating duct of the hall emerges at the apex of the pyramid, and on cold winter days, the building comes alive as it puffs hot air through the roof. The coloring inside is vivid to the point of gaudy, and the piers of the banquet hall are splayed into the shape of coffins—another edgy choice. The message a visitor takes away is not how clever the architect was but how noble the veterans were. In its heroic scale, exactness of plan, integration of the various arts, and profound expression of the institutional message, the Soldiers and Sailors hall is a textbook example of what a Beaux-Arts building was supposed to do.

Pittsburgh society has a longtime reputation for gregariousness. Church clubs, singing clubs, sports clubs, and general social clubs still number in the hundreds today, but only the half-dozen clubhouses (broadly defined) in Oakland constitute a British-style "clubland." The Pittsburgh Athletic Association (PAA), on Fifth Avenue at Bigelow Boulevard, represents clubhouse architecture at its best. Architect Benno Jannsen imagined the PAA as a Venetian Renaissance palace and used its giant-order pilasters and engaged columns as a screen in order to create five stories behind what reads as a two-story elevation. The Venetian precedents were probably Michele Sanmicheli's Palazzo Grimani and Jacopo Sansovino's Libreria on Piazza San Marco, but Janssen's synthesis creates something entirely new. The white limestone and terra-cotta exterior has weathered well, and the cutting of the architectural details and sculptural reliefs could not be better. The decoration inside includes large murals, a mildly homoerotic painting in the lobby, and heavily carved ceilings by the New York decorator Albert Herter.

Janssen added a companion to the PAA a few years later when he designed the Masonic Temple on Fifth Avenue at Lytton, today the University of Pittsburgh's Alumni Hall. This severe limestone rendering of a Greek temple for years accommodated the twenty-five thousand Masons in the Pittsburgh district with a complex series of meeting and ceremonial rooms. From the outside, the temple appears to be three stories high, but inside are four floors and two mezzanines. The second and third floors once contained chambers rendered in architectural motifs according to their names: Doric, Gothic, Ionic, Corinthian, Tudor, and Egyptian. The exterior is totally uninformative about these interior arrangements, as though to protect the secrecy of the rituals.

A theater and concert hall named Syria Mosque stood next to the PAA from 1915 until its demolition in 1994. This was a quirky building with a decidedly Hollywood view of Islamic culture, but its excellent acoustics served the city well. Concerts by Fritz Reiner and the Pittsburgh Symphony

373

in the 1930s gave way to rock bands in the 1980s, until the worthy structure was pulled down for a parking lot. Tearing down Syria Mosque was an act both cynical and comical, involving a fierce bidding war between two rival branches of the University of Pittsburgh. The only good result of the war was a rekindling of preservationist sentiment in town. The hall's chandeliers and its four silky bronze sphinxes by Giuseppe Moretti survive at the Shriners' current headquarters in Cheswick, northeast of Pittsburgh.

Benno Janssen showed particular wit in the design of the Twentieth Century Club at the intersection of Bigelow and Parkman. This women's club was founded in 1894 in the afterglow of the Women's Pavilion at the Chicago World's Fair of 1893, but the original quarters of 1910 proved shabby and inadequate after just twenty years. Invited to do something better, Janssen seems to have asked himself, "What historical precedent is there for cloaking a poor old building in the skin of a new one?" The answer was Michelangelo's rebuilding of the Capitoline Palace in Rome, and Janssen faithfully followed that model as he renovated the club. Another sort of club next door, at 4338 Bigelow, was the Historical Society of Western Pennsylvania, a jewel of a building from 1912 whose adaptive reuse has been held up by years of neighborhood dissent.

Henry Hornbostel's nearby University Club, built in 1926 at 123 University Place and now the University of Pittsburgh faculty club, is internally very effective in the usual clubby mode. Almost back-to-back with this block, at the corner of O'Hara and Thackeray streets, stands the former Central Turnverein, a prominent German singing and athletic club that disbanded after World War I, not long after the building went up. Between these two clubs stands another, the Concordia Club, at the corner of O'Hara and University Place. It moved here from Old Allegheny in 1913, and this structure is one of many instances of the Kaufmann family's patronage in architecture. Both the Concordia and the former Turnverein buildings are unremarkable two-story blocks of beige brick, but the latter is much enlivened by the Cubist-style cement decoration on the doorframe and between the windows, which seems to pick up Frank Lloyd Wright's ornamental work at Chicago's Midway Gardens. Secure as Oakland's clubs were on the eve of World War I, this bold and futuristic decoration suggests that even "clubland" was feeling the winds of change.

fig. 7.32
SOUTH OAKLAND,
AERIAL VIEW

fig. 7.33
ROBINSON STREET
HOMES

SOUTH OAKLAND

The upscale transformation of Craig Street and the additions to Carnegie Mellon, the University of Pittsburgh, and the medical center are the most recent in a series of changes that have come to Oakland since the 1830s. But along with these changes there remain stretches more characteristic of working-class neighborhoods. Modest homes are densely packed on Oakland Hill and in south Oakland, and these areas have an intense if often melancholy appeal of their own.

Chesterfield, Robinson, and Dunseith streets on the Oakland brow of the Hill are the best survivors from Oakland's years as a working-class village. Chesterfield, still paved in cobblestones, is one of the newer applications of an old development formula on these streets: a steep slope flanked by a hundred identical peaked wooden houses. The homes are saved from monotony by their lively rhythm as they sit two-by-two on their own serrated terraces, like teeth on a saw.

The long rows of brick houses on Dunseith and Robinson are older and squatter but still starkly effective. A nonprofit group called Breachmenders is a strong presence here; their focus is on improving living conditions in this section of Oakland by purchasing, renovating, and reselling houses to families in need of assistance. The agency seeks to minimize the breaches that occasionally open up in these rows—often the first sign of neighborhood decay. At the broad intersection of Robinson and Fifth Avenue sits a row of eight Italianate houses of the 1870s, half with porches and half with boldly protruding three-panel bay windows—but also one unsightly gap where a house was lost to fire. The townhouses create a lingering and effective memory of Oakland for travelers proceeding down this dramatic bend to lower Fifth Avenue and the Hill.

fig. 7.34
TOWNHOUSES,
FIFTH AVENUE,
OAKLAND

fig. 7.35
OAK HILL

This point of overlap between Oakland and the Hill was blighted for much of the twentieth century by ill-conceived housing projects such as Allequippa Terrace, which was developed in 1939 and largely abandoned by the 1990s. Starting in 1996, Allequippa Terrace was redeveloped into the mixed-income settlement of Oak Hill. A protracted battle ensued with the University of Pittsburgh for development rights to the land, but Oak Hill got most of it— a coup for any development so close to university territory.

Oak Hill's planners made a concerted effort to connect their new buildings to the surrounding neighborhood—something Allequippa Terrace had failed to do—by replacing the original winding street plan with a grid and realigning existing streets to extend into it. The homes, some wood-frame cottages and others high-style apartments, generally relate in scale and style to housing in the surrounding neighborhood, whereas the severe old blocks of Allequippa Terrace did not. Generous greenspace and sweeping views of Downtown and the Monongahela Valley complete this new vision of a revived neighborhood for middle-income Oakland residents.

For a century, Pittsburgh had few neighborhood portals as clear cut as the entrance to Oakland that one would use if coming up from the Golden Triangle. The long climb up Fifth or Forbes avenues ended, and the two streets leveled off and stretched broad and straight across the Oakland plain. At Forbes and Craft, the neighborhood guardian was St. Peter's Church, erected in 1852 after its congregation moved from Grant Street. This church and its alter ego, John Notman's St. Mark's in Philadelphia, were among the best products of the ecclesiological, or archaeologically correct, period of the Gothic Revival in America. Then, in the 1990s, St. Peter's was demolished a second time and gave way to a science building for Carlow University. The second Oakland portal, at the intersection of Fifth and Robinson, met a happier fate. That crucial entry into Oakland is still dominated by the brick mass of St. Agnes Roman Catholic Church (now the St. Agnes Center of Carlow University), which since 1917 has been strategically angled like a billboard to herald the entrance to a new neighborhood for visitors from Downtown.

South Oakland is a separate trapezoid bounded by Forbes Avenue, Bouquet and Bates streets, and the Monongahela riverbank. This remnant of old Oakland was largely unplanned, and it derives its character not from any monuments but from its unpretentious streets. Most of the houses were built by speculators in the thirty or forty years following the Civil War, when the Coltarts, Crafts, Halkets, Meyrans, and Atwoods were breaking up their estates into the long blocks that still bear those family names. The focus of Oakland after the Civil War was initially on the Jones & Laughlin works that dominated the Monongahela riverbank below the Oakland cliff. Passage to the Golden Triangle by horsecar began in 1859, but it was slow and expensive. Cable car service started in 1888 (the triangle formed by Cable and Semple streets marks the old turnaround), until Oakland was finally linked to Downtown by electric-powered trolleys in the 1890s.

Though somewhat roughly treated during the century in which Oakland has served—not always happily—as a college town, some intriguing monuments still line these streets. An important part of the neighborhood's entertainment constituency is the Pittsburgh Playhouse at Craft Avenue and Hamlet. It was built as the Tree of Life Synagogue by David Crone, son of the resident rabbi, in 1906, and for decades provided a theater complex for Point Park University. The neighboring street names—Elsinore, Hamlet, Ophelia, Romeo, and Juliet—are perfect complements. The main sanctuary of the synagogue was theatrical to begin with, featuring the bold mass of an octagonal pyramid and a porch of six oversized Tuscan columns.

The elegant old estate fronting the erstwhile synagogue has been transformed, too. Early in the nineteenth century it had sheltered the Maples, the striking Greek Revival mansion of shoe pioneer Asa Childs, later father-in-law to Henry Clay Frick. The influential Pittsburgh politician Christopher Lyman Magee later bought the grounds, erecting both a huge trolley barn for his public-transportation monopoly and an impressive Victorian mansion for himself. The mansion and grounds in turn became the core of what is today the UPMC Magee-Womens Hospital. A vaguely Egyptian-style wrought-iron fence still encircles part of the grounds, although the Magee mansion long ago ceded its place to the hospital.

The eight blocks of Forbes Avenue from Craft Avenue to the Cathedral of Learning are the heart of Oakland's separate existence as a college town. Fast-food places, bookstores, and CD outlets are the rule, but the Iroquois

377

Apartments building dominates the block of Forbes between Meyran and Atwood. The massive but bland Forbes Tower skyscraper went up behind the apartment block in 1996, and, luckily, it was just far enough back to make it invisible from Forbes Avenue. It housed the administrators of the UPMC health system before their move to the U.S. Steel tower in Downtown.

The Iroquois was developed by James Flannery, who in 1903 followed the lead of Nicola, with his Schenley Hotel, and created this luxurious apartment building, the first in town to include prestige shops on the ground floor. The Iroquois's shops are no longer prestigious, and its apartments are no longer residences but doctors' offices. Still, the building remains a fine piece of streetscape. It consists of five stories of brown glazed Roman brick, arranged as four separate wings over a commercial base. Frederick Osterling enlivened the huge block with exaggerated ornamental details, undulations in the façade, and a massive entablature. The Iroquois is a handsome addition to Forbes Avenue even on overcast days. When the sun catches Osterling's details, it becomes a universe unto itself.

Two other commercial buildings exude confidence in the same manner as the Iroquois: the former No. 4 Precinct Station at 3807 Forbes, which served for years as the King's Court Theater, and the former Isaly's Dairy on the Boulevard of the Allies at the intersection of Halket Street. The Victorian-era police station is an almost absurdly pretentious Romanesque Revival sandstone fortress that was evidently thought appropriate as a symbol of law and order, while Isaly's (today administrative offices for UPMC Magee-Womens Hospital) owes its commanding position to the sightlines that were created after the Boulevard of the Allies sliced Oakland in half in the 1920s.

There is a decidedly Roaring Twenties feel to the Isaly's façade, which is covered in Art Deco terra-cotta tiles. But there is also solemnity in the bold piers that recall the Egyptian temple of Saqqara, whose excavation by the French took place just before this south Oakland showpiece went up in 1930. Built as the main factory and retail outlet for the Isaly food chain, this radiant building was for years a temple to a different sort of cult: the chipped ham, the Klondike bars, and "skyscraper" ice cream cones that were traditional features of Pittsburgh's regional cuisine.

Immediately behind Isaly's is the enclave of Oak Cliff, reached where Craft Avenue points toward the Monongahela riverbank. This triangle of narrow streets ends in Lawn Street, a terrace so narrow that homes line only one side of it. Until the 1980s, the narrow grass strip (the "lawn" of the street's name) was hemmed in by the towers of the Jones & Laughlin Eliza Furnaces, as well as by a curtain of pollution. Today, nothing blocks Oak Cliff's superb vistas over the Monongahela to South Side and the skyscrapers Downtown.

fig. 7.36
ISALY'S DAIRY,
NOW PART OF
UPMC MAGEE-
WOMENS HOSPITAL

The crowding of Oakland's houses and the occasional flourish of an Italian-language sign give nearby Bates, Semple, and Dawson streets the flavor of Naples. Neapolitan for sure is the complexion of a score of tiny but dignified row houses of the 1920s, whose solariums stand just a few feet from the noisy corner of Bates Street and the Boulevard of the Allies. These streets of south Oakland, especially Atwood Street and Oakland Avenue, have also become the center for inexpensive ethnic dining in the city; Korean, Thai, Indian, and Mexican restaurants now offer permutations on the standard college fare of sandwiches and pizza.

Oakland Square, opening off Dawson Street, was created in 1890 by Charles Chance, chairman of the Oakland Board of Trade, as a Boston- or Paris-style grouping of two-family frame and brick houses with mansard roofs and oriel windows in a style close to that of Frank Furness. The square is sober and impressive, accentuated by the developer's generosity in leaving its east side open for a view of Schenley Park on the opposite bluff of Four Mile Run.

A half-dozen blocks away, on the far side of Boulevard of the Allies, stands the childhood home of Andy Warhol, where he also spent his college days attending school across the gully at Carnegie Mellon. The simple yellow brick double house (the Warhola family owned just the right side) stands at 3252 Dawson Street, between Swinburne and Frazier. In 2005, it became Warhola property once more.

7.37

7.38   7.39

         7.40

fig. 7.37
ANDY WARHOL'S
HOUSE, ON RIGHT

fig. 7.38
OAKLAND SQUARE
HOUSES OVERLOOKING
SCHENLEY PARK

fig. 7.39
INTERSECTION OF
FRAZIER AND ROMEO
STAIR-STREETS

fig. 7.40
SHRINE TO THE
BLESSED MOTHER,
OAKLAND

Dawson Street makes a sharp left turn into Bouquet Street, the jewel of which is the former S. Lorenzo di Gamberale Mutual Benefit Association clubhouse at 379 South Bouquet. Built in 1938 as the social center of an Italian community that had established itself a half-century earlier on this street and in Junction Hollow below, the churchlike assembly hall, now largely given over to rental units, is emblazoned with twin reliefs of dogs set in its scrubbed brick façade. The club members still live in homes precariously set on the slopes of Joncaire Street or along the public steps called Diulus Way. A descent deep into the haunting gully of Junction Hollow is a sobering conclusion to any study of Oakland, offering a vision of the ancient terrain before the effects of human intervention.

A few blocks toward the Monongahela there is an equivalent drop-off on Frazier Street, which also ends as public steps. Halfway toward the precipitous cliff by the Bates Street gully, the Frazier Street steps meet those of Romeo Street, itself part roadway and part public steps. Juliet Street is just a single block away, but those star-crossed lovers will never intersect, unlike Hamlet and Ophelia streets, which meet a few blocks over.

Oakland has, and always has had, a certain sacred dimension. It comes from the tightness of the neighborhood bonds, from the protective profile of the Cathedral of Learning that is visible from every street, and from the Virgin Mary statues standing on dozens of lawns, often with a sort of half-bathtub grotto sheltering them from the elements. The great mark of popular faith in the neighborhood is the Virgin of the Parkway (also known as the Shrine of the Blessed Mother, though the local Catholic hierarchy will have nothing to do with it). The fourteen Stations of the Cross were dug into the rocky bluff where the Oakland plateau drops several hundred feet to the inbound lanes of expressway I-376. One comes upon the shrine by a path at the end of Wakefield Street, itself reached from the Boulevard of the Allies via the full length of Ward Street; passersby offer directions to tourists. The shrine dates from 1956, but no one remembers who first thought to erect the crosses, the Nativity, the glass-encased Crucifix, and the concrete Virgin garlanded in artificial flowers. Some say the shrine's founder was a Jones & Laughlin steelworker; others say it was a nun or local woman. The grotto (for such it is, since water seeps from the rocks in all seasons) is painstakingly tended by neighborhood women, and extends its blessing to motorists stuck in traffic on the Parkway below, who can use it.

THE RIVER TOWNS: VALLEYS OF INDUSTRY

fig. 8.1
ON THE ALLEGHENY

The confluence of its three rivers prophesied Pittsburgh's rise as the dominant city of western Pennsylvania, but it took a while for that natural prophecy to be fulfilled. During its first century of existence, the town was little more than a regional coordinating center for the hundred agricultural settlements and river towns around it. Pittsburgh assumed dominant status over these other towns only with the coming of the railroad and the second industrial revolution that Jones & Laughlin, Carnegie, Westinghouse, the Mellons, PPG, and Alcoa fomented between 1850 and 1900. During those Gilded Age years, a single decision made in a Golden Triangle boardroom could radically transform old river towns like Hazelwood, Braddock, and McKeesport or create new industrial satellite towns overnight. Naming these new river towns was an art in itself. A. W. Mellon's 1890 steel-town of Donora, on the Monongahela River, jointly immortalizes Mellon's partner, William H. Donner, and Mellon's wife, Nora. Industrial towns constitute the most notable part of the urbanization of the three river valleys, but by no means all of it. Other settlements in the Monongahela, Ohio, and Allegheny river valleys include a utopian commune at Ambridge, a planned community by Walter Gropius at New Kensington, and Rachel Carson's ancestral home at Springdale.

Two stories from World War II give some idea of the global reach of the river towns of the Monongahela Valley. In Italy, old-timers still refer to Pittsburgh as the metropolis *"dove facevano le bombe"*—where they made all the bombs. And in Germany, Adolf Hitler supposedly told the Luftwaffe commanders that when they reached the United States to take out Washington first, Pittsburgh second.

For 130 years, from 1853 to 1983 (the dates of the creation and extinction of the Jones & Laughlin works in south Oakland), the Monongahela Valley meant "Steel Valley," not just in America but throughout the industrialized world. Ten huge steel mills were shoehorned into the twenty-three-mile segment of this serpentine valley between Pittsburgh and Clairton. A hundred thousand workers labored in these mills during World War II, though employment today is just a fraction of that.

While it lasted, this ribbon that smoldered by day and glowed by night was one of the sublime sights on earth. From the air, the smoke and fire of the Mon Valley was so distinctive that airplane pilots flying between New York and Chicago fixed their bearings by it. On the ground, the steeltowns could be bleak and ugly, but they bustled with the intensity of a gold rush. Like a gold rush, Pittsburgh's mills attracted workers from the British Isles; Central, Eastern, and Southern Europe; Scandinavia; the Middle East; the lands around the Mediterranean and Baltic seas; Mexico; and African American hamlets all over the South. Steelworkers labored at furnaces that could reach 3,000 degrees Fahrenheit, generally twelve hours a day for twenty-six days a month, with a swing shift of twenty-four hours every two weeks. They probably worked harder than any free people in history.

The Mon Valley achieved world dominance in steel because it was itself constituted as an immense assembly line that orchestrated the processing of iron ore from the north and west, coal and limestone from the south, and laborers from the east. Mass and energy were fused in a process that was physically brutal but intellectually elegant. Inventors in many countries contributed to steelmaking, but it became a golden goose in the hands of five immigrants to Pittsburgh: Benjamin Franklin Jones, James Laughlin, Andrew Carnegie, Henry Clay Frick, and Charles Schwab.

The Jones & Laughlin Pittsburgh Works (in its last stage part of the LTV conglomerate) served as the prototype: the rolling mills of B. F. Jones's American Iron Works on the South Side (1853) were linked to James Laughlin's Eliza blast furnaces across the Monongahela at south Oakland (1859) and their joint coke works upstream in Hazelwood (1884). Carnegie applied the same formula farther upriver on the Monongahela, where he started one steel mill (the Edgar Thomson works) and snared four others that earlier Pittsburgh entrepreneurs had built. These five, with two later mills, eventually became the Monongahela Valley works of U.S. Steel. Coke was produced at Clairton and sent downriver to the blast furnaces at McKeesport, Duquesne, Braddock, and Rankin. The pig iron from these mills was then charged in steelmaking furnaces, and the steel ingots produced were rolled and finished locally or sent on to the Homestead or Irvin plants for specialized work. Putting the mills along the river furnished the enormous quantities of water needed for steelmaking, assured cheap transportation for the raw and finished materials, gave access to plentiful hillside land where the workers could build their homes, and exploited the contiguous valleys where slag heaps could pile up.

The fragmentation of the Mon Valley works into independent units along the river would be unthinkable today and was a major cause of their decline, but it suited Carnegie, who ran his mills as two dozen separate companies before selling them all in 1901 to investors who formed what eventually became U.S. Steel. Fragmentation neutralized Carnegie's partners and prevented the unionization of his workers. Linked but not yoked, the plants had the flexibility to exploit fluctuations in the American economy. The steel rails produced in Braddock met the needs of the post–Civil War railroading boom of the 1870s, while the girders turned out in Homestead responded to (and made possible) the American skyscraper boom of the 1880s. In the 1890s, McKeesport rode the American oil boom as the world's greatest supplier of tubes and pipes; in 1938, as the Depression bottomed out, General Motors' metal stamping plant at West Mifflin, called the USS Irvin works, was established to supply flat-rolled steel to meet the demand for appliances and automobiles.

385

fig. 8.2
COKEWORKS,
CLAIRTON

For years, the technology of these plants was the most advanced anywhere, with succeeding generations of Bessemers and open-hearth, basic oxygen, and electric furnaces. Say what you will of the decline of Smokestack America and the Rust Belt: one hundred years ago, the Mon Valley was—except in labor relations—the perfection of enterprise in the United States. It remains the ideal, at least subliminally, that all later forms of American enterprise have tried to emulate.

The Steel Valley begins where it was invented, at Pittsburgh. Second Avenue, which starts underneath the Boulevard of the Allies ramp at Grant Street, was extended along the east bank of the Monongahela to Hazelwood early in the nineteenth century, then pushed on as a plank road to Braddock. At that point, where south Oakland met the Monongahela waterfront, stood James Laughlin's Eliza Furnaces, named for the daughter who passed on her inherited wealth and her taste in art to her son, the pioneering modern art collector Duncan Phillips.

There is no hint of steelmaking in the dozen gleaming buildings of the Pittsburgh Technology Center research park that rehabilitated the Jones & Laughlin mill brownfield site on Second Avenue. Nonetheless, you can grasp how huge the J&L mill was by walking, biking, or roller-blading the Eliza Furnace Trail—the recycled B&O Railroad track line that linked Pittsburgh and McKeesport from the 1870s to the 1980s. The trail was an early component of Pittsburgh's twenty-four-mile river promenade—the best environmental news in Pittsburgh since the antipollution laws of the mid-twentieth century. A new bridge links the Eliza Furnace Trail (generally called the "Jail Trail" because it passes the Allegheny County Jail on its way Downtown) with the old Hot Metal Bridge. For a hundred years this twin-span structure ferried molten iron from the Eliza Furnaces over the river to the J&L steel mill on the South Side. Now one span is reserved for pedestrians and cyclists—the latter potentially able to ride all the way to Washington, DC, via the Great Allegheny Passage.

fig. 8.3
PITTSBURGH
TECHNOLOGY
CENTER, ON THE
SITE OF THE
ELIZA FURNACES

The Monongahela

Hazelwood has legally been part of Pittsburgh since 1869, though its grim brick rows and hillside cottages give it the look of an independent steeltown. As "Scotch Bottoms," it had its share of summer estates until shortly after the Civil War, when its industrial transformation took place. That alchemy is vividly documented by what happened to a house that stands at 4527 Irvine Street (an offshoot of Second Avenue), between Tullymet and Mobile, at the entrance to the neighborhood. This Italianate villa might be called a "mansion-factory," since it was put up as a summer resort in pre–Civil War days but was caught up in such rapid industrialization that it ended up serving as a factory.

Nearby, two blocks up Hazelwood Hill, stands the John Woods house, at the corner of Monongahela Street and Tullymet. It was built around 1784 by the son of the surveyor who laid out Pittsburgh in the same decade. Though crudely built of erratically squared sandstone, the house carries recognizably Georgian lines.

At the base of the slope, Hazelwood's badly decayed commercial strip unfolds along Second Avenue. Below that, for a hundred years, rose the Jones & Laughlin Hazelwood coke works, marked by gigantic coal bunkers and lorry cars that rode back and forth as they fed batteries of coke ovens. The structures covered 178 acres, and in those structures were ovens; quenching stations; spike and chain factories; cold-finishing mills; rail yards; and paint, welding, pipe, and carpentry shops. All of this was flattened in the first years of the new millennium, but the world has not heard the last from the brownfields of Hazelwood. The ALMONO consortium (the name combines the names of Pittsburgh's three rivers), formed by the Heinz, Mellon, Benedum, and McCune foundations, bought the entire site and intends to make it a model development for the best recreational and aesthetic uses of the Pittsburgh waterfronts.

Like all steeltowns, Hazelwood had two classes of public monuments: its factories and its churches. The oldest of the churches to survive (several churches and a synagogue did not) is the Episcopal Church of the Good Shepherd on Second Avenue at Johnston Street. A wealthy and ritualistic Anglo-Catholic congregation was founded here in 1870, and two decades later it put up this surprisingly playful building, with a fantastic pagoda spire that is scalloped in five stages. About 150 congregants can fit in its intimate sanctuary, over which hovers a richly detailed hammer-beam roof.

If Good Shepherd represents Hazelwood's mill owners, then St. Stephen's Church on Second Avenue at East Elizabeth represents its Irish-origin middle managers and laborers. The congregation chose a ponderous Baroque Style

fig. 8.4
4527 IRVINE
STREET,
HAZELWOOD

for the façade, then rendered it in buff industrial brick with decorative trim formed in molds filled with fine-grained cement. Opened to worship in 1902, the interior of St. Stephen's uses a good deal of poured concrete, which links it to the industrial-finish churches that Auguste Perret would build in France a few decades later.

The Eastern European work force of Hazelwood is represented by the First Hungarian Reformed Church at 221 Johnston, near Gertrude. The elegant Art Nouveau letters on its cornerstone show that it was laid in 1903 and that the architect was the fiercely original Titus de Bobula. The church is small, with sandstone in front but buff factory brick on the sides. The step-gabled façade is perforated by two strange ovoid windows left and right of the central tower. The Art Nouveau Style is particularly marked in the windows and in the flower shape of the light fixtures inside.

Who was Titus de Bobula? We have relatively scant information on him beyond three Pittsburgh churches that survive, a photograph of one that does not, and designs for a group of free-flowing monuments that, if executed, might have made him a sensation among American architects. We also have his photograph in *Palmer's Pictorial Pittsburgh*, from 1905; he peers from its pages rather enigmatically from under a hat, like Toulouse-Lautrec.

In the spontaneity of his style, particularly his languid, sinuous curves, the clashing of smooth and rough materials, and his sometimes outrageous handling of the Classical orders, Titus de Bobula must be regarded as an authentic Art Nouveau architect—perhaps the only true devotee of that style in the United States. De Bobula was Hungarian, and his style suggests that he was trained in the Vienna secession school. He worked in Pittsburgh from around 1900 to 1910 and is next heard from in 1920, designing a house in New York. His fifteen minutes of fame came three years later, when he was arrested for participating in a failed attempt to overthrow the Hungarian government on the same day as Adolf Hitler's attempted *putsch* in Munich.

The industrial river towns of Homestead, West Homestead, and Munhall were laid out on the south bank of the Monongahela River, one bend upriver from Hazelwood. The three contiguous boroughs are reached from Hazelwood over the Glenwood Bridge or from Squirrel Hill over the Homestead Grays Bridge. There is also a long but lovely drive on the Monongahela waterfront from the South Side along East Carson Street, which offers views of such calm water and pristine woods that a motorist might momentarily forget that the Industrial Revolution ever happened.

The East Carson Street drive brings you first to West Homestead and to the great bulk of what used to be the Mesta Machine Company plant, between

Seventh Avenue and the river. For a generation, this was the world's largest machine shop under one roof, and Mesta was hailed as the most versatile creator of machinery in the world. Its supreme product was the seven-story, fifty-thousand-ton hydraulic press that was used to form the sheet metal for air force jets in the mid-1950s. George Mesta built the factory here in 1898; it was rebuilt after he died in 1925, and for a half-century it yielded rich profits, until the company's collapse in 1983. The West Homestead plant was purchased by the Park Corporation, which runs it as their WHEMCO manufacturing facility. Several acres closer to the Monongahela were turned to lighter purposes—waterslides at the Sandcastle amusement park.

A more personal example of Mesta's glory days is the nearby George and Perle Mesta house at 540 Doyle Avenue, in West Homestead. This clapboarded Colonial Revival mansion from around 1890 forms part of a fine hillside terrace where the Mesta superintendents lived. After three generations as a boardinghouse, it was attractively restored in 2007 as a single-family dwelling. On the left side of the house is the elaborate and beautifully scaled ballroom that launched Perle Mesta's career as a hostess, not more than a quarter-mile from her husband's factory.

In 1879, the boroughs of Homestead and Munhall filled up overnight with the homes of seven thousand workers when the Pittsburgh Bessemer Steel Company set up its steel blast furnaces and blooming mill there. Carnegie bought the operation in 1883 after he drove it into near bankruptcy, and then he linked it to the blast furnaces he had built at Braddock a decade earlier. The Homestead works grew phenomenally after the first open-hearth furnaces were added in 1886. Its work force then shot up to twenty thousand, and the mill eventually stretched three miles along the Monongahela, with its hundreds of buildings jammed crazily into a 430-acre site. Over the lifetime of the complex, its rolling mills yielded 200 million tons of steel. Some came out as rails and railroad cars, and much was produced as armor plate for battleships and tanks, after Carnegie decided he was no longer a pacifist. But the exalted product at these works was structural steel. The columns, girders, and beams rolled in Homestead supported the top floors of the Home Insurance Building in Chicago—the first true skyscraper—as well as the Empire State Building in New York, the massive Hancock and Sears towers in Chicago, the locks of the Panama Canal, and the Gateway Arch in St. Louis. There was hardly a more productive spot on the face of the planet.

Yet Homestead had two kinds of fame. Some books recount its key role in construction history, while to others it is infamous for the labor strike in 1892. The Amalgamated Association of Iron & Steel Workers (AAISW) union,

fig. 8.5
SAWTOOTH
ROW HOUSES,
HOMESTEAD

formed in 1876, had reluctantly agreed in 1889 to a new wage scale in exchange for official recognition by the company. (The old wage scale was tied to productivity, but when production soared, Carnegie ordered the men paid by the hour instead.) When the 1889 contract with the AAISW expired, Henry Clay Frick, as chairman of Carnegie Steel, vowed to break the union. He hired three hundred Pinkerton men to open the mill to strikebreakers, and on July 6, 1892, sixteen Pinkertons and strikers died during a fierce battle. The union lost that strike and also the next, in 1919, after which U.S. Steel issued a poster of Uncle Sam telling the men to get back to work, in eight different languages. The union was not certified until the 1930s.

This story is well told in the Rivers of Steel Heritage Area visitors center in the Bost Building, at 623 East Eighth Avenue. The structure had just gone up in 1892 as a hotel when it was taken over by the steelworkers' strike committee. Restored in 2002, the elaborate model of the Homestead works inside makes that complex manufacturing site surprisingly comprehensible.

Anyone who goes looking for some physical evidence of the Homestead works today will be disappointed because there is next to nothing left of it. In 1986, U.S. Steel closed the Homestead works, then sold it—or perhaps secretly

fig. 8.6
A HOMESTEAD
DEAD END. THE
VENTING STACKS
WERE PART OF
THE HOMESTEAD
WORKS.

sold it before the closure—to the Park Corporation. Park tore down almost all of the mill structures, shipped some working parts to South Korea, sold the rest as scrap, and thus transformed America's busiest steel complex into a vast brownfield.

Today, two ingot molds stand on a lorry car in a tiny park on Eighth Avenue to remind drivers coming across the Monongahela what had once been produced on that site. Some artifacts survive as curiosities at the mill site itself, notably twelve towering stacks that used to vent heat from the red-hot steel ingots waiting to be reshaped in the slab mill. In 1999, the rest of the site became the Waterfront, a 265-acre big-box shopping mall that masquerades as an old-fashioned main street, with the Loews Waterfront Theater acting as a kind of courthouse. On the margins are restaurants, some apartments, a hotel, office space, and a trail along the river.

Tellingly, the Waterfront is not integrated into the three communities that form it. It ramps over Homestead on the Homestead Grays Bridge to plug directly into the affluence of Squirrel Hill, on the opposite side of the Monongahela. Two active rail lines cut the mall off from most of West Homestead, Homestead, and Munhall. Those communities get a cut of the Waterfront's sales tax receipts but nonetheless languish in unemployment and decay.

You can see Homestead borough fighting for its life just a street or two from the Waterfront. The row of once-colorful mom-and-pop stores along Eighth Avenue, particularly the three blocks between West and McClure streets, was a gold mine in the days when thousands of steelworkers and their families crowded this street on payday. The more prosperous steelworkers lived in small brick and frame houses built by Carnegie's land company. These houses still survive by the hundreds, along with a score of larger homes for the mill managers. One of the latter stands nearby at 201 East Tenth Avenue, at the corner of Amity. It is an incongruously bright blue and red stick-style clapboard cottage from the 1880s, with a set of false gables rising from the eaves.

Homestead no longer bears any sign of its notorious tenements or "courts" for the immigrant workers, where fifteen people would crowd into a flat and a hundred would drink the fetid water from a single pump. What testifies to the immigrant experience today is the houses of worship that are clustered within a two-block radius of the intersection of Ann Street and East Tenth Avenue. There are sixteen in all, giving Homestead a sacred density to rival Rome and Jerusalem. Two churches and a synagogue are now deconsecrated; of the thirteen still in use, just over half serve congregations of African Americans and ethnic Hungarians (two), Russians, Italians, Slovaks, and Carpatho-Ruthenians.

The prize for highest visibility among these houses of worship goes to St. Mary Magdalene Roman Catholic Church at Amity Street and East Tenth Avenue. Its 1890s architecture is commonplace, but the church has superbly intricate brickwork in checkered and herringbone patterns (bricklaying was important to steelmaking because of the constant need to reline the blast furnaces). Inside, along with religious stories, the stained-glass windows honor Pittsburgh and the labor movement.

The Carpatho-Ruthenian community erected St. John the Baptist Greek Catholic Cathedral in 1903 just over the line in Munhall, at the corner of East Tenth Avenue and Dickson. The Art Nouveau design of this structure, now the National Carpatho-Rusyn Cultural and Educational Center, is one of the more erratically brilliant buildings in Pittsburgh. Its façade is marked by two fantastic towers that begin in arches of exaggerated sandstone voussoirs and end in Neoclassical columned *tholoi*. The towers are bridged by a cavelike arch in the basement and by two columnar walkways. In both this structure and the parish house next door, Titus de Bobula jumbled Classical and industrial elements in a style that recalls fin-de-siècle Vienna (or a location even farther east: scholar Kenneth Kolson suggests a specific attempt to recall the cathedral of Uzhorod). But the complex is American in its assemblage of bits and pieces of architectural history. De Bobula would have been an ideal partner for Bernard Maybeck, who was building in the same spirit around San Francisco, or for Julia Morgan as she concocted William Randolph Hearst's castle at San Simeon, high above the Pacific.

Another outstanding church in the area is the Slovak community's St. Michael the Archangel, just over the line in Munhall on East Ninth Avenue at Library Place. Constructed in 1927, it presents the dramatic integration of traditional European church types and modern styling. Not surprisingly, a church built by steelworkers has religious iconography particular to them. Perched high on the belltower, Frank Vittor's statue of St. Joseph depicts the patron saint of workers not as a carpenter but as a steelworker,

8.7
8.8   8.9
        8.10

surmounting four miniature Bessemer converters that are coating the globe in molten steel.

One final church possesses exceptional vividness. The Orthodox church of St. Gregory the Theologian, uphill at the corner of East Fifteenth Street and Maple, is among the more recent Homestead churches, from 1950, but it carries the weight of an exalted Byzantine tradition. It consists of nine bays forming one square, with three east-west bays intersecting three oriented north-south and a glistening metal dome surmounting the central bay. Extremely compact, St. Gregory carries the authority of a building ten times its size—another powerful legacy to Pittsburgh from Eastern Europe.

The dominant secular monument of the district is Carnegie Library of Homestead, at 510 Tenth Avenue. Dedicated in 1898, it is Andrew Carnegie's conciliatory gift to his striking workers in the form of a French Renaissance palace with a music hall, library, gymnasium, swimming pool, and four lanes of duckpin bowling alleys. In the ordered universe of a steeltown, the visual fiction of Homestead suggested that everyone lived in harmony: the workers in the low rows of diminutive flats on Tenth Avenue, behind St. Michael's; the middle managers in middle-size brick homes on Twelfth Avenue; and the bosses in twenty-room houses on "superintendents' row" on Eleventh Avenue, above and alongside the library. Several of those superintendents' mansions survive. Lest anyone forget who was the boss of all bosses, the three main cross-streets still bear the names Andrew, Louise, and Margaret, for Carnegie, his wife, and his mother.

The National Historic Park of the Steel Industry, destined to become the single most riveting sight for visitors to Pittsburgh, is being prepared on the north bank of the Monongahela, upriver and diagonally across from Homestead. Here stand the industrial towns of Swissvale and Rankin and the mesmerizing remains of the Carrie Furnaces, which began operations in 1884. (Carrie Moorhead's family started the enterprise before the brothers Henry and William Fownes took it over.) The blast furnaces were purchased and expanded by Andrew Carnegie in 1898 as an additional source of pig iron for his steelmaking furnaces at Homestead. The Homestead and Carrie mills were then joined in 1900 by the Rankin Hot Metal Bridge, which still connects the two sites. Carnegie had furnaces 6 and 7 constructed in 1906 and 1907; today, they offer the only examples of pre–World War II blast furnaces in the United States.

The six immense "hot stoves," three of them feeding superheated air to each of the furnaces, rise ninety-two feet, but they are still eclipsed by the blast furnaces and their draft stacks. Alongside the furnaces is the ore bridge that conveyed

coke, ore, and limestone to the furnaces in case regular railroad cars were unable to feed the furnaces in wintertime. Everything is preserved, visible, and accessible in this fascinating complex, including the skip cars that fed the furnaces and the huge pipes that brought coke gas from the coke ovens at Clairton, fourteen miles downriver. Nearly indescribable is the sensation of standing at the base of the actual furnaces, from which rivers of molten iron poured out day and night in troughs. The town of Rankin occupies a dramatic hillside site above the mill, with the three gilded onion domes of St. Michael the Archangel Greek Catholic Church on Third Avenue standing out against the slope of the hill. Higher up, green cemeteries are set like laurel wreaths at the hill's crest.

The broad floodplain of Braddock, the next town upriver from Rankin, entered history in 1755, when it provided a perfect musket range for the French and Indian massacre of General Edward Braddock and his Coldstream Guards. Braddock's defeat was an epochal event; it launched the Seven Years' War and the military career of George Washington, the general's aide-de-camp. The massacre was also an indirect but important cause of the American Revolution. This seemingly easy victory encouraged American Indian tribes throughout the frontier to attack the white settlers who were encroaching on their lands. To appease the Indians and prevent further clashes, Parliament issued the Proclamation of 1763, which forbade British colonists from settling on Indian-occupied territory. The proclamation angered the American settlers who had fought in the French and Indian War for the right to settle west of the Appalachians. The issue was the first of many that would ultimately separate the American colonies from Britain. In addition, the British defeat in western Pennsylvania made the colonists wonder whether the mother country could even protect them.

The war stories of 1755 were directly related to Andrew Carnegie's purchase in 1873 of one hundred acres where the historic floodplain was bisected by Turtle Creek and three railroad lines. Carnegie's mentor William Coleman was a history buff who would crisscross the battlefield, picking up the odd redcoat brass button surviving from the carnage of a century before. It was Coleman who told Carnegie that the site fully answered his requirements for an integrated steel mill that would introduce the Bessemer converter to America.

Carnegie called in Alexander L. Holley as engineer for what is now the U.S. Steel Edgar Thomson works, with its main gate on Braddock Avenue at Thirteenth Street. Along with Edison's electric light and Bell's telephone in the same decade, the opening of this mill in 1875 was one of the great leaps forward in American technology. The mill still functions for U.S. Steel; its recent production of 3 million tons of steel a year actually surpasses its output levels in the old days. The heightened productivity began in 1992 with the installation of a continuous caster that cuts steel slabs directly rather than having them rolled out from reheated ingots.

Many a Pittsburgh fortune was made in the hundred shops that line Braddock Avenue in the blocks leading up to the mill. Trees now grow between these boarded-up shops, and the population has shriveled to just one-fifth of its peak of twenty-two thousand. Without a dramatic reversal, the only record of Braddock a generation from now may be three works of art: the heroic painting entitled *Braddock's Defeat*, now in Carnegie Library, by Emanuel Leutze, the artist who created *Washington Crossing the Delaware*; Thomas Bell's 1941 novel *Out of This Furnace*; and a set of *cinéma verité* films on Braddock made by local filmmaker Tony Buba.

What explains the devastation on the main street and the even more forlorn aspect of the side streets? Among the answers are globalization, since China and South Korea make steel for a fraction of what it costs locally; political fragmentation, which put the steel mill not in Braddock but in the separate town of North Braddock; and the lure of shopping malls and upscale housing—both of which today's high-paid steelworkers can afford—less than half a mile away, in suburbs such as Monroeville. Further damage was done when Allegheny County put subsidized housing blocks in a community that was too weak to reject them. The final threat comes from a half-finished Monongahela Valley expressway that in a decade or two might flatten these blocks anyway. Not that Braddock's plight is hopeless. The moderne-style Ohringer Building at Braddock Avenue and Seventh, a furniture store from the 1930s, for a while offered free working space for artists in the hope of spurring an arts revival within the community. The project is on hold, but with an infusion of funds perhaps the building's five curved glass-block windows will someday carry projected images of Braddock landmarks and pertinent texts.

fig. 8.13
U.S. STEEL EDGAR THOMSON WORKS, BRADDOCK

fig. 8.14
STOREFRONT ANGEL, BRADDOCK

Overall, it is Braddock's architectural and industrial heritage that makes it memorable, so its old buildings will necessarily play a major role in any economic revival. A small miracle has already reinvigorated Carnegie Library of Braddock on Library Street, just uphill from Braddock Avenue. With its sandstone blocks now liberated from decades of black soot, this magnificent Romanesque Revival design would be the envy of any city in the country. Opened in 1888, Braddock's is the earliest of Carnegie's libraries, except for the small building he endowed in his hometown of Dumfermline in Scotland in 1881. Braddock's gift from Carnegie was more than just a building for books. It had a gym, pool, baths, music hall, and billiards room, and it set the

fig. 8.15
CARNEGIE LIBRARY,
BRADDOCK

fig. 8.16
CHARLES SCHWAB
MANSION

pattern for the score of other Carnegie libraries in Pittsburgh area's milltowns and the thousands of others that sprang up worldwide. The designers broke up the mass of the building into five separate components to express its various functions, but those constituents also make the library resemble a rich man's private house and subliminally propagate the image of Carnegie as a benevolent father living in the midst of his workers. Barely surviving the 1970s and 1980s, in the 1990s the library made a brilliant comeback thanks to the efforts of passionate volunteers.

Carnegie left Pittsburgh in 1867, but the region always formed nearly the totality of his industrial empire, and he insisted that his superintendents live hard by the mills. The Charles M. Schwab house at 541 Jones Avenue, a few blocks uphill from the library, is a charmless Queen Anne hulk that Schwab built in 1891, the year he was made superintendent of the Braddock works. Carnegie's most flamboyant associate, Schwab was then twenty-seven; just six years had passed since he joined the plant as a laborer at a dollar a day. The presidencies of both U.S. Steel and Bethlehem Steel still lay ahead of him, but this castle, now brilliantly restored, shows Schwab already seized by a mania for opulence. This mansion in Braddock turned out to be a practice run for the Riverside Drive palace Schwab built twelve years later in New York, with its six elevators and ninety guest bedrooms.

The so-called Superintendent's House at 817 Kirkpatrick, a block from Schwab's house, presents itself as an opulent Queen Anne essay in wood, with art-glass windows, fishscale shingles in the dormers, and protuberances both circular and octagonal to the left of the main block. Other prodigy houses survive around Braddock, with some astonishingly elaborate Catholic and Eastern Orthodox churches and two synagogues—one in operation and one not.

A mile out of town, Braddock Avenue passes under the George Westinghouse Memorial Bridge, over which passes the Penn-Lincoln Highway (state route 30) into Pittsburgh. The five-span bridge acts also as the portal to the Turtle Creek Valley and the huge electric works that George Westinghouse opened in 1894. The Westinghouse Bridge was a sensation when it opened in 1934, with the longest reinforced-concrete arch in the world (still the longest in the United States). Westinghouse stands as a paradigm of what a good bridge should be. Even after repeated viewings, one does not tire of the elegant proportions of the piers, the effortlessness of the semi-elliptical arches, Frank Vittor's heroic Art Deco reliefs, and the perfect match of the natural wonder and inspired ingenuity of the site.

A second reminder of George Westinghouse is the Westinghouse Electric Corporation East Pittsburgh Works, which extends about two miles along Turtle Creek, near the Westinghouse Bridge. This goliath turbine works, constructed in 1894, was the outgrowth of the first practical application of alternating current for electric power transmission (not Westinghouse's own invention, but that of Nikola Tesla). That application was first demonstrated in 1886, with a wire running between the Golden Triangle and Lawrenceville. Realizing what an immense demand his system would create for generators and electric machinery, Westinghouse purchased five hundred acres of land in the Turtle Creek Valley in 1887 as the site for a giant factory complex, but fierce opposition from Edison and the partisans of direct current electricity forced him to put the project on hold for six years. In 1893, Westinghouse scored two decisive triumphs over Edison by supplying AC electricity to the Chicago World's Fair and exploiting the power of Niagara Falls. The next year, the East Pittsburgh works opened to national and international acclaim. Photographers loved to shoot inside its colossal volumes; one manufacturing aisle was seven stories high and three football fields in length.

The East Pittsburgh plant employed twenty thousand workers at its peak, many of whom lived in the small homes that the Westinghouse land company built for them nearby in the valleys and on the mesa tops. An impressive group of these wooden homes and boardinghouses stands north of the plant on Brown Avenue, toward Churchill. From the efforts of the engineers and workers at the plant came the world's first electric locomotive, the first regular radio broadcast (on Pittsburgh's KDKA), and the first electronic television camera. Much of the old complex was clad in a metal skin in 1957, but Thomas Rodd's French Renaissance–style administration building, where Westinghouse himself worked, is still intact. The sprawling manufacturing plant is now the Keystone Commons business incubator, housing traditional manufacturing companies such as tool and die makers, various types of administrative offices, and high-tech ventures. It is still immense; buses routinely ride through it as though it were a city street.

fig. 8.17
GEORGE WESTINGHOUSE
BRIDGE, SHORTLY
AFTER COMPLETION

It is two miles from the old Westinghouse Electric plant to the slightly earlier Westinghouse Air-Brake Works in Wilmerding. The architect Frederick Osterling, barely out of his teens, designed these impressive brick foundries and machine shops in 1890, with Westinghouse himself closely supervising the enterprise. The best survivor of the original complex is the machine shop alongside the Pennsylvania Railroad tracks, at 325 Commerce Street. This building is used by Wabtec, the reorganized Westinghouse Air Brake Technologies Corporation, still a global leader in manufacturing equipment for locomotives, freight cars, and passenger transit vehicles. Once preserved in the foundry building, but gone now, were the "traveling tables" that brought work to the artisan, rather than the artisan moving from location to location. Detailed articles in 1890 in *Railroad Gazette* and *Scientific American* and in the *Railway News-Record* in 1892 described Westinghouse's revolutionary innovation. Henry Ford read the articles and adapted the "traveling tables," coming up with assembly lines for manufacturing automobiles.

Around the factories, Westinghouse laid out a model industrial town called Wilmerding in honor of Johanna Wilmerding Negley, whose family farmed in the valley for generations. Worker houses survive by the hundreds in Wilmerding: long brick rows with ample wood porches on Middle Avenue and, on Air Brake Avenue, double or single cottages as well as homes with more elaborate gabled terraces. Along Air Brake Avenue, the ancient Turtle Creek now flows as an industrial canal.

For a small town, Wilmerding is oddly confusing in layout, being bisected both by the rail tracks and the industrial canal. In 1890, atop a little rise that overlooks the mills, Westinghouse had Frederick Osterling put up the superbly towered Westinghouse Air-Brake General Office Building. It was originally a

fig. 8.18
WESTINGHOUSE
AIR-BRAKE
MACHINE SHOP

civic building (and still looks the part); inside it had a library and community center with a swimming pool and baths, on the same lines as Carnegie's proto-type at Braddock. When the library burned in 1896, Westinghouse directed Osterling to rebuild it in still grander style, but he closed it to the public. On the left side of the building, Janssen & Cocken added an even fancier wing, in French Renaissance Style, in 1927. "The Castle," as locals refer to it, remains the final image of a fascinating inventor and his paternalistic but sincere con-cern for his workers.

The Yellow Belt (state routes 130 and 148 south) connects Wilmerding with McKeesport, an old river town at the confluence of the Monongahela and Youghiogheny rivers, 3.7 miles to the south. As the home of major sup-pliers of tubes and pipes to the oil industry, McKeesport grew in spurts with the various oil booms but always along the lines of the grid that its founding father John McKee and his surveyor Andrew McCullock had set down for it in 1795. Once linked to Pittsburgh by rail and trolley, McKeesport was none-theless far enough away to create its own vigorous economy and culture. Jenny Lind, the singing sensation of the nineteenth century, did not perform just in Pittsburgh when she toured; she also sang in the McKeesport Opera House.

McKeesport was always dominated visually by the blast furnaces of the National Tube Company, which set up operations locally in 1872. The "hot end" of the riverside mill was shut down in 1987, and just a fraction was left standing. One rehabbed unit operates today as a telecommunications center, clad outside in startling pastels. The downtown area preserves an excellent set of pompous Beaux-Arts buildings that manifest how rich a town this once was; a few smaller mills and rows of worker houses still testify to its industrial past.

McKeesport is one of a sextet of industrial towns that cluster around a pronounced double S-curve in the Monongahela River and its Youghiogheny River offshoot. Two rail lines once snaked along the north and south banks of the Youghiogheny. CSX trains still run on the old B&O line on the north bank, but the Western Maryland Railroad line on the south bank was abandoned and now serves as part of the Great Allegheny Passage biking trail to Washington. Just outside McKeesport, in the hamlet of Boston on the Youghiogheny bank, there is a lively strip where cycling enthusiasts gather before starting out on that trek, now made a good deal less arduous by the bed-and-breakfast inns that dot the route every ten or twenty miles.

On the Monongahela bank itself, south of McKeesport, lies Glassport, a town created by the U.S. Glass Company when it was still a rival to PPG. About a mile upriver lies the once-flourishing village of Elizabeth, a major force in boat building in the late eighteenth century, when the town's well-preserved grid was laid out. Though there is conflicting documentation, it appears that one of the secondary boats of the Lewis and Clark expedition was constructed here, to join the bigger craft that Meriwether Lewis was building in Pittsburgh. The shoreline at Elizabeth is entirely peaceful today, given over to nothing more strenuous than fishing.

Quite a different scene prevails on the opposite bank of the Monongahela from Elizabeth, which is dense with the industrial towns of Dravosburg, Duquesne, and Clairton and the U.S. Steel Irvin works. Clairton, immediately opposite Elizabeth but a world away from that quiet town, grew up around H. C. Frick's St. Clair Steel Company and the coke plant that Frick created in 1900. Until the 1970s, it was the largest coke plant anywhere; 13 percent of the world's coke was produced in this one complex. The mill is still active, belching forth huge plumes of steam ("quenches") day and night. Mountains of coal are piled up, awaiting the processing that will turn it into coke. Unlike most riverfront steeltowns, Clairton has no significant "lower town," apart from the mill; the whole city is built on a high terrace above the Monongahela.

Six miles north, still hewing to the Monongahela bank (or reached directly from McKeesport over the McKeesport Bridge), lies the former steeltown of Duquesne. The Duquesne Furnace & Steel Works created the instant company town of Duquesne in 1888, before being taken over by Carnegie two years later. For half a century the town was dominated by a mountainous twenty-eight-story blast furnace named Dorothy Six, which was pulled down in 1986. Now the mill site is leveled, except for the few industrial basilicas—surprisingly handsome and even costly in their architecture—that survive as incubators for small tenant firms. On the main road through what is now Duquesne's research park stands a mournful shrine of steel-cut steelworker effigies looking like industrial scarecrows. The city of Duquesne itself has held up proudly despite the harsh blows it took from the

fig. 8.19
Industrial
scarecrows,
Duquesne

closing of the mill. In the upper town, the yellow brick roads are still intact, and long tree-shaded streets still yield superb views over the Monongahela. One senses a community waiting for the other shoe to drop.

Along with its devotion to work, the Mon Valley permitted itself a single installation made for fun. Kennywood Park, immediately north of Duquesne in the direction of Homestead, rises at 4800 Kennywood Boulevard in the borough of West Mifflin. The chief promoter here was — of all people — A. W. Mellon, who created Kennywood in 1899 to boost ridership on his Monongahela Street Railway. The park's engineer was George S. Davidson, the design engineer for a dozen or more of Pittsburgh's most distinguished bridges.

Kennywood flourished long after Mellon's trolley line folded, and its one hundred acres are packed with revelers all summer long. The carousel here is an Art Nouveau period piece, and the main restaurant is a remake of the even older Shingle-style casino. Connoisseurs of such things rate the Thunderbolt roller coaster as one of the classics in the nation. One is not obliged to ride it, but the careful student of the Mon Valley should, because just before the cars take their sickening downward plunge, they stop for an instant at the top. From that height, as though lifted up by an angel, one can look directly across the Monongahela to the steel mill at Braddock. Who is to say that the ghosts of Jones and Laughlin, and of Carnegie, Schwab, and Frick, do not hover there also?

More towns dot the Monongahela banks upriver, toward the West Virginia state line. South of Elizabeth, the local road that hugs the east bank of the Monongahela is so little used that a visitor may think it is the trace of some forgotten colonial highway. The route is nonetheless a lively mix of old river towns like Belle Vernon and Monongahela and the newer industrial towns of Donora, Monessen, and Charleroi.

The eighteenth century reasserts itself twenty-three miles upriver at Brownsville, an enticing river town that kept up its busy steamship traffic with Pittsburgh as late as the 1930s. After its fort and trading post gave way to a town in 1785, Brownsville became an important Monongahela River port. It declined in the 1850s, when the railroad eclipsed that function, but its erstwhile prosperity is apparent in the wall-to-wall storefronts downtown and in three remarkable structures. The oldest of these structures is the curious Nemacolin's or Bowman's Castle, an eccentric remake of a trading post of the 1790s. The most significant structure in national terms is the Dunlap Creek Bridge of 1836–1839. This, the first metal-arch bridge in the United States, was a major leap forward in engineering at the time. A decade newer, but evoking a millennial tradition, is the rugged Gothic Revival St. Peter's Roman

fig. 8.20
KENNYWOOD AMUSEMENT PARK

fig. 8.21
OLDEST METAL-ARCH BRIDGE IN AMERICA, BROWNSVILLE

fig. 8.22
ST. PETER'S CHURCH, BROWNSVILLE

Catholic Church of 1845, uptown. The church and its graveyard are superbly sited for a wide-ranging view of the Monongahela Valley, but it is the original parish's lofty ambitions that are so memorable. The evidence of those ambitions lies inside St. Peter's, where arrangements were made to give the church the function and status of a cathedral the moment the pope elevated it to the see of the diocese of western Pennsylvania. That honor went instead to Pittsburgh, in 1853, but Brownsville holds on to what is still an exceptional church.

Twenty miles south of Brownsville lie the last two Monongahela river towns before one reaches Pennsylvania's southern boundary: New Geneva and Point Marion. New Geneva was established by the remarkable Swiss immigrant Albert Gallatin, whose political career took him to the office of secretary of the treasury under Presidents Jefferson and Madison. The early glassworks and gun factory that Gallatin started in New Geneva declined, but his elaborate home at Friendship Hill, from 1789, survives on the Monongahela waterfront. A few miles south, the Monongahela cuts the Mason-Dixon line, and West Virginia begins.

ON THE OHIO

The Ohio River is the lifeblood that linked Pittsburgh to the rest of the world when water travel was the only way to go. A barge traveling down the Ohio and Mississippi rivers could cover the eighteen hundred miles to the Gulf of Mexico with relative ease. The Ohio begins at the confluence of the Monongahela and Allegheny rivers, just as generations of schoolchildren were taught, but it does not really look like the Ohio until a mile downriver from the Point, where it flows under the West End Bridge. The striking 770-foot parabolic arch of this 1930s structure seems to leap in the air above the river and above the modest houses on both banks.

The plan for the West End Pedestrian Bridge, projected to hang off the West End Bridge by 2010, will allow pedestrians and bicyclists to move easily between the North Side and the West End and thus be linked to the loop of waterfront trails around Pittsburgh. The sweeping curved addition will hug the original structure, affording views upriver and downriver without altering the appearance of the bridge from the shore. This clever piece of structural technology also affirms Pittsburgh's commitment to a vigorous lifestyle and a reduced carbon footprint.

Pittsburgh's West End is no more homogeneous than is its East End and actually a good deal less so. There are a dozen hilly neighborhoods, such as Elliott and Sheraden, all occupying a high plateau that was eroded over the

fig. 8.23
WEST END BRIDGE

centuries by the turbulent Chartiers Creek and the smaller but still treacherous Saw Mill Run. The former marks the northern and western boundaries of the West End; Saw Mill Run and the Parkway West (I-376 West) provide the southern boundary, and the eastern limit is the Ohio River itself.

The West End developed as the beginning of the thirty-five-mile Steubenville Pike, which led westward from Pittsburgh along an old Indian trail across a narrow strip of West Virginia to Steubenville, Ohio. Saw Mill Run got its name from the water-powered sawmill that in 1760 cut the logs for Fort Pitt, and it was thus the military precursor of local manufacturing activity that included saltworks, glassworks, iron mills, oil refineries, and railroad shops. Steuben Street follows the irregular route of the Steubenville Pike from the West End Bridge through West End Village, a neighborhood once known as Temperanceville. In 1837, reformers John Warden and John Alexander established an alcohol-free refuge on the site, and some ten years later it was expanded into the hundred-acre village of Temperanceville on the flats next to Saw Mill Run. The experiment failed, and, legendarily at least, Temperanceville had more bars than any other part of the city. In its current revitalization, the neighborhood has dropped the name Temperanceville in favor of West End Village.

Steuben Street winds uphill and branches off at a sharp angle to Chartiers Avenue, the main West End thoroughfare. Chartiers Avenue and Lorenz Street form the baselines of a hilly checkerboard grid of streets on which sit the attractive but modest wood cottages of the separate neighborhood of Elliott. At the top of this grid, toward the Ohio, lies the fashionably named Rue Grande Vue, which gives visitors the broadest and best of all the views of Pittsburgh, particularly at dawn and in the late afternoon. Downtown Pittsburgh rests at the confluence of the three rivers to the right, with Manchester and the rest of the North Side directly ahead and the Ohio River flowing vast and broad to the left.

Chartiers Avenue meanders through the working-class neighborhoods of Sheraden and Esplen, then descends through the newer suburban-style neighborhoods of Windgap and Chartiers City before intersecting Windgap Avenue and crossing over Chartiers Creek on the Windgap Bridge. Here the road resumes the name Chartiers Avenue and becomes one of the main streets of McKees Rocks.

The main part of Steuben Street does not turn uphill but continues straight toward the boroughs of Crafton, Thornburg, and Ingram. Steuben Street also bridges Chartiers Creek several miles upstream from the creek's final dash into the Ohio River at McKees Rocks.

The attractiveness of the Chartiers Valley (the name derives from a French Canadian, Pierre Chartiers, who set up a trading post at the mouth of this valley in 1743) was noted as early as 1777, when Brigadier General Edward Hand established a hospital on the Steubenville trail next to what is now the Crafton Athletic Field on Steuben Street. Numerous other settlers followed after the trail became a full-fledged turnpike in 1818.

One of the farming villages along the Steubenville Pike transformed itself into a suburb in the 1860s on the initiative of James Craft, whose family had first subdivided its Oakland estate (Craft Avenue today) before moving out to the western countryside. Craft promoted the building of the Pittsburgh, Chartiers & Youghiogheny Railroad through the valley and left a substantial tract of land to his son, Charles, who laid out the village of Crafton around 1873.

West of Crafton, West Steuben Street (state route 60 west) crosses a bridge high over Chartiers Creek, after which it resumes its historic name of Steubenville Pike. Immediately beyond the bridge, a road on the left leads to the early twentieth-century settlement of Thornburg. This hamlet was laid out in 1899 on the model of the Los Angeles suburb of Pasadena, which members of the Thornburg family had visited. The settlement was developed by Samuel Thornburg McClarren, who designed several of the homes, and his cousin Frank Thornburg, both grandsons of the Thomas Thornburg who had farmed a thousand acres in the area during the early republic. With its score of ample mansions, curving streets named for early colleges, a direct rail link to Pittsburgh, and a private golf course, Thornburg was one of the prestige addresses of Pittsburgh during the first decade of the twentieth century.

A number of Thornburg's homes remain attractive today. Prominent is a Shingle-style house from around 1905 at 1137 Cornell Avenue, at the corner of Hamilton, with Queen Anne details, a high Dutch gambrel roof, and a striking cobblestone chimney. The Colonial Revival mansion at 1080 Stanford Road, at the corner of Yale, is a faithful copy of the Morris-Jumel mansion in New York's Harlem Heights, from 1765. Farther uphill is the Frank Thornburg house, at 1132 Lehigh, a handsome, distinctively horizontal Richardsonian Romanesque house that has an uncoursed fieldstone base but is shingled above in the manner of the Newport-area homes of McKim, Mead & White.

Diagonally opposite Thornburg, on the east side of Chartiers Creek, the borough of Ingram developed in much the same way as its two neighbors. In this case it was Thomas Ingram who laid out a town in 1880 on the hill his grandfather had bought as farmland in 1823. Ingram and West Prospect avenues are its two main arteries, the former in the valley and the latter high on a hill.

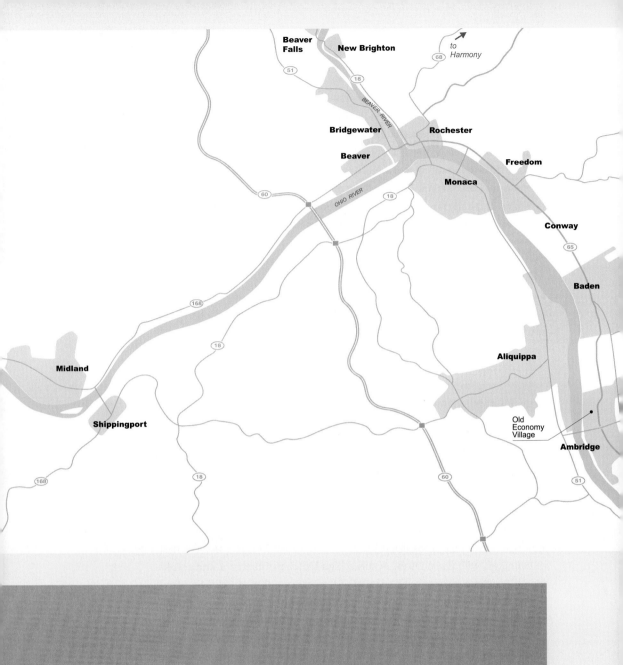

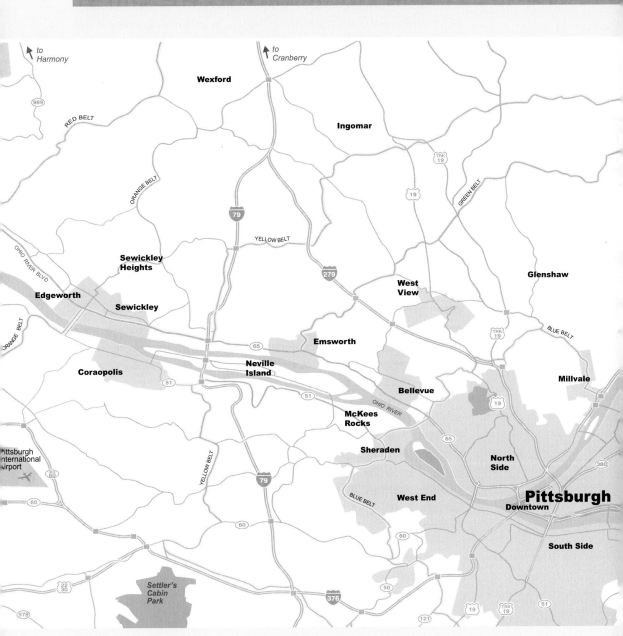

to Harmony

to Cranberry

Wexford

Ingomar

989

RED BELT

ORANGE BELT

TRK 19

79

YELLOW BELT

19

GREEN BELT

OHIO RIVER BLVD

Sewickley
Heights

279

West
View

Glenshaw

Edgeworth

Sewickley

TRK 19

BLUE BELT

ORANGE BELT

65

Emsworth

Coraopolis

Neville
Island

Millvale

51

Bellevue

19

51

OHIO RIVER

McKees
Rocks

65

Pittsburgh
International
Airport

Sheraden

North
Side

380

60

BLUE BELT

West End

Pittsburgh
Downtown

60

60

50

South Side

79

YELLOW BELT

Settler's
Cabin
Park

60

22
30

978

376

19

TRK 19

51

121

The Ohio

The dramatic views over the Chartiers Valley induced several suburban-
ites to build elaborate Italianate and Gothic Revival villas on West Prospect
Avenue. The street dips at its west end to a sumptuous turn-of-the-century
Colonial Revival home at 315 West Prospect, which now serves as the
Allegheny Valley School–Patricia Hillman Miller Campus. Another house of
distinction in Ingram stands high on a hill at 80 Berry Street, near the intersection of Berry and West Prospect. This cruciform-shaped summer house of
the 1870s features a number of favorite motifs in High Victorian Gothic Style,
one example being sunburst brackets. The structure seems to derive from
suggestions in the indispensable Victorian handbook, Charles Locke Eastlake's
Hints on Household Taste, published in London in 1868 and republished with
great success in Boston four years later. A half-block downhill from the house,
Berry intersects Windgap Avenue, which in turn enters McKees Rocks.

Not many people come to study McKees Rocks, but those who do find
in it the marriage of a superb natural site and powerful industrial buildings,
making it almost a paradigm of the Pittsburgh steeltown. The actual rock in
McKees Rocks is a huge sandstone outcrop on the Ohio, so prominent that
in 1758 members of the Ohio Company of Virginia proposed using it rather
than the Point as the location of Fort Pitt. When Colonel Alexander McKee
took possession of the rock in 1766 as part of a 728-acre land grant in payment
for military services, it consisted of both the natural formation and a human-
shaped mound that the Adena and Hopewell culture Indians had erected and
used from the first millennium BCE until after 500. The site was quarried for
years, to the point that the Indian mound is entirely gone now, and the natural
rock formation is engirdled by an oil refinery and an asphalt plant.

Alexander McKee enjoyed his rock only briefly because, being a Tory, he
fled Pittsburgh during the Revolution. It fell to his brother James to lay out a
town on "the Bottoms." The town became a major industrial center but was
hard hit by postindustrialization. Today, McKees Rocks may appear to be just
another depressed working-class town, but there remains in it a sense of loyalty
and pride that many outsiders would envy.

One learns the most about McKees Rocks by entering it from the mile-
long McKees Rocks Bridge over the Ohio, from state route 65 north on the
Pittsburgh side of the river. The bridge, from 1931, is as impressive as the
river, with its central through-arch of steel backing up against four noble
pylons of stone. The bridge leads to Island Avenue (state route 51 south) and
Chartiers Avenue in the McKees Rocks upper town; below the bridge lie the
industrial buildings, houses, and churches of the town's markedly different
lower section.

fig. 8.24
PITTSBURGH &
LAKE ERIE RAILROAD
LOCOMOTIVE SHOPS

The packed streets of McKees Rocks, with their jumble of frame and brick homes, provide the perfect foil for its public and industrial architecture. The key landmark of the upper town is St. Mary's Church on St. John Street, from 1901. This Gothic Revival design with three needle spires and a façade of deep-toned brick stands out compellingly over the rows of worker houses. Less effusive but beautifully rendered alongside is its former convent from the 1930s, today a residence for the elderly. This little but self-possessed stone building shaped like a medieval bishop's palace stands right next to the Chartiers & Youghiogheny Railroad tracks but seems wholly oblivious to the twenty-first century.

Back on Chartiers Avenue, at the corner of Margaret, one is a little astonished at St. Francis de Sales Church, a dramatic if somewhat preposterous 1899 design melding an Alberti-derived sandstone portico with a high nave of irregularly coursed rock-faced stone and a cupola that miniaturizes the dome of Santa Maria del Fiore in Florence. Unneeded as a church today, it functions as an events facility under the name of Cathedral Hall.

McKees Rocks was the town in which the Pittsburgh & Lake Erie Railroad (P&LE) concentrated its dozen switching and maintenance buildings. The most impressive of these is still standing, functioning as the Pittsburgh & Lake Erie Railroad Locomotive Repair Shop (originally the erecting and machine shop), just over the tracks at the end of Linden Street. H. L. Turner, probably a company engineer, is credited as superintending this leviathan, in 1903, but the consulting engineer for the McClintic-Marshall Construction Company, which constructed the building, was Albert Lucius of New York.

In this shop, steam locomotives were cared for in a twenty-four-bay basilica that exudes true Roman magnificence in its 500-foot length and grandly scaled thermal windows worthy of an emperor. The exacting nature of the structure is already revealed on the outside, where the walls begin with a cast concrete base, over which is stone and then the brick walls into which steel trusses were set. The interior is still more remarkable; 170 feet wide, it consists of an immense "nave," then two side aisles that are roofed over together. Down the entire length of this industrial basilica moved two huge traveling cranes; one had the capacity of 120 tons and could pick up entire locomotives. There were six traveling cranes in all; today, just one or two are in working order, but everything else could be restored. Over each of the traveling cranes rode lorry cars that would whiz back and forth like robots.

The P&LE Railroad used the facility regularly until 1961 and sold it in 1981 to its current owners, who use it only for warehousing steel plates. It currently rains inside the structure, and the owners wish to sell it. One potential use for the basilica would be a working museum of railroading. This is a practical consideration since there is a working steam locomotive next door, and the P&LE (now CSX) rail line passes right by the building on its way to Station Square in Pittsburgh.

Another example of McKees Rocks' innovative but underemployed industrial architecture is the Taylor-Wilson Manufacturing Company, today Pennsylvania Drilling Company, at 500 Thompson Avenue, immediately adjacent to Chartiers Creek. Taylor-Wilson's mix of concrete and glass seems typical for a factory from the outside, but the remarkable part is inside, where the three-story vaulted ceiling and large windows create a vast uninterrupted space that glows with natural light.

This light and airy structure, opened in 1905, is strikingly different from all other Pittsburgh-area factories and has global importance as part of the first generation of reinforced concrete factories anywhere. Its designer, Robert A. Cummings, was born in Britain and evidently in contact with Ernest Ransome, the British-born world leader in reinforced concrete. Just a year before Cummings erected Taylor-Wilson, Ransome completed his pioneering reinforced-concrete factory at Greensburg, east of Pittsburgh. The evidence of their contact is still circumstantial at this point (for example, Cummings owned a copy of Ransome's most important book on reinforced concrete), but it is almost unimaginable that two contemporaries, both British immigrants, could work so near one another and not have some contact. That makes the industrial pedigree of Taylor-Wilson impressive indeed, and the factory—used as nothing more than a warehouse today—warrants the highest possible priority for preservation.

fig. 8.27
St. Nicholas
Russian
Orthodox
Church,
McKees Rocks

A separate world is the packed neighborhood called the McKees Rocks bottoms, reached by (and at the same time isolated by) ramps leading to the McKees Rocks Bridge. The bottoms once had railroad shops, ironworks of a dozen firms, more churches, hundreds of homes, and Helen Street, one of McKees Rocks' two commercial strips (the upper town had Chartiers Avenue as its commercial street).

Helen Street is tired today, its monotony broken only by bars, domed Orthodox churches, and funeral homes, but fifty years ago it was a flourishing retail district. Just one block to the west, parallel to Helen, is Munson Street, with an ecumenical sacred precinct that encompasses St. Mark's Roman Catholic Church and St. Nicholas Russian Orthodox Church, from 1914. The latter is marked by six onion-domed towers outside and a brilliant fresco treatment of the walls inside. Until 1980, the grouping of religious houses concluded with a picturesque Baroque Revival synagogue next to St. Mark's, but today the site is a park.

The neighborhood at the Pittsburgh end of the McKees Rocks Bridge is Brighton Heights, the city's northernmost district before the suburbs start. All is standard near-suburbia here except for the Cesarespada house at 1138 Stanford Road, where believers follow a liturgical prototype that goes back nearly as far as Jesus and the Apostles. Thousands of house-churches *(domus ecclesiae)* once functioned in Mediterranean regions until the fourth century, when Christianity was legalized and Christians no longer had to worship in secret. The modern-day house-church here owes its existence to the miracle claimed by the homeowner, Delfina del Russo Cesarespada. In 1963, Mrs. Cesarespada was presumed dead at Shadyside Hospital, but she recovered and claimed to have been resurrected by the intercession of Blessed Nunzio

Sulpizio, a man who had lived a short, exemplary life in nineteenth-century Naples. Mrs. Cesarespada lived thirty more years, and the bishop of Pittsburgh authorized a priest to celebrate a public mass once a month at her home. This still takes place, in what used to be Delfina Cesarespada's living room.

The Pittsburgh-area river town par excellence is Sewickley, which lies eight miles downriver on the Ohio from Brighton Heights. One reaches Sewickley either by water or, more commonly, by Ohio River Boulevard (state route 65 north). The boulevard—itself a dramatic work of 1920s engineering—incorporates parts of a centuries-old road to Beaver that was in turn based on an Indian trail. The drive offers a dramatic mix of industrial and natural views through a district that was the heart of the Depreciation Lands that Pennsylvania parceled out in three-hundred-acre lots in 1784 as compensation to its unpaid Revolutionary War veterans. (The term "Depreciation" stuck because the land was next to worthless.)

Ohio River Boulevard borders the suburbs of Bellevue, Avalon, Ben Avon, and Emsworth, with their many large Italianate and Shingle-style homes. In the Ohio River sits Neville Island, five miles of farmland once so rich that, as late as 1926, the old Waldorf-Astoria Hotel in New York featured Neville Island asparagus on its menu. The island experienced frenetic industrial growth in World War II when the Dravo Corporation began launching hundreds of landing craft from its shipyards. By the 1970s, there were more than fifty different firms in heavy industry on the island; today, these plants are either vacant or dedicated to other uses, but the coke ovens of Shenango, Inc., soldier on.

fig. 8.28
ANNOUNCING
BELLEVUE,
OHIO RIVER
BOULEVARD

Several miles downriver from Neville Island, Beaver Street splits off from Ohio River Boulevard, and several handsome blocks of High Victorian Gothic and Shingle-style homes mark the boundary of Sewickley. It started as an eighteenth-century river town that prospered as a summer refuge when the railroad reached it in 1851. Sewickley and the neighboring, interlocking boroughs of Edgeworth and Sewickley Heights then flourished as an autonomous settlement, making it today an open-air museum of nineteenth-century houses and churches.

Like Pittsburgh's Shadyside district, which it resembles in age, physical area, and wealth, Sewickley works hard at retaining a small-town atmosphere. It keeps up a number of fine churches. Prime among these are St. Stephen's Episcopal, on Frederick Avenue at Broad Street, a vigorous, uncoursed brownstone approximation of early English Gothic, and Sewickley Presbyterian, on Grant at Beaver Street, a regularly coursed, hammer-dressed design of austere Gothic with an elegant and airy country-church interior.

Among the notable private homes, 66 Beaver Street, at the corner of Grant and opposite the Presbyterian church, is a handsome Gothic cottage of the Civil War period with picturesque irregular turrets and gables. Diagonally across from St. Stephen's, at 246 Broad Street, stands an elaborate Italianate villa, dressed with clapboards and shingling, from 1877 that served for years as an American Legion hall. Alongside St. Stephen's are two excellent Gothic Revival cottages: a board-and-batten wood frame house at 424 Frederick, from around 1845, and the Atwell-Christy house at 403 Frederick, an intimately proportioned Gothic Revival cottage of tightly lapped vertical wood siding, from 1862.

Pine Road, just north of Sewickley Presbyterian Church, extends northeast from Beaver Street as a link to tree-lined Woodland Road in the neighboring borough of Edgeworth. The homes on Woodland bear the distinguished pedigrees of society architects such as Charles Barton Keen, Brandon Smith, and Benno Janssen, but they are relatively new, from the 1910s and 1920s. The older homes of Edgeworth line Beaver Road, a block closer to the Ohio riverbank. The John Way house at Beaver and Quaker roads dates from the Federal period, around 1810, with a Greek Revival addition; the adjoining Abishai Way house at 108 Beaver, on the Edgeworth borough limit, is an elegant brick house with Greek Revival portico, from 1838, built for a successful Pittsburgh merchant and business agent for the communitarian Harmony Society. The Ways resided in these homes for generations, and their descendants still live nearby.

Of even greater duration is the seven-generation ownership of the mansion called Newington, at the intersection of Beaver Road and Shields Lane. Daniel Leet, from Washington, Pennsylvania, surveyed Edgeworth in 1776, when it was claimed by Virginia. He surveyed it again in 1783–1784, that time on behalf of Pennsylvania, for the Depreciation Lands grants. Pennsylvania gave Leet the Newington land for services rendered, and he passed it on to his son-in-law, David Shields. Shields built the modest first block of Newington in 1816 and added a large Federal-style house seven years later.

It was this house and its luxurious eleven acres of gardens that set the model for the grander homes that the iron and steel barons later built on the Sewickley hills, much as Judge William Wilkins's mansion was the lightning rod that drew many men of the same class to locate their city homes around Point Breeze. Wilkins enjoyed Homewood for only thirty years, however, while the Leet-Shields family has been at Newington for more than two hundred. The clan worships together one block to the south, in Grace Episcopal

Church's Shields Chapel, on Church Lane. They bury their dead in the Romanesque Revival Shields Mausoleum next door.

The borough of Sewickley Heights, a mile inland from the Ohio River, shelters fewer than a thousand residents on its forty-six hundred acres. This people-to-acreage ratio by itself marks Sewickley Heights as a wealthy district, if no longer one of the most affluent in the nation the way it was in the 1930s. The luxurious summer estates of the Thaw, Oliver, Scaife, Walker, Snyder, Jones, Rea, Singer, and other families of the industrial aristocracy are just fragments now, together with a number of pioneer log houses, but the care taken with the environment endures.

Sewickley Heights does not wish to be viewed, so there is not much to see except the stone walls and wood fences that keep visitors out. A suggestion of its past and present opulence is offered, however, by a two-mile drive on Blackburn Road (the Orange Belt), which starts a few blocks from the Ohio. The Edith Oliver Rea estate, once on this road, was famed for its great size and beautiful gardens before it was dismembered and turned into subdivisions. On the left side of Blackburn, a half-dozen servant houses still stand from Benjamin Franklin Jones Jr.'s Fairacres estate (the name is still incised on the handsome gateway). On the right, just beyond the turn for the Allegheny Country Club, another service unit of the Jones estate survives as Fox Hill Farm, keeping up the Joneses' stables and their water tower.

Wilpen Hall, the William Penn Snyder estate, survives in impeccable condition on the trapezoid between Blackburn, Scaife, and Waterworks Road, and it is best viewed from Waterworks. George Orth, who designed Wilpen in 1898, offered up an image reminiscent of Noah's Ark coming to rest on the top of Mount Ararat. It is a huge Shingle-style mansion at the top of its own hill, with brownstone walls and shingled gables that rise over a rough stone base and are capped by a mammoth Dutch gambrel roof and a dozen chimneys. From this point, Scaife Road winds back 1.3 miles through a score of other estates to rejoin Blackburn as it meanders east to the I-79 expressway.

For years it was hard not to lapse into clichés at the contrast between the austere homes of the communitarian settlement of Old Economy at Ambridge, on the east bank of the Ohio some six miles downriver from Sewickley, and the massive scale of the Aliquippa works of LTV Steel, which once stood directly opposite on the west bank. One might have thought the mill would outlast the delicate structures of Old Economy by centuries, but it was the steelworks that was demolished first. Even when the LTV works was belching smoke and fire, however, the difference between the two riverbanks was less than met the eye. Pittsburgh's passion for industry affected even the utopian

8.29
8.30   8.31
8.32

ideals of Economy, which, communitarian or not, became one of the important industrial centers of the early republic.

The story of Economy begins with the emergence of Johann Georg Rapp, or Father Rapp, his title as leader of the pietistic Harmony Society in the German city of Württemberg around 1785. Seeking an end to religious restrictions, Rapp brought his flock to America in 1804, and from 1805 to 1815, several hundred of them lived on nine thousand acres of land centered at the town of Harmony, twenty miles northeast of Old Economy. The Harmonists then migrated to New Harmony, Indiana, where they lived another decade before selling to a fellow Utopian, Robert Owen. On their return to Pennsylvania, they settled at Economy in 1824 and had most of their buildings up by 1831. The designer was Father Rapp's architect son, Frederick.

The fervor of Economy proved to be as commercial as it was spiritual. In Economy and in nearby satellite communities, the Harmonists operated some of the first steam-driven textile mills in America, flourished in the winemaking and distilling trades, and even began drilling for oil immediately after Colonel Edwin Drake made his important strike at Titusville. The Harmony Society owned stock in five different railroads, and the Harmonists soon amassed enough shares in the Pittsburgh & Lake Erie Railroad that they could install their leader Jacob Henrici as its president in 1881.

A celibate sect, the Harmonists died out, depopulated but rich, in 1905. By then, the American Bridge Division of U.S. Steel had built the world's largest bridge and structural steel and fabricating plant over much of their land—hence its current name of Ambridge. The Commonwealth of Pennsylvania took over the remaining seventeen buildings of Economy in 1919, and Charles Stotz restored them as a museum twenty years later.

The publicly accessible buildings of the Harmonists are bounded by Ohio River Boulevard, Thirteenth, and Church streets in Ambridge, with several score more Harmonist houses now in private hands. The buildings are in the finely proportioned Federal Style that was in vogue when the sect came to America, but there are numerous overlays of German vernacular architecture. The mix is immediately recognizable in the village chapel, now St. John's Lutheran Church, with its distinctive bell-shaped lantern over an otherwise standard bell tower and Protestant church sanctuary. The half-timbered stone base of the Granary is another unambiguous throwback to medieval Germany. The Granary was one of Economy's most substantial structures because the settlers kept a full year's supply of food to live on during the period of "tribulations" that they believed would precede the Second Coming of Christ. Elsewhere in the settlement are workshops, stores, dormitories, the Feast Hall (where the eight hundred adherents would gather for "love feasts" about eight times a year), a formal garden, an herb garden, and the Great House, which was the residence of Father Rapp.

The exquisite octagonal cut-stone Garden Pavilion was created as a focal point around which the community would develop. Inside, the Garden Pavilion originally housed a wooden figure (its replacement is carved of stone), which stood in a fountain and from whose fingers water flowed. A hundred feet away stands the Grotto, a marvelous sight with its walls of rough-hewn stone and thatched roof—a probable allusion to the Garden of Eden. The stylish Adamesque interior could not be more different; it alludes to the Harmonists' view of human beings as rough on the outside but gentle inside, yet it seems emblematic also of their wider difficulty of living in two cultures.

Harmony, the original toehold of the Harmonists in North America, is not a river town, but its link to Old Economy is so tight that the two settlements are generally thought of together. It is reached in a half hour's drive from Ambridge by state routes 989 and 68 north. Visitors are greeted by a well-preserved cluster of approximately seventy-five brick and log houses that date from the founding of the colony in 1805 or from its later takeover by the Mennonites. The town plan is a grid, like Economy's, set alongside Connoquenessing Creek. Father Rapp's architect son Frederick erected a delicate house in the center of the village in 1811, with the modern address of 523 Main Street, its finely laid brick and white trim evocative of Federal Style.

The house at 516 Main Street is particularly representative of those times. It is a pioneer American log house, built by Christian and Elizabeth Waldmann in 1804, that was extended a few years later in half-timbered brick, in conformity with medieval German tradition. This return to "old country" modes shows that the process of architectural assimilation could work inversely to what we might expect. In this case, old-style construction followed the new and not vice versa. On the outskirts of the village is an affecting walled cemetery, and close by lies the agreeable town of Zelienople, laid out by a German baron in 1802.

Beaver County, in which Old Economy is located, contains a series of historic river towns on both the Ohio and the tributary Beaver River. The riverbank immediately across the Ohio from Ambridge was occupied for close to a century by the astonishing mass of the Jones & Laughlin Aliquippa Works (LTV in its last years). This miles-long facility occupied 725 acres on a site that extended all the way toward Monaca, at the bend of the Ohio River. It was built in 1907–1912 and was extensively modernized several times.

The steelworks at Aliquippa was built around five blast furnaces. Manufacturing followed a totally integrated process, with on-site coke ovens, blast furnaces for making pig iron, steel furnaces, and a cold-rolling mill that spun out sheet steel at the speed of seventy miles an hour. It employed fourteen thousand workers, and as late as 1981, it shipped out 3 million tons of steel a year. Nothing is left of it now.

It would be simplistic to speculate how such a disaster could so suddenly overtake a magnificent steelworks, but the architectural history of the plant suggests that its rise was as quick as its fall. Before 1907, Aliquippa had been a small village called Woodlawn, the only attractions of which were a small steelworks and an amusement park that was run by the P&LE Railroad. When Jones & Laughlin took over the site in 1907, it temporarily placed its administrative offices in what had been the dance hall of the amusement park. Three-quarters of a century later, those temporary offices were still there.

The town of Aliquippa has always been secondary to the steelworks, but even in its current depressed state, it is an interesting place. Its chief monument—copying Carnegie—is the B. F. Jones Memorial Library at 663 Franklin Street, by the society architect Brandon Smith. The company paid to erect this flawless Renaissance marble and limestone *palazzetto* in 1929.

The Jones & Laughlin land company was responsible for laying out the entire town of Aliquippa. It devised thirteen districts, each with a specific house type and each designated for a different ethnic group according to their rank in the social hierarchy. Every house was made to fit a specific income bracket so that, as advertised, every man could afford a house on his salary. This layout was seemingly ideal, since every worker could own a house in a neighborhood where his language and customs would be undisturbed, but there was little or no room for advancement. The income brackets laid out by Jones & Laughlin were a product of that era's racial and ethnic stereotypes, with white Anglo-Saxon Protestants at the top and Eastern Europeans and African Americans at the bottom. Aliquippa remains a working-class community today, but it is a good deal more diverse than it once was. There abides a strong sense of loyalty to the town, and residents still return to the churches, businesses, and community events even after they have moved away. Hard as the work of steelmaking was, there was a rich social and cultural life in these steeltowns. Famed movie theme composer Henry Mancini got his start performing in a band that accompanied street processions to the Italian church in Aliquippa.

Just north of Aliquippa, Beaver County preserves another cluster of early industrial installations near the confluence of the Ohio and Beaver rivers, at

425

Beaver Falls and New Brighton. Like a score of early Pennsylvania towns, the county seat of Beaver took Philadelphia as its urban model when it was laid out in 1792; it even adopted Philadelphia's large central square and four subsidiary squares in each corner of town. Unlike Philadelphia, however, Beaver never grew, which means that a visitor can stand in its broad streets and imagine both Philadelphia and Pittsburgh as they would have been in the eighteenth or early nineteenth centuries.

All of the river towns in this area were originally conceived as agricultural centers where farmers would bring their produce to the river for sale or shipping. Ultimately, though, the towns in Beaver and the contiguous counties proved more fertile for industry than agriculture. Just two miles upriver on the Ohio from Beaver, at Shippingport, the world's first nuclear-fueled electric power plant for commercial use was started up in 1957, while inland to the northeast lies Titusville, where Edwin Drake ushered in another energy age by pumping oil in 1859.

ON THE ALLEGHENY

The Allegheny is neither so heroic a river as the Ohio nor so important to industry as the Monongahela, but it is beloved by the boaters who cruise its swift-flowing waters. While the Monongahela River is almost entirely dedicated to work, the Allegheny even more than the Ohio alternates points of making money with elegant venues for spending it.

In Pittsburgh, the Allegheny's south bank was significantly industrialized at one time, and pockets of industry persist, but recreation and luxury became the main bywords for the district in the 1920s with the construction of Allegheny River Boulevard (state route 130, part of the Green Belt). This majestic early motorcar road provides an easy passage of five miles along the river from Pittsburgh to Verona and Oakmont. The Nadine Road intersection is marked by the Beaux-Arts–era Nadine Pump House, which takes in water from the Allegheny, filters it, and pumps it to about 100,000 people in a radius of approximately three miles.

Driving up Nadine Road gives a visitor the special pleasure of inspecting the Longue Vue Club, just west of the intersection of Nadine and Lincoln roads. Longue Vue was another of Benno Janssen's genial inspirations: a Cotswold-style rambling structure in the shape of a stretched and curved double H, with two bridge-tunnels that allow cars to pass through it to the parking lot in the rear. By turns formless and formal, the clubhouse rises at points in great peaked chimneys and elsewhere hugs the rolling hills. The walls are made of local sandstone, often thinly sliced like Roman bricks, and set in thick cement beds as if for a peasant farmhouse. The Vermont slate on the roof is likewise thick and richly textured. The whole building is brilliantly choreographed, and it was most likely Richard King Mellon's appreciation of it that led him to choose Janssen as the architect for his opulent Rolling Rock Club at Ligonier about a year later. But Janssen's expressive work at Longue Vue has more surprises. The two huge arches he created when he bridged the roadways under the clubhouse are not merely passages but sightlines. They point the viewer to the edge of the parking lot, which affords a delicious view of the limpid and clear Allegheny River, seemingly untouched by human settlement.

Three miles upriver from the Longue Vue Club is the former railroading town of Verona, whose name is a melodic corruption of that of the town's founder, James Verner. A mile upstream on the Allegheny lies Oakmont, which also began as an industrial settlement and mill town by the river but developed instead into an elegant residential quarter.

Oakmont was founded in 1889 and preserves a good many relics of it earliest years, such as St. Thomas Memorial Episcopal Church at the corner of Delaware Avenue and Fourth, from 1907, and the Oakmont Carnegie Library on Allegheny River Boulevard at the intersection with Pennsylvania Avenue. Oakmont can be justifiably proud of this library. The branch built in 1901 was adequate and in some ways elegant, but minimal. The wing added in 1998–2006 represents an astute contextual intervention. The library was functionally reoriented toward Pennsylvania Avenue, with the new wing being a learned restatement of the original building and the new features, such as eyebrow dormers and a pseudo-spindled verandah, having a certain wit.

Oakmont has done equally well with the half-dozen blocks that constitute its commercial strip on Allegheny River Boulevard. What was in origin nothing more than a railroad right-of-way has been transformed into an elegant promenade on either side of the tracks, with attractive street furniture for walkers and bicyclists to use during their breaks. The town center, including a classic movie theater from the 1920s, is unusually coherent, and the sound the cars make as they rumble over the brick streets is somehow satisfying.

The fourteen rooms of the Dr. Thomas R. Kerr Memorial Museum, at Delaware Avenue and Fourth, give a good indication of upper-middle-class life in Oakmont between 1897 and 1910. Other historically notable homes are the half-timbered house by Brandon Smith at 728 Hulton, the Colonial Revival Wade house at 833 Hulton, and a reworked but still alluring stucco-walled home from 1907 by Frederick Scheibler at 1204 Hulton. These are no

fig. 8.33
ALLEGHENY RIVER,
VIEWED FROM
LONGUE VUE CLUB

fig. 8.34
LONGUE VUE
CLUBHOUSE

more than the merest sampling of hundreds of excellent homes in Oakmont, where there is also intelligent urban design. A road like Twelfth Street, off Hulton, shows that the often-boring grid system for laying out cities and towns can have significant payoffs. Fox Chapel, on the opposite bank of the Allegheny, is a generation younger than Oakmont and notably richer, but its luxurious houses set on irregular winding streets have only a fraction of the effect of the magnificent homes on Oakmont's Twelfth Street. A person driving through Fox Chapel sees nothing of its homes, which is part of their prestige. By contrast, you see everything of the homes in Oakmont. The individual achievements of the various homes are impressive, but more impressive overall is their collective success.

The urban development of Oakmont depended on neither industry nor on bourgeois life, but on golf. The Pittsburgh industrialist Henry C. Fownes (1856–1935), who established the Carrie blast furnaces in Rankin and Swissvale, among other achievements, moved out to Oakmont around 1900 and took up golf for his health. The Scots-born Andrew Carnegie was already mad for golf and taught Fownes the game. Fownes then determined to lay out the finest golf course in the country. He, not some employee, personally designed the grounds of the Oakmont Country Club on Hulton Road, to which the pseudo-Tudor clubhouse, from 1904, is just a pleasant appendage. It was the treacherousness and speed of Oakmont's clay-based course that made it world famous in just a few years. In tribute, the U.S. Open has been held at the Oakmont course seven times, more than at any other venue; the U.S. Amateurs, five times; the PGA Championships, three times; and the U.S. Women's Open, once.

Though the towns on the south bank of the Allegheny River are for the most part leisurely and residential, those on its north bank are resolute and

fig. 8.35
CLUBHOUSE
AND GROUNDS
AT OAKMONT
COUNTRY CLUB

industrial. This is made immediately clear by the names borne by the first two of these towns: the hardworking Millvale and the volcanic Etna. Millvale's residents are mainly of Central European heritage, but there is also a heavy presence of residents who are Croatian in origin. The workers who were Millvale's founding residents left two monuments: their own homes, perched tenaciously on the sides of a valley that opens like a vast amphitheater on the Allegheny riverbank, and the frescoes inside St. Nicholas Catholic Church at 24 Maryland Avenue, high up on a promontory over town. The factory-brick church is unexceptional as architecture but memorable for the murals that were executed here by the Croatian painter Maximilian Vanka in 1937–1938 and—after a break attributed to his being tormented by a ghost on the scaffolding—finished in 1941. In these vivid scenes, Vanka combined socialist realism, the expressionism of Mexican contemporaries such as Orozco, and traditional Byzantine iconography. Among the most affecting scenes are those in the transepts, showing some of the disasters that befell Croatia in the twentieth century. Vanka painted visions of war and death in the homeland on one side of the church and equally terrifying explosions amid the blast furnaces of Pittsburgh on the other.

Roughly two miles upstream on the Allegheny, Etna was wittily named for Mount Etna in Sicily, and the town proved worthy of its namesake, being a volcano of industrial activity in the years following the Civil War, particularly 1885 to 1915. It was in this small town that H. S. Spang & Son opened the Etna Iron Works in 1829. Later, Charles Spang, Charles Herron, and John Chalfant controlled both the Spang-Chalfant Company, which ran the first pipe mill in America, and the Isabella Furnace (the one that had a long-running rivalry with Carnegie's Lucy Furnace across the river). The three were also founders of the Duquesne Club in downtown Pittsburgh, but they

fig. 8.36
MURAL IN
ST. NICHOLAS
CHURCH,
MILLVALE

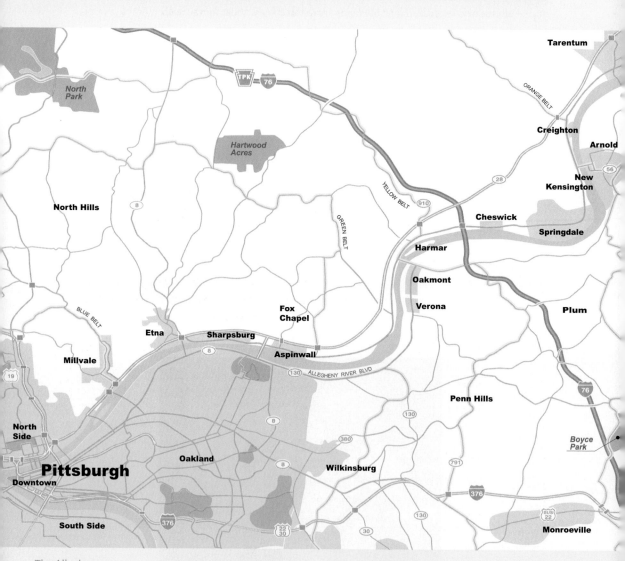

The Allegheny

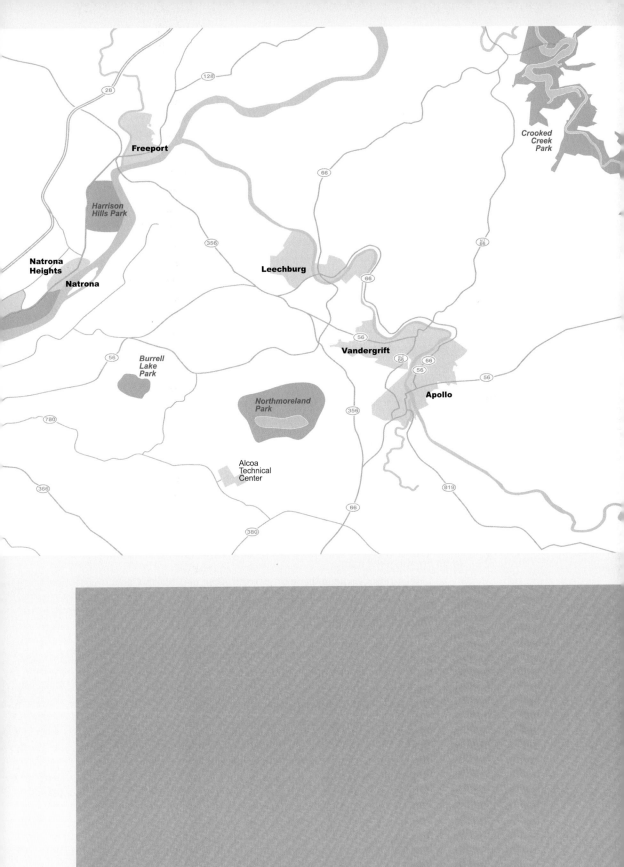

conducted some of their negotiations with J. P. Morgan and Carnegie in Etna's Union Hotel. The days when Etna's mills and furnaces were some of the most important in the United States are long over, but the town has had a modest revival as a residential community and incubator for small businesses.

Etna is one of three tightly linked Allegheny river towns, the other two being Sharpsburg and Aspinwall. Even motorists speeding past Sharpsburg on the Allegheny Valley Expressway (state route 28) pay attention to this remarkable settlement. The huge smokestack of the former Fort Pitt Brewery on Mary's Avenue thrusts into the air at twice the height of the homes and stores around it, but Sharpsburg's skyline shows marks of spirituality, too. The needle spire of Grace United Methodist Church on North Canal Street, from 1872, pierces the sky at the midpoint of the town, and an answering echo comes from the huge limestone basilica of St. Mary's Church, from 1916, on Garner Street, just a stone's throw from the highway. The austerity of the first church bespeaks native Protestantism; the magnificence of the second carries echoes of the Counter-Reformation in Europe.

What brought Sharpsburg the wealth that financed these fine monuments was the Pennsylvania Canal, which passed through the town between 1829 and 1852. The canal was sold to the railroads in 1857, filled with earth in 1861, and replaced by trains in 1866, but by then Sharpsburg was well launched as a rich town. There may be more excellent houses of the 1830s in Sharpsburg than anyplace else in western Pennsylvania. One of the first stands at the west end of town, at North Main and Garner streets, with a characteristic double-flue chimney. At 1420 North Main, at the corner of Fourteenth Street, a similarly proportioned five-bay brick house with a fanlight over the door sits on a high podium. A triple house at 532–536 North Main has the same traits.

More surprises come at the fork of North Main and North Canal streets, in a plaza dedicated to H. J. Heinz. Heinz was born in Pittsburgh's South Side in 1844—the only major Pittsburgh industrialist actually born in town—then moved to Sharpsburg with his parents when he was five. His parents' home still stands at 1623 Main Street; Heinz's own boyhood house was purchased by Henry Ford to become part of Ford's Greenfield Village in Dearborn, Michigan. Heinz left Sharpsburg for Pittsburgh in 1877 but returned two years later and stayed until he was obliged to live the life of a Pittsburgh lord in the 1890s. The reciprocal loyalty of the man and the town was clearly steadfast.

In 1896, Heinz paid for a statue that was erected in the plaza to commemorate Guyasuta, the Seneca tribal chief who controlled all of this district north of the Allegheny. Guyasuta entered history by meeting and befriending

fig. 8.37
CANAL-ERA
HOUSE,
SHARPSBURG

fig. 8.38
H. J. HEINZ
TEACHING
SUNDAY SCHOOL,
SHARPSBURG

George Washington in 1753. In his old age, Guyasuta lived in a log cabin near the Sharpsburg end of the Highland Park Bridge, and he died there in 1795. The statue that Heinz dedicated in 1896 had to be recast twice after vehicles hit it; what is there now dates from 1985.

On the back wall of the plaza is another sculptural composition, this one by Emil Fuchs showing H. J. Heinz teaching Sunday school at Grace United Methodist Church. Fuchs sculpted it in 1924 for the rotunda of the main Heinz administration building; it was reinstalled in the plaza in the 1950s. Alongside this main relief are secondary reliefs of the Christian principles by which Heinz lived. The whole image is not only well executed but affecting.

The original Heinz plant was built in Sharpsburg in 1869 on Main Street near Seventeenth Street, employing two women at first. But Heinz not only made food products; he also ran his own glassworks in Sharpsburg to ensure that the bottling was up to his specifications. Just off Fifteenth Street is another of Sharpsburg's numerous links with Heinz, in Heinz Terrace. These half-dozen Shingle-style homes erected before World War I were used by Heinz executives who, even after the plant left Sharpsburg for Pittsburgh, were not far away from their offices. What grabs one's attention right away is a Buddhist temple lantern, possibly hundreds of years old, and of good to fine quality, standing at the center of this grouping of houses. Heinz was a collector of Chinese antiquities, and this stone lantern seems to mark still another of his contributions to his hometown.

fig. 8.39
FREDERICK SAUER
HOUSES, ASPINWALL

There is nothing historic to Aspinwall, unlike so much of Sharpsburg. The brick-paved streets are laid out in an unexciting grid between the riverbank Freeport Road and the Allegheny Valley Expressway. But one architectural complex breaks out of the mold. Halfway up the steep hill of Center Avenue, immediately above the expressway overpass, stand the Frederick Sauer houses, from 615 to 627 Center, which must constitute the most eccentric residential colony in western Pennsylvania. Sauer was one of the many German-born or German-origin architects who dominated the middle ranks of Pittsburgh designers early in the last century. He was a native of Heidelberg, and these hillside houses not far from the Allegheny River may be Sauer's after-image of the famous ruined castle in his hometown.

Sauer got his architectural education in Stuttgart, then came to Pittsburgh around 1880 and built a dozen Catholic churches. In 1904, he began to construct rental properties on this plot of land in Aspinwall, acting as his own designer, mason, bricklayer, and carpenter. Sauer designed the first house, at 625 Center, in fairly conventional fashion out of ordinary Kittanning brick (the regional brick center of Kittaning lies thirty-six miles to the northeast) on a four-square Colonial Revival footprint. He continued to build through the 1920s and 1930s, with each new structure more fantastic than the last.

Sauer's usual materials were irregularly coursed stone and yellow brick, to which he added hundreds of strange inserts: lopsided keystones, turkeys and eagles, lions and Roman gods, roundels of Benjamin Franklin. All contribute to the whimsical nature of this miniaturized village. The buildings are a little more stolid than the supreme American fantasy structure, which is Simon Rodia's Watts Tower, from the 1920s, in Los Angeles, but only because they had to serve a practical purpose. They are somewhat dilapidated today, even though some portions have been restored. Each apartment unit grows in an easy organic manner out of its designated materials and out of its hillside niche. The whole group culminates in a fantastic mailbox that seems to have been made by hobbits from J. R. R. Tolkien's *Lord of the Rings*.

Springdale lies upriver from Aspinwall, past a great bend in the Allegheny and is recognizable from several miles away by the huge steam-powered electricity plant that the West Penn Power Company built at the waterfront to take advantage of the coal that was mined for the plant directly across the river, in Plum Borough.

What draws visitors from around the world to Springdale is not the power plant but the Rachel Carson Homestead at the top of Colfax Hill, at 613 Marion Avenue. The modest frame farmhouse was built by Rachel Carson's ancestors around 1840 at the center of their forty-three-acre farm. Carson was born there in 1907, graduated from high school in New Kensington in 1925, and took her science degree from what is today Chatham University in Squirrel Hill.

The Carson house is preserved as it was when Rachel left it to go to college in the 1920s. It is a low-ceilinged house with tiny bedrooms and presents the same forthright integrity as its famous occupant. Carson did not write her epochal *Silent Spring* of 1962 in this house, but the site may have nonetheless served to raise her ecological consciousness. The hilltop provides a striking view of the green mantle of the Allegheny Valley that is despoiled only by the red-and-white striped smokestack of the Springdale power plant. The plant that spoils this sylvan view went up in 1920, when Carson was at the impressionable age of thirteen.

New Kensington occupies the opposite bank of the Allegheny another few miles and one more bend upriver from Springdale. It is laid out like Springdale: a grid of streets starting at the river and extending uphill. Its distinction for more than half a century was industrial, as the world capital of

fig. 8.40
RACHEL CARSON'S
HOUSE, SPRINGDALE

aluminum processing. Aluminum came to New Kensington not because anyone thought its hills contained bauxite or its river might provide hydro-electric power but because Pittsburgh entrepreneurs agreed to back Charles Martin Hall's new aluminum-extraction process after Boston capitalists had rejected it. In 1891, three years after its beginnings in Pittsburgh's Strip District, the Aluminum Company of America (Alcoa) moved production to New Kensington, to a giant plant that once extended over many acres of the Allegheny riverbank. Production later left Pittsburgh, drawn by cheap and plentiful hydroelectric power available in places as diverse as Niagara Falls, Tennessee, and parts of Canada, but the New Kensington finishing plant remained in operation until after World War II.

Today, the operations that Alcoa conducts in and around New Kensington are exclusively in research. The Alcoa Technical Center here specializes in automotive, aerospace, and basic aluminum products. Indicative of this trend from production to research is the 1930s Alcoa Research Station that Henry Hornbostel designed for the hilltop at the intersection of Freeport and Edge-wood roads. Out of service, fenced off, and boarded up since the 1950s, the Neoclassical structure once held a commanding position overlooking New Kensington, but today's travelers pass it by without curiosity.

One highly significant monument from the years when Alcoa employed seven thousand workers in New Kensington remains in active use. This is Aluminum City Terrace, from 1941, designed by Walter Gropius and Marcel Breuer. The settlement stands on East Hill Drive, uphill from the core of New Kensington via Seventh Street and its continuation as Powers Drive. Contrary to its rural aspect, the site is within the municipal boundaries of New Kensington.

fig. 8.41
ALUMINUM CITY
TERRACE,
NEW KENSINGTON

Much of the fame that Walter Gropius enjoyed when Harvard University brought him to the United States in 1937 was derived from his 1920s housing estates at Dessau and Berlin, but Aluminum City Terrace is the only housing project he built once he got to America. Made for wartime workers in the nearby aluminum plant, it reflected its low budget (thirty-two hundred dollars per unit) in its austere use of brick and wood and in the spartan dimensions of each unit. Gropius and Breuer broke their 250 units into thirty-eight rows that seem to be scattered at random over the uneven ground. What Gropius and Breuer were looking for, however, was social interaction among the residents of the rows, as well as optimum positioning for sun and shade.

These International Style rows originally reflected the clarity and unblinking rigor of the European designers, but in 1962, they were radically Americanized. To yield more privacy, renovators transformed the backs of the rows into their fronts by adding porches and demarcating private gardens. This about-face also put residents closer to their cars in the nearby parking lots—something the European designers would never have done. Also during this renovation, the early, inefficient wooden sunshades were replaced with aluminum ones. With these changes, the residents effectively became their own architects, and today, the unit owners (Aluminum City Terrace became a cooperative in 1948) take great pleasure in their homes. The restructuring of Aluminum City Terrace represents a conflict between its European architects and its American residents in one way, but in another way it can be seen as a partnership between the two parties to forge what Gropius sought to promote all his life—a real sense of community.

For millennia, the ancient technique of glassmaking resisted large-scale production. In the nineteenth century, a glassmaking industry blossomed in Pittsburgh, where for the first time glassmaking was fired by coal and then by natural gas. It was also in Pittsburgh that the industry took many critical steps toward mechanization; for example, all of the early machines that produced Coca-Cola bottles were made in Pittsburgh.

It was the presence of coal mines on both sides of the Allegheny that led the directors of the newly constituted Pittsburgh Plate Glass (PPG) firm to build a huge glassworks in 1883 on the north bank of the Allegheny at Creighton, some two miles upriver from New Kensington. PPG became the world's first successful producer of plate glass, and within a decade, some six thousand workers labored in several score buildings. All of the old mills, with their distinctive peaked roofs (to dissipate the intense heat), have been leveled to accommodate the current glass plant, which is the huge structure seen from state route 28 north. PPG now produces glass all over the world, but

439

locally it maintains just this plant at Creighton, a coating plant in Springdale, a research center closer to Pittsburgh, in Harmar Township, and its Downtown world headquarters.

Three river towns in the nine-mile stretch between New Kensington and the northern boundary of Allegheny County supported three key American innovations of the nineteenth century: aluminum in New Kensington, plate glass in Creighton, and oil in Natrona. Of the three towns, Natrona is the most interesting by far, in both visual and social terms. Its distinctions are two: it was America's first significant oil producer, and it is a rare survivor among mid-nineteenth-century company towns. In 1850, the Pennsylvania Salt Manufacturing Company set up an important plant in Natrona for the production of caustic soda through the heating of salt brine (the town's name derives from the Greek word for salt). The location by the Allegheny's north bank was ideal, with bounteous salt wells nearby and ample coal to fire the boilers and reduce the brine to salt. Just as fortunately, the Pennsylvania Canal flowed through the area, giving the company a constant supply of laborers from Pittsburgh and giving its salt direct access to markets in Philadelphia and the East Coast. The company used the canal as the center-line of its new town; in 1852, the Pennsylvania Railroad laid its tracks directly over the filled-in canal bed.

Along with industrial buildings, Penn Salt constructed about 150 worker houses in wood and brick between 1850 and 1857. For nearly a century, the company rented the homes to its employees, then sold them in 1941 when it left town. Most of those homes are still standing, wedged between the river, the towering plants of Allegheny Ludlum Steel at either end of town, and a massive slag heap inland. The oldest units stand on Blue Ridge Avenue, facing the old Pennsylvania Railroad tracks. Long grim rowhouses of brick, they are an unintentional parody of the elegant rowhouse-lined Philadelphia streets that the company founders had left behind. The wooden houses a few blocks over, particularly those on Federal Street (known to the residents as "Pigeon Row") are almost unimaginably small, with just two rooms below and one above. Still, the wood houses are detached, as though cottages, and bespeak a certain independence in their gabled peaks and—in the few units that were not modernized—their vertical board-and-batten siding.

The salt wells of Natrona were also the birthplace of the American oil industry a decade before Drake drilled his well in Titusville. In 1849, annoyed at the petroleum seeping into his salt wells, the industrialist Thomas Kier helped his son Samuel bottle it as "Kier's Petroleum or Rock Oil." Young Kier sold what he could of the petroleum as medicinal oil and as a lubricant, and

441

fig. 8.42
"Pigeon Row"
worker houses,
Natrona

in 1853, he began to refine it as an illuminant. Kier produced twenty-five barrels of "carbon oil" a day at his still on Grant Street in the Golden Triangle. The next year, Samuel Kier drilled more wells, some four hundred feet deep, in Natrona and nearby Tarentum, and pumped oil out of these, too. By 1860, Kier was exporting oil as far as London. Although Edwin Drake, attracted by Kier's success, brought in oil in much greater quantity at Titusville in 1859, the heart of the industry in its early years lay in the refineries of Pittsburgh. It was the Mellons' familiarity with the local oil business that induced them to prospect for oil on a global scale with their Gulf operations in Texas and abroad.

Besides Natrona, aficionados of American industrial archaeology can find a second significant company town northeast of Pittsburgh. This is Vandergrift, in adjoining Westmoreland County. Vandergrift is also a river town, in this case located on a sharp bend in the Kiskiminetas River, a few miles before it flows into the Allegheny. The town was the work of the country's most distinguished urban design firm at the close of the nineteenth century: the Boston-based Olmsted Brothers, under the direction of two sons of the valorous Frederick Law Olmsted, father of landscape architecture in America.

Vandergrift was a spin-off of the Apollo Iron & Steel Company, which, emerging from labor strife in 1894, wanted to reward its nonunion workers with model housing yet also keep them tractable. Not for long did the town hold to the gentle contours and generous land allotment projected by the Olmsted firm: later additions follow conventional grids. Nonetheless, a remarkable amount of the Olmsteds' original city plan does survive, along with the city hall and civic center called the Casino, which makes Vandergrift one of the more impressive company towns in the country.

THE PITTSBURGH PERIPHERY:
SUBURBIA, HISTORY, AND RENEWAL

fig. 9.1
Cranberry:
an Aerial view

Pittsburgh is so resolutely urban that it is hard to think of it as a suburban experience, too. But starting in 1851, with the establishment of America's first "romantic," or picturesque, suburb at Evergreen Hamlet, the city's strong urban context created an equally strong suburban response. Many of the suburbs grafted themselves onto old country churches that went back to Revolutionary War days; that was the case for Churchill, Bethel Park, and Mt. Lebanon, with a later church serving as the core of Fox Chapel. Being harder to reach in their hilly locations than the industrial satellites in the three river valleys, these dozens of middle-class or affluent clusters did not grow until they were linked to Pittsburgh by the trolley and the motorcar. Allegheny County put in special motorcar roads along the Allegheny and Ohio rivers to serve some of the suburbs in the 1920s and 1930s; others had to wait for the turnpike and the interstates to thread through the region's hills between the 1940s and the 1990s. There has been plenty of sprawl, but overall Pittsburgh's suburbs are like the city itself and maintain an urban logic that leaves little room for disorder. The suburbs may signify nothing but sprawl to their detractors, but for half a million Pittsburghers, their towns or townships are not anti-neighborhoods; they *are* neighborhoods.

Disposed around Pittsburgh today are the three smaller cities, eighty-four boroughs, and forty-two townships that together form Allegheny County. The county covers 728 square miles (an area half the size of Rhode Island) and has a population of about 1.3 million. Symmetrically disposed around Allegheny County are the eight other counties of southwestern Pennsylvania: Beaver, Lawrence, Butler, and Armstrong to the north; Westmoreland to the east; and Fayette, Greene, and Washington to the south and west.

These suburbs, exurbs, and towns make Pittsburgh the de facto capital of western Pennsylvania. In the Middle Ages, it was common wisdom that a town like Dante's Florence could not achieve greatness without distinguished supporting towns in the *contado*, or hinterland. The towns that ring Pittsburgh were once flourishing, too, but most were badly hit by the collapse of heavy industry. When the towns were prospering, Pittsburgh treated its surrounding countryside not in the modern American way, as something inferior that buckles under urban sprawl, but in the medieval European way, as a partner in a development of mutual benefit. Pittsburgh's satellite towns are neither inferior nor superior to the city, but they are necessary to it. Pittsburgh would not be Pittsburgh without them.

There are perennial complaints about how hard it is to get around Pittsburgh by car since the major roads do not circle the metropolis but instead extend from the center to the periphery like the arms of an octopus. (Allegheny County offers some help by designating five "color belts" that link the secondary roads by means of color-coded signs.) Pittsburgh never got the circular beltway that characterizes so many American cities, but it compensates with two expressway triangles around the city. The inner triangle is composed of the Pennsylvania Turnpike (I-76), the north-south I-79, and the east-west Parkway (now designated I-376). The outer triangle uses the east-west I-70 as its base and I-76 and I-79 as its two sides. As a result, we could say that contemporary Pittsburgh—in a cultural but not a legal sense—stretches north to Butler, east to Greensburg, west to East Liverpool, Ohio, and south to Morgantown, West Virginia.

It is also illuminating to look beyond the suburbs. Up to a certain point, the farther you move out from Pittsburgh, the newer things become. But beyond that point, the farther you move out, the older things become and we find places and events that go back in time before Pittsburgh itself. Thus, well to the north of the city we find the path taken by George Washington in 1753 on his way to parley with the French—as it passes in front of brand-new suburban malls. Then to the southeast there are equally new housing developments in the region rubbing shoulders with some of the oldest villages or forts, such as Fort Necessity, where Washington and his troops were badly beaten in a skirmish with French forces in 1754.

SETTLEMENTS SOUTH AND WEST

There is a crescent of agricultural land that stretches for about twenty-five miles between and beyond the industrial developments in the Monongahela and Ohio valleys. For a century, this agricultural district was isolated from Pittsburgh by the Monongahela River, the fast-flowing Chartiers Creek, and the bulk of Mount Washington. It was strongly influenced by Virginia, which claimed and briefly administered the settlements in this area in the 1770s. In 1871, however, the Pittsburgh & Castle Shannon Railroad cut into the heart of the South Hills with a track that was later connected to an inclined plane over Mount Washington. Other train and streetcar lines followed, either going over Mount Washington or around it along Saw Mill Run.

It was the inauguration of the Mt. Washington Transit Tunnel in 1904 that turned the South Hills into a full-fledged suburban extension of Pittsburgh. Brentwood, Whitehall, Castle Shannon, Dormont, and Mt. Lebanon developed as trolley suburbs, while West Mifflin, Pleasant Hills, Bethel Park, and Upper St. Clair grew later as motorcar suburbs, following the opening of the Liberty Tunnels below Mount Washington in 1924. The South Hills preserves several monuments of what might be termed the pioneer phase of suburbia in America. These include an early shopping center, a pioneer airport, a cloverleaf traffic circle from the 1930s, and early tract houses erected near Bridgeville by Edward M. Ryan, whose family firm later built suburban homes all over the United States.

Being suburbia, the South Hills has no distinct gateway, but it has certain landmarks. One of the most prominent is its airport, not the huge international airport west of town but a miniature one that now serves only private and corporate jets. This is the 1930s Allegheny County Airport in the borough of West Mifflin, where Lebanon Church Road meets state route 885. The terminal is standard Beaux-Arts in its symmetry, but the more fanciful Art Deco Style emerges in the overlay of Aztec designs and the streamlined corners of the building. Especially memorable are the green and black terracotta planters decorated with eagles, propellers, and squadrons of planes.

West Mifflin also contains three outstanding homes from the years 1939 and 1947–1950 by two of Frank Lloyd Wright's most distinguished disciples. The prime mover behind Meadow Circles was Cornelia Brierley, since it was a commission from her two aunts; there may also have been design input from her husband, Peter Berndtson. The little Wrightian colony stands 1.3 miles north of the airport, reached by state route 885 north, Noble Drive, and Irwin Run Road to the winding Lutz Lane. Brierley's 1939 Notz house is at

fig. 9.2
THE ALLEGHENY
COUNTY AIRPORT

number 125 Lutz Lane, and the Katz and Bear houses of 1947–1950 are at 111 and 120 Lutz Lane. All three homes have survived in relatively good condition.

West Mifflin's most imposing monument is not a building but an anti-building. Brown's Dump is a heap of 70 million tons of slag that nearby U.S. Steel plants for years poured out in red-hot streams into a deep valley south of the airport, between parallel state routes 885 and 51 south. Local teenagers would park nearby and watch the hell-fire dumping as a cheap Saturday night date. By the time the liquid pouring ceased in 1969 and the dumping of hard slag was halted a few years later, what was once a valley had become a towering mountain. In 1979, the Century III Mall was built over the partially flattened lower slopes of the mountain. The psychic Jeanne Dixon predicted an awful catastrophe would result, but so far the only awful thing there is the mall architecture that rose over the slag.

Just a mile north of the once hellish slag pouring on state route 51 (Clairton Boulevard), is a vision of the heavenly Jerusalem in Holy Trinity Serbian Orthodox Cathedral in the borough of Whitehall. In 1971, architect John Tomich, neither ignoring nor slavishly imitating the historical precedents for Orthodox churches, fashioned a Brutalist poured-concrete structure that has an extraordinary degree of self-assurance and nobility. Tomich's basic scheme is a rectangle with three apses, recalling the triconch plan used in the time of the emperors Constantine and Justinian. The rectangle is surmounted by two intersecting barrel vaults and a high watchtower. The façade also has an isolated barrel vault that recalls Alberti's Sant'Andrea at Mantua. The detailing is thoughtful and engaging—for example, in the thin panels of glass that separate the apses from the main rectangle. Not everything at Holy Trinity is successful, however; the interior effects were never resolved, and the wing housing the social hall and school is perhaps too overtly modeled on the work of Louis Kahn. But the church is one of the majestic buildings of postwar Pittsburgh, and it should endure when the minor structures around it have returned to pasture.

Suburbia would not be suburbia without highway cloverleafs, and the South Hills area has a particularly early example. This is the Pleasant Hills cloverleaf, where Curry Hollow Road and Lebanon Church Road intersect state route 51. This was the first cloverleaf in western Pennsylvania and among the pioneers in the nation (its dedication plaque, from 1939, quaintly calls it a "grade separation bridge"). Next to it stands another milestone of Pittsburgh suburbia, the Bill Green Shopping Center, gateway to the borough of Pleasant Hills. While not large in population (about eighty-four hundred), Pleasant Hills stands out as the first Pittsburgh district to be developed entirely

fig. 9.3
HOLY TRINITY
SERBIAN
ORTHODOX
CHURCH,
WHITEHALL

as tract housing, with a half-dozen different projects established between 1929 and the early 1970s. In its period of greatest growth during the Eisenhower years, the developers put a new home under roof every three days.

Pittsburgh's most famous recent citizen lies buried five miles west of the cloverleaf, where St. John the Baptist Byzantine Catholic Cemetery shelters the grave of Andy Warhol (1928–1987). To get from the cloverleaf to the cemetery, one must take Curry Hollow Road and Broughton Road west for five miles, then state route 88 north (Library Road) a half-mile north to its T-junction with Connor Road, just inside the borough of Bethel Park. Warhol may have made his name in New York, but he lies buried in his hometown, a few feet from his parents' graves in this hillside; the artist's tomb is easily visible in the upper tier of graves. The gravestone is frequently the site of offerings, the faithful leaving coins and the occasional Campbell's soup can.

The crown jewel of the South Hills in terms of nature's glory is the two thousand acres of South Park, immediately south of the St. John the Baptist cemetery and at the intersection of state route 88 and Corrigan Drive. This fine greenspace and its twin, North Park in the North Hills, were established in the 1920s by Edward V. Babcock, who was mayor of Pittsburgh before becoming an Allegheny County commissioner. Taking his cue from Pittsburgh's park pioneer, E. M. Bigelow, Babcock bought much of the land using his personal funds and then turned it over to the county.

South Park has significant historical value, too, in the pioneer Oliver Miller homestead on Stone Manse Drive. This stone house, designed on Georgian lines similar to the profile of the John Woods house in Hazelwood, was built by James Miller in 1808 on the site of his father's log house of a generation earlier. The father, Oliver Miller, has the distinction of being the first casualty in the Whiskey Rebellion gun battle that resulted in the burning of John Neville's Bower Hill plantation house in 1794. The rebellion was sparked by the excise tax that the federal government tried to impose on western Pennsylvania distillers, and it was the first significant ripple of discontent and show of force in the fledgling republic. To the right of the original house, the later addition of 1830 is marked by an enormous rubble chimney. The building was inhabited by five generations of Millers until 1927, after which the interior was preserved as a museum. The barn alongside the house is new but well worth inspection, since it follows the precepts of western Pennsylvania barn construction, which were specific to the region.

Bethel Park is rich in other structures evocative of early America. The wooden Peter Boyer house at 5679 Library Road, a mile south of the South Park main gate, exhibits a visual pride of place. Built in the late 1840s, this

447

fig. 9.4
ANDY WARHOL'S
TOMB, BETHEL PARK

fig. 9.5
OLIVER MILLER
HOMESTEAD,
SOUTH PARK

structure is one of the best Greek Revival homes in the Pittsburgh district, with a striking two-level Ionic portico and meticulously carved wooden moldings. About a mile northwest stands a core building of the area: Bethel Presbyterian Church, at 2999 Bethel Church Road. This is the fifth house of worship for a congregation that was organized in 1776. Next to the church stretches an ample graveyard, with fourteen tombs of Revolutionary War veterans. Pioneer days are also remembered nearby in the elegant brick George Marshall house, at the intersection of Oakhurst and Marshall roads. Dating from 1838, except for an anachronistic giant-order portico that was added in the 1930s, the original structure was built by the pastor of the church, who was a grandson of President John Adams.

Mt. Lebanon, the borough adjoining Bethel Park on the north, is the archetype of the wealthy Pittsburgh suburb. Just six miles separate Mt. Lebanon from the Golden Triangle, but the town has always acted as though it was much farther away. Settlement of the borough began in the 1770s, when it was a tavern stop on the Washington Pike, one of two routes between Pittsburgh and the town of Washington, Pennsylvania. The traditional explanation for the name Lebanon is that some cedars of Lebanon were brought from the Holy Land in the nineteenth century and planted along the pike.

The population grew as access to Pittsburgh improved, with railroad tracks installed to the north and south in 1871 and 1878, a trolley link to Saw Mill Run in 1902, and the streetcar tunnel under Mount Washington in 1904. These public transit routes broke down Mt. Lebanon's isolation, and between 1918 and 1941 the borough grew tenfold, from two thousand to twenty thousand residents. Today, its six square miles sustain a population of about thirty-three thousand.

In 1901, Mt. Lebanon saw its first large housing project, one that was urban rather than suburban in character and close to the projected trolley line on Washington Road. The next wave of housing construction, following World War I, took place east of Cochran Road and was designed for homeowners with cars; a third wave, in the 1920s and 1930s, created the more fastidious homes of the Mission Hills, Virginia Manor, Beverly Heights, and Hoodridge and Terrace Drive districts. In these areas, Mt. Lebanon's early grid gave way to contoured streets, and the homes changed from standard builders' vernacular to Cotswold, Neoclassical, or Federal designs. Mission Hills was directly modeled on the namesake development that went up outside Kansas City in the 1920s.

Despite their elevated prices, the houses in Mission Hills and the related tracts were still part of a "development"; most of them were designed by a half-dozen architects retained by the developers, and their stone and slate came exclusively from quarries controlled by those developers. Successive complexes filled up the unbuilt areas of the borough between the 1940s and the 1960s, with the remaining empty spaces being developed until recently. In all, about forty separate tract housing projects were built in Mt. Lebanon over a period of eighty years. But Mt. Lebanon was not a Levittown of western Pennsylvania; the home prices were too high, the architecture was too varied, the streets too irreproachably landscaped. And there was Washington Road to provide a "main drag" that holds the municipality together even today. The movie theater here is dark now, but the churches, restaurants, and Art Deco and Tudor Revival storefronts along Washington Road are flourishing. The town also has a civic presence in the Mt. Lebanon Municipal Building at 710 Washington Road, from 1930. This structure presents itself in the stylish moderne idiom of the time, asserting its authority with an octagonal stepped pyramid termination outside and mural paintings of Mt. Lebanon inside.

Three fine Washington Road churches give spiritual authority to the district from the summit of Mt. Lebanon Hill. The three stand in the triangle formed by Scott and Washington roads and the Mt. Lebanon Cemetery, each an accomplished variant in Gothic Revival Style. They are the rock-faced Mt. Lebanon Methodist Church from 1923; Mt. Lebanon United Presbyterian Church, from 1929, in English decorated Gothic Style, modeled on York Minster; and—the best of the group—the muscular but delicately colored St. Bernard's Roman Catholic Church at 311 Washington Road. Constructed and decorated between 1933 and 1947 in transitional Romanesque-Gothic Style, St. Bernard's is a cathedral in everything but title. Its siting on the crest of a hill reminds visitors that there really is a "Mount Lebanon," and the church's excellent sightlines show off its huge mass a mile or more away. The stonework outside is locally unsurpassed in color and cutting. Inside, lead designer William Perry showed his knowledge of Romanesque precedent (he had traveled the Pilgrimage Road in France and Spain a decade before). The highly original sculpture, painting, and glass inside work well with the architecture to deliver a rare spiritual impact.

Mt. Lebanon's trio of churches stands opposite Bower Hill Road, a curving route that snakes 4.4 miles down the sides of the Chartiers Valley and has along it a number of reminders of the era when Pittsburgh was founded. Around 1790, Brigadier General John Neville built the most opulent mansion in western Pennsylvania on Bower Hill, in what is now the borough of Bridgeville, only to see it torched during the Whiskey Rebellion in 1794. Neville, an aristocratic Virginian, had earlier commanded Fort Pitt, but in his

451

fig. 9.6
St. Bernard's
Church

later capacity as collector of the excise tax on whiskey, the local farmers who relied on distilling their grain for cash vented their fury at him.

Still surviving from the Neville family patrimony is Woodville, the superb plantation house the family had built earlier, in the 1780s. The house stands at 1375 Washington Pike (state route 50), halfway between the towns of Heidelberg and Bridgeville. Woodville was a Virginia plantation house in both form and function, since it was built to replace the simple log house John Neville had erected on land alongside Chartiers Creek around 1780. Neville expanded the house in the Tidewater Virginia hall-and-parlor tradition a few years later, by which time it had become the center and showpiece of the seven thousand acres he owned in the Chartiers Valley. The original log house was retained as the kitchen, and its old fireplace was extended in a Y shape to serve two adjacent rooms.

Neville went on to build the ill-fated mansion on Bower Hill, and after its destruction by the mob, he lived out his days at his estate on Neville Island in the Ohio River. Woodville passed to his son Presley and his descendants, who added the early Gothic Revival dormers and the gently swelling eaves that give the house a profile one might expect to find in Mississippi or Tennessee. In 1973, after the house had passed through six generations of Nevilles and the parlor had acquired sixteen coats of paint, Woodville was purchased by the Pittsburgh History & Landmarks Foundation (today, a local history association maintains it). A unique feature of the house is the group of names of guests and the dates of their visits scratched into the window glass, the earliest

fig. 9.7
WOODVILLE,
THE NEVILLE
PLANTATION
HOUSE

inscription being from 1811. In 1825, a well-known Revolutionary War commander came to visit Presley Neville, his former aide, and he, too, followed this custom. The glass pane into which the noted visitor etched his signature was lost or stolen a generation ago, but until then one could clearly make out the signature of the Marquis de Lafayette.

Half a mile back toward Pittsburgh, on the east side of Chartiers Creek, where Washington Pike enters Scott Township, stands another evocative monument of the pioneer days of Pittsburgh. This is St. Luke's Episcopal Church, at the corner of Old Washington Pike and Church Street. This rustic Gothic Revival church in uncoursed masonry was constructed in 1852 as the third building of a congregation that was organized around 1770. The Pittsburgh specialist James Van Trump attributed the design to John Notman, who came to Pittsburgh in 1851 to superintend construction on another Episcopal church: St. Peter's, Downtown. St. Luke's is a skillfully crafted building with a board-and-batten wood vestibule (reproduced from photographs), an impressively severe aspect inside, and a graveyard full of evocative tombstones going back to the Revolutionary War.

Today, Washington Pike leads without incident to Bridgeville, a lively old town on a great bend in Chartiers Creek, then southwest to Washington, Pennsylvania, about ten miles distant. The seat of Washington County, "Little Washington" was laid out in 1781, nine years before Washington, DC. The name was bestowed both to honor the general and to recognize his extensive land holdings in the area. Washington, Pennsylvania, is a distinctive hill town full of Greek Revival townhouses in the city's core, all grouped around the effusive Washington County Courthouse that Frederick Osterling erected in the middle of town in 1900. In the wider suburban radius, Shingle-style and other more informal homes predominate, particularly around the campus of Washington and Jefferson College, the main building of which dates from 1793.

A few miles northwest of Washington lie two testimonies to western Pennsylvania's early days. One is the village of West Middletown, eleven miles up state route 844 from Washington. Though no longer quite so fine as it was as late as the 1970s, the town still preserves numerous eighteenth- and nine-teenth-century houses on its spacious tree-lined streets. On the outskirts is Plantation Plenty, a perfectly conserved Federal-era brick farmhouse and out-buildings that for more than two centuries have served the descendants of the Rhode Island–born settler Isaac Manchester, who completed construction on the main house in 1815. The same era is evoked near the village of Avella, just a few miles distant and reached easily from Pittsburgh on I-79 south, then state route 50 west. This is the Meadowcroft Museum of Rural Life, a Colonial Williamsburg–type collection of several dozen pioneer homes, shops, and artisan workshops that were moved here to simulate a frontier village.

Avella also offers something vastly more ancient, from perhaps the continent's earliest human inhabitants. It is here that, in 1973, University of Pittsburgh archaeologists began excavating the Meadowcroft Rockshelter, which has since then yielded a million human and animal bones, 2 million human artifacts, and millions more plant remains. Through radiocarbon dating, the scientists have traced human visits to the site over the course of sixteen millennia—the longest documented human occupation record in North America. A modest but effective visitors center has provided public access to the site since 2008, under the auspices of the Heinz History Center in Pittsburgh. It is no small thrill to encounter this account of ancient life just thirty-five miles from a metropolis.

The same fast-moving (and occasionally deadly) Chartiers Creek that passes by Woodville and forms the boundaries for several boroughs here was also a key factor in the settlement of the working-class borough of Carnegie, four miles west of Pittsburgh. The primary industrial town of the Chartiers Valley, Carnegie received its name in 1894 when two settlements, Chartiers and Mansfield, merged to form a new identity. The severe stone Greek Revival Mansfield Brown house of 1822 survives, thus commemorating the major landowner of the district. It stands near the center of town at 602 Poplar Alley, behind the Episcopal Church of the Atonement.

At the heart of town, in a dense industrial and residential district, stands another of Titus de Bobula's exuberant bulbous-domed churches. This is St. Peter and St. Paul Ukrainian Orthodox Church at 200 Walnut, at the corner of Mansfield Boulevard. This brilliantly crafted building of concrete and industrial brick from 1906 sports two side domes and a high central octagonal belfry that is crowned by a sequence of fragmented onion domes. Similar to the way that McKees Rocks clustered several houses of worship in a single zone, the town of Carnegie created a sacred district so that this church and two others were located in an unbroken row. The ecclesiastical neighbors are St. Paul A.M.E. Zion Church, from 1927, an African American congregation, and the Holy Virgin Russian Orthodox Church, from 1920.

Carnegie has another extraordinary feature, which is a sort of acropolis that rises south of Main Street. On this height, mill superintendents once lived in the elegant Colonial Revival houses that survive on Beechwood and Library avenues. The slopes of the hill are eroded and overgrown with vegetation now, so this acropolis does not make the dramatic statement it must have made in the days of Pierre Chartiers. But this acropolis actually does feature a temple, in this case, the pompous Renaissance-style Andrew Carnegie Free Library, from 1899.

The town of Carnegie marks the most memorable point on the Parkway West, where drivers follow the highway as it drops into the Chartiers Valley, a spot fourteen miles southeast of Pittsburgh International Airport and a few miles from Downtown. The location chosen for the previous iteration of Pittsburgh's commercial airport terminal, which was a gracious retro deco building of 1952, and the simultaneous construction of the Parkway leading to it, fueled an explosion of office building construction in what had been the least developed area of the Pittsburgh region. High-tech companies began to set up shop there, either in the two office parks of the Regional Industrial Development Corporation, west and north of the airport, or in private clusters, such as those of Bayer Chemical Corporation, Penn Center West, Foster Plaza, or the Parkway Center. These buildings were the nucleus of a corporate suburbia that is physically close but conceptually remote from the soot-blackened steeltowns in which many of these firms had their beginnings.

Pittsburgh International Airport replaced its predecessor in 1992. Its twelve thousand acres completely cover the site of that previous facility, which was itself the fourth airfield Pittsburgh had constructed since 1919. Using the same runways as the 1992 structure, the newer Midfield Terminal consists of separate landside and airside terminals. The airport's X-shaped layout attempts

fig. 9.8
CHURCH ROW,
CARNEGIE

to move the traveler from parking lot to plane and back in the least painful manner. People-movers transport passengers under the tarmac to the airside terminal, where they reach their gates on automated sidewalks. In-transit visitors to the airport use only the airside terminal while awaiting connecting flights. There, they ease their wait in an air mall of about a hundred retail outlets (the terminal consistently ranks in the top tier of airports worldwide). The airport design is nothing if not earnest in its poured-concrete barrel vaults, clerestories, and skylights, culminating in a gravity-defying mobile by Alexander Calder, which hangs at the center of the X. But in the end the gigantic building satisfies only functional needs, and its large expanses of concrete and tile simply overpower. Nonetheless, and even though the airport dropped the word "Greater" from its name, the size and efficiency of the airport make it one of the few recent civic buildings that appropriately matches the contemporary scale of greater Pittsburgh.

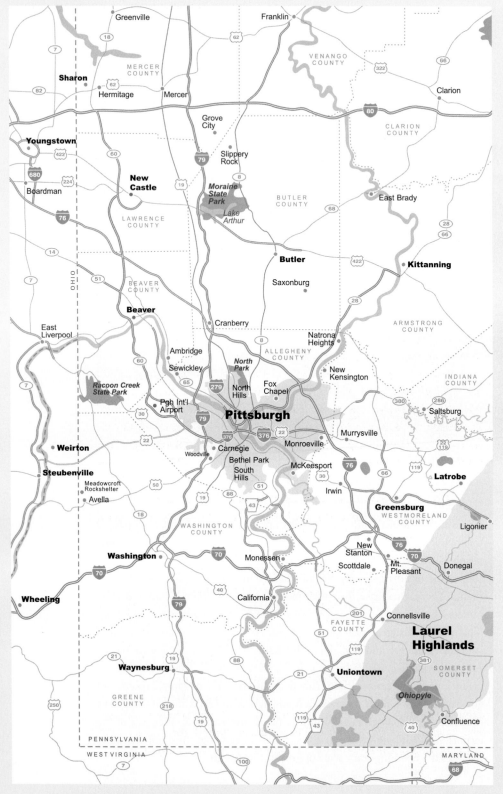

Southwestern Pennsylvania

SETTLEMENTS NORTH

Though broad, the inland district that lies between the Ohio and the Allegheny rivers forms a triangle with enough topographic and chronological coherence that Pittsburghers refer to all of this land as the North Hills. The North Hills proper consists of a dozen postwar suburbs that are located in or adjacent to McCandless, Hampton, Ross, Shaler, and several smaller townships. At its widest, the North Hills encompasses the whole triangle between the Allegheny and Ohio rivers, up to the northern boundary of Allegheny County. The population of the district is about 150,000—smaller than that of the eastern or southern suburbs, but growing at a faster pace.

The growth of the North Hills may be measured by certain milestones. The first was the transformation in 1796 of the old Venango Indian footpath from Pittsburgh to Lake Erie into the wider Franklin Road for horses and wagons. This was the same trail used by George Washington in 1753 when he made an arduous winter journey from the Forks of the Ohio to the settlement of Venango (now Franklin) and then up French Creek to the enemy outpost of Fort LeBoeuf. Very nearly killed not once but twice in the process, Washington was on a mission to assess French imperial intentions toward British interests in North America. The intelligence Washington successfully gathered was directly responsible for the outbreak of the Seven Years War, better known to Americans as the French and Indian War. (The path he took is now marked by signs along stretches of modern-day routes 19 and 528 in Butler County.) A second improvement to the trail came in 1805, which was marked by its new name as the Pittsburgh-Mercer Road. Today the same road operates under a third name, the Perry Highway (state route 19). Other North Hills milestones were the opening in 1823 of the Butler Road (state route 8, now in part the William Flinn Highway), which linked Sharpsburg and Etna on the Allegheny with the seat of Butler County; the construction of the railroad to Erie in 1864; a local oil boom from 1890 to 1915; the creation of North Park in 1927; and the emergence of the McKnight Road (truck route 19) commercial strip in the 1930s. Banal as most of the roads are, there is profit in studying them because each road etched a distinctive character onto its domain according to its particular time and space.

The second half of the twentieth century saw the addition of the three expressways that now crisscross the North Hills: I-79, which crosses the Ohio River not far from the airport and heads due north to Lake Erie; its I-279 offshoot, crossing the Allegheny in Downtown and cutting through the North

Side until linking with the main road; and the Pennsylvania Turnpike (I-76), which crosses the Allegheny at Oakmont, then twists northwest to intersect with I-79. (The direct connection of the latter two roads was delayed for three decades by the dithering of politicians and highway engineers.) There are, in addition, some purely local roads that link to settlements along the Allegheny: Babcock Boulevard, coming out of Millvale; Mount Royal Road, coming out of Etna; and Fox Chapel Road, coming out of the Allegheny river town of Aspinwall.

Evergreen Hamlet, just off Babcock and a few miles north of the Allegheny, has a valid, if slightly tenuous, claim to being the first suburb, at least the first "romantic" suburb, in the United States. Established in 1851, the settlement of about eighty-five acres sits high on Rock Ridge Road, which meets Babcock Boulevard at a sharp bend just north of that road's intersection with Evergreen and Peoples Plank Road.

The question of when and where Americans created a community that was neither urban nor rural is of major significance for the nation's social history. The usual answer is Alexander Jackson Davis's Llewellyn Park at West Orange, New Jersey, from 1853. That colony appears to have trailed behind Evergreen, however, since seven lots were purchased at Evergreen in 1851, and four homes were ready the next year. Although the Evergreen experiment parallels Thoreau's communion with nature at Walden Pond in the same years, its leaders were not philosophers but businessmen, including William Scaife, William Shinn, Robert Sellers, William Hill, and Wade Hampton.

Unlike the earlier extensions of the Golden Triangle into the Hill or Oakland, Evergreen Hamlet was not just an offshoot of something else but a true suburb. Its isolation on a mountaintop six miles from Pittsburgh was deemed ideal both for the social benefits of the site and for its picturesque view of the Allegheny Valley some 250 feet below. The colony was laid out (by Heastings & Preiser, Pittsburgh surveyors) in conformity with the natural contours of the hill. It was not a mere summer colony, however, since the Allegheny Valley Railroad started operations on the opposite bank of the Allegheny River in 1856, which strongly suggests that Evergreen Hamlet's promoters knew in advance that they would have to wait only a few years before they would enjoy speedy daily conveyance to their businesses in the Golden Triangle. The men living in Evergreen Hamlet were prototype commuters; they left their homes every morning and returned each evening, as millions of Americans have done ever since.

Evergreen Hamlet may go down in American history as the first suburb, but it was not a successful one; only four villas were actually built. The architect

fig. 9.9
SHINN HOUSE,
EVERGREEN HAMLET

of record for those four was Joseph W. Kerr, but their real inspiration was
Andrew Jackson Downing, author of *Treatise on the Theory and Practice of
Landscape Gardening* (1841), *Cottage Residences* (1842), and *The Architecture
of Country Houses* (1851). All three of Downing's books paint the picture
of Americans living harmoniously with nature in villas that expressed their
personal individuality.

Two of the four surviving villas at Evergreen Hamlet followed Downing's
program only in part. The Wade Hampton and Robert Sellers houses are
four-square Regency-style villas of formidable bearing inside and out. They
do not really correspond to Downing's philosophy, although the latter house
has a relaxed latticework verandah. The William Shinn house is by contrast a
more adventurous building, almost a Swiss chalet, with drooping bargeboard
ornaments and a pronounced verticality to its board-and-batten frame construction. Its design is an amalgam of various A. J. Davis plans that Downing
had published. The cross-gable roof was an important element in the Gothic
Revival home because (one theory holds) homeowners of the era thought the
"sign of the cross" feature would ensure domestic purity.

Grander than the other three villas is the William Hill house, again in
board-and-batten and today correctly painted in pastels rather than the white
that Downing despised. It is nonetheless a big and formal house, with a library
and parlor opening left and right of the central hall to create a cross-axis fifty-
seven feet long. The plan mixes features of two different plans in Downing's
Architecture of Country Houses, but the house may also carry references to

Jefferson's Monticello in the half-octagonal dining room and in the closing off of the stairs behind closet doors. All four villas are beautifully maintained, and a visit to Evergreen is mandatory preparation for a trip to America's foremost villa, at Fallingwater, since Frank Lloyd Wright was himself a child of the mid-Victorian passion to escape the city.

Another four miles up Babcock Road lies Swan Acres, another groundbreaking Pittsburgh suburb. Swan Acres had its moment of fame in the 1930s as the first totally modern housing development in the nation. The original twelve of these thirty-six houses were built between 1934 and 1936, mainly to the designs of Pittsburgh architect Harry C. Clepper and his young collaborator, Quentin Beck. Set on thirty-five acres of wooded drives, the colony was to be a "Planned Community in the Country," as the *Pittsburgh Press* proclaimed on opening day in 1936.

The homes have the unadorned walls, flat roofs, glass block, casement windows, and rounded corners that were the hallmarks of the International Style of the 1920s and the 1930s. Each home is different (their prices ranged from twelve thousand to twenty-two thousand dollars), but most derive from a basic formula. The home at 111 Circle Drive is unusual in being of stone rather than concrete, and 127 Circle Drive is different from the rest in being derivative of Frank Lloyd Wright in its brickwork and intersecting planes. Forgotten today even in Pittsburgh, and looking somewhat timid compared to the radical modernism of Le Corbusier in the same years, Swan Acres is still a fascinating footnote to the nationwide battle between architectural traditionalists and modernists in those years.

A vote for architectural traditionalism is unequivocally expressed on state route 8, the next major road to parallel Babcock. This was the 639-acre Mary Flinn Lawrence estate, six miles inland from Etna via state route 8 and Saxonburg Boulevard. With elaborate stables and a mansion designed in what is sometimes called "stockbroker Tudor" by Alfred Hopkins in 1929, the mansion is in equal parts huge and uninteresting. Those stables and a towering hayloft are borderline brilliant in their picturesqueness, however. The estate serves as a cultural center by hosting plays and free concerts all summer long, drawing thousands of spectators.

Affluence is still the rule in Fox Chapel, which is inland from the Allegheny River town of Aspinwall via Fox Chapel Road. It was for years the second-wealthiest Pittsburgh suburb after Sewickley Heights. The old distinction was that the CEOs of the Pittsburgh corporations lived in Fox Chapel, while the families who had founded those firms preferred Sewickley. Today, Fox Chapel has edged out Sewickley as the wealthiest district in western Pennsylvania.

In terms of urban development, what is remarkable is not Fox Chapel's wealth but the rapidity with which it assembled all the urban institutions that usually take generations to develop in a new area. Like Sewickley, which expanded as a successor to Allegheny City downriver on the Ohio, Fox Chapel replicates much of Pittsburgh's East End as it was on the eve of World War I. The district began as part of the Depreciation Lands of 1784, but within a generation much of it fell within the twelve-hundred-acre estate of the financial speculator and U.S. senator, James Ross.

A Methodist chapel donated in 1889 in memory of early settler John Fox was the nucleus of the future suburb. Fox's chapel now stands rebuilt at the north end of the borough under the name Faith United Methodist Church, at 261 West Chapel Ridge Road. That first congregation was joined by two others: the neo-Georgian Fox Chapel Presbyterian Church, at the crossing of Fox Chapel and Field Club roads, and Fox Chapel Episcopal Church, at 630 Squaw Run Road East. The latter began life as a house designed by Brandon Smith, a disciple of Stanford White who in the 1920s and 1930s was among Pittsburgh's top society architects.

Secular institutions migrated from Pittsburgh along with the spiritual: the Pittsburgh Field Club, founded in Point Breeze in 1882 and relocated to Fox Chapel in 1915, and Shady Side Academy, which followed suit in 1922. In 1923, the newly formed Fox Chapel Golf Club was organized. Several of these clubhouses stand on Fox Chapel Road or its offshoot, Field Club Road. The most significant of the institutional buildings in the district are those belonging to Shady Side Academy, at 423 Fox Chapel Road. Approaching the campus on its winding yellow brick driveway, visitors come around a bend and enter an Ivy League–style central mall, perhaps feeling as though they had walked into the setting of *A Separate Peace*, John Knowles's coming-of-age novel. The architecture is conventional neo-Georgian from the 1920s, but the landscaping by Ezra Stiles creates a memorable and stately atmosphere.

Though many remain secluded in the woods, some of Fox Chapel's traditional-style homes are visible on Field Club Road and its continuation as Guyasuta Road, southwest of Squaw Run Road. Here, particularly on the steep hill south of Guyasuta, are superbly rendered homes by Brandon Smith, Theodore Eichholz, and Benno Janssen. At any moment one might expect Douglas Fairbanks, Greta Garbo, or the great Gatsby to come out of these elegant doorways.

The best of these residences is the Edgar and Liliane Kaufmann house, known as La Tourelle, Benno Janssen's 1925 escape for the future builder of Fallingwater. Its current address is 8 La-Tourelle Lane, off Pasadena Drive,

fig. 9.10
La Tourelle,
E. J. Kaufmann's
house, Fox Chapel

fig. 9.11
Frederick Meeder
farm, Cranberry

fig. 9.12
"McMansion"
subdivisions in
Cranberry

because the estate no longer includes its original approach road and twenty acres that contained stables, barns, and kennels. What is left is nonetheless outstanding: a brick mansion with a costly slate roof, the whole looking like three different fragments of a Cistercian monastery that have been randomly stuck together. La Tourelle is also famous for its guests: both Frank Lloyd Wright and Albert Einstein stayed with the Kaufmanns in December 1934. It was there, that same month, in the highly conservative living room, that Wright and Kaufmann planned Fallingwater.

In urbanism, as in anything else, the future sometimes comes in unexpected packages. Today's residents of Pittsburgh's older districts may not be ready to acknowledge Cranberry Township as a local neighborhood. One reason for skepticism, even resentment, about Cranberry is its location, since this fastest-growing of all Pennsylvania municipalities does not lie in Allegheny County but just over its northern boundary in Butler County, some twenty-five miles north of Downtown. But the greater objection stems from *what* Cranberry is. Pittsburghers often mutter "Cranberry" as a shorthand reference to everything they hate about urban sprawl, but in fact, administrators across the whole of Pennsylvania laud Cranberry Township for using state-of-the-art technology to monitor and shape its development.

The Township of Cranberry was founded in 1804, but as late as the 1970s, it was mainly farmland, which included the last of the cranberry bogs. The township consisted of a few hundred farm families, with a nucleus called Criders Corners at the intersection of state routes 19 and 228 (Freedom Road). Growth took off at the end of the 1980s, and the population grew from 14,816 in 1990 to nearly twice that ten years later. One reason for the township's unbridled growth is Butler County's tax rate, appreciably lower than Allegheny County's.

However, the main reason Cranberry is growing so fast is the classic real estate mantra of location, location, location. Cranberry lies at the nexus of the east-west Pennsylvania Turnpike (I-76) and the north-south I-79, which links Pittsburgh and Erie. (Travel between Pittsburgh and Cranberry was reduced to about half an hour in 1989 when I-279 was created as a shortcut to the metropolis—a shortcut that proved highly damaging to Pittsburgh's North Side, as mentioned earlier.) The farmland that is daily giving way to development is mainly flat, hence quick and easy to build over, and new construction orients itself easily to the two cross-axial main streets: the north-south state route 19 and east-west route 228, exactly where the nineteenth-century settlement began.

Cranberry preserves the occasional farmhouse, such as the Frederick Meeder house at the intersection of route 19 and Rochester Road, from 1869. Beyond that, nearly everything in Cranberry is new. The sequence of strip malls and cookie-cutter tract housing tends to the monotonous, but the buildings are not entirely without wit. The Cranberry Township Municipal Building at 2525 Rochester Road, off route 19, is a former industrial structure that in 1992 was reconfigured with a light touch to create a kind of village-within-a-village. In this miniature neighborhood, the municipal offices, plus the public library, facilities for infants, teens, and seniors, and offices for state and local lawmakers all present themselves not as officious counters but as welcoming dollhouse buildings. Enjoying these civic amenities, one could reasonably ask whether western civilization has not come to rest in suburbia.

Suburbs rarely present anything monumental, but Cranberry does, in not one but two instances. The first case is the ninety-five-acre campus of the Swedish telecommunications giant Ericsson, which was begun in 1997 for FORE Systems, a local start-up that later went through several mergers. The Ericsson campus is not part of Cranberry physically, since it lies a mile south, in Warrendale, at the northwest corner of Allegheny County. But its four buildings share the visual style of Cranberry, and the way they spread atop a mesa with perfect visibility from the I-79 expressway makes them effective heralds to Cranberry.

FORE Systems was born as a Carnegie Mellon software spin-off when it developed a superior ATM computer switch. Needing space, and needing to attract to Pittsburgh the kinds of employees who were used to a West Coast lifestyle, the four original partners called in a West Coast design firm to create a nontraditional research campus. The four buildings represent western Pennsylvania's prime venture into deconstructivism, which here deliberately distorts both perspective and form to create an edgy but not unpleasant sense of instability. These structures, which seem to be lurching because of the 45-degree angles, succeed in giving a new culture to the stereotypical corporate research park. The Ericsson buildings start out like conventional three-story blocks, then get uncannily transformed. Building One bears twisted (but still functional) sunshades, Building Two sets its tartan plaid volumes at teetering angles, Building Three houses a glass-enclosed cafeteria under a steel arch (the menu is a bit atypical in featuring South Asian along with standard American fare), and Building Four provides a fitness center as well as offices. Each structure is marked inside by galvanized air-conditioning and heating ducts that zigzag across the steel structural rafters. In contrast, the office spaces stand out as austere cubicles broken up by communal "breakout points."

The dot-com bust in the year 2000 had considerable impact on the high-tech mesa. Ericsson's staff dropped from 1,600 researchers to just a fifth of that, and construction halted on a fifth building, which stands in a skeletal state. Buildings One and Two were rented out to the Heinz Innovation Center, whose 350 R&D employees staff scientific labs for product development and a mini-supermarket that tests consumer preferences.

Can the progressive attitudes of West Coast corporate culture be grafted onto the conservative stock of western Pennsylvania? The answer may be found in the past: Andrew Carnegie demanded tremendous innovation in the physical layout of his workplaces, and George Westinghouse and H. J. Heinz were even more innovative in caring for the social and economic well-being of their employees. The Ericsson-Heinz deconstructivist campus can be seen as just one more step in an old Pittsburgh tradition.

Still underway is a second campus of three interlocked buildings for the Westinghouse Electric world headquarters in Cranberry Woods, near the intersection of I-79 with state route 228. This, too, is a partial mesa that until recently was left untouched by Mine Safety Appliances, which, however, included the possibility of such a giant development (three to five thousand employees needing office space within about three years).

Cranberry's detractors associate it with sprawl, but even the most superficial examination of the municipality would show its devotion to careful planning. The most surprising feature of the township's urban planning initiative is the administrators' devotion to traditional neighborhood configurations and even to pedestrians and cyclists. Cranberry's critics would be surprised to learn that the township's current growth models are old Pittsburgh neighborhoods such as Squirrel Hill and "new urbanism" developments such as Summerset at Frick Park, locally, and Celebration and Kentlands, in Florida and Maryland, respectively. The central concern for planners in Cranberry is shared across the whole of western Pennsylvania: how to attract "knowledge workers" and keep the ones that are already in place.

To its critics, Cranberry is just one more instance of urban cannibalism; they contend that its growth hastens the decay of Pittsburgh's older districts. But perhaps it was always so. It was Pittsburgh that stole Allegheny City's political status as county seat back in 1788, when that town had just been founded. It was Allegheny City that annexed all its North Side neighbors before it was in turn seized by Pittsburgh in 1907. True, by luring the Westinghouse Electric world headquarters, Cranberry is siphoning jobs and people from Monroeville, its counterpart "edge city" east of Pittsburgh. But these complaints are nothing new. The residents of Rome's Palatine Hill were

fig. 9.13
ERICSSON
CORPORATE CAMPUS

furious when palaces started to go up on the Aventine, and the whole of
Rome let out a howl of envy when Emperor Constantine shifted the imperial
capital to Constantinople. Everything is a question of perspective. As orders
for European and Asian nuclear plants pour into the Westinghouse facility in
Cranberry, they return Pittsburgh to the status it has not had for years: a
center of global importance.

Butler County is not unfamiliar with innovation of global importance, as
we find in the little town of Saxonburg, which lies nineteen miles northeast of
Cranberry. Visitors will find Saxonburg to be one of the outstandingly preserved early nineteenth-century towns anywhere in the commonwealth, but
its importance lies in the work done there by its founder and most famous
citizen, the engineering genius John Augustus Roebling (1816–1869). After
Roebling was forced to flee Berlin because of political unrest, he and his
brother Carl came to western Pennsylvania in 1831 and purchased 1,583
acres of Butler County land for about $1.50 an acre. They placed their village
in typical German medieval fashion, on the spine of a hill, and called it
Germania at first, then Sachsenburg (the Roeblings came from Mühlhausen,
in Saxony). The Main Street vista closes in a dramatic manner at the façade
of the former German Evangelical Church (now Saxonburg Memorial
United Presbyterian Church). The structure dates from 1837, with later
modifications. It is tightly integrated into the plan of the town, since John
Roebling oriented both the settlement and its church precisely east-west. The
orientation means the church façade lights up in dramatic fashion as the
morning sunrise hits Main Street.

The careful thought that John Roebling put into the organization of
Saxonburg also went into his engineering career, which would bring him
international fame. Roebling in fact later declared that he chose to settle in
western Pennsylvania because he was certain Pittsburgh would emerge as the
capital of the industrial world. Educated by two of the leading intellectuals
of the day, the philosopher Georg Hegel and the architect Karl Friedrich

fig. 9.14
MAIN STREET,
SAXONBURG

fig. 9.15
ROEBLING'S
WIRE-ROPE
WORKSHOP

Schinkel, Roebling would spend only five years farming the soil of Butler County. By 1837, he had found work as an engineer on the Pennsylvania Canal. It was for that ambitious effort that Roebling first improved on the concept of "wire rope" in 1841. The iron cables hauled barges out of the water and set them on the tracks of a portage railroad, by which manner the barges could cross over the Alleghenies (it was a madcap system, but it worked, and Charles Dickens left a full description of it).

Roebling's cable design was destined to revolutionize suspension bridges the world over. Four times Roebling tested his cables in Pittsburgh: in 1844, on the world's first suspension aqueduct bridge, which carried the Pennsylvania Canal over the Allegheny River; on the suspension bridge over the Monongahela to South Side, in 1846; on the Sixth Street suspension bridge to the North Side, in 1859; and on the Monongahela Incline up Mount Washington, in 1870. After these tests in Pittsburgh and elsewhere, Roebling was ready to design the project that brought him immortal fame: the Brooklyn Bridge.

The wire rope factory that Roebling used from 1842 until his move to Trenton, New Jersey, still stands relatively unscathed on North Rebecca Street, though it was moved about two hundred feet south of its original foundations a generation ago. The building is an unpretentious houselike structure of one story plus an attic, whose only grace notes outside are the Federal-style side lights by the door. Inside, Roebling's German heritage is evident in the horse-hair binding in the plaster, which is reinforced by diagonal wooden struts. The workshop—virtually untouched—is empty now but deeply affecting. It is one of a score of places where a genius came to the Pittsburgh region and began work that changed the whole world.

SETTLEMENTS EAST

So much of what was important to Pittsburgh came from the east—the British troops that conquered it, the railway that transformed it, and the immigrants who peopled it—that by rights the eastern suburbs should be the region's oldest and most settled district. Instead, there is much that is old but little that could be called settled in the seven-mile stretch between Wilkinsburg (the easternmost of Pittsburgh's "city suburbs") and the Pennsylvania Turnpike.

A century ago, George Westinghouse put a premium on research in his various plants in the Turtle Creek Valley. As the ranks of manual laborers in the valley declined, the number of scientists and engineers at the Westinghouse laboratories grew to the thousands. Much of their work was in nuclear energy, in which Pittsburgh has long been the global leader. One of the poignant reminders of those heady days is the Westinghouse atom smasher, built in 1937. Although decommissioned, it is reverently preserved in Forest Hills on the grounds of the old Westinghouse Research Laboratories and easily visible at the intersection of North Avenue in Chalfant borough and West Street in Forest Hills.

The atom smasher—properly termed a Van de Graaff nuclear accelerator —is a benign-looking steel tank shaped like an upturned pear. It was the first testing ground anywhere for the industrial application of nuclear physics and was used to observe the action of particles that were shot through a vacuum tube at 100 million miles an hour. From it came the first fission of uranium atoms by gamma rays, an important step in the science of nuclear energy. Based on the discoveries made at this facility, in 1957 Pittsburgh became the world's first nuclear-powered city (the nuclear plant providing the city's power was decommissioned about twenty years later). It is auspicious that Westinghouse preserved the historic atom smasher rather than scrapping it. Today, ground zero at Hiroshima symbolizes the birth of the nuclear age, but should the peaceful applications of the atom prevail over the military ones, the appropriate symbol of the nuclear age may be this steel tank in Pittsburgh.

This area also witnessed a number of pioneering efforts in the formation of religious congregations. Pittsburgh's Beulah Presbyterian Church, Sri Venkateswara Temple, and Hindu-Jain Temple were all built by pioneer congregations: the first in 1837 on the hill where a group of settlers first gathered to pray in 1758 and the second and third by the Indian scientific and professional community of Pittsburgh, in 1976 and 1988, respectively. The elaborate features of the two temples contrast well with the sturdy lines of Beulah Church, which stands at the intersection of Beulah and McCrady roads at the Churchill interchange of the Parkway East. This was where British troops made their last encampment before marching on Fort Duquesne in November 1758. One contingent remained behind to tend the army's cattle supply, and they built a church and laid out a graveyard in the years that followed. The graveyard was legally incorporated by 1773, and thirty-four veterans of the Revolutionary War were eventually buried there. The congregation was formally organized in 1784; two log-walled churches followed, and the congregation built the current structure in 1837.

The Flemish-bond brick walls, the gentle slope of the roof, and the two-door arrangement of the façade show the church builders thinking in terms of the older Federal Style, although the newer Greek Revival makes its appearance in the slender window frames. This is one of the perfect works of architecture in the Pittsburgh region: sensitively cradled in the earth, superbly

fig. 9.16
WESTINGHOUSE
ATOM SMASHER,
FOREST HILLS

fig. 9.17
BEULAH
PRESBYTERIAN
CHURCH,
CHURCHILL

proportioned, and vigilantly preserved. Most of the glass panes are original, and the only concession to modern taste are the cushions on the hard wooden pews.

It is about a mile from Beulah Church to the Sri Venkateswara Temple at 1230 South McCully Drive in Penn Hills. Set on the forested west slope of the cool and humid Thompson Run Valley, the temple commands attention from motorists driving into Pittsburgh on I-376. This was the second Hindu temple in the nation, modeled on the Tirupathi shrine of the seventh century in southern India. The two spire towers, or *sikhara*, and the two domes are made of inch-thick stucco over a brick and concrete base. When the sun catches the encrusted walls, they light up like a white-hot fire. Inside, a skylighted atrium leads to the central sanctuary and three recessed shrines for the images of Vishnu and the goddesses Padmavathi and Andal. A lotus pond completes the temple in the conch of the hill below.

The Hindu-Jain Temple, at 615 Illini Drive in Monroeville, also has a number of noteworthy cultural and architectural elements. Begun in 1988, construction faced some delays and continued into the 1990s. The temple is in the tenth-century Nagradi Style of northern and central India. Rose-colored bricks form coursings of varying thickness to shape the façade, augmented by ornate moldings around the windows and portals. In an exploit that would alarm a western builder, no construction documents were used to create the seven red conical towers that dominate the roof; instead, master masons from India worked from memory to achieve the correct proportions. Not so effective in a cross-cultural or geographic sense was the fact that the temple builders mixed the mortar to resist an Indian summer rather than a Pennsylvania winter, so thousands of hand-carved bricks have had to be replaced. Nonetheless, the temple is both a stunning architectural and diplomatic triumph, since its construction required the cooperation of seven different Hindu denominations.

It would be a mistake to imagine that all of Monroeville is as serene as the temple, because the borough has always been the child of highways. The first was the Northern Pike of 1810, fragments of which still survive; the second was the William Penn Highway of 1924 and its Old William Penn Highway predecessor, both of which continue to be active roadways. Then, in the 1950s, Monroeville became the nexus for the Pennsylvania Turnpike (I-76) and the Parkway East (I-376), which linked the turnpike to Pittsburgh.

Amid these busy roads, at the intersection of Monroeville Boulevard and Stroschein Road, stands a key historic site: the Cross Roads Presbyterian Church. A congregation was organized on this hillock in 1836, with the farmer Andrew Mellon—grandfather of the financier of the same name—as one of

fig. 9.18
HINDU-JAIN
TEMPLE,
MONROEVILLE

its elders; the cemetery next to the church dates from a generation earlier. The current church building is distinguished by the bell tower dedicated to George Westinghouse and his collaborator, the electrical genius Nikola Tesla. Cross Roads is a hearty survivor, and it has resisted the encroachment of three high-speed boulevards, several fast food outlets, a trailer park, and the high-tech gloss of a neighboring office block.

Monroeville is the perfect example of an "edge city," according to the definition provided by Joel Garreau in his book *Edge City: Life on the New Frontier* (1991). Its conjunction of expressways lures shoppers away from Pittsburgh to feed its shopping malls. But such urban cannibalism is risky; as mentioned earlier, Monroeville has lost its Westinghouse nuclear research labs to Cranberry, whose explosive growth now makes Monroeville look sedate.

As it adjusts to its unaccustomed role as historic artifact, Monroeville can find solace in the venerable Monroeville Mall, once among the biggest of U.S. shopping centers but now so old (it dates from 1969) that mini-malls are growing out of it like barnacles. The mall won countercultural fame as the setting for George Romero's 1978 film *Dawn of the Dead* and draws a thousand would-be zombies to assemble every Halloween. Amid all the commercial activity is a bust of the mall's developer, Harry Soffer, gazing out from a perch on the lower floor with the impassivity of a Roman emperor. Rephrasing Sir Christopher Wren's epitaph at his tomb in St. Paul's Cathedral in London (*si monumentum requiris circumspice*, or "if you seek his monument, look around you"), this inscription reads, "A Man Whose Vision and Foresight Made All That You See Here Possible."

When the first portion of the Pennsylvania Turnpike opened in 1940, it did not yet extend to Monroeville but terminated at the old town of Irwin, a few miles to the south, because from there cars could reach Pittsburgh via state route 30. That highway had ancient antecedents. It began as the Raystown Path Indian trail, but colonial settlers knew it better as the Forbes Road, because its enlargement by British engineers allowed General John Forbes to march his troops to victory over the French at Fort Duquesne in 1758. The route had a third incarnation around 1821, when it was improved and renamed the Greensburg or Pennsylvania Turnpike. A fourth incarnation followed a century later, when it was incorporated into the Lincoln Highway, the nation's first transcontinental road for motor vehicles.

Southwestern Pennsylvania has an equally ancient road in state route 40. Cutting diagonally through Fayette and Washington counties, the Nemacolin Trail, named for the American Indian chief who blazed it, was the route taken by General Edward Braddock during his failed expedition to dislodge the

French from the Forks of the Ohio in 1755. It, too, had a revival when it became part of the National Road or National Pike. When Albert Gallatin, living close to the Nemacolin Trail, joined the Jefferson administration as treasury secretary in 1801, he lobbied for the transformation of the road into the first highway in the United States. Ordered by Congress in 1806 and completed within the boundaries of Pennsylvania between 1811 and 1820, the National Road eventually stretched from Baltimore almost to St. Louis.

It is Lincoln Highway (state route 30) that connects Pittsburgh to Greensburg, thirty-one miles to the southeast. Greensburg (the name celebrates Revolutionary War general Nathanael Greene) was laid out as the seat of Westmoreland County in 1785. Some of the early settlement can still be made out, but far more dramatic is the monumental architecture that traces the industrial growth of Greensburg in the decades between 1880 and World War I.

Greensburg is a hill town, like Little Washington. The grid of 1785 survives in the town's central artery, which runs roughly ten blocks along Pittsburgh Street east to west and then turns and runs the same number of blocks along Main Street, north to south. Greensburg's architecture and urbanism are particularly rich in symbolism. The Westmoreland County courthouse has always stood at the midpoint of town, the intersection of Main and Pittsburgh

fig. 9.19
WESTMORELAND
COUNTY
COURTHOUSE,
GREENSBURG

streets. First were the two simple courthouses of 1787 and 1798, then the elaborate Greek Revival structure of 1854, and finally the monumental fourth courthouse, of 1906. This midpoint in town is not the highest point, but the courthouse gives this site the greatest visual prominence. A traveler entering Greensburg along West Pittsburgh Street sees the courthouse in full outline from the top of a hill, but then the road takes a considerable dip downhill, so as the same traveler ascends a second hill to reach Main Street, the courthouse looms above in unparalleled majesty.

The role of the courthouse as the social keystone of Greensburg is equally significant. All the prominent buildings in town seem to assert themselves in terms of their proximity to it: the Masonic temple and Presbyterian church are closest, the Episcopal and Methodist churches a bit farther away, then finally the synagogue and the Catholic cathedral—though the latter is magnificent and superbly sited—still farther out. On its own lookout stands the Westmoreland Museum of American Art, an excellent collection of the arts of western Pennsylvania.

fig. 9.20
TRIBUNE-REVIEW PLANT,
BEFORE ADDITIONS,
GREENSBURG

Sadly, what architectural historians deem the most significant building of Greensburg's industrial era is lost. This was the Kelly and Jones machine shop in south Greensburg, from 1903, the structure in which Ernest Ransome achieved the world's first wholly integrated reinforced concrete building. The machine shop became part of the Walworth firm's south Greensburg works, and it stood for close to a century at the intersection of Huff Avenue and state route 119 until it was pulled down around 1980.

Not of world importance, but still a regional treasure, is the fortresslike Greensburg Tribune-Review building on Cabin Hill Drive, off Main Street, from 1961. Here Louis Kahn, who was on the cusp of becoming the most important American architect of the second half of the twentieth century, struggled with a sloping site and a perplexing program. His task was to integrate editorial offices with a printing plant that would generate severe vibrations because of the presses and the turning of huge rolls of newsprint. Kahn was not entirely successful in his solution, for he was better at searching for answers than finding them.

With its tight budget and difficult site, the Tribune-Review building design was not ideal, but one cannot help but be astonished at what Kahn was able to achieve with an interplay of solids and voids, lights and darks, and the exploitation of ordinary materials like poured and cast concrete. Outside, what at first look to be simple slit windows actually combine three different kinds of concrete blocks plus a finer type of stone for the sill. Inside, there is real nobility in the design of the stairs, and Kahn must have been dreaming of ancient Greece when he designed the basement's concrete columns with their industrial capitals. Though the Tribune-Review company has treated Kahn's design somewhat roughly, it is not entirely unaware of its artistic heritage. An old photograph of Kahn discussing his design with the newspaper managers still hangs at one of the loading docks, and nearby hangs a reproduction of one of his sketches.

Greensburg lies at the intersection of the two main roads that cut through Westmoreland and Fayette counties, which cover an area collectively known as the Laurel Highlands. State route 30 leads eighteen miles farther east to Ligonier, and state route 119 points south to Connellsville and Uniontown. The town of Ligonier owes its start to Fort Ligonier, the main staging base for the British in 1758 just before they took Fort Duquesne. The reconstruction east of town presents a dramatic sight, especially in the sharpened staves splayed out from the wooden stockade.

Ligonier came into its own around 1905, when Richard Beatty Mellon organized his private Rolling Rock Club there. The Mellons had farmed the district early in the nineteenth century, then returned to Ligonier to buy and expand its local rail lines. Today, the western approach to Ligonier is heralded by lush forests along Loyalhanna Creek, giving a hint of the town in its preindustrial days. A score of Mellon heirs and several hundred heirs to other Pittsburgh fortunes still live around Ligonier or at nearby Laughlintown and Rector.

The Rolling Rock Club and adjacent lands extend for about a thousand acres along state route 381, off state route 30, east of town. The Georgian-style clubhouse is a 1920s work by Edward Purcell Mellon, the family's in-house designer. The environment is opulent but predictably traditional, with its best feature being a water tower disguised as a Romanesque fortress. The star of

fig. 9.21
FORT LIGONIER
RECONSTRUCTION

fig. 9.22
THE HUNT STABLES
AT THE ROLLING
ROCK CLUB

Rolling Rock is a Cotswold-style complex of stables and kennels designed by Benno Janssen and dating from 1928. This complex is the best work of Janssen's notable career, with so timeless and impeccable an aspect that, like the fox hunting that once took place at the club, nothing in England could touch it. The kennels and stables were converted into condominiums in 1986.

If you drew a partial circle with a radius of about twenty-five miles from southeast of Greensburg to southwest of the town, this arc would capture not only two centuries of industrial sites but also memories of presidents from Franklin Roosevelt back to George Washington. The Rooseveltian presence emerges at Norvelt, southeast of Greensburg on state route 130. This exceptional settlement was a commune that the federal government created for 250 families in 1934. Called Westmoreland Homesteads, the hamlet renamed itself in 1937 after Eleanor Roosevelt visited there. (A similar commune called Penn-Craft survives in neighboring Fayette County.) The men of Norvelt farmed land that was held in common while the women made handicrafts for sale in their homes. The modest Cape Cod–style homes were designed by Greensburg's Paul Bartholomew; the communal buildings were added by WPA architect Alfred Marks. Enough of both survive to make Norvelt a significant historic site, one of the few places in the country in which the Depression turns from an abstraction into something you can actually see.

fig. 9.23
ABRAHAM OVERHOLT'S GRISTMILL, WEST OVERTON

Norvelt has a double about ten miles to the southwest, in the mid-nineteenth-century industrial village of West Overton, outside the town of Scottdale. Here, in 1834, the Mennonite farmer Abraham Overholt created a settlement with a score of farm and distillery buildings to produce his Old Farm brand rye whiskey. Contrary to myth, Overholt did not himself turn out Old Overholt Whiskey, produced by his son Jacob from a distillery alongside the Youghiogheny River, just below Connellsville. Jacob did put his father's portrait on his label, however, and it remains there today.

It would be a mistake to think of West Overton as nothing more than an elaborate farm. It was a prototype industrial site, as demonstrated by the spur railroad line that Overholt constructed to serve his property. The introduction of the railroad to Westmoreland and Fayette counties meant that agricultural products could reach their markets to the east at accelerated speed. It was his exploitation of the railroads that ultimately made Overholt the "Squire of Westmoreland County," as neighbors called him.

The center of Overholt's plantation is the elaborate brick house he built himself in 1838 and his impressive gristmill of 1859. Both still stand, as museums, together with the rustic two-room springhouse in which Overholt's grandson, Henry Clay Frick, was born in 1849. A reconstructed beehive coke oven recalls the thousands of ovens that Frick later built in the vicinity. The springhouse is a poignant sight, not least because its shabby interior strikingly resembles the cramped home in which Frick's arch-rival Carnegie was born a decade earlier, halfway around the world in Scotland.

Having been born in the heart of the Pittsburgh coal region, Frick was quick to capitalize on the heightened demand for coke to fuel Pittsburgh's steel mills. An advertisement published for the Frick Coke Company around 1880 numbered Frick's coke ovens at eight thousand, but eventually he operated forty thousand ovens in Fayette County alone. To work the coal mines, the Frick Coke Company and others created hundreds of Laurel Highlands towns known as coal patches. One of the better preserved villages today is Shoaf, in Fayette County's Georges Township, southwest of Uniontown, where several coke batteries also remain standing. The coal patch towns were certainly rudimentary in terms of urbanism, but they had one fascinating element: they provided a model for the worker housing that would go up in larger towns. George Westinghouse, for example, probably looked at the coal patch villages before laying out his model industrial city at Wilmerding.

To the southwest of Overholt's village (ten miles by air, twenty-six by road) is another exceptional piece of urbanism, that of Perryopolis, just off state route 51. Perryopolis sits on land that George Washington bought in 1769. It was just a fraction of the thousands of acres he owned in western Pennsylvania, though Washington regarded his land as part of Virginia (the boundaries were not officially defined until 1786). Because of its connection to Washington, one hears hugely exaggerated tales about Perryopolis: for example, that Washington wanted it to be the nation's capital instead of the site on the Potomac. In actuality, he never saw Perryopolis, since it was drawn up sometime after 1812, well after Washington's sale of these lands in 1789 and his death a decade later. But the promoters of Perryopolis clearly exploited the Washington connection, and they did indeed make their town plan rival that of Washington, DC, with every road emerging from a central square either at a right angle or diagonally. Perryopolis is a miniature town of just a few hundred residents, however, and covers only a few acres. What look to be boulevards on the original plan or in aerial views turn out to be barely wider than alleyways.

The gristmill Washington erected here in 1774 was the major structure for miles around. The mill was wood over a stone base: a close counterpart to Washington's stone gristmill at Mount Vernon. The mill was operational until 1917 but was allowed to deteriorate into ruins soon after. The stone foundations were re-mortared by teams of jail inmates in 1993, then a crew of Amish carpenters, the youngest just twelve years old, re-created the wooden super-

fig. 9.24
GEORGE
WASHINGTON'S
MILL,
PERRYOPOLIS

structure in 1999, and the waterwheel was added a few years later. A stone's throw from the gristmill, never ruined and so never substantially restored, stands an ancient distillery. The distillery postdates Washington's ownership of the mill, but it provides another echo of our first president, whose distillery was the biggest income producer at Mount Vernon.

Isaac Meason (1743–1818) was another Virginian with extensive land-holdings in Fayette County, but unlike Washington, Meason struck it rich in western Pennsylvania, not in grain but in iron. As settlers moved in, there was a demand for home implements like iron pans and iron bars for building reinforcement. Since the area was thickly wooded and iron ore was available in some quantity, smelting operations began almost immediately. But the great local monument from those early years of the Industrial Revolution is not industrial but domestic, specifically, the cut-stone mansion that the English

fig. 9.25
ISAAC MEASON
HOUSE, NORTH
OF UNIONTOWN

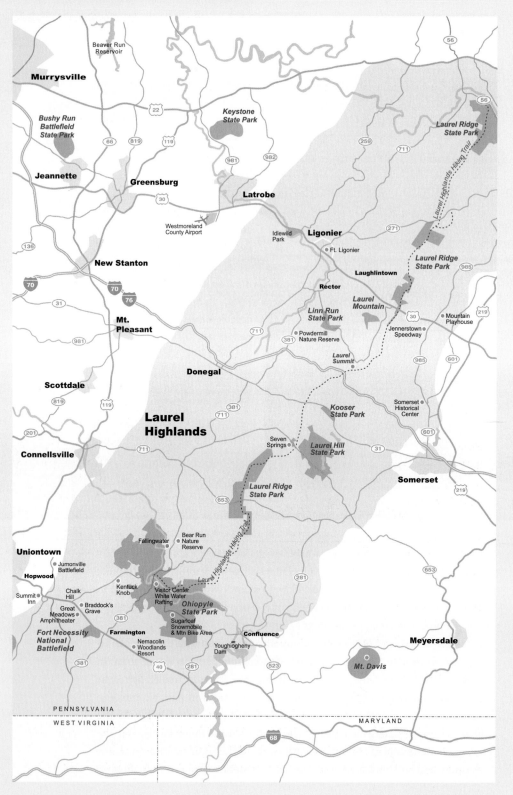

The Laurel Highlands

builder Adam Wilson designed for Meason in 1802. Meason had interviewed Wilson in England for the much more challenging task of erecting three iron bridges nearby: one over the Youghiogheny at Connellsville; a second over the same river at West Newtown, close to Pittsburgh; and a third over Jacobs Creek, to the north. Designing Meason's house was only a secondary task for Wilson, but it is the only example of his art to survive anywhere.

Mt. Braddock, the name Meason gave his house, stands just a minute's drive or two off state route 119, seven miles northeast of Uniontown. The Meason house is not only the most important early house in western Pennsylvania but also one of the most significant homes dating from the early republic anywhere in the country. Yet no attempt has so far been successful in guaranteeing the preservation of this building as a public trust. The house now stands about three hundred feet from an automobile graveyard in front, while long-wall strip mining recently came within about five hundred feet of the house in the back.

The technical claim to fame of the Meason house is that it is the only seven-part home ever built in the United States. A visitor finds that the main block of the house has two passageways leading to attached side buildings and then two outrider buildings, making seven units in all. The claim to uniqueness for its seven-part layout is, however, less important than the elegance of the house, which is manifest to even the most casual visitor. The house is somewhat old-fashioned in nature, looking more like a Virginia plantation house of the 1770s, but it is beautifully executed both in woodwork and in the labor-intensive stone carving in the pediment.

Meason's industrial activity is best represented today by the Ross Furnace, one of a dozen iron furnaces surviving in the Laurel Highlands. Ross Furnace stands in Westmoreland County's Fairfield Township, off state route 711, northeast of Ligonier on state route 1002. Meason had been building similar small pyramidal furnaces since the 1790s; his involvement as a partner at Ross Furnace dates from 1814, close to the end of his life.

Traveling from Perryopolis to Uniontown, the seat of Fayette County, one follows state route 51. The twenty-mile stretch of the National Road from Uniontown to the Maryland state line carries significant architecture of the early republic. Some of this architecture was specific to the National Road, like Searight's Tollhouse, from the 1830s, on state route 40, four miles west of Uniontown. This structure is an exceptionally elegant octagon, considering that tollbooths are not normally counted as monumental architecture. There was a great deal of auxiliary construction, too, such as the handsome Federal-style Mount Washington Tavern from 1827, on state route 40 east of Uniontown at Farmington, close to Fort Necessity.

fig. 9.26
NEMACOLIN
WOODLANDS
RESORT

One of the peculiarities of Fayette County, which is among the poorest districts of Pennsylvania, is how attractive it has been to the rich people who have lived, worked, or vacationed there, from George Washington and Albert Gallatin to Isaac Meason and Henry Clay Frick. That tradition continues today in the Nemacolin Woodlands Spa and Resort, on state route 40 at Farmington, which has marvelous *faux* buildings, from a pseudo–French Renaissance château to a Fallingwater knock-off. Credit for broadcasting to a wealthy audience the natural beauty of the Laurel Highlands belongs to a band of landscape painters who in the 1860s and 1870s set up camp at Scalp Level in adjoining Cambria County. Those painters immortalized the local landscape and indirectly laid the basis for the region's current tourism industry. The first artistically significant painting that Henry Clay Frick purchased, for example, was an 1882 landscape by George Hetzel.

But the creative artist who did the most to publicize the natural setting of the southwestern corner of Pennsylvania was Frank Lloyd Wright, and his creations were Fallingwater and Kentuck Knob, two residences that thrillingly exploited Laurel Highlands sites. Both Wright houses are reached from state route 381, which branches north off state route 40.

Fallingwater is the most publicized private home of the twentieth century, but much less well known is how intimately it is tied into the ecological and social warp and woof of the Laurel Highlands. It was designed by Wright for Edgar and Liliane Kaufmann in 1936–1937 for their fifteen-hundred-acre estate on Bear Run, a tributary of the Youghiogheny River. But Edgar was not the first member of his clan to see the turbulent waterfall in the woods over which the house was built. His uncles Jacob and Isaac Kaufmann saw it in the 1860s, when they canvassed this district as peddlers. Edgar Kaufmann knew the territory intimately, too; around 1909, when he discovered the land for himself, he was running a general store in Connellsville. The Kaufmann property had another element that distinguished it from a typical rich man's estate: it was originally a rest-and-relaxation camp for employees of Kaufmann's Department Store in Pittsburgh.

Frank Lloyd Wright understood the intimate links the local people had with the land, even back to tales of the American Indians who set campfires on the giant boulders by the waterfall. His design was expressive of architectural trends of the 1930s, as it had to be, but beyond that it is an exceptionally adroit summation of American architecture from colonial New England (inside) to the adobe pueblos of the Southwest (outside).

Fallingwater is also reflective of Pittsburgh in that it utilizes great quantities of its steel, concrete, and plate glass. Some of these references a visitor to Fallingwater will grasp immediately while others one can sense only fleetingly. In that respect, Fallingwater works very much the way H. H. Richardson's Allegheny County Courthouse does, since both buildings go beyond mere style to offer something sublime. How exceptional that two of the top masterpieces of American architecture stand not more than forty-five air miles distant from each other.

E. J. Kaufmann the retailer also imagined himself a dairy farmer, and it was through his cows that he came into contact with I. N. Hagen, who ran the main dairy in Uniontown. Kaufmann and Hagen got to discussing the subject of Frank Lloyd Wright, and that discussion led to another architectural masterpiece for the region, the house called Kentuck Knob. Built in 1954, Kentuck Knob is a half-hour's drive from Fallingwater (on state road 2010 from Ohiopyle to Chalk Hill, off state route 381). Kentuck Knob got its first name from an eastern pioneer who had intended to settle in Kentucky but settled for western Pennsylvania instead; its second name comes from its position on an outcrop of Chestnut Ridge, the westernmost hill of the Laurel Highlands. Here again there is a rightness in the balance between the natural and the built environments, with Wright refusing to place this fine villa on the height of Chestnut Ridge and setting it instead well down from the brow. In Kentuck Knob, Wright exploited not just the local sandstone but also local wood, especially in the marvelous overhang to the viewing platform that looks over Chestnut Ridge. The home's theme of living with nature is augmented by the internal furnishings, some by the distinguished Pennsylvania woodworker George Nakashima.

fig. 9.30
KENTUCK KNOB

In 2006, these two important Wright houses were unexpectedly joined by a third, giving the Laurel Highlands a holy trinity of Wrightian designs. The new house was Wright's prefabricated Duncan house, which went up in 1957 in Lisle, Illinois, but was rebuilt in Polymath Park Resort, near the village of Acme, in Westmoreland County. Polymath Park lies about five miles from the Donegal exit of the Pennsylvania Turnpike, less than twenty miles from Fallingwater. The Duncan house stands alongside the Blum and Balter houses, two designs from the 1960s by Wright's excellent Pittsburgh disciple, Peter Berndtson. For a fee, overnight stays are available in any of the three.

487

Route 40 affords two final reflections of the young George Washington, though not at his best. In June 1754, Washington and his small band of American Indian allies massacred a scouting party of French soldiers at Jumonville, on the heights of Chestnut Ridge. A high metal cross on state road 2021 marks the approximate spot, a few minutes' drive off route 40. Washington got his payback the next month, when he was surrounded by a larger French party at the Great Meadows along the Nemacolin Trail, where state route 381 from Fallingwater intersects route 40. The English colonials threw up a stockade known as Fort Necessity, but they could not avoid surrender to the French. Though the current fort is a reconstruction, the meadow seems unchanged from two centuries ago. It was peculiar that Washington later bought this exact spot as personal property. Whether his purchase was attributable to sentiment or to expedience (so that no political enemy could raise the issue of his ignominious loss to the French) is unknown.

fig. 9.31
FORT NECESSITY,
SITE OF
WASHINGTON'S
EPIC DEFEAT
IN 1754

The most interesting of the myths concerning Washington's landholdings in western Pennsylvania is the legend that he owned Bear Run, the site of Fallingwater. The Kaufmanns believed that he had, and since Bear Run lies only about thirteen miles from Fort Necessity, the myth is not entirely preposterous. For years, all the guides at Fallingwater would begin their tours by saying that the house stood on land once owned by our founding father. The myth might even be true, though the vagaries of deed research in eighteenth-century documents from the frontier will never confirm nor disprove it. Even if apocryphal, the idea that George Washington once owned the land under Fallingwater has a fine ring to it. It allows Pittsburgh's biographical history to recycle once again, now from Frank Lloyd Wright back to Washington. Here is a fitting conclusion to the Pittsburgh periphery, a remarkable region that is rich in inventiveness as well as in natural riches and the perfect foil to a remarkable city.

SIGNIFICANT BUILDINGS OF PITTSBURGH

The purpose of this appendix is to provide the reader with concise information about the sites discussed in the body of the text, including the location, and, when known, the architect and year of completion. Sites are listed by chapter (excluding the introductory chapter), categorized by type, and then alphabetized by common name. Those buildings no longer in existence are marked by a † symbol.

Chapter 2: Downtown

Public and Government Buildings

Allegheny County Courthouse and Jail, Grant Street at Forbes Avenue; H. H. Richardson, architect; completed by Shepley, Rutan & Coolidge; 1888

Allegheny County Jail, 950 Second Avenue; Tasso Katselas Associates, architects; 1995

Allegheny County Morgue, 542 Fourth Avenue; Frederick Osterling, architect; 1900

CAPA, the Pittsburgh Public High School for the Creative and Performing Arts, Fort Duquesne Boulevard at Ninth Street; MacLachlan Cornelius and Filoni, architects; 2003

Carnegie Library, Downtown Branch, 612 Smithfield Street, adaptive reuse by Burt Hill, architects; 2006

City-County Building, Grant Street at Forbes Avenue; Henry Hornbostel with Edward B. Lee, architects, 1917; sculpture of Mayor Richard Caliguiri by Robert Berks, 1990

County Office Building, Ross Street at Forbes Avenue; Stanley Roush, architect; 1931

Moorhead (William S.) Federal Building, Grant Street and Liberty Avenue; Altenhof and Brown, architects; 1964

United States Post Office and Federal Courts Building, Grant Street at Seventh Avenue; Trowbridge and Livingston, architects, with J. A. Wetmore; 1932

Corporate and Business Buildings

Arbuthnot Stephenson Building, Penn Avenue at Garrison Alley; W. S. Fraser, architect; 1890

Arrott Building, Fourth and Wood; Frederick Osterling, architect; 1902

† **Bank of Pittsburgh**, Fourth Avenue; George Post, architect; 1896

Benedum-Trees Building, formerly Machesney tower; 221 Fourth Avenue; Thomas H. Scott, architect; 1905

Buhl Building, formerly Nicola Building; 205 Fifth Avenue; Benno Janssen, architect; 1913

Burke Building, 209 Fourth Avenue; John Chislett, architect; 1836

The Carlyle, formerly Union National Bank; 306 Fourth Avenue; MacClure and Spahr, architects, 1906; and Commonwealth Trust, 312 Fourth Avenue; Frederick Osterling, architect, 1907; renovation by Berardi and Partners, architects; 2007

Century Building, 130 Seventh Street; Rutan & Russell, architects, 1907; adaptive reuse by Julie Eizenberg and Hans Koning, architects; 2008

Chatham Center, Washington Place at Fifth Avenue; William Lescaze, architect, 1964; expanded by Burt Hill Kosar Rittelmann, architects, 1981

Citizens Bank, formerly Mellon Bank; 525 William Penn Place; Harrison & Abramovitz, architects, with W. Y. Cocken; 1952

Clark Building, Seventh Street at Liberty Avenue; Hoffman and Henon, architects, 1928; restoration by MacLachlan Cornelius and Filoni, architects, 1987

Colonial Trust Company, Forbes and Fourth avenues; Frederick Osterling, architect; 1902

Conestoga Building, Fort Pitt Boulevard and Wood Street; Longfellow, Alden & Harlow, architects; 1890

Diamond Savings Bank Building, Fifth Avenue at Liberty; MacClure and Spahr, architects; 1904

Dollar Bank, Fourth Avenue at Smithfield; Isaac Hobbs and Sons, architects, 1868–1871; wings by James Steen, architect; 1906

Eiben & Irr Building, 940 Penn Avenue; John Barr, architect; 1888

Ewart Building, 921–925 Liberty; Charles Bickel, architect; 1891

† **Farmers' Deposit National Bank**, Fourth Avenue; Frank Furness, architect; 1884

Federal Reserve Bank of Cleveland–Pittsburgh branch, 717 Grant Street; Walker and Weeks, architects, with Henry Hornbostel and Eric Fisher Wood, architects; 1931

Fidelity Trust, 341 Fourth Avenue; James Steen, architect; 1889

Fifth Avenue Place, 120 Fifth Avenue, bordered by Stanwix Street and Penn and Liberty avenues; Stubbins Associates, architects; 1988

Four Gateway Building, Harrison & Abramovitz, architects; 1960

Freehold Building, 93–95 Fourth Avenue; 1893

Frick Building, 437 Grant Street; Daniel Burnham, architect; 1902

General Nutrition Building, formerly Spear & Company Department Store; 915–921 Penn Avenue; Charles Bickel, architect; 1910

Granite Building, formerly German Savings Bank; 301–313 Sixth Avenue, corner Wood; Bickel and Brennan, architects; 1890

Grant Building, 330 Grant Street; Henry Hornbostel with Eric Fisher Wood, architects; 1929

Gulf Building, Grant Street at Seventh Avenue; Trowbridge and Livingston, architects, with E. P. Mellon; 1932

Heinz 57 Center, formerly Kaufmann & Baer's, then Gimbel's department store; Smithfield at Sixth Avenue; Starrett and Van Vleck, architects; 1914

Homes Building, 121–123 Seventh Street, ca. 1905

Industrial Bank, 333 Fourth Avenue; Charles M. Bartberger, architect; 1903

Investment Building, formerly Insurance Exchange; 239 Fourth Avenue; John Donn, architect; 1927

Keystone Bank, 324 Fourth Avenue; MacClure and Spahr, architects; 1903

Koppers Building, Grant Street at Seventh Avenue; Graham, Anderson, Probst and White, architects, with E. P. Mellon; 1929

Landmark Tavern, 24 Market Place, 1902; restoration by UDA Architects, 1982

Lord and Taylor, formerly Mellon Bank; Fifth Avenue at Smithfield; Trowbridge and Livingston, architects, with E. P. Mellon; 1924

Macy's, formerly Kaufmann's department store, Smithfield Street at Fifth Avenue; Benno Janssen, architect, 1910, incorporating earlier wings from the 1890s

Maginnis Building, 913–915 Liberty Avenue; 1891

Midtown Towers, formerly Keenan Building; 643 Liberty Avenue; Thomas Hannah, architect; 1907

National City Center, Stanwix Street at Fort Pitt Boulevard; Skidmore, Owings & Merrill, architects; 1983

Nicholas Coffee, 23 Market Place; restoration by UDA Architects, 1982

Oliver Building, Smithfield Street opposite Mellon Square; Daniel Burnham, architect; 1910

One Mellon Center, Grant Street at Fifth Avenue; Welton Beckett Associates, architects; 1983

One PNC Plaza, formerly Pittsburgh National Bank; Fifth Avenue at Wood Street; Welton Beckett Associates, architects; 1972

Oxford Centre, Grant Street at Fourth Avenue; Hellmuth, Obata, Kassabaum/HOK, architects; 1983

Park Building, Fifth Avenue at Smithfield; George B. Post, architect; 1896

Parkvale Bank, formerly People's Savings Bank; Fourth and Wood; Alden & Harlow, architects; 1901

Philadelphia Traction Company 435 Sixth Avenue; MacClure and Spahr, architects; 1902

Piatt Place, formerly Lazarus Department Store; Fifth Avenue at Wood Street; 1998; adaptive reuse by Strada Architects, 2007

Pittsburgh Engineers' Society, formerly Union Trust Company; 337 Fourth Avenue; Daniel Burnham, architect; 1898

Port Authority of Allegheny County, formerly Monongahela National Bank, then Azen's Furriers; Wood Street and Liberty and Sixth avenues; Edward Stotz, architect; 1928

Porter Building, William Penn Place at Sixth Avenue; Harrison & Abramovitz, architects; 1958

PNC Firstside Center, Grant Street at First Avenue; Astorino, architects; 2001

PPG Place, Stanwix Street, Third and Fourth avenues; Philip Johnson and John Burgee, architects, 1984; water feature designed by WET Design of Universal City in collaboration with the SWA Group, 2003

Regional Enterprise Tower, formerly Alcoa Building; Mellon Square; Harrison & Abramovitz, architects, with Altenhof and Brown and Mitchell and Ritchey, architects; 1953

Renaissance Pittsburgh Hotel, formerly Fulton Building; 107 Sixth Street; Grosvenor Atterbury, architect; 1906

625 Liberty Avenue, formerly CNG Tower and Dominion Tower; Kohn Pedersen Fox, architects; 1985

Standard Life Building, formerly Pittsburgh Bank for Savings; 345 Fourth Avenue; Alden & Harlow, architects; 1903

300 Sixth Avenue Building, formerly McCreery's Department Store, and Spear & Company; Sixth Avenue at Wood; Daniel Burnham, architect; 1904

Three PNC Plaza, Fifth and Liberty avenues; Gensler Associates and Astorino, architects; 2009

Times Building, 336 Fourth Avenue; Frederick Osterling, architect; 1892

Triangle Building, Liberty Avenue and Smithfield Street; Andrew Peebles, architect; 1884

United States Steel Corporation Building, Grant Street at Seventh Avenue; Harrison & Abramovitz and Abbe, architects; 1971

United Steelworkers Building, formerly IBM; 60 Boulevard of the Allies at Stanwix Street; Curtis and Davis, architects; 1964

Verizon, formerly Bell Telephone Building; 416–420 Seventh Avenue; Frederick Osterling, architect; 1890

Westinghouse Electric Corporation, former world headquarters, 11 Stanwix Street; Harrison & Abramovitz, architects; 1968

West Penn Building, 14 Wood Street; Charles Bickel, architect; 1907

William Penn Hotel, William Penn Place at Sixth Avenue; Janssen and Abbot, architects, 1916; expanded by Janssen and Cocken with Joseph Urban, 1929

Industrial and Engineering Works

First Avenue Garage and Station, 600 First Avenue; IKM architects; 2001

Grant Street Transportation Center, Eleventh Street and Liberty Avenue; IKM architects; 2009

The Pennsylvanian, formerly Penn or Union Station; 1100 Liberty Avenue; Daniel Burnham, architect; 1902

Wood-Allies Garage, 224 Boulevard of the Allies; Burt Hill Kosar Rittelmann Associates, architects; 1984

College and University Buildings

Point Park University administration building, formerly Pittsburgh Athletic Club; 201 Wood Street; Janssen and Cocken, architects; 1929

Point Park University Center, Wood Street, Forbes and Fourth avenues; Press C. Dowler and other architects, 1890s–1927; renovation by Damianos + Anthony, architects; 1997

Religious Buildings

First Lutheran Church, formerly First English Evangelical; 615 Grant Street; Andrew Peebles, architect; 1888

First Presbyterian Church, 320 Sixth Avenue, Theophilus P. Chandler Jr., architect; 1905

Smithfield United Church, 620 Smithfield; Henry Hornbostel, architect; 1925

St. Mary of Mercy Church, Stanwix Street at Fourth Avenue; William Hutchins, architect; 1936

Trinity Cathedral and Graveyard, 328 Sixth Avenue; Gordon W. Lloyd, architect; 1872

489

Residential Buildings

Encore on Seventh, Seventh Street at Fort Duquesne Boulevard, 2007

151 FirstSide, 151 Fort Pitt Boulevard; Indovina Associates; 2007

Museums, Clubs, and Recreational Venues

August Wilson Center for African American Culture, Liberty Avenue at William Penn Way; Allison G. Williams, architect; 2009

Benedum Center for the Performing Arts, formerly Stanley Theater; Seventh Street at Penn Avenue; Hoffman and Henon, architects; 1928

David L. Lawrence Convention Center, Penn Avenue between Tenth and Eleventh streets; Rafael Viñoly, architect; 2003

Duquesne Club, 325 Sixth Avenue; Longfellow, Alden & Harlow, architects, 1889; expansions by Alden & Harlow, 1902; Janssen and Cocken, architects; 1931

Fort Pitt Museum, 101 Commonwealth Place; Charles Stotz, architect; 1972

Harris Theater, formerly Art Cinema; 809 Liberty; ca. 1930

Harvard-Yale-Princeton Club, William Penn Place at Strawberry Way, 1894; renovation by Edward B. Lee, architect; 1930

Heinz Hall, formerly Penn Theater; Sixth Street at Penn Avenue; C. W. Rapp and George Rapp, architects, 1926; restoration by Stotz Hess MacLachlan and Fosner, architects; 1971

O'Reilly Theater, 621 Penn Avenue; Michael Graves, architect; 1999

YWCA, Wood Street at Third Avenue; Skidmore, Owings and Merrill, architects; 1963

Chapter 3: The North Side

Public and Government Buildings

Allegheny General Hospital, 320 East North Avenue; York & Sawyer, architects; 1936

Allegheny Observatory, 159 Riverview Avenue; Thorsten E. Billquist, architect; 1900–1912

Carnegie Library, Allegheny Regional Branch and Carnegie Hall, Allegheny Square; Smithmeyer & Pelz, architects; 1889; Carnegie Hall restoration by Sylvester Damianos, architect, 1976

Engine Company No. 3, 1416 Arch Street, corner Jacksonia; Bailey and Anglin, architects; 1877

Corporate and Business Buildings

Alcoa Corporate Center, 201 Isabella Street; The Design Alliance, architects, with Rusli Associates; 1998

Allegheny Center, Deeter Ritchey Sippel, architects; 1966; Four Allegheny Center Building, formerly IBM; I. M. Pei Associates, architects; ca. 1965

Allegheny Commons East, 255 East Ohio Street at East Commons; Tasso Katselas, architect; 1972

Babb Inc., formerly William Penn Snyder house; 850 Ridge Avenue, corner Galveston; George Orth and Brother, architects; 1911

Bidwell Training Center and Manchester Craftsmen's Guild, 1815 Metropolitan Street; Tasso Katselas, architect; 1985

Del Monte Center, 375 North Shore Drive; Strada Architects; 2004

Equitable Resources, 225 North Shore Drive; Strada Architects; 2004

Hughes Funeral Home, formerly John Ober house; 1501 Lowrie Street; 1877

Osterling (Frederick) architectural studio, 228 Isabella Street; Frederick Osterling, architect; 1917

SMS/Schloemann-Siemag, 100 Sandusky Street; UDA Architects; 1994

Industrial and Engineering Works

The Brewery, formerly Eberhardt-Ober Brewery; 800 Vinial Street; Joseph Stillburg, architect; 1897

Religious Buildings

Calvary United Methodist Church, 971 Beech Avenue at Allegheny; Vrydaugh and Shepherd, with T. B. Wolfe, architects; 1895

Emmanuel Episcopal Church, 957 West North Avenue at Allegheny Avenue; H. H. Richardson, architect; 1886

Most Holy Name of Jesus Church, 1500 Claim Street at Harpster; 1863

Most Holy Name of Jesus parish rectory, formerly Suitbert Mollinger house; 1700 Harpster Street; 1876

Original Church of God Deliverance Center, formerly St. Joseph's Church; Liverpool and Fulton streets; Frederick Sauer, architect; 1898

Spring Hill United Church of Christ, 1620 Rhine, opposite Yetta Street; 1902

Western Theological Seminary, 809 Ridge Avenue; Thomas Hannah, architect; 1912

Residential Buildings

Allegheny Widows' Home, formerly Orphan Asylum of Pittsburgh and Allegheny; 308 and 310–322 North Taylor Avenue; John Chislett, architect; 1838

Anderson (James) house, 1423 Liverpool Street; ca. 1830

Brashear (John) telescope workshop, 2016 Perrysville Avenue; ca. 1885

Byers-Lyon house, 901 Ridge Avenue; Alden & Harlow, architects; 1898

Frazier (William G. and Mary Lea) house, 1414 Pennsylvania Avenue; 1876

Heathside Cottage, 416 Catoma Street at Myler; attributed to Joseph Kerr, architect; ca. 1865

Heinz Lofts, formerly the Heinz food processing plant; 300 Heinz Street, bounded by the Allegheny River and East Ohio Street; 1890s; additions by Albert Kahn, 1930; Skidmore, Owings & Merrill, 1953; adaptive reuse by Sandvick Architects, 2005

Heinz (Sarah) House, Heinz and East Ohio streets; R. Maurice Trimble, architect; 1913

Henderson cottage, 1521 Warren Street; ca. 1860

Henderson house, 1516 Warren Street, ca. 1860; restoration by Tai+Lee, 1984

Jones (Benjamin Franklin Jr.) house, 808 Ridge Avenue at Brighton Road; Rutan & Russell, architects; 1908

Langenheim (Gustav) house, 1315 Liverpool Street; Frederick Osterling, architect; 1884

Parador Inn, formerly Joshua and Eliza Rhodes house; 939 Western Avenue; ca. 1866 and 1875

Reineman house, 1515–1517 Lowrie Street; ca. 1870

Rinehart (Mary Roberts) house, 954 Beech Avenue; ca. 1880

Stein (Gertrude) house, 850 Beech Avenue; ca. 1870

Stifel house, 1319 Liverpool Street; Charles M. Bartberger, architect; 1885

Thaw (William Jr.) house, 930 Lincoln Avenue; ca. 1870

Wertheimer-Sipe house, 1220 West North Avenue; 1892

Museums, Clubs, and Recreational Venues

Andy Warhol Museum, formerly Frick & Lindsay, and Volkwein Music; 117 Sandusky at Robinson Street; Joseph Franklin Kuntz for the William G. Wilkins Co. Ltd., architects, 1911; expanded by O. M. Topp, 1918 and 1922; adaptive reuse by Richard Gluckman and Associates and UDA Architects, 1994

Carnegie Science Center, 1 Allegheny Avenue; Tasso Katselas Associates, architect; 1991

Children's Museum of Pittsburgh, formerly Allegheny City Post Office; Allegheny Square; William M. Aiken, architect, 1897; with Buhl Planetarium and Institute of Popular Science by Ingham, Pratt and Boyd, architects, 1939; and Green Museum by Konig Eizenberg and Perkins Eastman, architects, 2004

Heinz Field, 100 Art Rooney Avenue; Hellmuth, Obata, Kassabaum/HOK, architects; 2001

Rivers Casino, North Shore Drive at West End Bridge; Strada Architects; projected for 2010

Mattress Factory, formerly Stearns & Foster; 500 Sampsonia Way; renovation by Joel Kranich, architect, 1991; addition by Landmarks Design Associates, 2003

National Aviary, formerly Phipps Conservatory, 1887; West Park; rebuilding by Lawrence Wolfe, 1952; Lawrence and Anthony Wolfe, with Simonds and Simonds, landscape architects, 1969; renovation by Studio DeLisio Architecture and Design, 1997

PNC Park, Robinson and Federal streets; Hellmuth, Obata, Kassabaum/HOK, architects; 2001

Chapter 4: The South Side

Public and Government Buildings

Arlington Fire Station, Arlington Street at St. Patrick; Astorino, architects; 1981

Carnegie Library, Knoxville Branch, 400 Brownsville Road; Paul Schweikher, architect; 1966

Carnegie Library, Mt. Washington Branch, 315 Grandview; Longfellow, Alden & Harlow, architects; 1900

Corporate and Business Buildings

Carson City Saloon, formerly German Savings Deposit Bank, and Mellon Bank; 1401 East Carson Street; possible attribution to Charles Bickel, architect; 1896

Double Wide Grill, formerly Texaco service station; East Carson at Twenty-fourth Street

Iron and Glass Bank, 1114 East Carson; 1926

Maul Building, East Carson at Seventeenth Street; W. G. Wilkins Company, architects; 1910

PNC South Side Branch, formerly People's Trust; 1736 East Carson; 1902

SouthSide Works, East Carson Street from Twenty-sixth to Hot Metal Bridge Street; 2000 and ongoing

Station Square, Monongahela riverfront at West Carson Street; master plan by UDA Architects; restoration and conversion by Landmarks Design Associates, 1975

Industrial and Engineering Works

Duquesne Brewery, South Twenty-first Street at Mary; 1899 and later

Pittsburgh and Lake Erie Railroad Terminal, Monongahela riverfront at Smithfield Street Bridge; William George Burns, architect; 1901

Religious Buildings

Cleaves Temple Christian Methodist Episcopal Church, 1005 East Carson, near South Tenth Street; J. O. Keller, builder; 1913

Grace Episcopal Church, Bertha at West Sycamore avenues; original from 1852; rebuilt by J. Stewart, architect, 1926

South Side Presbyterian Church, Sarah and South Twentieth streets; 1869; rebuilt 1893

St. Adalbert's Church, South Fifteenth Street at CSX railroad tracks; 1889

St. Casimir's Roman Catholic Church, Sarah at South Twenty-second Street; 1901; adjacent school from 1913

St. George's Roman Catholic Church, Allen Street at Climax; Herman Lang, architect; 1910

St. John the Baptist Ukrainian Catholic Church, East Carson at South Seventh Street; Beezer Brothers, architects and builders, 1895; expanded 1917

St. Mary of the Mount Church, 403 Grandview; Frederick Sauer, architect; 1896

St. Michael's Roman Catholic Church and community center, Pius Street; church, 1861, and community center, 1897; convent and girls school from 1874; rebuilt 1900

St. Paul of the Cross Monastery, 148 Monastery Avenue; Charles F. Bartberger, architect; 1853

Talmud Torah Synagogue, 1908 Sarah Street; ca. 1920s

Residential Buildings

Angel's Arms Condominiums, formerly St. Michael's Roman Catholic Church; Pius and Brosville streets; Charles M. Bartberger, architect; 1861; parish rectory by Frederick Sauer, 1889; adaptive reuse by Hanson Design Group, 2006

Bedford School Lofts, formerly Bedford Public School; 910 Bingham Street; 1850; adaptive reuse by Edge Studios, 1997

Fox Way Commons, 1700 Wharton Street; Perkins Eastman, architects; 1997

Hilf (Daniel) houses, Volk's Way, off 224 Kearsarge; ca. 1910

South Side Recreational Center, formerly South Side Market House; Bedford Square; Charles Bickel, architect; 1893; restored 1915

491

Trautman (George) house, 94 South Eighteenth Steet; ca. 1880s

Trimont Condominiums, 1 Trimont Lane at Grandview Avenue; Astorino, architects; 1985

Museums, Clubs, and Recreational Venues

City Theater, formerly Birmingham Methodist Church; Bingham and Thirteenth streets; ca. 1860s

Lithuanian Hall, 1721 Jane Street; formerly a German social club; ca. 1870s

Chapter 5: Penn Avenue

Public and Government Buildings

Carnegie Library, Homewood Branch, 7101 Hamilton Avenue; Alden & Harlow, architects; 1910; historic rehabilitation by Pfaffmann + Associates, architects, 2004

Carnegie Library, Lawrenceville Branch, 279 Fisk Street; Alden & Harlow, architects; 1898

East Hills Elementary Magnet School, 2150 East Hills Drive; Tasso Katselas, architect; 1966

Edgewood Municipal Building, 2 Race Street; Clifford Lake, architect; 1932

Friendship School, 5501 Friendship; Charles M. Bartberger, architect; 1899

Lemington Elementary School, 7060 Lemington Avenue, opposite Paulson; Edward J. Weber and Marion M. Steen, architects; 1937

Lincoln-Larimer Fire Station, formerly Lemington Engine House No. 38; Lemington Avenue at Missouri Street; Kiehnel & Elliott, architects; 1908

Mellor (C. C.) Library and Edgewood Club, West Swissvale and Pennwood; Edward B. Lee, architect; 1916

Waldorf School, formerly Henry Lynch house, Ursuline Academy, and Victoria Hall; 201 South Winebiddle; possible attribution to Isaac Hobbs, architect; 1868

Western Pennsylvania School for the Deaf, Swissvale and Walnut avenues, Wilkinsburg; Alden & Harlow, architects; 1903

Corporate and Business Buildings

Church Brew Works, formerly St. John the Baptist Church; 3501 Liberty; John Comes for Beezer Brothers, architects; 1902–1907

Desmone & Associates, formerly Pennsylvania National Bank; Doughboy Square; Beezer Brothers, architects, 1902; adaptive reuse by Desmone & Associates, 1992

Highland Building, 121 South Highland; Daniel Burnham, architect; 1910

Lawrenceville Technology Center, AVRR to Hatfield Street, between Forty-third and Forty-eighth streets

PNC Lawrenceville Branch, formerly Metropolitan National Bank; 4105 Butler Street; Beezer Brothers, architects; 1903

Sack Store Fixture Company, 1201 Penn Avenue; ca. 1890

Industrial and Engineering Works

Allegheny Arsenal, Allegheny River to Penn Avenue at Fortieth Street; master plan and earliest buildings by Benjamin Henry Latrobe; 1813

Black Diamond Steel Works, counting house, formerly Park Brothers; 2949 Smallman; ca. 1870

Byrnes & Kiefer Company, 1133 Penn Avenue; Frederick Osterling, architect; 1892

Day's Baum Boulevard Dodge Chrysler Jeep, 5625 Baum Boulevard; Albert Kahn, architect; 1934

Edgewood Railroad Station, 101 East Swissvale Avenue at the Conrail tracks; Frank Furness, architect; 1903

Ford Motor Company assembly plant, Baum Boulevard at Morewood; John Graham Sr., architect; 1916

Otto Milk, formerly Phoenix Brewery; Smallman at Twenty-fourth Street; 1893

Pennsylvania Railroad Fruit Auction & Sales Building, Smallman Street at Sixteenth Street Bridge; 1926; renovation by The Design Alliance, 1983

Pittsburgh Brewery, formerly Iron City Brewery; 3340 Liberty Avenue; 1888

Pittsburgh Glass Center, 5472 Penn Avenue; adaptive reuse by dggp, now FortyEighty Architecture with Bruce Lindsey, architect; 2001

Ralph Meyer Company, formerly Park Brothers, Kloman-Phipps works, Union Iron Mills, and Black Diamond Steel Works; Smallman and Thirty-First streets; ca. 1860

Westinghouse Air-Brake Company, 2401–2425 Liberty Avenue; 1870

Religious Buildings

B'nai Israel Synagogue, 327 North Negley Avenue; Henry Hornbostel with Alexander Sharove and Philip Friedman, architects; 1923

Cornerstone Baptist Church, formerly St. Walburga's; Lincoln and Campania avenues; 1928

East Liberty Presbyterian Church, Penn Avenue at South Highland; Ralph Adams Cram, architect; 1931–1935

Eastminster United Presbyterian Church, 250 North Highland Avenue; William Fraser, architect; 1893

Emory United Methodist Church, 325 North Highland Avenue; Stotz, Hess, MacLachlin & Fosner, architects; 1973

First Presbyterian Church of Edgewood, 120 East Swissvale Avenue; Thomas Hannah, architect; 1918

Holy Rosary Roman Catholic Church, 7160 Kelly; Ralph Adams Cram, architect; 1928

Immaculate Heart of Mary Church, 3058 Brereton Street; William P. Ginther, architect; 1905

Our Lady Help of Christians Church, 6513 Meadow Street; 1898

Pittsburgh Theological Seminary, 616 North Highland Avenue; 1954 and ongoing

Reformed Presbyterian Theological Seminary, formerly The Gables (the Horne estate); 7418 Penn Avenue; attributed to Charles Tattersall Ingham, architect; ca. 1890

St. Augustine's Roman Catholic Church, 220 Thirty-seventh Street; John T. Comes for Rutan & Russell, architects; 1901

St. Elizabeth of Hungary Church, 1620 Penn Avenue; 1895

St. Joseph's Roman Catholic Church, 4712 Liberty; Adolphus or Adoulf Druiding, architect; 1886

St. Patrick's Church, 1711 Liberty; last rebuilt 1935

St. Stanislaus Kostka Church, Twenty-first Street at Smallman; Frederick Sauer, architect; 1892

Sts. Peter and Paul Roman Catholic Church, 130 Larimer Avenue; 1890

Residential Buildings

Alpha Terrace, 700 block of North Beatty Street; attributed to James Steen, architect; 1889–1894

Bartberger (Charles M.) house, 408 South Pacific; Charles M. Bartberger, architect; 1883

Baywood, the Alexander King estate, 5501 Elgin Street; ca. 1870s and later

Bendet house, 1321 Cordova Road; Theodore Eichholz, architect; ca. 1927

Bennett Place, Bennett and Sterrett streets; Lubetz Architects; 1988

Cinderella Apartments, Penn Avenue at Thirty-seventh Street; John Fink, builder; 1903

Clayton, the Henry Clay Frick estate, 7200 Penn Avenue; 1860s; rebuilt by Andrew Peebles, architect, 1883; then by Frederick Osterling, architect; 1891

Cork Factory Lofts, formerly Armstrong Cork Factory; AVRR, between Twenty-third and Twenty-fourth streets; Frederick Osterling, architect, 1901–1912; adaptive reuse by Antunovich and Carr Associates, architects; 2007

The Crescent, 724–734 Kelly Avenue, Wilkinsburg; ca. 1905

Elliot house, 935 North Highland Avenue; 1891

Fairmont Apartments, 5461 Penn Avenue; Rothschild Doyno, architect; 2007

Fraser (William) house, 5655 Stanton Avenue; William Fraser, architect; 1891

Gardner-Bailey house, 124 West Swissvale Avenue; 1864

Grubbs-Kerr house, 235 West Swissvale Avenue; ca. 1860

Henius (Lillian) house, 1315 Cordova Road; Kiehnel & Elliott, architects; 1918

Klages house, 5525 Beverly Place; Frederick Scheibler, architect; 1922

Kloman (Andrew) house, 3600 Penn Avenue; 1864

Lawrence Square Apartments, 3417–3429 Liberty; ca. 1890

Lawrenceville Bathhouse, 3445 Butler Street; 1904

Linwood Apartments, 6801 McPherson Avenue; Frederick Scheibler, architect; 1907

Mueller (Sebastian) house, 944 Sheridan Avenue; 1901

Negley (Mary Ann Berkstresser) house, Heberton and Grafton streets; core building ca. 1819

Old Heidelberg Apartments, 401–423 South Braddock at Waverly; Frederick Scheibler, architect; 1905 and 1908

Parkstone Dwellings, 6937–6943 Penn Avenue; Frederick Scheibler, architect; 1922

† **Peacock (Alexander) house,** Rowanlea, formerly at Highland Avenue and Bryant; 1892

Rebecca House and Jane Holmes Residence, 900 Rebecca and 441 Swissvale avenues; Barr and Moser, architects; 1871 and 1882

Schoolhouse Lofts, formerly a school; 3052 Smallman Street; ca. 1870

Singer (John) house, 1318 Singer Place, Wilkinsburg; 1863–1869

Stanton Castle, 5652 Stanton Avenue at St. Clair; ca. 1910

Syria and Kismet Apartments, 7430–7434 Bennett; Frederick Scheibler, architect; 1904

Tim (J. W.) house, 1317 North Sheridan Avenue; 1861

201 East End Avenue Apartments, Frederick Scheibler, architect; 1907

Winebiddle house, 340 South Winebiddle; ca. 1885

Museums, Clubs, and Recreational Venues

Kelly-Strayhorn Theater, formerly Regent Theater; 5941 Penn Avenue; Harry Blair, architect; 1914

Pittsburgh Zoo and PPG Aquarium, Highland Park; 1898; aquarium by Indovina Associates, architects; 2000

Senator John Heinz History Center, formerly Chautauqua Lake Ice Company icehouse; 1212 Smallman Street; attributed to Frederick Osterling, architect, 1898; adaptive reuse by Bohlin Cywinski Jackson, architects, 1996; Pittsburgh Sports Museum wing by Astorino, architects; 2004

Chapter 6: Fifth Avenue

Public and Government Buildings

Carnegie Library, Hill District Branch, 2177 Centre Avenue at Kirkpatrick Street; Pfaffman + Associates, architects; 2008

Carnegie Library, Squirrel Hill Branch, Forbes and Murray avenues; Liff, Justh & Chetlin, architects, 1972; rebuilt by Lubetz Architects; 2006

Central Catholic High School, 4720 Fifth Avenue; Link, Weber & Bowers, architects; 1927

Fifth Avenue High School, 1800 Fifth at Dinwiddie; Edward Stotz, architect; 1894

Mercy Hospital, Locust and Pride streets; original complex by Haden Smith, builder; 1847

Taylor Allderdice High School, Shady at Forward avenues; Robert Maurice Trimble, architect; 1927

Corporate and Business Buildings

Crawford Grill, formerly Sochatoff Building; 2141 Wylie Avenue at Elmore; 1917

WQED Multimedia, 4802 Fifth Avenue; Paul Schweikher, architect; 1970

College and University Buildings

Mellon (Andrew W.) Hall, formerly the George Laughlin house; Woodland Road, Chatham University; MacClure and Spahr, 1907; expanded by E. P. Mellon, architect, 1917

Mudge Graduate House, formerly Pauline and Edmund Mudge house; 1000 Morewood Avenue at Fifth, Carnegie Mellon; Henry D. Gilchrist, architect; 1922

Religious Buildings

Beth Shalom Synagogue, 5915 Beacon Street; Alexander Sharove and Philip Friedman, architects, with Henry Hornbostel, architect; 1922 and later

Brown (Mary S.) Memorial Methodist Church, 3424 Beechwood; George Orth, architect; 1903

Calvary Episcopal Church, Shady at Walnut avenues; Ralph Adams Cram, architect; 1907

493

Christian Church of North America, formerly Shady Presbyterian; 241 Shady Avenue, corner Aurelia; ca. 1890

Enon Baptist Church, formerly Anshe Lubovitch Synagogue; 110 Erin; ca. 1920

Epiphany Roman Catholic Church, Washington Place at Centre Avenue; Edward Stotz, architect, with John Comes; 1903

Episcopal Church of the Ascension, 4729 Ellsworth Avenue; William Halsey Wood, architect; 1898

First Church of Christ, Scientist, now University of Pittsburgh Child Center; 623 Clyde Street; S. S. Beman, architect; 1904

First Mosque of Pittsburgh, formerly a Carnegie library; 1911 Wylie; Alden & Harlow, architects; 1899

Holy Spirit Catholic Church, Byzantine Rite, Fifth Avenue at Clyde; 1961

Jewish Community Center, 5738 Forbes Avenue; UDA Architects; 1986 and later

Miller Street Baptist Church, formerly Beth David/Shaaray Tefillah Synagogue; 23–25 Miller, ca. 1916; church school formerly the Labor Lyceum of the Arbeter Ring/ Workmen's Circle, 1916

Poale Zedek Synagogue, Shady and Phillips avenues; Alexander Sharove and Philip Friedman, architects; 1928

Rodef Shalom Temple, Fifth Avenue at Morewood; Henry Hornbostel, architect, 1907; renovation by the Ehrenkrantz Group and Eckstut, 1989

Sacred Heart Church, Shady at Walnut avenues; Carlton Strong, architect; 1924 and later

Shadyside Presbyterian Church, 807 Amberson Avenue at Westminster Place; Shepley, Rutan & Coolidge, architects; 1889–1892

Sixth Presbyterian Church, Forbes and Murray avenues; William Fraser, architect; ca. 1895

St. Benedict the Moor Roman Catholic Church, formerly Holy Trinity, then St. Brigid's; Centre Avenue at Crawford; Henry Moser, architect; 1894

St. Joachim's Church, Boundary Street at Four Mile Run Road; 1910

St. John Chrysostom Byzantine Catholic Church, 506 Saline Street at Anthony; W. Ward William, architect; 1931–1935

St. Michael's Russian Orthodox Cathedral, 43 Reed, corner Vine; 1903 and 1910

St. Rosalia's Church, 411 Greenfield Avenue at Lydia; Alfred Link, architect; 1923

Temple Sinai, formerly John Worthington house; 5505 Forbes Avenue; Louis Stevens, architect; 1909

Third Presbyterian Church, Fifth and Negley; Theophilus P. Chandler Jr., architect; 1896–1905

Young Peoples Synagogue, 6401 Forbes Avenue; ca. 1915

Zion Hill Baptist Church, formerly Kether Torah–Agudas Achim Synagogue; 2043 Webster Avenue, corner Erin; 1920

Residential Buildings

Aaron (Marcus) house, 5564 Aylesboro Avenue, corner Wightman; ca. 1910

Abbott and Marshall house, 920 St. James Street, ca. 1860

Abrams (Betty and Irving) house, 118A Woodland Road; Robert Venturi, architect; 1983

Aiken (David Jr.) house, 5020 Amberson Place; 1864

The Amberson, formerly Willis McCook house; 925 Fifth Avenue; Carpenter and Crocker, architects; 1906

Babcock (Edward V.) house, 5135 Ellsworth; George Orth, architect, 1898

Beacon Gardens, formerly Hamilton Cottages; 5635–5663 Beacon Street; Frederick Scheibler, architect; 1914

Brown (Louis) house, 704 Amberson; Edward Weber, architect; 1913

Childs House, 718 Devonshire; Peabody and Stearns, architects; 1896

College Place rowhouses, 5800 block of Pierce Avenue, between College and Maryland streets; ca. 1910

Frank (Robert and Cecilia) house, 96 East Woodland Road; Walter Gropius and Marcel Breuer, architects; 1939–1940

Gardner (William) house, 914–916 St. James Street; William Gardner, builder; 1890

Giovanitti (Frank) house, 118 Woodland Road; Richard Meier, architect; 1983

Gwinner-Harter house, formerly William B. Negley house; 5061 Fifth Avenue; ca. 1871

Harter house, 2557 Beechwood Boulevard; Frederick Scheibler, architect; 1923

Heinz (Howard) house, 5090 Warwick Terrace; Vrydaugh and Wolfe, architects; 1910 and 1923

Highland Towers, 340–342 South Highland Avenue; Frederick Scheibler, architect; 1913

Hillman house, formerly James Rees house; 5045 Fifth Avenue; 1878; rebuilt by E. P. Mellon, architect, 1926

Hunt (Alfred) house, 4875 Ellsworth, corner Devonshire; Edward Grenzbach, architect; 1976

Hunt (Roy) house, 5050 Amberson Place; Maximilian Nirdlinger, architect; 1913

Kingsbaker (Louis) house, 5530 Aylesboro

The Legacy, between Centre, Wylie, Erin, and Elmore; Rothschild Doyno Architects; 2008

MacBeth (George) house, 717 Amberson; Charles M. Bartberger and E. G. W. Dietrich, architects; 1884

McClung (Judge Samuel) house, 1180 Murray Hill Avenue; ca. 1895

†**Mellon (Richard B.) house,** formerly at Fifth Avenue and Beechwood Boulevard, now Mellon Park; Alden & Harlow, architects; Gilmore D. Clarke, landscape architect; 1907

Minnetonka Apartments, 5425–5431 Walnut, corner Copeland; Frederick Scheibler, architect; 1908

Moreland-Hoffstot house, 5057 Fifth Avenue; Paul Irwin, architect; 1914

Myler house, divided into 1331 and 1333 Bennington Avenue; Bertram Grosvenor Goodhue, architect; 1921

Neill (Robert) log house, Serpentine Drive, Schenley Park; 1769

Newton (Ambrose) log house, Serpentine Drive, Schenley Park; ca. 1764

Pfeiffer house, 5553 Northumberland Street; Lubetz Architects; 1982

Sellers (Francis) house, or Sellers-Carnahan house, Shady at Walnut avenues; 1858

Spencer (Charles) house, 719 Amberson; George Orth, architect; 1886

Speyer (Tillie) house, Wightman at Northumberland streets; A. James Speyer, architect; 1963

Sunnyledge Hotel, formerly Sunnyledge, the James McClelland estate; 5124 Fifth Avenue at Wilkins; Alexander Longfellow Jr. for Longfellow, Alden & Harlow, architects; 1887

Taylor (Charles) houses, 4735 and 4737 Bayard Street; 1842 and later

Washington Plaza Apartments, Centre Avenue at Crawford Street; I. M. Pei, architect; 1964

Willow Cottage, formerly Howe-Childs gatehouse to the Thomas Howe estate; Fifth Avenue at Woodland Road; ca. 1865

Wilson (August) house, 1727 Bedford Avenue, ca. 1910

Museums, Clubs, and Recreational Venues

Blakey Program Center, formerly Hebrew Institute; 1908 Wylie Avenue; 1915

James F. Henry Hill House Center, formerly, in part, the Irene Kaufmann Settlement auditorium; 1835 Centre Avenue; Edward Stotz, architect, 1928; new construction by Walter Roberts, architect, 1973

Madison School, Milwaukee and Orion streets; Ulysses Peoples, architect; 1902

Mellon Arena, formerly Civic Arena, 66 Mario Lemieux Place; James Mitchell and Dahlen Ritchey, architects; Ammann and Whitney and Robert Zern, engineers; 1962

New Granada Theater, formerly Pythian Temple; 2007–2013 Centre Avenue; Louis Bellinger, architect, 1927; reconstruction by Alfred M. Marks, architect, 1937

Pittsburgh Center for the Arts, mansion formerly the Charles Marshall house; Fifth Avenue at Shady; Charles Barton Keen, architect, 1911; auxiliary building formerly the Alan and Sarah Scaife house; Shady Avenue; Alden & Harlow, architects, 1904; renovated 1927

Pittsburgh Golf Club, Northumberland Street at Schenley Park; Alden & Harlow, architects; 1896

Chapter 7: Oakland

Public and Government Buildings

Board of Education, 341 South Bellefield; Ingham and Boyd, architects; 1927

Carnegie Library Main and Carnegie Museums of Pittsburgh building, 4400 Forbes Avenue; Longfellow, Alden & Harlow, architects, 1895; Alden & Harlow, 1907; Scaife Gallery by Edward Larabee Barnes, architect, 1974; Heinz Architectural Center by Cicognani Kalla Architects, 1993; library remodeled by Edge Studios, 2004; Dinosaur Hall expanded by Verner Johnson Associates with Burt Hill Kosar Rittelmann, architects, 2007

Children's Hospital, until 2009; Fifth Avenue at De Soto; York and Sawyer, architects, with E. P. Mellon; 1927

Detre Building, (Western Psychiatric Institute and Clinic), O'Hara Street at De Soto; Marlier and Stevens, architects; 1942

Falk Clinic, Fifth Avenue at Lothrop; E. P. Mellon, architect; 1930

Magee-Womens Hospital, incorporating the Maples, the former Christopher Lyman Magee estate; Forbes, Halket, and Craft avenues; original hospital by Thorsten E. Billquist, architect; 1915

Magee-Womens Hospital administration building, formerly Isaly's Dairy; 3380 Boulevard of the Allies; the McCormick Company, architects and builders; 1930

Montefiore Hospital, Fifth Avenue at Darragh; Schmidt, Garden & Erickson, architects, with Henry Hornbostel; 1929 and later

Pittsburgh Athletic Association, Fifth Avenue at Bigelow; Janssen and Abbott, architects; 1911

Presbyterian-University Hospital, De Soto Street at O'Hara; York and Sawyer, architects, with E. P. Mellon; 1930–1938

Schenley High School, Bigelow Boulevard at Centre; Edward Stotz, architect; 1916

Veterans Affairs Medical Center, University Drive C; ca. 1955

Western Pennsylvania School for Blind Children, Bigelow Boulevard at Bayard; George Orth, architect; 1894

Corporate and Business Buildings

King's Court Theater, formerly No. 4 Precinct Station; 3807 Forbes Avenue; Bickel and Brennan, architects; 1889

Lubetz Architecture Studio, 357 North Craig Street; adaptive reuse by Lubetz Architects; 1982

Software Engineering Institute, 4500 Fifth Avenue; Bohlin Powell Larkin Cywinski and Burt Hill Kosar Rittelmann, architects; 1987

Industrial and Engineering Works

Bellefield Boiler Plant, Boundary Street; Alden & Harlow, architects; 1907

College and University Buildings

CARLOW UNIVERSITY BUILDINGS

St. Agnes Center, formerly St. Agnes Roman Catholic Church; Fifth Avenue at Robinson, Carlow University; John Comes, architect; 1917

CARNEGIE MELLON UNIVERSITY BUILDINGS

College of Fine Arts, originally School of Applied Design; Henry Hornbostel, architect; 1912 and 1916

East Campus, master plan Dennis, Clark, & Associates with TAMS Consultants, Michael Dennis & Associates, architects, 1987

Gates Center for Computer Science, Mack Scogin Merrill Elam Architects, 2009

Hamburg Hall, originally U.S. Bureau of Mines; Henry Hornbostel, architect, 1912; Roberts Engineering Hall added by Payette Associates, architects; 1994

Hamerschlag, originally Machinery Hall, Henry Hornbostel, architect; 1912

Hunt Library, Lawrie & Green, architects; 1961

Kraus Campo, Mel Bochner and Michael Van Valkenburgh Associates, 2001–2003

Margaret Morrison Carnegie Hall, Henry Hornbostel, architect, 1907; extended by Hornbostel, 1914; Intelligent Workplace added by Bohlen Cywinksi Jackson, with Pierre Zoelly, architects; 1991

Mellon Institute, Fifth Avenue at Bellefield; Janssen and Cocken, architects; 1937

Porter, Baker, and Doherty halls, Henry Hornbostel, architect, 1905 and 1914

Purnell Center for the Arts, DDF Associates, Michael Dennis & Associates, Damianos + Anthony, and John Sergio Fisher & Associates, architects, 1999

Tepper School of Business, B. Kenneth Johnstone, architect, 1955; extended as Posner Hall by Kallmann, McKinnell and Wood, architects, 1992

University Center, Michael Dennis & Associates and UDA Architects, 1995

University Computing Center, Deeter Ritchey Sippel, architects; 1984

Walking to the Sky, art installation by Jonathan Borofsky, sculptor, 2006

Warner Hall, Charles Luckman, architect, 1966

Wean Hall, Deeter Ritchey Sippel, architects; 1971

UNIVERSITY OF PITTSBURGH BUILDINGS

Allen Hall, formerly Mellon Institute of Industrial Research; O'Hara Street; J. H. Giesey, architect; 1915

Alumni Hall, formerly Masonic Temple; Fifth Avenue at Lytton; Janssen and Abbott, architects; 1914

Bellefield Hall, formerly YMHA; 315 S. Bellefield; Janssen and Cocken, architects; 1924

Bellefield Towers, Fifth Avenue at Bellefield; UDA Associates, architects; 1987

Cathedral of Learning, Bigelow Boulevard between Forbes and Fifth avenues; Charles Klauder, architect; 1926–1937

Eberly Hall, formerly Alumni Hall; University Drive; Benno Janssen, architect; 1920

Frick (Henry Clay) Fine Arts Building, Schenley Drive; B. Kenneth Johnstone Associates, architects; interior murals by Nicholas Lochoff; 1965

Heinz Memorial Chapel, Fifth and Bellefield avenues; Charles Klauder, architect; 1938

Learning Research and Development Center, 3939 O'Hara Street; Harrison & Abramovitz, architects; 1974

Mervis Hall, Roberto Clemente Drive; IKM/SGE, architects; 1983

Pitt (William) Student Union, formerly Schenley Hotel; Forbes Avenue at Bigelow Boulevard; Rutan & Russell, architects, 1898; renovation by Williams Trebilcock Whitehead, architect; 1983

Salk (Jonas E.) Hall, formerly Municipal Hospital; Terrace Street at De Soto; Richard Irving and Theodore Eichholz, architects; 1940

Schenley Quadrangle dormitories, formerly Schenley Apartments; between Forbes and Fifth avenues east of Bouquet; Henry Hornbostel and Eric Fisher Wood, architects; 1923

School of Information Science, 135 North Bellefield; Tasso Katselas, architect; 1965

Thaw Hall, 3943 O'Hara Street; Henry Hornbostel, architect; 1909

Religious Buildings

First Baptist Church, 159 North Bellefield Avenue at Bayard; Bertram Grosvenor Goodhue for Cram, Goodhue & Ferguson, architects; 1912

St. Nicholas Greek Orthodox Cathedral, formerly the First Congregational Church; Dithridge Street at Forbes; Struthers and Hannah, architects; 1904

St. Paul Cathedral, Fifth Avenue at Craig; Egan and Prindeville, architects, 1906; Synod Hall by Edward J. Weber, 1914; parish rectory by Carlton Strong, architect, 1927

† **St. Peter's Church,** formerly at Forbes Avenue and Craft; John Notman, architect; 1852

Residential Buildings

Bellefield Dwellings, Centre Avenue between Bellefield and Dithridge; Carlton Strong, architect; 1904

Cathedral Mansions, 4716 Ellsworth Avenue; John Donn, architect; 1927

Central Turnverein, former headquarters, O'Hara and Thackeray streets; Kiehnel & Elliott, architects; 1912

The Fairfax, 4614 Fifth Avenue; Philip M. Julien, architect; 1926

Hampton Hall, 166 North Dithridge near Bayard; H. C. Hodgkins, architect; 1928

Iroquois Apartments, Forbes Avenue at Atwood; Frederick Osterling, architect, 1903; expansion into Forbes Tower, Tasso Katselas Associates, architects, 1996

King Edward Apartments, Bayard Street at Melville; H. C. Hodgkins, architect, 1914; expanded by Walter Perry, 1930

Metropolitan Shadyside condominiums, 537 North Neville; Astorino, architects; 2007

Moorhead (William S.) Tower, Craig Street at Baum Boulevard; Lubetz Architects; 1981

Neville House, 552 North Neville Street; Tasso Katselas, architect; 1958

Oak Hill housing development, Terrace and Burrows streets, Oak Hill Drive, and adjoining streets; Beacon/Corcoran Jennison, developers; Goody/Clancy Associates, architects; 1996 and later

Royal York Apartments, Bigelow Boulevard at Dithridge Street; Frederick Stanton, architect; 1937

Warhol (Andy) house, 3252 Dawson Street, between Swinburne and Frazier

Webster Hall Apartments, Fifth Avenue at Dithridge; Henry Hornbostel and Eric Fisher Wood, architects; 1925

Winchester Condominiums, 540 North Neville; Herbert Seigel, architect; 1971

Museums, Clubs, and Recreational Venues

Historical Society of Western Pennsylvania, former headquarters, 4338 Bigelow Boulevard; Ingham and Boyd, architects; 1912

The Oratory, Ryan Catholic Newman Center, Bayard Street at Dithridge, and Gailliot Center for Newman Studies, 211 North Dithridge; David Vater, architect; 1997 and 2007

Phipps Conservatory, Schenley Drive; Lord and Burnham, architects, 1893; expanded by IKM Architects, 2005

Pittsburgh Playhouse, formerly Tree of Life Synagogue; Craft Avenue at Hamlet; David Crone, architect; 1906

S. Lorenzo di Gamberale Mutual Benefit Association clubhouse, 379 South Bouquet; 1938

Soldiers and Sailors Memorial Hall and Museum, formerly Allegheny County Soldiers' and Sailors' Memorial Hall; 4141 Fifth Avenue, Henry Hornbostel, architect; 1910

Twentieth Century Club, Bigelow at Parkman; original building by G. H. Schwan, architect, 1910; restructured by Janssen and Cocken, architects; 1930

Chapter 8: The River Towns

Public and Government Buildings

Carnegie Library, Braddock Branch, 419 Library Street, Braddock; William Halsey Wood, architect, 1888; music hall added by Longfellow, Alden & Harlow, 1893

Carnegie Library, Homestead Branch, 510 Tenth Avenue, Munhall; Alden & Harlow, architects; 1898

Carnegie Library, Oakmont Branch, 700 Allegheny River Boulevard, Oakmont; Alden & Harlow, architects, 1901; expanded by Integrated Architectural Services, 1998–2006

Jones (B. F.) Memorial Library, 663 Franklin Street, Aliquippa; Brandon Smith, architect; 1929

Corporate and Business Buildings

Alcoa Research Station, Freeport and Edgewood roads, New Kensington; Henry Hornbostel, architect; ca. 1930

Bost Building, 623 East Eighth Avenue, Homestead; 1892

Ohringer Building, 640 Braddock Avenue at Seventh, Braddock; ca. 1935

Industrial and Engineering Works

Fort Pitt Brewery, 1600 Mary's Avenue, Sharpsburg

Pennsylvania Drilling Company, formerly Taylor-Wilson Manufacturing; 500 Thompson Avenue, McKees Rocks; Robert A. Cummings, engineer; 1905

Pittsburgh and Lake Erie Railroad Locomotive Repair Shop, end of Linden Street, McKees Rocks; Albert Lucius, engineer; H. L. Turner, superintendent; 1903

Pittsburgh Technology Center, Second Avenue, Hazelwood; various architects; ongoing since 1983

U.S. Steel Edgar Thomson Works, Thirteenth Street at Braddock Avenue, North Braddock; Alexander L. Holley, engineer for the earliest buildings; 1875

Wabtec, formerly Westinghouse Air-Brake Works; 325 Commerce, Wilmerding; Frederick Osterling, architect; 1890

Westinghouse Air-Brake general office building, Wilmerding; Frederick Osterling, architect, 1890; expanded by Janssen and Cocken, architects; 1927

Westinghouse Electric Corporation East Pittsburgh Works, state route 130 at Brown Avenue; Thomas Rodd, architect; 1894

WHEMCO plant, formerly Mesta Machine Company; Seventh Avenue, West Homestead; 1898; rebuilt 1925

Religious Buildings

Cathedral Hall, formerly St. Francis de Sales Church; Chartiers Avenue at Margaret, McKees Rocks; Marius Rousseau, architect; 1899

Cesarespada House-Church, 1138 Stanford Road, Brighton Heights/Pittsburgh

Episcopal Church of the Good Shepherd, Second Avenue at Johnston Street, Hazelwood; William Halsey Wood, architect; 1891

First Hungarian Reformed Church, 221 Johnston, near Gertrude, Hazelwood; Titus de Bobula, architect; 1903

Grace Episcopal Church, formerly Shields Chapel; Church Lane, Sewickley; Joseph W. Kerr, architect; 1868

Grace United Methodist Church, 1512 North Canal Street, Sharpsburg; 1872

Sewickley Presbyterian Church, Grant and Beaver streets, Sewickley; Joseph W. Kerr, architect; 1859

Shields Mausoleum, Church Lane, Sewickley; John U. Barr, architect; 1893

St. Gregory the Theologian Orthodox Church, East Fifteenth Street at Maple, Homestead; Basil Verkoskow, architect; 1950

St. Mark's Roman Catholic Church, Munson Street, McKees Rocks

St. Mary Magdalene Roman Catholic Church, 1008 Amity Street, Homestead; Frederick Sauer, architect, 1895; expanded by Button and MacLean, architects; 1936

St. Mary's Church, Penn and Garnier streets; Sharpsburg; Peter Dedrichs, architect; 1916

St. Mary's Church, St. John Street, McKees Rocks; William P. Ginther, architect, 1901; convent added by Comes, Perry & McMullen, architects, 1930

St. Michael the Archangel Church, East Ninth Avenue at Library Place, Munhall; Comes, Perry & McMullen, architects; 1927

St. Michael the Archangel Greek Catholic Church, 146 Third Avenue, Rankin; 1910

St. Nicholas Roman Catholic Church, 24 Maryland Avenue, Millvale; Frederick Sauer, architect, 1901 and 1922; Maximilian Vanka, painter, 1937 and 1941

St. Nicholas Russian Orthodox Church, Munson Street, McKees Rocks; 1914

St. Stephen's Church, 5115 Second Avenue, corner East Elizabeth, Hazelwood; Frederick Sauer, architect; 1902

St. Stephen's Episcopal Church, Frederick Avenue at Broad Street, Sewickley; Charles M. Bartberger, architect; 1894

St. Thomas Memorial Episcopal Church, 378 Delaware Avenue, Oakmont; Robert Maurice Trimble, architect; 1907

Residential Buildings

Aluminum City Terrace, East Hill Drive, New Kensington; Walter Gropius and Marcel Breuer, architects; 1941

Atwell-Christy house, 403 Frederick, Sewickley; 1862

Economy, Old Economy Harmonist settlement, Ambridge; Frederick Rapp, main architect for St. John's Lutheran Church, Feast Hall, Garden Pavilion, and Grotto, 1820s; restored by Charles Stotz, architect; 1939

817 Kirkpatrick, North Braddock; ca. 1890

Mesta (George and Perle) house, 540 Doyle Avenue, West Homestead; ca. 1900

Rachel Carson Homestead, 613 Marion Avenue, Springdale; ca. 1840

Sauer (Frederick) houses, 615–627 Center Avenue, Aspinwall; 1894–1942

Schwab (Charles M.) house, 541 Jones Avenue, North Braddock; Frederick Osterling, architect, 1889

Thornburg (Frank) house, 1132 Lehigh, Thornburg; Samuel McClarren, architect; 1906

Way (Abishai) House, 108 Beaver Road, Edgeworth; ca. 1810

Woods (John) house, 4604 Monongahela Street at Tullymet, Hazelwood; ca. 1784

Museums, Clubs, and Recreational Venues

Kerr (Dr. Thomas R.) Memorial Museum, 402 Delaware Avenue, Oakmont; 1897

Longue Vue Club, 400 Longue Vue Drive, Penn Hills; Janssen and Cocken, architects; with Albert D. Taylor, landscape architect; 1923

National Carpatho-Rusyn Cultural and Educational Center, formerly St. John the Baptist Greek Catholic Cathedral; 427 East Tenth Avenue, corner Dickson, Munhall; Titus de Bobula, architect; 1903

Oakmont Country Club, 1233 Hulton Road, Oakmont; clubhouse by Edward Stotz, architect, 1904; Henry C. Fownes, landscape architect

Chapter 9:
The Pittsburgh Periphery

Public and Government Buildings

Allegheny County Airport, Lebanon Church Road at state route 885, West Mifflin; Stanley Roush, architect, 1931; expanded by Henry Hornbostel, architect, 1936

Cranberry Township Municipal Building, 2525 Rochester Road, Cranberry; adaptive reuse by Ross, Shonder, Sterzinger, Cupcheck, architects; 1992

Mt. Lebanon Municipal Building, 710 Washington Road, Mt. Lebanon; William H. King Jr., architect; 1930

Shady Side Academy, 423 Fox Chapel Road; Edward P. Mellon, founding architect; Ezra Stiles, landscape architect; 1922

Washington County Courthouse, Beau and Main streets, Washington; Frederick Osterling, architect; 1900

Westmoreland County Courthouse, Pittsburgh and Main streets, Greensburg; William Kauffman, architect; 1906

Corporate and Business Buildings

Ericsson Communications, formerly FORE Systems, then Marconi; 5000 Ericsson Road, Warrendale; Studios Architecture; 1997

Greensburg Tribune-Review Building, Cabin Hill Drive, Greensburg; Louis I. Kahn, architect; 1961

Monroeville Mall, 200 Monroeville Mall, off William Penn Highway, Monroeville; ca. 1960

Westinghouse Electric Corporation world headquarters, state route 228 near I-79, Cranberry Woods, Cranberry Township; IKM architects and LLI engineers; 2010 and ongoing

Westinghouse Research Laboratories and atom smasher, intersection of North Avenue, Chalfant Borough, and West Street, Forest Hills; 1937

Industrial and Engineering Works

Roebling wire rope manufactory, North Rebecca Street, Saxonburg; 1842

Religious Buildings

Bethel Presbyterian Church, 2999 Bethel Church Road, Bethel Park; 1838 and ca. 1930

Beulah Presbyterian Church, Beulah Road at McCrady, Churchill; 1837

Cross Roads Presbyterian Church, intersection of Monroeville Boulevard and Stroschein Road, Monroeville; ca. 1890

Faith United Methodist Church, 261 West Chapel Ridge Road, Fox Chapel; ca. 1890

Fox Chapel Episcopal Church, formerly the Gould house; 630 Squaw Run Road East, Fox Chapel; Brandon Smith, architect; ca. 1920

Hindu-Jain Temple, 615 Illini Drive, Monroeville; Sashi Patel, architect; 1988

Holy Trinity Serbian Orthodox Cathedral, 450 Maxwell Drive, Whitehall; John Tomich, architect; 1971

Holy Virgin Russian Orthodox Church, 214 Mansfield Boulevard, Carnegie; 1920

Mt. Lebanon Methodist Church, 3319 West Liberty Avenue, Mt. Lebanon; Charles W. Bier, architect; 1923

Mt. Lebanon United Presbyterian Church, 255 Washington Road, Mt. Lebanon; J. Lewis Beatty, architect; 1929

Saxonburg Memorial United Presbyterian Church, formerly German Evangelical Church; 100 East Main Street, Saxonburg; John Roebling, probable architect; 1837

Sri Venkateswara Temple, 1230 South McCully Drive, Penn Hills; Sashi Patel, architect; 1976

St. Luke's Episcopal Church, Old Washington Pike at Church Street, Scott Township; attributed to John Notman, architect; 1852

St. Paul A.M.E. Zion Church, 216 Mansfield Boulevard, Carnegie; 1927

St. Peter and St. Paul Ukrainian Orthodox Church, 200 Walnut, corner Mansfield Boulevard, Carnegie; Titus de Bobula, architect; 1906

Residential Buildings

Boyer (Peter) house, 5679 Library Road, Bethel Park; ca. late 1840s

Duncan house, Acme, Westmoreland County; Frank Lloyd Wright, architect; 1957

Fallingwater, E. J. Kaufmann Sr. estate, Fayette County; Frank Lloyd Wright, architect; 1937

Kentuck Knob, I. N. Hagen estate, Chalk Hill, Fayette County; Frank Lloyd Wright, architect; 1954

Marshall (George) house, 3000 Oakhurst Road, Bethel Park; 1838

Miller (Oliver) homestead, Stone Manse Drive, South Park; 1808

Swan Acres housing development, Circle Drive off Babock Boulevard, Ross Township; Harry C. Clepper and Quentin Beck, architects; 1934 and 1936

Museums, Clubs, and Recreational Venues

Meadowcroft Museum of Rural Life, 401 Meadowcroft Road, Avella

Meadowcroft Rock Shelter Visitors' Center, Avella; Pfaffmann + Associates, architects, 2007

Rolling Rock Club, state route 30, east of Ligonier; clubhouse by Edward Purcell Mellon, ca. 1920; stables and kennels by Benno Janssen, architect, 1928; adaptive reuse by Al Filoni of MacLachlan Cornelius & Filoni, 1986

FURTHER READING

Alberts, Robert. *The Good Provider: H. J. Heinz and His 57 Varieties.* Boston: Houghton Mifflin, 1973.

———. *Pitt: The Story of the University of Pittsburgh, 1787–1987.* Pittsburgh: University of Pittsburgh Press, 1987.

———. *The Shaping of the Point: Pittsburgh's Renaissance Park.* Pittsburgh: University of Pittsburgh Press, 1980.

"Allegheny County Survey." Unpublished manuscript, 1979–1984, Pittsburgh History & Landmarks Foundation. Copy at the Pennsylvania Historical and Museum Commission, Harrisburg, PA.

Aurand, Martin. *A Campus Renewed: A Decade of Building at Carnegie Mellon, 1986–1996.* Pittsburgh, 1996.

———. *Pittsburgh Architecture: A Guide to Research.* Pittsburgh: Carnegie Mellon University Architecture Archives, 1991; online updates at http://www.library.cmu.edu/Research/ArchArch/PGHARCHres.

———. "Prairie School Architecture in Pittsburgh." *Pittsburgh History* 78, no. 1 (spring 1995): 5–20.

———. *The Progressive Architecture of Frederick G. Scheibler, Jr.* Pittsburgh: University of Pittsburgh Press, 1994.

———. *The Spectator and the Topographical City.* Pittsburgh: University of Pittsburgh Press, 2006.

Baldwin, Leland. *Pittsburgh: The Story of a City, 1750–1865.* 1937. Reprint, Pittsburgh: University of Pittsburgh Press, 1970.

Barnett, Jonathan. "Designing Downtown Pittsburgh." *Architectural Record* 170, no. 1 (January 1982): 90–107.

Bauman, John, and Edward Muller. *Before Renaissance: Planning in Pittsburgh, 1889–1943.* Pittsburgh: University of Pittsburgh Press, 2006.

Becher, Bernd, and Hilla Becher. *Industrial Landscapes.* Cambridge, MA: MIT Press, 2002.

Bell, Thomas. *Out of This Furnace.* 1941. Reprint, Pittsburgh: University of Pittsburgh Press, 1976.

Bodnar, John. *Steelton: Immigration and Industrialization, 1870–1940.* 1977. Reprint, Pittsburgh: University of Pittsburgh Press, 1990.

———, Roger Simon, and Michael Weber, eds. *Lives of Their Own: Blacks, Italians, and Poles in Pittsburgh, 1900–1960.* Urbana: University of Illinois Press, 1982.

Bolden, Frank E., Lawrence A. Glasco, and Eliza Smith Brown, eds. *A Legacy in Bricks and Mortar: African American Landmarks in Allegheny County.* Pittsburgh: Pittsburgh History & Landmarks Foundation, 1995.

Borkowski, Joseph. *Miscellaneous History of Lawrenceville.* Pittsburgh, 1989.

Boucher, John N., ed. *A Century and a Half of Pittsburg and Her People.* 4 vols. New York: Lewis Publishing, 1908.

Brashear, John A. *A Man Who Loved the Stars: The Autobiography of John A. Brashear.* 1924. Reprint, Pittsburgh: University of Pittsburgh Press, 1988.

Brown, Mark, Lu Donnelly, and David G. Wilkins. *The History of the Duquesne Club.* Pittsburgh: Art and Library Committee, Duquesne Club, 1989.

Buck, Solon, and Elizabeth Buck. *The Planting of Civilization in Western Pennsylvania.* 1939. Reprint, Pittsburgh: University of Pittsburgh Press, 1969.

Buckley, Gail Lumet. *The Hornes: An American Family.* New York, 1986.

Burgoyne, Arthur. *The Homestead Strike of 1892.* 1893. Reprint, Pittsburgh: University of Pittsburgh Press, 1979.

Buvinger, Bruce. "The Origin, Development, and Persistence of Street Patterns in Pittsburgh, Pennsylvania." MA thesis, University of Pittsburgh, 1972.

Cannadine, David. *Mellon: An American Life.* New York: Knopf, 2006.

Carlisle, Ronald. *The Story of "Woodville": The History, Architecture, and Archaeology of a Western Pennsylvania Farm.* Pittsburgh: Pittsburgh History & Landmarks Foundation, 1998.

Carnegie, Andrew. *The Autobiography of Andrew Carnegie.* Boston: Houghton Mifflin, 1920.

———. "Value of the World's Fair to the American People." *Engineering Magazine* 6 (January 1894): 417–22.

Cather, Willa. *Collected Short Fiction, 1892–1912.* Edited by Virginia Faulkner. Rev. ed. Lincoln: University of Nebraska Press, 1970.

Couvares, Francis G. *The Remaking of Pittsburgh: Class and Culture in an Industrializing City, 1877–1919.* Albany: State University of New York Press, 1984.

Cowin, Verna. *Pittsburgh Archaeological Resources and National Register Survey.* Pittsburgh: Carnegie Museum of Natural History, Pennsylvania Historical and Museum Commission, and Pittsburgh Dept. of City Planning, 1989.

Davenport, Marcia. *The Valley of Decision.* 1942. Reprint, Pittsburgh: University of Pittsburgh Press, 1989.

Demarest, David, Jr., ed. *From These Hills, From These Valleys: Selected Fiction about Western Pennsylvania.* Pittsburgh: University of Pittsburgh Press, 1976.

———. "A Relict Industrial Landscape: Pittsburgh's Coke Region." *Landscape* 29, no. 2 (1986): 29–36.

———. "Touring the Coke Region." *Pittsburgh History* 74 (1991): 100–13.

———, and Eugene Levy. "Remnants of an Industrial Landscape." *Pittsburgh History* 72 (1989): 128–39.

Dennis, Neal. *Historic Houses of the Sewickley Valley.* Sewickley, PA: White Oak Publishing, 1996.

Dickens, Charles. *American Notes.* London, 1843.

Dienstag, Eleanor. *In Good Company: 125 Years of the Heinz Table.* New York: Warner Books, 1994.

Dillard, Annie. *An American Childhood.* New York: Harper & Row, 1987.

499

Donnelly, Lu, H. David Brumble IV, and Franklin Toker. *Buildings of Pennsylvania: Pittsburgh and Western Pennsylvania*. Charlottesville: University of Virginia Press, 2009.

Duffus, R. L. "Is Pittsburgh Civilized?" *Harper's,* 16 October 1930.

Elkus, Leonore, ed. *Famous Men and Women of Pittsburgh*. Pittsburgh: Pittsburgh History & Landmarks Foundation, 1981.

Emerson, Ken. *Doo-dah! Stephen Foster and the Rise of American Popular Culture*. New York: Simon & Schuster, 1997.

Engineering Society of Western Pennsylvania. *Pittsburgh*. Pittsburgh, 1930.

Fenves, Steven J. "A History of Pittsburgh's Bridges." *Pittsburgh Engineer* (May–June 1989): 14–18, 32–36.

Fitch, John. *The Steel Workers*. 1910. Reprint, Pittsburgh: University of Pittsburgh Press, 1989.

Fleming, George. *Pittsburgh: How to See It*. Pittsburgh: W. G. Johnston, 1916.

Floyd, Margaret Henderson. *Architecture after Richardson: Regionalism before Modernism; Longfellow, Alden, & Harlow in Boston and Pittsburgh*. Chicago: University of Chicago Press in association with the Pittsburgh History & Landmarks Foundation, 1994.

Fullilove, Mindy Thompson. *Root Shock: How Tearing Up City Neighborhoods Hurts America and What We Can Do about It*. New York: One World/Ballantine Books, 2004.

Gay, Vernon, and Marilyn Evert. *Discovering Pittsburgh Sculpture*. Pittsburgh: University of Pittsburgh Press, 1983.

Grash, Valerie. "The Commercial Skyscrapers of Pittsburgh: Industrialists and Financiers, 1885–1932." PhD dissertation, Pennsylvania State University, 1998.

Hannegan, Barry. "Pittsburgh's Emerald Necklace." *PHLF News,* August 1996, 8–12.

———. "Surrey-on-Forbes." *PHLF News,* September 1998, 1–4.

Hellerstedt, Kahren Jones, et al. *Clayton: The Pittsburgh Home of Henry Clay Frick; Art and Furnishings*. Pittsburgh: Helen Clay Frick Foundation, 1988.

Hersh, Burton. *The Mellon Family: A Fortune in History*. New York: Morrow, 1978.

Hessen, Robert. *Steel Titan: The Life of Charles M. Schwab*. New York: Oxford University Press, 1975.

Hoerr, John P. *And the Wolf Finally Came: The Decline of the American Steel Industry*. Pittsburgh: University of Pittsburgh Press, 1988.

Hoffmann, Donald. *Frank Lloyd Wright's Fallingwater: The House and Its History*. New York: Dover Publications, 1978.

Hopkins, G. M., and Company. *Atlas of the Cities of Pittsburgh, Allegheny, and the Adjoining Boroughs*. Philadelphia, 1872–1939; http://digital.library.pitt.edu/maps/1872ind.html.

Ingham, John N. *The Iron Barons: A Social Analysis of an American Urban Elite, 1874–1965*. Westport, CT: Greenwood Press, 1978.

———. *Making Iron and Steel: Independent Mills of Pittsburgh, 1820–1920*. Columbus: Ohio State University Press, 1991.

Jucha, Robert. "The Anatomy of a Streetcar Suburb: A Development History of Shadyside." *Western Pennsylvania Historical Magazine* 62 (1979): 301–19.

Kelly, J. M. *Handbook of Greater Pittsburg*. Pittsburgh: J. M. Kelly Company, 1895.

Kidney, Walter. *Allegheny Cemetery: A Romantic Landscape in Pittsburgh*. Pittsburgh: Pittsburgh History & Landmarks Foundation, 1990.

———. *Henry Hornbostel: An Architect's Master Touch*. Pittsburgh: Pittsburgh History & Landmarks Foundation in cooperation with Robert Rinehart Publishers, 2002.

———. *Landmark Architecture: Pittsburgh and Allegheny County*. Pittsburgh: Pittsburgh History & Landmarks Foundation, 1985.

———. *Pittsburgh's Bridges: Architecture and Engineering*. Pittsburgh: Pittsburgh History & Landmarks Foundation, 1999.

———. *Pittsburgh's Landmark Architecture: The Historic Buildings of Pittsburgh and Allegheny County*. Pittsburgh: Pittsburgh History & Landmarks Foundation, 1997.

———, and Arthur Ziegler Jr. *Allegheny*. Pittsburgh: Pittsburgh History & Landmarks Foundation, 1975.

Killikelly, Sarah H. *The History of Pittsburgh: Its Rise and Progress*. Pittsburgh: B. C. & Gordon Montgomery Company, 1906.

Klukas, Arnold. "H. H. Richardson's Designs for the Emmanuel Episcopal Church, Pittsburgh." *American Art Review* 2 (July–August 1975): 64–76.

Koskoff, David. *The Mellons: The Chronicle of America's Richest Family*. New York: Crowell, 1978.

Krass, Peter. *Carnegie*. Hoboken, NJ: John Wiley & Sons, 2002.

Lane, Christopher. *A Panorama of Pittsburgh: Nineteenth-Century Printed Views*. Pittsburgh: Frick Art & Historical Center, 2008.

Long, Haniel. *Pittsburgh Memoranda*. 1935. Reprint, Pittsburgh: University of Pittsburgh Press, 1990.

Lorant, Stefan. *Pittsburgh: The Story of an American City*. 1964. 5th ed., updated and enlarged, millennium ed., Pittsburgh: Esselmont Books, 1999. The Pittsburgh chronology from this book is available online at http://digital.library.pitt.edu/chronology.

Lubove, Roy, ed. *Pittsburgh*. New York: New Viewpoints, 1976.

———. *Twentieth Century Pittsburgh: Government, Business, and Environmental Change*. 1969. Reprint, Pittsburgh: University of Pittsburgh Press, 1996.

———. *Twentieth Century Pittsburgh: The Post-Steel Era.* Pittsburgh: University of Pittsburgh Press, 1996.

Macdonald, Dwight. "Pittsburgh: What a City Shouldn't Be." *Forum,* 10 August 1938.

McHugh, Jeanne. *Alexander Holley and the Makers of Steel.* Baltimore: Johns Hopkins University Press, 1980.

McLean, Robert, III. *Countdown to Renaissance II: The New Way Corporate America Builds.* Pittsburgh: Urban Marketing Associates, 1984.

Mellon, Thomas. *Thomas Mellon and His Times.* 1885. 2nd ed., Pittsburgh: University of Pittsburgh Press, 1994.

Miller, Annie Clark. *Chronicles of Families, Houses and Estates of Pittsburgh and Its Environs.* Pittsburgh, 1927.

Miller, Donald. *The Architecture of Benno Janssen.* Pittsburgh: Carnegie Mellon University, 1997.

———, and Aaron Sheon. *Organic Vision: The Architecture of Peter Berndtson.* Pittsburgh: Hexagon Press, 1980.

Moorhead, Elizabeth. *Pittsburgh Portraits.* Pittsburgh: Boxwood Press, 1955.

Mosher, Anne. *Capital's Utopia: Vandergrift, Pennsylvania, 1855–1916.* Baltimore: Johns Hopkins University Press, 2004.

Nasaw, David. *Andrew Carnegie.* New York: Penguin Press, 2006.

The Olden Triangle: A Sequence of Forgotten History. Pittsburgh: Urban Design Associates, 1977.

Orr, C. Prentiss, et al., eds. *Pittsburgh Born, Pittsburgh Bred: 500 of the More Famous People Who Have Called Pittsburgh Home.* Pittsburgh: Published in cooperation with the Senator John Heinz History Center, 2008.

Palmer, Robert. *Palmer's Pictorial Pittsburgh.* Pittsburgh, 1905 and rev. eds.

Parton, James. "Pittsburg." *Atlantic Monthly* 21 (January 1868): 17–36.

Pennsylvania: A Guide to the Keystone State, Compiled by Workers of the Writers' Program of the Work Projects Administration in the State of Pennsylvania. New York: Oxford University Press, 1940.

The Pittsburgh Survey. 6 vols. Charity Organization Society of the City of New York and Russell Sage Foundation. New York, 1909–1914.

Regan, Bob. *The Bridges of Pittsburgh.* Pittsburgh: Local History Company, 2006.

———. *The Steps of Pittsburgh: Portrait of a City.* Pittsburgh: Local History Company, 2004.

Sanger, Martha Frick Symington. *Helen Clay Frick: Bittersweet Heiress.* Pittsburgh: University of Pittsburgh Press, 2007.

———. *Henry Clay Frick: An Intimate Portrait.* New York: Abbeville Press, 1998.

Schuyler, Montgomery. "The Buildings of Pittsburgh." *Architectural Record* 30, no. 3 (September 1911): 204–82.

Shribman, David, and Angelika Kane, eds. *Pittsburgh Lives: Men and Women Who Shaped Our City.* Chicago: Triumph Books, 2006.

Smith, George David. *From Monopoly to Competition: The Transformations of Alcoa, 1888–1986.* Cambridge: Cambridge University Press, 1988.

Spencer, Ethel. *The Spencers of Amberson Avenue: A Turn-of-the-Century Memoir.* Edited by Michael Weber and Peter Stearns. Pittsburgh: University of Pittsburgh Press, 1983.

Standiford, Les. *Meet You in Hell: Andrew Carnegie, Henry Clay Frick, and the Partnership That Transformed America.* New York: Crown, 2005.

Story of Old Allegheny City, Compiled by Workers of the Writers' Program of the Works [sic] Projects Administration in the Commonwealth of Pennsylvania. Pittsburgh: Allegheny Centennial Committee, 1941.

Stotz, Charles. *The Early Architecture of Western Pennsylvania.* 1936. Reprint, Pittsburgh: University of Pittsburgh Press, 1995; reissued as *The Architectural Heritage of Early Western Pennsylvania.* Pittsburgh: University of Pittsburgh Press, 1966.

Stryker, Roy, and Mel Seidenberg. *A Pittsburgh Album, 1758–1958.* Pittsburgh, 1959.

Sturgess, Louise King, Albert Tannler, and David Vater, eds. *Whirlwind Walk: Architecture and Urban Spaces in Downtown Pittsburgh.* Pittsburgh: Pittsburgh History & Landmarks Foundation, 2008.

Swetnam, George, and Helene Smith. *A Guidebook to Historic Western Pennsylvania.* Rev. ed. Pittsburgh: University of Pittsburgh Press, 1991.

Tannler, Albert. *A List of Pittsburgh and Allegheny County Buildings and Architects, 1950–2005.* 3rd ed. Pittsburgh: Pittsburgh History & Landmarks Foundation, 2005.

———. *Pittsburgh's Landmark Architecture, 1785–1950: A Concise Bibliography.* Pittsburgh: Pittsburgh History & Landmarks Foundation, 1994.

Thomas, Clarke. *They Came to Pittsburgh.* Pittsburgh: Pittsburgh Post-Gazette, 1983.

Toker, Franklin. *The Buildings of Pittsburgh.* Charlottesville: University of Virginia Press, 2007.

———. *Fallingwater Rising: Frank Lloyd Wright, E. J. Kaufmann, and America's Most Extraordinary House.* New York: Knopf, 2003.

———. "In the Grand Manner: The P&LE Station in Pittsburgh." *Carnegie Magazine* 53, no. 3 (March 1979): 4–21.

———. "A Magnet for Good Architecture: The Laurel Highlands from Meason House to Fallingwater—and Beyond." *Westmoreland History* 11, no. 3 (2007): 22–36.

———. "Philip Johnson and PPG: A Date with History." *Progressive Architecture* 60 (July 1979): 60–61.

————. *Pittsburgh: An Urban Portrait.* 1986. Reprint, Pittsburgh: University of Pittsburgh Press, 1994.

————. "Reversing an Urban Image: New Architecture in Pittsburgh, 1890–1980." In *Pittsburgh-Sheffield Sister Cities: Proceedings of the Pittsburgh-Sheffield Symposium on Industrial Cities,* edited by Joel A. Tarr. Pittsburgh: College of Fine Arts, Carnegie Mellon University, 1986.

————. "Richardson *en concours:* The Pittsburgh Courthouse." *Carnegie Magazine* 51, no. 9 (November 1977): 13–29.

Uhl, Lorraine, and Tracy Coffing. *Pittsburgh's Strip District: Around the World in a Neighborhood.* Pittsburgh: Historical Society of Western Pennsylvania, 2003.

Urban Design International 5, no. 1 (spring 1984). Issue on urban planning in Pittsburgh with contributions by Jonathan Barnett, David Lewis, Robert Lurcott, and Franklin Toker.

Van Slyck, Abigail A. *Free to All: Carnegie Libraries and American Culture: 1890–1920.* Chicago: University of Chicago Press, 1995.

Van Trump, James. *An American Palace of Culture: The Carnegie Institute and Carnegie Library of Pittsburgh.* Pittsburgh: Carnegie Institute, 1970.

————. *Life and Architecture in Pittsburgh.* Pittsburgh: Pittsburgh History & Landmarks Foundation, 1983.

————. *Majesty of the Law: The Court Houses of Allegheny County.* Pittsburgh: Pittsburgh History & Landmarks Foundation, 1988.

————, and Arthur Ziegler Jr. *Landmark Architecture of Allegheny County, Pennsylvania.* Pittsburgh: Pittsburgh History & Landmarks Foundation, 1967.

Vexler, Robert. *Pittsburgh: A Chronological and Documentary History, 1682–1976.* Dobbs Ferry, NY: Oceana Publications, 1977.

Wall, Joseph. *Andrew Carnegie.* New York: Oxford University Press, 1970.

Warhol, Andy. *The Philosophy of Andy Warhol from A to B and Back Again.* New York: Harcourt Brace Jovanovich, 1975.

Warner, A., ed. *History of Allegheny County, Pennsylvania.* 2 vols. Chicago: A. Warner and Company, 1889.

Warren, Kenneth. *Triumphant Capitalism: Henry Clay Frick and the Industrial Transformation of America.* Pittsburgh: University of Pittsburgh Press, 1996.

————. *Industrial Genius: The Working Life of Charles Michael Schwab.* Pittsburgh: University of Pittsburgh Press, 2007.

Weisberg, Gabriel, et al. *Collecting in the Gilded Age: Art Patronage in Pittsburgh, 1890–1910.* Pittsburgh: Frick Art & Historical Center, 1997.

Wilkins, David, ed. *A Reflection of Faith: St. Paul Cathedral, Pittsburgh.* Pittsburgh: Saint Paul Cathedral Centennial Book Committee, 2007.

Wilson, August. *Three Plays.* Pittsburgh: University of Pittsburgh Press, 1991 (plus the individual plays, released from 1985 through 2007).

Wilson, Erasmus. *Standard History of Pittsburgh.* Chicago: H. R. Cornell & Company, 1898.

Wollman, David, and Donald Inman. *Portraits of Steel: An Illustrated History of Jones and Laughlin Steel Corporation.* Kent, OH: Kent State University Press, 1999.

Works of F. J. Osterling, Architect, Pittsburg. Compiled by J. Franklin Nelson. Pittsburgh, 1904.

507

511

PHOTO CREDITS

All photographs in this book are taken by and appear courtesy of Franklin Toker, except as noted below:

Allegheny County Department of Public Works: 1.13

Armstrong, Christopher Drew: 3.1, 5.16

August Wilson Center: 2.34

British Library: 1.5, 1.7

Carnegie Library of Pittsburgh: 1.6, 1.11, 4.1

Carnegie Mellon University: 7.1

Carnegie Museums of Pittsburgh: 7.13

Carnegie Museum of Art: 5.27, 7.15

Corante, Hector: 2.18, 2.24, 3.12, 3.22, 3.23, 4.5, 4.6, 4.10, 4.11, 4.15, 5.5, 5.11, 5.21, 5.28, 6.7, 6.12, 6.29, 6.30, 7.9, 7.12, 7.21, 8.3

Cork Factory Lofts: 5.6

Cranberry Township: 9.1

Duquesne University: 6.3

Elliot, John: 8.17 (courtesy Library of Congress, HABS)

Engleman, Tim: 6.23 (courtesy Shadyside Presbyterian Church)

Ferguson, Herb: 1.18, 2.19, 2.21, 2.25, 2.32, 2.42, 2.43, 2.44, 3.6, 7.3, 7.4, 7.5, 7.7

Finer, Chad: 1.22, 2.3, 2.10, 2.11, 2.12, 2.13, 2.14, 2.23, 2.26, 2.27, 2.33, 2.39, 2.41, 5.2, 6.2

Frank Lloyd Wright Foundation: 1.17

Friendship Development Associates: 5.1

Goody Clancy Architects: 7.35

Greene, Jonathan: 7.19

Hare, Clyde: 2.46, 2.48, 2.50, 2.52

Hillman Company: 1.8, 1.10

Joseph, Carl: 6.31 (courtesy Howard Hanna Real Estate)

Judkis, Jim: 4.12

Kaulen, Tim: 7.24 (courtesy Carnegie Mellon University)

Landesberg Design: 3.25, 8.20

Library of Congress, HABS: 2.7, 2.20, 2.51, 3.15, 5.12, 8.17, 8.21

Macy's, Inc.: 2.16

Massery, Ed: 1.4 (courtesy Heinz History Center), 6.36 (courtesy Lubetz Architects)

McNaugher, Melinda: 7.16 (courtesy Carnegie Museum of Natural History)

Milmoe, James: 1.16

Mull, Heather: 1.19

National Aeronautics and Space Administration: 1.3

Novelly, Laura: 3.5, 3.7

Penberthy, William J.: 8.30, 8.32 (courtesy Sewickley Valley Historical Society)

Pittsburgh History & Landmarks Foundation: 1.2, 2.4, 2.37, 2.40, 2.47

Pittsburgh Penguins: 6.6

Pittsburgh Post-Gazette: 2.17, 2.45, 8.1

Preis, Chris: 8.25

Reed, Lindsay: 5.39

Ruschak, Robert: 9.30

Sapp, Darrell: 1.21, 4.4 (courtesy *Pittsburgh Post-Gazette*)

Shuppy, Elliott: 8.7

Society to Preserve the Millvale Murals of Maxo Vanka: 8.36

Spooner, Sharon: 7.25

Strovers, Robert D.: 9.6

Tierney, Maurice: 5.15, 5.31, 8.23

Traub, Nicholas: 2.20, 2.51, 5.12 (courtesy Library of Congress, HABS)

Tye, Tony: 4.20 (courtesy *Pittsburgh Post-Gazette*)

Uhl, Charles: 3.2

University of Pittsburgh: 1.12, 3.11, 7.6

VisitPittsburgh: 2.1, 2.2, 2.28, 2.36, 3.24, 3.26, 5.3, 5.35

Western Pennsylvania Conservancy: 9.27, 9.28, 9.29

Walter, Zach: 8.40